D1236515

STUDIES AND NOTES SUPPLEMENTARY TO STUBBS' CONSTITUTIONAL HISTORY

BIBLIOGRAPHICAL NOTE

Part I of STUDIES AND NOTES SUPPLEMENTARY TO STUBBS' CONSTITUTIONAL HISTORY, translated by the late W. E. RHODES, M.A., was issued separately in 1908. Part II, translated by W. T. WAUGH, M.A., appeared in 1914. Both volumes were edited by JAMES TAIT, Litt.D., F.B.A. Part III, translated by MARION E. I. ROBERTSON, M.A., D-es-L., and R. F. TREHARNE, M.A., Ph.D., was published during 1929 under the editorship of F. M. POWICKE, Litt.D., F.B.A.

STUDIES AND NOTES
SUPPLEMENTARY TO STUBBS'
CONSTITUTIONAL HISTORY

BY

CH. PETIT-DUTAILLIS, D-ᴇs-L.

AND

GEORGES LEFEBVRE

MANCHESTER UNIVERSITY PRESS
BARNES & NOBLE INC., NEW YORK

© 1930 MANCHESTER UNIVERSITY PRESS
Published by the University of Manchester at
THE UNIVERSITY PRESS
316–324 Oxford Road, Manchester 13

U.S.A.
BARNES & NOBLE, INC.
105 Fifth Avenue, New York, N.Y. 10003

First published 1930
Reprinted 1968

G.B. SBN 7190 0341 5

Printed in Great Britain by Lowe & Brydone (Printers) Ltd.,
London

EXTRACTS FROM THE AUTHOR'S PREFACE.

THE French edition of the " Constitutional History " of William Stubbs is intended for the use of the students of our Faculties of Arts and Law. . . . The " Constitutional History " is a classic and the readers of the " Bibliothèque internationale de Droit public " [1] have seen it more than once quoted as a book, the authority of which is accepted without discussion. It seems desirable, however, to emphasize the exceptional merits of this great work as well as to draw attention to its weak points and, as it is not an adaptation but a translation—complete and reverent—that is given here, to explain why we have thought some additions indispensable. . . . All that we know of Stubbs inspires confidence, confidence in the solidity and extent of his knowledge, the honesty of his criticism, the sureness of his judgment, the depth of his practical experience of men and things. Despite the merit of his other works, and especially of the prefaces which he wrote for the " Chronicles " he edited, Stubbs only showed the full measure of his powers in the " Constitutional History." It is the fruit of prodigious labour, of a thorough investigation of the printed sources which a historian could consult at the period when these three bulky volumes successively appeared. It is an admirable storehouse of facts, well chosen, and set forth with scrupulous good faith. The word " Constitution " is taken in its widest sense. How the England of the Renascence with its strong Monarchy, its House of Lords, its local institutions, its Church, its Nobility, its towns, its freeholders and its villeins was evolved from the old Anglo-Saxon Britain, this is the subject of the author's enquiry. With the exception of diplomatic and military history he touches upon the most diverse subjects. His book is at once a scientific manual of institutions and, at least from the Norman Conquest onwards, a continuous history of every reign. Mr. Maitland has called attention to the advantages of the plan which by combining narrative and analysis allows no detail of importance to escape, and gives a marvellously concrete impression of the development of the nation.[2]

[1] In which the translation is included.
[2] Maitland, *Eng. Hist. Rev.*, xvi., 1901, p. 422.

v

Does this imply that the perusal of the " Constitutional History" leaves us nothing to desire ? The French who have kept the " classical " spirit and reserve their full admiration for that which is perfectly clear, will doubtless find that his thought is very often obscure and his conclusions undecided. This is really one result of the vast erudition and the good faith of the author. This honest historian is so careful not to neglect any document, so impressed with the complexity of the phenomena that he does not always succeed in disposing them in an absolutely coherent synthesis. . . .

But inconsistencies of view and the relative obscurity of certain passages are not the only fault which impairs Stubbs' work. There is another, at once more serious and more easily remedied, a fault which is particularly felt in the first volume. The book is no longer up to date. The chapters dealing with the Anglo-Saxon period, especially, have become obsolete on many points. The revisions affected by Stubbs in the successive editions which he published down to his death, are insufficient. They do not always give an accurate idea of the progress made by research, and they are not even executed with all the attention to details which is desirable. Although the author had not ceased to be interested in history the task of revision obviously repelled him. The " Constitutional History " has grown out of date in yet another way. Stubbs wrote history on lines on which it is no longer written by the great mediævalists of to-day. He belonged to the liberal generation which had seen and assisted in the attainment of electoral reforms in England and of revolutionary and nationalist movements on the Continent. He had formed himself, in his youth, under the discipline of the patriotic German scholars who saw in the primitive German institutions the source of all human dignity and of all political independence. He thought he saw in the development of the English Constitution the magnificent and unique expansion of these first germs of self-government, and England was for him " the messenger of liberty to the world." The degree to which this optimistic and patriotic conception of English history could falsify, despite the author's scrupulous conscientiousness, his interpretation of the sources, is manifest in the pages which he devoted to the Great Charter. Nowadays when so many illusions have been dissipated, when parliamentary institutions, set up by almost every civilized nation, have more openly revealed, as they developed, their inevitable littlenesses and when the formation of nationalities has turned Europe into a camp, history is written with less enthusiasm. The motive of the deeds accomplished by our forefathers are scrutinized with cold impartiality, minute care is taken to grasp the precise significance which they had at the time when they were done, and lastly the economic conception of history exercises a certain influence even over those who do not admit its principles. Open the " History of English Law " of Sir Frederick Pollock and Mr. Maitland, the masterpiece of contemporary English learning, written twenty years after the " Constitutional History " and note the difference of tone.

This French edition being intended for the use of students and persons little versed in mediæval history, it was necessary to let them know that the work is not always abreast of the progress of research and we have thought it possible to furnish them, although in a very modest measure, with the means of acquiring supplementary information. . . .[3]

I have specially written for this publication a dozen studies and additional notes. Some of these lay claim to no originality, and their only purpose is to summarize celebrated controversies or to call attention to recent discoveries. In others a study of English history of some duration has allowed me to express a personal opinion on certain questions. The problems most discussed by the scholars who are now investigating the Anglo-Saxon, Norman and Angevin periods have thus been re-stated with a bibliography which may be useful. . . .

M. Bémont, the Frenchman who has the best knowledge of mediæval England, has been good enough to read the proofs of the additional studies.

[3] M. Petit-Dutaillis proceeds to state that he has added to Stubbs' notes references to works and editions by French scholars " which he was unacquainted with, or at least treated as non-existent," and has referred the reader to better editions of English Chronicles and other sources where Stubbs was content to use inferior ones, or where critical editions have appeared since his death.

CH. PETIT-DUTAILLIS.

PREFACE TO THE ENGLISH TRANSLATION OF PART I.

THE twelve studies and notes here printed have been translated from the French of Professor Ch. Petit-Dutaillis in order to provide the English student with a supplement to the first volume of bishop Stubbs' " Constitutional History of England." The recent appearance of the first volume of a French translation of that classical work, more than thirty years after the publication of the corresponding volume of the original, is good evidence that it still remains the standard treatise on its subject. At the same time, the fact that M. Petit-Dutaillis, the editor of the French edition, has found it necessary to append over 130 closely printed pages by way of addition and correction shows that the early part of the book, at all events, has not escaped the ravages of time. The thirty years which have elapsed since it appeared have seen much fruitful research both in England and abroad upon the period which it covers. Continental scholars such as Fustel de Coulanges and Meitzen and in this country, Maitland, Seebohm, Round, Vinogradoff, and others have added greatly to our knowledge of the origin and early history of English institutions. The results of this research so far as it had proceeded in Stubbs' lifetime were very imperfectly incorporated by him in the successive editions of his book. Moreover, as M. Petit-Dutaillis points out in his preface, the study of these institutions is now approached from a standpoint different from that which was taken by Stubbs and his contemporaries. Some portions of the first volume of the " Constitutional History " have, therefore, become obsolete and others require correction and readjustment.

Teachers and students of English constitutional history have long been embarrassed by a text-book which, while indispensable as a whole, is in many points out of date. Hitherto thay have had to go for newer light to a great variety of books and periodicals. English historians were apparently too much engrossed with detailed research to stop and sum up the advances that had been made. It has been left to a French scholar to supply the

viii

much-needed survey. M. Petit-Dutaillis, who was, at the time when he brought out the first volume of his edition, Professor of History in the University of Lille, but has quite recently been appointed Rector of the University of Grenoble, had already shown an intimate and scholarly acquaintance with certain periods of English history in his " Etude sur la vie et le régne de Louis VIII." and in his elaborate introduction to the work of his friend André Réville on the Peasants' Revolt of 1381. The twelve " additional studies and notes " in which he brings the first volume of the " Constitutional History " abreast of more recent research meet so obvious a need, and, in their French dress, have been so warmly welcomed by English scholars, that it has been thought desirable to make them easily accessible to the many students of history who may not wish to purchase the rather expensive volume of the French edition in which they are included.

M. Petit-Dutaillis willingly acceded to the suggestion and has read the proofs of the translation. The extracts from his preface, given elsewhere, explain more fully than has been done above the reasons for and the nature of the revision of Stubbs' work which he has carried out.

As M. Petit-Dutaillis observes, in speaking of the French version of the " Constitutional History," the translation of books of this kind can only be competently executed by historians. It has in this case been entrusted to a graduate of the University of Manchester, Mr. W. E. Rhodes, who has himself done good historical work. I have carefully revised it, corrected, with the author's approval, one or two small slips in the French text, substituted for its references to the French translation of the " Constitutional History " direct references to the last edition (1903) of the first volume of the original, and added in square brackets a few references to Professor Vinogradoff's " English Society in the Eleventh Century," which appeared after the publication of the French edition. The index has been adapted by Mr. Rhodes from the one made by M. Lefebvre for that edition.

JAMES TAIT.

THE UNIVERSITY,
  MANCHESTER,
    September 8th, 1908.

PREFACE TO THE ENGLISH TRANSLATION OF PART II.

As was foreshadowed in M. Petit-Dutaillis' preface to the French translation of the first volume of the " Constitutional History " of bishop Stubbs, the second volume, of which the French version appeared last year, has been found to need much less revision of the kind for which footnotes are inadequate. Instead of the twelve additional Studies and Notes of volume I., which were translated by Mr. W. E. Rhodes and published under my editorship by the Manchester University Press in 1908, M. Petit-Dutaillis has thought it unnecessary to append to volume II. more than two such studies. The subjects with which they deal, " The Forest " and " The Causes and General Characteristics of the Rising of 1381 " are, however, treated with such thoroughness as to provide sufficient matter for another volume of " Supplementary Studies." In his preface M. Petit-Dutaillis holds out the hope that his additions to the third volume of Stubbs' work will be concerned with questions more directly constitutional ; but the Forest played a part in the contest between the English Crown and people which makes the inclusion of the first essay in these studies quite appropriate, while the many additions that have been made to our knowledge of the Peasants' Revolt since Stubbs wrote constitute a sufficient justification for the second. The translation of the two studies has been made by my friend and colleague Mr. W. T. Waugh, and my duties as editor have been exceedingly light. As in the first volume, a few footnotes have been added in square brackets, in most cases by Mr. Waugh, who has also adapted the index from the one made by M. Lefebvre for the French edition.

JAMES TAIT.

THE UNIVERSITY,
MANCHESTER,
July 10*th*, 1914.

PREFACE TO THE ENGLISH TRANSLATION OF PART III.

In 1908 and 1913 the Manchester University Press published an English translation of the " Studies and Notes supplementary to Stubbs' Constitutional History," which M. Petit-Dutaillis had added to the French edition of the first two volumes of Stubbs' work. The appearance of the third volume of the French edition was delayed by the war and the preoccupations of M. Petit-Dutaillis. He was able to secure the co-operation of M. Georges Lefebvre, who made himself responsible for the additional essays, while M. Petit-Dutaillis wrote a long introduction. An English translation of the essays of both scholars is given in this volume. The authors have kindly discussed a few difficult or doubtful points with the translators and myself, but, with their full consent, we are responsible for such changes as have been made. These are not numerous. Where possible, references to recent work strictly bearing upon the subject matter have been added. The paging continues that of parts one and two of the English translation.

After some hesitation we decided not to add in the footnotes references to the third and fourth volumes of Professor Tout's " Chapters in the Administrative History of Mediæval England " which unfortunately appeared too late to be used by M. Lefebvre. If we had done this we should have added considerably to the length of the volume without being able to do justice to Dr. Tout's work. M. Lefebvre has made much use of the scattered essays and lectures in which Dr. Tout anticipated his most important conclusions, and for other matters, such as his striking pages on the characteristics of the central element in parliament which came to be called the House of Lords, we must be content to direct the reader's attention to the book itself. Similarly we have not referred to the series of articles in which Mr. H. G. Richardson and Mr. G. O. Sayles are investigating with minute care the early records of the English Parliaments. These papers must be studied as a whole. The writers insist upon the judicial character of parliament, give careful lists of the parliaments of Edward I. and Edward II. and a much needed analysis of the original records which lie behind Ryley's " Placita Parliamentaria " and the printed

" Rotuli Parliamentorum." [1] The value of their work is obvious, but it is too early to estimate the extent to which it will modify the views generally accepted since the appearance of Maitland's edition of the Memoranda of the parliament of 1305.

The studies in this volume differ from their predecessors in one respect : they have little relation to the chapters of Stubbs to which they were added. The third volume of the Constitutional History was devoted to the history of the fifteenth century, to comprehensive studies in ecclesiastical and social history, and to the antiquities of parliament. M. Petit-Dutaillis and M. Lefebvre have confined themselves almost entirely to the development of administration and parliamentary institutions in the thirteenth and fourteenth centuries. We do not think that their readers will regret this departure from the plan of the earlier studies, for it is most helpful to have, upon so complicated a series of problems, some of which will be the occasion of discussion and dispute for many years to come, the impressions of scholars who are experts in French history and can look at our English history without any of our prepossessions. Even if we continue to differ—and I must confess that my own outlook upon English history is not the same as that of M. Petit-Dutaillis—we can learn much from them. At the same time we cannot but wish that it had been possible to include in this series a number of studies upon the aspects of our history which Stubbs discussed in his last volume. Much has been written, since he wrote, upon the relations between secular and ecclesiastical authority, upon local government, the development of municipal institutions, and the importance in constitutional history of economic progress. However, the writings of Maitland, Fueter, Workman, Tait, Unwin, Miss Putnam and others are not hard of access ; [2] and we have every reason to be thankful to M. Petit-Dutaillis and M. Lefebvre for what they have given us.

[1] The " Early records of the English Parliaments " in the *Bulletin of the Institute of Historical Research*, v. 129—154 (Feb. 1928), vi. 71—88 (Nov. 1928), 129—155 (Feb. 1929). To these should be added " Scottish Parliaments of Edward I." in *The Scottish Historical Review*, xxv. 300—327 (July 1928), " The Irish Parliaments of Edward I." in *The Proceedings of the Royal Irish Academy*, xxxviii. section C, 128—147 (Jan. 1929), and Mr. Richardson's paper " The Origins of Parliaments " in *Transactions of the Royal Historical Society*, 4th series, xi. 137—183 (1928).

[2] A useful short biography of English Constitutional History has recently been prepared for the Historical Association by Miss Helen Cam and Mr. A. S. Turberville (published for the Historical Association by G. Bell and Sons., 1929).

OXFORD,   F. M. POWICKE.
April, 1929.

CONTENTS

LIST OF ABBREVIATIONS USED IN FOOTNOTES OF PART III.

Adams. *The Origin of the English Constitution.* G. B. Adams. Yale University Press, 1912.

Amer. Hist. Rev. American Historical Review.

Baldwin. *The King's Council in England during the Middle Ages.* J. F. Baldwin. Oxford, Clarendon Press, 1913.

Bibl. de l'Ec. des Chartes. Bibliothéque de l'Ecole des Chartes.

Commemoration Essays. Magna Carta Commemoration Essays. Edited H. E. Malden. London, 1917.

Const. Hist. The Constitutional History of England. W. Stubbs. Oxford.

E. H. R. English Historical Review.

J. R. B. Bulletin of the John Rylands Library. Manchester.

Luchaire, *Inst. mon. Histoire des institutions monarchiques de la France sous les premiers Capétiens* (987—1180). D. J. A. Luchaire. Paris, 1883.

Luchaire, *Manuel. Manuel des institutions françaises, période des Capétiens directs.* D. J. A. Luchaire. Paris, 1892.

McIlwain. *The High Court of Parliament and its Supremacy.* C. H. McIlwain. Yale University Press, 1910.

McKechnie. *Magna Carta : a commentary.* W. S. McKechnie. London, 1914 (2nd edition).

Maitland. *Memoranda de Parliamento : Records of the Parliaments holden at Westminster, A.D. 1305.* Ed. F. W. Maitland, (Rolls Series), London 1893.

Pasquet. *An Essay on the Origin of the House of Commons.* D. Pasquet (trans. R. G. D. Laffan). Cambridge, 1925.

Picot. *Documents rélatifs aux Etats Généraux et assemblés réunies sous Philippe le Bel (1302—1308).* Picot, 1900.

Pollard, *Evolution of Parliament. The Evolution of Parliament.* A. F. Pollard. London, 1920.

Rot. Parl. Rotuli Parliamentorum. (Record Commission.) London.

Statutes. Statutes of the Realm. (Record Commission.) London.

Studies. Studies and Notes Supplementary to Stubbs' Constitutional History (i and ii). Ch. Petit-Dutaillis (trans. Rhodes and Waugh). Manchester University Press, 1915.

Tout. *Chapters. Chapters in the Administrative History of Mediæval England.* (Vols. i and ii.) T. F. Tout. Manchester University Press, 1920.

Tout. *Place Edward II. The Place of the Reign of Edward II. in English History.* T. F. Tout. Manchester University Press, 1914.

Tout. *Some Conflicting Tendencies.* "Some Conflicting Tendencies in English Administrative History during the XIVth Century." (*Bulletin of the John Rylands Library*, 1924.) T. F. Tout.

Tout, T. F. Essays presented to. Essays in Mediæval History presented to Thomas Frederick Tout. (Ed. A. G. Little and F. M. Powicke.) Manchester University Press, 1925.

Viollet. *Hist. des Inst. pol. et admin.* "Histoire des Institutions politiques et administratives de la France." P. Viollet.

Wylie. *Henry IV. History of England under Henry IV.* J. H. Wylie. London.

Wylie. *Henry V. The Reign of Henry V.* J. H. Wylie. Cambridge University Press, 1914—1919.

I.

THE EVOLUTION OF THE RURAL CLASSES IN ENGLAND AND THE ORIGIN OF THE MANOR.

AT the end of the Middle Ages, rural England was divided into estates, which were known by the Norman name of *manors*.[1] The manor, a purely private division,[2] a unit in the eyes of its lord, did not necessarily coincide with the township or village, a legal division of the hundred and a unit in the eyes of the king; but, except in certain counties,[3] the two areas were normally identical. In each of his manors, the lord of the manor retained some lands in demesne, which he cultivated with the aid of labour services, and he let the remainder in return for fixed dues, to the tenants, free or villein, who formed the village community.[4] Agriculture and cattle-rearing

The manor at the end of the Middle Ages

1. The term is not absolutely general. At the end of the 12th century it is not used in the Boldon Book, the land-book of the Bishop of Durham; the rural unit, in this document, is the *villa*, though in reality the manorial organisation existed. (Lapsley, in *Victoria History of the Counties of England, Durham*, i, 1905, pp. 262, 268.)

2. Maitland, *Select Pleas in Manorial Courts*, 1889, i, p. xxxix.

3. In the counties of Cambridge, Essex, Suffolk, Norfolk, Lincoln, Nottingham and Derby, and in some parts of Yorkshire, the village was frequently divided between three or four Norman lords, at least at the date of *Domesday Book* (Maitland, *Domesday Book and Beyond*, 1897, pp. 22–23). The co-existence of several manors in the territory of one village sometimes brought about the partition of the village; or on the other hand it persisted, and was the cause of frequent disputes; see on this subject Vinogradoff, *The Growth of the Manor*, 1905, pp. 304 sqq.; *Villainage in England*, 1892, pp. 393 sqq.; Maitland, *Domesday Book and Beyond*, pp. 129 sqq.

4. See the description of the manorial organisation in Vinogradoff, *Growth of the Manor*, pp. 307 sqq., and *Villainage*, pp. 223 sqq. [Cf. also his *English Society in the Eleventh Century*, 1908, pp 353 sqq.] Mr. Maitland his published an excellent monograph on the Manor of Wilburton in the *English Historical Review*, 1894, pp. 417 sqq. Numerous monographs of this kind would be very useful.

B

were carried on according to the system of the unenclosed field, the open field.[1] In the manor
The Open Field
there were several fields alternatively left
fallow or sown with different crops.[2] Each of these fields,
instead of belonging as a whole to a single tenant, was
divided, by means of balks of turf, into narrow strips of
land, whose length represented the traditional length of
furrow made by the plough before it was turned round.
The normal holding of a peasant was made up of strips
of arable land scattered in the different fields, customary
rights in the common lands, and a part of the fodder
produced by the meadows of the village. Once the
harvest had been reaped in the fields and the hay got
in in the meadows, the beasts were sent there for
common pasture. Every one had to conform to the same
rules, to the same method of rotation of crops; even the
lord of the manor, who often had a part of his private
demesne situated in the open field.

Whatever progress individualism had made in the
13th century, the inhabitant of a village was a member
The Village of a community whose rights and interests
Community. restricted his own, and which, in its relation
to the lord of the manor, still remained powerful.[3]
Common business was discussed periodically in the *hall*
of the manor, and the villeins, the English term for
the serfs, attended the *halimot* just as much as the free
tenants; although the villeins were in a majority, the
free tenants were amenable to this court in which we see
the peasants themselves " presenting " the members of

1. The English open-field system has been often studied. The starting
point is Nasse's essay *Zur Geschichte der mittelalterlichen Feldgemein-
schaft in England*, 1869. F. Seebohm revived the subject in his celebrated book, to which we shall have to refer again : *The English Village
Community*, 1883, pp. 1 sqq. See *ibid.*, pp. 2 and 4, the map and sketch
made from nature—for there still exist some relics of these methods of
cultivation. Cf. Mr. Vinogradoff's chapter on the Open-field System, in
The Growth of the Manor, pp. 165 sqq. ; Stubbs, i, pp. 52 sqq., 89 sqq.
2. For example : corn-barley or oats,—fallow.
3. See Vinogradoff, *Growth of the Manor*, pp. 318 sqq., 361 sqq. and
passim ; *Villainage*, pp. 354 sqq.

the community who had done their work ill. The reason is that the community as a whole was answerable to its lord. Sometimes, moreover, the village, like the free towns, farmed the dues and paid a fixed lump sum to its lord. It was, then, a juridical person.[1] Finally, the village had its share in local government, police and the royal courts of justice.[2]

Thus the English manor, like a French rural domain of the same period, was dependent on a lord; and the lord claimed dues from his tenants and day-work to till the land which he cultivated himself. But the customs to which the exercise of the right of ownership had to defer, the methods of husbandry and pasturage, the importance of the interests of all kinds entrusted to the peasants themselves, showed the singular strength of the English rural community.

What was the origin of this manorial organization, of the usages of the open field, of the condition of the freeman and villeins, of this village community which had the rights of a juridical person and formed the primordial unit of local government?

The question of the origin of the seignorial and manorial system, which, in the history of the whole of Obscurity of particularly obscure and complex in the question the West, is a subject of controversy, is of origins England, because England underwent only a partial Romanisation which is imperfectly known, and the exact extent and character of which it is impossible to estimate.

The " Romanists " and " Germanists " of the other side of the Channel engage in battles in which analogy and hypothesis are the principal weapons; and the projectiles are not mortal to either of the two armies.

The Germanists deny any importance in the develop-

---

1. We adopt on this point the views of Mr. Vinogradoff, *Growth of the Manor*, pp. 322 sqq.
2. Stubbs, *Const. Hist.*, i, pp. 88 sqq., 102, 115, 128, etc.

ment of English institutions to the Roman element, as indeed also to the Celtic. The earliest of them sought to explain the formation of the rural community and even that of the manor by the Mark theory.[1] Several years before the appearance of the famous works of G. L. von Maurer on the *Markverfassung in Deutschland,* Kemble in his *Saxons in England,* drew a picture, somewhat vague in outline it is true, of a Saxon England divided into *marks,* inhabited by communities of free Saxons, associated of their own free will for the cultivation of the soil and exercising collective rights of ownership in the lands of their mark. In this " paradise of yeomen " the free husbandman is judged only in the court of the mark, submits to the customs of the mark alone, acknowledges no other head but the " first marksman," hereditary or elected, or the powerful warrior who secures the safety of the mark. This head, however, ends, thanks to his prerogatives and usurpations, by reducing the members of the community to economic dependence. The lands not yet exploited, which should have remained as a reserve fund at the disposal of the people, fall into the hands of the chief men. This capital phenomenon fully explains the formation of the feudal and manorial system.[2]

The Germanist thesis.
The Mark

Kemble had the merit of raising questions which are still debated at the present day; unfortunately, his structure is a creation of fancy. Maurer, on the contrary, founded his Mark theory on a thorough study of the German village of the Middle Ages. But Fustel de Coulanges has accused him of having " attributed to ancient Germany

The Mark theory has been partially abandoned

---

1. A summary of this controversy may be found in Vinogradoff, *Villainage in England*, pp. 16 sqq.; C. M. Andrews, *Old English Manor* (Baltimore, 1892) *Introduction*; E. A. Bryan, *The Mark in Europe and America* (Berlin, 1893), etc.

2. Kemble, *Saxons in England*, ed. W. de Gray Birch, 1876, vol. i, especially pp. 53 sqq., 176 sqq.

usages whose existence can only be verified twelve centuries later,"[1] and has partly succeeded in overthrowing the " mark-system." The Germanists can no longer maintain that the mark is " the original basis on which all Teutonic societies are founded,"[2] and even Stubbs, who appears to be unacquainted with the works of Fustel, and quotes those of Maurer with unqualified praise, makes some prudent reservations. He does not admit that the mark is a " fundamental constitutional element." But he thinks that the English village " represents the principle of the mark," and in the pages which he devotes to the township and the manor, he allows no place to Roman or Celtic influences.[3] The majority of the best-known English historians of his generation and ours, Henry Summer Maine, Freeman, Green, Maitland,[4] are, like him, decided Germanists. In the same camp are ranged the German scholars who have studied or approached the problem of the origin of English civilization on any side, such as Konrad Maurer, Nasse, Gneist and Meitzen.

Until 1883, the Romanists had not given uneasiness to the English scholars of the Germanist school. The The analogies and suppositions which were Romanists work of Coote [5] was built in the air, on often extravagant; it is difficult to take seriously his theories on the fiscal survey of the whole of Britain, on the persistence of the Roman *Comes* and on the Roman origin of the shire. The book in which Fustel de

1. *De la marche germanique* in *Recherches sur quelques problèmes d'histoire*, 1885, p. 356. Cf. *Le problème des origines de la propriété foncière*, in *Questions Historiques*, ed. Jullian, 1893, p. 21 sqq.
2. Kemble, *Saxons*, p. 53.
3. *Const. Hist.*, i, pp. 35 sqq., 52 sqq., 89 sqq., 97 sqq. For Stubbs' general views on the Germanic origin of English institutions, see *ibid.*, pp. 2 sqq., 65, 68.
4. Mr. Maitland, however, entirely rejects the term ' mark ' as applicable to the English village community. See *Domesday Book and Beyond*, pp. 354–355.
5. *The Romans of Britain*, 1878.

Coulanges had studied Roman Gaul was little known on
the other side of the Channel; nor would it have shaken
the conviction of scholars who consider that English
institutions have had an absolutely original development
and are the "purest product of the primitive genius of
the Germans." In 1883, the famous work of Mr.
F. Seebohm appeared to disturb the tranquility of the
Germanists.

Mr. Seebohm set himself to examine "The English
Village Community in its relations to the manorial and
tribal systems and to the common or open field system
of husbandry." Such was the title of the book; the
problem to be solved was indicated in the preface thus:
"whether the village communities of England were
originally free and this liberty degenerated into serfdom,
or whether they were at the dawn of history in serfdom
under the authority of a lord, and the 'manor' already
in existence."

The author proceeds from the known to the unknown;
his starting point is a description of the remains of
open field cultivation which he has himself observed in
England. He has no difficulty in proving that this
system was already employed at the end of the Middle
Ages, and co-existed with the manorial organisation
and villeinage. He then goes back to the period of
the Norman Conquest.. According to him, when the
Normans arrived in England, they brought with them no
new principle in the management of estates. Already,
tempore regis Edwardi, we find the manor, with a lord's
demesne and a village community composed of serfs,
whom the lord has provided with indivisible holdings;
the Domesday Book of the astern counties speaks
indeed of *liberi homines* and *sochemanni,* but they were
Danes or Normans: the natives were not free tenants.
Earlier still, in the time of King Ine or Ini, at the end
of the seventh century, the usages of the open field
existed, the *ham* and the *tun* were manors, the *thegn*

or *hlaford* was the lord of a manor, the *ceorl* was a serf. And as in the laws of Ethelbert a century older, there is mention of *hams* or *tuns* belonging to private individuals or to the king, the manor must already have existed at the end of the sixth century. Now, the Anglo-Saxons, at that time, had scarcely completed the conquest of the island; it is impossible, therefore, that the free village community, conforming to the mark system, can have been introduced by them into England, since the first documents that we have on their social condition prove that this free community did not exist. Therefore either the Saxons brought the system of the manor and the servile community into England, or else they found it already established there, and made no change in it. This second hypothesis is

The manor and villeinage of Roman origin the more probable; the manorial and servile organisation must go back to the period of Roman domination in Britain. It will be objected that the Romans were few in number, that the Britons were Celts, and that, in the countries where Celtic civilization persisted, Wales and Ireland, the manorial organisation did not exist in the Middle Ages. The Celtic tribal community was entirely unacquainted with the fixed and indivisible holding which is one of the essential features of the manor. But, declares Mr. Seebohm, there is nothing to prove that before the arrival of the Anglo-Saxons the whole of Briton was still under the empire of the customs of pastoral and tribal civilization. The evidence of Cæsar proves that the inhabitants of the south-east had already passed out of this stage. The Romans found subjects accustomed to a settled life. They had no difficulty in establishing in their new province the régime of the ' villa,' the great estate, that is to say, the manor : and the administrative abuses of the Lower Empire hastened the formation of the seignorial authority and the enslavement of the free husbandmen, Germans for the most part, whom the emperors had imported in large numbers to colonise the country. The Romans, for the rest, improved agriculture and introduced the use of the triple rotation of crops; they thus gave to the open field system, which the Britons had only practised until then in its most rudimentary form, its definitive constitution.

As for the hypothesis according to which the open field system with triple rotation and lordship with servile, indivisible holdings, was introduced after the fall of the Roman domination, by the Anglo-Saxons, it is not indefensible, but only upon condition that the Anglo-Saxons came from Southern Germany, which had undergone contact with Roman civilization, and not, as is generally thought, from Northern Germany, where the triple rotation of crops was unknown. Mr. Seebohm does not reject this supposition, which, indeed, does not exclude the first hypothesis. Half Romanised Germans may have found in England the system of husbandry with which they were already acquainted on the Continent. In either case the English manor has a Roman origin.

Mr. Seebohm's work compels attention by the skill with which the author sets forth his ideas and puts fresh life into the subject. As we shall see, it **Objections** has obliged the Germanists to make important concessions. But the theory, taken as a whole, is untenable. We are struck, in reading it, by the viciousness of his general method, by the missing links in **The Roman** his chain of proof, by the poverty of many **origin is not** of his arguments. The method of working **proved** back adopted by Mr. Seebohm is extremely fallacious; it falsifies the historical perspective, and the author is inevitably led to reason in most cases by analogy. By such a method, if some day the documents of modern history disappear bodily, a scholar might undertake to connect the trades unions of the nineteenth century with the Roman *Collegia*. " No amount of analogy between two systems," says Stubbs wisely, " can by itself prove the actual derivation of one from the other." [1]

Mr. Seebohm juggles with texts and centuries very adroitly, but not by any means enough to create the illusion of continuity which he claims to see himself in going back through the course of the ages. There are yawning gaps in his demonstration.

The alleged proof drawn from the laws of Ethelbert amounts to nothing; the thesis of a Roman England entirely divided into great estates is an absurd improbability; the same is true of the supposition that the Saxon pirates could have come from the centre of Europe. Even when Mr. Seebohm treads on ground which appears more solid, and quotes his documents, he is unconvincing. In fact, from the time that he arrives, in his backward march, at Domesday Book, he loses hold on realities and allows himself to be duped by his fixed idea. He is the sport of a veritable historical mirage, when he sees the whole of England in the eleventh century, covered with manors like those of the thirteenth and cultivated by serfs. Still more misleading is the illusion by which England presents itself to him under the same aspect during the Anglo-Saxon period. According to him, the ceorl is a serf; he is the conquered native; the Saxon conquerors are the lords of manors, the successors of great Roman landowners. He takes no account of the texts which prove the freedom of the ceorl, and the existence of the small landholder; he does not explain at all what became of the mass of the German immigrants who had crossed the North Sea in sufficient numbers to impose their language on the Britons. His mistake is as huge as that of Boulainvilliers, who sought the origin of the French nobility and of feudalism in the supremacy of the Frank conquerors and the subjection of the Gallo-Romans.

1. Stubbs, *op. cit.*, 1, p. 227

Mr. Seebohm's Romanist thesis, despite a brilliant success in the book market, has, in short, turned out but a spent shot. Among English historians of mark Mr. Ashley now stands alone, and with many reservations too, as its defender.[1] But it has had the merit of stimulating the critical spirit and of inducing the moderate Germanists, such as Green or Mr. Vinogradoff, to make concessions which we think justified.

There is, in fact, no necessity to range oneself in either Camp, to be " Germanist " or " Romanist," to **The true** neglect completely, as Stubbs has set the **method** regrettable example of doing, all facts anterior to the Germanic conquest, or to fall, like Coote or Mr. Seebohm, into the opposite extreme.

It is not reasonable to seek a single origin for English institutions, and to pretend to explain by one formula a very complex state of things, which was bound to vary not only in time, but also in space. The eclectic method adopted by Mr. Vinogradoff in his recent work on the " Origin of the Manor," appears to us a very judicious one, and we believe it alone to be capable of leading to the real solution.

To begin with, room must certainly be left for an original element which the uncompromising Germanists **The Celtic** and Romanists alike have, by common **element** consent, ruled out of the discussion : the Celtic element.[2]

1. *The origin of Property in Land*, by Fustel de Coulanges, translated by Margaret Ashley, with an introductory chapter on the English Manor, by W. J. Ashley, 1891; 2nd edition, 1892.—*An introduction to English Economic History*, vol. 1, 3rd edition, 1894, translated by P. Bondois and corrected by the author, under the title of *Hist. des doctrines économiques de l'Angleterre*, 1900, vol. i, pp. 30 sqq.

2. We do not mean to say that England, before the arrival of the Romans and Germans, was peopled by Celts only. There were pre-Celtic populations, perhaps more important as regards numbers, but the Celtic civilization predominated. See a very interesting general sketch of the English races in H. J. Mackinder, *Britain and the British Seas*, 1902, pp. 179 sqq. A summary bibliography of works relative to the Prehistoric and Celtic periods will be found in Gross, *Sources and Literature of English History*, 1900, pp. 157 sqq.

We can get an approximate idea of its character and creative action,—on condition of being content with general conclusions,—by consulting the much later and indirect sources which we possess on Celtic tribal civilization : the Welsh laws especially, the Irish laws, and the information we have on the Scottish clan, or on the Celts of the Continent.[1]

Whatever Mr. Seebohm may say, it is allowable to believe that the Britons, as Pytheas or even Cæsar knew them,[2] had not passed, from an economic point of view, the stage of tribal and still semi-pastoral civilization. Judging by the general history of the Celts and the data of comparative history, they knew nothing similar to the manor. The inferior class called *taeogs* dwelt apart, and did not work for the benefit of the free men. There was neither servile tenure nor even private property in the strict sense of the word. Their principal resource was cattle-rearing ; Celtic agriculture was an extensive superficial agriculture, which required neither careful work, nor capital for the improvement of the soil. It was little fitted to inspire the feeling of individual proprietorship.

On the other hand the method of labour required the spirit of co-operation. The plough was large and heavy ; eight oxen were usually yoked to **Origin of the Open Field** it ; it was so costly a thing that it could only belong to a group of persons, and it is for this reason that, according to the Welsh laws, the land was divided into parcels assigned to the members of each plough-association, one supplying the plough-share, others the oxen, others undertaking to plough and lead the team.[3] An understanding between

1. For all that follows, cf. Vinogradoff, *Growth of the Manor*, pp. 3 sqq.
2. For the fragments of the journal of Pytheas, preserved in various ancient authors, and for Cæsar's description, see J. Rhys, *Celtic Britain*, 2nd edition, 1884, pp. 5 sqq., 53 sqq.
3. Seebohm, *English Village Community*, pp. 122 sqq

the workers being indispensable for ploughing, and individual effort being reduced to a minimum, the conception of private property could not be the same as with our peasantry. The assignation of shares by lot, and the frequent redistribution of these shares were quite

Idea of property

natural things. Finally, the great importance of sheep and cattle rearing, of hunting and fishing was very apt to preserve communist habits. Everything inclines us to believe that in England the English village community and the open field system have their roots in the Celtic tribal civilization.[1]

This probability cannot be rejected unless it can be proved that the Britons were exterminated and their agricultural usages completely rooted out, either by the Romans or by the Anglo-Saxons; and that is a thing which is impossible of proof.

The Romans did not exterminate the Britons, and recent archæological excavations appear to prove that

The Roman element

the manner of living of the native lower classes, their way of constructing their villages and of burying their dead, remained quite unaffected by contact with Roman civilization.[2]

Many regions of Britain entirely escaped this contact, none underwent it very thoroughly. The emperors' chief care was to occupy Britain in a military sense, in order to protect Gaul, and its foggy climate attracted few immigrants.[3]

1. I do not claim, it must be understood, that primitively the open field was peculiar to the Celts. Mr. Vinogradoff is of opinion that the system originated in habits of husbandry common to all the peoples of the North (*Growth of the Manor*, p. 106, Note 58). Mr. Gomme likewise thinks that the village community existed among all the Aryan peoples (*The Village Community*, 1890). This goes to show that these institutions had not been brought into England by foreigners, within historical times.

2. See A. H. L. F. Pitt Rivers, *Excavations in Cranborne Chase*, 1887—1898.

3. These characteristics of the Roman occupation are very well brought out and explained by Green, *Making of England*, 5th edition, 1900, pp. 5 sqq. Mr. Haverfield somewhat exaggerates the Romanisation of

Still the Roman domination lasted for three and a half centuries on the other side of the Channel, and every year English archæologists bring to light some comfortable or luxurious villa, with pavements in mosaic, painted stucco, hypocausts and baths.[1]

Evidently, the Roman officials, like the English in India to-day, knew how to make themselves comfortable;

The Villa they brought with them industries and arts which pleased the higher ranks of the Britons. And this at least must be retained out of the hazardous theories of Mr. Seebohm, that the estate organised on the Italian model, the great landowner living in a fine country house, having the part he had reserved for himself cultivated by slaves, and letting out the rest of his property to *coloni*, were by no means unknown in Britain. By the side of the free Britons grouped in communities, there was a landed aristocracy.

The disturbance caused by the German conquest, by the wholesale immigration of the Angles and Saxons

The Anglo-Saxon element was no doubt immense. Stubbs is justified in appealing to the philological argument; the fact that the Celtic and Latin languages disappeared before Anglo-Saxon is sufficient to prove how thoroughly England was Germanised. But Stubbs is mistaken in looking upon England at the arrival of the Germans as a *tabula rasa*. Wht he calls the ' Anglo-Saxon system ' was not built up on ground that was levelled and bare. It was the interest of the conquerors

---

Britain in the *Introductory Sketch of Roman Britain*, printed at the beginning of the excellent studies which he has written for the *Victoria History of the Counties of England*; for instance, in the *Victoria History of Hampshire*, vol. 1, 1900. See also his *Romanization of Roman Britain* in the *Proceedings of the British Academy*, vol. ii (1905–6). Cf. on the Roman occupation; Vinogradoff, *Growth of the Manor*, pp. 37 sqq., and the chapter by Mr. Thomas Hodgkin, in vol. i of the *Political History of England*, edited by W. Hunt and R. L. Poole, 1906, pp. 52 sqq.

1. See Mr. Haverfield's studies : *Victoria History of Hampshire*, vol. i, 1900 ; *Worcester*, vol. i, 1901 ; *Norfolk*, vol. i, 1901 ; *Northamptonshire*, vol. i, 1902 ; *Warwickshire*, vol. i, 1904 ; *Derbyshire*, vol. i, 1905, etc.

to utilise the remains of Roman civilization. Nor is it by

Persistence of the earlier agrarian customs

any means proved that where they settled they exterminated the native population.[1] They had no aversion to the usages of the open field, and could quickly accustom themselves to live side by side with the British peasants. The Celtic tribal communities would be absorbed in the village communities formed by the *ceorls*. At the same time, the very great inequality which prevailed among the Anglo-Saxons, the development of royal dynasties and ealdorman families richly endowed with land, and, lastly, the grants made to the Church, necessarily preserved the great estate, cultivated with the help of ' theows ' or slaves and of *coloni*.

Nevertheless, for the establishment of the seignorial system in England it was not enough that there were

Tendencies towards a new classification of society

rich men and ' theows.' The predominance of the small freehold, the existence of numerous ' ceorls ' cultivating their hide[2] and members of independent communities, were incompatible with the general estab-

lishment of the manorial system. A new classification of

1. J. Rhys, *Celtic Britain*, pp. 109–110. See also R. A. Smith in the *Victoria History of Hampshire*, vol. i, p. 376; he gives the bibliography of the question.

2. The hide has been the subject of numberless controversies. There is a whole literature on the question, and the subject is not exhausted, for the good reason that the term has several meanings, and the hide was not, as a matter of fact, a fixed measure. Stubbs states that the hide of the Norman period " was no doubt a hundred and twenty or a hundred acres " (*Const. Hist.*, i, p. 79). But he should have drawn a distinction between the fiscal hide, which was a unit of taxation, and the real or field hide. Mr. Round (*Feudal England*, 1895, pp. 36 sqq.; see also *Victoria History of Bedfordshire*, 1904, vol. i, pp. 191—193) and Professor Maitland (*Domesday Book and Beyond*, pp. 357 sqq.) have shown the artificial character of the Domesday hide. This hide was very generally divided into 120 fractions called acres [for fiscal hides of fewer acres see Vinogradoff, *Growth of the Manor*, p. 155], but these appellations did not correspond to any fixed reality, any more than did the " ploughland " (*carrucata*) and the " sulung " or the French "hearths" of the Middle Ages. The *hide* (or *hiwisc, hiwshp*), in its other sense, the primitive one, which it continued to retain alongside its fiscal sense, denoted the quantity (obviously variable according to locality) of

society had to come into existence; some freemen had to descend in the social scale, while others raised themselves. This transformation was inevitable in an age in which the old bonds of tribe and family no longer sufficed to give security to the individual, and in which the royal power was not yet able to ensure it. Throughout Christendom patronage and commendation, along with private appropriation of public powers, paved the way for a new political and social system.

The Anglo-Saxon kings, under the pressure of necessities which were not peculiar to them, at an early period bestowed on their thegns and on churches either lands or the rights which they possessed over some village and the community of freemen who dwelt there. Thenceforward such thegns or churches levied on their own account the taxes, dues and supplies hitherto due to the king; for example, the profitable *firma unius noctis*. Armed with this right the recipient became the lord of the free village, the peasants commended themselves to him,[1] and the parcel of land or the house which he possessed in the neighbourhood became a centre of manorial organisation; the lands of the peasants who had commended themselves came ultimately to be considered as in some way held of him. The grant of judicial rights (*sac and soc*) was also a powerful instrument of subjection. When a church or thegn received a grant of sac and soc in a district the rights

Gifts of land and royal rights to thegns and churches

Commendation

Sac and Soc

arable land and rights of common necessary for the maintenance of a family. The actual number of acres in the real hide was often 120, but not always. The hide is not therefore an agrarian measure; it is the unit of landed property, the *terra familiae*, and we must doubtless conclude that the hundred was an aggregation of a hundred of these hides. See Vinogradoff, *Growth of the Manor*, pp. 141, 151 sqq., 170, 250, Note 33. Stubbs says elsewhere (*op. cit.* p. 185) that "the hide is the provision of a family." He ought to have adhered to that definition.

1. On Anglo-Saxon commendation, see Maitland, *Domesday Book and Beyond*, p. 69; Pollock and Maitland, *History of English Law*, vol. i, pp. 30, 31.

so conferred were exercised, either in the court of the hundred or in whatever popular court it pleased the grantee to set up; the reeve of the church or thegn presided over the court and received the fines. Stubbs ascribes the beginning of grants of sac and soc to the reign of Canute; but Mr. Maitland makes them go back to the seventh century.[1]

The evolution which was carrying England towards the seignorial régime became a very much speedier process in consequence of the struggles against the Danes in the ninth and tenth centuries. Professional soldiers, expensively armed, were alone capable of arresting this new wave of barbarians, and they necessarily became privileged persons. Military service was henceforth the obligation and attribute of thegns. Most of them had at least five hides, that is to say, landed property five times as large as the old normal family holding, and the revenue of their estates allowed them, with the serjeants whom they maintained (*geneats, radknights, drengs*) to devote themselves entirely to the profession of arms. A deeply defined division began to show itself between these thegns or *twelfhynd-men* and the simple *ceorls* or *twyhynd-men*,[2] who continued to till the land and lost their old warlike character, that is to say, their best title to the privileges of a freeman. There remained soldiers on the one hand and tillers of the soil on the other. Labour in the fields had been formerly the occupation of every freeman; it was henceforward a sign of inferiority. At the same time the old tradition of the inalienable family holding grew weaker, many of the ceorls no longer had the hide necessary for maintaining a household and the

Results of the struggle against the Danes

Military and landed aristocracy

1. Maitland, *Domesday Book and Beyond*, pp. 80 sqq., 226 sqq., 236 sqq., 258 sqq., 318 sqq.; Vinogradoff, *Growth of the Manor*, pp. 212 sqq.

2. On the meaning of the terms *twelfhynd-men* and *twyhynd-men*, see below, pp. 36 sqq.

virgate, the quarter of a hide,[1] became the common type of small freehold. To escape calamity therefore men were obliged to abase themselves before some powerful neighbour. Little by little, for reasons at once economic and political, the bonds of dependence were drawn closer between the "liber pauper" and the thegn, rich, esteemed, endowed by the king with a portion of public authority, and become, as it were, his responsible representative in the district.[2] This formation of a military and landed aristocracy is a general phenomenon in the history of the West, which explains, in France as in England, the decay of the small freeholders and the definitive entrance of the seignorial system.

Domesday Book, drawn up twenty years after the Norman invasion, allows us to form some idea of the state of rural England at the end of the Anglo-Saxon period. It is a document bristling with difficulties, and of baffling obscurity. But, since the appearance of the ' Constitutional History,' it has been the subject of a number of admirable studies, some of which were known to Stubbs and might have been utilised more by him in the last editions of his work. Mr. Round has elucidated some particularly thorny questions in his *Feudal England,* and he and other scholars are at present furnishing the editors of the *Victoria History of the Counties of England* with a detailed examination, county by county, of all the historical information that *Domesday* Book contains. Mr. Maitland has drawn a masterly picture of Anglo-Saxon society in the eleventh century in his *Domesday Book and Beyond,* an at times daring but extremely suggestive synthesis, one of the finest books which

The England of Domesday Book

---

1. On the Virgate, see Vinogradoff, *Villainage*, p. 239; J. Tait, *Hides and virgates at Battle Abbey*, in *English Historical Review*, xviii, 1903, pp. 705 sqq.
2. Maitland, *Domesday Book*, pp. 163 sqq.; Vinogradoff, *Growth of the Manor*, pp. 216 sqq.: A. G. Little, *Gesiths and Thegns*, in *English Historical Review*, iv, 1889, pp. 723 sqq.

C

English scholarship has produced. Finally Mr. Vinogradoff, in his *Villainage in England* and his quite recent *Growth of the Manor* [and *English Society in the Eleventh Century*], has put forth solutions which deserve the most favourable attention.

The very nature of the document, the end King William had in view in commanding this great inquest, are sufficiently mysterious to begin with.

Difficulties of interpretation For Mr. Round and Mr. Maitland, Domesday is a fiscal document, a " Geld-Book " designed to facilitate an equitable imposition of the Danegeld. Mr. Vinogradoff reverts to an older and more comprehensive definition, and believes that the royal commissioners wished not only to prepare the way for the collection of the tax, but also to discriminate the ties which united the subjects of the king to one another, and to know, from one end of England to the other, from whom each piece of land was held ; in this way alone the political and administrative responsibilities of the lords in their relation to the king could be fixed.[1] We now understand why England, as the commissioners describe it, seems to be already divided into manors. Mr. Seebohm allowed himself to be misled by this appearance.[2] In reality the agents of the king spoke of manors where there were none, where there was nothing but a piece of land with a barn, capable of becoming some day a centre of manorial organisation ; for it was of importance for the schemes of the Norman monarchy that the seignorial system should be extended everywhere.

1. *Growth of the Manor*, pp. 292 sqq.
2. Mr. Maitland, on the contrary, puts in sharp relief the contrast which exists between the manor of *Domesday Book* and the manor of the 13th century. He concludes that the manor of *Domesday* is not the seignorial estate, but the place at which the geld is received (*Domesday Book and Beyond*, pp. 119 sqq.). This theory is untenable. See J. Tait, in *English Historical Review*, xii, 1897, pp. 770—772 ; Round, *ibidem*, xv, 1900, pp. 293 sqq., *Victoria History of Hampshire*, i, 443, *Victoria History of Bedfordshire*, i, 210 ; Lapsley, *Vict. Hist. of Durham*, i, 260 ; Salzmann, *Vict. Hist. of Sussex*, i, 355 ; Vinogradoff, *Growth of the Manor*, pp. 300 sqq.

Moreover, the nomenclature used is a source of perplexity and mistakes; the compilers often use Norman terms; the names they choose sometimes change their meaning later, so much so that they have become subject of controversy amongst modern scholars.

The difficulty, then, of an exact interpretation of *Domesday Book* is great. And even when the necessary
Social precautions have been taken, it is a
complexity peculiarly arduous task to elicit from the document a clear description of Anglo-Saxon society *tempore regis Edwardi.*

Stubbs shows well how extraordinary was its complexity, what variety the ties created by commendation and gifts of land presented, and how diverse the personal and territorial relations were. The small freehold still existed side by side with the great estate; the most populous region, the Danelaw,[1] was a country of free husbandmen, of village communities.[2] Not only were there lands which belonged neither to thegns nor to churches, but there were, in the England of Edward the Confessor, whole villages, and in large numbers, in which the fiscal and judicial rights of the king had not fallen into private hands, nor did such villages form part of the royal demesne properly so called.
Ties of But the free husbandmen were for all that
Dependence involved in the ties of dependence, as, indeed, were their lords, for the thegns were themselves thegns of an ealdorman, or a church, or another thegn, or the queen, or the king.[3]

1. On the extent of the Danelaw or Danish district, see a note of Mr. Hodgkin, in the *Political History of England,* edited by R. L. Poole and W. Hunt, i, 1906, pp. 315—317 [and Chadwick, *Anglo-Saxon Institutions,* p. 198].

2. Mr. Maitland remarks on the need of guarding against the temptation that assails those who have read Domesday Book, to see great estates everywhere at the end of the Anglo-Saxon period (*Domesday Book and Beyond,* pp. 64, 168 sqq.).

3. Maitland, *Domesday Book,* p. 162. Upon the *láen-lands* granted by the Church to the thegns, see *ibidem,* pp. 301 sqq.

The same personal or territorial ties which attached the members of the military aristocracy to one another established infinitely varied relations between them and the rest of the free population. The *liberi homines commendatione tantum* could leave their lord when they wished, for they had not subjected their land to him, and they had the right to " recedere cum terra sua absque licentia domini sui." [1] Sometimes, on the other hand, the *commendatio* attached the land to the lord, and if the land was sold, it remained under the commendation of the same lord. In certain cases the land belongs to a *soc,* and he who buys it has to recognise the judicial rights of the lord. Finally, the Freeman may hold a *terra consuetudinaria* and owe dues or agricultural services; such are the *sochemanni cum omni consuetudine* [2] in the eastern counties, whom the compilers of *Domesday Book* would have called *villani* in another part of England.[3]

This last expression has been the source of mistaken theories which Messrs. Maitland and Vinogradoff have
The villeins of Domesday Book fully succeeded in clearing out of the way. In the eyes of Mr. Seebohm especially all the *villani* of *Domesday Book* were villeins in the sense which the word acquired later on in England, that is, peasants subject to personal servitude.[4] In reality, the term has no legal sense here; *villanus* is the translation of *tunesman,* man of the village; he is, according to Mr. Vinogradoff, a member of the village community, who possesses the normal share in the open field. He has the same wergild as the *sochemannus*

1. See the numerous passages quoted by Round, *Feudal England,* pp. 24 sqq.
2. *Ibidem,* pp. 31 sqq.
3. On the sokeman of *Domesday Book,* see Maitland, *Domesday Book and Beyond,* pp. 66, 104 sqq.; Vinogradoff, *Manor,* p. 341; [*English Society,* pp. 124, 431.]
4. *English Village Community,* pp. 89—104. In his *Tribal Custom in Anglo-Saxon Law,* 1902, p. 504, Mr. Seebohm begs that this servitude may not be confounded with slavery.

and, like him, owes only agricultural services fixed by custom and very light; by the side of the land he holds from a lord he may have an independent holding. In a general way at least, the *villein* of *Domesday* is a free man, a descendant of the ceorl, the twyhynd-man.[1]

This social state, further complicated by the persistence of slavery, was the natural product of very remote

The Norman element

antecedents, the fruit of the development and friction of several superimposed races, the spontaneous and varied forces, in a country where the pressure of the central power was extremely feeble. Neither the adventurers who followed William the Bastard is order to obtain a fine ' guerdon,' nor the servants of the Norman monarchy were disposed to respect this composite and bizarre edifice on which so many centuries had left their mark. They left standing only what was useful to them or did not inconvenience them. The Norman Conquest, begun by brutal soldiers and completed by jurists of orderly and logical mind, was to have for its effect the systematizing of the social grouping and its simplification at the expense of the weakest.

In fact and in law, the most original features of Anglo-Saxon society disappeared. In fact, during the hard

Result of the conquest for the native rural classes

years which followed the landing of William the natives who were not massacred or expelled from their dwelling [2] had to

---

1. Maitland, *op. cit.* pp. 38 sqq. ; Vinogradoff, *Manor*, pp. 339 sqq. Mr. Maitland remarks also, with reason, that the conception of personal liberty is extremely difficult to fix in this period and throughout the whole of the Middle Ages; cf. the remarks of Stubbs (*Const. Hist.*, i, 83). See also Seebohm, *Tribal Custom*, p. 430.

2. Here is an example of the expulsion of a humble peasant : "Ricardus de Tonebrige tenet de hoc manerio unam virgatam cum silva unde abstulit rusticum qui ibi manebat " (*Domesday*, quoted by Maitland, *op. cit.* p. 61, note 5). The difficulty is to know if these cases, which cannot all have been mentioned in Domesday, were numerous. Stubbs has preferred to discuss this difficult question of the spoliation of the Anglo-Saxon proprietors, and the transfer of their lands to the companions of the Conqueror, only incidentally and without dwelling upon it. To what

accept the conquerors' terms.   The small freeholders were
reduced to a subordinate condition.   The lands they held
without being accountable for them to anyone were given

degree were the native English deprived of their estates?   What were
the new families which were established in England.   At the time when
Stubbs wrote his book, *Domesday Book* had perhaps not been studied
enough for it to be possible to reply to questions like these.   Stubbs
speaks with great reserve while giving proof of his habitual perspicacity.
Augustin Thierry believed in an expropriation *en masse*, without however
basing his thesis on serious arguments.   Reacting against this view,
Freeman claimed that a large number of natives kept their lands; as is
well known, he generally tries to reduce to a minimum the results of
the Norman Conquest.   Stubbs notes (vol. i, p. 281, note 2) the confiscation with which William punished the declared partisans of
Harold and quotes on that head the passage in the *Dialogus de
Scaccario* (i, c. x; ed. Hughes, etc., p. 100); but he does not believe
that the bulk of the small owners were dispossessed.   " The actual
amount of dispossession was greatest in the higher ranks; the smaller
owners to a large extent remained in a mediatised position on their
estates."   Mr. Round, in the studies which the *Victoria History* is at
present publishing, hesitates to formulate a very decided opinion on
this difficult subject; but he rejects the view of Freeman more
completely than does Stubbs : " So far as we can judge all but a few
specially favoured individuals were deprived of the lands they had held,
or at most were allowed to retain a fragment or were placed in subjection to a Norman lord.   And even the exceptions, there is reason to
believe, were further reduced after Domesday " (*Victoria Hist of Bedfordshire*, i, 1904, pp. 206–207).   He confesses elsewhere that "great
obscurity still surrounds the process by which the English holders were
dispossessed by the strangers.   The magnates, no doubt, were dispossessed either at the opening of William's reign or, on various pretexts,
in the course of it " (*Vict. Hist. of Warwickshire*, i, 1904, p. 282).   Mr.
Round, it is obvious, does not believe in an immediate and methodical
dispossession, but he considers that the cases in which an Englishman
was fortunate enough to escape the storm were rare.   Certain natives,
like Oda of Winchester, particularly favoured by the Conqueror, lost
their old estates and received others in their place : " In this, no doubt,
there was deep policy; for they would henceforth hold by his own grant
alone, and would be led, moreover, to support his rule against the
English holders they had dispossessed " (*Vict. Hist of Hampshire*, i,
1900, pp. 427–428.   See also *Essex*, i, 1903, pp. 354–355; *Buckinghamshire*, i, 1905, p. 217).   Saving these not very numerous exceptions, the
Conquest, in Mr. Round's opinion, was a great misfortune for all the
English.   Let us remark that it is necessary to distinguish between the
counties, and that on the borders of the kingdom, dispossession was
more difficult.   Mr. W. Farrer (*Victoria Hist. of Lancashire*, i, 1906,
283) considers that, in the region which under Henry II became the
county of Lancaster, the greater number of the manors were held in the
12th century by descendants of the old Anglo-Saxon owners.   With
regard to the families from the Continent who were endowed with lands
in England, many new details and rectifications will be found in Mr.
Round's articles.   He rightly insists in the pages he devote to Northamptonshire, that the conquerers were far from being all Normans; in
Northampshire, there were many Flemings and Picards (*Vict. History
of Northamptonshire*, i, 1902, pp. 289 sqq.).

to Norman lords, and they could only continue to cultivate them by submitting to an oppressive system of dues and services; the same heavy burdens, of course, pressed upon the estates formerly held in dependence on a thegn, where rents and services had still been light.[1]

Domesday Book shows us a certain Ailric, who had a fine estate of four hides, now obliged to hold it at farm from a Norman lord, " graviter et miserabiliter;"[2] it speaks of free men forcibly incorporated in a manor, " ad perficiendum manerium,"[3] of the creation of new dues and the augmentation of the old. The diminution in the number of the *sochemanni* in the first twenty years of William's reign is characteristic : in the county of Cambridge there are no more than 213 of them instead of 900; 700 have descended to an inferior social rank.[4] In the county of Hertford the decadence of this class is equally striking.[5]   In short, small free ownership has received a mortal blow, and the anarchy of Stephen's reign will complete the founding of the seignorial or manorial system.[6]

In law, the legal theory of ownership changed. All land, outside the royal demesne, was held of some one,
New theory of ownership. Tenure   was a tenement, that is, the subject of a dependent tenure, and the principle of " no land without a lord " was introduced into England.   In addition every tenure involved

1. Upon the whole of this question and upon the arguments drawn from the later condition of the peasants of the Ancient Demesne of the Crown and of Kent, see Maitland, *Domesday Book*, pp. 60 sqq.; Vinogradoff, *Villainage*, pp. 89 sqq., 205 sqq.; *Growth of the Manor*, pp. 295 sqq., 316 sqq.

2. Passage quoted by Maitland, *op. cit.* p. 61, note 3.

3. *Ibidem*, pp. 127–128.

4. *Ibidem*, pp. 62, 63.   On these statistics of *Domesday*, see Maitland, *op. cit.* p. 17; Round, *Victoria History of Hampshire*, i, p. 433.

5. Round, in *Victoria History of Hertfordshire*, i, 1902, pp. 265 sqq.

6. On the troubles of Stephen's reign, see Stubbs, *Const. Hist.*, i, 353 sqq.; H. W. C. Davis, *The Anarchy of Stephen's reign*, in *English Historical Review*, xviii, 1903, pp. 630 sqq.; Vinogradoff, *Villainage*, pp. 218–219.

some service. The military class definitively constituted itself in England in the eleventh and twelfth centuries, based on the very simple rule that a fief carries with it service in the army. In the same way the peasants were all tenants owing dues and generally manual labour; the conditions of their tenure became the essential criterion of their social rank. The manifold distinctions which divide the rural population in the Anglo-Saxon perod, and of which traces remain in *Domesday Book,* were effaced under the double pressure of the seignorial authority and the common law. Slavery, which was repugnant to the habits of the Normans, and was in no sort of harmony with the principles of manorial exploitation,[1] completely disappeared. In the thirteenth century there are on the land only freeholders, perhaps in small numbers,[2] and villeins. It is, above all, the burdens of tenure in villeinage which constitute villein status, and the legal presumption of villeinage; he is not free who performs for his lord a " servile work," such as manuring the land or cleaning the ditches.[3]

Two kinds of rural tenure

1. See Maitland, *Domesday Book*, pp. 35–36.
2. See the case of the manor of Wilburton in Mr. Maitland's monograph, *English Historical Review*, ix, 1894, p. 418.
3. It is true that, if we examine the legal and manorial records relative to villeinage, matters are not so simple. The lawyers considered the villein as in a state of personal servitude towards his lord. *Servus, nativus, villanus,* are the same thing. The villein belongs, body and chattels, to his lord, has not the right to leave him, must pay *merchetum* when he marries his daughter. The reason is that the villeins of the thirteenth century were not descended only from the ancient Anglo-Saxon ceorls, the *villani* of *Domesday Book*, free men whom the troubles of the times had compelled to enter into the manorial organisation, to accept an aggravation of dues and services; there were also many villeins descended from Anglo-Saxon slaves (*theows*; *servi* of *Domesday*). The villein class of the English Middle Ages sprang from this fusion. The Norman lord treated the ceorls burdened with labour-services and the theows alike; the theows gained thereby, but the ceorls lost; by contact with the slaves who became their equals they contracted some of the marks of servitude which degraded their companions, and the dying institution of slavery did not disappear without leaving stains behind it. Nevertheless, in practice, this personal servitude to which the villeins and not the freeholders are subject has no great importance. The conditions of tenure are the important thing. And here is a striking

For the rest, we must not exaggerate the difference which, in the thirteenth century, separated the tenant in villeinage and the tenant in socage. From the economic point of view, their burdens differ in quality and quantity, but they are very nearly equivalent. From the point of view of the defence of his rights the freeholder is protected by the royal courts, while the villein has generally no action against his lord; but, in fact, he is perfectly protected against arbitrary treatment by the custom of the manor. Finally, as we have seen, he forms part of the village community by the same title as the freeholder.[1]

Slight differ-
ence between
these two kinds
of tenure

We have thus arrived again at the point from which we started. We have seen how the masters of English mediæval scholarship reply just now to the questions we put to ourselves. Even if we put on one side those who claim to explain the problems of the manor, the open field, villeinage and the village community by a Romanist theory which certainly cannot be accepted, these historians are far from being in agreement on all points. Mr. Maitland is a Germanist after the manner of Stubbs; the internal development of Anglo-Saxon society seems to him to be the key to all these mysteries; he willingly recognises the effects of the great catastrophe of 1066; but, for him, the seignorial system already existed in England at the end of the

Conclusion

proof : the free peasants who have succeeded in not allowing themselves to be assimilated to the *servi*, the freeholders, or tenants in *socage*, are considered free as long as they have a free holding, burdened only with light and occasional services; if they accept a villein tenement, they come to be considered as serfs, personally dependent on their lord, pay the merchetum and are even called villeins, like the others. They can lawfully leave their holding, but they do not avail themselves of this right of renouncing their means of existence; and thus the tenement in villeinage imposes the status of a villein on him who takes it up. On the whole question, see Vinogradoff, *Villainage*, pp. 43 sqq., 127 sqq.; *Growth of the Manor*, pp. 296 sqq., 343 sqq.; Pollock and Maitland, *History of English Law*, 2nd edition, 1898, i, pp. 356 sqq.

1. Vinogradoff, *Villainage*, pp. 81 sqq., 308 sqq.

Saxon period, as well as feudalism. Mr. Round has not approached these great questions as a whole, and has only thrown light on certain aspects of them; without doubt he looks on them from an entirely different point of view to that of Mr. Maitland.[1]

Finally, Mr. Vinogradoff refuses to begin the history of the English rural classes at the invasion of the Anglo-Saxon pirates. According to him, the village community and the customs of the open field had their roots in a distant antiquity, and maintained themselves without great change throughout all catastrophes, as very humble things, which do not inconvenience the conquerors and adapt themselves to their plans, can do. The pattern of the great manorial estate was set in England as early as the Roman period, but the 'manor' did not become general until very much later, as a result of the formation of a rich military aristocracy, which as early as the Anglo-Saxon period began to establish its economic and political dominance over the remainder of the freemen, and was replaced, after the Conquest of 1066, by the powerful Norman feudal baronage. With the triumph of the manorial system coincided perforce the disappearance of small free ownership and the appearance of villeinage.

This last solution is the one which we believe to conform most closely to the documents as a whole, to the data of general history, and to common sense. It is, nevertheless, only a provisional solution. It must be supported by more thorough and extensive study of documents, and it will be beyond all doubt rectified on more than one point. The question of the origin of the English village community particularly still remains very obscure. To resolve it, we must be better informed than we are about the Anglo-Saxon village. As Mr. Vinogradoff has remarked, its organisation was not changed by way of

Doubts concerning the village community

1. See *Feudal England*, p. 262.

legislation, and the modest concerns discussed by the
ceorls did not excite the curiosity of the historians of
that day, so that neither the laws nor the chronicles give
us sufficient information on the rural community. It
existed undoubtedly; it watched over the collective concerns; but in what degree was it organised? Have we
any right to apply to the Anglo-Saxon township what we
know of the township of the thirteenth and fourteenth
centuries, as Mr. Vinogradoff has boldly done?[1] Mr.
Maitland advises caution, and without doubt he is right.
He remarks that the communal affairs that had to be
transacted in a free village were very few in number
and that many of these villages were very small.[2]

We do not know what influence the Norman Conquest
had upon the development of the rural communities.

**The Norman
point of view**
Did it curtail their freedom, or, on the
other hand, did the Norman lords think it
profitable to their interests to organise the
village more thoroughly. We must discuss the
question afresh, as Mr. Round, we shall see, has done
in the case of military tenure, placing ourselves at the
Norman point of view. English historians would do
well to give more serious attention to M. Leopold
Delisle's book on the agricultural class in Normandy.
It is well to remember that servitude disappeared very
early on the Norman estates; that the communities of
inhabitants " exercised most of the rights appertaining
to the true communes," that in the twelfth century some
of them had the services which their lord could demand
of them legally recognised, and that as early as the
time of William the Conqueror we see the peasants of
Benouville acting in a body and giving their church to
the nuns of the Trinity at Caen.[3] It would be desirable,

1. *Growth of the Manor*, p. 185 sqq.
2. *Domesday Book and Beyond*, pp. 20, 21, 148 sqq.
3. Delisle, *Etude sur la condition de la classe agricole en Normandie,*
1851, pp. 137 sqq.

also, to keep in mind that " the companions of William, in whom many people see nothing but the spoilers of the wealth of the Anglo-Savons, in more than one way renewed the face of England. We must not forget that most of them were great agriculturists."[1]

1. *Ibid.*, p. 251.

II.

FOLKLAND.

WAS THERE A " PUBLIC LAND " AMONG THE ANGLO-SAXONS ?

FOLLOWING Allen,[1] and along with all the scholars who have dealt with this question after Allen,[2] up to but
Mistake of Allen
exluding Mr. Vinogradoff, Stubbs in the earlier editions of his book, gave to the Anglo-Saxon expression *folk-land* the meaning of "land of the people," *ager publicus,* and expounded a whole theory of this alleged institution. In 1893, Mr. Vinogradoff showed decisively that Allen was mistaken.[3] To this conclusive refutation Mr. Maitland, 1897, added new arguments; he adopted, reproduced and completed it in a chapter of his *Domesday Book and Beyond.*[4]

Stubbs was evidently acquainted with the works of these two great jurists, although he does not expressly
Attitude of Stubbs
quote them; in the last edition of his *Constitutional History* he alludes to the new explanation of the word *folkland,* given by " legal antiquaries,"[5] and has even obviously altered some passages of his work, in which he spoke incidentally of

1. John Allen, *Inquiry into the rise and progress of the royal prerogative in England*, 1830; 2nd ed., 1849, pp. 125—153.
2. Kemble, Freeman, Thorpe, Lodge, Pollock, Gneist, Waitz, Sohm, Brunner, etc.
3. P. Vinogradoff, *Folkland* in *English Historical Review*, viii, 1893, pp. 1—17. Cf. Stubbs' somewhat ambiguous note (*Const. Hist.*, i, p. 81). See also Vinogradoff, *The Growth of the Manor*, 1905, pp. 142–143 and 244–245.
4. *Book-land and Folk-land*, in *Domesday Book and Beyond*, pp. 244–258.
5. Stubbs, i, p. 81, note 2.

folkland.[1] But his readers may ask themselves whether he accepts the opinion of Professors Vinogradoff and Maitland or no even as regards the meaning of the word. For, in several other passages, he lets the older interpretation of Allen [2] stand; elsewhere he tells us that " the change of learned opinion as to the meaning of *folkland* involves certain alterations in the terminology, but does not seem to militate against the idea of the public land ";[3] and he maintains his theory on the Anglo-Saxon *ager publicus,* when in reality it is impossible to admit its existence, if we adopt the conclusions of Mr. Vinogradoff on the meaning of the word folkland, as we are bound to do. An extraordinary confusion results from this hesitation of Stubbs, which, in view of the great and legitimate authority of the *Constitutional History,* will contribute to uphold a view of whose erroneousness there can be no doubt.[4]

It is important to warn readers of Stubbs that : (1) folkland does not mean public land ; (2) that there was not in Anglo-Saxon England any " public land " distinct from the royal demesne.

The term *folkland* is to be found in three texts only ; a law and two charters. According to a law of Edward
the Elder (900—924 ?) it appears that all
Use of the word folkland suits concerning landed property might be classed in two categories : suits regarding folkland, and suits regarding bookland.[5] One of the

1. Compare especially the editions of 1891 and 1903 in § § 54 (p. 144) and 75 (p. 209).
2. See in the edition of 1903, the unfortunate use of the word *folkland* on pages 100, 118, 131, 138 and above all on page 202. This use is in contradiction with the previous explanation of the term in note 2 on. p. 81. It is evident that Stubbs would have substituted *public land* for *folkland,* if these passages had not escaped him in his revision.
3. *Ibid.,* i, p. 83, note 2.
4. The old mistake about folkland is reproduced in Mr. Ballard's recent book, *Domesday Boroughs,* 1904, p. 124.
5. Edward I, 2, in Liebermann, *Gesetze der Angelsachsen,* I, pp. 140–141.

two charters is a charter of exchange, granted by King
Ethelbert in 858; it is in Latin; in the text there is no
mention of folkland, but a note in Anglo-Saxon on the
back of the document indicates that the king has
converted into folkland a piece of land which he has
received in exchange for another.[1] The third document
is the will of the ealdorman Alfred, a document from the
last third of the ninth century; it deals with a piece of
land which is folkland and which the ealdorman wished
to pass on to his son (according to all appearances an
illegitimate son). He recognises that his son cannot enter
into possession of this land unless the king consents.[2]

In these three documents folkland is opposed not to
private property, but to bookland, that is to say, land

**" Folkland "
opposed to
" bookland "** held by charter. All sorts of difficulties
begin to appear if we understand by folk-
land the " land of the people," and, as
Mr. Vinogradoff has ingeniously shown, the scholars
who have followed Allen's interpretation have made
additions to it, in order to maintain it intact, by which
it has been rendered, really, more and more unacceptable. These difficulties vanish and the three texts
become as clear as possible if we return to the
explanation of the word folkland proposed in the
seventeenth century by Spelman. Folk-

**and signifies
land held by
custom** land signifies not the land of the people,
public land, but the land held by popular
custom, by folk-right. Bookland is the
land held under franchises formally expressed in a
charter, a *book* : under the influence of the Church and
in consequence of the laws enacted by the king and the
witenagemot, this more recent kind of property escaped
old usages, and he who held it might dispose of it at
his will, whilst folkland, at least in principle, was
inalienable. It becomes clear to us that the law of

1. Kemble, *Codex diplomaticus aevi Saxonici*, ii, pp. 64—66, No. 281.
2. *Ibidem*, p. 120, No. 317.

Edward the Elder classifies every kind of property under the two rubrics of land held by custom and land held by a charter,[1] that King Ethelbert is converting a newly-acquired estate into folkland, inalienable property ; that the consent of the king is necessary for the transmission to a bastard of folkland, a family estate subject to customary restrictions.

Thus folkland does not mean " public land." Stubbs gives his adhesion to this view a little unwillingly, it would seem,[2] in the passages he has carefully revised and corrected. But he maintains that there existed, at least until the end of the period of the Heptarchy,[3] a public land belonging to the people and distinct from the royal demesne. It was " the whole area, which was not at the original allotment assigned either to individuals or to communities. . . . It constituted the standing treasury of the country ; no alienation of any part of it could be made without the consent of the national council. . . . Estates for life were created out of the public land . . . the benficiary could express a

Stubbs maintains that there was a public land

1. The classification of the law of Edward, which recognises only folkland and bookland, *oththe on bóclande oththe on folclande*, would be incomplete and surprisingly erroneous, if folkland signified "land of the people." It would leave out of account family property transmitted hereditarily, as distinguished from holdings burdened with services ; yet such property certainly existed then. It is doubtless this difficulty which has led certain defenders of Allen's thesis to suppose, without a shadow of proof, that the hereditary family estate had disappeared at an early date. There was another difficulty : this land, had existed in any case ; was it not strange that no term denoting it specially was to be found in the Anglo-Saxon texts? This objection had already struck Kemble. As they did not realise that family landed property was called in Anglo-Saxon *folkland*, they sought for a name for it. Hence the terms *ethel* (invented by Kemble), *yrfeland* (invented by Pollock), to which Stubbs has made the mistake of giving currency. (See *Const. Hist.*, p. 81, note 2 ; compare, however, p. 80, note 1, restriction of the word *ethel*.) These appellations are not and cannot be founded on the authorities, for the good reason that the word denoting this kind of property was *folkland*.

2. In note 3 of vol. i, p. 81. Stubbs appears to hesitate and speaks of the "much contested term *folkland*."

3. " The public land," Stubbs supposes, " was becoming virtually king's land from the moment the West-Saxon monarch became sole ruler of the English." (*op. cit.* p. 212, cf. p. 100.)

wish concerning their destination in his will, but an express act of the king and the *witan* was necessary to give legal force to such a disposition. . . . . . The tribute derived from what remained of the public land and the revenue of the royal demesne sufficed for the greater part of the expenses of the royal house, etc." [1]

On what authorities is this theory founded? Stubbs, usually so precise, does not quote his authorities in his notes, speaks vaguely of "charters." It is easy to see that, whilst appearing to accept the interpretation of the word folkland which Mr. Vinogradoff rediscovered in Spelman, Stubbs retains a historical theory founded principally on the three texts of which we have just been speaking and on the erroneous explanation of the word folkland. His expression, quoted above, respecting the possessor of an estate in public land, who expresses a desire in his will with regard to the destination of that estate, is founded solely on the will of ealdorman Alfred; [2] now, as we have seen, Alfred expresses a wish relative to his *folkland,* which as a matter of fact is a family estate, and not a portion of *ager publicus.*

It has been claimed, it is true, that other documents in which the term folkland is not used, attest the existence of an Anglo-Saxon *ager publicus.* Mr.
Letter from Bede to Egbert Vinogradoff has clearly shown how unjustifiable such an interpretation is. The most celebrated of these documents is a letter of Bede to Egbert: the pseudo-monasteries of his time had caused so many estates, *tot. loca,* to be given to them, that there did not remain enough to endow the sons of the nobles and warriors, *ut omnino desit locus ubi filii nobilium aut emeritorum militum possessionem accipere possint.* Stubbs concludes from this that "the sons of

---

1. See especially *Const. Hist.,* i, pp. 82-83, 202-203, 212. See also pp. 118, 127, note 4, 131, 138, 159, 302, etc.
2. It may be noted too that, in the document, there is mention of the consent of the king, but the *witan* are not referred to.

the nobles and the warriors who had earned their rest looked for at least a life estate out of the, public land.[1] Who can fail to see that this translation of the words *loca, locus,* has arisen from a preconceived idea? It is perfectly allowable to suppose that the grants of which Bede speaks were made from the royal demesne. In England, as in France, men complained of the alienations from the royal demesne, or at least of the manner in which they were effected. That is all that Bede's letter proves.

It was doubtless with a view to restraining the imprudence of which Bede speaks that in the following century the witan intervened in matters of alienation of the demesne. The consent of the Witenagemot to alienations of land is an incontestable and interesting fact, but it has not the significance Stubbs attributes to it. We must begin by remarking with Mr. Maitland that this consent is at first very seldom expressed,—four times only in charters anterior to 750; it becomes habitual in the ninth century, then falls in desuetude, and from about 900 or 925 onwards is replaced by the mere mention of the confirmation by witnesses.[2] Again, there is no reason to attach a very special importance to the intervention of the witan in cases of alienation, since they dealt with all kinds of business; their very extensive political rôle is one of the characteristic features of Anglo-Saxon institutions. Finally, the mention we have of the consent of the witan in no wise confers more probability on the theory that there existed a public land distinct from the royal demesne. In the often quoted charter of 858 the land which Ethelbert alienates with the consent of his witan is called *terra juric mei.* We have no document in

Consent of Witenagemot to alienations of land

---

1. *op. cit.* p. 171. The passage in Bede [ed. Plummer, 1, 415] is quoted in note (2).

2. Cf. Stubbs, *Const. Hist.,* i, p. 212.

which the land alienation of which the witan confirm or revoke appears as a part of the *ager publicus*.

Thus there is no ground for distinguishing between public land and royal demesne. The Anglo-Saxon kings had evidently in that respect ideas as vague and blurred in outline as our Merovingians, and it would be very singular if they had established a distinction between two things so difficult not to confound.

Stubbs' theory about Anglo-Saxon public land is therefore a weak part of his work. He was often enough unfortunate when he founded general theories on the work of others. But he was a scholar of incomparable perspicacity and sobriety when he studied the sources himself; this was most frequently the case, and it is for that reason that his book maintains its position.

III.

TWELFHYND-MAN AND TWYHYND-MAN.

A New Theory Respecting Family Solidarity among the Anglo-Saxons.

ACCORDING to the usual interpretation which has been adopted by Stubbs,[1] the twelfhynd-man is the man who
Usual interpretation has a wergild of 1,200 shillings, and the twyhynd-man is the simple ceorl, who has a wergild of one-sixth of that amount. Similarly the oath of the twelfhynd-man, in a court of justice, is worth six times that of the ceorl. The intermediate class of sixhynd-men possessed a wergild of 600 shillings. *Hynd, hynden* is *hund,* a hundred. Twelfhynd-man ought to be translated man of twelve hundreds, twyhynd-man by man of two hundreds, etc.

In a fairly recent book, which is moreover a work of absorbing interest, Mr. F. Seebohm proposes an entirely
Interpretation of Mr. Seebohm different explanation, which serves him as the foundation of his theory as to the importance of family solidarity in the formation of Anglo-Saxon society.[2] According to him the term *hynden,* which we find in the 54th chapter of the laws of King Ini or Ine, has no numerical significance, and denotes the compurgators who support with their oath a kinsman accused of murder. The judicial oath of full value, which can aid a man most effectively to purge himself of an accusation, is the oath taken by the twelve oath-helpers of his kindred, having each a complete family. In primitive times a great number of relatives is an unquestionable advantage.

1. *Const. Hist.,* i, pp. 128, note 4. 175, 178.
2. *Tribal Custom in Anglo-Saxon law,* 1902, pp. 406 sqq., 499 sqq.

The kindred aids the accused with the weight of its oath, or else by fighting for him when private war is inevitable, or else again by paying a share of his wergild. The *twelfhynd-man*, then, is the man in possession of a full kindred, which assures him the maximum of credit in the court of justice, and enables him to produce " twelve hyndens," that is to say, twelve kinsmen representing twelve groups ready to defend him. The *twyhynd-man* is the man who does not enjoy this advantage; he can only produce two oath-helpers, or at least those whom he produces are worth only " two hyndens," carry only one-sixth of the weight of the oath-helpers of the twelfhynd-man. Whether he be, by origin, an emancipated slave or a free man of low condition, or a native belonging to the conquered race, or an immigrant foreigner, he is in every case a man who has not a family sufficiently numerous to protect him when he is accused. The result for him is that he is obliged to seek the protection of a magnate, an act fraught with great consequences; the twyhynd-men thus form the class of tenants dependent on a lord, who at critical times takes the place, for his men, of the powerful kindred, which is at once the pride and the support of the twelfhynd-man.

The unfortunate thing is that Mr. Seebohm offers no convincing reasons for the new translation which he

Objections

gives of the *hynden* of Ini. There is no reason for rejecting in this passage its ordinary meaning : *hund,* a hundred.[1] Moreover, we

1. Chapter 54 of Ini (see Liebermann, *Gesetze* i, pp. 112—115) is, moreover, very obscure. Mr. Chadwick in his *Studies on Anglo-Saxon Institutions* (1905), pp. 134—151 has minutely studied the question of the value of the oath expressed in hides. A relatively satisfactory interpretation of chapter 54 can be deduced from his laborious researches, an interpretation which very nearly agrees with the translation proposed by Liebermann in his edition. The first clause of the chapter would signify : when a man is accused of murder and wishes to purge himself of the accusation by oath, it is necessary that for each hundred shillings (which the composition he is threatened with having to pay comprises) an oath should intervene " of the value of thirty hides." This oath of the value of thirty hides is that of the twelfhynd-man; it is worth six times that

have an authentic document on the scale of wergilds :
twelfhynd-man and *twyhynd-man* are explained in it in
the clearest manner ; *hynd* and *hund* are brought together
in a manner which leaves no room for doubt.[1]

The traditional opinion implicitly accepted by Stubbs,
and adopted also in the most recent works[2] ought then
to be retained.[3] This remark does not, however, at all
diminish the importance which Mr. Seebohm so justly
attaches to the social results of family solidarity. The
participation of the kindred in the burdens and profits
of the wergild is a fact of considerable significance in the
history of law and manners, and the very terms whose
meaning we have just been discussing sufficiently prove
what a large share the wergild, with all its consequences,
had in the formation of the Germanic communities.

of the twyhynd-man or simple ceorl. For example, if the composition to
be paid is 200 shillings, an oath proferred by two twelfhynd-men is
necessary. But Mr. Chadwick has not succeeded on explaining the origin
of the expression "oath of thirty hides." Mr. Seebohm, *op. cit.* pp.
379 sqq., quotes and comments on a passage from the *Dialogue of archbishop Egbert*, in which the hides are replaced by *tributarii* : a priest
swears "secundum numerum cxx tributariorum." Mr. Seebohm concludes
from this that the hide of the laws of Ini is " the fiscal unit, paying
gafol, which is designated by the *familia* of Bede." Mr. Hodgkin (in
the *Political History of England*, edited by W. Hunt and R. L. Poole,
i, 1906, p. 230) remarks that usually the ceorl did not possess five hides,
and that the thegns were far from all having the immense estates which
the different documents relative to the oaths seem to presuppose. According to him, the figures of hides given in these documents were entirely
conventional. On the meaning of *hyndena* and *hynden-man*, cf. Athelstan
vi, 3, in Liebermann, *Gesetze*, i, p. 175.

1. " Twelfhyndes mannes wer is twelf hund scyllinga. Twyhyndes
mannes wer is twa hund scill' " (Liebermann, *Gesetze*, i, p. 392). That
is to say the wergild of a twelve-hundred-man is twelve hundred
shillings, the wergild of a two-hundred-man is two hundred shillings.

2. Besides Chadwick, op. cit., see P. Vinogradoff, *The Growth of the
Manor*, p. 125.

3. " The *six-hynd-man*," says Stubbs (*Const. Hist.*, i, p. 179, note 3)
" is a difficulty." Mr. Chadwick (op. cit., pp. 87 sqq.) proposes a fairly
satisfactory solution. The *sixhynd-man* would be sometimes a gesithcund
who can ride on horseback in the service of the king, without, however,
possessing the five hides necessary to be a *twelfhynd-man*,—sometimes
again a landowner having five hides, but of Welsh origin, and " worth"
in consequence only one half an English owner of five hides. This class
of *sixhynd-men* was doubtless hereditary and did not increase either
from above or below, since, at the end of the Anglo-Saxon period, there
is no longer any mention of it, and we must suppose it to have disappeared. Cf. Seebohm, op. cit., pp. 396 sqq.

IV.

THE "BURH-GEAT-SETL."

STUBBS understands by the expression *burh-geat-setl* a right of jurisdiction without giving any further explanation.[1] It has been shown recently

The reading is incorrect

that the text to which he refers, the little treatise which he alludes to, following Thorpe, under the name of *Ranks,* and which is entitled in the *Quadripartitus:* "De veteri consuetudine promotionum," has been badly read. There should be a comma after *burh-geat* and *setl* should be taken with the words *on cynges healle* which come after.[2] It is thus that the phrase was understood in the old Latin translations. The compiler of the *Quadripartitus* says : "Et si villanus excrevisset, ut haberet plenarie quinque hidas terre sue proprie, ecclesiam et coquinam, timpanarium et *januam, sedem* et sundernotam in aula regis, deinceps erat taini lege dignus." The compiler of the *Instituta Cnuti* also writes : " . . . . et ecclesiam propriam et clocarium et coquinam et portam, sedem et privatum profectum in aula regis, etc." It is true that these Latin translations have not an indisputable

---

1. *Const. Hist.*, i, pp. 86, 120, 210. H. Sweet, *Dictionary of Anglo-Saxon* (1897) says more explicitly : "Law-court held at city gate." Similarly Bosworth-Toller, *Anglo-Saxon Dictionary* : "a town gate-seat, where a court was held for trying causes of family and tenants, ad urbis portam sedes." As a matter of fact there is certainly no question of a tribunal held at the gates of a town. Mr. Maitland in *Domesday Book and Beyond* (p. 190 ; cf. p. 196, note 1) made a different mistake, and translated burh-geat-setl by "a house in the gate or street of the burh." 'Geat' cannot signify street. Mr. Maitland has given up this translation. See below.

2. The passage is as follows : "And gif ceorl getheah, thæt he hæfde fullice fif hida agenes landes, cirican and kycenan, bellhus and burhgeat, setl and sundernote on cynges healle. . . ." (Liebermann, *Gesetze*, i, pp. 456—457.)

authority. But Mr. Liebermann and before him Mr. W. H. Stevenson[1] have pointed out that the palæographic mark of punctuation by which the word *geat* is followed (a full stop having the value of a comma), and the rhythm of the whole passage, equally forbid us to take *setl* with *burh-geat*.

Setl, a very vague word, denotes in a general way a place; *geat* is the gate, and *burh* a fortified place, town, or house. The passage signifies therefore that, among the conditions necessary before a ceorl could become a thegn, he must have an assigned place and a special office (*sundernote*) in the hall, the court of the king, and also a belfry (*bell-hus*) and a " burh-gate." What does this "burh-gate" mean ? Mr. W. H. Stevenson, the learned editor of the *Crawford Charters* and of the *Annales* of Asser, sees in it nothing but a rhetorical figure : the part is taken for the whole, and the " burh-gate " means simply the " burh," the fortified house. All idea of jurisdiction ought therefore to be laid aside. Stubbs and the other scholars who have made use of the passage not only, in Mr. Stevenson's opinion, retained an undoubted misreading but interpreted the expression badly. Mr. Maitland has rejected this last conclusion.[2] Mr. Stevenson's article having been published in the most widely-circulated English historical review, and Mr. Maitland's refutation having possibly escaped the notice of many readers, it seemed necessary to note here that on the whole Stubbs was not mistaken as regards the meaning of " burh-geat." Mr. Maitland points out, in fact, the following clause in a charter granted to Robert Fitz-Harding :[3] " Cum tol et them et zoch et sache et belle et burgiet et infankenethef." The words

Meaning of Burh-geat

<hr/>

1. W. H. Stevenson. ' Burh-geat-setl,' in *English Historical Review*, xii, 1897, pp. 489 sqq.
2. *Township and Borough*, 1898, Appendix, pp. 209–210.
3. Printed in John Smyth, *Lives of the Berkeleys*, i, p. 22 (quoted by Maitland).

which surround " burgiet " here prove that there is
question of an " outward and visible sign of jurisdiction
or lordly power." The gate of the burh had become,
like the belfry, a symbol of the right of justice.
But for what reason ? Miss Mary Bateson has quite
recently completed and simplified the explanation.[1]
She shows that the seignorial court was often held near
to the gate of the castle and to the belfry, and that a
natural relation thus established itself between the gate,
the belfry and jurisdictional power.

1. *Borough Customs*, ii, 1906, p. xvi, note 1.

V.

THE CEREMONY OF "DUBBING TO KNIGHTHOOD."

The Reciprocal Influences of the Anglo-Saxon and Frankish Civilizations.

Stubbs believes rightly that the practice of "dubbing to knighthood" was derived from a primitive and very widespread custom, and allows that an analogous usage may have existed among the Anglo-Saxons; but he is inclined to believe that they borrowed it from the Franks.[1] Recently the converse hypothesis has been put forth.

Origin of ceremony

M. Guilhiermoz, in his fine *Essai sur l'origine de la Noblesse,* studies the history of dubbing.[2] He notices that the Germanic custom of the delivery of arms to the young man come to adult age, a custom described in the famous 13th chapter of the *De Moribus Germanorum,* is still to be distinguished, among the Ostrogoths, at the beginning of the sixth century; but afterwards it seems to disappear. Until the end of the eighth century the documents only speak of another ceremony, equally marking the majority of the young man, the *barbatoria,* the first cutting of the beard. From the end of the eighth century onwards, the ceremony of investiture reappears in the documents, while the *barbatoria* seems to fall into desuetude. Two explanations are possible; either the investiture took place, from the sixth to the

Theory of M. Guilhiermoz

1. *Const. Hist.,* i, pp. 396-397, and note 1, p. 396.
2. *Essai sur l'origine de la Noblesse en France au Moyen Age* (1902), pp. 393 sqq.; see particularly p. 411, note 60.

eighth century, at the same time as the *barbatoria,*
though it is not mentioned in the sources; that is the
hypothesis which M. Guilhiermoz regards as most
probable; or, on the other hand, " we might perhaps
suppose that the solemn arming had disappeared among
the Franks and that it only came into vogue again with
them to replace the *barbatoria* as a practice borrowed
from a Germanic people who had preserved it better . . .
A passage in the life of St. Wilfrid of York, by Eddi,
seems to allude to the custom of arming among the
Anglo-Saxons at the end of the seventh century."[1]

    Thus the Anglo-Saxons, who kept many Germanic
institutions which the Franks had dropped, are
Influence of Anglo-Saxon civilization on the continent supposed to have preserved the primitive
usage described by Tacitus and to have
transmitted it, towards the end of the
eighth century, to Charlemagne and his
subjects. The hypothesis is an interesting one, and
connects itself with a class of considerations which
Stubbs perhaps did wrong to neglect. As M.
Guilhiermoz says, "a certain number of facts show
the influence exercised in the Frank empire by Anglo-
Saxon usages in the seventh and eighth centuries."
The anointing of the kings in France, Brunner has
noticed, was an Anglo-Saxon importation; so also was
the custom of entrusting the young people brought up
at the palace to the care of the queen.[2]

    The part that the scholars of the school of York
played in the Carolingian Renaissance is well known.
Carolingian painting, whose origins are complex and
obscure, is beyond a doubt derived, in large part, from
the early Anglo-Saxon art of miniature; and when we

---

1. " Principes quoque saeculares viri nobiles, filios suos ad erudiendum
sibi (to St. Wilfrid) dederunt, ut aut Deo servirent, si eligerent, aut
adultos, si maluissent, regi *armatos* commendaret." M. Guilhiermoz
takes this passage from Raine, *Historians of the Church of York,*
i, p. 32.
2. Guilhiermoz, *loc. cit.* and pp. 92, 93.

compare the strange and striking productions of English painting in the tenth century with those of the Rheims school in the ninth, we may ask ourselves whether, far from having inspired Anglo-Saxon art a century after, the famous psalter of Hautvillers, or " Utrecht psalter," was not painted in France by Englishmen.

Stubbs has shown forcibly the influence of Carolingian institutions on English institutions.[1] It would be well, perhaps, to insist equally on the expansion of Anglo-Saxon civilization, which is in certain respects remarkable.

1. An influence which was only however very powerful in the 12th century. Stubbs describes this phenomenon of tardy imitation, with much learning, in his account of the reforms of Henry II (*Const. Hist.* 1, 656—7).

VI.

THE ORIGIN OF THE EXCHEQUER.

SEVERAL scholars, since Stubbs, have examined the perhaps insoluble question of the origin of the Exchequer, notably Mr. Round and quite recently Messrs. Hughes, Crump and Johnson.[1] These latter come to the conclusion that the financial organisation described in the celebrated treatise of Richard Fitz-Neal proceeded both from Anglo-Saxon and from Norman institutions. We should have in it therefore a typical example of that process of combination which formed the strength of the Norman monarchy, and which Stubbs has put in so clear a light. But in the searching study which he made of the Exchequer Stubbs refrained from distinguishing the elements of this institution with a precision that the sources did not appear to him to justify. Are there grounds for speaking with more assurance that he did? Let us see what we have learnt for certain which he has not told us.

The Exchequer, it will be remembered, comprised two Chambers, the *Inferius Scaccarium,* a Treasury, to which the sheriffs came to pay the *rma comitatus* and other revenues of the king, and the *Superius Scaccarium,* a Court of Accounts staffed by the great officers of the crown and personages having the confidence of the king, whose business it was to verify the accounts of the sheriffs on the " exchequer," and also to give judgment in certain suits. The thesis of Messrs. Hughes, Crump and Johnson is that the Treasury, the *firma comitatus* and the system of payment employed in the first years

Recent work on the question (marginal note)

1. In the introduction which they have prefixed to their critical edition of the *Dialogues de Scaccario* (1902), pp. 13—42.

after the Conquest, were of Anglo-Saxon origin, while the verification on the exchequer and the constitution of the staff of the Court of Accounts were of Norman origin. In short, an upper chamber of foreign origin was superimposed on a lower chamber already established before the Norman invasion.[1]

The Anglo-Saxon kings could not do without a Treasury. Stubbs admitted the existence of a "central

Anglo-Saxon elements of the Exchequer

department of finance" before the Conquest,[2] and the latest editors of the *Dialogus* will meet with no contradiction on that head. Let us add that we know even the name of the treasurer of Edward the Confessor. An inquest relative to the rights of the king over Winchester, made between 1103 and 1115, speaks of "Henricus, thesaurarius," who, in the time of Edward the Confessor, had a house in that town, at which the Norman kings themselves for a long time kept their treasure.[3] Two offices mentioned in the *Dialogus,* those of weigher (*miles argentarius*) and melter (*fusor*), appear to be anterior in origin to the constitution of the Exchequer properly so called, and evidently date, like that of the treasurer, from the Anglo-Saxon period.[4] Stubbs himself tells us that the *farm* paid by the sheriffs was tested by fire and weighed, and that this operation could not have a Norman origin. Thus the offices of treasurer, weigher, and melter, the *firma comitatus* and the method of verifying the value of the money date from the pre-Norman period. Mr. Round has pointed out

1. Hughes, Crump and Johnson, *op. cit.*, pp. 14, 28.
2. *Const. Hist.*, i, p. 408, note 1.
3. Round, *The officers of Edward the Confessor* in *English Histor. Review*, 1904, p. 92. Upon this inquest, see an article by the same author, in the *Victoria History of the Counties of England. Hampshire*, i, pp. 527 sqq.
4. In the time of Henry II., they were dependent on no other officer, and the author of the *Dialogus* was not sure whether he ought to connect them with the Lower Exchequer or the Upper Exchequer (*Dialogus*, i, 3; ed. Hughes, etc., p. 62). [Modern writers following Madox generally call the weigher pesour.]

that, contrary to an erroneous assertion of Stubbs, the "blanch-farm" is mentioned several times in *Domesday Book*.[1] Stubbs' proof might have been more complete and more exact, but on the whole his conclusion remains inexpugnable. No one is entitled to say, with Gneist and Brunner, that "the court of Exchequer was brought bodily over from Normandy." The pre-Norman origin of a part of the financial organisation of thè twelfth century is a settled point.

Shall we now try to distinguish, with Messrs. Hughes, Crump and Johnson, the elements imported from abroad? "The arithmetic of the Exchequer, like the main portion of the staff of the Upper Exchequer, is," they say, "clearly of foregn origin."[2] The 'clearness' they give us on that point is not dazzling. Let us see what it amounts to.

The "exchequer" was a cloth divided into squares by lines, with seven columns, each column including several squares; according to the place it occupied at one or the other extremity a counter might signify one penny or 10,000 pounds.[3] This arrangement suggested the idea of a game played between the treasurer and the sheriff,[4] and, according to Mr. Round, was intended to strike the eyes of the ignorant and to make the business easy to such unskilful accounters as were the sheriffs of the time of Henry I. It was out of the question to demand writings on parchment from them.[5]

Origin of the arithmetical system of the Exchequer

The editors of the *Dialogus* think, on the contrary, that the system required "skilled calculators," and suppose

1. *The Origin of the Exchequer*, in : *The Commune of London and other Studies*, p. 66.
2. *Op cit.*, p. 43.
3. See the description, *op. cit.*, pp. 38 sqq.
4. "Inter duos principaliter conflictus est et pugna committitur, thesaurarium scilicet et vicecomitem qui assidet ad compotum, residentibus aliis tanquam judicibus ut videant et judicent." (*Dialogus*, i, 3; p. 61 of edition quoted.)
5. *Commune of London*, p. 75.

that the Anglo-Saxons were ignorant of it. Personally we share the opinion expressed by Mr. Round, and we find a difficulty in admitting that the English were not acquainted with the use of the abacus before the Norman Conquest. But let us approach the problem more directly. Can we determine the provenance of the arithmetical system described in the *Dialogus*? Stubbs notices that the term *Scaccarium* comes into use only in the reign of Henry I.,[1] and that until then the financial administration is called *Thesaurus* or *Fiscus*. Mr. Round quotes[2] a curious passage from the Cartulary of Abingdon, which records a lawsuit tried in the *Curia Regis* at Winchester, in the Treasury: "apud Wintoniam, in Thesauro;" we must perhaps conclude from this that at that moment, that is to say, in the first years of the reign of Henry I., the institution described later by the author of the *Dialogus* already existed in its essential features, with its attributes at once financial and judicial, but that the accounts of the sheriffs were not yet received on the chequered cloth, since the term *Scaccarium* has not yet replaced the term *Thesaurus*. Doubtless the sheriffs were accounted with by means of "tallies," the notched sticks of which Stubbs speaks. The author of the *Dialogus* tells us indeed: "Quod autem hodie dicitur ad scaccarium, olim dicebatur ad taleas."[3] It must then have been in the course of the reign of Henry I. that the substitution of the one system for the other was effected; henceforth the financial court called previously *Thesaurus* took, by extension, the name of *Scaccarium,* which denoted the table of account now in use, and which had been suggested by the appearance of the chequered cloth.[4]

1. *Const. Hist.*, i, p. 407.
2. *Commune of London*, p. 94.
3. *Dialogus*, i, 1 (Ed. Hughes, etc., p. 60.
4. "Licet autem tabula talis scaccarium dicatur, transumitur tamen hoc nomen, ut ipsa quoque curia, que consedente scaccario est, scaccarium dicatur. . . . Que est ratio huius nominis?—Nulla mihi verior ad presens occurrit quam quia scaccarii lusilis similem habet formam." (*Ibidem.*)

This is the very probable view accepted by Mr. Round. But we do not see that anyone is justified in concluding from it that "the arithmetic of the Exchequer is clearly of foreign origin." It would be necessary indeed to prove: (1) that this system of accounting was not known previously in England; we have already expressed our doubt on this head; (2) that it was employed previously on the Continent. The term Exchequer is only found in the countries occupied by the Normans, but it in no wise follows that it is of Norman origin. It may equally well be of English origin. The considerations brought forward on that point by Stubbs retain all their force even since the discovery by Mr. Round in a Merton Cartulary of proof that there was an Exchequer in Normandy in 1130 at the very latest.[1] Indeed there is nothing to preclude the adoption of the chequered cloth in England being anterior by some years to this date.

The foreign origin of the Exchequer is not proved

The Norman origin, therefore, of the arithmetic employed in the twelfth century is very far from being proved. As regards the staff of the Upper Exchequer, it is true that the great officers who sit there bear essentially French titles. When we compare the little work entitled *Constitutio Domus Regis* with the *Dialogus de Scaccario,* we note that "with a few exceptions every important officer in the financial department has his place in the household. It may

The staff of the Upper Exchequer may have been formed before the Conquest

1. *Bernard the King's scribe,* in *English Historical Review,* xiv, 1899, pp. 425 sqq. The document in question relates to a lawsuit regarding a Norman estate claimed by Serlo the Deaf from Bernard the Scribe. The suit was tried at the Exchequer: " Et ibi positus fuit Serlo in misericordia regis per judicium baronum de Scaccario, quia excoluerat terram illam super saisinam Bernardi, quam ante placitum istud disracionaverat per judicium episcopi Luxoviensis et Roberti de Haia et multorum ad Scaccarium, etc." The document as a whole shows that we have to do with a Norman Exchequer. The bishop of Lisieux, who presided over it, it seems, resided uninterruptedly in his diocese, and Robert de la Haie was seneschal of Normandy.

be added that the constitution of the household is so clearly of Frankish origin that it is not possible even to doubt that its organization was originally imported from abroad." [1] But again, we must be agreed on the nature of the point at issue. The important thing, be it remembered, is to distinguish what influence the Norman Conquest can have had on the development of the financial organization.

We have just seen that the method of verification of the accounts and even the name Exchequer may have arisen simultaneously in England and in Normandy or in England even earlier than in Normandy. As far as concerns the great officers sitting in the financial court, the Conquest of 1066 may have equally had no influence—for the good reason that these great officers existed in England before the Conquest of 1066, and that the court of Edward the Confessor was already profoundly "Normanised." Mr. Round, whom we have constantly to quote, has shown that this king had a marshal (named Alfred), a constable (Bondig), a senchal (Eadnoth), a butler (Wigod), a chamberlain (Hugh), a treasurer (Henry), a chancellor (Regenbald), in short the same great officers who figured at the court of the Norman dukes.[2] Did these personages take part in financial administration? It would be rash to affirm it at present. But all that we know of the monarchical institutions of the West at that period equally forbids us to deny it.

To sum up, we see that some new documents have been contributed to the discussion, but without throwing any decisive light upon it. The description which Stubbs gave, thirty years ago, of the operations of the Exchequer, has been rectified and the details filled in, but his cautious conclusions upon the

Conclusion

---

1. Hughes, Crump and Johnson, Introduction, p. 14.

2. Round, *The officers of Edward the Confessor*, in *Engl. Hist. Review*, xix, 1904, pp. 90—92.

origin of the institution remain intact. He may have happened on other points to have underestimated excessively the effects of the Conquest of 1066 on the political development of England, but he appears to have been right in thinking that while the Exchequer manifestly contains certain Anglo-Saxon elements we cannot discern with certainty any element the introduction of which was the direct result of the Norman Conquest.[1]

1. See the bibliography of works relating to the Exchequer in Gross, *Sources*, § 50, and in the edition of the *Dialogus* referred to above, pp. vii—viii. The chief things to read are the article published by Mr. Round, in *The Commune of London and Other Studies*, and the introduction of Messrs. Hughes, Crump and Johnson, the merit of which we do not think of disputing. Mr. Round has brought to light the feudal, "tenurial" character of the two offices of Chamberlain and studied the mode of payment *ad scalam* and the *ad pensum* system; he has discovered also that the whole of the receipts and expenses did not appear in the Pipe Rolls, and that besides the Exchequer, the Treasury, which for a long time had its seat at Winchester, had its special accounts and its chequered cloth to verify them.

VII.

ENGLISH SOCIETY DURING THE FEUDAL PERIOD.

The Tenurial System and the Origin of Tenure by Military Service.

In certain pages of his work Stubbs, either in dealing with the Norman Conquest or in order to give an understanding of the elements which **Differences from Continental Society** composed the solemn assemblies of the *Curia Regis,* incidentally explains what an earl, a baron and a freeholder were, and expresses his opinion on the origin of tenure by knight-service.[1] We shall consider here the question as a whole, and at a slightly different angle, in order that the reader may the more clearly account for the differences which separate English and French society during that period.

In spite of the " feudalization " of England by the Normans, the principles which distinguished men from one another in England were not the same as on the Continent. Differences of terminology already warn us that the institutions are not identical. The word *vassallus* is very seldom met with ; *alodium,* in *Domesday Book,* does not denote an estate not held of a lord ; but doubtless simply a piece of land transmissible to a man's heirs ; it is very nearly the sense of *feodum,* which has a very vague meaning in English documents. It is said that So-and-So " tenet in feodo," if his rights are heritable, even when he has only the obligations of an agricultural tenant towards his lord.[2]

1. *Const. Hist.,* i, pp. 283 sqq., 389 sqq., 604 sqq.
2. Maitland, *Domesday Book and Beyond,* pp. 152 sqq.; Pollock and Maitland, *History of English Law,* i, pp. 234 sqq., 297. It is to this last work that we chiefly refer the reader for all that follows. He will find there a notable exposition of what we call the "feudal institutions" of England. [On *feudum* and *alodium* in Domesday, cf. Vinogradoff, *English Society in the Eleventh Century,* pp. 232—8.]

And, indeed, there is, properly speaking, no distinct feudal law in England. There, " feudal law is not a special law applicable only to one fairly definite set of relationships, or applicable only to one class or estate of men ; it is just the common law of England."[1] The English nobility is not therefore separated from the non-noble class, as in France, by a whole body of customs which constitutes for it a special private law. It is public law which gives it a place apart and a superiority very different, for the rest, from those which the French baronage claimed. The English baronage was founded by the Norman monarchy, and owed its riches and privileges to it.

No distinct feudal law

The *barones majores* are those whom the king has endowed with rich estates[2] and whom he summons to

---

1. Pollock and Maitland, *English Law*, i, pp. 235–236.

2. It is well-known that these estates, instead of forming compact principalities like those of the French dukes and counts, were generally scattered over several counties. Mr. Round has proved that this disposition, a singularly favourable one to the monarchy and attributed by historians to the political genius of William the Conqueror, frequently originated in the uncompactness of the properties of the Anglo-Saxon thegns. " It is often urged," he says, " that William deliberately scattered a fief over several counties in order to weaken its holder's power. But this scattering might be only the result of granting the estate of a given thegn. Thus, in Hampshire, Alured of Marlborough had, in both his manors, succeeded a certain Carle, who was also his ' antecessor' in Surrey and Somerset, and in the bulk of his Wiltshire lands. Arnul de Hesdin had for his predecessor, in his two Hampshire manors, an Edric, who was clearly also his ' predecessor' in the three he held in Somerset, and in some of his lands in Gloucestershire, Wilts. and Dorset. In like manner Nigel the physician held lands in Wiltshire, Herefordshire and Shropshire, as well as in Hampshire, because in all four counties he had succeeded Spirtes, a rich and favoured English priest. On the other hand, a Domesday tenant-in-chief may have received a *congeries* of manors lying in a single shire. Of this there is a very striking instance in the fief of Hugh de Port. Except for two manors in Cambridgeshire, and one apiece in Bucks and Dorset, the whole fief lay in Hampshire," where he held fifty-six manors from the crown, and thirteen from the bishop of Bayeux. (*Victoria History of Hampshire*, i. 421—422; cf. *Hertfordshire*, i, 1902, p. 277; cf. also the case quoted by F. M. Stenton, *Vict. Hist. of Derbyshire*, i, 1905, p. 305).

Mr. Round admits also that side by side with the cases in which the companions of William received the entire estates of rich Englishmen, we have examples of Anglo-Saxon estates divided between several Normans, and estates formed for Normans from numerous small English estates. (*Vict. Hist. of Essex*, i, 353.)

The barons the *Commune Concilium* by individual letters; some of them are honoured by him with the title of earl and bear the sword of the earldom. The English aristocracy is to be a political aristocracy, a high nobility formed of privileged individuals, transmitting their power to the eldest son.[1]

In the same way the knights who are to play so important a rôle in constitutional history, do not enjoy a very peculiar personal status; but, as **The knights** Stubbs shows, the carrying into effect of the judicial system inaugurated by Henry II. depends on their loyal co-operation; they are a class of notables, charged with judicial functions which can only be devolved upon men of trust. Apart from this distinctive feature, no barrier separates the knights from the rest of the freemen; military service is not strictly confined to the tenure by knight service, and the knight's fee might even be held by a freeman who was not a knight.

To sum up, in England there is no legal *personal* distinction except between the free and the un-free; but *liber* does not mean noble, although this **Meaning of** has been lately maintained.[2] In its *liber homo* narrower meaning, at least in certain passages, the *liber homo* of the English realm, far from designating the noble in opposition to the non-noble person, designates the non-noble freeman as opposed to the noble.[3] In its wider significance, *liber homo* means : one who is not a serf; it is in this sense that the Great Charter is granted to the *liberi homines* of the realm. It

1. On all this comments will be found, which, if not original, are at least formulated with much precision and vigour, in E. Boutmy, *Développement de la Constitution et de la Société politique en Angleterre*, pp. 13 sqq., and English Translation by I. M. Eaden (*The English Constitution*), 1891, pp. 3 sqq.

2. According to M. Guilhiermoz, *Origines de la Noblesse*, p. 364, in England, *liberi homines* signifies *gentilshommes*, and *liberi tenentes* signifies possessors of noble fiefs or holdings. This theory is no truer of England than it is of France.

3. See the case of 1222 quoted by W. E. Rhodes, *Engl. Histor. Review*, xviii, 1903, p. 770 : the rate of the contribution paid for the deliverance of the Holy Land is 1s. for the knight and 1d. only for the *liber homo*.

is as *liber homo,* not as noble, that the noble has personal rights.[1]

Tenure

But social relations in England rested, above all, on another principle—that of *tenure,* which was applied to almost the whole of the population, from the king, from whom every tenure depends mediately or immediately, down to the humblest serf cultivating the land of his lord.[2] There was not an inch of English soil which was not subjected to this single formula : ' Z. tenet terram illam de . . . . domino rege,' Z. being either *tenens in capite* or separated from the king by more or less numerous intermediaries. This formula applies to all those who have a parcel of land, even to the farmer, even to the serf *cotter,* and it equally applies to the religious communities who hold land from a donor without owing him anything in return save prayers. Vagabonds and proletarians excepted, who must, I imagine, have existed always and everywhere in country and town,[3] all the English of the Middle Ages were tenants, and tenure, in the eyes of the lawyers, was much more important than personal status.[4] The distinction even between free and non-free in this country was practically a distinction between tenures much more than a distinction between persons.[5]

1. See the exposition and applcation of this fact in Pollock and Maitland, i, pp. 408 sqq.
2. See above, p. 23.
3. On the floating population of the country, the " undersette " and the " levingmen " see Vinogradoff, *Villainage,* pp. 213, 214.
4. Let us add that one and the same person might have tenements of different categories. Pollock and Maitland, *English Law,* i, p. 296, quote the instance of Robert d'Aguilon, who held lands from different lords, by military service, in sergeanty, in socage, etc.
5. See Pollock and Maitland, i, p. 322 sqq., 356 sqq., 407. The customs which we call feudal, such as rights of relief of wardship, of marriage, etc., attached themselves not to the person but to the tenure by knight service. In practice, of course, they were subjects of the keenest interest for members of the nobility, and it is for this reason, that, in the Great Charter, the baronage took particular precautions to prevent the crown from abusing them. Pollock and Maitland, pp. 307 sqq., study these customs and try to determine in what measure they were peculiar to the tenure by knight service. Sometimes tenure in socage was subject to the rights of wardship and of marriage.

Let us leave aside servile tenures, of which we have spoken in studying the problem of the manor. The free tenures at the end of the historical period dealt with in Stubbs' first volume may be grouped into the following principal types : —

Free tenures

1. Tenure in *frankalmoin, in liberam elemosinam,* in free alms. It is theoretically the land given to the Church, without any temporal service being demanded in return ; it is agreed or understood that the community will pray for the donor. In practice, tenure in frankalmoin admits of certain temporal services, and its clearest characteristic, at the end of the twelfth century, is that judicially it is subject only to the ecclesiastical forum.

Tenure in frankalmoin

2. Tenure by knight service, *per servitium militare.* The holder of a knight's fee owes in theory military service for forty days. In the twelfth century the king often demanded, instead of personal service, a tax called scutage.[1] The usual rate was two marks on the knight's fee, and it has been pointed out that that sum was equal to the

Tenure by knight service

1. Stubbs discusses scutage in several passages; see vol. i, pp. 491-492, 494, 624-625. He rightly remarks that this term did not always denote a tax to replace military service. But, both in regard to the origin of scutage and in regard to the obligations imposed, when it was levied, on those who held land by knight service, he should have taken account of recent work and not have contented himself with referring in a single line to Mr. Round's article which is in absolute contradiction with some of the conclusions to which Stubbs continued to adhere. Mr. Round took up the question of scutage again, in the course of a bitter controversy with Mr. Hubert Hall, editor of the *Red Book of the Exchequer.* (See the bibliography in Gross, No. 1917.) An excellent piece of work by an American scholar, J. F. Baldwin, should also be read : *The scutage and knight service in England,* Chicago, 1897. Briefly, there is no ground for considering scutage as an innovation of the reign of Henry II.; the tax in substitution for military service and even the word *scutagium* already existed under Henry I. On the other hand, scutage only dispensed from military service if the king thought fit : his subjects had not the right to choose. (See Pollock and Maitland, *English Law,* i, pp. 267 sqq.) Scutage, from the beginning of the 13th century, came to be a tax like any other; no exemption was granted in exchange. Mr. Baldwin shows, moreover, that its financial importance has been exaggerated The question of scutage will be definitely elucidated when all the Pipe Rolls anterior to the middle of the 13th century, the period at which scutage fell into desuetude, have been published and studied.

pay of a knight hired for forty days. The king's servants reckoned, in the thirteenth century, that William the Conqueror had created 32,000 knights' fees. It has been calculated that in reality the king of England could not count on more than 5,000 knights.[1] Legally, military service was a *regale servitium*. The right of private war was not recognised. In practice, the lords reckoned on the knights whom they had enfeoffed to sustain their personal quarrels and not merely to provide the service demanded by the king from each of his tenants-in-chief; there were some even who maintained more knights than their obligations towards the king required.

3. Tenure in serjeanty. The *servientes,* serjeants (officers of every kind from the seneschal or the constable

Tenure in serjeanty to the cook or messenger), received land from the king or the lord whom they served on a tenure called *serjanteria.* The obligations of this tenure were sometimes agricultural, sometimes military. Holders of military serjeanties only differed from knights by their lighter equipment.

4. Tenure in free socage, *in socagio.* From the end of the twelfth century it can be said that all free tenure

Tenure in socage which is neither frankalmoin nor knight service nor serjeanty, is tenure in socage. Land can be held in socage by the most diverse persons; by a younger son of a family, who has received it from his father, by a great personage who holds it of the king on condition of a rent or of agricultural services, or, finally, a very ordinary case, by free peasants. These last owe the lord a rent or services, and their economic condition frequently approaches that of the un-free villeins; but these freeholders are bound directly to the king by an oath of allegiance, often take even an actual oath of homage to their lord and form part of the county court and the juries.

1. Round, *Feudal England*, pp. 264—265, 292.

In the category of tenure in socage we may class the tenure in burgage, peculiar to the burgesses of the towns with charters. What is the origin of the English tenures? The systematization, the symmetrical simplification and the legal theory of tenure are due to the Norman lawyers; this is not disputed. The difficulty, as we have already seen in studying the evolution of the agricultural classes, is to ascertain in what proportions the feudal and seignorial principles brought from the Continent by the Norman invaders underwent admixture with Anglo-Saxon traditions in order to produce, in the world of reality, the new régime. Stubbs approached the problem from several sides, but never stated it with all the clearness desirable. We have already said that several scholars of our generation, notably Messrs. Maitland and Round, have done much to define its terms and advance its solution, although they are far from being always in agreement.

Tenure in burgage

Origin of English tenures

We have treated of the origin of peasant tenures above. There is another side to the problem, if not as interesting at least as obscure : this is the origin of feudal military service and of tenure by knight service. Mr. Round seems to have definitively elucidated this difficult subject. It is another reason for giving it our attention for some moments; Stubbs was content to refer, in a note, to Mr. Round's article, without modifying, as he should have done, the rather confused and hesitating pages which he devotes to the knight's fee and knight service.

Problem of military service and of tenure by knight service

Stubbs, and with him the historians of the Germanist school, such as Gneist, Freeman, and, in our own day, Mr. Maitland, have more or less a tendency to see in the military organization of the last Anglo-Saxon centuries " a strong impulse towards a national feudalism."[1]

Germanist theory. Anglo-Saxon origin

1. *Const. Hist.*, i, p. 208.

The king's warrior is the thegn, that is to say, according to Stubbs, the man who possesses five hides of land of his own;[1] moreover, we see that in Berkshire, in the reign of Edward the Confessor, it was the custom to furnish a warrior (*miles*) for every five hides. Military service is not yet attached to a special tenure, but the military obligation is linked already with the possession of land instead of being, as formerly, a personal obligation of the whole free population. Stubbs thinks that, England once subjected by the Normans, " the obligation of national defence was incumbent as of old on all landowners, and the customary service of one fully-armed man for each five hides was probably the rate at which the newly-endowed follower of the king would be expected to discharge his duty."[2]

Unit of service in the host

According to Gneist, William the Conqueror made this Anglo-Saxon usage into a legal rule which he imposed " on the entire body of old and new possessors of the land;" but the rate of five hides was only an approximate indication, and in reality military obligations were fixed according to the productive value of the estates (Gneist even thinks that the principal object of *Domesday Book* was to permit of this fixing of military obligations). The *feuda militum*, the knights' fees, were units worth £20 a year.

Stubbs takes the same view, adding that nevertheless

1. Stubbs, adopting the views of K. Maurer, claims (i, p. 173) that the name of *thegn* was given to all those who possessed the proper quantity of land, that is to say five hides. This theory is inadmissible. It is founded on two wrongly interpreted texts. One of them is that which we have quoted above in our note on the *Burh-geat*, p. 39 note 2. We need only read it as a whole to perceive that more than the possession of five hides was required in order to become a thegn. The holding of five hides was doubtless the normal and traditional estate of the thegn, but there were *rustici* who possessed as much or more land, without thereby becoming thegns. See A. G. Little, *Gesiths and Thegns*, in *English Histor. Review*, iv, 1889, pp. 726—729.
2. *Const. Hist.*, i, pp. 284 sqq. We are trying here to give a coherent account of the thesis of the Germanists, and we shall not bring out the contradictions in detail which Stubbs' argument presents; Mr. Round does this (*op. cit.*, pp. 232-233).

"it must not be assumed that the establishment of the knight's fee was other than gradual."

Gradual formation of the system William the Conqueror did not create the knights' fees at a stroke; there is, as regards this, a great difference between the state of things which is described in *Domesday* and that which the charter of Henry I. allows us to divine, and we may even say that the formation of the military fiefs took more than a century to accomplish, and was not yet completed in the reign of Henry II. It was the subject of a long series of arrangements.[1]

Thus Anglo-Norman military tenure would be derived from the Anglo-Saxon usages, and nevertheless would only have been established very slowly.

Mr. Round's objections Mr. Round[2] has no difficulty in showing the weakness of these theories. If the number of knights which each great vassal had to furnish to the king depended on the number of hides in his estates or on their value in annual revenue, if the king required a knight for each unit of five hides, or for a land unit producing £20 a year, and if the knight's fee represented that unit precisely, what remained for the baron? Obliged to divide the whole of his estate into military fiefs, was he then despoiled of all? The supposition is absurd; the argument of Stubbs and Gneist, however, leads directly to it. Moreover, the alleged slowness with which the feudal military system constituted itself is not seriously proved. The argument *ex silentio* drawn from *Domesday Book* is worth nothing, first, because the object of Domesday was fiscal not military, and secondly, because a closer study of that document demonstrates beyond question the existence of military tenure. We are told that under the first Norman kings certain great estates were not yet divided into knights' fees; but we must not conclude from this that they were

1. *Const. Hist.*, i, pp. 285 sqq., 468 sqq.
2. *Introduction of knight service into England in Feudal England*, pp. 225 sqq.; cf. his *Geoffrey de Mandeville*, p. 103, and *Vict. Hist. Worc.*, i, 250.

not subject to military obligations; here lies the chief flaw in Stubbs' argument.   On his reasoning it would seem that the existence of feudal military service and the existence of knights' fees were bound up together, and that the king had himself to devise a rule for the formation of these fees.   But this was not the case. In order to form his host, the king addressed himself to his barons,[1] his tenants-in-chief alone, and demanded from each of them so many knights; but the manner in which each of them procured them did not concern him directly.

Gneist, Stubbs and Freeman, Mr. Round very rightly remarks, lose sight of the real problem to be solved, and immerse themselves in generalisations and vague writing about the " gradual evolution " of the institution. " For them," he writes,[2] " the introduction of knight-service means the process of sub-infeudation on the several fiefs; for me it means the grant of fiefs to be held from the crown by knight-service.   Thus the process which absorbs the attention of the school whose views I am opposing is for me a matter of mere secondary importance.   The whole question turns upon the point whether or not the tenant-in-chief received their fiefs to hold the crown by a quota of military service, or not.   If they did, it would depend simply on their individual inclinations, whether, or how far, they had recourse to sub-infeudation.   It was not a matter of principle at all; it was, as Dr. Stubbs himself puts it, " a matter of convenience," a mere detail.   What we have to consider is not the relation between the tenant-in-chief and his under-tenants, but that between the king and his tenants-in-chief : for this was the primary relation that determined all below it."

1. I use " baron " here in the sense which it generally has of direct vassal, tenant-in-chief.   Mr. Tait (*Mediæval Manchester*, 1904, pp. 14 sqq., 182 sqq.) observes that in the 11th and early part of the 12th century any considerable military tenant might be called a baron whether he held of the crown or not. Little by little the appellation was restricted to the tenants-in-chief.

2. *Feudal England*, p. 247.

Mr. Round next asks himself what were the obligations imposed by William upon his tenant-in-chief; he concludes that the Conqueror,

It was William the Conqueror who established feudal service

without issuing any written grants or charters, nevertheless fixed the obligations of each great vassal and himself settled the *servitium debitum.*[1]

Examining, elsewhere, the replies given by the barons in 1166 to the inquest ordered by Henry II.,[2] he remarks that, save for rare exceptions which cannot invalidate the principle, the barons and the bishops owe to the king a number of knights varying from 10 to 100,[3] and which is always a multiple of 10 or of 5. If the assessment of the *servitium debitum* conformed to a precise estimate of the value of the barony, the

The amount fixed in relation to the unit of the host

adoption of these round figures is incomprehensible; we can understand it on the contrary, if we observe that the English *consta-*

1. Mr. Round chiefly invokes the testimony of the monastic chroniclers. He quotes in addition the following unpublished writ, which he dates 1072 : " W. rex Anglorum, Athew' abbati de Evesham salutem. Precipio tibi quod submoneas omnes illos qui sub ballia et justitia sunt, quatinus omnes milites quo[s] mihi debent paratos habeant ante me ad octavas Pentecostes apud Clarendunam. Tu etiam illo die ad me venias et illos quique milites quos de abbatia tua mihi debes tecum paratos adducas. Teste Eudone dapifero. Apud Wintoniam." (*Feudal England*, p. 304.)

2. The object of the inquest of 1166 was to fix and as far as possible increase the resources which might be expected from scutage. which was paid, as is well known, on the *scutum* or knight's fee. Mr. Round has shown very well how the replies of the barons were always interpreted to their disadvantage. These *cartae* of the barons, transcribed in the *Black Book* and the *Red Book* of the Exchequer, answered the following questions : How many knights had been provided with a knight's fee in the barony before the death of king Henry I.? How many since? If the number of knights' fees created was not equal to the number of knights to be furnished, how many knights *on the demesne*, that is to say, not enfeoffed, did the baron furnish? What were the names of the knights? Apropos of the expression *super dominium*, Mr. Round (p. 246, note 57) points out one of the "marvellously rare" lapses, which can be found in Stubbs; the latter has wrongly interpreted (see *Const. Hist.*, i, p. 285, note 3) the reply of the bishop of Durham. This prelate, as a matter of fact, declared that he had already created more than 70 knights' fees. Upon the tenures of the bishopric of Durham, see an article by G. T. Lapsley, on the *Boldon Book*, in *Victoria History of the County of Durham*, i, 1905, pp. 309 sqq.

3. Robert, son of Henry I. alone furnished 100 knights. It is even rare for the *servitum debitum* to reach 60 knights : the most frequent figures are 30 and under.

bularia consisted of ten knights, and that the Normans,
were already, at the time of the Conquest, acquainted with
the military unit of ten knights. It was natural that the
demands of the king from his barons should be based,
not with exactitude on their resources, which, moreover, it
was impossible for him to know with complete precision,
but on the necessities and customs of the military system.
" As against the theory that the military obligation of
the Anglo-Norman tenant-in-chief was determined by
the assessment of his holding, whether in hidage or in
value, I maintain that the extent of that obligation was
not determined by his holding, but was fixed in relation
to, and expressed in terms of, the *constabularia,* of ten
knights, the unit of the feudal host. And I, consequently, hold that his military service was in no way
derived or developed from that of the Anglo-Saxons,
but was arbitrarily fixed by the king, from whom he
received his fief." We believe, with Mr. Round, that
this solution is correct, and that it " removes all
difficulties."

To go back to the question which has drawn us into
following Mr. Round in his long discussion, we see that
the origin of military tenure or tenure by
knight service is a double one : the barony
was as a general rule a military holding
conferred by the king from the first days of
the Conquest, in return for the service of so many
knights ; the lands enfeoffed by the barons to knights in
order to be able to fulfil the said obligation towards the
king constituted a second series of military holdings.[1]

Origin of the
two series of
military
holdings

This second series was formed slowly, gradually, as
Stubbs says, and the crown only began to concern itself
directly with them and claim to regulate the number
of these sub-tenancies after the lapse of a century, at
the time of the inquest of 1166, at a moment when the

1. Mr. Round, pp. 293 sqq., admits that the knight's fee was normally
an estate yielding an annual revenue of 20 pounds.

tax for the redemption of service, the *scutage* of one or two marks on the knight's fee attracted the attention of the financiers of the exchequer. It seems as if the inquest of 1166 might have given military tenure a precision and stability which it had not as yet; but the fiscal aims which the officials of the Exchequer pursued were very soon to take from tenure by knight service its primitive reason for existence and its true character. In the thirteenth century military tenure will be simply the tenure which involves payment of scutage; thus it began to decline from the time it was regularised, a fairly frequent phenomenon in the history of institutions.

What view are we to take now as regards the links some have sought to discover between the Norman military tenure and the service of the Anglo-Saxon thegn? Mr. Round rejects every idea of filiation, and even declares that his theory on the introduction of knight service into England opens the way to the examination, on a fresh basis, of kindred problems, which should be viewed from the feudal point of view, and not with the set purpose of seeing Anglo-Saxon influences everywhere. Mr. Maitland, who has since published his *Domesday Book and Beyond,* and the second edition of his *History of English Law,* admits, as proved in the " convincing papers " of Mr. Round, that the number of knights furnished by each barony was actually fixed by William the Conqueror. But he questions whether the Normans really thus introduced into England a principle which was not already applied there. Even the notion of a contract between him who receives a piece of land and him who gives it in return for military servce was not foreign to the English. The ecclesiastical administrators who granted land to thegns were not squandering the fortune of the saints for nothing : they evidently intended to provide themselves with the warriors whom

Mr. Maitland's theory respecting Anglo-Saxon military service

their land owed to the king. Such a state of things might adapt itself to a feudal explanation; perhaps even it might give rise to it. We do not know what system was practised in the east of Saxon England, where the seignorial power was weak; but in the west the substance even of the knight's fee already existed. The Bishop of Worcester held 300 hides over which he had *sac and soc*; he had to furnish 60 *milites*; now at the beginning of the reign of Henry II., it is the same number of 60 knights which is imposed upon him.[1]

We find it difficult and even somewhat futile to choose between the view of Mr. Round and that of Mr. Maitland.

No direct influence upon Anglo-Norman service in the host

It is probable that the Normans, at the moment of the Conquest, were entirely ignorant of the very complex and varied institutions of the Anglo-Saxons, and that, if they had found nothing in England analogous to the feudal system, they would none the less have imposed their feudal ideas and customs, conquerors as they were, and but little capable, moreover, of rapidly grasping new social and political forms. On this ground, and if we ask ourselves for what reasons William the Conqueror brought over into England the system of service in the host as it existed in France, Mr. Round may quite legitimately deny all filiation between tenure by knight-service and the five hides of the thegn about which, doubtless, the Conqueror did not trouble himself.[2]

But England was prepared by her past to receive and develop the feudal organisation on her soil. She was

---

1. *Domesday Book and Beyond*, pp. 156 sqq.; see also pp. 294, 307–309, 317. Pollock and Maitland, *History of English Law*, i, pp. 258–259.

2. King's thegns still exist in the reign of William the Conqueror. But they do not rank with the tenants-in-chief by military service. In Domesday they are placed after the serjeants of the shire. As a distinct social class, they disappear during the reigns of the Conqueror's sons. (See the article by F. M. Stenton on the *Domesday* of the county of Derby in *Vict. History of Derbyshire*, i, 195, p. 307).

F

acquainted with commendation, with land held from a lord or from several lords superimposed, with military service due to a lord; under the form of the heriot, she was acquainted even with the right of relief; seignorial justice was widely established.[1]

The feudal régime finds a favourable soil for original development

England, therefore, easily accepted the seignorial and feudal régime; but of necessity she impressed her stamp upon it. Anglo-Norman society in the twelfth century differed from French society in very important points. Words and things show this clearly; tenure in socage, which little by little absorbed all the free tenures of the Middle Ages and still exists to-day, is an Anglo-Saxon term and is derived from the status of the *sochemanni*. It has been said that the Anglo-Saxon régime had only produced dismemberment and anarchy, and that the Norman Conquest arrested this disintegration by the introduction of the feudal system; but did not this dismemberment and this anarchy proclaim the spontaneous formation of a native feudal system? What the Norman Conquest brought to England, which England had not at all, either in reality or germ, was not feudalism, it was a monarchic despotism based on administrative centralisation.

1. Mr. Round in the studies which the editors of the *Victoria History* are publishing, insists on the divergences between the Norman feudal system and Anglo-Saxon institutions (*Victoria History of Surrey*, i, 1902, p. 288, *Hertfordshire*, i, 1902, p. 278; *Buckinghamshire*, i, 1905, p. 218). Mr. Maitland, however, does not pretend to deny these divergences.

VIII.

THE ORIGIN OF THE TOWNS IN ENGLAND.

THERE exists no satisfactory general account of the origin of the towns in England.[1] The pages devoted to this question by Stubbs, in three of the chapters of Vol. I.,[2] have long been the safest guide to consult. But during the last fifteen years this problem has been the subject of studies based on thorough research which have advanced its solution, and even those with which Stubbs was able to make himself acquainted and which he has quoted sometimes in the notes to his later editions might have been turned to greater profit by him. The researches of Mr. Gross, the ingenious and disputable theories of Mr. Maitland, the discoveries of Mr. Round and Miss Mary Bateson, notably, deserve to be known by our readers. With their help we must now draw out a summary sketch, in which we shall make it our chief endeavour to give the history of the English towns its proper place in the framework of the general history of the towns of the west.

France in the Middle Ages was acquainted with infinitely varied forms of free or privileged towns, and very diverse too are the names which were used to designate them from North to South. In England the degrees of urban enfranchise-

Novelty of the question (marginal note)

The "borough" (marginal note)

---

1. For the bibliography, see Ch. Gross, *Bibliography of British Municipal History*, 1897. It is an excellent repertory. But since 1897, some very important works have appeared, notably those of Miss Mary Bateson. Some years ago, English municipal history was backward compared with that of France; but the activity now displayed in that respect by scholars on the other side of the Channel contrasts with the present scarcity of good monographs on the French towns.

2. *Const. Hist.*, i, pp. 99—102, 438—462, and 667—676.

ment are less numerous,—the upper degrees are wanting—and, in addition, a somewhat peculiar term is applied to the privileged town in the later centuries of the Middle Ages : in opposition to the *villa,* to the *township,* it is called *burgus, borough,* and the municipal charters often contain in their first line the charactertistic formula : " Quod sit liber burgus." [1]   Hence in the works of English scholars who concern themselves with the origin of municipal liberties, the word borough is constantly made use of.   It seems to us necessary, however, to get rid of this word, which uselessly complicates and confuses the problem to be solved, and it is well to give our reasons at the outset.

The first idea that the word *borough* summons up is that of the " bonne ville " as it used to be called in **The difficulty of defining the borough** France ; that is to say, the town which sent representatives to the assemblies of the three estates.   In fact, in the fourteenth and fifteenth centuries, the borough is the town which is represented in the House of Commons.   But if we are not content to stop short at this external characteristic, and if we enquire in virtue of what principles a town is **The parliamentary criterion** selected to be represented in Parliament, we are obliged to recognise that such principles do not exist, that the list of boroughs is arbitrarily drawn up by the sheriffs, and that it even varies to a certain extent.   In the period before the application of the parliamentary system, is the boundary line which separates the boroughs from the simple market towns and villages any clearer?

Already, in his valuable book on the gild merchant, which is so full of ideas, facts and documents, Mr. Gross had observed that the term *liber burgus* is a very vague one, applying to a group of franchises the number of which gradually grew in the course of centuries, and

---

1. See, for example, in Stubbs' *Select Charters.* 8th edition, pp. 311, 313, etc. Upon this expression see below, page 69, note 2.

none of which, if we examine carefully the relative position of the *burgi* and the *villae*, was rigorously reserved to the *burgi*, or indispensable to constitute a *burgus*.[1] First among them was judicial independence :
The judicial the burgesses of the *liber burgus*[2] had not
criterion to appear before the courts of the shire and the hundred.[3]

In a quite recent work Miss Mary Bateson expresses the opinion that we have there in fact the characteristic of the borough : it is by its court of justice that the *borough*, detached from the hundred and forming as it were a hundred by itself, is distinguished from the Norman period onwards, from the township and the market town. It may have been originally a township, it may continue to be a manor in the eyes of its lord ; it is none the less, from a legal point of view, an entirely special institution, which has its place outside the shire and the hundred. It is not a slow evolution, it is a formal act, which gives it this place apart, and which makes of the word borough a technical term corresponding to a definite legal conception.[4] Undoubtedly there is much

1. Gross, *Gild Merchant*, 1890, i, pp. 5 sqq. Cf. A. Ballard, *English boroughs in the reign of John*, in *English Histor. Review*, xiv, 1899, p. 104.

2. According to Mr. Tait (*Mediæval Manchester*, p. 62; Cf. Pollock and Maitland, *History of English Law*, i, 639) the expression *liber burgus* would denote simply the substitution of the tenure in *burgagium* and its customs for the villein services and *merchetum* of the rural manor; and where it does not appear in the charter, it is because burgage-tenure existed before the granting of the charter. We do not think that this interpretation is sufficiently broad. *Liber burgus* often has a much more general sense, notably in the following document of the year 1200 relating to the town of Ipswich (published in Gross, *Gild Merchant*, ii, p. 117 : " Item eodem die ordinatum est per commune concilium dicte villate quod de cetero sint in burgo predicto duodecim capitales portmenni jurati, *sicut in aliis liberis burgis Anglie* sunt, et quod habeant plenam potestatem pro se et tota villata ad gubernandum et manutenendum predictum burgum et omnes libertates ejusdem burgi, etc."

3. Upon the great importance of the jurisdiction of the English towns in the early period, a jurisdiction which extended to " causae majores," see Mary Bateson, *Borough Customs*, ii, 1906, p. xx.

4. Mary Bateson, *Mediæval England*, 1903, pp. 124, 125; cf. the same author's *Borough Customs*, i, 1904, pp. xii sqq.; controversy with Mr. Ballard in *English Historical Review*, xx, 1905, pp. 146 sqq.

truth in this theory. But we cannot decidedly accept it in its entirety. The court of justice did not suffice, any more than the tenure in *burgagium* or the *firma burgi,* to constitute a *borough,* at the period at which men claimed to distinguish clearly between the *boroughs* and the market towns.[1] And, *a fortiori,* this must have been the case during the Norman period.

The criterion of "incorporation" We might be tempted to admit, with Mr. Maitland, that it is the character of a corporation,[2] which is the essential part in the conception of a *borough.* But "incorporation" is a legal notion, for which the facts no doubt prepared the way, but which was not stated in precise form until towards the end of the thirteenth century. For the twelfth and preceding centuries we must give up the attempt to find an exact definition of *burgus.* During the Anglo-Saxon period, and even in the eleventh century, the word *burh* had an extremely general signification. It does not even exclusively denote a town, but is also applied to a fortified house, a manor, a farm surrounded by walls.[3]

It should be observed that the important towns are also designated, for example in *Domesday Book,* by the name of *civitates;* like almost all the words in the language of the Middle Ages, *civitas* and *burgus* have no precise and strict application.[4] The difficulty would be the same, or nearly so, if one attempted to define the French *commune* not in an *a priori* fashion but after comparison of all the passages in which the word is

1. See the case of Manchester : Tait, op. cit., pp. 52 sqq. Cf. Pollock and Maitland, *English Law,* i, 640.
2. *Corpus corporatum et politicum, communitas,* etc. See Gross, *Gild Merchant,* i, pp. 93 sqq.; Pollock and Maitland, i, pp. 669 sqq.; and above all Maitland, *Township and Borough,* 1898.
3. W. H. Stevenson, in *English Historical Review,* xii, 1897, p. 491.
4. In France, *civitas* denotes a bishop's see; and this is often the case in England, but not uniformly. Cf. Maitland, *Domesday Book and Beyond,* 1897, p. 183, note 1; *Township and Borough,* p. 91; Round, in *Victoria History of the Counties, Essex,* i, 1903, pp. 414, 415. Upon the definition of the modern city, see G. W. Wilton, *The county of the city* in the *Juridica Review* (Edinburgh), April, 1906, pp. 65 sqq.

employed. In the same way that there is an advantage
in making use of this convenient word to denote our
most independent towns, it may be of service to use the

**Necessity of
laying aside
this term**   word *borough*, when we are studying the
English towns of the end of the Middle
Ages. But, for the period of origins, which
is the only one we have before us at present, it is better
not to embarrass ourselves with this expression which by
its misleading technical appearance has perhaps greatly
contributed to plunge certain English scholars into
blind alleys. It will be enough to ask ourselves how
the towns were formed which have a court of justice and
a market, which have a trading burgess population,
which have sooner or later obtained a royal or baronial
charter, and which, both by a variable body of privileges
and by their economic development, have distinguished
themselves from the simple agricultural groups; whether
they were destined to be called boroughs or market towns
matters little.

There is no imperious necessity for formulating the
problem any differently from the way it has been
formulated for the towns of the Continent, and it is for
this reason that we have not entitled this essay : *The
Origin of the Borough*. The question which directly
interests general history is to know how the English
towns were formed. It is doubtful whether this problem
can ever be solved with absolute certainty,[1] but that is
no reason for not approaching it at all.[2]

1. Cf. the reflections of Mrs. Green, *Town Life in the fifteenth
century*, 1894, Preface, p. xi. Mrs. Green appears to think that it is
better to lay aside for the present the study of municipal origins.

2. We make no pretence of treating here of the problem of the origin
of municipal liberties, or of explaining what those liberties were. Stubbs
has dealt very fully with the question, and we should risk repeating
him. A systematic enumeration of the privileges of the " boroughs " will
be found in Pollock and Maitland, *English Law*, i, pp. 643 sqq., and the
excellent book of Ch. Gross, *The Gild Merchant*, may be read with the
greatest profit; the second volume of this work is composed of original
documents of the highest interest for English municipal history as a
whole.

Domesday Book alone can give a solid point of departure for this study. The relatively abundant sources of the Anglo-Saxon period, laws, charters or chronicles, furnish only a very meagre quota to what we know of the towns before the Conquest. It is fortunate again that the " tempus regis Edwardi " was a matter of interest to the commissioners of King William, that we can project the light emanating from *Domesday* on the later times of Anglo-Saxon rule,—obscured though that light may often be.[1]

The sources

The most serious gap in our sources may be guessed : we have no information as to the filiation which may exist between certain English towns of the Middle Ages, and the towns founded on the same site by the Roman conquerors.[2] During the period of the Roman domination there were no great towns in England.[3] It is believed that Varulamium (St. Albans, in Hertfordshire) was a *municipium*; only four *coloniae* are known : Colchester, Lincoln, Gloucester and York. London was already the principal commercial centre, but we know almost nothing about it. There was without doubt a fairly large number of little towns; the names of some thirty of them have come down to us. Winchester, Canterbury, Rochester, Dorchester, Exeter, Leicester, etc., existed, and doubtless had a germ of municipal organisation. But, in the first place, we know nothing of this organisation, no important municipal

The question of Roman origin

Roman towns in England

1. On the mainly fiscal nature of Domesday, in which, moreover, a certain number of very important towns do not figure, see Maitland, *Domesday Book and Beyond*, pp. 1 sqq.; and A. Ballard, *Domesday Boroughs*, 1904, pp. 1 sqq.; above p. 18.
2. We have still less information, naturally, respecting Celtic origins. London seems to have arisen from a small, pre-Roman town. It is well known that the first mention of London is to be found in the *Annales* of Tacitus, bk. xiv, c. 33. ad ann. 61 : " Londinium . . . . copia negotiatorum et commeatuum maxime celebre. . . ."
3. See the works cited above, p. 12, note 3. On the places at which the Romans built towns see Haverfield, *Romano-British Warwickshire*, in *Victoria History of Warwickshire*, i, 1904, p. 228.

inscription having been preserved.   Again, we have no idea what became of the Romano-British towns during the tempest of the invasions.   At least the precise knowledge which we possess only relates to the disappearance of certain of them, burnt by the Anglo-Saxons, or else completely abandoned, like that curious

Silchester   Calleva Attrebatum (near the present village of Silchester, in Hampshire), of which it has become possible to say—so much have excavations been facilitated in our day by this rapid and definitive abandonment—that it is the best known archæologically of all the Roman provincial towns.   Calleva Attrebatum, after the extinction of the imperial government (about 407), was still inhabited for about a century ; a recent discovery has shown that they had again begun to speak and write the Celtic language there ; then, at the approach of the Germanic invaders the town was completely evacuated, and has never since been inhabited.[1] Other towns, such as Winchester (Venta Belgarum), appear, on the contrary, to have survived the catas-trophes of the sixth century ; but we know nothing of their ancient institutions.[2]   It is more than probable that they resembled those of the Roman towns of the

Romanist **theories**   Continent, and in consequence differed essentially from the municipal franchises of the Middle Ages.   Nevertheless Th. Wright[3] and H. C. Coote[4] have asserted the continuity of mnicipal life in England, the filiation of the urban institutions of

1. See the very interesting articles by Mr. Haverfield : *The last days of Silchester*, in *English Histor. Review*, xix, 1904, pp. 625 sqq. ; *Silchester* in the *Vict. Hist. of Hampshire*, i, pp. 271 sqq. Cf. *ibidem*, pp. 350 sqq., the archæological description by G. E. Fox and W. H. St. John Hope. See also the description of Castor, near Peterborough, in *Victoria History of Northamptonshire*, i, 1902, pp. 166 sqq. Mr. Haverfield believes that Castor was an old Celtic settlement.

2. See Haverfield, *Victoria History of Hampshire*, i, pp. 285 sqq.

3. *The Celt, the Roman and the Saxon, illustrated by ancient remains*, 1st edition, 1852, 4th edition, 1885.

4. *A neglected fact in English History*, 1864 ; *The Romans of Britain*, 1878.

the Middle Ages and of the Roman period. We can only repeat what Stubbs says of this same theory which he found again in Pearson's *History of England*. All the analogies on which the Romanists rely are susceptible of a different and much more probable explanation.[1] He might have added that most French scholars agree to-day in rejecting this filiation as far as concerns even the most profoundly and anciently Romanised parts of Gaul where municipal life was most intense.[2] What chance remains of there having been continuity in a country like Great Britain in which the imperial domination was much less solidly established? The humble village, with its tenacious agricultural customs, was able to maintain itself as it was, so it is supposed, in the storm of the Germanic conquest, but not the municipality with its institutions.

Certain towns, however, in the material sense of the word, were able, I repeat, to survive the great catastrophe. In spite of the disdain of the Germans for fortified refuges, the ramparts of the Roman towns and imperial fortresses must have been utilised, doubtess even kept in repair for a certain time by the invaders as well as by the invaded,[3] and certain Anglo-Saxon *burhs* must have been only the continuation or the resurrection of Roman fortified places. Such may have been the case with Winchester, Lincoln, Canterbury. In Gaul, a great number of Roman towns perished during the invasion; others, in spite of terrible misfortunes continued to be inhabited, while losing every vestige of their ancient political institutions; life concentrated itself in some particularly favourable quarter, easy of defence, or, with the materials of the abandoned houses, a square *castrum*

Probable persistence of some settlements

1. *Const. Hist.*, i, p. 99, note 3.
2. See Flach, *Orig. de l'ancienne France*, ii, pp. 227 sqq.
3. One of the most ancient Anglo-Saxon charters, No. 1 of the *Codex Diplomaticus* of Kemble, dated 604, speaks of a rampart (wealles).

was constructed, to which the sadly reduced population confined itself.[1] It is probable that this phenomenon of the preservation of fragments of urban life occurred in Britain as elsewhere, and the Germanists have no serious grounds for denying its possibility. In the material sense of the word, certain English urban groups may have continued the Roman town.

Stubbs, as we have seen, does not put this supposition absolutely aside. For the rest, if his study of the Anglo-Saxon town is a little wanting in clearness and vigour, at any rate it avoids thereby the faults of too systematic an exposition, and when he examines the formation of the *burh,* which, in his eyes, is nothing but " a more strictly organised form of the township," [2] he assigns a great share to the most diverse influences, and the wealth and variety of the information which his text and notes furnish has not perhaps been sufficiently noticed or turned to profit. We believe with him that in England, as in France, many of the urban communities grew out of pre-existent villages.[3] The rural, agricultural character of the town is particularly remarkable in England during the whole of the Middle Ages. Those who study its history, " have fields and pastures on their hands." [4] Part of the townsmen—doubtless the descendants of the most ancient inhabitants—are

Formation of English towns. Different influences

Towns born from villages

---

1. See Flach, *op. cit.,* pp. 238–9; Pirenne, *Orig. des constitutions urbaines,* in *Rev. Historique,* lvii, pp. 59 sqq.

2. We may guess what reading and comparisons inspired Stubbs with this theory, which derives the institutions of the town from those of the village, and which is rejected to-day by most scholars, doubtless in too absolute a manner : G. L. von Maurer, whose ideas had so much influence on him, alleges in his *Geschichte der Städteverfassung in Deutschland* (1869—1871) that every town is derived from a mark community. Since then, von Below has adopted the theory again in a less inadmissible form (*Ursprung der deutschen Stadtverfassung,* 1892) ; cf. Vinogradoff, *Growth of the Manor,* p. 148.

3. See the case of Derby in F. M. Stenton's article on the Domesday of Derbyshire, *Victoria History of Derbyshire,* i, 1905, pp. 308, 309.

4. Maitland, *Township and Borough,* p. 9.

husbandmen, the cultivated lands are sometimes found even inside the walls, and whatever may have been said to the contrary there are lands belonging to the community of burgesses.[1]

But the towns must have developed above all " in the places pointed out by nature as suited for trade," [2] **Influence of commerce** whether these places were still uninhabited or whether ancient Roman towns or villages existed there already. It was the interest of the kings and magnates to create markets there, which brought them in good revenues, and to guarantee the security of trade ;[3] merchants perhaps founded colonies there, as in **The monasteries** Germany and France. The " great monasteries in which the Anglo-Saxon bishops had their sees," were also by their economic importance, by the industrial and commercial needs, which the service of religion gave rise to, by the attraction which celebrated relics exercised, centres of urban concentration and work, and Stubbs notes that in the Anglo-Saxon version of Bede the equivalent given for *urbana loca* is *mynster-stowe*.[4]

Throughout the West the castles also formed the nuclei of urban groupings; they offered a refuge in **Military origins** case of attack, and it was the lord's interest to have for his neighbours artisans and

1. Cf. Maitland, *op. cit.* and *Domesday Book and Beyond*, pp. 200 sqq. ; .J. Tait, *English Historical Review*, xii, 1897, p. 776; and Ballard, *Domesday Boroughs*, pp. 87 sqq.

2. Stubbs. *Const. Hist.*, i, 99.

3. On the creation of markets, the prohibition of buying and selling elsewhere, the idea of preventing the sale of stolen objects, the market peace, etc., see Maitland, *Domesday Book and Beyond*, pp. 192 cqq.

4. The inventory of the rents and dues owing to the Abbey of St. Biquier (Hariulf, *Chron. de Saint Riquier*, ed. Ferd. Lot, 1894, Appendix vii) shows us, as early as the year 831, a numerous population of lay artisans grouped in streets according to their trades around that abbey, and in return for lands which are granted to them, furnishing some, tools, others bindings, or clothes or articles of food, etc. This very curious document has, it seems to us, the value of a general explanation, in the history of the monasteries and the monastic towns of the West.

merchants who could supply him with cheap goods.[1] It must have been the same in England. In any case it is quite clear that at one period every English town took on a military character. We may assume that this transformation which was to complete the constitution of towns clearly distinct from villages, took place in the time of Alfred. Until then the word *burh* denoted not a town, but a fortified house belonging to a king or a magnate.[2] In the eighth century the urban settlements, old or new, with the exception perhaps of those which may have grown up around one of these fortified houses, no longer had or never had any serious defence; so that the Danes, when they invaded eastern England in the ninth century, occupied the towns without resistance. By constructing military works for their own use they completed the lesson they were giving the English.

1. The formation of the town of Bruges is quite characteristic. It was, doubtless, the favourable geographical situation of the castle of the count, which caused the town to become a great commercial city instead of remaining an insignificant market town like so many of those which arose around castles (Cf. Pirenne, *op. cit.*, Revue Historique, lvii, p. 65). But there are many favourable sites to be met with where no town has ever been founded. It was the castle of Bruges which, to all appearance, determined the formation of the town; see the very typical passage from Jean le Long reproduced in Fagniez, *Docum, relat. à l' Hist. de l'industrie et du commerce en France*, 1898, i, No. 95 : " Post hoc ad opus seu necessitates illorum de castello ceperunt ante portam ad pontem castelli confluere mercemanni, id est cariorum rerum mercatores, deinde tabernarii, deinde hospitarii pro victu et hospicio eorum qui negocia coram principe, qui ibidem sepe erat, prosequebantur, domus construere et hospicia preparare, ubi se recipiebant illi qui non poterant intra castellum hospitari ; et erat verbum eorum : "Vadamus ad pontem" : ubi tantum accreverunt habitaciones, ut statim fieret villa magna, que adhuc in vulgari suo nomen pontis habet, nempe *Brugghe* in eorum vulgari pontem sonat." True—and M. Fagniez should have pointed this out to his readers—Jean le Long flourished in the fourteenth century ; and, as Dom Brial observes *(Historiens de France*, xviii, p. 593), he is not always able to distinguish the false from the true in the sources he consults. But there is every reason to accept his account of the construction of the castle of Bruges by Baldwin 'Bras de fer,' count of Flanders, in the time of Charles the Bald, and consequently the tradition which he recounts concerning the foundation of the town deserves attention.

2. On the ancient significance of the word *burh* and the *burh-bryce*, see Maitland, *Domesday Book*, p. 183. On the manner in which the *burhs* were fortified, see Round, *The Castles of the Norman Conquest*, in *Archæologia*, lviii, 1903.

Alfred (871—900) knew how to profit by it and created fortified places; and it is from his time that the word *burh,* instead of only denoting fortified houses, is also employed in the sense of town. We see in the Anglo-Saxon chronicle that the valiant warriors, the *burh-ware,* of Chichester and of London, contributed greatly to the success of the war against the Danes. Edward the Elder, son of Alfred (900—924), continued to found *burhs.*[1] We understand henceforth why the documents tell us of *cnihts* dwelling in the towns, and why the first city gilds are *cnihtengilds.*

Mr. Maitland has thrown a flood of light upon this foundation of military towns, which occupy a special place in the county, bear the same name as the county throughout the greater part of England,[2] and in some cases are planted at its geographical centre. The strategic value of these new towns explains why some of them are so small; it is not commercial prosperity nor density of population that gives the latter the special institutions which distinguish them from villages which are sometimes much larger; it is the fact that they are fortified places.

The county towns

Mr. Maitland goes further. He seeks to explain by purely military causes the differentiation which took place between the township and what he calls the borough; on a study of *Domesday Book,* which is certainly ingenious and suggestive, he bases a hypothesis which has been called the " garrison theory "; and he has been followed by another scholar, Mr. Ballard, who systematizes and exaggerates his theory.

The " garrison theory "

1. In 923, Manchester was fortified and occupied by a garrison, and this is the first mention which we have of that town (Tait, *Mediæval Manchester*, pp. 1 sqq.).

2. The counties lying to the North of the Thames nearly all bear the name of their county-towns; for example Oxford-shire (see list of counties in Stubbs, i, p. 107). Upon this question, see Ballard, *Domesday Boroughs,* pp. 4 sqq.

Certain towns described in *Domesday Book*, these two scholars observe, are characterised by tenurial hetero-
The passages
on which it
is founded
geneity, being composed of houses which belong, some (the majority) to the king, others to this or that Norman lord, lay or ecclesiastic; and these houses before the Conquest belonged, some to the king, others to some thegn or other. Thus at Oxford the *burgenses* and their houses or *haws* appertain in some cases to the king, in others to a prelate (the Archbishop of Canterbury, the Bishops of Winchester, of Lincoln, of Hereford, of Bayeux, of Coutances, the Abbot of Abingdon, etc., in others again to a Norman lord (the Count of Mortain, the Count of Evreux, Walter Giffard, etc.). *Domesday* affords evidence that this is not a Norman innovation for it gives us a list of *thegns* of the county of Oxford who, before the Conquest, so held houses in the " borough " of Wallingford. Moreover, the possession of many of these houses was in direct relation with the possession of such and such a manor in the rural part of the county; indeed the *Domesday* compiler frequently mentions the manor instead of the lord, and indicates how many houses the manor has in the borough; for example, the manor of Doddington has five haws in Canterbury. It is specified that before the Conquest, " tempore regis Edwardi," there were in Canterbury 259 houses thus attached to manors; and the rural estates possessing houses in Canterbury numbered thirteen. Not only houses but burgesses appertained to manors : eighty burgesses of Dunwich appertain to one of the manors of Ely, twenty-four burgesses of Leicester to the manor of Ansty, etc. These statements which puzzle the reader of *Domesday*, become intelligible and coherent if we suppose that every town characterised by tenurial heterogeneity dated from the period at which the Danish invasion had to be repelled, that it was originally essentially a military post, and that its

garrison and the upkeep of its ramparts were the concern of the whole county. We can understand then why, side by side with ordinary houses, there are houses which are appurtenances of rural estates, and why, at

Mural houses

Oxford, these houses bear the name of *mansiones murales,* and are burdened with the special charge of maintaining the fortifications of the town.[1] Freemen are in fact subject to the *trinoda necessitas,* the triple duty of repairing bridges, serving in war, and maintaining fortifications; the great rural proprietors who wish to acquit themselves of this last obligation without displacing their men, have a house in the town, furnished with *burgenses,* who when the king gives the order, will put in a state of defence the part of the ramparts the care of which is their charge. Many of the *burgenses,* moreover, are warriors, *cnihts,* and are maintained by the king and the great proprietors of the surrounding countryside : in this way is to be explained the mention in *Domesday* of *burgenses* attached to such and such a rural manor. In short, the primitive " borough " is essentially a fortress kept in a state of defence by the inhabitants of the county.

Later, at the end of the Anglo-Saxon period, the military spirit in the borough became enfeebled, a

Decay of the system. The homogeneous boroughs

fact which explains the relative ease of the Norman Conquest and the difficulty which we have in reconstituting the real character of the earliest towns. In addition there grew up on the royal demesne, or upon the estates of powerful men, urban groups which obtained tardily, perhaps subsequently to the Conquest, the privileges which the simple townships did not enjoy. These are the homogeneous ' boroughs,' which are dependent on a single lord; for example, Steyning, which belongs to the Abbot of Fécamp, and whose

---

1. The service of *burh-bot* and the custom of Oxford are noted by Stubbs, *op. cit.,* i, p. 102, note 4.

burgesses are all the Abbot of Fécamp's men. But the real 'borough,' the primitive *burgus,* is that which, at the date of *Domesday Book,* is still dependent on numerous lords.[1]

This theory is confronted unfortunately by unsurmountable objections.[2] If the inhabitants of a county ought to "contribute" to the upkeep of the ramparts and of the garrison of a particular "borough," and if it is thus that we must explain the mention of houses and burgesses appurtenant to rural manors, how comes it that *Domesday Book* speaks of houses appurtenant to manors which are not situated in the same county as the "borough" in which these houses stand? Why is it impossible to establish a proportion between the number of burgesses furnished by a manor and the extent of that manor, and how is the fact to be explained that a single manor of the Church of Ely maintains eighty burgesses at Dunwich?[3] Why are there so many manors exempt from the burden of maintenance, why are there only three which have duties towards the town of Chester? Moreover, the peculiarities of *Domesday Book,* which

Objections (margin note)

1. Mr. Maitland (*Domesday Book and Beyond,* pp. 176 sqq.) only considers specially characteristic the boroughs described in Domesday at the beginning of their county, apart from the general arrangement of fiefs, and so to speak in direct relation with the county itself. It is these that he calls *county towns,* and Mr. Ballard (*Domesday Boroughs,* p. 5) calls *county boroughs.* But according to Mr. Ballard (p. 43) there are other "boroughs" (he gives them the queer name of *quasi county boroughs*) which are not separately described at the beginning of the county, and which yet ought, from the point of view which he is taking, to be classed with the first category; the difference which separates them is of a fiscal nature, and does not directly concern the "garrison theory."

2. See the reviews of *Domesday Book and Beyond* by J. Tait, and of Ballard's work by Miss Mary Bateson, in the *English Historical Review,* xii, 1897, pp. 772 sqq. and xx, 1905, pp. 144 sqq. Cf. Round, in *Victoria History of Surrey,* i, 1902, pp. 285-286; *Hertfordshire,* i, 1902, p. 295; *Essex,* i, 1903, p. 385; *Berkshire,* i, 1906, pp. 310 sqq. Mr. Round more particularly corrects the mistakes of Mr. Ballard.

3. Dunwich, moreover, is simply described as a manor, *manerium,* in *Domesday Book.* But Mr. Ballard inserts in his list of "boroughs" all the localities to which *Domesday Book* attributes *burgenses,* and applies the garrison-theory to all of them .

G

the garrison theory claims to render intelligible, are for the most part capable of a simpler interpretation. Miss Bateson has elucidated the position of the *burgenses* appurtenant to rural manors in a very satisfactory manner. They were evidently non-resident burgesses, country people, who, with a view to gain, bought the freedom of a town, in which they might do a profitable trade. The eighty *burgenses* of Dunwich, appurtenant to a manor of the abbey of Ely, had doubtless bought their title, in order to come and buy the herrings which the monks needed, in that port. The houses appertaining to rural lords might serve as occasional lodgings, storehouses, etc. . . . We may add that comparative history does not allow us to consider the " tenurial heterogeneity " of so many English towns very surprising. Material and political dismemberment is the dominant feature of the French and German towns up to the eleventh century. The town was nothing but a juxtaposition of patchwork, of fragments of great estates.[1] There is no reason for attributing an absolutely original growth to the English towns, and it is, in our view, singularly rash to spin theories on their origin without constantly recalling to mind the conditions under which the towns of the Continent appear to have developed.

We propose then to accept the views of Mr. Maitland on the foundation of numerous fortified places in the time of Alfred and his successors, but to reject his theory, made even less acceptable as systematized by Mr. Ballard, on the alleged distinction, of a purely military character, between the " borough " and the township. The creative element of this distinction was doubtless, in England as on the Continent, commerce. Even at the period of the creation of the military *burhs* the economic factor must

Early importance of commerce

1. Flach, *Orig. de l'ancienne France*, ii, pp. 243 sqq. ; Pirenne, in *Revue Historique*, lvii, pp. 62 sqq.

have played its part; except in some cases in which
strategic considerations stood in the way, the king
doubtless chose trading places, which it was all important
to defend and convert into defensive centres, for
fortification and the development in them of the
military spirit : such was evidently the
case with London. It is evident, besides,
that the transformation of a town into
a *burh* must have singularly facilitated the development
of its trade, since the king's peace specially protected
burhs. A good situation on a navigable river or
on an old Roman road, and commercial traditions, on
the one hand, the special security due to the ramparts,
the garrison, the king's peace, on the other hand,
may have thus had a reciprocal action. The military
occupation of the towns thus completed and did nothing
but complete the work accomplished under the powerful
stimulus of commercial and industrial needs. And it is
signficant that, in the Anglo-Saxon laws, we sometimes
find the town designated by the name of *port*,[1] and that
numerous charters tell us of a town's officer called port-
reeve or port-gerefa.[2] The *port* is the
place of commerce; it is the old name for
a town in Flanders, where civic origins have a clearly
economic character.[3]

Thus the Anglo-Saxon towns, like the towns of the

Reciprocal influences

The " port "

1. Notably in a passage in the laws of Athelstan, in which *port* is
clearly synonymous with *burh* (Liebermann, *Gasetze*, i, pp. 155—159,
§ § 14 and 14, 2).
2. Stubbs, *op. cit.* i, 100, 439, 440, 451, note 2. There is also the
port-moot or *port-man-moot*, the *port-men*, etc. These words apply to
inland towns as well as to sea-ports.
3. The different causes which favoured the growth of towns can be
clearly distinguished in the county of Durham. According to the
Boldon-Book, this county possessed five towns at the end of the 12th
century. The external conditions which had determined their development were : at Durham, the castle and the church; at Norham, the
castle; at Wearmouth, the sea-port; at Darlington, the high-road; at
Gateshead, the close vicinity, on the other bank of the Tyne, of the
town of Newcastle, of which Gateshead was in some sort the suburb.
See the article by Lapsley on the *Boldon-Book*, in *Victoria History of
Durham*, i, pp. 306 sqq.

Continent, were formed in the places in which the
insufficiency of agricultural life made itself
felt, where the chance of leading a less
laborious, more spacious, even safer life
than that of the peasant offered itself.
In England, as elsewhere, the monastery and the
castle served as nuclei of urban concentration. There
as elsewhere the creation of markets attracted colonies
of traders, and, thanks to the special protection of
the king, the town was an abode of peace, a peace
safeguarded by a doubtless rigorous penal code. There
as elsewhere walls gave the citizens a security unknown
to the rustic population. The Anglo-Saxon town, it is
true, possesses a special franchise : it is a hundred by
itself, it has its *moot,* its court of pustice. It owes this
point of superiority over the French town to the surival
of the Germanic institution of the hundred among the
Anglo-Saxons. But, like the towns of the Continent at
the same period, it is heterogeneous, split up, and its
judicial unity is interfered with by private jurisdictions;
sac and *soc* correspond to immunity.[1] It has no corporate
unity : it has indeed associations, gilds; but these are
pious or charitable brotherhoods, clubs whose main
business is to brew beer and drink it at the common
expense ;[2] they are not corporations taking part in the
government of the town. Of merchant gilds, whose

*Features of
resemblance to
the continental
towns*

1. Whilst attaching due importance to the interesting popular institution of the *moot,* we should remember that in the continental towns,
justice had not entirely fallen into private hands, and that the cases of
the merchants escaped the immunists. Already, in the Carolingian
empire merchants were protected by the public authority, and it followed
that disputes in matters of weights and measures and business transactions
continued to belong to the public jurisdiction. Many merchants, moreover, were subject to no private jurisdiction, from any point of view.
See Pirenne, *op. cit., Revue histor.,* lvii, pp. 78 sqq., and pp. 86 sqq., for
the importance of the *jus mercatorum,* [of which a useful account is given
in Mitchell's *Law Merchant* (1904)]. Upon this last point, cf. L. Vander-
kindere. *La première phase de l'évolution constitutionelle des communes
flamandes,* in *Annales de l'Est et du Nord,* année 1905, pp. 365 sqq.

2. See the article by J. H. Round on the inquest of Winchester, in
Victoria History of Hampshire, i, p. 532.

interest it would be to manage common affairs, there is
as yet no trace either in the documents or the Anglo-
Saxon period or even in *Domesday*; it has been proved,
moreover, that later, when there were merchant gilds,
they did not constitute the kernel of municipal administration.   And this is another feature common to the
towns of England and those of the Continent, that the
gild, while it was an element of progress and of joint
defence against oppression, was not the creative element
of civic self-government.[1]

From what Stubbs says it is evident that we are as
badly informed respecting the inner life of the primitive
**Urban
institutions** English towns as respecting that of the
towns of the Continent.[2] We know
nothing which allows us to assert the
existence of a true municipal patriciate; there is not
proof that the possessors of sac and soc, such as the
lagemen of Lincoln, had administrative powers. We
see clearly what the burdens weighing upon the
' burgenses ' are : payment of *geld* and dues in kind
(*firma unius noctis* and others) to the king, payment of
gafol to the lord of the manor, military service, etc.; but
we do not see what their liberties are. It is true that the
description of such liberties was not one of the objects
for which the Anglo-Saxon charters and *Domesday
Book* were drawn up. It is very probable, moreover,
that, as early as the eleventh century, the burgesses,
emboldened by wealth and peace, had sought for safeguards against the financial tyranny of the royal officers,
had dreamed of independence; they had evidently more
cohesion and strength than the inhabitants of the
country. They asked to be allowed to pay the sheriff
an annual fixed sum, instead of numerous little imposts
which made exactions easy; at Northampton the *firma*

1. See Gross, *Gild Merchant*, i, pp. 77 sqq.; Hegel, *Staedte und Gilden*
(1891).

2. Stubbs, *Const. Hist.*, i, p. 100 sqq.

burgi already exists at the time of *Domesday*. At this period, the movement of revolt against seignorial oppression has already begun in some continental towns. Everywhere the increase of moveable wealth created a powerful class of townsmen, careful to safeguard their material interests and able to enforce their claims.

It would perhaps be allowable to say that from that time forward divergences show themselves between the towns of England and those of the rest of the West. And yet, while it is true that city-republics analogous to those of Italy or Flanders are not found across the Channel, we must not think that the island was not open to continental influences. The present generation of English scholars has only quite recently set itself to determine these influences, and the results obtained have already changed all received ideas as to the development of the English towns. " Our characteristic belief that every sort of ' liberty ' was born of ideas inherently English," writes one of these scholars,[1] " must receive another check, and must once more be modified to meet certain facts that have failed to obtain due recognition."

Mr. Round has shown that the maritime towns forming the confederation of the Cinque Ports had, with their mayor and their council of twelve *jurats,* a constitution of French origin, that they were acquainted with the essentially Flemish and Picard penalty of demolition of the offender's house,[2] and he thinks that the very idea of this confederation—

(marginal notes: Continental influences after the conquest; The Cinque Ports)

1. Miss Mary Bateson, *The Laws of Breteuil*, in *English Histor. Review*, xv, 1900, p. 73.
2. Mr. Round is wrong, however, in saying that this punishment existed in England only in the Cinque Ports. I find it in the Customs of Preston : "Pretor de curia colliget firmam domini regis ad quatuor terminos anni, et ibit semel propter firmam, et alia vice, si placuerit ei, *deponet hostium cujuslibet burgensis, etc.*" (*Engl. Histor. Review*, xv, 1900, p. 497). Other instances have been quoted by Miss Bateson in her *Borough Customs*, i, pp. 30, 264, 280 and ii, pp. 38—40.

analogous to certain French collective communes and christened, moreover, by the French name of " Cinque Ports,"—was borrowed from Picardy.[1]

We shall summarize and discuss further on Mr. Round's articles on the history of London; according to that scholar we have there an example of communal revolution analogous to those of France and suggested by them. Finally, a more certain fact, the Norman

---

1. *Feudal England*, pp. 552 sqq. Professor Burrows, in his *Cinque Ports* (Historic Towns), held that this privileged confederation was in existence before the Norman conquest. Mr. Round, *op. cit.*, vigorously disputes this assertion. He appears to us to have proved that Edward I, in his charter of 1278, does not mention any charter of Edward the Confessor relative to the Cinque Ports. He also shows that we do not possess any royal charter granting privileges to the Cinque Ports as a body, anterior to that of 1278. He recognises that the charter of Edward I did not create the confederation, did nothing but sanction the relations already existing between the maritime towns of the south-east. But he asserts that " even so late as the days of John the Ports had individual relations with the crown, although their relations *inter se* were becoming of a closer character, as was illustrated by the fact that their several charters were all obtained at the same time (in 1205). Hastings alone, as yet, had rights at Yarmouth recognised : hers were the only portsmen styled " barons " by the crown." It is surprising to find a scholar like Mr. Round in error. Formal documents, which are very accessible, refute his view. I have collected, in my *Etude sur la vie et le règne de Louis VIII,* a fair number of documents concerning the Cinque Ports in the time of John Lackland and Henry III (see my index at the word Cinque Ports.) They prove that, not only did the Cinque Ports in the eyes of the contemporary chroniclers, of the Pope and of the legate, form an official confederation, but John and the counsellors of his infant son treated them as such, and did not reserve the name of barons to the inhabitants of Hastings alone. It will suffice to quote a letter patent of 26 May, 1216, in which John Lackland institutes Earl Warenne as warden of the Cinque Ports, whose " barons," moreover, had decided to take the side of Lewis of France : " Rex baronibus de Quinque Portubus. Quia nolumus quemquam alienigenam vobis capud vel magistrum prefici, mittimus ad vos deiictum nobis et fidelem W. comitem Warenniae, consanguineum nostrum, ut presit vobis ex parte nostra ad vos custodiendum et defendendum." (*Rotuli litt. Pat.* i, p. 184, col. 1). Since when had this confederation existed ? I do not know whether the question can ever be settled. Mr. Round recognises that the problem is difficult, and Samuel Jeake (*Charters of the Cinque-Ports*, 1728, p. 121) already said that the origin of the Cinque-Ports and their members was a very obscure question. We cannot, in any case, discuss it with any chance of success until all the documents bearing upon it have been got together. Works such as the book—a very artistic production it may be admitted—of Mr. F. M. Hueffer (*The Cinque Ports, a historical and descriptive record*, 1900) are useless to the scholar, owing to the absence of any serious study of the sources.

conquerors created towns to secure their domination, and gave these towns French customs. This very interesting discovery was made by Miss Mary Bateson.[1]

It was thought until recently that the customs of Bristol had served as a model to a great number of English towns;[2] it was, in most of the cases, a mistake, arising from a faulty translation of the place-name Britolium.

The diffusion of the customs of Breteuil

Miss Bateson has shown that at least seventeen towns of England, Wales and Ireland, perhaps twenty-five,[3] had been granted the customs and franchises of the little Norman town of Breteuil, that several of these seventeen towns—Hereford, Rhuddlan and Shrewsbury—served in their turn as models to others, had daughter towns, even grand-daughter towns. Thus Breteuil played the same part in England as Lorris or Beaumont-en-Argonne in France, or Freiburg-im-Breisgau in Germany. It was not a very ancient or very celebrated town; it first appears in history about 1060 when Duke William built a castle there; but William Fitz-Osbern, to whom the castle of Breteuil was entrusted, became one of the greatest personages of Norman England,[4] and it is to him and his powerful family that the diffusion of the custom of Breteuil is due. This diffusion took place principally in the March of Wales, and its history shows how, by

1. 'The Laws of Breteuil,' in *English Histor. Review*, xv, 1900, and xvi, 1901. Aug. de Prévost, *Mém pour servir à l'hist. du départ. de l'Eure*, 1862, i, pp. 430 sqq., had already given useful information on this subject. See also R. Génestal, *La tenure en bourgage dans les pays régis par la coutume de Normandie*, 1900, pp. 237 sqq.

2. Mr. Gross enumerates thirty-one towns "affiliated" to Bristol (*Gild Merchant*, i, pp. 244 sqq.); eleven only, amongst these thirty-one, were so in reality.

3. Hereford, Rhuddlan, Shrewsbury, Nether Weare, Bideford, Drogheda in Meath and Drogheda Bridge, Ludlow, Rathmore, Dungarvan, Chipping Sodbury, Lichfield, Ellesmere, Burford, Ruyton, Welshpool, Llanvyllin, Preston. The eight less certain cases are those of Stratford-on-Avon, Trim, Kells, Duleek, Old Leighlin, Cashel, Kilmaclenan, Kilmeaden.

4. Stubbs, i, p. 389.

the creation of castles and of free towns the Norman

Process of urban colonisation
barons definitely colonised and subjected regions far from the centre of government where the pressure of the royal power was comparatively weak. The castle was generally constructed near an already existing village; the village was converted into a free town, or even in some cases a new town was built beside the village. The creation of a market, the assured custom of the garrison, the bait of the franchises of Breteuil, attracted settlers. The former inhabitants of the village continued to cultivate the land, whilst the new population, endowed with very small holdings, comprising, for example, a house and a garden, gave themselves up to industry and commerce. At times even a third element placed itself side by side with the two others; at Shrewsbury, for instance, there was a colony of French merchants, who lived apart and under a régime which had some special features. The article of the customs of Breteuil to which the burgesses attached the most value was doubtless that which reduced the maximum fine to 12 pence. It is to be found in the customs of many towns of Wales, Ireland, Devon, Cornwall, etc., which did not enjoy the rest of the franchises of Breteuil.

Thus the process of urban colonisation, employed throughout the whole extent of France by the church, the feudal baronage and the crown, employed also to civilize Germany, at first by Charlemagne, then by the emperors and princes of the twelfth and thirteenth centuries, was also applied in England. The " ville neuve " is to be found there [1] with franchises borrowed from a French prototype.

It cannot, however, be denied that the development of the English towns had a somewhat peculiar character,—

---

1. See what M. Luchaire says about the ‘villes neuves’ : *Manuel des institutions françaises*, pp. 445—450.

Original features of the English towns

above all, because it was slower than on the Continent and was incomplete. The English towns never attained complete independence; during the whole of the Middle Ages they remained rather small urban groups. Must we conclude from this that the Anglo-Saxon genius was ill-adapted for city life, and was only at its ease in the organisation of the village and the agricultural group?[1] We will not invoke the " genius of the race;" it is better to explain this fact by the economic conditions peculiar to mediæval England and by the extraordinary power of its monarchy.[2]

1. This is what Mr. Round says in a passage which, however, is concerned only with the Anglo-Saxon period (*Commune of London*, 1899, p. 221).
2. It will suffice to recall the case of the most important of English towns, London, whose mediocre liberties were unceasingly at the mercy of the kings. See below.

NOTE BY EDITOR.—Since this chapter was written a valuable survey of recent investigations into the origin of English municipal institutions has been contributed by Mr. H. W. C. Davis to the *Quarterly Review*, Jan., 1908 (vol. ccviii, p. 54).

IX.

LONDON IN THE TWELFTH CENTURY.

ACCORDING to Stubbs,[1] the charter of Henry I., granted
to the Londoners in the first years of the twelfth century [2]
profoundly altered the organisation of
London. The "complex system of gild
and franchise" gave place to the system of
the county; the city became a county in itself, and the
county of Middlesex, in which it lay, was let at farm to
the Londoners by Henry I.; henceforth London had its
own sheriff. But Henry I.'s favours were ephemeral;
the *Pipe Roll* of 1130 bears witness to it. The suppression of such precious privileges, the disappearance of
the port-reeve, the conversion of the *cnihten-gild* into a
religious house, "signify, perhaps, a municipal revolution the history of which is lost."

The charter
of Henry I.

Such a statement of the facts treats the searching
studies of Mr. Round as if they had never been.[3]

It is to them that, pending the appearance of a good
history of London, which does not yet exist,[4] we must

1. *Const. Hist.*, i, p. 439 sqq.; 673 sqq.
2. *Ibid.*, p. 674.
3. *The early administration of London*, in *Geoffrey de Mandeville*
(1892), "Appendix P," pp. 347—373;—*London under Stephen*, in *The
Commune of London* (1899), pp. 97—124. Stubbs quotes (p. 440, note 1)
the first of these two articles for a detail concerning a misreading of the
charter of Henry I, and he adds that "the whole history of London at
this period is treated there," but in spite of this admission, he has not
rectified his certainly erroneous interpretation of the charter of Henry I.
4. We await with impatience the volumes dealing wih London, which
are to form a special series in the *Victoria History* of the counties.
Quite recently there has appeared the first volume of a description of
London in the Middle Ages by Sir Walter Besant (*Mediæval London*,
1906, i). There is scarcely a mention in this first volume of the municipal institutions which are to be studied in vol. ii. Sir Walter Besant's
work is unprovided with any notes or *apparatus criticus*.

look for an exact and intelligible interpretation of the charter of Henry I.

"Sciatis me concessisse civibus meis Londoniarum tenendum Middlesex ad firmam pro ccc libris ad compotum, ipsis et haeredibus suis, de me et haeredibus meis, ita quod ipsi cives ponent vicecomitem qualem voluerint de se ipsis."[1]

Several scholars, notably Freeman,—Stubbs has not taken sides clearly on this point—have thought that by this clause Henry I. gave Middlesex in some sort to the Londoners, made of it a district subject to London, in its fiscal relations. Mr. Round has shown, that *Middlesex* here signifies London and Middlesex which surrounds it, that London and Middlesex formed but a single unit for the farm of taxation, and that this state of things, far from having been created by the charter of Henry I., existed long before. It was natural, indeed, that the smallest of the English counties should form one body with the greatest of English towns, which it contained. It is also a mistake to believe that the office of sheriff was created by the charter of Henry. The sheriff (*shire-reeve*) existed before, but, as here the town (*port*) was more important than the county (*shire*), that officer was called the *port-reeve* and not the *shire-reeve*. The *vicecomes* is no other than the *port-reeve* of London, who was, perhaps, called *shire-reeve*, sheriff when dealing with the affairs of Middlesex. The title of *port-reeve* disappeared in the 12th century, but not the office.[2]

Henry I., then, neither constituted London a county, **Real object of the Charter** nor subjected Middlesex to London, nor created the office of sheriff of London.[3]

1. *Select Charters*, p. 108.
2. As for the "conversion of the *cnihten-gild* into a religious house" accepted by Stubbs, Coote, and Loftie, it is, Mr. Round has shown, pure imagination.
3. Was the office of justiciar of London, on the contrary, a novelty? Henry I. says in his charter: ". . . ipsi cives ponent . . . . justitiarium qualem voluerint de seipsis, ad custodiendum placita coronae meae et eadem placitanda, et nullus alius erit justitiarius super ipsos homines

But the Londoners, who had evidently suffered from the exactions of the royal sheriffs, by the charter in question obtained the entire disposal of the office, in other words they paid the farm of the City and of Middlesex to the king themselves.

In addition, the farm, which Henry I. had increased to £500, was brought down to the previous figure of £300.

There is nothing to compel us to believe that the charter of Henry I., whose date is unknown, is earlier **No corporate** than the *Pipe Roll* of 1130, which bears **unity** witness to an organisation much less advantageous to the citizens; it was this unfavourable organisation that, in all probability, the charter granted by Henry remedied. But there was still nothing, it seems, in the capital, which resembled a municipality;[1] as Stubbs says, London was nothing but an " assemblage of little communities, manors, parishes, ecclesias-

---

Londoniarum." Mr. Round asserts that this office, which arose from a dismemberment of the sheriffdom, was, as far as London is concerned, created by the charter of Henry I (*Geoffrey de Mandeville*, pp. 106 sqq. and Append. P, p. 373). Nevertheless Mr. Round has himself republished a charter of 1141, in which King Stephen confers on Geoffrey de Mandeville " *justicias* et vicecomitatum de Londonia et de Middlesexa in feodo et hereditate *eadem firma qua Gaufridus de Mannavilla avus suus eas tenuit, scilicet pro C C C libris*" (*Ibidem*, pp. 141–142). The office existed, therefore, at the end of the preceding century (cf. *ibidem*, p. 373), unless we assume that the charter of 1141 mentions separately two offices which were still united in one in the time of Geoffrey de Mandeville the grandfather. We should like, however, to draw attention to the fact that this is pure hypothesis, and that there is nothing in the charter of Henry I to show that the office was a new one. This office is several times mentioned in the collection of London municipal documents, contained in the Additional MS. 14, 252, which Miss Bateson has analysed in *E. H. R.* Unfortunately, these documents are for the most part undated. The justiciar is there called *justicia* in Latin, *justise* in French. (*E. H. R.*, xvii, 1902, pp. 707, 711.)

1. Dr. Liebermann has, indeed, drawn attention to a phrase in the little tract entitled *De injusta vexatione Willelmi Dunelmensis*, of which Stubbs had occasion to make use for another purpose (see Stubbs, i. p. 476). We find mention there of the "meliores duodecim cives " of London, and it may be asked whether there is not a reference here to a body of twelve notables governing London as early as the end of the 11th century (Cf. Mary Bateson, in *E. H. R.*, xvii, 1902, p. 730, note 105.)

tical jurisdictions and gilds," and each of these organisms had a life of its own. The corporate unity of London was prepared for only by some common institutions: I mean the financial system of the royal farm, the *folkmoot,*—an assembly of little importance which had met from time immemorial,—and above all the weekly court of Danish origin, the *husting.* The misfortunes and anarchy of Stephen's reign showed the value and necessity of this corporate unity, without however bringing about its definitive realisation.

The Londoners, who had taken part in the election of Stephen, and who, during the disorder of the civil war,

The "communio" of 1141 saw the monarchical power dissolve and the king's peace disappear, were too proud, too careful for the security of their persons and their property, not to aspire to the unity alone capable of securing their independence and rendering them redoubtable. They were in constant relations with the communities of the Continent. The idea came quite naturally to them of imitating these. It appears that in 1141, the year in which they made a *conspiratio* to drive out the Empress Matilda, they formed a sort of sworn commune; William of Malmesbury speaks of a *communio* and says that barons had been received into this association.[1]

There would seem, then, to have been a revolutionary movement in London analogous to those which agitated certain towns of the Continent. But it very often happened that the leagues formed under oath, in French or German towns had no lasting result.[2]

1. " Feria quarta venerunt Londoniensis, et, in concilium introducti, causam suam eatenus egerunt ut dicerent missos se a communione quam vocant Londoniarum, non certamina sed preces offere, ut dominus suus rex de captione liberaretur. Hoc omnes barones, qui in eorum communionem jamdudum recepti fuerant, summopere flagitare a domino legato." (Will of Malmesbury, *Hist. Novella*, Ed. Stubbs, ii, p. 576.) Cf. the account given by Stubbs, *Const. Hist.*, i, p. 442.

2. For example, the league formed in 958 by the people of Cambray to prevent their bishop from returning to their town : " Cives Cameraci male consulti *conspirationem* multo tempore susurratam et diu desideratam

This was what took place in the case of the "communio" of 1141, whatever may have been its precise character.

Far from granting new privileges to the Londoners, who had just rendered him a splendid service, Stephen was, in fact, obliged by circumstances to favour the powerful Geoffrey de Mandeville at their expense, and to take from them even the advantages which had been granted to them by Henry I., or at least those which they valued most. As early as Christmas of this same year 1141, the offices of sheriff and justiciar of London were conferred on or rather restored by Stephen to, the house of Mandeville, which had already enjoyed them, at the end of the preceding century, in return for a farm of £300.[1]

King Stephen and London

In the reign of Henry II., the sheriffs of London and of Middlesex are named by the king, and the farm rises to the figure of £500 or even more. The office of justiciar, doubtless incompatible with the circuits of the itinerant justices, disappears. The charter cf 1155 marks a reaction from the charter of Henry I. The reign of the most powerful sovereign, of the most despotic statesman perhaps who had yet governed the English had just begun, and the son of Matilda could not easily pardon the Londoners either for the support they had given Stephen against the empress, or for their aspirations to independence.

Henry II. and London

---

juraverunt *communiam*. Adeo sunt inter se sacramento conjuncti, quod nisi factam concederet *conjurationem*, denegarent universi introitum Cameraci reversuro pontifici." This phrase of the *Gesta episcoporum Cameracensium* (*Monum. Germ.* SS. vii, p. 498) recalls the *communio* and the *conspiratio* of London in 1141. But it proves (*nisi factam concederet conjurationem*) that the Cambresians demanded liberties, while we know absolutely nothing of the end aimed at by the *communio* of the Londoners, and their *conspiratio* of the month of June 1141 seems to have had for its sole object the expulsion of Matilda

1. Sir Walter Besant does not seem to have been acquainted with this charter of Stephen in favour of the Mandevilles. (Cf. *Mediæval London*, i, p. 4.)

Exactly half-a-century after the episode of 1141, when Henry II. was dead, when Richard was fighting in the Holy Land, and civil troubles were beginning again in England, the Londoners took advantage of the conflict between William Longchamp and John Lackland to renew the attempt to establish a commune. This time, they succeeded, and John took an oath to the *communa* of London on the 8th of October.[1] It was a real commune, a " seigneurie collective populaire" in the French fashion. The famous invective of Richard of Devizes proves this fact very clearly.[2] The commune of London doubtless organised itself immediately. In any case—we learn this from a text which Dr. Liebermann had pointed out and Mr. Round first made full use of,—as early as 1193, it had a mayor. At that date, indeed, the members of the commune of London swear to remain faithful to Richard, who is a prisoner in Germany; they swear also to adhere to the commune, and obey the mayor of the city of London and the *skivini* (*échevins*) of the commune, and give consideration to the mayor and *skivini* and other *probi homines* who shall be with them.[3]

The commons of 1191

The mayor of London

Stubbs, who was not acquainted with this document,

1. See the very brief account in Stubbs, i, p. 673.

2. " Concessa est ipsa die et instituta communia Londoniensium, in quam universi regni magnates et ipsi etiam ipsius provinciae episcopi jurare coguntur. Nunc primum in indulta sibi conjuratione regno regem deesse cognovit Londonia, quam nec rex ipse Ricardus, nec praedecessor et pater ejus Henricus pro mille millibus marcarum argenti fieri permisisset. Quanta quippe mala ex conjuratione proveniant ex ipsa poterit diffinitione perpendi, quae talis est : communia est tumor plebis, timor regni, tepor sacerdotii " (Ed. Howlett in *Chronicles of the reigns of Stephen, etc.* (Rolls Ser.), iii, p. 416.)

3. "*Sacramentum commune tempore regis Ricardi quando detentus erat Alemaniam* (sic.).—Quod fidem portabunt domino regi Ricardo de vita sua et de membris et de terreno honore suo contra omnes homines et feminas qui vivere possunt aut mori et quod pacem suam servabunt et adjuvabunt servare, et quod communam tenebunt et obedientes erunt maiori civitatis Lond[onie] et skivin[is] ejusdem commune in fide regis et quod sequentur et tenebunt considerationem maioris et skivinorum et aliorum proborum hominum qui cum illis erunt salvo honore Dei et sancte Ecclesie et fide domini regis Ricardi et salvis per omnia libertatibus civitatis Lond[onie]." (Round, *Commune of London*, pp. 235–236.)

had divined the character of the revolution of 1191. He
notes the French origin of the office of
mayor, and of the commune. He only
touches lightly on the question in his
Constitutional History. But, in one of the substantial
notices with which he has accompanied his *Select
Charters*, he writes : " The mayoralty of London dates
from the earliest years of Richard I., probably from the
foundation of that *communa* which was confirmed on
the occasion of William Longchamp's downfall. The
name of that officer, as well as that of the *communa*
itself, is French. That the incorporation under this
form was held to imply very considerable municipal
independence may be inferred from the fact that one of
the charges brought by William Fitz-Osbert against
Richard Fitz-Osbert, was that he had not forbidden the
saying : *quodcunque eat vel veniat quod nunquam
habeant Londonienses alium regem quam majorem
Londoniarum.*" [1]

The influence of French institutions on the establishment of this commune of London is not matter of
doubt, any more than is the high degree of
independence to which the citizens laid
claim. It is more than probable that they
had chosen their mayor themselves. But what are the
skivini and *probi homines* who appear in the oath of the
commune in 1193 ? The mention which is made of them
has suggested to Mr. Round a very ingenious hypothesis. It is that the constitution of London was
modelled upon the *Etablissements* of Rouen [2] and that
London, like Rouen, had a council of twelve *skivini*
and twelve other persons (the *duodecim consultores* of
Rouen, the *alii probi homines* of the oath of 1193), to
administer justice. And, in fact, adds Mr. Round, we

The marginal notes read:
Character of this revolution according to Stubbs

Hypotheses of Mr. Round

1. *Select Charters*, 8th edition, p. 308.
2. Mr. Round makes a correction of M. Giry's book on the *Etablissements* of Rouen and proves that they are anterior to the year 1183
(*Commune of London*, pp. 247—251.)

H

have the text of an oath sworn to King John in 1205—
1206 by twenty-four persons charged with the administration of justice in London; these twenty-four are not
the aldermen, who are simply heads of wards.   The
twenty-four can only have been councillórs elected by
the mass of the burgesses.

**And of
Mr. Adams**   Mr. G. B. Adams has sought to complete and follow up Mr. Round's hypothesis.[1]

According to him, the commune created in 1191 was
a commune in the technical sense, a "seigneurie
collective," a vassal of the king, like the great French
communes.   King Richard did not allow London thus
to quit his demesne, and by becoming his vassal escape
the domanial claims and took this privilege away from
it as soon as he returned, whilst leaving it its mayor and
its *skivini*.   London thus ceases to be a commune until
the day when John is forced to seek its support.   By
article 12 of the Great Charter he formally recognises
the feudal character of the city, for he admits that it
owes to him the *auxilium*, that is to say the feudal aid,
the aid of the nobles.   A document of the reign of
Henry III. shows, in fact, that London claimed only to
give the king an aid, and refused to pay the tallage;[2]
this pretension was however rejected by the counsellors
of Henry III.   London did not succeed in obtaining a
lasting recognition of its legal right to a commune.

We cannot subscribe wholly to either the theory of
Mr. Round or that of Mr. Adams.   Miss Mary
Bateson has studied from beginning to end
**No filiation
with Rouen**   the collection of municipal documents in
which Mr. Round found the oath of 1193,
and has discovered in it texts which render untenable

---

1. *London and the Commune*, in *E. H. R.*, xix, 1904, pp. 702 sqq.
2. Mr. Adams contents himself with analysing this important text.
There is some advantage in reading it *in extenso*; it is printed by Madox,
Exchequer, i, p. 712, note a (edition of 1769).   See the abstract and
fragments of it we give below.

the hypothesis of a filiation between London and Rouen.[1] We see, in fact, there that the aldermen sat in the husting, that they declared the law there,[2] and beyond doubt the twenty-four who are mentioned in the text of 1205-6 are aldermen, and not a self-styled council of twelve *skivini* and twelve *probi homines*. For the rest, it is quite likely that the *skivini* mentioned in the text of 1193—without their number being specified—are simply the twenty-four aldermen; *skivini* was an exotic term which a scribe may have used to designate the aldermen; and it is remarkable that it is not found afterwards, in any text relating to London. As for the *probi homines*—whose number Mr. Round, with no more reason than in the case of the *skivini*, fixes at *twelve*,—they were, in the most vague and general sense, notables, who advised and aided the mayor, and on occasion this term doubtless served to denote the aldermen themselves. There were *probi homines* sitting in the husting,[3] and it is not surprising that the burgesses, in 1193, swear to respect them; it is noticeable, moreover, that they do not swear to obey them.[4]

We shall only, therefore, admit that London formed itself into a commune in 1191, and that it had— immediately doubtless—a mayor. We

Richard certainly did not recognise the commune

shall also admit with Mr. Round and Mr. Adams that Richard Cœur-de-Lion suppressed the commune (or at least that he took no account of the oath of 1191), while

1. Mary Bateson, *A London Municipal Collection of the reign of John*, in *E. H. R.*, xvii, 1902, pp. 480 sqq., 707 sqq.

2. "E les aldremans dirunt si le rei deit aveir le plai u le vescunte . . . Les aldermans en durunt dreit." (*Ibidem*, p. 493.)

3. " . . . . Dunc deit le veskunte predre quatre prudomes dedenz les quatre bancs del husteng . . . ." (*Ibidem*, p. 493.) Respecting these "quatre bancs," see Mary Bateson, *Borough Customs*, ii, 1906, p. cxlvii.

4. *E. H. R.*, xvii, pp. 510–511.   On pages 727–728 of the same volume Miss Bateson prints a text which fully confirms her view : "Item de omni redditu forinsecorum capiatur de singulis libris xiid. exceptis redditibus ecclesiasticis. Item ad hanc pecuniam colligendam et recipiendam eligantur iiii *probi ac discreti homines* de qualibet custodia." *Probi homines* is used in no more technical or precise sense than *discreti homines*.

maintaining a mayor, who kept his office for life. John Lackland, indeed at his accession, granted to the Londoners their old privilege of holding the sheriffdom of London and Middlesex, for a farm of 300 pounds; this privilege for which the Londoners paid King John a sum of 3,000 marks, they would have had no need to buy if they had been at that time an independent commune, protected, by the liberties it had won, against the royal sheriffs and the financial pressure of the crown. Moreover, in the three charters granted to the Londoners at this period there is no mention made of the commune.

Was the commune of London restored afterwards by John Lackland, when he had need of the support of **Did John** the inhabitants? Such is, we have seen, **recognise it?** the opinion of Mr. Adams based on article 12 of the Great Charter and a document of the time of Henry III. Mr. McKechnie, for his part, is of opinion that the charter of the 9th May, 1215, granting to the Londoners the right of electing their mayor annually, is an official recognition of the commune.[1] Let us look at these documents more closely, and, if possible, throw light on them by others.

Miss Bateson discovered a list of nine articles, which seems to be a summary of a petition presented by the **The Nine** Londoners before the granting of the **Articles** charter of the 9th of May, 1215; the annual mayoralty is mentioned.[2] There is no mention of a commune; no mention is made of it either in the charter of the 9th of May. By this last document,[3] John only grants to his " barons " of the city of **The charter of** **9 May, 1215** London the right to elect every year from their own number a mayor " faithful to the

1. " The charter of May, 1215, by officially recognizing the mayor, placed the commune over which he presided on a legal footing. The revolutionary civic constitution, sworn to in 1191, was now confirmed." (McKechnie, *Magna Carta*, 1905, p. 289.)

2. " De majore habendo, de anno in annum, per folkesmot, et quod prium juret." (*English Histor. Review*, xvii, 1902, p. 726; art. 7).

3. *Select Charters*, pp. 314–315 (8th edition).

king, discreet and suitable for the government of the city " who is to be "presented" to the king, or, in his absence, to the justiciar, and swear fealty to him. At the end of a year the Londoners might keep the same mayor, or change him. The liberties of London are confirmed in vague terms.[1] Unquestionably the right of electing the mayor annually was extremely important, and this right was actually exercised by the Londoners. But it cannot be claimed that it was sufficient to constitute a commune in the French sense of the word.

As for article 12 of the Great Charter, it is obscure and we may be allowed to quote it in its exact form :

London and the Great Charter " Nullum scutagium vel auxilium ponatur in regno nostro, nisi per commune consilium regni nostri, nisi ad corpus nostrum redimendum, et primogenitum filium nostrum militem faciendum, et ad filiam nostram primogenitam semel maritandam, et ad hec non fiat nisi racionabile auxilium ; simili modo fiat de auxiliis de civitate London." Article 13 goes on :[2] " Et civitas London, habeat omnes antiquas libertates et liberas consuetudines suas, tam per terras quam per aquas. Preterea volumus et concedimus quod omnes alie civitates et burgi et ville et portus habeant omnes libertates et liberas consuetudines suas."[3] By article 12, John Lackland pledges himself not to levy any scutage or aid beyond the three occasions provided for by feudal law, without the consent of the assembly of tenants-in-chief, and the aid in these three cases is to be levied on a reasonable scale. But what does the

1. " Concessimus etiam eisdem baronibus nostris et carta nostra confirmavimus quod habeant bene et in pace, libere, quiete et integre, omnes libertates suas quibus hactenus usi sunt, tam in civitate Londoniarum quam extra, et tam in aquis quam in terris, et omnibus aliis locis, salva nobis chamberlengeria nostra." These last words signify that the purveyors of the king's household shall have the right of making their choice, first of all, from the goods brought in by foreign merchants.

2. It is not without interest to remember that this division into articles does not exist in the original.

3. Bémont, *Chartes des Libertés Anglaises*, p. 29.

obscure phrase relative to the aids of the city of London mean ? Must we conclude from it with Mr. Adams that John Lackland identified the aids of London with the feudal aids, and thus recognised its character of a " seigneurie collective populaire ? "

We do not think so. In order to understand this phrase we must go back to article 32 of the *Articuli*
London and the Petition of the Barons
Baronum, a petition presented by the barons to John Lackland some days before the granting of the Great Charter : " Ne scutagium vel auxilium ponatur in regno, nisi per commune consilium regni, nisi ad corpus regis redimendum, et primogenitum filium suum militem faciendum, et filiam suam primogenitam semel maritandam ; et ad hoc fiat rationabile auxilium. *Simili modo fiat de taillagiis et auxiliis de civitate London.* et de aliis civitatibus que inde habent libertates, et ut civitas London. plene habeat antiquas libertates et liberas consuetudines suas tam per aquas, quam per terras." [1] Mr. Adams declares that this article of the petition of the barons was badly drafted, whilst the corresponding article of the Great Charter was drafted with care. We believe, on the contrary, that the article of the petition
What the Londoners wanted
of the barons alone represents the precise wishes of the Londoners. They desired a guarantee against royal arbitrariness, and did not wish any longer to have to pay ruinous taxes, either in the form of *tallage* or in the form of *aids*,—an extremely elastic term, which had very diverse meanings and was in nowise reserved for the feudal aid.[2]

1. Bémont, *op. cit.*, p. 19.
2. The author of the *Dialogue concerning the Exchequer*, ii, c. xiii (Edition of Hughes, Crump and Johnson, p. 145), speaks formally of the *donum* or *auxilium* of the towns : " de auxiliis vel donis civitatum seu burgorum." And, in fact, in the first half of the 12th century, when the Danegeld was still collected, the sum furnished by Middlesex was paid under the name of *Danegeld*, that paid by London was paid under the name of *donum* or *auxilium*. See on this point Round, *Commune of London*, pp. 257 sqq. We may read in Stubbs (i, p. 620, note 2), a writ of 1207, in which John demands an *auxilium* from the archdeacons

The tallage was the tax which bore upon the inhabitants of the royal demesne, and the towns possessing a royal charter were considered as forming part of the demesne. The aid was in theory a gift made to the king, and the townsmen did not escape from the ill-defined obligation to this gratuity, any more than the clergy or the nobility. The Londoners feared the tallage even more than the aid.[1] A text to which attention has never been paid until now proves this. In this list of nine articles, of which I was speaking just now, I read as follows : " De omnibus taillagiis delendis nisi per communem assensum regni et civitatis." Thus, before obtaining their private charter of the 9th of May, the Londoners already demanded that they might not be subjected to the tallage without the consent of the *regnum,* that is to say, evidently, the assembly of the tenants-in-chief. The silence of the charter of the 9th of May proves that John did not wish to give up any part of his prerogative upon this point. The following month the barons, who had great obligations towards the townsmen of the realm, and particularly towards the Londoners, included in their petition article 32, which secured London and the towns having the same liberties as London against the abuses of zeal for the interests of the royal treasury,—in so far as the consent of an assembly of barons could be a security. Comparison of the petition of the barons and the Great Charter shows that in this question, as in many others, John Lackland exacted a compromise.[2] He refused to put any other town in the position of London, and even to London he only granted a derisive satisfaction. The

John's illusory concession

of the realm, and expresses the desire that the rest of the clergy may be influenced by the example of the archdeacons to pay an *auxilium* also. The word was therefore used in a very wide sense. Cf. Stubbs, i, pp. 626—628.

1. They had just paid, in the year 1214–15, a tallage of 2,000 marks : " Anna ejusdem Johannis sextodecimo, talliati fuerunt praedicti cives Londoniae ad duo millia marcarum." (Madox. *Hist. of Exchequer,* i, p. 712, note a.)

2. This is well put by McKechnie, *Magna Carta,* pp. 277 sqq.

suppression of the words *de taillagiis* allowed him to tallage the Londoners at his pleasure; on these conditions he could do without their *auxilia*. Such, in our opinion, is the true explanation of article 12 of the Great Charter.

The argument which Mr. Adams draws from the text published by Madox is more specious. It may be asked

Why London claimed exemption from tallage

why the Londoners were so particular about paying an *auxilium* and not a *tallagium*.[1] But the context supplies a very simple answer to this question. Henry III. levies a tallage of three thousand marks on the Londoners. They refuse to pay it and offer an aid of two thousand marks.[2] They are told that they may pay, if they wish, a composition of three thousand marks in place of the tallage,[3] but if they refuse the tallage shall be assessed on the town in the form of a capitation. The Londoners still resist, and then arises the dispute over the use of the word *tallagium*; the inquest proves the baselessness of their pretension, they recognise themselves as tallageable and pay the three thousand marks. For them it was clearly a question of not paying in its entirety the large sum demanded by the king, and, as they knew well that they could not discuss the amount of a tallage, they had hit on this expedient of saying that they were not tallageable, and of offering an " aid " of two thousand marks only. For an aid is, professedly, a voluntary gift to the sovereign, and it is recognised by the king's officers that the assessment

---

1. " Et cum contencio esset, utrum hoc dici deberet tallagium vel auxilium, rex scrutari fecit rotulos suos, utrum ipsi aliquid dederunt regi vel antecessoribus suis nomine tallagii. . . ." An inquest proved that the Londoners had paid a tallage of 2,000 marks in 1214–1215, and several tallages in the reign of Henry III. " Postea in crastino . . . . venerunt praedicti Radulfus major et cives et recognoverunt se esse talliabiles." (Madox, *op. cit.*, i, p. 712, note a.)

2. "Rex petebat ab eis tria millia marcarum nomine tallagii, et illi . . . optulerunt regi duo millia marcarum nomine auxilii, et dixerunt praecise quod plus non poterunt dare nec darent."

3. Finem trium millium marcarum pro tallagio."

cannot be left to his arbitrary discretion.[1] The king was not particular about the name provided he had the thing, and he offered to abandon the tallage if they would pay him its equivalent; as the Londoners did not comply and haggled over the terms, he forced them to recognise that they were tallageable. They never dreamed of asserting that they constituted a commune and that because of this they owed nothing but a feudal aid; there is nothing of the kind in the text, and Mr. Adams's argument will not hold water.

Not only was the " Commune of London " not recognised by John Lackland, but the burgesses did not

London did not demand the recognition of the commune

even show any desire for such recognition. They asked for nothing of the sort in the nine articles, or in the petition of the barons. I will add that such a claim is equally absent from their demands, some months later, when Lewis of France, son of Philip Augustus, landed in England, and this fact appears to me decisive. The Londoners were the most faithful allies of Lewis, his allies from first to last. The pretender could have refused them nothing. Now, there is no question of the recognition of the commune either in the engagements he entered into with them on his arrival nor in the negotiations and stipulations of the peace which preceded his definitive departure.[2]

1. In a very interesting passage, which Mr. Adams has not had present in his memory, the author of the *Dialogue concerning the Exchequer* (Bk. ii, c. xiii, Edn. of Hughes, Crump and Johnson, p. 145) discusses the case in which the *donum vel auxilium* of the towns was imposed by the officers of the king in the form of a capitation (observe that this is the procedure with which Henry III threatens the Londoners, if they do not give way), and the case in which it consists of a round sum, offered by the burgesses, and accepted as " principe digna." In the eyes of the author of the *Dialogue*, there is no reason for reserving for this offer "worthy of the prince" the name of *auxilium*, and calling *tallagium* only the tax imposed in the form of a capitation. In the thirteenth century, men become more subtle, the burgesses try to make distinctions to their profit; but they have no idea of claiming that London ought to be treated as a feudal person, nor do they invoke article 12 of the Great Charter to prove it.

2. See my *Etude sur la vie et le règne de Louis VIII.*, especially pp. 102 and 160 (Cf. the word *Londres* in the index).   According to the

We must neither exaggerate or deprecate the status
of London at this period. The city was not a commune
in the French sense of the word; it had
Actual status
of London
only been so for a very brief space, during
the absence of Richard Cœur de Lion. It
was not bound to the king by that mutual oath which,
according to the historians was characteristic of the
French *seigneurie collective populaire:* this bilateral
oath had only been taken in 1191, and since the return
of Richard Cœur-de-Lion there had been no longer
question of anything but the oath taken by the burgesses
or their mayor. The city had not, in the matter of
finance and justice, the independence of the popular
republics of the Continent.[1] Nevertheless it was very
powerful, and rival parties disputed its alliance. Its
inhabitants were " barons." *Londonienses, qui sunt
quasi optimates, pro magnitudine civitatis,* said William
of Malmesbuhy, who wrote in the time of King Stephen ;
since that time, thanks to the difficulties of the reign of
Richard I. and the crisis of 1215, London had gradually
gained one of the principal municipal liberties, that of
having an annually elected mayor. And perhaps, after
all, it is puerile to investigate whether London in 1215
was or was not a commune; the Londoners of that day
did not trouble themselves about it ; and without doubt
we attach too much importance to words which we
have made technical terms for the convenience of our
historical studies.

account of several chroniclers, Lewis, on his arrival, 3 June, 1216,
received the 'homage' of the citizens, and in return promised to give
back to the Londoners good laws : " Juravit quod *singulis eorum* bonas
leges redderet, simul et amissas hereditates." But the reference here is
only to the mutual pledge quite natural under the circumstances, and
not to the oath of the commune. See the passages quoted *ibidem*, p. 102,
note 2.

1. Four times at least in eleven years, Henry III. seized the town of
London into his hands, notably for false judgement in the husting
(Pollock and Maitland, *Hist. of English Law*, i, p. 668.)

X.

THE TWO TRIALS OF JOHN LACKLAND.

ACCORDING to the narrative of Stubbs, John Lackland was twice condemned as contumacious by the court **Narrative of** of Philip Augustus—in 1202 and in 1203. **Stubbs** After his first condemnation, in 1202, his nephew Arthur, "taking advantage of the confusion, raised a force and besieged his grandmother in the castle of Mirabel, where he was captured by John, and, after some mysterious transactions, he disappeared finally on the 3rd of April, 1203. Philip, who believed with the rest of the world that John had murdered him, summoned him again to be tried on the accusation made by the barons of Brittany. Again John was contumacious, and this time Philip himself undertook to enforce the sentence of the court" and conquered Normandy.[1] It is singular that so careful a scholar as Stubbs should have summarised these celebrated events with so much negligence;[2] it is still more surprising that he took no account, in the successive editions of his book, of the opinion accepted and expressed, for a score of years, by all the

1. *Const. Hist.*, i, p. 556.
2. To speak only of quite well known and indisputable facts. Stubbs appears not to know that, as early as the month of June 1202, long before the death of Arthur, and in execution of the first sentence of the court of France, Philip-Augustus had taken up arms and invaded Normandy. If he had narrated these events with more exactitude he would, no doubt, have been led to see the improbability of the view that there were two condemnations, which M. Bémont has so thoroughly refuted. In the otherwise very remarkable preface, written for his edition of the *Historical collections of Walter of Coventry* (Rolls Series; ii, p. xxxii, note 3) he only noted that the earliest mention of the condemnation of 1203 was to be found in the manifesto launched by Lewis of France in 1216.

French, German and English scholars, with one exception, who have given their opinion on the alleged trial of April, 1203. M. Bémont demonstrated in 1884, by the most cogent arguments, that the condemnation of John Lackland in 1203 for the murder of Arthur was a fable, invented by the court of France in 1216, in order to justify the pretensions of Lewis of France to the crown of England.[1] The attempt made in 1899 by M. Guilhiermoz to refute the thesis of M. Bémont has not met with acceptance.[2] We have examined and contested it on a previous occasion. We will content ourselves with quoting the views of two scholars who

The now accepted opinion upon the second trial

1. *De Johanne cognomine sine Terra Angliae rege Lutetiae Parisiorum anno 1202 condemnato*, 1884; French edition : *De la Condemnation de Jean sans Terre par la cour des pairs de France en 1202* in the *Revue Historique*, xxxii, 1886. Cf. Ch. Petit-Dutaillis, *Etude sur la vie et le règne de Louis VIII*, 1894, pp. 77 sqq. M. Guilhiermoz remarks that the conclusions of M. Bémont "appear to have been universally accepted," and he quotes MM. Ch. V. Langlois, Beautemps-Beaupré, Luchaire, Lot, etc.

2. Guilhiermoz, *Les deux condemnations de Jean sans Terre par la cour de Philippe-Auguste*, in *Bibl. de l'Ecole des Chartes*, 1899. Cf. his controversy with M. Bémont in the same volume, and with MM. Petit-Dutaillis and G. Monod, in *Rev. Historique*, lxxi and lxxii (1899—1900), and a new article by him in the *Nouv. Rev. hist. de droit français et étranger* (1904), p. 786 sqq. I am bound to say that on a reperusal of the article in which I refuted M. Guilhiermoz's thesis, my only regret is that I did not put my conclusion more strongly. For the rest, M. Guilhiermoz has found no supporters. See a luminous summary of the question by M. Luchaire, *Séances et Travaux de l'Acad. des Sc. Morales*, liii, 1900 ; F. Lot, *Fidèles ou vassaux* (1904), pp. 89, note 3, 223 sqq.; R. Holtzmann, *Der Prozess gegen Johann ohne Land und die Anfänge des französischen Pairhofes*, in the *Historische Zeitschrift*, Neue Folge, lix. (1905). M. J. Lehmann, *Johann ohne Land*, in the *Historische Studien* published by E. Ebering, Pt. 45, 1904, goes beyond M. Bémont's thesis and puts forth the singular view that the documents of 1216, in which the trial of 1203 is referred to, are not authentic. I am only acquainted with the summary of this article given by M. Holtzmann, *op. cit.*, p. 32, n. 3. In England, Sir James Ramsay (*The Angevin Empire*, 1903, pp. 393 and 397) does not believe in the condemnation of 1203; but he thinks there was a citation; he interprets the documents quite wrongly and obscures the question instead of throwing light on it. An American scholar, Mr. G. B. Adams, entrusted with the treatment of this period in the *Political History of England* (ii, 1905), declares, p. 399, that he is not convinced by M. Guilhiermoz. So, too, Miss Kate Norgate in the article referred to below, and in her *John Lackland* (1902), pp. 91–92; as we shall see, Miss Norgate goes farther than M. Bémont, and assuredly much too far.

not having been brought into the controversy by M. Guilhiermoz, have expressed an opinion the impartiality of which no one will dispute. M. Luchaire declares that " he adheres until further proof is forthcoming to the conclusions of M. Bémont"; quite recently M. Holtzmann stated that the vehement polemic of M. Guilhiermoz has made no impression; it appears to him to be based rather on " a lawyer's argument than on a critical examination of the sources."

In a work devoted to English institutions I cannot dwell any longer on this point, and Stubbs' excuse is just this, that it is a matter of little importance for the subject of which he is treating whether M. Bémont is right or wrong as far as concerns the reality of the second trial of John Lackland.

But it is important to know whether M. Bémont was right in believing in the reality of the first trial; the loss of Normandy had such consequences in the

Miss Kate Norgate's theory respecting the first trial constitutional history of England that it is a matter of interest, even here, to determine whether it was the result of a sentence of the court of France. The publication of M. Bémont's article did not affect the belief that Normandy was confiscated by legal process; only the date or dates of the confiscation were matters of controversy. But a new theory has grafted itself on that of M. Bémont. According to an article published in 1900 by Miss Kate Norgate[1] John Lackland was no more condemned by the court of Philip Augustus for refusing to redress the wrongs he had inflicted on the Poitevin barons, than for having put to death his nephew Arthur, and the "alleged condemnation " of 1202 was invented in 1204-5 by Philip Augustus, in order to overcome the scruples of the Norman clergy and justify the conquest of

---

1. *The alleged condemnation of King John by the Court of France in 1202*, in *Transactions of the Royal Historical Society*, New series, xiv, 1900, pp. 53—67.

Normandy. It seems to me expedient to examine this theory closely.

Miss Norgate's argument is as follows. Five contemporary documents narrate the citation of John Lackland before the court of France in 1202 : the French chronicles of Rigord and Guillaume le Breton, the English chronicles of Gervase of Canterbury and Ralph of Coggeshall, and finally a letter addressed by Pope Innocent III. to John Lackland on the 31st of October, 1203. Roger of Wendover does not speak of the citation at all.[1] And the later chroniclers who accepted the discredited trial of 1203 are silent as to that of 1202. The five documents mentioned above supplement one another and present no contradiction amongst themselves, as far as concerns the citation, and the relations of the two kings before the trial ; but Ralph of Coggeshall alone declares that John Lackland was condemned by default,[2] and the alleged sentence of 1202 rests in reality on his single testimony. It is improbable that this abbot of an obscure monastery in Essex was better informed than Gervase of Canterbury, Rigord, Guillaume le

1. I do not quite understand why Miss Norgate limits her study to six documents in all, including Roger of Wendover. Robert of Auxerre is a contemporary of the events and his testimony has great value ; he does not speak of a citation either, but he says nothing to prevent us from believing in one. See the passage in *Historiens de France*, xviii, p. 266.

2. " Tandem vero curia regis Franciae adunata adjudicavit regem Angliae tota terra sua privandum, quam hactenus de regibus Franciae ipse et progenitores sui tenuerant, eo quod fere omnia servitia eisdem terris debita per longum jam tempus facere contempserant, nec domino suo fere in aliquibus obtemperare volebant." (R. de Coggeshale, *Chronicon Anglicanum*, ed. Stevenson, p. 136). It will be observed that the sentence is based upon the faults committed by *John and by his ancestors*, towards their suzerains the kings of France. This, it seems to me, has escaped the scholars who have quoted this passage ; M. Bémont (*op. cit.*, p. 54 and p. 307) and M. Luchaire (*Hist. de France*, publiée sous la direction de M. Lavisse, iii, 1re partie, 1901, pp. 128-129) translate it inaccurately. Sir James Ramsay (*op. cit.*, p. 393) and Miss Norgate (*John Lackland*, p. 84) pass over in silence the reasons given in the sentence, as our chronicler relates them. As for M. Guilhiermoz (*Bibl. de l'Ec. des Chartes*, 1899, pp. 48, 65), he makes very free with the text of Ralph of Coggeshall, which he interprets in the most arbitrary manner.

Breton, and the Pope himself. The testimony of Ralph of Coggeshall cannot prevail against their silence. Innocent III., to whom it was Philip Augustus's strong interest to give information respecting the trial and three chroniclers well situated for hearing it spoken of were ignorant of the condemnation; consequently it never occurred.

The very first reading of this argument reveals one of its weak points; Miss Norgate's scepticism is highly **Exaggerated** exaggerated, it is " hypercriticism." If we **scepticism** had to reject all the historical facts which are only known to us from one source, a great part of our knowledge of the past would crumble away. And Miss Norgate would be obliged to suppress many pages of her works, notably of her *John Lackland*, where she often confides in the unsupported testimony of the biographer who wrote the metrical life of William the Marshal. Given the weakness of historical science and the mediocrity of the materials at its disposal, it is necessary to admit information derived from a single document, on the double condition that the general veracity of that document has been tested on other points, and that on the particular point in question it is not in contradiction with our other sources.

Now this twofold condition is fulfilled as far as concerns the testimony of Ralph of Coggeshall. His **Great value of** chronicle is indisputably one of the most **the evidence of** precise and most exact that we have for the **Coggeshall** first twenty-five years of the thirteenth century. On the other hand, Rigord, Guillaume le Briton and Gervase of Canterbury, whose narrative, be it remarked, is much briefer than Ralph's, say nothing which forbids us to accept the condemnation. All three state that John failed to appear, and suppressing mention of the sentence, relate afterwards, like Ralph of Coggeshall, how Philip Augustus invaded Normandy

and destroyed the castle of Boutavant.[1] It is clear that
the details of the trial did not interest them. Just as they
do not speak of the dilatory pleas put forward by John,
of which Ralph of Coggeshall informs us,[2] they have
omitted to relate that a condemnation by default had
been pronounced; was not this condemnation a matter
of course, and why should the court of Philip Augustus
have abstained from passing this sentence the necessity
of which was self-evident? The event was so natural
that there was hardly need to describe it.

As for the letter addressed by Innocent III. to John
Lackland on the 31st of October, 1203, a year and a half
after these events and seven months after
the death of Arthur, it appears to us not
only to be reconcilable with the statements
of Ralph of Coggeshall, but to absolutely corroborate
them, and this document, in which Miss Norgate seeks
her most decisive arguments, appears to be the one which
definitively rebuts her thesis.

Innocent III's
letter proves it

In this celebrated letter,[3] the Pope communicates to the
king of England the reasons which Philip Augustus has
placed before the Holy See, "per suas literas et nuntios,"
to justify his conduct. Evidently, Innocent III., being
impartial, must have faithfully reproduced these reasons.
Now the justification put forward by the king of France,
as the Pope summarizes it, confirms the narrative of
Ralph de Coggeshall almost word for word, even on the
precise point under discussion in Miss Norgate's article;

1. This was a castle which John had promised to deliver up as a
pledge of his appearance at the court of Philip Augustus; he had
refused to fulfil his promise (Guillaume le Breton, ed. Delaborde, i, pp.
207, 209, 210). The destruction of the castle of Boutavant was therefore
a logical consequence of the condemnation; and we may even say that it
implies it. Ralph of Coggeshall says with the precision which distinguishes his whole narrative : " Hoc igitur curiae suae judicium rex
Philippus gratanter acceptans et approbans, coadunato exercitu, con-
festim invasit castellum Butavant " (Ed. Stevenson, p. 136).

2. Guillaume le Breton gives them only a single word, " post multos
defectus."

3. Potthast, *Regesta Pontificum Romanorum*, No. 2013. Miss Norgate
dates it by mistake the 29th October.

and it is curious that that scholar was not struck by the singular agreement of the two documents. In both we see that it is on an appeal of vassals that Philip Augustus acted; that he first repeatedly required King John to make peace with his vassals; that, not being able to get any satisfaction, he cited him before his court, with his barons' concurrence. From this point the two narratives differ somewhat; Ralph of Coggeshall insists on the privilege alleged by the King of England, who claimed to have the right not to appear at Paris, while Philip Augustus, in the letter summarized by Innocent III., insists on his attempts at accommodation. But Miss Norgate failed to see, and I do not know whether anybody has yet observed, that the bull of Innocent III. contains a clear allusion to the condemnation : *Although the king of France,* writes the Pope, *had defied you* (*diffidasset*) *by the counsel of his barons and his men* and war had broken out, he sent you again four of his knights, charged to ascertain whether you were willing to repair the wrongs committed towards him, and to cause you to know that in the contrary case he would henceforth conclude alliance against you with your men, wherever he could. And you have **The " defiance "** avoided those who sought you. . . ." **proves previous sentence** The term *diffidare* has here evidently its full and formal sense : it is the solemn rupture of the feudal relationship; now, as M. Luchaire says in his *Manuel des Institutions françaises,*[1] " defiance can only take place between suzerain and vassal after the suzerain has summoned his feudatory to appear before his court and *has had him condemned there,* either present or by default." The moment that Philip declares he has defied John Lackland there is proof that the court has previously given its sentence.[2]

1. *Manuel des Institutions françaises* (1892), p. 230.
2. The pope adds that Philip Augustus acknowledges having, after these events, received the homage of certain vassals of the king of England, " quod *contumaciae tuae* asserit imputandum."

I

It is not surprising that Philip Augustus did not give the Pope circumstantial details respecting the condemnation by default and the text of the sentence. It was not his interest to do this in a letter in which he strove above everything to convince the Pope of his conciliatory spirit; and he contented himself therefore with telling the Pope that by the counsel of his barons and his men, *de baronum et hominum suorum consilio,* he had broken the feudal tie which bound him to John, *diffidasset.* This is why, in his letter of the 7th of March, 1205, to the Norman bishops,[1] a letter on which Miss Norgate has no right to found an argument, Innocent III., ill-informed upon the trial of 1202, maintains an attitude of reserve. Philip Augustus is requiring the bishops to swear fealty to him because he has acquired Normandy upon a sentence of his court : *asserens quod, justitia praeeunte, per sententiam curiae suae Normanniam acquisivit;* the Pope, consulted by the bishops as to what they ought to do, cannot give them an answer in default of sufficient information : *quia vero nec de jure, nec de consuetudine nobis constat, utpote qui causam, modum et ordinem, aliasque circumstantias ignoramus.* He does not say that he has never heard of this condemnation of 1202; but he is ignorant of its precise tenour and the circumstances, and he is not well acquainted with the custom of France.

The letter to the Norman Bishops

The letter of the 31st October, 1203, is in short the most important text which we possess for the solution of the problem of the two trials of John Lackland. By the absolute silence it maintains respecting the death of Arthur it proves convincingly that seven months after John's alleged condemnation by the peers of France as the murderer of his nephew, nothing was known at Rome either of the death of the young prince or of the

1. Potthast, *op. cit.,* No. 2434.

condemnation which was its supposed consequence. By the summary which it gives of the apology which the King of France had made for his conduct, it confirms the assertions of the very exact Ralph de Coggeshall.

M. Bémont's conclusions then still hold the field. John Lackland was not condemned to death by the

M. Bémont's conclusions hold their ground

court of France as murderer of Arthur in 1203, but he was condemned in 1202 by default, to the loss of his French fief, for disobedience and refusal of service to his suzerain.

The appeal of the Poitevin barons, a fine opportunity for preparing annexations, eagerly seized by Philip

Constitutional importance of the question

Augustus, was thus the indirect cause of the separation of Normandy and England; an event of immense importance for the English constitution as well as for French policy; for the monarchy of the Plantagenets was suddenly detached from a province from which it had derived a part of its institutions and its administrative staff, and, on the other hand, as Stubbs says, "the king found himself face to face with the English people."

XI.

AN "UNKNOWN CHARTER OF LIBERTIES."

THERE exists in our *Trésor des Chartes* a list of "concessions of King John" to his barons, which was printed as early as 1863 by Teulet, in his *Layettes*.[1] This document had completely escaped scholars working upon English history until the moment at which it was "discovered" by Mr. Round in a copy forming part of the *Rymer Transcripts,* and published by him in the *English Historical Review*.[2] It is celebrated now under the name, inaccurate it will be seen, which Mr. Round has given to it of the "Unknown Charter of Liberties." As this so-called "Unknown Charter of English Liberties," certainly interesting, has only been studied since 1893, as Stubbs does not quote a single line of it, as he did not insert it in the last edition of his *Select Charters,* and as it is not to be found correctly transcribed in any of the books which French libraries usually possess, we reproduce it here.[3]

History of "unknown charter"

The manuscript, the writing of which is French and dates from the first quarter of the thirteenth century, contains, first, a copy of the charter of Henry I., preceded by these words: "Charta quam Henricus, communi baronum consilio rex coronatus, eisdem et prelatis regni Angliae

Copy of the charter of Henry I.

1. *Layettes du Trésor des Chartes,* publ. par A. Teulet, i, 1863, p. 423.
2. J. H. Round, *An unknown Charter of Liberties, English Histor. Review,* viii, 1893, pp. 288 sqq.
3. We shall follow the text given by Mr. McKechnie, *Magna Carta,* pp. 569-570.

plurima privilegia concedit," and followed by the note :
" Hec est carta regis Henrici per quam barones querunt
liberatates, et hec consequentia concedit rex Johannes.[1]

Next follows the list of the " concessions of King
John," here given ; we shall indicate for
each clause[2] the analogous clauses of the
charter of Henry I.,[3] of the *Articuli Baronum* (June,
1215)[4] and of the Great Charter :[5]

Text of the document

1. " Concedit rex Johannes quod non capiet hominem
absque judicio, nec aliquid accipiet pro justitia, nec
injustitiam faciet " (Cf. *Articles of the Barons*, art. 29
and 30; *Great Charter*, art. 39 and 40.[6])

2. " Et si contingat quod meus baro vel homo meus
moriatur et heres suus sit in etate, terram suam debeo
ei reddere per rectum releveium absque magis capiendi."
(Cf. *Charter of Henry I.*, 2 ; *Articles of the Barons*, 1 ;
Great Charter, 2.)

3. " Et si ita sit quod heres sit infra etatem, debeo
quatuor militibus de legalioribus feodi terram bajulare
in custodia, et illi cum meo famulo debent mihi reddere
exitus terre sine venditione nemorum et sine redemptione
hominum et sine destructione parci et vivarii ; et tunc
quando ille heres erit in etate, terram ei reddam quietam."
(Cf. *Articles of the Barons*, 2—3 ; *Charter*, 3—4.)

4. " Si femina sit heres terre, debeo eam maritare,
consilio generis sui, ita non sit disparagiata. Et si una
vice eam dedero, amplius eam dare non possum, sed se

---

1. Round, *loc. cit.*, p. 288, and H. Hall, quoting a letter of M. Bémont,
in *English Histor. Review*, ix, 1894, p. 327.
2. The division into clauses does not exist in the original any more
than it does in the Great Charter.
3. Liebermann, *Gesetze*, i, pp. 521 sqq., or Bémont, *Chartes des
libertés anglaises*, pp. 3 sqq.
4. Bémont, pp. 15 sqq. The true title is : *Capitula que barones petunt
et dominus rex concedit.*
5. Bémont, pp. 26 sqq.
6. Cf. also the letter patent of the 10th of May, 1215, in Rymer, Rec.
edition, i, p. 128, and the excellent commentary which Mr. McKechnie
gives on article 39 of the Great Charter (*Magna Carta*, pp. 436 sqq.).

maritabit ad libitum suum, sed non inimicis meis."
(Cf. *Henry I.*, 3; *Articles*, 3 and 17; *Charter*, 6 and 8.)

5. " Si contingat quod baro aut homo meus moriatur, concedo ut pecunia sua dividatur sicut ipse diviserit; et si preoccupatus fuerit aut armis aut infirmitate improvisa, uxor ejus, aut liberi, aut parentes et amici propinquiores, pro ejus anima, dividant." (Cf. *Henry I.*, 7; *Articles*, 15—16; *Charter*, 26—27.)

6. " Et uxor ejus non abibit de hospitio infra XL dies et donec dotem suam decenter habuerit, et maritagium habebit." (Cf. *Henry I.*, 4; *Articles*, 4; *Charter*, 7.)

7. "Adhuc hominibus meis concedo ne eant in exercitu extra Anglia nisi in Normanniam et in Britanniam et hoc decenter; quod si aliquis debet inde servitium decem militum, consilio baronum meorum alleviabitur."

8. " Et si scutagium evenerit in terra, una marca argenti capietur de feodo militis; et si gravamen[1] exercitus contigerit, amplius caperetur consilio baronum regni." (Cf. *Articles*, 32; *Charter*, 12.)

9. "Adhuc concedo ut omnes forestas quas pater meus et frater meus et ego afforestavimus, deafforesto." (Cf. *Henry I.*, 10; *Articles*, 47; *Charter*, 47, 53.)

10. "Adhuc concedo ut milites qui in antiquis forestis meis suum nemus habent, habeant nemus amodo ad herbergagia sua et ad ardendum; et habeant foresterium suum; et ego tantum modo unum qui servet pecudes meas." (Cf. *Articles*, 39; *Charter*, 47.)

11. " Et si aliquis hominum meorum moriatur qui Judeis debeat, debitum non usurabit quamdiu heres ejus sit infra etatem." (Cf. *Articles*, 34; *Charter*, 10.)

12. " Et concedo ne homo perdat pro pecude vitam neque membra." (Cf. *Articles*, 39; *Charter*, 47; *Charter of the Forest*, of 1217, article 10.)

What is this document? What is its origin, what does it represent?

1. Mr. Hubert Hall, *loc. cit.*, p. 329, proposes the correction : alle-vamen.

None of the numerous hypotheses formulated so far by English scholars quite satisfies us. We must put aside to begin with, as untenable, the idea **Different suppositions** of a charter granted by John, in 1213, to the barons of the North, to the " Norois,"[1] and the supposition of a forged coronation charter of John Lackland, fabricated in 1216—1217 to legitimize the pretensions of Lewis of France.[2]

Mr. Prothero's theory is less unacceptable; it is that it was a charter of liberties offered by the king to the baronage, in the first four months of the year 1215, in order to calm the discontent and uneasiness of the nobles, in the same way that he had wished to appease the clergy by granting them liberty of election.[3]

Mr. Prothero remarks with reason that this list of concessions interests almost exclusively the nobility. But, even admitting that the form of the document authorises this supposition, it would be very singular that no chronicler should have made any allusion to so important an offer; very singular that the nobility should have rejected it; very singular, finally, that John should have spontaneously offered never to require the military service of the English knights, for his expeditions in the centre and south of France, seeing that this weighty concession is not mentioned in the Great Charter itself. Mr. McKechnie makes the converse supposition; that we have here not an offer of the king, but a preparatory schedule proposed by the barons in the month of April, 1215, and mentioned moreover by Roger of Wendover.[4]

But Roger of Wendover says that this schedule was

1. This is the explanation proposed, with all reserves, by Mr. Round, *English Historical Review*, viii, 1893, pp. 292 sqq. See the decisive objections of Mr. Prothero, *ibidem*, ix, 1894, pp. 118 sqq.
2. See the article by Mr. Hubert Hall, *ibidem*, ix, 1894, pp. 326 sqq.
3. Prothero, *Note on an unknown Charter of Liberties*, *ibidem*, ix, 1894, p. 120.
4. McKechnie, *Magna Carta*, p. 204.

rejected by the king,[1] and our text runs: "hec consequentia *concedit* rex Johannes."

In these explanations, too, no account is taken of the singularly clumsy form which this document assumes. **Neither an authentic nor an apocryphal charter** We have seen that it commences thus: "concedit rex Johannes quod . . . ," and that in the following sentence the king begins to speak, expressing himself in the first person: he even expresses himself in the first person singular, contrary to the usage of John Lackland's chancery. If we had to do with a charter offered by the king, or a document proposed by the barons, or even with a forged charter fabricated by the French, these anomalies would not present themselves.

We believe, therefore, with Mr. H. W. C. Davis, who has quite recently studied the problem afresh,[2] **It is a report** that the so-called "unknown charter" is not a charter, but an informal report of the negotiations which ended in the drawing up of the Great Charter. By whom was it drawn up and at what exact moment? We will not say with Mr. Davis, that the author, having transcribed the charter of Henry I. with so pious a respect was evidently a partisan of the barons; that his Latin betrays an English rather than a French origin;[3] that the composition of article 12 reveals the humbleness of his rank;[4] nor that the documents must have been drawn up during the three

1. "Affirmavit tandem cum juramento furibundus, quod nunquam tales illis concederet libertates, unde ipse efficeretur servus" (Wendover, in Matt. Paris, *Chron. Maj.*; ed. Luard (Rolls series), ii, p. 586).
2. In the *English Historical Review*, xx, 1905, pp. 719 sqq.
3. Mr. Hubert Hall, *loc. cit.*, p. 333, on the contrary, points out "Gallicisms" in it. These hypotheses seem to me very unprofitable.
4. The author, according to Mr. Davis, declaims in literary rather than legal phrase, against the Forest Law, so hard upon poor people. Mr. Davis does not notice that: (1) The Forest Law also greatly injured the interests of the barons; (2) The Charter of the Forest, of 1217, contains an article drawn up in very similar terms (Art. 10 in Bémont, p. 67): "Nullus de cetero amittat vitam vel membra pro venacione nostra."

days[1] which passed between the acceptance of the *Articuli Baronum* and the publication of the Great Charter. To us it seems possible to affirm this, and this only :

1. The document is in close relation with the *Articuli Baronum* and the Great Charter. Only the article relative to the service in the host abroad and two complementary clauses touching the Forest, have no equivalent in the *Articuli Baronum,* or the Charter.

2. Our document is not an official text. It is a memorandum, it is notes taken by a spectator. He is well informed; he is struck by the importance attached by the barons to the charter of Henry I., to the extent of transcribing that charter entire at the beginning of his minute; he reports certain of the king's concessions almost in the terms in which they were officially drafted. But he is neither a jurist, for his diction is at times very loose,[2] nor a personage directly interested in the concessions made, for he often does not understand the sense of them and distorts them in the summary he gives of them.[3]

---

1. McKechnie, *Magna Carta*, p. 45, has proved that the *Articuli Baronum* were accepted by the king and sealed with his seal on the 15th of June (the date borne by the Great Charter itself) and that the Great Charter was sealed and published on the 19th.

2. Cf. the inexact drafting of article 1; the *cum meo famulo* of article 3, etc.

3. Clause 1 is a vague and inaccurate summary of the pretensions so clearly formuated in the *Articles of the Barons* and the *Great Charter.* One would not suspect, in reading it, that what the barons really wished for was a return to feudal justice, as it existed before the great legal and judicial revolution of the reign of Henry II. In article 5 the demands of the barons as regards inheritances have not been well understood; the main object was to prevent the king's servants from carrying out wrongful seizures; the true sense of clauses 26–27 of the Great Charter does no appear here. Similarly, in article 11, the author of our document does not perhaps understand that the barons, as far as concerns debts to the Jews, chiefly wished to protect themselves against the greed of the king. Mr. Hubert Hall (see above, p. 118, note 1) thinks that in article 8 the scribe has replaced *allevamen* by *gravamen*; in our opinion it is not a question of an error of transcription; the French agent, who, let us believe, was the author of the document, must have supposed that scutage was a simple tax in substitution for military service, such as existed in France for the " roturiers " in the

3. Our document exists in the original in the *Trésor des Chartes,* in which our kings preserved the records which directly interested the Crown of France, its rights and its designs. The handwriting is French, and there is no strong reason for believing that the compiler was an Englishman. Still, as Mr. Davis has recognised, he might have been an Englishman in the service of the king of France.

The work of an agent of Philip Augustus

However this may be, it appears to us beyond question that the manuscript has been shut up in the *layettes* of the *Trésor* since the times of Philip Augustus. That prince, as we know, had agencies on the other side of the Channel; he offered succour to the rebel barons, sent the pirate Eustace the Monk to convey war machines to them, and this attitude helped to bring about the concession of the Great Charter.[1]

Evidently he had confidential agents who kept him informed respecting the negotiations taking place between John Lackland and his barons. The alleged " unknown charter of English Liberties " is the report of an agent of Philip Augustus.

4. The very character of our document forbids us to assign a precise date to it. We can only say that it is a little anterior to the *Articuli Baronum,* and dates from a moment at which the agreement between the king and the barons already appears as certain, without being definite. Everything inclines us to believe that negotiations were entered upon before the Runnymede interview, and we have before us an account of these negotiations, at a moment when the rumour ran that such and such

---

time of Philip Augustus (see Borrelli de Serres, *Recherches sur divers services publics,* i, 1895, pp. 467 sqq.) and that the tax became heavier if the service in the host required was more exacting. *Allevamen exercitus,* proposed by Mr. Hubert Hall, would make the meaning as follows : If there is exemption from services the tax to pay on this count (and to add to the scutage) shall be determined upon the advice of the barons.

1. See my *Etude sur la vie et le règne de Louis VIII.,* p. 69.

concessions had been granted by the king. If Philip Augustus' agent had written after the publication of the *Articuli Baronum* or of the Great Charter, he would have contented himself with sending into France a copy of the official text.

Is this as much as to say that the " unknown charter " has no historical interest? Far from it. It has a new proof of the curiosity with which events in England were followed in France; a new proof also of the part played by the spirit of tradition and of the prestige exercised by the charter of Henry I. In addition, it contains a clause which does not occur either in the *Articles of the Barons* or in the *Great Charter,* and clauses which are only to be found there in a very altered form; in this way it enlightens us respecting the hesitations and mutual concessions of the two parties, and explains better why the barons gave this or that form to certain of their claims. This is what the scholars who have studied it up till now have not sufficiently observed.

Interest of the document

The clauses on the repression of judicial abuses committed by the king (article 1), on the amount of the feudal relief (article 2), on the right of wardship (article 3), on the debts of minors to the Jews (article 11), on the marriage of heiresses (article 4), on dowry and the dower of widows (article 6), on the disposal of pecuniary inheritances after the decease of the testator or intestate person (article 5), are to be found again, in a more technical and generally a more complete form, in the Great Charter.[1] Some of them resemble more the *Articuli Baronum,* others the definitive charter. There is no need to insist at length on the details of the wording, as the differences may depend on the varying care and success with which the author of our document has summarized what he intended to report, and, I repeat, he

1. On the subject of clause 5, see Miss Mary Bateson, *Borough Customs,* ii, 1906, p. cxliii.

appears not to have always understood the exact sense of the clauses which he noted.

What is more interesting is this : articles 9, 10, and 12 touching the Royal forest, give us light upon the concessions which the barons had at first intended to wrest from the king.[1] According to clause 9, John would appear to have engaged to disafforest the forests created by himself, by Richard, and by Henry II. In clause 47 of the *Articuli Baronum* and of the Great Charter, it is only the forests created in the reign of John that are to be disafforested. Article 53 of the Charter proves however that the king had pledged himself to enquire whether certain forests of Richard and Henry II. ought not to be disafforested; our document is useful therefore for the understanding of article 53 of the Great Charter. Articles 10 and 12 of our document establish that the knights who possess a wood in the royal forests of ancient date, may henceforth cut trees and branches there for building and fuel; they shall have in their wood a forester in their service, and the king can only place a single forester there, for the purpose of protecting the game. According to article 12, no one may be condemned to death or to mutilation, for an offence touching the royal game. Important as were these concessions, the barons were not content with them; they preferred, in clause 39 of the Articuli and clause 48 of the Great Charter, to demand the constitution of elective juries in each county, to make enquiry concerning all the " evil customs " of the royal forests. The " evil customs " denounced by these juries of

Articles touching the Forest

1. Stubbs (i, p. 434 sqq.) has explained what the Royal Forest was and how it was administered. Cf. G. J. Turner, Preface to the *Select pleas of the Forest* (1901) and the good summary of McKechnie, *Magna Carta*, pp. 482 sqq. This irritating question of the Forest interested the baronage as well as the popular classes. It was the people of small consequence who suffered most from the abuse of power of the royal foresters; but the barons who had lands comprised within the forest bounds also submitted with impatience to the prohibitions of every kind issued to protect the trees and game.

inquest were to be immediately abolished; a plan very dangerous to the royal authority, and which would have ended in the complete suppression of a prerogative to which the Norman and Angevin kings attached the highest value. As a matter of fact, the civil war prevented these juries from completing their work. The council of regency of Henry III., in 1217, granted a Forest Charter : in article 10, the penalty of death and mutilation is abolished for poaching offences. We see that as early as 1215 the barons had demanded the abolition of these cruel penalties.

According to articles 7 and 8 of our document, the men of the king do not owe military service outside England, except in Normandy and in Brittany, and even then under certain conditions (*et hoc decenter*); if any one owes the service of ten knights, the assembly of the barons will grant him an " alleviation."[1] If the king levies a scutage, he will only take a mark of silver from each knight's fee.[2]

Foreign service and scutage

These clauses are very interesting. All that is said in the *Articuli Baronum* (art. 32) and in the *Great Charter* (art. 12) is that, beyond the aid in the three cases, no scutage can be levied without the consent of the *Commune Consilium regni,* and they were contented with specifying that the rate should be " reasonable." At the time to which our document belongs, we see that the barons did not think of preventing the king from freely levying the scutage of one mark. On the other hand, it seems that, by means of mutual concessions,

1. That is to say, according to Mr. Hall's interpretation (*loc. cit.*, p. 327), instead of furnishing knights he will pay a composition.

2. The text adds : if there is an increase of military obligations, a higher scutage may be collected, but on the counsel of the barons of the realm. As we have said above (p. 121, n. 3), there must be a mistake here. Scutage was not a mere tax for providing substitutes as Stubbs tended to believe; at any rate, in the reign of John, it was an addition to the effective military service, and did not exempt from it. See above, p. 56, note 1, a note on scutage.

they had come to an agreement with the king for the settlement of the troublesome question of military service in France; they agreed to accompany him in the provinces bordering on the Channel, but not beyond. Why is any clause of this kind wanting in the *Articuli Baronum* and the Great Charter? We may conjecture that neither the king nor the barons cared to make engagements on this head and to maintain the ephemeral concessions the memory of which is preserved in the notes we have just analysed.

Such is the supposed " unknown charter of English liberties." It will be observed that there is no question **Almost all these** either of the clergy or the merchants, or **concessions** the towns, and that the royal concessions **relate to the** it contains are made entirely or almost **nobility alone** entirely to the nobility. Was it because in the eyes of the French agent who drew up these notes, the negotiations between the king and the barons concerned very specially the particular interests of the latter? And, if this hypothesis is correct, was the French agent wrong? That is a question we shall now have to discuss.

XII.

THE GREAT CHARTER.

It will be well to describe here the ideas which appear to prevail to-day, in regard to the constitutional importance of the Great Charter; they are not at all in agreement with the classical, "orthodox" exposition of Stubbs.

Importance of the Great Charter

The bishop of Oxford considers that the Great Charter is the work of the whole nation joined in a coalition against the king : " The demands of the barons," he cries in an almost lyrical tone, " were no selfish exaction of privilege for themselves. . . . . They maintain and secure the right of the whole people as against themselves as well as against their master; clause by clause, the rights of the commons are provided for as well as the rights of the nobles. . . . . The Great Charter is the first great public act of the nation after it has realised its own identity." The 12th and following articles, concerning the levy of scutages and aids and the summons of the *Magnum Concilium* are " those to which the greatest constitutional interest belongs; for they admit the right of the nation to ordain taxation." [1]

According to Stubbs it is the work of the nation

Hallam,[2] Gneist,[3] Green,[4] M. Glasson,[5] Boutmy,[6]

1. Stubbs, *Const. Hist.*, i, 570, 571, 573, 579. Cf. Stubbs. preface to the *Historical Collections of Walter of Coventry* (Rolls series), ii, p. lxxi sqq.
2. *Middle Ages*, ii, 447; quoted by McKechnie, *Magna Carta*, p. 134.
3. *History of Engl. Parliament*; English translation by A. H. Keane, 4th edition, 1895, p. 103.
4. *Short History of the English People*, illus. ed., i, 240 sqq.
5. *Hist. du droit et des instit. de l'Angleterre*, iii, 1882, p. 6.
6. *Développement de la Constitution de la Soc. politique en Angleterre*, 1887, p. 55, and English translation by I. M. Eaden (*The English Constitution*, 1891), p. 29.

also regard the Great Charter as a constitutional victory gained by the nation as a whole over the king. The majority of English historians of the 19th century exalted the Great Charter with the same fervour, and the "sentimental force" which the course of historical events has given to this contract between King John, the English church, and the *liberi homines* of the kingdom is not yet exhausted.

Texts have to be read, however, without preoccupying ourselves with the importance which has been attributed to them in later ages, and if we apply a **Reaction in modern criticism** like method to the study of the Great Charter, we form a very different judgment upon it. Without claiming to have been the initiator of this reaction,[1] I may be allowed to recall, that, in a work published in 1894, I drew very different conclusions from the study of the sources used by Stubbs and also of documents which he had not utilised, and that I wrote as follows : " The barons had no suspicion that they would one day be called the founders of English liberty. The patriotism of writers on the other side of the Channel has singularly misrepresented the nature of this crisis. They extol the *noble simplicity* with which the people asserted its rights. But the authors of the Great Charter had no theories or general ideas at all. They were guided by a crowd of small and very practical motives in extorting this form of security from John Lackland."[2]

A decade ago the Great Charter underwent in England itself a critical examination which was not favourable to it. In their admirable *History of English Law* of which

1. Hallam said : " It has been lately the fashion to depreciate the value of Magna Carta, as if it had sprung from the private ambition of a few selfish barons, and redressed only some feudal abuses " (quoted by McKechnie, *Magna Carta*, p. 134). I do not know what authors are alluded to in this passage, and there is no use in trying to find out. In any case this " depreciation " is excessive. The Great Charter did not do nothing but "redress some feudal abuses." As we shall see, it struck at all the abuses of the royal power, from which the nobility had to suffer, directly or indirectly.

2. *Etude sur la vie et le règne de Louis VIII.*, pp. 57-58.

the first edition appeared in 1895, Sir Frederick Pollock
and Mr. Maitland observe very justly that it contains
almost no novelty. It is essentially a conservative or
even reactionary document. Its most salient characteristic is the restoration of the old feudal
law, violated by John Lackland, and
perhaps its practically most important
clauses, because they could be really
applied, were, that for example which
limited the right of relief, or that which forbad the king
to keep the land of a felon for more than a year and a
day, to the detriment of the lord. Upon other points,
the Great Charter marks an ecclesiastical and aristocratic
reaction against the growth of the crown.[1] Sir
Frederick Pollock and Mr. Maitland express this opinion
with discretion, and without denying the high value of
the Great Charter. Another jurist, Mr. Edward Jenks,
has shown less reserve : he sees in the movement of 1215
nothing but an attempt at a feudal reaction, and showers
the bolts of his ionoclastic zeal on the " myth of the
Great Charter."[2]

Miss Kate Norgate in her *John Lackland,* gives only
a brief and superficial analysis of the Great Charter.
But at least she shows very clearly that the
authors of this " peace " were, not the body
of the English baronage, but to use the
evidently very exact words of Ralph of
Coggeshall, " the archbishop of Canterbury, several
bishops and some barons." The attitude of the barons
before the crisis of 1215 and after the conclusion of
the pact of Runnymede, proves clearly, she says, that
the mass of the baronage were incapable of rising to the

Conservative and reactionary character of the Great Charter

Political incapacity of the Baronage

1. Pollock and Maitland, *History of English Law,* 2nd edition, 1898,
i, pp. 171 sqq. See also McKechnie, *op. cit.*; this careful commentator
has shown that as a whole the Great Charter restores custom; by that
very fact, it is at times reactionary ; on some points only, it marks a
step in advance.
2. *The Myths of Magna Carta* in the *Independent Review,* Nov., 1904.

K

conception of a contract between the king and all the free classes of the nation. Before the crisis of 1215, the barons had let John persecute the Church without doing anything to defend it ; after the signature of the Charter, these pretended champions of Right did not even know how to respect their plighted faith.[1] Mr. Pollard, in his *Henry VIII.*, has developed an analogous idea : vigorously and thoroughly enquiring why the Tudors were able to reign despotically, he finds only one possible explanation. We must renounce that idea—an idea so dear to Stubbs—that for seven hundred years England has been the messenger of liberty in the world.

England has not always been eager for liberty

The English were but men and, in a general way, "the English ideal was closely subordinated to the passion for material prosperity," and not to the love of liberty for its own sake. That the English have always burned with enthusiasm for parliamentary government, is a legend invented by modern doctrinaires. The Great Charter, the symbol of this alleged political genius of the Anglo-Saxon race, only became in reality the " palladium of English liberty " in the 17th century, to serve the necessities of the anti-monarchical opposition, and for that purpose it was greatly distorted and travestied. In the 16th century, it did not so to speak come into question, it had been forgotten : Shakespeare does not say a word about it in his " King John."[2]

We are now a long way off from the panegyrics in which the Great Charter is represented as the source of all the greatness and all the political institutions of England, far even from the more measured appreciation of Stubbs. Whatever the respect with which we must regard the work of that eminent scholar, it is clear that, upon the causes of the crisis of

1. *John Lackland* (1902), pp. 219, 234, 236 sqq., and *passim*.
2. A. F. Pollard, *Henry VIII*, ed. in 18mo (1905), p. 33 sqq.

1215, upon the character of the compact, upon the conceptions and the state of mind which engendered it, upon the influence it has had in the development of English liberties, we can no longer profess in all respects the same opinion as he did. Recently a new and learned commentary on the Great Charter has been published[1] of which we shall have to speak again; in reading this work of Mr. McKechnie, the most thorough and balanced which has been written on the subject, we receive the impression that Stubbs was the dupe of many illusions, and that the historians of his generation have had difficulty in guarding themselves against the legends created by the exaltation of patriotism and by political strife.

It is quite clear that history is written to-day with more sobriety; but we must add that we are better informed respecting the crisis of 1215

New light on the subject than they were or could be at the time at which the first volume of the *Constitutional History* appeared. In the course of a quarter of a century, English, German, and French scholarship, has thrown much light on most of the questions which are touched on in the Great Charter, and it cannot now be interpreted as it used to be. Moreover, we are enlightened by new documents.

The term " new document " cannot, to speak exactly, be applied to the most important of those of which I am thinking : the *Histoire des ducs de Normandie et des rois d'Angleterre,*

Narrative of the " Histoire des ducs de Normandie " published in 1840 by Francisque Michel. But Stubbs and his contemporaries, who somewhat strangely neglected works of French scholarship, were not acquainted with this chronicle and never utilised it. I believe myself to have been the first to make use of it, at least as far as regards

1. W. S. McKechnie, *Magna Carta,* 1905.

the history of England.[1]   It was written about 1220 by a
minstrel attached to Robert of Béthune, who was one of
King John's familiars.   It is interesting to see how this
contemporary summarizes events, and what he recollects
of the Great Charter.   The barons, he says : "decided
to demand of the king that he should observe in regard
to them the charters which King Henry, who was his
father's grandfather, had granted to their ancestors, and
which King Stephen had confirmed to them; and if
he refused to do this, they would all throw off their
allegiance to him and make war upon him until he was
forced to do it.   So he had to make such a peace there as
the barons wished; there he was forced to agree that a
woman should never be married in a quarter where she
would be disparaged.   This was the best agreement
which he made with them, had it been well kept.   In
addition he had to agree that he would never cause a man
to lose member or life for any wild beast that he took;
but that he should be able to atone for it by a fine; these
two things could readily be tolerated.   The reliefs of
lands, which were too high, he had to fix at such a rate
as they willed to have them.   The highest powers of
jurisdiction they insisted on having in their lands.
Many other things they demanded with much reason, of
which I am unable to inform you.   Over and above all
this they desired that 25 barons should be chosen, and
by the judgment of these 25 the king should govern
them in all things, and through them redress all the
wrongs he should do to them, and they also, on the other
hand, would through them redress all the wrongs that
they should do to him.   Also they further desired, along
with all this, that the king should never have power to
appoint a bailiff in his land except through the 25.   All
this the king was forced to concede.   For the observance
of this peace the king gave his charter to the barons as
one who could not help himself."

1. See my *Etude sur la vie et le règne de Louis VIII.*, Introduction,
pp. xx–xxi.

It will be convenient to subjoin the original text of the passages here translated :

[Li baron] deviserent que il demanderoient al roi que il lor tenist les chartres que il rois Henris qui fu ayous son père avoit données a lor ancissours et que li rois Estievenes lor avoit confremées; et se il faire ne le voloit, il le desfieroient tout ensamble, et le guerroieroient tant que il par force le feroit . . . . . Si li couvint là tel pais faire comme li baron vaurrent; là li couvint-il avoir en couvent à force que jamais feme ne maricroit ou liu ù elle fust desparagie. Chou fu la miudre couvenence que il lor fist, s'elle fust bien tenue. O tout chou li couvint-il avoir en couvent ke jamais ne feroit pierdre home menbre ne vie por bieste sauvage k'il presist;[1] mais raiembre le pooit : ces deus choses pooit-on bien soufrir. Les rachas des tierres, qui trop grant estoient, li couvint metre à tel fuer comme il vaurrent deviser. Toutes hautes justices vaurrent-il avoir en lor tierres. Mainte autre chose lor requisent ù assés ot de raison, que je ne vous sai pas nommer. Desus tout chou vorrent-il que XXV baron fussent esliut, et par le jugement de ces XXV les menast li rois de toutes choses, et toz les tors que il lor feroit lor adreçast par eus, et il autresi de l'autre part li adreceroient toz les tors que il li feroient par eus. Et si vorrent encore avoec tout chou que li rois ne peust jamais metre en sa tierre bailliu, se par les XXV non. Tout chou couvint le roi otriier à force. De cele pais tenir donna li rois sa chartre as barons, comme chil qui amender ne le pot.[2]

In this summary, which is very incomplete, but accurate enough on the whole, the Great Charter appears as a purely feudal compact. What struck

Author's conception of the Great Charter

the minstrel, what evidently struck the men of his time, is that the king, under force and compulsion, had to promise not to disparage heiresses, to diminish the rights of relief, to renounce the strict laws which protected his forests, to respect the rights of justice of the feudal lords, and to recognise the existence of a commission of twenty-five barons, charged to bring to his notice the grievances of the nobility. Not a word of the alleged alliance between the baronage and

1. This clause does not exist textually in the Great Charter. Cf. above, p. 125.

2. *Histoire des ducs de Normandie*, pp. 145–146, 149–150.

the rest of the nation. The barons are proud, puffed up with their importance, and think only of themselves. "On the strength of this wretched peace they treated him with such pride as must move all the world to pity. They required him to observe quite faithfully what he had agreed with them; *but what they had previously agreed with their men they were unwilling to observe.*"[1]

The biographer of William the Marshal, in the celebrated poem discovered by Paul Meyer, says in two words " That the barons for their franchises came to the king "[2] and afterwards relates at great length the war which followed the annulling of the Great Charter. But he says not a word about the Great Charter itself, does not even quote it.

" History of William the Marshal "

These are, it is true, chronicles written by minstrels and heralds who are only interested in the doings of the nobles and in feats of arms. But the " unknown charter " which we have recited and commented on above has by no means that character. It is a summary of negotiations between John and his adversaries, the work no doubt of an agent of Philip Augustus, and that king had the greatest interest in knowing the real grounds of the quarrel. Now we have seen that it is concerned almost exclusively with concessions granted to the nobles.

The "Unknown Charter "

That the Great Charter was drawn up for the baronage and not for the nation as a whole is therefore our deduction from documents which Stubbs did not make use of. But it is also the deduction to be drawn from the chronicles which he used, and, lastly, from the Charter itself. Let us read again without preconcep-

The classical narratives— Wendover, Coggeshall, Barnwell

1. Avoec toute la vilaine pair, li moustroient-il tel orguel que tous li mons en deust avoir pitié. Il voloient que il moult bien lor tenist chou que en couvent lor avoit; *mais chou que il avoient en covent à lor homes avant ne voloient-il tenir (Ibidem,* p. 151.)

2. Que li baron por lor franchises vindrent al rei . . . *Histoire de Guillaume le Maréchal,* ed. Paul Meyer, (*Soc. de l'Histoire de France,*) ii, pp. 177 sqq.

tion the three principal narratives of the crisis of 1215, those of Roger of Wendover,[1] of Ralph of Coggeshall[2] and of the Canon of Barnwell.[3] We see there that the insurrection is an entirely feudal one; they record only the complicity of the Archbishop of Canterbury and certain bishops and of the " rich men "[4] of London. The insurgents wished to revive the liberties expressed in the charter of King Henry I.,"[5] which guaranteed the Church and the baronage against a certain number of royal abuses.

These chroniclers speak neither of consent to taxation nor of national union against the king. The Runnymede assembly is composed of "tota Angliae nobilitas regni,"[6] and the Great Charter is a " quasi pax inter regem et barones."[7] The chroniclers are perfectly in agreement with Innocent III., who, in his bull of the 24th August, 1215,[8] speaks of the rebellion of the "magnates et nobiles Angliae," and with John Lackland himself, who calls the crisis the " discordia inter nos et barones nostros," and recognises that he is signing a sort of treaty of peace with his barons.[9]

Let us take the text of the Great Charter, not to recommence clause by clause an analysis already made

1. In the edition of the *Chronica Majora* of Matthew Paris, (Rolls Ser.), ii, pp. 582, 583, 584—589.

2. Ed. Stevenson (Rolls series), pp. 170—173.

3. In the *Historical Collections of Walter of Coventry*, ed. Stubbs (Rolls series), ii, pp. 217—221.

4. " Favebant enim baronibus divites civitatis, et ideo pauperes obmurmurare (or : obloqui) metuebant " (Wendover, p. 587).

5. " Chartam regis Henrici primi proferunt quae libertates exprimit quas proceres, olim abolitas, nunc resuscitare contendunt " (Coggeshall, p. 170).

6. Wendover, p. 589.

7. Coggeshall, p. 172.

8. Printed by (among others) Bémont, *Chartes des Libertés Anglaises* pp. 41 sqq.

9. " Ad melius sopiendum discordiam inter nos et barones nostros motam " (Great Charter, art. 61; see also art. 1). Cf. art. 52 : " in securitate pacis. . . ."

by Stubbs,[1] but to investigate whether in reality " the barons maintain and secure the rights of the whole people as against themselves as well as against their master," and whether "the rights of the commons are provided for as well as the rights of the nobles," whether, again, the famous articles 12 and 14 " admit the right of the nation to ordain taxation."[2]

Of the sixty-three clauses into which modern editors divide the provisions, often somewhat ill arranged, of the charter of the 15th of June, 1215,[3] about

fourteen are temporary articles or relate to the execution of the agreement. Of the forty-nine which remain two concern the clergy,[4] twenty-four specially secure the baronage against the abuse which the king made of his rights as suzerain.[5] These articles, placed for the most

---

1. *Const. Hist.*, i, pp. 572—579. This analysis is in general faithful and exact; but on many points, the interpretation is no longer acceptable. We refer our readers once for all to the excellent commentary by McKechnie.

2. *Const. Hist.*, i, 570 and 573.

3. We shall quote the Great Charter and the Articles of the Barons (which preceded it and form a sort of first draft of it authentic and approved by the king), from the excellent collection of *Chartes des Libertés Anglaises* of M. Bémont.

4. Arts. 1 and 22.

5. Art. 2 to 12, 14 to 16, 21, 26, 27, 29, 32, 34, 37, 39, 43, 46. These articles of feudal law precise and well drafted restore ancient custom; two of them, articles 34 and 39, would to some extent have ruined the royal system of justice and the legal progress accomplished since the reign of Henry II., had they been applied in their letter and their spirit, and it is of them above all that we have been thinking in speaking of the reactionary character of the Great Charter : article 34 in fact forbade the king to call up suits touching property, and article 39 restored judgement by peers. They were evidently evoked by the disquieting development of royal justice at the expense of seignorial justice, and by the executions without sentence with which John Lackland had threatened the barons : " Nec super eum ibimus, nec super eum mittemus, nisi per legale judicium parium suorum vel per legem terre." I do not, however, believe that article 39 was drafted with the intention of denying the competence of the professional judges (Cf. article 18 on the iters), and Mr. McKechnie seems to me to be wrong in seeing in the *lex terre* the old national procedure by battle, compurgation, and ordeal. The *lex terre*, is doubtless the custom of

part at the beginning of the document, are evidently its fundamental clauses in the minds of the authors of the agreement. Ten others concern the general

General clauses against the abuse of royal power

exercise of the royal justice.[1] The benefit of them could not be confined to the barons alone; but it is clear that it was of themselves that the barons were thinking when exacting these guarantees, which, without exception, have for them, directly or indirectly, a powerful interest.[2] It is the same with the important articles which set a limit to the exactions of the sheriffs, to abuses of purveyance, etc. The special régime of the royal Forest was particularly hard on the poor people, but it very much annoyed and irritated the barons themselves.[3]

In conclusion, let us take the clauses which appear to be drafted specially in favour of the people of the towns and villages. It is by a study of them that we can verify whether the Great Charter was made " to secure as well the rights of the common people as those of the nobles," and whether " the demands of the barons were no selfish exaction of privilege for themselves."

" Let the city of London," says article 13, " have all its ancient liberties and free customs as well on land

the realm in a general sense, the *lex regni*; cf. the charter granted to the barons on the 10th of May, to settle the same question : "nec super eos per vim vel per arma ibimus, nisi *per legem regni nostri*, etc." (Bémont, p. 33, note).

1. Art. : 17, 18, 19, 20, 24, 36, 38, 40, 45, 54.

2. Clause 20, for example, which might seem " democratic," had a financial interest for the lords. See below. Article 17 similarly seems made for the smaller litigants : " Communia placita non sequantur curiam nostram, set teneantur in aliquo loco certo." But this definite fixing of the court of common pleas (that is to say of the suits which did not interest the king personally) at Westminster was not important for the smaller litigants only. The barons might be ruined by the journeys they were until then obliged to make in order to obtain justice. The case of Richard of *Anesty*, who had to follow the king and his court through England, Normandy, Aquitaine and Anjou for five years, is quite characteristic (See McKechnie, pp. 309–310, and Stubbs, i, 642 and note 1. *Anesty* is Anstey in the county of Hertford ; see Round, in *Victoria History of Essex*, i, p. 379.)

3. Clauses 23, 25, 28, 30, 31, 33, 35, 41, 44, 47, 48.

Clauses for the towns

as on water."[1] Such is the vague and commonplace concession obtained by the Londoners as the price of their aid. As for the free customs of the other towns, the barons did not even ask, in their *Articuli,* that the king should confirm them. It was only at the time of the definitive drafting of the Great Charter that, perhaps in order to further weaken by generalising the value of the promises made to the Londoners, this phrase was added : " In addition we wish and grant that all the other cities, boroughs, towns and ports may have all their liberties and free customs." It is quite obvious that these " other towns " had taken no active part in the quarrel between the king and the barons, and that they derived no real profit from it.

But the merchants, it will be said, obtain substantial guarantees against arbitrary treatment. By article 20

Clauses concerning the merchants

they are assured that their merchandise will not be confiscated, under the pretext of fines to be paid. According to article 41, they may go out of, come into and travel in England without paying exhorbitant customs; in article 35 they are promised uniformity of weights and measures. All these concessions were in reality made in the interests of the barons. They saw clearly that the king, by inflicting ruinous fines on the merchants, diminished by so much, to the sole profit of his treasury, the wealth of the lordships to which the condemned men belonged.

1. As for the passage relating to the aids paid by the Londoners (see the text and what we have said above, pp. 101 sqq.) it is very obscure. If this passage means, as some scholars have conjectured, that the aid ought to be *reasonable,* it is too vague to form a guarantee; if it means that every aid levied on the Londoners (except the three feudal aids) must be assented to by the Common Council of the realm, it will be obsrved that this Common Council, by the terms of article 14, includes only the barons, prelates and tenants-in-chief of the king. It is true that there were ' barons ' of London in the Common Council (see Stubbs, p. 398). According to the list given by Matthew Paris (*Chron. Maj.* (Rolls series), ii, pp. 604–605), William Hardel, mayor of London, figures in the Committee of Twenty-five barons elected to keep the king under surveillance in conformity with article 61 of the Great Charter : " quod barones eligant viginti quinque barones de regno quos voluerint."

Article 41, as the context proves, was merely designed to meet the case of the alien merchants who came to visit England to the great convenience of buyers, but were hated and hunted by the native producers. Similarly the uniformity of weights and measures, a reform well calculated to frustrate the frauds of the merchants, was desired by consumers only.

Stubbs wonders that the implements and working beasts of the serf should be exempted from arbitrary **Clause touching** fines. But the text reads: ' Et villanus **the " wainage "** eodem modo amercietur salvo waynagio **of the villeins** suo, si inciderint *in misericordium nostram*." What does this engagement made by the king mean ? It means that the " wainage " of a serf prosecuted *before a royal tribunal* shall not be confiscated; only serfs who do not belong to the king and fines imposed by royal officers are in question;[1] the guarantee is given not to the serfs but to the lords; the Charter only concerns itself with these serfs because their " wainage " is the lord's property. It does not protect them against the fines of seignorial courts. Moreover, it does not protect them against arbitrary tallage, and it is clearly specified that the securities relative to royal requisitions are granted only to freemen. Similarly the first article says : " Concessimus *omnibus liberis hominibus* regni nostri omnes libertates subscriptas. . . ." It might be queried whether the burgesses of the towns are included among the *liberi homines;* it is open to question; but that the serfs or *villani* (we have seen that these are equivalent terms in England in the thirteenth century) were in no wise *liberi homines,* and that by this very fact the great majority of the English population found itself excluded from the benefit of the Great Charter, is a fact which does not admit of doubt.

1. This is proved by the slightly different and more precise wording adopted in the confirmations of 1217 and of 1225 : " Villanus alterius quam noster eodem modo amercietur, etc." (Bémont, p. 52). No security is granted to the villeins of the royal demesne; for the rest, their lot was in general better than that of the seignorial villeins.

It is undoubtedly from this standpoint that we must interpret article 60 : "All these aforesaid customs and

Clause concerning the sub-tenants liberties which we have conceded to be observed in our kingdom in our relations with our men (*ergo nostros*), all those of our kingdom, as well clerk as lay, shall observe in their relations with their men (*erga suos*)." This clause manifestly does not concern, as Thomson in his commentary thought, the whole of the English people, but only the freemen who did not hold their land directly from the king, and who also wished to be protected against the violence of their lords and the exactions of their agents. In order to understand article 60 we must compare it with article 15, in which the king declares that, just as he will not levy any extraordinary aid on his tenants-in-chief without the consent of the Common Council of the realm, in the same way he will no longer sell any writ authorising a lord to levy an aid on his free tenants, *de liberis hominibus suis*) beyond the three cases recognised by English custom. To sum up, besides the prelates, barons and tenants-in-chief of the king, the only class which obtains precise guarantees is the class of free tenants who are only mediately tenants of the king, and I imagine that this means only the freeholders holding by military service and not simple peasants holding in socage. It was the body of knights, direct and indirect vassals of the king, who had risen against him to obtain " liberties "; it was to them that the barons had made their appeal.[1] It was for them as well as for the barons that the Great Charter was drafted. The Great Charter was essentially a document of feudal law.

This being so, it is very difficult to believe that it contains some new political germ, and institutes the

1. It was probably in 1215 that an appeal was issued of which we have no more than the following mention : " Charta baronum Anglie missa tenentibus Northumbriam, Cumbriam, Westmorelandiam, contra Johannem regem Anglie " (Ayloffe, *Calendar of Ancient Charters*, 1774, p. 328).

The alleged consent to taxation principle of consent to taxation. It is, moreover, the expression and the reflection of a social state in which taxation, properly speaking, is not known. At irregular intervals the king, who is supposed to content himself with the revenues of his demesne for his ordinary necessities, levies an extraordinary tax on some class or other of his subjects; for example, a feudal aid, notably under the form of " scutage," on the knights,—or a carucage on the other freeholders,—or a tallage on the peasants and towns of the crown. Is it said in the Great Charter that whatever may be the form which it takes " taxation " should be assented to? Not in the least. The authors of the compact are not acquainted, let us repeat, **True bearing of the text** with " taxation " in general, and they wish solely to take cognisance of scutage or feudal aids : " That no scutage or aid[1] be established in our kingdom, unless it be to pay our ransom or for the knighting of our eldest son, or for the first marriage of our eldest daughter, and that in these three cases a reasonable aid only be levied." And to please the Londoners these words were added, the obscurity of which we have pointed out : " Let it be the same with regard to the aids of the City of London." Article 14 then specifies the rules for the summons of the Common Council, and, as Stubbs says, evidently does nothing but expressly

---

1. The barons bring together here, as if to confound them, the *auxilium* and the *scutagium*. The *auxilium* is the aid due to the suzerain in virtue of one of the most general principles of feudal law. In France, it is understood that the vassals cannot refuse the *aid in the four cases* : when the suzerain is a prisoner and put to ransom, or when he makes his son a knight, or when he marries his daughter, or when he sets out on the Crusade; in England this last case is not recognised by custom. The *scutagium* in the 12th century was generally a tax levied in lieu of military service, and such is the significance that modern historians, for the most part, give to scutage; but (1) the term might be applied differently, and might have, as early as this period, the general sense of a feudal aid; there are examples of aids in the three cases being called scutage; (2) John Lackland raised scutage which did not dispense from military service (see above, p. 56, note 1, and p. 125). The barons were then justified in assimilating the scutage to the aid.

confirm the previous custom. The king had not the right to levy a feudal aid by his own authority except in the three fixed cases ; outside these three cases he had to consult his barons and tenants-in-chief. John Lackland had ignored this usage, or at least he had levied at his discretion, almost every year, a tax, the scutage, to which Henry II. had only resorted seven times and at a more moderate rate. The barons, as the wording of the clause proves, considered scutage as a sort of aid, and the uncertainty of terminology justified them in doing so. In any case the object of article 12 was to remind the king of the custom which regulated the feudal aid in the three cases, and to submit scutage expressly to the same restrictions. When John Lackland had disappeared, this clause was not reproduced in the confirmation of the Great Charter granted on the 12th of November, 1216. We must not conclude from this that the question had no importance in the eyes of the barons, for it was said in article 42 of that confirmation that, upon divers grave and doubtful clauses of the Great Charter, notably on the *levy of scutages and aids,* more ample deliberation was to be taken.[1] It was perhaps the assimilation of the scutage to the feudal aid in the three cases, which was contested by the king's advisers. However this may be, in the confirmations of 1217 and of 1225, clause 12 was replaced by the following one in which no mention is

Text adopted in the confirmations

made of the feudal aid in the three cases : " That scutage be henceforth taken as it was accustomed to be taken in the time of King Henry II."[2] This wording clearly proves that the barons had no idea of a parliamentary system, and only wished to be secured, in some way or other, against the too frequent return and the raising of the rate of scutage. Article 14 of the document of 1215, touching

1. "Quia vero quedam capitula in priori carta continebantur que gravia et dubitabilia videbantur, scilicet de scutagiis et auxiliis assidendis . . ." (Bémont, p. 58, n. 4).
2. Article 37 (Bémont, p. 57).

the summons of the Common Council is not to be found
again in any of the confirmations, and our opinion is
that it had been introduced into the Great Charter by
desire of the king,[1] and not in the least by desire of the
barons. The more so as it does not figure in the
Articles of the Barons.

The Great Charter of 1215, as we see, was not a
political statute, inaugurating constitutional guarantees
unknown until then.   On the other hand,
far from being a national work, it was
manifestly conceived in the interests of a
class.   What is to be our conclusion?
Sir Frederick Pollock and Mr. Maitland,
after having pointed out a great number of defects
in the Great Charter, add : "And yet with all its
faults this document becomes, and rightly becomes, a
sacred text, the nearest approach to an irrepealable,
' fundamental statute ' that England has ever had.   For
in brief it means this, that the king is and shall be below
the law."[2]   That again, it seems to us, is to assign too
glorious a rôle to the baronage of John Lackland and to its
political conceptions, which are childish and anarchical.
The English nobility of that day has not the idea of law
at all.   Powerless to prevent the growth of a very strong
royal power which has enveloped the country with the
network of its administration and its courts, it seeks only
to secure itself against financial exactions and the
violence of a cruel and tyrannical king.   It does not
succeed in discovering, and it perhaps does not seek for

(margin note: The Great Charter is not a national work.)

1. The end of the clause specifies that " the business should be transacted on the day assigned, by the counsel of those who are present,
although all the persons summoned are not come."   This is a precaution
taken by the king against those who claimed only to pay the tax if
they had consented to it in person, and the insertion of this rule is
doubtless the principal motive which dictated the insertion of the article.
No one, besides, thought that the consecrated usage of the *Common
Council* could be abolished and when article 14 disappeared from the
confirmations of the Great Charter, assemblies of barons and prelates
continued none the less to be convoked.
2. *History of English Law*, i, p. 173.

Does not organise the reign of law any "legal" means of controlling his acts and preventing abuses, it does not think of organising the "Common Council," it forgets even to speak of it in the *Articles* which it asks the king to accept. In order to force the king to respect his engagements, what expedient does it devise? The most naïf, the most barbarous procedure, **Appeal to civil war** the procedure of civil war: "The barons shall elect twenty-five barons of the kingdom, who shall with all their power observe, keep and cause to be observed the peace and liberties granted," and in case of need, if the king refuse to repair the wrongs he has committed, "compel and molest him in every way that they can, by taking of his castles, of his lands and of his possessions" with the aid "of the commune of all the land," that is to say, with the aid of all those who are accustomed to bear arms. There is no question, in the Great Charter of John Lackland,[1] of the reign of law; it is merely a question of engagements taken by the king towards his nobles, respect for which is only imposed on him by the perpetual threat of rebellion.

The importance of the Great Charter is in reality due to its fullness, its comprehensiveness, to the variety of **Reasons of the constitutional importance of the Great Charter** the problems which it attempts to solve. It does not differ fundamentally from the charters of liberties which preceded it in the twelfth century, but it is much more explicit. It is five times longer than that of Henry I., it regulates a much greater number of questions, and, being posterior to the capital reforms of Henry II., it is more adapted to the conditions of life and to the state of Law. In passing, and

---

1. It is quite understood that our remarks cannot apply in their entirety except to the Great Charter of John Lackland. The clause respecting the twenty-five barons has disappeared from the Great Charter of 1225, which has a constitutional importance of the first order, while it is less interesting and less characteristic in the eyes of the historian than that of 1215.

accessorily it enunciates in favour of chartered towns, the merchants and the seignorial villeins, certain promises of which there is no question in the documents conceded at their accession by Henry I., Stephen and Henry II.; although we must reduce the scope of these clauses to its just proportions, the share here assigned to civic liberties is evidently a new and striking fact. Finally, the Great Charter was the result of a celebrated crisis. The aristocracy in arms wrested it by main force from a prince as redoubtable by his intelligence as by his vices, and its publication was followed by a terrible civil war, which ended in its solemn confirmation. It thus became a symbol of successful struggle against royal tyranny; men have discovered in it, in the course of centuries, all sorts of principles of which its authors had not the least notion, and have made of it the " Bible of the Constitution."[1] False interpretations of some of its articles have not been without influence on the development of English liberties. There is no need to seek elsewhere the causes of its success in the Middle Ages and of its long popularity in modern times.

1. Speech of William Pitt, quoted by Bémont, *Chartes*, p. lxix, note 1.

L

THE FOREST.

THE institution of the Forest, established by the Norman
kings and maintained by the Plantagenets, has strong
claims on the attention of the historian. Not
only, as an institution very characteristic of
the times, does it throw valuable light on
certain features of mediæval society, law, and administration; but the fact of its existence led to important
results in the constitutional crises of the thirteenth and
fourteenth centuries. One may regard the Forest as a
melancholy and decisive witness to the brutality of the
Norman Conquest, as an illustration of the despotic
authority of the Norman and Angevin kings, as a cause
of the hostility of the barons and higher clergy towards
the crown, or as a ground for the hatred felt by the
people towards the king's officers. But from every
point of view the Forest is equally worthy of study.

Stubbs did no more than touch upon the subject, and,
as far as we know, the history of the Forest in mediæval
England has never been treated in its entirety on the
general lines which we wish to follow. Our intention is
to set forth the most important of the results that have
been achieved. We have used such printed records—
whether published in full or calendared—as we have
been able to consult, and several valuable works of
modern scholarship, among which special mention
should be made of Dr. F. Liebermann's critical essay
on the *Constitutiones de Foresta* ascribed to Cnut, and

Mr. G. J. Turner's study on the Forest in its legal aspect during the thirteenth century. In addition, the interest of the task has led us to make cautious expeditions into the realm of comparative history. In seeking the origins of the English Forest we have turned to the Continent, where they are certainly to be found, and occasionally we have drawn a parallel between the evolution of the Forest in England and the corresponding process in France.

Use of the comparative method

THE FOREST AND THE RIGHT OF THE CHASE IN MEDIÆVAL ENGLAND.—ORGANISATION OF THE FOREST.

We have first to ask what meaning was attached in England to the word " Forest," in its legal sense,[1] as used, for example, in the phrase " Forestas retinui " in the charter of Henry I, or in such expressions as " bosci afforestati," " manere extra forestam," which appear in the charter of 1217.

Meaning of the word "forest"

As early as the time of Henry II, Richard Fitz-Neal, in his *Dialogus de Scaccario,* gave a very clear definition of the Forest. It consists, he says, in preserves which the king has kept for himself in certain well-wooded counties where there is good pasture for the venison. There the king goes to forget his cares in the chase ; there he enjoys quiet and freedom : consequently those who commit an offence against the Forest lay themselves open to the personal vengeance of the king. Their punishment is no concern of the ordinary courts, but depends entirely on the king, or his specially appointed delegate. The laws of the Forest spring " not from the common law of the realm, but from the will of princes ; so that what is done in accordance with them is said not to be just absolutely, but just according to the forest law." [2] The nature of the Forest could not be more clearly stated, and the definitions given by Manwood in the sixteenth century and Sir Edward Coke in

Definition in the " Dialogus de Scaccario"

1. The word is also used, even by lawyers, in its modern sense of a tract covered with trees ; the author of the *Dialogus de Scaccario* writes, "Reddit compotum. . . . de censu *illius nemoris vel foreste.* . . ." (*Dialogus de Scaccario,* II. xi ; ed. Hughes, Crump, and Johnson, 1902, p. 141).
2. *Dial. de Scacc.* I. xi, xii ; ed. cit. 105 sqq.

the seventeenth, are based on those formulated by Richard Fitz-Neal.[1]

The word *Forest,* adds the author of the *Dialogus,* comes from *fera,* wild beast, *e* being changed to *o.*

The Forest is a hunting-preserve Fanciful though it be, this derivation is deduced from a perfectly correct notion : in law and in fact, if not in etymology, the Forest owed its origin to sport. The Forest or the Forests—the word was used, in the middle ages, in both the plural and the singular—consisted of a number of game-preserves protected by a special law. They were mostly covered with woods, but also included moorland, pasture, and even agricultural land and villages.[2]

The Forest, as such, belonged to the king. It must not, indeed, be confused with the royal demesne : for

In what sense does the Forest belong to the crown ? there were royal woods which were not Forest, and on the other hand, a forest often comprised estates which were the property of subjects, even of great lords. But it belonged to the king in the sense that it was created for his benefit, that within its limits none save himself and those authorised by him might hunt the red deer, the fallow deer, the roe, and the wild boar,[3] and

1. " A forrest doth chiefly consist of these foure things, that is to say, of vert, venison, particuler lawes and priviledges, and of certen meet officers appointed for that purpose, to thend that the same may the better be preserved and kept for a place of recreation and pastime, meet for the royall dignitie of a prince " (Manwood, *Treatise of the Lawes of the Forrest,* 1598, f. 1) ; " A Forest doth consist of eight things, videlicet of soil, covert, laws, courts, judges, officers, game, and certain bounds " (Coke, *Fourth part of the Institutes of the Laws of England,* ed. 1644, p. 289).

2. The word *forestis, foresta,* which is found in Merovingian documents of the seventh century, comes, according to Diez, from the Latin *foris,* and already meant a district placed *outside,* or preserved, by royal command. This etymology is quite in accordance with the sense of the word Forest in England, but after a careful study of Merovingian records, I am doubtful whether to accept it.

3. These four were generally considered to be the "beasts of the Forest" to which the forest law applied. The list varied somewhat in different times and places. See the very learned and sound paper of F. Liebermann, *Ueber Pseudo-Cnuts Constitutiones de Foresta,* 1894, p. 20 ; G. J. Turner, *Select Pleas of the Forest* (Selden Society, 1901), x sqq. From the time of the first Norman kings neither the wolf nor the fox was regarded as a beast of the forest. John of Salisbury says that they were not hunted according to the rules of venery (Liebermann, p. 23).

that it was subjected, throughout its extent, to very severe laws, enacted arbitrarily by the kings for the protection of the "vert and venison," that is to say for the preservation of the beasts of the Forest and the vegetation which gave them cover and food.[1]

In mediæval documents mention is also made of the king's *parks* and *warrens,* and sometimes of his *chase.*

Chases and royal parks There was, in our opinion, no real difference between the king's chase and the Forest.[2]

Parks were distinguished by the fact that they were enclosed by a wall[3] or fence.[4] But the records published by Mr. Turner show that the royal parks formed part of the Forest,[5] that they were under the oversight of foresters,[6] and that offences committed in them were punished in the same way as forest offences :[7] and in these respects isolated royal parks must have been in the same case as those surrounded by Forest. As the king's object in making a park was the better preservation of his game, it would be absurd if the forest law were not applicable to it. It is well to insist on this point, for English historians have vied with one another

1. If the king alienated a part of his Forest the forest law might still be applied to it for the benefit of the new owner. This was the case in the forests held by the earls of Lancaster in the fourteenth century (Turner, pp. ix, cxi sqq.). But as a rule the forest, in such an event, became a chase (see below, p. 154).

2. According to W. H. P. Greswell, *Forests and Deer Parks of the County of Somerset* (1905), p. 244, the chase was not subject to the forest law. He gives no proof of this, and admits that in certain documents the Forest of Exmoor is called the Chase of Exmoor. Kingswood Forest in Essex is another case in point. In 1328 J. le Warre complained that some years before the "gardeins de la chace" had put his manor "en la chace de Kingeswode et de Fulwode "; so that he no longer had the right to cut his wood (*Rotuli Parliamentorum,* ii, 29). Kingswood was part of the forest of Essex (Turner, p. 69). Mr. Turner's remarks on chases (*ibid.,* pp. cix sqq.) apply only to the chases of feudal lords.

3. " Fregit murum parci et intravit eum cum canibus " (Turner, p. 40).

4. " Operarii in parco predicto ad reparandum palicium " (*ibid.,* p. 55).

5. " Venacio data per dominum regem : . . . comes Cornubye venit in foresta de Rokingham . . . et cepit in parco et extra parcum bestias ad placitum. . . . . " (*ibid.,* p. 91).

6. " Willelmus, forestarius pedes in parco de Bricstoke " (*ibid.,* p. 83). These foresters were sometimes styled parkers (*ibid.,* p. 55).

7. *Ibid.,* pp. 4, 54 sqq., etc.

in repeating that parks were not subject to the forest law.[1] In this general form, the statement is false : a distinction should be made between the royal parks and those of the lords.[2]

The position of the royal warrens has never, as it seems to me, been accurately stated. It is clear that the word bore another meaning than the one **Royal warrens** it had in France,[3] and was applied especially to land reserved for hare-hunting. It would, however, be too much to say that royal warrens were entirely exempt from the forest law,[4] for in the *Placita foreste* we find thefts of hares from a warren judged by the same process as poaching in the Forest.[5] Even in Middlesex there was

1. See, e.g., W. S. Holdsworth, *History of English Law* (1903), i, 346 ; MacKechnie, *Magna Carta* (1905), p. 493.

2. The treatise of Mr. Turner, who possesses well-deserved authority on the subject of the forest law, does not tend to prevent this confusion. Although royal parks often appear in the documents he has edited, he deals in his introduction only with the parks of subjects. It is of these that he is speaking when he says (p. cxxii) : " The park was not subject to the forest law."

3. In France itself the meaning of the word changed—a fact which has caused many blunders. It was only in the sixteenth century that " garenne " acquired the almost exclusive sense of rabbit-preserve. See the remarks of Olivier de Serres, *Théâtre d'Agriculture,* ed. 1805, II., 62 sqq. There were certainly "garennes à connins" in the Middle Ages, but the word " garenne " had the quite general meaning of " game preserve." See, among others, a document published in De Maulde, *Condition forestière de l'Orléanais,* p. 491 : " . . . ius habendi garennam ad *grossum animal* "; and an *arrêt* of the Parlement of Paris, dated 1270, in *Olim,* I., 835, no. xlix : " . . . in loco ubi rex habet garennam suam ad grossam bestiam et minutam."

4. As Mr. MacKechnie asserts (*Magna Carta,* p. 493).

5. From the examples in the documents published by Mr. Turner, we have selected three of different periods : i. In 1209, in the pleas of the Forest held at Shrewsbury, Hamon Fitz-Marescat was tried for stealing hares in the warren of Bulridge (Turner, p. 10).—ii. In 1255 : the offence was the theft of four hares in the warren of Somerton ; the presentment was made by the verderers ; the chief offender being a clerk of the king's court, the case was adjourned. The inquisition had been held in the ordinary way (pp. 41 sqq.). The title of the document from which this illustration is drawn runs : *Placita foreste in comitatu Sumerset,* and the sub-title : *Placita de warrena de Sumerton.* The document also summarises an inquisition held concerning a hare found dead, and conducted like inquisitions on beasts of the Forest found dead.—iii. In 1286 : *Placita Foreste apud Huntyndone. . . . Placita warrenne de Cantebrigge* (pp. 129—131). This record is the most elaborate of the three,

a warren which was entirely subject to the forest law.[1]
Such cases were, however, exceptional. Offences against
rights of warren had, as a rule, to be tried in the ordinary
courts of law.

The question whether all the royal demesne was
regarded as warren has been investigated by Mr. Turner,
who concludes that the king would pro-
bably not consider his own lands to be
warren unless they were sufficiently well
stocked with game to make hunting worth while.[2]
Nevertheless we find Edward I taking care to specify in
1305 that he had right of warren on all his demesne
lands.[3] From the beginning of the Norman period,
moreover, private warrens had existed only by royal
grant. It may safely be inferred from this that the king
could claim right of warren over the whole realm. And
as a matter of fact, he did establish warrens for himself
in all parts : as late as the end of the thirteenth century
he is found defending his right of warren in lands which
did not belong to his demesne.[4]

In short, the king apparently claimed the right of the

The king's right of warren

---

and also the most striking, for it certainly looks as if this Cambridge
warren lay quite apart from any forest. Evidently a large number of
arrears had to be cleared off and delicate points decided. The
justices of the Forest, sitting at Huntingdon, tried a large number of
cases of hare-poaching and gave decisions on claims put forward by
the inhabitants. See below, n. 4.

1. In 1227 Henry III disafforested the warren of Staines, in Middlesex.
His charter shows that the warren had been subject to the forest law
(Turner, p. cviii ; cf. *Rot. Lit. Claus.* II., 197).

2. Turner, p. cxxxiii.

3. *Statutes of the Realm,* i, 144.

4. We have a very characteristic document of 1286 concerning the royal
warren at Cambridge : " Johannes Extraneus, dominus de Middilton,
Warinus de Insula, dominus de Ramton, et templarii de Daneye clamant
habere libertatem warrenne in terris suis infra warrenam predictam
domini regis ; et sepius cum leporariis suis ceperunt plures lepores in
eisdem terris suis pro voluntate sua. . . . Ideo preceptum est vice-
comiti quod faciat venire predictos Johannem et Warinum et pre-
ceptorem ad ostendendum warantum si quod inde habeant, vel ad satis-
faciendum domino regi de transgressione predicta . . . " (Turner, pp.
130—131.) See also (p. 131) the claim of the Abbot of Ramsey.

chase in every part of his realm.[1]   In his view, this right
entitled him to hunt small game, not only on the whole
of his demesne, but also in the warrens which he had on
the estates of his barons.   But he preferred a nobler
quarry, and so set apart for himself vast preserves for
larger game.   These were called Forests or Chases, and
Parks when they were enclosed; and he established a
code of forest law to protect them.

We now come to the hunting-rights possessed by the
king's subjects.   Apart from royal grants of the right to
hunt in the Forest,[2] the barons and prelates
Hunting had " chases," " parks," and " warrens "
rights of the of their own.   The chases of the lords were
king's subjects generally parts of the Forest which had
been alienated by the king : in a sense the grant did not
involve complete disafforestment, for the burdens imposed
on the inhabitants were maintained, at least in part, for
the benefit of the recipient.[3]   The parks of the lords, on

1. The matter is obscure, and in our opinion was a question of fact
rather than of law.   English writers on feudal law have tried to formulate
theories about it.   Blackstone asserts that all the game in the realm
belongs to the king, and that nobody therefore may hunt without his
permission.   Christian, however, in his notes on Blackstone, cites documents which contradict this view, notably the following ancient pronounce-
ments of English law : " Quant beastes savages le roye aler hors del
forrest, le property est hors del roy . . . s'ilz sount hors del parke,
capienti conceditur " (Blackstone, *Commentaries,* 17th ed., bk. II., cap.
xxvii, n. 10).
The following passages leave the impression that contemporaries had
rather vague notions as to the rights of the king over game which had
strayed from forests and parks : " Quedam dama evasit de parco domini
regis . . . et venit quidam homo domine Hugeline de Neville cum
duobus leporariis, et prosequebatur dictam damam et cepit eam in campo
de Pizeford, et duxit dictam venacionem secum in domo domine Hugeline.   Set non possunt attachiari quia manent extra forestam." As an
inquisition was held, it was evidently thought that an offence had been
committed   (Turner, p. 90, under the year 1250).   " Dicunt per sacramentum suum quod homines comitis de Ferrariis fugaverunt unum
brokettum dami infra libertatem usque ad aquam subtus Wodeford.   Et
brokettus ibi transivit aquam et resistit in quodam butimine extra Wodeford, et ibi custoditus fuit per villatam quousque Ricardus de Audewincle,
viridarius, venit et per ipsum et per villatam ductus fuit ad forestam
salvus et sanus " (*ibid.,* p. 105, under the year 1252).
2. Numerous examples of these grants are to be found in the close rolls.
3. Turner, pp. cix sqq.

the other hand, though they were sometimes situated in districts which had formerly been forest, were not under the forest law. Provided that the king's hunting was not injured, a landowner was at liberty to make a park and hunt there at his pleasure.[1] Sometimes the king made a gracious present of bucks and does to stock a park.[2] As for the warrens in private hands, they were unenclosed tracts on a lord's demesne,[3] where he hunted other game than the beasts of the Forest—hares in particular, but also rabbits, foxes, wild cats, partridges, pheasants, and so forth. If noble game, like a buck, took refuge in a warren, the hunters might follow it there from outside without restriction, for it was not a beast of the warren. Warrens, as we have already said, were established by royal charter. Thus the abbot and monks of Battle had right of warren on all their lands by charter of William the Conqueror : they alone, that is to say, might hunt the beasts of the warren. It was laid down in these charters, that every breach of the right of warren was punishable by a fine of ten pounds to the king.[4]

Outside these various preserves, royal and other, it appears that the chase was free in England during the middle ages. On this point the evidence, though naturally meagre, is sufficiently convincing.[5] It was

1. Turner, pp. cxv sqq.
2. " Per breve, magister Simon de Wauton fecit capere in foresta de Rokingham octo damas et quatuor damos vivos, de dono domini regis, ad parcum suum instaurandum " (Anno 1253, *ibid.*, p. 106).
3. The king was in general opposed to the " elargacio " of a seignorial warren over the lands of the lord's free tenants or the lands of his neighbours (Turner, p. cxxv).
4. *Ibid.*, pp. cxxiii sqq. ; cf. *Rot. Parl.* ii, 75 b.
5. As to lands where the chase was free, besides the documents cited by Turner (pp. cxxiii, n. 1, cxxviii, cxxx, cxxxiii) see *Rot. Parl.* i, 330a, no. 207, and in particular certain charters of disafforestment granted by John, notably the one in which he concedes the disafforestment of a district in Essex : " ita quod tota foresta infra predictas metas contenta et homines ibi manentes et heredes eorum sint deaforestati et liberi et soluti et quieti in perpetuum de nobis et heredibus nostris de omnibus que ad forestam et forestarios pertinent, *et quod capiant et habeant omnimodam venationem quam capere poterint infra predictas metas*" (*Rot. Chartarum*, ed. Hardy, p. 123. Cf. *ibid.*, pp. 122, 128, 132, 206).

only at the end of the fourteenth century that the idea—
long entertained by the nobility[1]—of depriving the
common people of the right to hunt game, made its
appearance in English law.

In order to form an accurate estimate of the extent and
validity of the grievances of the nation against the crown,

Importance of the question of the right of the chase
future writers on the Forest will have to
dispel the obscurity which surrounds this
question of the right of the chase in England. And with their treatment of the
Forest they must combine that of the warrens, just as the
two are connected in article 48 of the Great Charter.[2]

We come now to a subject which is better known—
the organisation of the Forest at the time of its highest

The forest organisation
development, that is, during the rule of the
first Plantagenets. Stubbs dealt with the
subject;[3] but Mr. Turner's excellent study
has given us more exact knowledge and corrected certain
mistakes. From it we have drawn most of the short
sketch which follows, and the reader may be referred to
it for all that concerns the details of forest procedure.

Nobody had the right, without royal permission,[4] to
take any of the game, wood, or pasture of the Forest—

The protection of the Forest
not even the baron or freeholder on his
own land, if that land lay within the bounds
of a forest. " Those who dwell within the
Forest," writes the author of the *Dialogus de Scaccario*,
" do not take of their own wood, even for the necessities
of their house, except under the view of those who are
appointed to keep the Forest." [5] The right of cutting

1. Cf. Liebermann, *Pseudo-Cnut*, pp. 45, 47.

2. " Omnes male consuetudines de forestis et warennis, et de
forestariis et warennariis . . . "

3. *Const. Hist.*, vol. i (ed. 1903), pp. 434 sqq.

4. For authorisations to make clearings or enclosures, and the preliminary inquiries, see W. R. Fisher, *Forest of Essex*, pp. 321-2. On permission to take game see below, pp. 187-188.

5. *Dialogus*, I. xi, pp. 102-3.

wood, whether for fuel or making repairs,
was narrowly restricted : anyone who
exceeded his customary rights committed
the crime of " waste " (*vastum*); he had to
pay a composition in order to keep the wood he had cut,
and was amerced whenever the itinerant justices came
round, until the damaged trees had grown to their former
state. If trees were uprooted to turn woodland into
arable or merely to gain a few square feet of soil, a fine
was inflicted ; and though the offender was not required
to plant other trees, he had to pay a composition on
every crop raised on this " assart." This system of
converting a punishment into an annual rent and an
offence into a permanent source of revenue is extremely
characteristic. The chase was certainly the parent of
the Forest, but it is nevertheless true that this institution
quickly acquired a financial significance :[1] the king was
even more concerned to secure an income at the expense
of the inhabitants of the Forest than to prevent the
destruction of wood. Furthermore, there was the crime
of " purpresture," committed whenever, by enlarging a
field, making a mill or a fishpond, a hedge or a ditch,
anyone encroached on the domain of the king's deer or
restricted their movements.[2] The offender was fined, and
might only keep the land he had gained, or the works
he had constructed, by payment of a further
sum. As for the destruction of game, it was
punished more or less severely, according to
the period, and it was guarded against by
vexatious rules to which we shall return later.

Trespasses to the vert : waste, assart, and purpresture

Trespasses to the venison

1. [Much welcome light is thrown on forest finance by Miss Margaret
L. Bazeley in her recently-published monograph, *The Forest of Dean in
its Relations with the Crown during the Twelfth and Thirteenth Centuries*
(Transactions of the Bristol and Gloucestershire Archæological Society,
vol. xxxiii, pp. 153 sqq.). It appears that the financial resources of this
forest were not properly exploited until the 13th century.]
2. *Porprestura* has the general meaning of " encroachment," " usurpation." See the passage from Glanvill cited by Du Cange, s.v. *porpren-
dere*. A clear distinction was not always made between the offence of
" assart " and that of " purpresture."

The supervision of the Forest and the punishment of offences were provided for by a complicated system of officials and institutions—functionaries appointed by the king, commissioners and jurors chosen by election, officers who held their posts by hereditary right, investigations by commissions of enquiry, local courts, and eyres of itinerant justices.

The forest officials

At the head of the forest administration we find the *capitalis forestarius* mentioned in the charter of 1217, or else two high dignitaries, who in the thirteenth century had the title of justices. From 1238 onward, it was usual for the Forest to be administered in this way by two justices, one for the district north, the other for that south, of the Trent.[1]

The head of the administration

Each of the forests, or each group of forests, was administered by an official who was called warden, bailiff, seneschal, or chief forester.[2] His post was sometimes hereditary,[3] but even in this case he might be removed. When the warden was appointed by letters patent, the same document often conferred on him the custody of the castle of the district.[4]

The wardens

Besides the warden, there were in most of the large forests one or more *forestarii de feodo, foresters de fé,* who likewise saw to the preservation of the vert and the venison, and executed the decisions of the itinerant justices. They

The foresters-in-fee

1. Turner, pp. xiv sqq. [Mr. Turner has printed a list of the justices of the forests south of the Trent (1217-1821) in *Eng. Hist. Rev.* 1903, pp. 112-116.]

2. Turner, pp. xvi sqq. On the rights possessed by the wardens see *ibid.*, pp. 66-7, and the passage quoted in the Introduction, p. xxi, n. 1. Cf. an interesting document of the fourteenth century (*Rot. Parl.* ii, 79). [In the French the official under discussion is termed the *chef-forestier.* Following Mr. Turner (Introd., p. xvi) I shall refer to him as the "warden."]

3. As in the case of John Fitz-Nigel, whose duties and rights were determined by an inquisition of 1266. In return for the profits which were guaranteed to him, he paid the king forty shillings a year and kept the forest of Bernwood (Turner, pp. 121-2).

4. Turner, *Introd.*, p. xvii. [See also Miss Bazeley's excellent account of the rights and duties of the warden in the Forest of Dean (*op. cit.* pp. 175—191).]

possessed certain rights over the Forest. Some, but not all, paid a ferm to the king.[1] They were not always bound to obey the warden.[2] Some, without doubt, had been enfeoffed by the king, and owed submission to him only; others had been enfeoffed by the warden.[3] Occasionally a whole forest would be put under the custody of a forester-in-fee; his office would then be merged in that of warden. An instance was the office of forester-in-fee of the forests of Somerset, which was held in the fourteenth century by the family of Mortimer.[4]

The ordinary foresters were game-keepers who pursued and arrested offenders. A distinction is often made **Under-foresters** between mounted foresters and under-foresters who went on foot.[5] They were chosen by the wardens, or, in some districts, by the foresters-in-fee, but they took an oath of fidelity to the king. There were also private foresters, **Woodwards** called woodwards, who guarded the woods held by subjects within the limits of the Forest: they were bound by oath to preserve the vert and venison for the king's hunting; and if they failed to do so, the wood was confiscated. Each forest, moreover, had as **Agisters** a rule four *agistatores,* charged with the oversight of the *agistment* of the cattle and swine in the

1. Turner, pp. xxiii-iv, only touches upon the question of foresters-in-fee. Interesting details will be found in Greswell, *Forests of Somerset,* pp. 136 sqq. In *Fleta,* a legal treatise written about 1290, there are curious rules for the conduct of inquisitions concerning foresters-in-fee (*Fleta,* lib. ii. c. 41, § 30). [Miss Bazeley gives some particularly interesting information about the nine foresters-in-fee of the Forest of Dean (pp. 191 sqq.). See especially p. 194, where their possessions and obligations are tabulated. All paid an annual ferm to the king; but in the thirteenth century they could assert no warrant for their jurisdiction " nisi antiqua tenura."]

2. A warden, Henry Sturmy, declared in 1334 that all the *forestarii de feodo* in his forest owed him obedience (*Rot. Parl.* ii. 79). This was therefore not the invariable rule.

3. " Hugo de Stratford, quondam forestarius de feodo de balliva de Wakefeud, reddidit per annum domino Johanni de Nevyle, tunc senescallo foreste, pro predicta balliva, ad firmam, duas marcas et dimidiam," etc. (Turner, p. 123).

4. Greswell, pp. 150 sqq.

5. Fisher, *Forest of Essex,* p. 137; Greswell, p. 144.

woods and fields, and with the collection of the rents exacted for pasturage.[1]

The verderers belong to another class. They were knights or substantial landowners who had property in the Forest. They were elected in the county court, generally to the number of four in each forest, to attend the forest courts of justice. Once elected, they as a rule retained office for life.[2]

Verderers

Regarders

Finally, the regarders were sworn knights,[3] charged with a temporary commission of enquiry. The functions of the verderers and regarders can best be understood by an examination of the working of the forest courts.[4]

Stubbs' sketch of the administration of justice in the Forest[5] is rather meagre and even wanting in accuracy.

Forest justice. The swanimote

The swanimote, which he represents as a court of justice corresponding to the county court, was only an assembly of the foresters, held to make arrangements about the pasture, to receive the rents which it brought in, and to take precautions against injury to the deer during the fawning season.[6] There were really only two kinds of tribunals—the court of attachment, *attachiamentum*, held as a rule in each forest every six weeks, and the court of the itinerant justices of the forests, *justiciarii itinerantes ad placita foreste*, who held an eyre in each forest every few years. The functions of the court of attachment were rather

The court of attachment

1. Turner, pp. xx sqq., xxiv sqq., xxvi. Du Cange, s.v. *agistare*.
2. Turner, pp. xix-xx, xxvi.
3. [Turner, pp. lxxv sqq.]
4. In regard to the following section, see the details given by Coke, *Fourth Institute,* ed. 1644, ch. lxxiii, pp. 289—320; Turner, pp. xxvii sqq. A very clear summary is given by W. S. Holdsworth, *History of English Law,* i, 342 sqq.
5. Stubbs, *Const. Hist.,* i. 437 sqq.
6. This appears clearly from § 8 of Henry III's Charter of the Forest. The misapprehension as to the nature of the swanimote originated with Manwood; cf. Turner, pp. xxvii sqq. The term " swanimote " is, however, sometimes applied to the courts of attachment and to the forest inquisitions.

administrative than judicial.[1] Only minor trespasses against the vert were punished there : people who had cut boughs, for instance, might be sentenced to a fine of a few pence. Important cases concerning the vert, and all concerning the venison, went before the justices in eyre.

We must now glance at the preliminary proceedings in the cases which were brought before the itinerant

The court of the itinerant justices: preliminary proceedings

justices. When the offender was not caught in the act by the foresters, there were several types of inquisition by which he might be discovered. As early as the twelfth century and perhaps before, there took place every three years the *visitatio nemorum* or

The regard

" regard."[2] The regarders were twelve knights, appointed by the sheriff at the instance of the king. This commission of enquiry had to visit the Forest and investigate any offences that had been committed, basing their procedure on a list of questions which were called " chapters of the regard."[3]   The chief chapters were those on assart, waste, and purpresture : others concerned the pasture on the demesne, the eyries of falcons and hawks, honey, forges and mines,[4] harbours,[5] the weapons and dogs of the inhabitants of the Forest.

1. *Attachiamentum* was the obligation to appear. The court of attachment was so called because its chief function was to " view the attachments " made by the foresters. " Et praeterea singulis annis quadraginta diebus per totum annum conveniant viridarii et forestarii ad videndum attachiamenta de foresta, tam de viridi quam de venacione, per presentacionem ipsorum forestariorum et coram ipsis attachiatis " (*Charter of the Forest,* § 8). At this court the attachments were enrolled, and the offenders found sureties for their appearance before the itinerant justices. Notwithstanding § 8 of the charter, Mr. Turner (pp. xxxv-vi) holds that as a rule the nomination of sureties was performed in the court of attachment only for trespasses against the vert, and not for those against the venison. See also p. xl.

2. " Imminente visitatione nemorum, quam reguardam vulgo dicunt, que tertio anno fit . . " (*Dial. de Scacc.* I. xi).

3. Turner, pp. lxxv-vi, mentions several versions of the chapters of the regard.

4. Because wood was needed to work forges and mines.

5. The records furnish instances of wood being stolen in a forest near the sea, and put on shipboard.

M

As for poaching, at least from the beginning of the thirteenth century, and probably before, it was the occasion of special inquisitions which involved the whole countryside in trouble. If a beast of the Forest was found dead, an inquisition to discover the offender must be held by the four townships nearest the spot.

The special inquisition

Poachers detected by the inquisition of the four townships, or surprised in the fact, were generally kept under arrest until they had found sureties for their appearance before the justices in eyre. In this way they sometimes spent a year or more in gaol. Persons accused of trespasses to the vert might also, in certain cases, be kept in detention.[1]

Imprisonment and pledges

The visitations of the justices were arranged by royal writ, nominating *justiciarii itinerantes* to hear and determine the pleas of the Forest in a particular county or group of counties. In the twelfth century the eyres occurred once in three years, since the regards took place at that interval and were held in view of the coming of the justices. In the time of Henry III they occurred about every seven years, like the eyres of crown pleas and common pleas; and the intervals between them became longer and longer.[2] The justices were persons of some eminence. One of the two Justices of the Forest was always of their number.

Frequency of the eyre

---

1. On this last point, see the details given by Turner, pp. xxiii sqq. According to the Assize attributed to Edward I, offenders against the vert were not liable to arrest and imprisonment until after their third "attachiamentum." (For the meaning of this word, see above.) " Post tercium attachiamentum corpus debet attachiari et retineri " (*Statutes,* i. 243). As a matter of fact, the itinerant justices of Edward I gave instructions in conformity with this rule : see the Provisions of the justices, at Nottingham, in 1287 (Turner, p. 63). Cf. the Assizes of Henry II and Richard I, cited below.

2. [See Miss Bazeley's list of eyres in Gloucestershire during the twelfth and thirteenth centuries (*op. cit.* p. 214). They were more frequent under Henry II than afterwards, though even at this early time, the intervals between them varied greatly. With respect to the thirteenth century, the list confirms the generalisations in the text.]

The itinerant justices dealt separately with the pleas of the vert and the pleas of the venison. The *presentment* was made by the foresters and verderers, not by a regular jury. The report of the inquisition was generally taken as sufficient proof of the facts ; and it was seldom that the townships which had made the inquisition were required to come and confirm the evidence orally. In the thirteenth century convicted delinquents were fined, and if they did not pay, were sent back to prison till they found the money. If anyone cited failed to appear, he was summoned in the county court, and if he remained contumacious, was outlawed.

Procedure at the forest eyre

Punishments inflicted

To give a clear impression of the effects of this system of administration, it would be necessary to draw a map of the Forest at the beginning of the thirteenth century. In the present state of our knowledge this is impossible. But there is no doubt that the Forest comprised a good part of the realm. Foreigners and travellers noted with astonishment its enormous extent. The Italian Polydore Vergil, who crossed the Channel at the beginning of the sixteenth century, asserted that a third of England consisted of parks and forest, and a century later Moryson could still write that there were more deer in England than in all the rest of Europe.[1] The statement of Polydore Vergil is evidently a serious exaggeration, for it refers to a period subsequent to extensive disafforestments. But it might not be far from the truth if applied to the beginning of the thirteenth century. At that time indeed, before the disafforestments carried out by John, Henry III, and the three Edwards, there were only six counties out of thirty-nine which contained no Forest.[2] These consisted of a compact group of counties corresponding to the

Extent of the Forest

1. Authorities cited by Greswell, p. 242.
2. Cf. the lists of counties in *Parl. Writs,* ed. Palgrave, i. 90-1, 396-7 ; and Turner, pp. xcvi n. 1, xcvii n. 3, xcix sqq., ciii n. 5, cvi sqq.

ancient East Anglia and its marches—Norfolk, Suffolk, Cambridgeshire, Bedfordshire, and Hertfordshire.[1] In another quarter there was Kent, to which one might, strictly speaking, add Middlesex.[2] In Kent, Norfolk and Suffolk, more than anywhere else, the rural population maintained its freedom after the Conquest,[3] and these were precisely the districts free from the forest law. On the other hand, thirty-three counties, representing six-sevenths of the area of the realm, contained forests, often of great extent. Essex, which was indeed an exceptional case, was entirely forest in the days of Henry I and Henry II.[4]

We can imagine the result of the state of things just described. The forests swarmed with game, and even in time of famine it was unlawful to touch it.

Effects of the forest system : i. economic It had freedom and protection, and might ravage the crops without fear of arrows.

The very owners of the soil were forbidden to make clearings, on pain of fines and yearly compositions. A tenant was not allowed to follow his own wishes in the development of his land, even to the extent of making a hedge or ditch. The ancient customary rights which had formerly ensured to the Saxon peasant many advantages and some prosperity, were now pretexts for the infliction of fines ; at a time when the cultivation of forage-crops was seldom practised, the law forbade the use of the grass-land and woods for the feeding of cattle ; and one might not cut down a tree or a bough on one's own property, except under the surveillance of the all-powerful forester, with his vexatious restrictions and demands. It was within his power to make a family's

1. It is, however, not quite certain that the three last contained no forest. See on this Turner, p. cviii.
2. As we have seen, Middlesex contained a warren, which was under the forest law. It was suppressed in 1227 (Turner, p. cviii). There was no forest properly so called in the county.
3. Vinogradoff, *Villainage in England,* pp. 205 sqq., 218 sqq., 316.
4. J. H. Round, *Forest of Essex,* in the *Journal of the British Archæological Association,* new series, iii, 39.

lot intolerable, and in the event of opposition, to summon its members time after time before the court of attachment and ruin them by countless fines.

It was not only in the economic sphere that the forest law made its effects felt.   From a legal and political

ii. political standpoint, the forests were a dangerous anomaly.   They were withdrawn from the operation of the common law and of the custom of the realm, and governed by rules laid down in special assizes and ordinances.   In them, too, there lived troops of royal officers, who alone were allowed to bear arms and who were pledged by oath to serve the interests of the king. The Forest was the stronghold of arbitrary power.

Such was the character of the Forest at the time of its greatest extent and influence.   We thought it best to begin by describing it : we have now to account for its existence, and to trace its history from its rise to its decline.   We shall be concerned in particular to show how the Forest, a natural outcome of the Conquest, became perhaps the most oppressive and the most hated of the institutions which the Norman and Angevin kings sought to impose on their subjects, and how it consequently strengthened the hostility of the barons, and furthered the union of the English against the despotic power of the crown.

ORIGIN OF THE FOREST. DEVELOPMENT OF THE SYSTEM UNDER THE FIRST THREE NORMAN KINGS.

Like all the rulers of their time, the Anglo-Saxon kings loved the chase and possessed game-preserves. They did In origin the not, however, establish a forest jurisdic-
Forest was not
an English insti- tion, with an administrative organisation,
tution courts, and special laws.[1] It was from the continent that the forest system came, and it was the Norman conquerors who brought it over. It is in Frankish and Norman records that its origin should have been sought by English historians.[2]

No one can study the Carolingian capitularies which relate to the *Forestis* without being struck by the but analogy or rather the clear connection which
Frankish exists between them and the English Assizes of the Forest. Under Charles the Great and his immediate successors, the Forest was essentially a royal institution. The wood and the game were protected by " forestarii," and " if the king has given to any man one or more beasts in the Forest, he ought not to take more than has been given."[3] This Frankish institution of the *Forestis* did not disappear with the Carolingians. In the tenth and eleventh centuries the dukes and counts among whom Gaul was divided evidently revived it to their own advantage in all districts where there was plenty of wood

1. Liebermann, *Ueber Pseudo-Cnuts Constitutiones de Foresta*, pp. 14 sqq. Details in regard to Anglo-Saxon hunting will be found in Greswell, *op. cit.*, pp. 24 sqq.
2. See (in the recently-published *Mélanges* dedicated to M. Charles Bémont) an essay in which we devote special attention to the Franco-Norman Origins of the English Forest. A German scholar, Herr Hermann Thimme, has argued that the Frankish Forest consisted of arable and pastoral lands from which the inhabitants of the " mark " were excluded. (*Forestis, Königsgut, und Königsrecht*, in the *Archiv für Urkundenforschung*, vol. ii, 1909, pp. 101–154). This paradox, we think, has been completely refuted in an essay which we have just written, and which we hope to publish in the *Bibliothèque de l'Ecole des Chartes*.
3. Boretius, *Capitul*, i, 172 ; see also pp. 86 sqq., 98, 291 ; vol. ii, 355.

and game.   At all events, the dukes of Normandy had a Forest before the conquest of England.

Norman records of the eleventh century are meagre and scarce.   They suffice to prove, however, that in certain woods, and even in woods granted by **and Norman** the duke to his subjects, larger game, such as the red-deer, roe, and wild-boar, was reserved for the duke's hunting, and the trees might be neither felled nor cut.[1]   There were pleas of the Forest[2] and a forest law, and in the reign of duke Richard II the peasants rebelled in the hope of securing the free use of the woods and waters, in spite of the *jus ante statutum.*[3]

When sources become more plentiful, at the beginning of the twelfth century, we find the administration of the Norman Forests very similar to the administration of those in England.[4]   It is true that, by the time from which our authorities date, Normandy might have taken in her turn certain institutions which had sprung up in England.   But in any case the beginnings of the Forest are prior to the union of Normandy and England; the Forest was a Frankish, not an Anglo-Saxon institution; and it was carried across the Channel by William I.

The forest system, introduced into England by a victorious dynasty which from the first was very powerful, soon made remarkable advances in **Brutal character** this country.   As we said in our study on **of the Norman** the origins of the manor, the Norman **conquest** Conquest was no passing storm for the

1. Charter of William the Conqueror for St. Etienne of Caen ; Delisle, *Cartulaire normand,* no. 326.

2. Duke Robert's charter to Cerisy : Dugdale, *Monasticon,* ed. 1846, vii. 1073.

3. Guill. de Jumièges, V. ii. in Duchesne, *Hist. Normann. Scriptores,* p. 249.   See also the *Cartulaire de St. Michel du Tréport,* ed. Laffleur de Karmaingant, no. 10.

4. See the studies by Leopold Delisle, *Des revenus publics en Normandie an xiie siècle,* Bibl. Ec. Chartes, vol. xi (1849) ; *Etude sur la condition de la classe agricole en Normandie,* (1851) ; M. Michel Prevost's monograph, *Etude sur la forêt de Roumare, Bull. de la Soc. d'émulation du Commerce et de l'Industrie de la Seine-Infér.,* 1903 (published separately, 1904) ; and also my study referred to above, p. 166, n. 2.

vanquished. Confiscations were numerous, and the small Saxon freeholder received a mortal blow.[1] This general estimate, which we adopt on the authority of the most learned students of the eleventh century, justifies us in regarding as probable and natural the accounts of chroniclers concerning the establishment of the Forest in England. The event which most im-

The creation of the New Forest pressed contemporaries was the making of the New Forest in Hampshire.[2] As everyone knows, William Rufus was killed by an arrow while hunting. Florence of Worcester, who died in 1118, declares that his fate was a stroke of divine vengeance, punishing the son for a sin committed by the father. For William the Conqueror, he says, to make the New Forest, had ruined a hitherto prosperous country, driven out the inhabitants, and destroyed houses

Discussion of Florence of Worcester's account and churches.[3] Later writers have enlarged on the same theme. Quite recently, however, the late Mr. F. H. M. Parker has called this story into question. According to him, William Rufus was the victim cf a conspiracy : Henry I's complicity was not beyond doubt : and the story about divine vengeance was invented to remove suspicion.[4] Long ago the worthy David Hoüard, in his commentary on Littleton, affirmed in his academic style that William the Conqueror " did not resort to the excesses which some English historians cast in his teeth," and that it was " the monks " who gave him his bad reputation.[5] No purpose would be served here by a detailed discussion of Parker's article, sound as many of his comments are. It is enough to point out that Florence

1. See above, pp. 21 sqq.
2. See the details given by Freeman, *History of the Norman Conquest,* iv. 611 sqq.
3. Florence of Worcester (ed. Thorpe, Eng. Hist. Soc.), ii. 44-5.
4. *The Forest Laws and the Death of William Rufus (Engl. Hist. Rev.,* 1912, pp. 26 sqq.).
5. *Anciennes loix des François conservées dans les coutumes angloises recueillies par Littleton* (ed. 1766), i. 448.

of Worcester wrote too soon after the creation of the New
Forest to risk so flagrant a falsehood, and that, even on
the theory of a conspiracy, such a lie would have been
very clumsy. William Rufus was universally hated,
regarded as an enemy to God and man; if, as Parker
supposes, there was a political motive for the circulation
of a story of divine vengeance, it would have sufficed to
recall the crimes and extortions of Rufus himself, and it
was as clumsy as dangerous to assert facts which the
enemies of the new king could have disproved. Finally,
Henry I was himself a great hunter, and if Florence had
been trying to please him, he would certainly have taken
care not to represent the creation of the New Forest as a
crime. His denunciations can therefore only be explained
on grounds altogether opposed to those suggested by
Mr. Parker. If, while on the subject of the death of
Rufus, he brought in the ravages perpetrated by William
the Conqueror, it was because contemporaries really
remembered them, and connected the misdeeds of the
father with the violent death of the son.

There is reason, however, for regarding the statement of
Florence as an exaggeration. It has been shown that the
district afforested in Hampshire was by
no means entirely an inhabited and
cultivated country. I am not speaking of
the negative argument put forward by
archæologists, who have found no traces of pre-Norman
villages in this region: archæological arguments are
only convincing when positive. But there is the evidence
of Domesday Book, which has been examined by Mr.
Baring. It shows that William I found in a corner of
Hampshire 75,000 acres of almost deserted country, and
of this he made a forest. He added, however, fifteen or
twenty thousand acres of inhabited land, on which there
were a score of villages and a dozen hamlets; and
doubtless through fear of poaching, he evicted five
hundred families, numbering about two thousand

*Evidence of
Domesday Book
regarding
the New Forest*

persons. Later, the New Forest was further increased by between ten and twenty thousand acres, which were mainly covered with wood and thinly populated.[1]

William the Conqueror and his sons, therefore, made forests at their pleasure, without troubling much about the distress they caused. Of the utterly **Arbitrary policy** arbitrary nature of their policy, we may **of the Norman** **kings** give another · illustration, reported at an inquisition in a most naïve and certainly most sincere style. While travelling through Leicestershire, Henry I saw five hinds in Riseborough wood : he decided to afforest the wood, and left one of his servants to guard the game, the office afterwards passing to a Leicestershire man who held land in the neighbourhood. The wood in question was in a populous and cultivated district.[2] The famous articles concerning the forests in the charters of Henry I and Stephen prove clearly that the Forest continued to grow during the **Continual growth** reigns of the first three Norman kings.[3] **of the Forest** Under Henry I, the whole of Essex was subject to the forest law, including the hundred of

1. Baring, *The Making of the New Forest* (*Engl. Hist. Rev.*, 1901, pp. 427 sqq.; 1912, pp. 513 sqq.) [The first article also separately in his *Domesday Tables* (1909), pp. 194—203.]

2. The inquisition was made in the reign of Henry III; the document is curious in more than one respect : " Cum rex Henricus primus . . . iturus fuisset versus partes aquilonares, transivit per quendam boscum, qui vocatur Riseberwe, qui boscus est in comitatu Leycestrie ; et ibi vidit quinque bissas ; qui statim precepit cuidam servienti suo nomine Pichardus quod in partibus illis moraretur usque ad reditum suum a partibus predictis et dictas bissas interim ad opus suum custodiret. Contigit autem quod infra annum illum dictus rex ibi non rediit ; infra quem annum dictus Pichardus associavit se cuidam servienti euisdem patrie, qui vocabatur Hascullus de Athelakeston, ad cuius domum sepius conversabatur. Finito vero anno illo, postquam predictus rex rediit a partibus aquilonaribus, adiit dictus Pichardus regem predictum, dicens se nolle amplius ballivam predictam custodire. Et tunc requisitus ab ipso rege quis esset idoneus ad dictam ballivam custodiendam, respondit dicens quod dictus Hascullus, qui terras ibidem habuit vicinas et manens erat in eadem balliva. Et tunc dictus rex commisit Hascullo predicto dictam ballivam custodiendam scilicet forestariam de comitatu Leycestrie et similiter Rotelandie, qui eam custodivit toto tempore suo " (Turner, p. 45).

3. See the passages quoted in Stubbs, *Const. Hist.*, i. 435, notes 1 and 2.

Tendring, which was afterwards disafforested.[1] Henry
I's contemporary, Ordericus Vitalis, asserts that he
" claimed for himself the hunting of the beasts of the
Forest in all England and hardly granted to a small
number of nobles and friends the privilege of coursing in
their own woods."[2] This is unquestionably a gross
exaggeration.[3] What is proved by this passage is that,
as other documents show, Henry extended the bounds of
the Forest, and thus restricted the exercise of the right of
hunting by reserving it to himself in lands which did not
belong to the royal demesne. His object was to secure
for himself the possession of huge game-preserves, and at
the same time, no doubt, a substantial income of fines for
forest offences.[4]

It is impossible, in the present state of our knowledge,
to estimate the territorial extent of the Forest reign by
reign. Nor is it much more possible to
The forest law
under William I
and William II
trace accurately the growth of the forest
law and organisation. The records are so
scanty, so vague, sometimes so difficult to
date, that no indisputable conclusions can be reached.
I am inclined to think that, in its essential features, the
forest law was already formulated in Normandy before
the Conquest and that William I established " the peace
of his beasts "[5] on lines which were in general followed

1. On the extent of the Forest in Essex, see Round, *The Forest of
Essex,* in the *Journal of the British Archæological Association,* new series,
iii. 37 sqq.
2. Ordericus Vitalis, ed. Aug. le Prevost, iv. 238.
3. Cf. the charter granted by Henry I to the citizens of London, *in
fine* : " Et cives habeant fugationes ad fugandum, sicut melius et plenius
habuerunt antecessores eorum, scilicet Ciltre et Middlesex et Sureie " (*Sel.
Charters,* ed. H. W. C. Davis, pp. 129 sqq.).
4. Mr. Round, who emphasises strongly the fiscal character of the
enlargement of the Forest, thinks that in the vast preserve constituted
by the county of Essex, the kings seldom hunted outside the district of
Waltham (*Forest of Essex,* p. 39).
5. This is stated by the Anglo-Saxon Chronicle (ed. Thorpe, i. 355).
From William I's letter to the Londoners, forbidding them, unless
individually authorised by the archbishop to chase the red-deer, roe,
or any other game in Lanfranc's manor of Harrow, it is clear that
besides the king, there were already subjects with special hunting rights.
See J. H. Round's edition of this charter (*Londoners and the Chase,* in the
Athenæum, 30 June, 1894, p. 838).

to the death of Henry I. The " baronies of the Forest " which he established for instance in Somerset, were no doubt instituted for purposes of political supervision, but they were also the origin of foresterships-in-fee which are found in existence in the next century.[1]

William Rufus unquestionably had officers who protected the game, made enquiry into encroachments, and imposed fines for trespasses against the venison, even in lands which were not part of the demesne.[2] In this reign the forest administration seemed so intolerable to small landowners and to the Saxon peasants, that William, to win their help against the rebellious Normans, promised, among other delusive concessions, to give up his forests; and with this hope before them, they supported him faithfully.[3]

We have rather more information as to the organisation of the Forest under Henry I. We must not indeed accept without hesitation the authority of the so-called *Leges Henrici Primi.* Dr. Liebermann, who has studied the collections of twelfth-century laws with great learning and insight, sees in them no more than traces of the legislation of Henry I.[4] He admits,[5] however, that, as the compiler states,[6] the Forest was reckoned as an appurtenance of the crown in the time of Henry I, and the seventeenth chapter of the *Leges,* composed of heads of chapters which summarise the powers of the forest courts, he considers to be a fragment of the instructions given by Henry to his justices of the Forest.[7] It appears

Documents of the reign of Henry I. The " Leges Henrici primi "

1. A *baronia Foreste,* held of William I *per servicium Foreste,* was the origin of the office of forester-in-fee in Somerset (Greswell, pp. 42 sqq., 85).
2. See the passages cited by Liebermann, *Ueber Pseudo-Cnuts Constitutiones de foresta,* p. 21.
3. See the passages cited in Stubbs, *Const. Hist.,* i. 321-2.
4. Liebermann, *op. cit.* p. 23.
5. *Ibid.*
6. " De iure regis. Hec sunt iura que rex Anglie solus et super omnes homines habet in terra sua . . . Foreste " (*Leges Hen. primi,* cap. x, § 1; in Liebermann, *Gesetze der Angelsachsen,* i. 556).
7. *Pseudo-Cnut,* p. 23.

from this chapter[1] that the holders of lands under the
forest law were exposed to countless annoyances : the
right of making clearings, of putting up buildings, of
cutting wood, of carrying weapons, of keeping dogs, was
already denied them or was subject to most irksome
restrictions : they had to attend the forest courts when
summoned, and to act as beaters when the king went
hunting.

Authentic documents of the time of Henry I, such as
charters and the pipe roll, confirm the impression made
by this chapter of the *Leges* and point to its
Charters of trustworthiness. The charters show that the
Henry I king had a staff of foresters, called *venatores,
servientes, ministri*,[2] who not only had oversight of the
royal Forest, but also strove to enlarge it, made themselves troublesome to the neighbouring landowners, and
prevented them from hunting on their own estates and
clearing their land.[3] The Charter of the Forest of 1217
proves that the " regard " was known in the days of
Henry I, since, according to the fifth article, the
" regarders " went " through the forests to make the
regard at the time of the first coronation of Henry II ";
and they had certainly not been instituted during the
period of anarchy which followed Henry I's death.[4]

1. It runs as follows : " De Placito Forestarum. Placitum quoque
forestarum multiplici satis est incommoditate vallatum : de essartis ; de
cesione ; de combustione ; de venacione ; de gestacione arcus et iaculorum
in foresta ; de misera canum expeditacione ; si quis ad stabilitam non
venit ; si quis pecuniam suam reclusam dimisit ; de edificiis in foresta ;
de summonicionibus supersessis ; de obviacione alicuius in foresta cum
canibus ; de corio vel carne inventa " (Liebermann, *Gesetze*, i. 559).

2. See the address of a charter of Henry I granting to the monastery of
Abingdon the tithe of the venison taken in Windsor Forest : " Willelmo
filio Walteri, et Croco venatori, et Ricardo servienti, et omnibus ministris
de foresta Windesores " (*Historia monasterii de Abingdon*, ed. J. Stevenson,
ii. 94).

3. " Henricus, rex Anglie, Croco venatori, salutem. Permitte lucrari
terram monachorum Abbendone de Civelea et de Ualingeforda, illam
scilicet que non noceat foreste mee et quod non sit de foresta mea "
(*ibid.*, ii. 83). " Silvas de Bacchleia et Cumenora iste abbas Faritius a
regis forestariorum causationibus funditus quietas et in eis capreorum
venationem, regio obtinuit decreto " (*ibid.*, ii. 113).

4. See also the passage from the *Chronicon abbatiae Rameseiensis*,
quoted below, p. 176, n. 4.

Finally the still extant pipe roll of the thirty-first year of Henry I's reign, claims particular attention.[1]

This valuable document makes occasional mention of fines inflicted at the pleas of the Forest,[2] and for the
The pipe roll counties of Essex and Hertford these form the matter of a special chapter entitled *De placitis foreste.*[3] The grounds for the sentence having no interest for the Exchequer, the accounts very seldom offer any valuable details. We find, however, evidence of collective fines paid by townships at the pleas of the Forest.[4] If these are compared with similar fines paid in the thirteenth century, they prove beyond question that, as early as the time of Henry I, when a beast of the Forest was found dead, the nearest township must discover the offender or else pay a fine. Such was evidently the content of the instructions concerning discoveries of the remains of game—under the heading : " De corio vel carne inventa "—in chapter xvii of the *Leges Henrici primi.*[5]

Finally these accounts prove beyond dispute that, under Henry I and perhaps before him, the justices of the Forest administered a written law, a forest
The forest Assize of Henry I assize, which contained a special prohibition against keeping greyhounds in the royal Forest.[6]

---

1. *Magnum rotulum Scaccarii vel magnum rotulum Pipae de anno 31° Henrici primi,* ed. Hunter, 1833.

2. For example, p. 49, under Surrey : " Albericus clericus compotum de xxxvis. viiid. de placitis Rad. Bass. de foresta."

3. Pp. 157-159. The counties of Essex and Hertford had a single sheriff. It is doubtful, as was said above, whether Hertfordshire contained any forest.

4. " Et de xxs de villata de Benflet . . . Et de dimidia marca de villata de Dunton. Et de dimidia marca de villata de Mucking. Et de xxs de villata de Neuport," etc. (*ibid.*, p. 158).

5. See above, p. 173, n. 1.

6. " Gilbertus de Mustiers reddidit compotum de viii li. xl d. pro leporariis habitis *contra assisam*" (p. 158). On the meaning of the word "Assize," see Stubbs, *Const. Hist.,* i. 614 and note. We do not think that this word can simply mean " custom."

It would not, we think, be impossible to reconstruct this assize with some approach to accuracy. We can form no theory as to its date, and there are no grounds for ascribing it to Henry I rather than to William the Conqueror. But some notion of its contents may be gained by a study of the so-called Assize of Woodstock, which certainly does not belong entirely to the reign of Henry II.

The Assize of Woodstock was several times edited by Stubbs. It is to be found in the *Gesta Henrici Secundi*

The Assize of Woodstock contains material of earlier date
ascribed to Benedict of Peterborough, and in the chronicle of Roger of Hoveden, while there are also separate copies of it.[1] Stubbs asserts that he failed to find a single satisfactory text, and indeed the wording of it is obscure, badly arranged, and sometimes inconsistent. It looks as if the text had never been officially fixed, and as if different copyists had strung together articles of various periods. The author of the *Gesta Henrici Secundi* gives only the earlier articles (1, 2, 3, 5 and 6). Roger of Hoveden does not quote the four last (13, 14, 15 and 16). In the first article the king announces his resolve to subject poachers to the cruel penalties of mutilation which had been inflicted in the time of his grandfather Henry I, whereas in the last he threatens them with imprisonment and fine only.

The twelfth article moreover begins with the words : *Apud Wodestoke rex precepit* . . . as if the preceding sections belonged to a period before the assembly at Woodstock. Stubbs believed that the version which appears in the *Gesta Henrici Secundi* was an ancient assize : additions would afterwards be made to it, and article 12 would be inserted last, at the time of the council

---

1. See the texts edited by Stubbs in *Gesta regis Henrici Secundi Benedicti abbatis* (R. S.), i. 323 ; *ibid.,* ii, Appendix iv, a text collated with two copies of the time of Elizabeth ; Roger of Hoveden, *Chronicle* (R. S.), ii. 245 sqq. ; *Sel. Charters,* pp. 186 sqq.

at Henry's hunting-lodge of Woodstock.

Clauses which date from the reign of Henry I

This view appears to me unconvincing. In my opinion, it would be more plausible to regard as ancient clauses, dating at least from the days of Henry I, those to which parallels can be found in the sources referred to above—charters and accounts, survivals of Henry I's legislation, and chronicles of the first Norman reigns. On this hypothesis, the assize mentioned in the pipe roll of Henry I will have contained the prohibition to carry arms and to keep greyhounds in the Forest,[1] the order to mutilate the paws of dogs in all places where the peace of the king's beasts was established,[2] the prohibition against destroying the woods in the Forest,[3] the order for the triennial inspection of assarts, purprestures, and waste,[4] and the command that all the inhabitants of the district shall attend the pleas of the Forest.[5] These early rules are preserved, we think, in articles 2, 14, 3, 5, 10 and 11, of the Assize of Woodstock. Finally article 1 of that assize evidently alludes to the fact that under Henry I poachers were punished by blinding and castration,[6] and the old assize

1. Assize of Woodstock, § 2 ; cf. the passages from the *Leges Hen. primi* cited above, p. 173, n. 1 (de gestacione arcus et iaculorum in foresta . . . de obviacione alicuius in foresta cum canibus), and the passage from the Pipe Roll, *supra*, p. 174, n. 6.

2. Assize of Woodstock, § 14 ; cf. *Leges Hen. primi* (de misera canum expeditacione) and Ordericus Vitalis, ed. cit., iv. 238, (in reference to Henry I) : " Pedes etiam canum, qui in vicino silvarum morabantur, ex parte precidi fecit." See also art. 6 of the Charter of the Forest of 1217, which mentions the practice as established at the accession of Henry II.

3. Assize of Woodstock, §§ 3 and 5 ; cf. *Leges Hen. primi* (de cesione, de combustione), and Henry I's writ to the huntsman Croc, *supra*, p. 173, n. 3.

4. Assize of Woodstock, § 10 ; cf. *Leges Hen. primi* (de essartis ; . . . . de edificiis in foresta), and art. 5 of the Charter of the Forest of 1217, which takes us back to the accession of Henry II. William Rufus asserted his right to have the forests of the abbeys inspected by his foresters " de bestiis et de essartis " (*Chron. abbatiae Rameseiensis*, ed. Macray, p. 210). Henry I exempted an estate of the abbey of Ramsey, " de visionibus forestarum et essartis " (*ibid.*, p. 214).

5. Assize of Woodstock, § 11 ; cf. *Leges Hen. primi* . . . " de summonicionibus supersessis."

6. The text of the Assize of Woodstock in the *Gesta Henrici Secundi* (i. 323) is the only one which specifies " ut amittat oculos et testiculos." In his *Select Charters*, Stubbs gives the milder version of other copyists.

perhaps enjoined this penalty. In any case it must have resembled the assizes of Henry II and Richard I in entirely forbidding any interference with the king's beasts.[1]

It is clear that Henry I was faithful to the declaration of his coronation Charter : he " retained the Forest in his hand." He moreover enlarged it and probably increased rather than lightened the severity of the forest law.

The exercise of the right of the chase, at the time when Henry I ruled in England and Louis VI was king of France, may be cited as a typical example of the power of the Norman kings and the weakness of the Capetians. In France the right belonged in theory to all the *hauts justiciers* and to those on whom they had conferred it ; but in practice it had often been acquired by force and in that case had no other foundation than immemorial possession, or " seisin." It was distributed in an extremely complicated and perplexing way, and was the object of numerous claims and negotiations. The king had forests and warrens, with an administrative system and foresters ; but with respect to the chase, his prerogative cannot be clearly differentiated from the rights of particular nobles, bishops, or even, in some cases, urban or rural communities. He might possess hunting rights on land outside his demesne, but within the demesne there were chases which did not belong to him. He had the privilege of hunting in many forests which belonged to the Church, but there were others of these where the hunting was in the hands of a lay lord. It was only after the beginning

Comparison with France

---

1. I do not venture to suggest a date for the remarkable thirteenth article, which lays down that every man dwelling "infra pacem venationis" shall at the age of twelve swear to the peace of the venison. The end of the clause (et clerici laicum feodum tenentes) is apparently a later addition, which may be attributed to Henry II. There is here an evident echo of Anglo-Saxon custom : according to the laws of Cnut, every man of the age of twelve must swear not to be a thief (Liebermann, *Gesetze*, i. 324-5).

of the reign of St. Louis that the king claimed superior rights in respect of warren.[1]

With the death of Henry I and the accession of Stephen, a chapter in the history of the Forest comes to an end. Up to this time, its bounds were continually advancing, and its law was becoming, as it seems, more and more oppressive. From now to the end of the Middle Ages, periods of decline and progress succeed one another, according as the power of the crown wanes or waxes. The "disafforestments" soon begin, interrupted by new afforestations. The forest law, systematised by the lawyers, but feebly defended by them—doubtless because it was scarcely defensible—soon undergoes violent attacks at the hands of the nobles, and from the reign of John gradually decays. Its history is now bound up with the history of the Constitution, until, having become harmless, it ceases to be the theme of complaints and falls into obscurity.

1. It is impossible to cite here the very numerous documents on which the last paragraph is based. They are drawn from royal records and those of the *Parlement* of Paris, from the *Enquêtes* of St. Louis, from Cartularies, and so forth. They will be cited in an essay on *The Forest and the Right of the Chase in France*, which we hope to publish in 1915.

(3)

THE FOREST UNDER THE ANGEVINS.

In the charter which he granted in March or April 1136, Stephen pledged himself to restore "to the churches and to the realm " the forests which Henry I had added to those of William I and William II.[1] It has been proved that he partially redeemed his promise, though he exacted payment for the disafforestments.[2] Soon, however, there was no need to buy his consent : the civil war reduced him to impotence; and everyone was free to chase the king's deer and make encroachments on his Forest.[3]

Disafforestment under Stephen

After these years of anarchy came a reign marked by the increase of royal power and the making of new laws. A great hunter, Henry II was at the same time an administrator, a jurist, and a vigorous and strong-willed ruler. In the charter which he issued after his coronation, he confirmed the liberties and grants bestowed by his grandfather, Henry I, but said nothing about those conceded by Stephen. His silence has been explained on the ground that he regarded as excessive the advantages conferred on the Church.[4] But without doubt he had equally strong objections to the disafforestments promised in Stephen's charter. Indeed he resumed the lands which, whether by virtue of the charter of 1136 or in the confusion of the civil war, had been disafforested in the reign of his feeble

Henry II restores the forest jurisdiction

1. Stubbs, *Const. Hist.*, i. 348 ; [*Sel. Charters*, pp. 143 sqq.]
2. Round, *Forest of Essex*, pp. 37–8. Stubbs' statement (*Const. Hist.*, i. 348) that Stephen " kept none of these promises," is therefore too strong. See also *op. cit.*, p. 349.
3. See the instances mentioned by Round, *Geoffrey de Mandeville*, p. 376, *Forest of Essex*, p. 39.
4. Bémont, *Chartes des libertés anglaises*, Introd. xv. n. 1.

predecessor; and he also made some entirely new additions to the Forest, which under his rule became larger
than ever.[1] The pipe rolls prove that he derived large
sums from it through judicial fines and rents exacted as
compensation for encroachments.[2]

The royal officials set themselves to formulate a legal
theory of the Forest. In the *Dialogus de Scaccario*, as
we have seen, Richard Fitz-Neal, the treasurer,
examined the forest organisation, though
without trying to justify it on other grounds
than the good pleasure of the king. The *Constitutiones
de Foresta* attributed to Cnut are an apocryphal work of
slightly different tendency, written probably at the end
of Henry II's reign by one of his foresters.[3] The Forest,
it seems, roused interest enough in the jurists for one of
them to devote himself to forging a document in its
honour.

In these conditions it was natural that a law-giving
king should publish an Assize of the Forest. This he
did at Woodstock in the latter part of his
reign. In a sixteenth-century copy the document is entitled : " Assize of the lord King
Henry touching his Forest and his venison, by the
counsel and consent of the' archbishops, bishops and
barons, earls, and nobles, at Woodstock." [4] We have

(marginal note) Theories of the lawyers

(marginal note) Henry II's Assize

1. Charter of the Forest of 1217, § 1 : " Omnes foreste quas Henricus
rex avus noster afforestavit." See below (p. 215, n. 4) the passage from
the royal letters of 1227 : " . . . tam bosci quos ipse ad forestam revocavit
quam illi quos de novo afforestavit." It is scarcely necessary to say that
in the reign of Henry II, as evidently at other times, the foresters played
a great part in determining the territorial extent of the Forest, and that
its continued growth was due in great measure to their initiative. Cf.
the letters of Henry III published by Turner, p. xcvi : " . . . et que foreste
afforestate fuerunt per Henricum regem avum nostrum tempore Alani de
Neville vel tempore aliorum forestariorum suorum, de voluntate ipsius
regis vel de voluntate aliorum forestariorum suorum."

2. Under the head of assarts, Essex in one year brought in 215 *l.* 18 *s.*
(Round, *Forest of Essex*, p. 39).

3. Liebermann, *Pseudo-Cnut*, pp. 32, 35, 37.

4. The title is given (of course in Latin) in *MS. Cotton Vespasian*, F. iv
(Roger of Hoveden, ed. Stubbs, ii. 245, n. 2).

tried to prove that part of this assize must have been derived from a more ancient assize mentioned in the pipe roll of the thirty-first year of Henry I.   But most of the articles certainly bear the mark of the **Check** administration of Henry II.   Such are articles **on the** **foresters** 4, 6, 7, 8, on the oversight of the Forests and the pledges demanded from the foresters, those included who were appointed by individuals to guard private woods within the forest boundaries. Henry II's foresters were zealous and greatly feared. Even villeins were at times appointed to the position.[1] Henry took care to protect his forest officials, and in 1175 four knights were hanged for killing one of them.[2]   At the same time he would tolerate no corrupt dealings, as is shown by the famous instructions which have been published under the title of the Inquest of Sheriffs.[3]   The **Penalties** first and the last articles of the Assize of Wood- stock probably belong also to the reign of Henry II, despite the fact that they contradict each other as to the punishment to be inflicted on poachers—a point to which we shall return later.   Article 12, which inflicts imprisonment on a delinquent after his third offence, begins with words—" at Woodstock the king ordained " —which leave no doubt as to its origin.   Finally, it was certainly Henry II who drew up article 9, one of the most characteristic and important of the assize—the article concerning clerical offenders.

1. " Ex servis forestarios super provincias constituit " (Ralph Niger, quoted by Liebermann, *Pseudo-Cnut,* p. 28).

2. *Gesta Henrici II,* i. 93-4.

3. *Inquest of Sheriffs,* art. 8, in *Sel. Charters,* p. 177 : "Et inquiratur quid vel quantum acceperint forestarii vel baillivi vel ministri eorum, post terminum praedictum, in baillivis suis, quocunque modo illud ceperint vel quacunque occasione ; et si quid perdonaverint de rectis regis pro praemio vel promissione vel pro amicitia aliqua . . . et si forestarii vel baillivi eorum aliquem ceperint vel attachiaverint per vadium et plegium, vel retaverint, et postea sine judicio per se relaxaverint . . ." On this Inquest, ordered by Henry II in 1170, after an absence of four years from England, see Stubbs, *Const. Hist.,* i. 510 sqq., and *Sel. Charters,* pp. 174 sqq.

The king, this article states, "forbids any clerk to trespass against his venison or his forests; he has strictly ordered his foresters, if they find clerks trespassing, to seize them without hesitation, keep them in custody and attach them; and he himself will be their warranty." Thus the clergy, though withdrawn from the jurisdiction of the common law, came under that of the Forest. Some years before, in 1175, Henry II had commanded that all persons should be sought out who, taking advantage of the rising of his sons, had chased the king's venison. Many clerks were accused and brought before the temporal courts; the papal legate, Hugo Pierleoni, raised no protest: it was understood between him and the king that the clergy, though in general exempt from secular justice, should lose their privilege in the case of forest offences.[1] Such was the origin of the ninth article of the Assize of Woodstock. From the point of view of Henry's interests, this clause was certainly unwise. The Church was the mistress of public opinion, and it was a mistake to arouse her enmity. The clergy never forgave the legate for his compliance,[2] and the forest system became a theme for clerical invective. So at least we may infer from a story told by Walter Map, one of Henry's itinerant justices. The bishop of Lincoln, St. Hugh, who had so great a moral influence at this time, said one day to Henry II that poor men oppressed by the foresters would enter paradise, but that the king and the

Marginal notes: Clerical offenders

Hostility of the Church towards the foresters

1. Ralph de Diceto, *Ymagines historiarum,* ed. Stubbs (R. S.), i. 402-3. See the passage from Henry II's letter to the pope quoted in Stubbs, *Const. Hist.,* i. 436, n. 4. On the severity with which the offences of 1175 were punished, cf. *ibid.,* p. 521.

2. *Gesta Hen. II,* i. 105 : " Praedictus cardinalis, qui in Angliam per mandatum regis venerat, concessit et dedit domino regi licentiam implacitandi clericos regni sui de forestis suis et de captione venationum. Ecce membrum Sathane ! Ecce ipsius Sathanae conductus satelles ! qui tam subito factus de pastore raptor, videns lupum venientem, fugit et dimisit oves sibi a summo pontifice commissas."

forestarii would remain *foris,* outside.[1] No doubt the pun had a great vogue, and reappeared in many sermons where the foresters were abused. The author of the *Magna vita sancti Hugonis* declares that in his zeal against the foresters, enemies of the liberties of the Church, St. Hugh went so far as to excommunicate Geoffrey, the *summus forestarius.*[2] If Henry II had winked at some of the deer-stealing and encroachments of the monks, he would perhaps have secured a little more peace for his successors.[3]

Richard I—or rather those who governed England for

1. " [The beginning is wanting] . . . verumtamen venatores hominum, quibus judicium est datum de vita vel de morte ferarum, mortiferi, comparatione quorum Minos est misericors, Rhadamanthus rationem amans, Aeacus aequanimis, nihil in his laetum nec letiferum. Hos Hugo, prior Selewude, iam electus Lincolniae, reperit repulsos ab ostio thalami regis quos ut obiurgare vidit insolenter et indigne ferre, miratus ait : ' Qui vos?' Responderunt : ' Forestarii sumus.' Ait illis ' Forestarii foris stent.' Quod rex interius audiens risit, et exivit obviam ei. Cui prior : ' Vos tangit haec parabola, quia, pauperibus quos hii torquent paradisum ingressis, cum forestariis foris stabitis.' Rex autem hoc verbum serium habuit pro ridiculo, et ut Salomon excelsa non abstulit, forestarios non delevit, sed adhuc nunc post mortem suam sitant coram leviatan carnes hominum et sanguinem bibunt; excelsa struunt, quae nisi Dominus in manu forti non destruxerit, non auferuntur hii. Dominum sibi praesentem timent et placant, dominum quem non vident offendere non metuentes. Non dico quin multi viri timorati, boni et iusti, nobiscum involvantur in curia, nec quia aliqui sint in hac valle miseriae iudices misericordiae, sed secundum maiorem et insaniorem loquor aciem." (Map, *De nugis curialium,* ed. Wright, pp. 7-8.) The author of the *Magna Vita Sancti Hugonis* reports the saint's pun, but without mentioning the king : " Recte homines isti et satis proprie nuncupantur forestarii, foris namque stabunt a regno Dei " (ed. Dimock, p. 176).

2. " Est . . . inter alias abusionum pestes, prima in regno Anglorum tyrannidis forestariorum pestis videlicet provinciales depopulans. Huic violentia pro lege est, rapina in laude, aequitas execrabilis, innocentia reatus. Huius immanitatem mali nulla conditio, gradus nullus, nec quisquam, ut totum breviter exprimamus, rege inferior, evasit indemnis, quem illius iniuriosa iurisdictio non saepe tentasset elidere. Hac cum pernicie primus Hugoni congressus fuit . . . Cum enim, more solito, ut in caeteros, ita et in suos homines, contra ecclesiae suae libertatem, forestarii debacchari coepissent, eo usque res tandem processit, ut summum regis forestarium, nomine Galfridum, excommunicationis vinculo innodaret. Quo rex comperto vehementem exarsit in iram " (*Magna vita S. Hugonis,* ed. cit., pp. 125-6).

3. On the procedure followed in the case of clerical offenders during the thirteenth century, and the complaints put forward by the clergy in 1257, see Turner, pp. lxxxvii sqq.

him during his long absences [1]—and his successor John
maintained the severities of the forest law,
and by extending the bounds of the forests
made it yet more burdensome.[2] When the
barons rose against John and had him at
their mercy, they contemplated demanding the immediate reform of the Forest. We have already reprinted and discussed certain notes of an agent of Philip
Augustus, which, under the title of " concessions of King John," throw much light
on the negotiations between the king and
the barons, and on the first demands presented by the
latter. Out of a dozen articles, three are concerned with
the Forest : and the impression of Philip's agent was
that the barons demanded the surrender of all the forests
created by John, Richard I, and Henry II; liberty for
individuals to take wood for their own use in the parts of
the Forest which they held; a rule as to the powers of
the foresters in these same private woods; and the abolition of punishment by death or mutilation for trespasses
to the venison.[3] The barons, however, let slip this
opportunity of ending the tyranny of the forest system.

As a matter of fact, they inserted in their petition and
in the Great Charter only two clauses specifically affect-

The Forest under Richard I and John

Original demands of the barons

1. On the Forest under Richard I, see Hoveden, iv. 63. At the pleas
of the Forest in 1198, the justices read certain "praecepta regis " which
repeated (see the text in Hoveden, pp. 63 sqq.) Henry II's Assize, and added
several articles to it (arts. xiii, xiv, xvi). Trespasses to the venison,
according to the Assize of 1198, were punished by blinding and castration
(art. xiv.) A charter of Richard in favour of Ramsey abbey (*Cartularium
monasterii de Rameseia,* ii. 296, no. 422) shows that the Church obtained
some relaxation of the forest law only as an exceptional privilege.

2. The Great Charter alludes to afforestations made by John and
Richard (arts. 47 and 53). In the " perambulationes " published by
Mr. Turner (pp. 116 sqq.) and by Mr. Greswell (*Forests of Somerset,*
pp. 272 sqq.) there are instances of afforestations made by John. On the
other hand, as we shall see later (pp. 212 sqq.), there were disafforestments
carried out by Richard and John, or at least promised by them, in return
for money.

3. See above, pp. 124 sqq.

ing the Forest : the king promised to
abandon the forests made by himself,[1]
without formally pledging himself to
abandon those made by Richard and Henry II ;[2] and,
secondly, the arbitrary summons to the pleas of the
Forest of those who dwelt outside its limits, was to be
forbidden.[3] In addition the barons adopted a plan which
threatened the whole system. They wanted to do away
with the abuses which made the Forest intolerable, and
which varied to a small extent in different parts ; and
fearing lest some might be overlooked and spared, they
demanded the appointment of elected juries to hold
inquisitions in every county regarding " all the evil
customs touching forests, warrens, foresters, and
warreners " ;[4] the twelve sworn knights were even charged
with the complete and irrevocable suppres-
sion of these evil customs within the fifteen
days following the inquisition. The king
had to accept this Draconian clause, and
only obtained, at the last moment, the concession that he
should receive notice before the abolition of any evil
custom was announced.[5] As early as 19 June, the real
date of the conclusion of peace between John and the
barons,[6] he called upon the sheriffs to cause these juries
to be elected in every county ;[7] and another writ of 27
June shows that the knights were at once chosen, and
that they were considered as local representatives of the
committee of twenty-five barons.[8]

Clauses in the Great Charter

Enquiry into the forests and warrens

1. Articles of the Barons, § 47 ; Magna Carta, § 47 : " Omnes foreste
que afforestate sunt tempore nostro statim deafforestentur."
2. He promised that complaints on this point should be impartially
considered after his return from crusade (Magna Carta, § 53).
3. Articles of the Barons, § 39 ; Magna Carta, § 44.
4. They added "and rivers." See also § 47 of the Articles and of Magna
Carta as to the disafforestment of rivers preserved by John. But the
question of fishing played only a minor part, and was put on one side in
the Charter of the Forest.
5. Articles of the Barons, § 39 ; Magna Carta, § 48.
6. MacKechnie, *Magna Carta*, p. 47.
7. *Sel. Charters*, p. 303 ; MacKechnie, *op. cit.*, pp. 576-7.
8. MacKechnie, p. 577 ; the French text is in Bémont, *Chartes*,
p. xxiv n.

There can be no doubt that the barons were aiming at little or nothing less than the suppression of the Forest jurisdiction. The king and his advisers were themselves so sure of it that they asked the clergy to step in to give article 48 the interpretation least injurious to the crown. Though assuredly the defence of the forest law was little to their interest, eight bishops agreed to sign a declaration which is preserved in the close rolls : they testify that this article was understood by the two parties in such a sense that all customs essential to the existence of the Forest ought to be maintained.[1]

Attempted abolition of the Forest

This conciliatory interpretation would certainly not have convinced the barons and the knights on the juries. It was the civil war and John's death that saved the Forest. In the confirmation of the Great Charter issued after the accession of Henry III (on 12 Nov. 1216), the immediate disafforestment of the forests made by John was promised : but the articles of Magna Carta concerning " forests and foresters, warrens and warreners " were placed among the "difficult and doubtful" clauses which demanded consideration.[2] Nothing more was heard of committing the reform of abuses to those who suffered from them and who would doubtless have left in existence next to nothing of an institution they detested.

The Forest saved by the civil war

1. " . . . Articulus iste ita intellectus fuit ex utraque parte, quum de eo tractabitur, et expressus, quod omnes consuetudines ille remanere debent, sine quibus foreste servari non possint : et hoc presentibus litteris protestamur." The signatures include the names of the bishops of Winchester, Worcester, and Bath, who to the end remained faithful to John, and of the archbishops of Canterbury and Dublin, and the bishops of London, Lincoln, and Coventry. (Rymer, ed. 1816, vol. i, pt. i, 134).

2. Charter of 1216, § 42, in *Sel. Charters*, p. 339.

(4)

THE CHARTER OF THE FOREST OF 1217.

The wise men who governed in behalf of the infant
Henry III made what concessions were
inevitable, and as early as 6 November,
1217, published the Charter of the Forest.[1]
An examination of this document is particularly instructive.

The Charter of the Forest: 6 Nov., 1217

The personal privileges of the king were curtailed by
articles 11 and 13. In the twelfth century, hunting was a
pleasure which certain kings were loth to
allow their barons to enjoy. Henry I was
accused of wishing to restrict it almost
entirely to himself. On the other hand,
John, notwithstanding certain vagaries [2]
which can be sufficiently explained by his capricious and
despotic character, made considerable use of the Forest to
reward services or gain partisans.[3] He went so far as to
permit his barons to hunt in the forest country administered by Brian de l'Isle, when they were passing through
it, adding : " We possess our forests and our venison not
for ourself only, but also for our subjects." He merely
ordered Brian de l'Isle to ascertain who made use of the
privilege and what was taken.[4] It may be said that

Royal rights curtailed.
i. Licence to hunt in the Forest

1. Bémont, *Chartes,* pp. 64 sqq. ; Stubbs, *Sel. Charters,* pp. 344 sqq. For
a refutation of Roger of Wendover's statement that the first Charter of the
Forest was published by John, see Richard Thomson's *Historical Essay
on the Magna Charta* (1829), pp. 237-8.

2. As when in 1209, for example, he forbade " the taking of birds
throughout all England." Cf. on this passage from Roger of Wendover,
Turner, p. ciii, and Greswell, p. 70.

3. For examples of these grants to individuals, see Fisher, *Forest of
Essex,* pp. 199 sqq.

4. *Rotuli Lit. Claus.* (ed. Hardy), i. 85.

the principle laid down in this letter was confirmed in the eleventh article of the Charter of the Forest : every archbishop, bishop, earl, or baron passing through the Forest, might take one or two head of venison under the oversight of the forester.

Another privilege of the king was that of reserving for himself, throughout the realm, the eyries of the fowl of the Forest—hawks, falcons, eagles, and herons—and the wild honey found in the woods. The Norman kings had in this case apparently brought over and converted into a royal prerogative a right which in France every lord seems to have enjoyed on his estates.[1] By article 13 of the Charter of the Forest, Henry III renounced these claims : every free man might have the eyries and the honey found in his woods. The high prices which were paid for the birds used in hawking, and the extensive use made of honey and wax, gave much importance to this concession.

ii. Eyries and honey

In the letter to Brian de l'Isle, mentioned above, John stated that the beasts of the Forest had more to fear from thieves than from the barons. All manner of precautions were taken against poaching by the inhabitants of the Forest or by dogs. In the pleas of 1209 which have been printed by Mr. Turner, we read of poachers chased by the foresters, of inhabitants of the Forest prosecuted for possessing arms without permission or for having eaten of the venison, and also of dogs which have been caught hunting on their own account and which are to be produced before the justices.[2] As on the continent, the

Measures against poachers maintained

1. *Capitul. de Villis*, § 36 (Boretius, i. 86); *Summa de legibus Normanniae* (13th century) in J. Tardif, *Coutumiers de Normandie*, ii. 12 sqq.; and an ordinance of Charles VI : " . . . Retinemus nobis . . . omnes nidos avium nobilium " (*Ordonnances*, viii. 162). If a swarm of bees was found, it became the property of the lord who had the exercise of *haut justice* (see De Maulde, *Condition Forestière de l'Orléanais*, p. 227; also a document of 1259 in *Layettes du Trésor des Chartes*, iii. no. 4474).

2. Turner, pp. 2 sqq.

forest law compelled the inhabitants of the Forest to mutilate the fore-paws of their dogs.[1] The foresters profited by this rule to levy arbitrary fines, and would confiscate a peasant's ox if his dog could still **Regulation of the lawing of dogs** trot, however haltingly. In the Charter of the Forest, the only alleviation granted was that the " lawing " of dogs should be confined to the districts where it was customary at the accession of Henry II; that it should be performed according to a fixed rule, and inspected by a jury at the time of the regards; and finally that no more than a three-shilling fine should be imposed on offenders. The law against carrying or possessing weapons remained in force for the inhabitants of the Forest.

Mention has been made of the annoyances inflicted on the pretext of protecting the trees and pastures. Articles 9 and 12 of the Charter, which were certainly **Change in the law on purpresture** regarded as among the most valuable, restored to dwellers in the Forest some of the rights of which they had been deprived. They might make mills, fish-ponds, pools, marl-pits, or ditches, clear their lands outside the covert (art. 12), and use at pleasure their own woods for feeding pigs **Amnesty for trespassers to the vert** (art. 9). Finally they were relieved of their annual payments to the Treasury for such purprestures, wastes, or assarts as had been made from the accession of Henry II to the second year of Henry III. But the law against touching the trees

1. On the "expeditatio canum," see Fisher, *Forest of Essex,* pp. 226 sqq. Du Cange, s.v. *expeditare,* cites only English authorities for this practice. But the custom of mutilating dogs, or at all events of hobbling them, on land preserved for hunting, was known on the continent. Cf. a charter of Aymeri, vicomte de Thouars, of the year 1229: "Canes vero rusticorum manencium infra metas garene nostre, de duabus magistris unciis unius pedis anterioris mutilabuntur " (*Cartulaires du Bas-Poitou,* published by Marchegay, p. 39). See also the custom of Hesdin in Richebourg, *Nouveau Coutumier Général,* vol. i, pt. i, 337; Sander Pierron, *Hist. de la Forêt de Soigne,* p. 253, etc. For Belgium, see on this subject, a work of A. Faider, which, however, is not on the whole to be recommended : *Hist. du droit de chasse et de la législation sur la chasse en Belgique, France, Angleterre, Allemagne, Italie, et Hollande,* pp. 32, 39, 71, 161.

was maintained, and new offences of waste or assart were to be punished by the usual amercements.[1]

There had been bitter complaints of the irregularity, the arbitrariness, and the abuses of forest justice. By article 16, custodians of castles and other local officers, who had their friends and enemies, were forbidden to hold the pleas of the Forest. The pleas of the vert and the venison, enrolled and attested by the seals of the verderers, were to be presented to the *capitalis forestarius* on eyre, and tried before him alone. The assizes of the twelfth century,[2] moreover, had insisted on the presence at the forest pleas of all the inhabitants of the county. Although this demand was liable to interpretations which diminished its rigour,[3] it clearly gave occasion for the levy of lucrative fines from various defaulters; and this was one of the abuses of which the suppression was demanded by the barons in their petition of 1215. They asked that the summons of the justices should not include inhabitants of the county dwelling outside the Forest, except those who were under accusation or had stood surety for offenders. This thirty-ninth article of the Petition was copied almost word for word in the Charter of the Forest (art. 2). In the same way, the meetings of the swanimote for the regulation of the pasture served as a pretext for fining the absent : but the presence of the

Safeguards against abuses

Attendance at the forest courts

1. " Qui de cetero vastum, purpresturam vel assartum sine licentia nostra in illis fecerint, de vastis et assartis respondeant " (art. 4). The words " de purpresturis " are omitted ; but there is no doubt that this is merely due to careless drafting. Article 12 did away in great measure with the crime of purpresture, but it did not authorise the making of new enclosures without permission ; in the thirteenth century the justices had the fences of such pulled down and amerced the offender ; see the examples in Turner, p. lxxxii.

2. Assize of Woodstock, § 11 (*Sel. Charters,* p. 188). Assize of Richard I, § 12 (Hoveden, iv. 64).

3. This is proved by the following verdict returned in 1209 at the pleas of Rutland and Leicestershire : "Veredictum militum comitatus Rotelandie quod ad summonicionem iusticiariorum de foresta venire debent ad placita foreste omnes de comitatu Leicestrie comuniter qui manent extra forestam ad distanciam duarum leucarum " (Turner, p. 6).

general public was not necessary, and the Charter lays down that they shall not be forced to attend (art. 8).

Among the most famous articles are 10 and 15, dealing with punishments and outlaws : "No one shall henceforth lose life or members for the sake of our venison; but if anyone has been arrested and convicted of the taking of venison, he shall pay a heavy ransom if he has wherewith to redeem himself ; and if he has not wherewith to redeem himself, he shall lie in our prison for a year and a day ; and if after a year and a day he can find pledges, he shall go out of prison ; but if not, he shall abjure the realm of England." " All who have been outlawed for the sake of the Forest only, from the time of king Henry our grandfather to our first coronation, shall come into our peace without hindrance, and shall find safe pledges that they will not henceforth offend against us touching our Forest." In future, then, banishment was the worst that could befall the poacher who had killed the king's deer ; and an amnesty threw the realm open to those who had previously been exiled for this offence.

Abandonment of the penalties of death and mutilation

It is possible to determine with more or less exactness the nature of the penalties actually inflicted in the twelfth century, and consequently the value of article 10 of the Charter. As for the barons, they had the privilege, in the twelfth as in the thirteenth century, of being tried only in the king's court : a heavy fine at the king's mercy was their worst possible fate if they hunted his deer.[1] It remains to enquire whether death, mutilation, or banishment awaited offenders who were not barons.

Previous practice

The barons

The chroniclers under the first Norman kings accuse William the Conqueror and Henry I of having punished

1. See the case of Robert Corbet in 1209 (*Select Pleas*, p. 8). See also *Gesta Hen. II*, i. 94. The author of the *Constitutiones Cnuti de foresta* states the principle which was applied in the twelfth and thirteenth centuries : " Episcopi, abbates, et barones mei . . . si regales [feras occiderint], restabunt rei regi pro libito suo, sine certa emendatione " (ed. Liebermann, § 26). Cf. *Capitul.* 802, § 39 (Boretius, i. 98).

Cruel punishments under the Norman kings

poachers by mutilation, and William Rufus of having put them to death.[1] Henry II and Richard I assert in their assizes that Henry I punished trespasses to the venison with blinding and castration.[2] These were the penalties used in the Carolingian Empire to punish crimes against the sovereign,[3] and the ferocity of penal law in the Middle Ages compels us to accept the statement of the assizes as most probably true. But on the accession of the Plantagenets, these severities were modified, and the object of the authorities was apparently to extract the largest possible fines from the delinquents. William of Newburgh says in fact that Henry II showed himself less cruel than his ancestors.[4]

Greater leniency under Henry II

In the Assize of Woodstock, the king asserts that he has hitherto been content with punishing the guilty through their goods.[5] It is true that he declares his resolve to apply henceforth the penalties in vogue under Henry I, but this was unquestionably a mere threat, intended to frighten the king's faithful subjects, to whom his officers had publicly to read the assize.[6] There is in any case a discrepancy between this declaration and articles 12 and 16. Article 12 lays down that for forest offences—

1. See the passages collected by Liebermann, *Pseudo-Cnut,* pp. 20-1 ; Freeman, *Norman Conquest,* iv. 610, v. 124-5.

2. Assize of Woodstock (text in the *Gesta Hen. II*), § 1 ; Assize of Richard I, § 1 (Hoveden, iv. 63).

3. Brunner, *Deutsche Rechtsgeschichte,* ii. 64, 78 ; cf. art. 10 of the so-called Statutes of William the Conqueror, compiled under Henry I, (Textus Roffensis) : "Interdico etiam ne quis occidatur aut suspendatur pro aliqua culpa, sed eruantur oculi et testiculi abscidantur " (*Sel. Charters,* p. 99). The Anglo-Saxon Chronicle, in speaking of the laws of William I for the preservation of game, mentions only blinding (i. 355).

4. " Venationis delicias, aeque ut avus, plus justo diligens, in puniendis tamen positarum pro feris legum transgressoribus avo mitior fuit : ille enim . . . homicidarum et fericidarum in publicis animadversionibus nullam vel parvam esse distantiam voluit ; hic autem huiusmodi transgressores carcerali custodia sive exsilio ad tempus coercuit " (*Historia rerum anglicarum,* lib. iii. cap. 26, in Howlett, *Chronicles of the reigns of Stephen,* etc. [R. S.], i. 280).

5. " Propter eorum catalla " (§ 1).

6. On this reading of the assize, see Hoveden, iv. 63.

trespasses to the venison included—sureties shall in the first instance be demanded, and that the delinquent shall not be imprisoned until the third offence. The sixteenth article concerns the crime, always regarded as particularly serious, of poaching by night : " no one shall hunt to take beasts by night, within the Forest or without,[1] in any place which the king's beasts frequent or where they have their peace, on pain of imprisonment for a year and of making fine at the king's pleasure." In the

Richard I's Assize

Assize of Richard I, which was drafted in more precise language, this last clause disappears, and offenders are simply threatened with the loss of eyes and castration.[2] But it is unlikely that this penalty was often inflicted : Roger of Wendover affirms that Richard I contented himself with the imprisonment or banishment of those who stole his deer.[3]

The jurists and judges of this period seem on the whole to have been mercifully inclined. To the author

Abandonment of corporal penalties in practice

of the *Constitutiones* the death penalty is limited to serfs and inflicted on them only if the beast has been killed.[4] The pleas of 1209, which are particularly interesting, contain no mention of the penalties of death and mutilation.

On the other hand these records show that people were imprisoned, not only on clear proof of an offence, but on

Severity of prison-life

suspicions that were sometimes extremely vague. Now prison discipline was commonly very severe during the Middle Ages.[5] A cer-

1. We shall try later to explain the words "extra forestam" (pp. 233 sqq.).
2. Assize of 1198, § 14, in Hoveden, iv. 65. Nevertheless, art. 17 of this assize quotes, without revoking it, art. 12 of the Assize of Woodstock : " . . . Idem rex Henricus statuit apud Wudestoke, quod quicunque forisfecerit ei de foresta sua semel de venatione sua, de seipso salvi plegii capiantur," etc.
3. Wendover, in Matthew Paris (ed. Luard, R. S.), iii. 213.
4. *Constitutiones de foresta,* ed. Liebermann, arts. 24-5.
5. Particularly in England ; cf. Jusserand, *English Wayfaring Life in the Middle Ages* (trans. by Miss Toulmin Smith), p. 266 ; Ch. Gross, *Coroners' Rolls (Selden Society)*, p. xxiv. n. 1.

o

tain Ralph Red of Siberton, imprisoned for having feasted on a doe, died in his cell. Roger Tocke, his friend, had been put in gaol also, although he was probably innocent : " he lay," we read, " a long time in prison, so that he is nearly dead." Such a prospect frightened the guilty, and numbers fled and were outlawed. One of these was Hugh the Scot : venison was found in his house ; he took sanctuary, kept to the church for a month, and escaped in women's clothes; he was pronounced *utlagatus*[1] As early as 1166 the Assize of Clarendon prescribed what measures should be adopted against those accused of forest offences who fled from one county to another.[2]

Imprisonment therefore awaited both those accused and those merely suspected.[3] It awaited also the penniless and friendless who failed to find **Cases in which imprisonment was imposed** sureties, and in some cases threatened even those who did. It would be unsound to urge that imprisonment was not, technically, a penalty; for, as we have seen, article 16 of the Assize of Woodstock punished nocturnal poaching with the *poena imprisonamenti unius anni*.

To sum up, during the reigns of the first three Plantagenets, poachers had to fear sometimes exile, but more often ruinous fines or very severe imprisonment; and the gaol was an object of such **Conclusion as to punishments before 1217** horror that often it seemed a greater evil than flight and the wretched lot of an outlaw. On the other hand, forest justice, organised with the main object of making money, was so regulated that it was impossible for the death penalty to be inflicted. This is sufficiently proved by the length of the procedure in capital cases and the long intervals between the eyres

1. Turner, pp. 1—3, 6, 9.
2. Art. 17 (*Sel. Charters*, p. 172).
3. According to article 12 of the Assize of Woodstock, delinquents could not be imprisoned till their third offence. It is probable that this article fell into disuse as far as trespasses to the venison were concerned. It is significant that it was confirmed by Edward I only so far as it touched trespasses to the vert (*Statutes*, i. 243).

of the justices. During this period, the execution or mutilation of an offender must have been an exceptional occurrence : these penalties, it is true, are mentioned in the negotiations which preceded the issue of Magna Carta; but neither in the Petition or Articles of the Barons, nor in the Charter itself, was it considered necessary to require their abolition.

It would therefore be a mistake to regard article 10 of the Charter of 1217 as a notable gain for the inhabitants of the Forest. It made very little difference to their actual position, and did nothing more than pronounce the royal blessing, so to speak, on previous practice. The taking of game was punished by a "heavy ransom"; the impecunious, it is true, were no longer liable to a year's imprisonment; but if they failed to find sureties, they were reduced at the end of this time to the miserable necessity of "abjuring the realm."[1] Still, the threats of dreadful punishments disappeared.

Article 10 confirms previous practice

In this last respect, English law was henceforward in advance of the customary law of France. Beaumanoir expressly states that those who poach by night in warrens are liable to be hanged,[2] though he adds that "some people" are not of this opinion. Enguerrand de Coucy having hanged "three young nobles for that they were found in his woods with bows and arrows, [but] without dogs and without other engines whereby they could have taken wild beasts," St. Louis forfeited the wood, which he gave to an abbey, and deprived Enguerrand of "all high justice of woods and fish-ponds, so that he can since that time neither imprison nor put to death for any offence committed there."[3] These passages prove that

Comparison with the law in France

1. That is, binding themselves by oath to leave England for ever. See A. Réville, *L'Abjuratio regni, Rev. historique*, Sept.-Oct. 1892, pp. 1 sqq. [See also Benham, *Red Paper Book of Colchester*, p. 33.]

2. Ed. Salmon, i. 474, art. 935. See also the texts of the Customs— for example, the 'Coutumier de Beaumont,' in E. Bonvalot, *Le Tiers Etat d'après la Charte de Beaumont*, Appendix, p. 10.

3. Guillaume de Saint-Pathus, *Vie de Saint-Louis*, ed. H. F. Delaborde, p. 136.

the penalty of death for poaching existed in thirteenth-century France, but that jurists did not unanimously countenance it and that the king controlled its application.

In England the consequences of poaching affected not only the poachers but also all their neighbours. In the pleas of 1209 we read of the amercement of numerous townships and tithings after the discovery of a dead beast or its remains : thus one township is amerced for not having " raised the hue and cry on evil-doers to the king " who have killed a hind ; another, because it has not found the offender or because it has gone back on its first evidence.[1] The Charter of the Forest made no change in this very remunerative system of collective responsibility, which must have been most unpopular.

Collective responsibility remains

As a rule the exactions of the foresters were for their own personal profit. The Charter of the Forest, therefore, provided safeguards against them. Many foresters made undue demands for sheaves of oats or wheat, for lambs, sucking-pigs, or money, and they also levied " scotale." [2] These extortions were forbidden, and it was agreed that the number of the foresters should be limited. The foresters-in-fee had the right of receiving " chiminage " in the woods of the demesne from the sellers of wood and charcoal : but, as they paid a ferm to the king and kept the revenues for themselves, they would extort very heavy sums, and even claim chiminage from poor folks carrying bundles of faggots or charcoal on their backs, demanding it too in woods outside the demesne. These abuses, which brought nothing to the Treasury, were to cease. [3]

Checks on extortion

1. Turner, pp. 1—9.
2. Regarding *scotale,* see Stubbs, *Const. Hist.,* i. 672 and notes, and below, p. 204.
3. Arts. 7, 14. Article 5 does not specify the abuses committed by the regarders. In the pleas of 1209 the references to them are equally obscure (Turner, pp. 6-7).

Frequently also the foresters strove to curtail the customary rights of the people.[1] They received a hint to respect the *communia de herbagio et aliis*

Protection of rights of common

in the demesne woods which were not to be disafforested.[2] They often prevented the inhabitants of the Forest from throwing open their pastures until the king's woods had been provided with swine : [3] henceforward every free man might "agist" his own woods at his pleasure, drive his pigs to pasture across the royal demesne, and receive the pannage due to him.[4]

These guarantees against the abuse of power by royal officials must have been warmly welcomed. The foresters were renowned for brutality, insolence, and greed. Those whom they had maltreated sometimes took a cruel revenge.[5] But a mere legal enactment was not enough to reform them, and they long remained deservedly unpopular.

The corruption and excessive zeal of the foresters were not peculiar to England. But what, in England, ren-

Disafforestment

dered intolerable these and all other abuses of the forest system, constituting them a national grievance against the king, was the fact that the Forest, though royal property and not divided among a number of magnates, was nevertheless larger in England than anywhere else, and that the kings kept on increasing it by arbitrary acts of afforestment. The question of disafforestment consequently seemed of the

1. On the somewhat obscure question of customary rights in the Forest, see Fisher, *Forest of Essex,* ch. v and vi. [Cf. Miss Bazeley, *op. cit.* p. 269.]

2. Art. 1.

3. This may at least be inferred from art. 7 of the Assize of Wood-stock (*Sel. Charters,* p. 187).

4. Art. 9.

5. The author of the *Magna Vita S. Hugonis* (p. 178) tells how, at the end of the preceding century, a forester was killed by men whom he had treated with extraordinary insolence. His body was cut into pieces which were carried to three different places. The huntsmen had the same evil reputation ; they were, says John of Salisbury, coarse, drunken, and licentious (*Policraticus,* lib. i. cap. iv, cited by Fisher, *Forest of Essex,* p. 199).

greatest importance, and took the foremost place in the Charter of 1217. It was the subject of the first and third articles. Nothing is said there about the forests made by the Norman kings; and in these therefore the forest law continued to be enforced. But the forests created by Henry II were to be viewed by "good and loyal men," and all the woods which he had afforested outside the royal demesne to the damage of their owners, were to be disafforested.[1] There was, moreover, to be an immediate disafforestment of all woods outside the demesne which had been made forest by Richard or John.[2] In granting these articles Henry's advisers were making a very great concession, which the barons had not explicitly demanded in 1215.

Such was the Charter of the Forest. It granted only part of the benefits hoped for in 1215. The extraordinary jurisdiction of the Forest remained. The inhabitants were still oppressed by hateful burdens, subject to irksome restrictions, and liable to heavy collective fines. But a good number of the evil customs from which they suffered, and from which the Great Charter of 1215 had vaguely promised to free them, were now suppressed by law, and, above all, some of them might confidently look forward to the disafforestment of their land and a return to normal conditions. Henceforth the English could appeal to a legal document. The rule of unmitigated despotism had ended, and the decline of the Forest was beginning.

Significance of the Charter

1. Art. 1.
2. Art. 3. Cf. above, p. 184. It will be seen that the interpretation of these articles might have been a matter of difficulty. Why select for disafforestment the woods which Henry II had afforested " ad dampnum illius cuius boscus fuerit "? How was this limitation to be understood? Moreover, was it possible to disafforest " statim," without inquisition, the woods afforested by Richard and John? In practice it appears that no difficulties were raised, and all the disafforestments were preceded by inquisitions. On this point see in particular the document published by Turner, p. xcvi. " Statim deafforestentur " was an injunction that could not be carried out, and no attempt was made to enforce it.

5

THE FOREST IN THE THIRTEENTH CENTURY.

The Select Pleas published by Mr. Turner prove that, notwithstanding the maintenance of the forest organisation and the rights which they had refused to surrender, the thirteenth-century kings, Henry III and Edward I, had great difficulty in keeping a hold on their hunting preserves and the revenues which they drew from the Forest.

Difficulty of defending the Forest

The Forest was a source of many temptations both to those who lived there and to those who were appointed to guard it. It is instructive to note the " chapters " of the great inquisition held in the royal forests in 1244-5 by Robert Passelewe.[1] The commissioners were to investigate the injuries done to the king by the inhabitants of the Forest, who had enlarged their fields at the expense of the vert, put up buildings, made parks and warrens, sold wood and charcoal, pastured cattle and horses, and all without any legal authorisation.[2] According to Matthew Paris, Robert Passelewe punished these offences severely, and despoiled of their goods, drove from their houses, imprisoned, banished, or reduced to beggary, a large number of people, both clergy and laymen, nobles and commons.[3]

i. Encroachments by the inhabitants

1. In regard to Passelewe, see Fisher, *op. cit.*, pp. 107-8.
2. *Inquisitiones de forisfactis diversis super foresta domini regis*, published in the *Additamenta* to the *Chronicle* of M. Paris (vi, 94 sqq.). On the frequency of trespasses to the vert in the 13th century, see Fisher, *Forest of Essex*, pp. 235-6.
3. M. Paris, iv, 400, 426–7. The pipe rolls of 29 Henry III preserve the financial results of this inquisition, and the pleas of 1255 furnish an example of a house built " to the damage of the Forest " in Huntingdonshire, which Passelewe ordered to be pulled down (Turner, p. 18).

Robert Passelewe had also to deal with corrupt foresters. Most of the instructions which he was to follow concern abuses committed by the foresters, and especially the consent which they had given, freely or otherwise, *gratia vel lucro,* to the illegalities of the inhabitants. They were also suspected of selling wood and hay, of wresting justice to their own profit, and of leasing forest land without authority.[1]

ii. Dishonest foresters

All these "chapters" of the inquisition were drawn up by men who understood their business. We know, moreover, of the malpractices laid in 1269 to the charge of Peter de Neville, warden of the forest in Rutland. According to the indictment brought against him by the verderers, the regarders, and twelve knights and loyal men, he had in thirteen years appropriated seven thousand trees, either for his personal use, or to sell them, give them to his friends, or make charcoal from them, and he had embezzled numerous fines and dues which ought to have gone to the Treasury, not to mention acts of extortion and violence against the inhabitants.[2] The pleas of the Forest likewise contain cases of subordinate foresters who allowed themselves to be bribed by offenders, or took the king's trees and game for their own benefit.[3]

Poaching was prevalent everywhere. Among those accused are to be found not only professionals, *consueti malefactores de venacione domini regis,*[4] but also university students,[5] a schoolmaster and his assistant,[6] numerous clerks and chaplains,[7] bailiffs and foresters both royal and private,[8] members

iii. Poaching

---

1. *Inquisitiones,* cap. 3, 6 sqq.
2. Turner, p. 44.   3. *Ibid.,* pp. 20–1, 24.   4. *Ibid.,* p. 43.
5. *Ibid.,* pp. 129 sqq.   6. *Ibid.,* p. 21.
7. *Ibid.,* 21, 33, 38, 79, 88, 94, 103, 112, etc. Clerical offenders were in the thirteenth century claimed by the spiritual courts, but they paid the king a composition fixed by the justices of the Forest (Turner, pp. lxxxvii sqq.).   8. *Ibid.,* pp. 20, 36, 39, 110.

of the king's household,[1] and lastly very great lords like
earl Ferrers[2] and the earl of Gloucester.[3]   There were
bands of poachers, up to a dozen strong,[4] hunting on
foot or on horseback,[5] with dogs and weapons of all
kinds.   They cared nothing for the gamekeepers, shot
at them, tied them to trees, and sometimes killed them ;[6]
and to such lengths did they go that to repress their
increasing boldness, the Parliament of 1293 decreed that
no proceedings should be taken against foresters, parkers,
and warreners if they killed poachers who would not
suffer themselves to be arrested.[7]   It was the more
difficult to catch the poacher that he had accomplices
everywhere.   He was popular : his exploits were sung
in ballads, and he was represented as a redresser of
wrongs, a friend of the king and the people.   Robin
Hood was the model hero.   He was an outlaw, he lived
on the venison of the Forest and on the superfluities of
the rich : but he was courteous ; he was religious, devoted
to Our Lady ; and he loved the king more than anyone
in the world.[8]   In the *Tale of Gamelyn,* the king gives
a good reception to Gamelyn, a brigand who sits in
judgment on judges and has them hanged, and appoints
him " chef justice of al his fre forest."[9]   In such ways
did popular poetry revenge itself on reality.   The king
is not responsible for the forest law ; he rather disap-
proves of it ; and he is full of indulgence for poachers.

During the thirteenth century, in fact, poaching was
not very severely treated.   Article 10 of the Charter was

1. Turner, pp. 34, 35, 42.   2. *Ibid.*, p. 40.   3. *Ibid.*, p. 34.
4. *Ibid.*, pp. 8, 17, 39, 77, 80, 99.
5. " Equites et pedites " (*ibid.*, p. 22).
6. *Ibid.*, pp. 8, 28, 38–9, 77, 80–1.
7. *Statutum de malefactoribus in parcis* (*Statutes* i, 111–2).   This
statute applies to the chases of the nobles as well as to the king's Forest.
8. See the cycle of the ballads of Robin Hood (12th—15th century) in
vol. v. of *English and Scottish Popular Ballads*, published by F. J. Child ;
cf. his introduction, p. 42.
9. This story, attributed to Chaucer, probably dates from the 13th
century.   Dr. Skeat has not included it in his edition of Chaucer, but
has published it separately.

leniently enforced. The " heavy ransom " was
Leniency towards poachers fixed in proportion to the means of the guilty
person, and seldom exceeded six or seven shil-
lings. The fine was really "heavy" only when
it was imposed on a delinquent of good family, or on an
official, a verderer for instance, who had betrayed his
trust by taking the king's beasts for himself. Poor men
were often pardoned or set at liberty in consideration of
the detention they had undergone before their trial.[1]
Poachers, in short, seem in the thirteenth century to have
been treated with a relative leniency which cannot have
made for the diminution of their numbers.

Nevertheless the administration and the justice of the
Forest remained irritating and unpopular because evil-
doers were not the only ones punished. To
The forest system still irksome pass through the Forest with hunting-dogs
which frightened the game was enough to
send a man to gaol.[2] One man was prose-
cuted for " having stupidly entered the forest with a bow
and arrows."[3] A boy found a dead fawn and carried it
away, not knowing that he was doing wrong; he was
kept in prison for over a year.[4] At the smallest indication of anything amiss, an inquisition was set on foot,
and the four nearest townships had to find and produce
the culprit. Whether it was a question of a landowner
who had let his dogs run loose or of a poacher who after
shooting a forester had fled under cover of darkness,
mattered nothing; if the townships "did not come fully,"
as it was put—that is to say, if they did not accuse
anyone—they had to pay a fine of at least 6s. 8d., and
often as much as six marks.[5]

Thus offenders who were caught got off lightly, and
the law-abiding inhabitants paid for those who escaped.

1. For details see Turner, pp. lxv–vi., [and also Miss Bazeley,
op. cit., pp. 109 sqq., where there is some extremely interesting matter on
poaching in the Forest of Dean in the 13th century.]
2. Turner, p. 31.   3. *Ibid.*, p. 17.   4. *Ibid.*, p. 29.
5. *Ibid.*, pp. 18, 28, etc., and Introduction, pp. xlviii, lxiii.

Tyranny and extortion of the foresters

The unpopularity of the whole forest system was rendered complete by the violence and exactions of the foresters. Some in their zeal collected illegal fines for the exchequer. Others were extortionate for their own advantage. In Rutland the warden of the Forest set the example : an extant record enumerates the arbitrary imprisonments inflicted by Peter de Neville to wring money from the inhabitants, and tells how on fanciful pretexts he levied fines, which he of course forgot to hand over to the exchequer.[1] The unlawful holding of pleas was also one of the most common complaints. Chapter XXI of the *Instructions* of 1244 concerns this abuse of power : "Item, to enquire if foresters-in-fee or others have held any plea of the vert or the venison, which belongs to the king and his chief justice ; to discover those who have thus received fines and amercements, and which and how much."[2] But the inhabitants had to suffer many other kinds of extortion, and the foresters-in-fee were not the only, or even the chief, offenders. Being well off, they were not much feared by the people,[3] who were far more afraid of the insatiable greed of the subordinate officers. Through desire of gain, the wardens of the forests appointed foresters in much greater numbers than were necessary ; these bought their offices and also paid an annual ferm to the warden.[4] Sometimes they were actually dismissed as soon as appointed, that their posts might be sold again to others.[5] Naturally, the under-foresters, liable to such extortions, were extortionate in their turn.

1. Turner, pp. 49 sqq.   2. M. Paris, vi, *Additamenta,* 98.
3. The inhabitants preferred the foresters-in-fee (Turner, p. cxxxix).
4. " La met le chef forester les foresters suz ly, a chival e a pe, a suen voler, saunz le veue de nuly, e plus ke ne suffist a garder la Forest dreyturele, par le lur donaunt sicum il puent finir pur aver baylye, a graunt damage e a grevaunce del pays " (*Grievances of the People of Somerset,* 1279, in Turner, p. 126, § 4 ; cf. also p. 128, § 8).
5. In the chapters of the Inquisition of 1244 this dishonest traffic is attributed to the foresters-in-fee, who indeed did in many places nominate the under-foresters (M. Paris, vi, *Additamenta,* 96 ; cf. *Fleta,* ii, c. 41, § 36).

The " grievances of the people and commonalty of the forests in Somerset " give us a clear idea of the abuses complained of in 1279 by the inhabitants of a single county. They speak only of acts contrary to the Charter of the Forest. They were forced to pay ancient dues for assart, waste, and purpresture, from which article 4 exempted them. In some districts they were deprived of the right of pasture.[1] They were summoned to the swanimote, with a view to the subsequent amercement of defaulters. The officers ordered the complete mutilation of the paws of their dogs. They levied tolls prohibited by the Charter. Furthermore, the unmounted foresters came to the villages in August claiming sheaves, lambs, young pigs, wool, and linen : with the grain given them they brewed beer and forced the peasants to buy it.[2] And after them came their mounted colleagues, and did the same.[3]

Grievances of the people of Somerset

It is not astonishing that the hatred of the peasants for the foresters continued unabated, and even led them to bring against their oppressors false accusations of stealing the king's deer and wood.[4]

On the subject of corrupt foresters, the king and the nation were necessarily in agreement, for, to use the ingenuous but weighty argument of the people of Somerset, " from these things the king has no profit."[5] That is why Henry III and Edward I ordered inquisitions into the conduct of the foresters. During his progress in 1244 and 1245, Robert Passelewe dealt with the case of the *prothoforestarius*, the justice John de Neville, whose place, moreover, he wanted to get. Notwithstanding the support he received,

Punishment of extortion

Inquisitions under Henry III

---

1. See also on the question of common of pasture, the grievances put forward by the people of Huntingdonshire in 1255 (Turner, pp. 25-6).
2. This is an example of the abuse of " scotale." See above, p. 196.
3. Turner, pp. 125 sqq.   4. " Odio et hatya " (*ibid.*, p. 37).
5. Turner, p. 128.

John was "shamefully convicted, and from being rich
became wretched"; he was pitied by nobody because he
had been without pity for others.[1] The inquisition of
1253 in Northamptonshire was concerned, among other
matters, with the conduct of the foresters.[2] The general
eyre of 1269—1271 was instituted mainly to deal with the
same subject, and it was then that discovery was made
of the peculation and extortion of Peter de Neville,
warden of the forest of Rutland. Peter de Neville
succeeded in getting out of his evil plight; and his
outlawry in 1273 was for another offence.[3]

It is well known with what thoroughness Edward I
administered his own affairs and those of his subjects.
Resolved as he was to keep in touch with every branch
of the administration, he turned his attention to the
Forest soon after he came back to England in 1274 and
assumed the reins of government. As early
Inquisitions under Edward I as 1277 he ordered a great inquisition in the
forests south of the Trent, declaring that he
wished the Charter of the Forest to be
observed in all its articles,[4] and in the following years
he instituted similar inquiries,[5] which sometimes led to
the removal of officers.[6] The lawyer who about 1290
wrote *Fleta* has preserved the list of the questions
which were put by the commissioners: they had in
particular to enquire if the foresters were too numerous,
if they levied illegal requisitions, and if they made profits
for themselves at the expense of the exchequer.[7]

These inquisitions of the first part of the reign
encouraged the presentation of lists of grievances, like

1. M. Paris, iv. 401, 427.
2. Turner, pp. 108 sqq.
3. *Ibid.*, pp. 43 sqq.; *Introduction,* pp. xvii, lxviii sqq.
4. The letters-patent are dated 1 March, 1277 (*C.P.R.* 1272-81, p. 237).
5. See an example of the thirteenth year of the reign (Turner, p. lxix, n. 4).
6. As, e.g., of Robert of Everingham, in Sherwood Forest (*ibid.*, p. 66).
7. *Fleta,* ch. 41.

the *Gravamina* of " the people of Somerset,"
and resulted—as early as 1278, if we are to
believe Manwood[1]—in the publication of the
Consuetudines et Assise de Foresta. This document
summarises very briefly the existing customs and laws
concerning trespasses to the vert and the venison, the
procedure of the courts, the duties of the inhabitants
and of the foresters with a view to the preservation of
the game, and so forth.[2] Theoretically, this forest code
was still in force in the sixteenth century, and Manwood
translated the whole of it in his treatise.

Edward I's Assize

The *Consuetudines et Assise* were intended to safeguard the rights of the king and not those of the
inhabitants of the Forest. We get the
impression that this was almost exclusively
Edward's aim when he instituted forest
inquisitions during the first part of his
reign. It was likewise the chief concern
of his itinerant justices. This is clearly shown by the
Provisions published in 1287 by William de Vescy,
justice of the Forest north of the Trent : their sole object
is to ensure the strict suppression of offences.[3]

Discontent with the forest administration under Edward I

Stubbs expresses astonishment at the violence of the
complaints raised in 1297, at the time when the king was
trying to collect money and troops in order to fight
Philip the Fair in Gascony and Flanders. In his
opinion, Edward I had governed according to the spirit
of the Charters and the charge of having violated them
was " vague declamation." [4] With regard to the Forest,
we have just seen that the royal administration was open

1. "There is no indication," says M. Bémont, "that Manwood imagined
this date" (*Chartes des lib. ang., Introd.*, p. lxv, n. 4).   Nevertheless Manwood may have simply assumed that the issue of the *Consuetudines* took
place immediately after the inquisition of 1277.   M. Bémont remarks
elsewhere (p. 97, n. 1) that in the old manuscript collections of statutes this
document is placed among those of 1290-91. Cf. Mr. Turner's observations
(p. xxxvii, n. 4).   According to him the first eleven articles date from the
beginning of the reign of Henry III, or even from the reign of John.
2. *Statutes*, i, 243 sqq.   3. Turner, pp. 62 sqq.
4. Stubbs, *Const. Hist.*, ed. 1896, ii, 150 sqq.

to criticism : it was not in agreement with the spirit of forbearance and equity which inspired the Charter of 1217 and guided Henry III's Council of Regency ; it was still, as under the personal rule of Henry III, narrowly jealous of its rights and careless of the sufferings endured by the inhabitants of the Forest. It was therefore natural that these should accuse Edward of not keeping the promises of his father, and that when in a moment of exasperation the nation drew up its list of grievances, they should add a clause of their own.

On 16 July, 1297, at the time when the marshal and the constable had just refused to serve overseas, arch-bishop Winchelsey summoned his clergy to deliberate on the need of a confirmation of the " great charters of liberties and of the Forest,"[1] and some days later the king promised to confirm them in return for an aid.[2] In a manifesto which was circulated at this juncture, the opposition complained of the violation of the Charter and of the Assize of the Forest, laying stress on illegal attachments.[3]

Crisis of 1297
The observance of the Charter of the Forest demanded

When the king had sailed for Flanders, his opponents succeeded in obtaining guarantees not only against arbitrary impositions, but against the severities of the

1. " . . . Articulus arduus videlicet de Magnis Cartis libertatum et Foreste salubriter innovandis, et de iuribus ac libertatibus ecclesie Anglicane, que hactenus deciderunt et adhuc continue decidunt in abusum, recuperandis a principe " (*Parl. Writs,* i, 53).

2. " . . . Pur aver le conferment de la graunt chartre des fraun-chises d'Engleterre et de la chartre de la Forest, lequeu confermement le roy leur ad graunté bonement, si li graunterent un commun doun tel com lui est mult besoygnable ou poynt de ore " (Royal proclamation of 12 Aug. 1297 : Bémont, *Chartes,* pp. 83-4). We have adopted the chronology established by M. Bémont in the excellent Introduction to his collection (p. xxxvii). It is, indeed, not at all probable that the reconciliation of the king and the archbishop occurred, as Stubbs supposes, on 14 July—that is to say, before the despatch of the summons cited above.

3. " . . . Preter hec, communitas terre sentit nimis se gravatam de assisa foreste, que non est custodita sicut consuevit, nec charta foreste observatur ; sed fiunt attachiamenta pro libitu extra assisam aliter quam fieri solebant " (*Articuli quos comites petierunt nomine communitatis,* art. 5 : Bémont, *op. cit.,* p. 78). On this manifesto, cf. Bémont, p. xxxviii, and Stubbs, *Const. Hist.,* ii, 143.

forest administration. As early as 10 October, the
regency granted them the *Confirmatio*
Confirmation *Cartarum;* the document was sent to
of the Charter
Edward, who surrounded by difficulties as
he was, could do nothing but agree to it. He sealed it
with the great seal at Ghent, on 5 November. In the
first article the king confirmed, along with Magna Carta,
the Charter of the Forest, gave orders that it should be
sent to all the counties and put into force by all officials
and justices, according to the Assize of the Forest, that
is to say, in agreement with the rules laid down in the
Consuetudines et Assise Foreste.[1] On 26 November he
initiated inquisitions in twenty-four counties; since they
were being made for the benefit of the inhabitants of the
Forest, these were to bear the expense.[2] But the *Confirmatio Cartarum* and this inquisition, like those which
had been held before, led to no radical change in the
forest system.

After experiencing so many disappointments, the
English had good reason to think that the only effectual
means of diminishing abuses was to diminish the Forest
itself. And indeed, after 1298, the quarrel about the
Forest, at the same time that it grew more bitter, became
a quarrel about disafforestment. Men were much less
concerned to obtain the punishment of guilty foresters
than to limit the operation of the evil by making the
Forest smaller. This question of disafforestment must
now be the chief object of our enquiry and the subject of
a separate chapter. But before showing its importance
at the end of the reign of Edward I, it will be necessary
to look back. In 1298 it had become a problem crying
for solution, but it had been in existence long before.
During the whole of the thirteenth century, the English
had never ceased to demand the execution of the promises
made on this matter in Magna Carta and the Charter of
the Forest.

1. Bémont, *op. cit.,* pp. 96 sqq. 2. *Parl. Writs,* i, 396–7.

6

THE STRUGGLE FOR DISAFFORESTMENT.

Despite a few picturesque details furnished by judicial records, what has just been said about the Forest in the reigns of Henry III and Edward I is in many respects somewhat commonplace and not at all peculiar to English history.

Analogies
between
England and
France

Encroachments at the expense of the Forest, the stealing of game, the annoyances experienced by the inhabitants, the exactions of the foresters, the intermittent efforts of the crown to obtain a better administration—these are facts which can for the most part be found in French documents of the same period, such as the reports of the inquisitors appointed by St. Louis, decisions of the *Parlement,* or royal letters. In France also a long peace, the increase of population, and agricultural prosperity, led to encroachments on the Forest by rural landholders. In France also there were poachers, both professional and amateur, and among them many ecclesiastics and foresters. In France also brutal means were used by the officials to protect the forests and warrens from unlawful injury. Trespasses were punished even more severely perhaps than in England, and without question more arbitrarily, for the machinery of forest justice worked with much less regularity, and complaints against unjust fines were innumerable. Encroachments were forbidden; compensation for purpresture was exacted; the extension of customary rights was opposed, and very often attempts were made to curtail those which had existed from time immemorial. In France also there were corrupt and oppressive foresters, and extortionate serjeants : and an inquisition concerning a verderer of the Forest of Brix[1] makes a fitting companion to the case of Peter de Neville.

In England, however, the history of the Forest has an importance which it entirely lacks in France. In England it plays a part in the history of the great constitutional crises. The reason is that immense tracts had been afforested to the advantage of the crown, whereas in France the hunting preserves of the Capetians were of modest extent. During the thirteenth century a problem which gave no trouble in France, was already causing serious disputes in England : the king wished to maintain his Forest, and his people demanded at least its partial surrender. It was principally the struggle for disafforestment which connected the history of the Forest with the history of the English constitution.

Why the Forest was of political importance in England alone

In resisting the demand, the king was not only fighting for his prerogative, for the continuance of the arbitrary jurisdiction so precisely defined by the author of the *Dialogus de Scaccario* : he was also fighting for his Treasury. He was loth to lose the fruits of forest justice, the rents for assarts, the great profits derived from the sale of game. It must not be overlooked that in the thirteenth century red deer, fallow deer, and roes, killed and salted by the king's huntsmen, were sold by the hundred.[2] The Forest was certainly the source of a large income. The whole of it was not necessary for the king's sport, for no king ever hunted in all his forests, but it was necessary if the royal budget was to balance.[3]

Why the king refused to surrender the Forest

1. *Cartulaire normand,* no. 1222 (A.D. 1272).

2. In a single day four hundred of these beasts were killed by Edward I and his huntsmen in the forest of Inglewood. The pipe rolls of Henry III record the wages paid for killing and salting, for instance, 235 roes, or 200 harts, or 200 hinds (F. H. M. Parker, *Forest Laws, Eng. Hist. Rev.,* 1912, p. 29). [See also the interesting details given by Miss Bazeley, p. 239.]

3. [In regard to the financial value of the Forest, see Miss Bazeley's careful analysis of the revenue derived from the Forest of Dean. She concludes that, between the years 1155 and 1307, the average income from this forest was about £75 per annum (*op. cit.,* chap. iii).]

In view of this, the king might justly have charged his opponents with putting forward two inconsistent claims : they grumbled because he kept his Forest, and, on the other hand, they called on him to refrain from extraordinary taxation, to " live of his own," and not to alienate the revenues of the crown.

But the forest system was excessively irksome, even in the thirteenth century, to all who held land within its sphere. Whether they were peasants or great landlords, they paid fines and rents, and were constantly exposed to interference, both in developing their property and in their daily lives. In general they had not even the satisfaction of hunting the game which fed on their lands; for, in the thirteenth century, licenses to hunt in the Forest were with few exceptions granted only within the narrow limits prescribed by the Charter.[1] The Assize of Edward I expressly mentions that the abbot of Peterborough has the right of hunting the hare, fox, and rabbit in the Forest and of keeping unlawed dogs, showing that at this time no other magnate enjoyed these privileges.[2] To estimate the discontent which must have been felt, we need only recall how great a part was played by the chase in the life of a mediæval man. It was the favourite sport of the nobles; in time of peace it offered a substitute for war, and was as dear to their hearts as the tournament itself. It likewise gave enjoyment to the middle and poorer classes. Moreover, for the people as well as for the king, hunting was not only a pastime but also a source of profit. The venison, the fur, the skins had much more value than now as food, clothing, and writing material. Every class of the nation was interested

All classes anxious for disafforestment

1. See the lists of game taken by bishops, earls, and barons in accordance with Article 2 of the Charter or by special writ, and also the references to gifts of game, in Turner, pp. 92–3, 95, 98, 102, 104, 105, 108, 113.

2. *Statutes*, i, 245. Edward I granted to the Bishop of Winchester the right to hunt in the Forest, but only within the limits of the episcopal demesne. (*Rot. Parl.*, i. 25).

in the curtailment of the Forest as a step towards its complete abolition.

Of all the inhabitants of the Forest, the small landholders no doubt suffered most from the law, but there is no ground for astonishment in the fact **Why the nobles took the lead in the struggle** that, as we shall see, the nobility almost always took the lead in the fight for disafforestment. They alone had enough authority to demand a diminution of the rights of the crown, and, in this particular case, they were directly interested in their object. The commons took no prominent part in the struggle, although it was a matter of intense importance to many poor people. Their inaction is the less remarkable if we remember the obstinate humility with which, during the Hundred Years' War, they constantly refused to express an opinion on the question of peace with France.

In the first quarter of the thirteenth century, it might have been thought that the Forest would be quickly reduced within reasonable limits. At first **Vicissitudes of the Forest in the 13th century** to cope with the pressing need of money, and afterwards to conciliate its enemies in very critical circumstances, the crown had made promises and had begun to execute them. But when Henry III came of age, a reaction set in, and disafforestment seemed so injurious to the royal finances that even some of the concessions that had been made were revoked.

The early history of disafforestment is lost in the night of time. It probably begins with the history of the Forest itself. In the Assize of Woodstock **Early disafforestments** Henry II speaks of "woods and other places disafforested by him and his ancestors."[1] It is clear that most of these ancient disafforestments had a financial motive. At all events, we know that Richard I had recourse to this method of

1. Art. 16; *Sel. Charters*, p. 188.

raising money[1] and that John followed his example. Roger of Wendover tells us that when Philip Augustus was conquering Normandy and Poitou, John, finding his subjects unwilling to follow him for the recovery of his lost heritage, oppressed them in a thousand ways.[2] The charter rolls prove that one of his devices for raising money was the surrender of parts of the Forest. We have a series of documents, dated March and May 1204, which disafforest the New Forest of Staffordshire, the Forest of Brewood in Shropshire, nearly all Cornwall and Devon, part of Essex, and other districts.[3] It is known that the *homines de Essexa* gave 500 marks for the disafforestments which were conceded to them,[4] and that, at the forest pleas of 1209, the inhabitants of Brewood Forest paid 100 marks to obtain the execution of the Charter of disafforestment granted in 1204.[5] During the crisis of 1215, three weeks before the granting of Magna Carta, when John was trying by a partial surrender to break up the coalition formed against him, he promised to abandon what remained of the Forest in Cornwall.[6] On the other hand, when Magna Carta was forced on him by the barons, he succeeded, as we have seen, in evading all compromising pledges on this subject.

Disafforestments of 1204

During the ten years after the death of John, Henry III's Council of Regency, having granted the Charter of the Forest, applied it faithfully, the articles on disafforestment included. They might have postponed the execution of these clauses, for it was a rule

Disafforestments during Henry III's minority

1. A reference in the pipe rolls of Richard I and the report of a perambulation made on 5 March, 1300, show that Richard at the beginning of his reign disafforested part of Surrey, and that in return the knights of that county gave him 300 marks. (The documents are published by Turner, pp. 117, 118, n. 1.)
2. Wendover in M. Paris, ed. cit. ii, 483.
3. *Rot. Chartarum* (ed. Hardy), pp. 122–3, 128, 132.
4. Round, *Forest of Essex, loc. cit.* pp. 40–1.
5. Turner, pp. 9, 10 n. 1.
6. See the charter of 22 April, 1215 (*Rot. Chart.,* p. 206).

of English law that a minor was not competent to make an irrevocable grant of land, and an ordinance of 1218 laid down that the young king could make no gift in perpetuity during his minority.[1] Now it was a considerable gift to surrender the forest rights of the crown over vast territories. Nevertheless, as early as 1218 and 1219, *perambulationes,* or *pourallées,* were instituted, in view of the impending disafforestments,[2] and others were set on foot when, on 11 February 1225, the Charter of the Forest was re-published. Some districts were certainly disafforested after these inquisitions, but there is little trace of their results.[3]

When on 9 January 1227, Henry III declared himself of age, did he intend, as Stubbs believes,[4] to revoke the Charter, or, at least, to demand money for executing the clauses concerning disafforestment? According to the narrative of Roger of Wendover, the earls who rebelled in July 1227, accused him of having "cancelled the charters of the liberties of the Forest."[5] In 1258 the "earls and barons" complained that he had "reafforested" woods and lands not contained within the bounds of the Forest : these woods and lands had been

Reaction when Henry came of age

Did Henry III revoke the Charter ?

1. G. J. Turner, *Minority of Henry III.,* in *Trans. Royal Hist. Soc., New Series,* xviii (1904), 280.   The ordinance is in Rymer, Record ed., i, pt. i, p. 152.

2. *Patent Rolls,* 1216-25, p. 162 : On 24 July, 1218, writs were sent to the sheriffs and letters-patent to John le Marshal, *capitalis iusticarius de Foresta Anglie,* commissioned to superintend the disafforestments in accordance with the charter ; see also (p. 178) the writ of 9 Nov., 1218, and (pp. 190 sqq., 193, 197 *et passim*) the letters of 1219 on disafforestments in various counties.

3. Turner, *Sel. Pleas,* pp. xciv sqq.   An extract from the pipe rolls (quoted *ibid.,* p. xcv, n. 8) proves that the cost of carrying out the disafforestments was borne by the inhabitants of the counties affected.

4. Stubbs, *Const. Hist.,* ii, 40.

5. "[Comites] addiderunt insuper, regi denuntiantes atrociter, ut cartas, quas nuper apud Oxoniam cancellaverat, de libertatibus forestae, sibi absque dilatione restitueret sigillatas.   Sin autem ipsi illum gladiis discurrentibus compellerent, ut sibi super his satisfaceret competenter.   Tunc rex statuit illis apud Norhamtonam tertio nonas Augusti diem, ut ibi faceret eis plenam rectitudinem exhiberi " (M. Paris, *ed. cit.,* iii. 125).

disafforested as a result of the " perambulation of good men " and in fulfilment of the promise made by the king[1] in return for the fifteenth of all the movable goods of his subjects. This complaint, which appears in the famous petition presented at the parliament of Oxford,[2] was well-founded, but it must not be thought that in 1227, as Wendover asserts, the Charter had been revoked.[3] What happened was this. In a certain number of counties, the knights charged with the perambulation had disafforested districts which had indeed been made forest by Henry II after his coronation, but which had already formed part of the Forest under Henry I, before the disafforestments of the reign of Stephen. Henry III considered that it was just to restore these districts to the Forest, and took measures accordingly.[4]

The explanation given by Stubbs, generally so accu-

1. The reference is to the confirmation of the Charter of the Forest dated 11 Feb., 1225. Henry explicitly stated that for this confirmation and that of the Great Charter his subjects had given him a fifteenth of their movable goods (see the document in Bémont, *Chartes*, p. 69, n. 5).

2. *Sel. Charters*, p. 374, art. 7.

3. Lingard (*History of England*, 6th ed., ii, 196, n. 3) and Pauli (*Geschichte von England*, ed. 1853, iii, 564, n. 3) observe that no document confirms this assertion and that some contradict it.

4. See the letters of the king to Henry de Neville, 9 Feb., 1227 : The knights charged with the perambulation in Leicestershire have admitted before the king " quod ipsi in perambulatione illa transgressi sunt, decepti ex eo quod breve nostrum de perambulatione illa facienda eis transmissum continebat quod ipsi deafforestarent omnes boscos quos H. rex avus noster afforestaverit, et non excepit eos qui ante tempus suum foresta fuerunt et quos ipse postea ad forestam revocavit ; unde credebant quod tam deafforestandi fuerunt bosci quos ipse ad forestam revocavit quam illi quos de novo afforestavit." There are similar letters concerning the perambulations in Rutland and Huntingdonshire (*Rot. Lit. Claus.*, ed. Hardy, ii, 169); also letters of 20 April, 1228, pardoning the knights charged with the perambulations in Lancashire, Staffordshire, Surrey, Salop, Northants, and Worcestershire, " qui recognoverunt quod ipsi in perambulatione illa erga nos per ignorantiam et errorem transgressi sunt" (*Pat. Rolls*, 1225-1232, p. 184). Cf. the similar letters for the commissioners in Yorkshire (*ibid.*, p. 225). It is significant that in 1220 the Council of Regency was already asking if the perambulation of the Forest between the Ouse and the Derwent could be accepted : " utrum perambulacio ipsius Foreste iuste facta fuerit" (*ibid.*, 1216-1226, 231). Doubts were also felt in 1226 (Turner, xcviii, n. 8).

rate, is therefore quite erroneous. He has confused—at

least by his method of stating them—facts belonging to different categories. In his eyes the revocation of the disafforestments in 1227 was " merely a means for raising money ; £100,000 was obtained by the repurchase of the grants imperilled ; a tallage was asked of the towns and demesne lands of the crown, and the charters remained in force." If reference be made to the authorities which he cites, neither those which relate to the confirmation of the concessions, nor those which concern the tallage, make any mention of disafforestment.

It is the more necessary to ascertain and remember the principle laid down by Henry III in 1227, because

his successors, Edward I in particular, appealed to it in their turn when defending the Forest. The Plantagenets, in short, claimed the right of keeping the districts which Henry I had afforested and which the weakness of Stephen had allowed to slip back for some years into the sphere of the common law. This claim was of doubtful validity. At his accession Stephen had solemnly renounced *all the forests made by Henry I,* and in article 1 of the Charter of 1217 it was simply said that the woods *afforested by Henry II* outside the demesne were to be disafforested. The opposition therefore had good grounds for arguing that the lands afforested under Henry I and disafforested under Stephen were no legal part of the Forest—those in the royal demesne excepted—and that lands disafforested by Stephen ought not to be retained in the Forest unless they had already belonged to it in the time of William Rufus. It is not certain, however, that the questions in dispute were so precisely stated, or that the validity of Stephen's charter was a subject of discussion.

At all events, the measures adopted by Henry III were regarded as a violation of the promises made in 1217.

Unpopularity of his action
When the limitation of an abuse has been granted, such vacillation in executing the reforms is not likely to be tolerated, whatever legal justification it may claim. Hence the indignation of the barons, whom Wendover represents as protesting, in July, 1227, against the abolition of the " Charters of the liberties of the Forest," demanding their restitution, and threatening the king with an appeal to arms. From this account, which is certainly inaccurate, nothing can be concluded except that the barons were annoyed at the announcement, made at the beginning of the year, that certain disafforestments were to be revoked. Henry may have given fair promises to appease them, but he none the less persisted in the resumption of districts which had been unduly disafforested.[1] Twenty years later this was still one of the complaints urged against him. At the Mad Parliament, as we have just said, the barons called upon him to surrender these districts once and for all. They complained also that the king had granted rights of warren on disafforested lands, maintaining that on these the chase should be free.[2] Their recriminations seem to have led to no result.

When Edward I came to the throne, articles 1 and 3 of the charter were still only in part carried out : the forests created since the accession of

The situation at Edward I's accession
Henry II had not all been disafforested.[3] Certain woods which ought to have been disafforested, say the people of Somerset in their complaints of 1279, remain in the Forest, " contrary to the Charter and to the grievance of the country."[4]

---

1. Turner, p. ci.   We have an example in the re-afforestation of Essex (Fisher, *Forest of Essex,* pp. 25 sqq.).
2. *Sel. Charters,* p. 374, arts. 7 and 9.
3. The only counties which had been entirely freed from the forest law by Henry III were Leicestershire and Sussex.   Middlesex may be added if we count the suppression of the warren of Staines (Turner, p. cvii).
4. Turner, p. 125.

In letters-patent of 1 March 1277,[1] as we have said above, Edward I announced his resolve to keep the

First perambulations of the reign

Charter of the Forest inviolably, and ordered an inquisition in the Forests south of the Trent. This inquisition was instituted not only to discover and repress abuses, but also to " make the perambulation," in obedience to the Charter. Nevertheless, the royal commissions and the juries were " to make a just perambulation, namely, that which was made in the time of the lord king Henry our father, which has not yet been impugned."[2] This clause meant that they had to limit themselves to decisions made by the commissioners of Henry III.[3] The king added that no executive measures were to be taken until reference had been made to him. In a word, he granted a perambulation, but he was resolved that the limits of the Forest should remain as they were fixed by his predecessor.

Edward's subjects refused to be satisfied with this illusory concession. The perambulations of Exmoor Forest, published by Mr. Greswell in an English translation, show that the struggle for disafforestment was already beginning to be waged between Edward and his people. In 1279 the jurors strove to prove that a large district, comprising at least half of this forest, ought to be disafforested. They alleged that this region had been included in the Forest by John, surrendered by Henry III, " when a fifteenth of the movable goods of all England was given him,"[4] and again afforested by the

---

1. *C.P.R.*, 1272–81, i, 237. One of these letters has been published in the Introduction to the *Select Pleas* (p. cii). Mr. Turner has not stated whether the inquisition led to any definite result, nor has he mentioned the very typical perambulations of the Forest of Exmoor, which are well worth publishing in their original text.

2. " . . . ut fiat perambulacio recta, illa scilicet que facta fuit tempore domini Henrici regis patris nostri, que nondum calumpniata fuit."

3. This is proved by a document cited by Greswell, *Forests of Somerset,* p. 275.

4. In 1225 ; see above, p. 215.

forester-in-fee, Richard de Wrotham, " to the great damage of the whole country and without profit to the king."
A second perambulation made in the same year by
another jury curtailed still further the part which the
king had a right to keep.   There is decisive documen-
tary evidence that Edward I retained Exmoor Forest in
its full extent.[1]   Throughout his life he was to play the
same game of granting and then taking back.   It is perhaps in this quarrel about disafforestment that his lean-
ing towards chicane and subterfuge appears most clearly.

In 1297 the departure of the king for Flanders left the
field clear for the opposition.   Like the Council which

Perambulations
authorised
by the regency
in 1297

had governed during the minority of
Henry III, the regents who were at the
head of affairs during Edward's absence
adopted a conciliatory policy.   Some days
after the grant of the *Confirmatio Cartarum,* and even
before it was ratified by the king, the regency ordered
perambulations to be made,[2] and it is at least certain that
they were carried out in Hampshire and Somerset.   Mr.
Greswell has published the record of the perambulations
made, in March and May, 1298, in the Somersetshire
forests of Selwood, Neroche, and Mendip.[3]   But just at
this moment Edward came back to England determined
on resistance.   Then began the great battle for disafforestment.

1. Greswell, *Forests of Somerset,* pp. 171 sqq.   See the map, p. 176.
Mr. Greswell is not sure that the perambulations of 1279 were not put
into effect : but the documents which he publishes on pp. 176–9 (perambulation of 1298) and pp. 199 sqq. (seizure of the wood of Dulverton in 1291)
prove clearly that they never were.—In 1280 Edward I disafforested Northumberland, but only in consideration of an annual rent of forty pounds
(Turner, p. cviii).   In 1300 this county appears among those which have
no forest (*Parl. Writs,* i, 91).

2. In the first instance, in the letters-patent of 16 Oct., 1297 (*C.P.R.*,
1292–1301, p. 312) the regent copied the wording of the letters of
1 March, 1277, which we have cited above, including the limitation of
the commissioners to the " perambulacio recta ;" but this restriction was
afterwards withdrawn.   See Turner, p. ciii.

3. *Op. cit.,* App. B, pp. 265 sqq.   The unpublished perambulation of
Hampshire is referred to by Turner, p. ciii, n. 6.

At Whitsuntide 1298, Edward's opponents, led by the earls of Norfolk and Hereford, demanded a new con-

The king's return

firmation of the charters and a general de-limitation of the Forest.[1] Now that the king was back, they expected that everything would have to be done over again. Edward justified their mistrust. First, he asked for time. Then, on 18 November, he appointed a commission, consisting of three bishops, two earls, and two knights, " to investigate and examine " the misdeeds of justices, foresters, verderers, and other officers of the forests throughout the realm. But nothing was said in the writ about dis-afforestment.[2] Next year, after much ter-

He pretends to yield

giversation, he appeared to be giving way before the threat of civil war,[3] and on 2 April he commanded the sheriffs[4] to enforce the observance of the Great Charter and the Charter of the Forest, the latter " according to the articles written below " : a copy of the charter was annexed, from which the articles regarding disafforestment were omitted.

His reservations

Edward added, it is true, that he wished the perambulation to be made, but *saving his oath and the rights of his crown,* and he intended to have the report of the commissioners submitted to him before any part of the Forest was surrendered. Finally, he asked for a further postponement of the perambulation : it should be made as soon as possible, when once he had completed the negotiations with the envoys who would shortly arrive from Rome on business which concerned all Christendom—namely, the Crusade.

These reservations and dilatory measures aroused an indignation which alarmed him. He gave way, as he

1. Blackstone, *Magna Carta,* Introd., p. lxviii. 2. *Parl. Writs,* i, 397. 3. At the Parliament of 8 March, 1299. Cf. Bémont, *Introd.,* pp. xliv sqq.
4. In the instructions, inserted in the statute rolls, which are known as the *Statutum de finibus levatis* (*Statutes,* i, 126 sqq.). See the passages cited by Bémont (p. lxv, n. 2) and Stubbs, *Const. Hist.,* ii, 154, n. 4.

Anger of the barons. Parliament of May, 1299 always did when he feared a complete breach with his subjects. On 3 May, he again called together the barons and prelates, whom he had just dismissed, and this time, according to a chronicler, he granted " everything " and pledged himself afresh to initiate a perambulation.[1] On 25 June, in a proclamation to his subjects, he complained of being so hardly pressed; he had to deal with urgent matters which would occupy him till the middle of July; the perambulation, moreover, could scarcely be made at the time of harvest; his people ought not to believe malicious reports, circulated to sow dissension between the king and his subjects; he promised that the commissioners for the perambulation should meet in Northampton at Michaelmas.[2] And on 23 September he did in fact nominate five of his most experienced judges, Roger de Brabazon, John de Berwick, Ralph de Hingham, William Inge, and John de Croxley,

Perambulation of 1299-1300 who during the winter were to make the perambulation in Northants, Huntingdonshire, Rutland, Oxfordshire, and Surrey.[3] The evidence of the juries appears to have been honestly given, and conscientiously recorded by the commission.[4]

Nevertheless, king and nation still distrusted each other, as is shown by the articles published after the Parliament of March, 1300. The king

Parliament of March, 1300 was forced to recognise that, for want of special safeguards, the charters had never been faithfully observed by the royal officials, and a demand was made for the appointment of elective commissions similar to those which had been forced on King

1. Trivet, *Annales,* ed. Hog, pp. 375–6.
2. *C.P.R.,* 1292–1301, p. 424; Blackstone, *op. cit.* p. lxix.
3. Turner, p. civ; the report of the perambulation in Rutland (7 Dec., 1299) is to be found on pp. 116–117; that for Surrey (5 March, 1300) on pp. 117–118.
4. In Rutland the jurors mentioned a district afforested by John. In Surrey they declared that they knew of no afforestment made since the accession of Henry II.

John. Though at heart determined to surrender nothing of his prerogative, Edward pretended to yield. In the *Articuli super Cartas,* he declared that the Charter of the Forest, as well as the Great Charter, ought to be kept, observed, and maintained in full, and read in every county four times a year; neither had " been kept or observed heretofore, because no penalties were hitherto established for offenders against the points of the aforesaid charters "; in future, therefore, every county should elect " three good men, knights or others, loyal, wise, and discreet, who shall be sworn as justices and commissioned by the king's letters patent under his great seal " to hear and determine, without delay, complaints against those who violate the two charters, and even to punish the guilty " by imprisonment, ransom, or amercement."[1] As early as 27 March writs were sent ordering the elections to be made,[2] and on 10 May Edward invested the commissioners with the powers specified in the *Articuli.*[3]

The "Articuli super Cartas"

It seems improbable that these commissioners were of much use, for it was laid down, both in the *Articuli* and in the writ of 10 May, that they were not to hold pleas " in cases where aforetime remedy was provided by writ according to the common law." It was contrary to the king's wishes " that prejudice should be caused to the common law, or to the aforesaid charters in any of their points." The commissioners were thus forewarned that they would run grave risk of committing illegalities and displeasing the king if they tried to perform their duties. The *Articuli,* moreover, ended with the inevitable reser-

The king still reserves his rights

1. *Articuli super cartas* (Bémont, pp. 99 sqq.).
2. Blackstone, *op. cit.* p. lxx.
3. *Parl. Writs,* i, 398 sqq. These writs were addressed to commissions of three in thirty-six counties. They concern the enforcement both of Magna Carta and the Charter of the Forest, and of the Statute of Winchester for the conservation of the peace. Among these thirty-six counties appears Kent, where there was no forest.

vation : " In all and each of the aforesaid matters, it is the will and intention of the king and of his council and of all those present when this ordinance was made, that the right and lordship of the crown shall be entirely preserved."

It was in the same spirit of pettifogging resistance that, on 1 April of the same year, the king appointed six new commissions to make perambula-
Perambulations of 1300 tions in eighteen counties. He still re-
served the rights of the crown, and he ordered Hugh le Despenser and Robert de Clifford, the two justices of the Forest, to be present at the perambulations in their respective jurisdictions, or to send a deputy : it was his wish that all the foresters-in-fee and verderers should be summoned, and everybody who could help in ascertaining the truth.[1] The commissioners no doubt understood what the king expected of them. The juries, however, did not allow themselves to be intimidated : so at least we can infer from the report of the perambulation in Warwickshire, where the jurors declared that there was no forest in the county at the accession of Henry II, and that the forests had been made by John, to the injury of the landholders.[2]

Edward was now reduced to the necessity of either accepting the result of these inquisitions, with the financial disasters that would follow, or run-
The king's attitude ning the risk of a complete breach with the opposition, now led with no little courage by Archbishop Winchelsey. Did the king really believe that he was being wronged, and that by his resistance he was upholding his rights? In this year 1300, after his recent experience of what had happened at the inquisitions, he was, we think, sincere. The assertions of the juries, it seemed to him, were based simply on " the

1. *Parl. Writs,* i, 397–8.
2. Perambulation of 29 June, 1300 (Turner, pp. 120–1).

common report of the country."[1]   It is indeed evident
that the imagination of the people, exasperated by the
rigour of the forest administration, had given birth to
legends. Unlikely misdeeds were attributed, for instance, to the wicked King John : the jurors of Somerset
affirmed that he had " afforested the whole of England."[2]
Was Edward, on the strength of traditions that were
often doubtful, to surrender part of his heritage ? Six
centuries later, and filled with the philanthropic notions
of to-day, we are apt to think that so great a king ought
to have suppressed so evil a system, or at all events, to
have loosened his grip and allowed the commissioners
to confine the evil within narrow limits.   But Edward
kept in mind his coronation oath, the solemn pledge
which he had given before God, that he would alienate
neither the rights nor the property of the crown.

Such was his attitude of mind when on 26 September
he summoned a parliament to meet at Lincoln on 20
January.   In the writs of summons he
Parliament   stated that he needed the advice of his
of Lincoln,   magnates and the commonalty of the realm,
Jan., 1301   in order that he might take counsel on the
reports of the commissions of disafforestment.[3] His intention was to transfer all responsibility to those who
demanded the acceptance of the findings of the inquisition.   Without doubt he was actuated simultaneously by
a conscientious scruple and a secret hope that he might
lead his subjects to think twice before taking action.
But the magnates, asked to declare that by confirming
the perambulations the king would not injure the crown
or violate his oath, refused to reply on this point, and
demanded immediate disafforestments.   All the records

1. Perambulation of 29 June, 1300 : " Iurati quesiti qualiter constat eis
quod predictus dominus Iohannes rex afforestaverit omnia maneria, villas
et hameletta predicta, dicunt quod ex relatu antecessorum suorum et per
commune dictum patrie " (Turner, p. 121).
2. " . . . quando afforestavit totam Angliam " (Turner, p. cii, n.).
3. *Parl. Writs,* i, 89.   See the detailed account in Stubbs, *Const. Hist.,*
ii, 156 sqq.

give the impression that the debate was very violent. Edward tried to indicate how seriously his dignity had been insulted by the " bill " of twelve articles which was addressed to him, and imprisoned the knight who had presented it : " those who brought us the bill from the Archbishop of Canterbury and from the others who unwarrantably importuned us at the Parliament of Lincoln," were the words he used in the writ ordering the imprisonment.[1] Nevertheless he gave way,
The king compelled to yield confirmed the Charter of the Forest, together with Magna Carta,[2] and granted the request that he should issue letters patent ratifying the disafforestments suggested in the reports of the perambulations.[3] But he had already shown that only force would make him yield.[4]

He waited till 1305 before freeing himself from engagements which in his eyes had no validity. He needed the support of the Holy See : and the election of the weak Clement V.[5] favoured his designs.

In 1305 Edward issued an Ordinance of the Forest, in which he did indeed recognise the disafforestments that had been carried out. But he was evidently in no gracious temper. He confirmed persons " put outside the Forest " in the right of being free from all " the things which the
The Ordinance of 1305

1. " Celi qui nous porta la bille de par l'ercevesqe de Cantebiris et de par les autres *qui nous presserent outraiousement* au parlement de Nichole." The document is quoted in Stubbs, *Const. Hist.*, ii. 158, n. 1. Cf. Rishanger, ed. Riley (R.S.), p. 198: " Rex . . . parliamentum tenuit Stamfordiae [*sic*], ad quod convenerunt comites et barones, cum equis et armis, eo, prout dicebatur, proposito, ut executionem Chartae de Foresta hactenus dilatam extorquerent ad plenum. Rex autem, eorum instantiam et importunitatem attendens, eorum voluntati in omnibus condescendit." See also *Flores Historiarum*, ed. Luard (R.S.), iii. 303.

2. Letters-patent of 14 Feb., 1301 (Bémont, p. 109).

3. Turner, p. cv, n. 3 ; Blackstone, *Magna Carta*, p. lxxii.

4. In letters-patent of 14 Oct., 1301, nominating commissioners to make a perambulation in the forests of Devon, Edward again inserted a reservation of the rights of the crown (*C.P.R.*, 1292-1301, p. 607).

5. Bertrand de Got, who became pope under this name, was archbishop of Bordeaux, and thus one of Edward's subjects. On his relations with Edward see W. W. Capes, *The English Church in the Fourteenth and Fifteenth Centuries*, pp. 38 sqq.

foresters demand of them," but denied to them, in their new state, the privilege " of having common within the bounds of the forests " : finally he was resolved to keep all his demesne in " the state of free chase and of free warren," so that in practice the inhabitants of disafforested lands on the royal demesne gained next to nothing by the change.[1] At the same time he was pressing on his negotiations with Rome, and on 20 December the pope published the desired bull.

In the preamble, Clement V. recalled the conspiracy formed in 1297, during the king's absence, to force him to make certain unjust concessions regarding " the forests and other rights which concerned the crown and the honour of his authority." The king's enemies had stirred up the people and sown scandal : he had been obliged to yield, and on his return he had again been forced, " by importunity and presumptuous instance," to renew his concessions. Now these tended to the injury of the royal prerogative, and the king's promises were incompatible with his pledge, given at his coronation, that he would defend the honour and rights of the crown. The pope therefore revoked and annulled the concessions absolutely, and forbade the English clergy to do anything contrary to this revocation. He added, however, that the rights of the English people should remain exactly as they had been before the concessions in question were extorted from the king.[2]

Clement V's bull, 20 Dec., 1305

A little later, in the Ordinance of the Forest of 27 May, 1306, the king on his part declared the disafforestments to be null and void : he had not granted them of his free will, and the sovereign pontiff had cancelled them.[3] At the same time, he obtained from the pope the suspension of Archbishop Winchelsey.

Ordinance of the Forest, May, 1306

1. *Statutes,* i, 144.   2. Bémont, pp. 110 sqq.
3. *Statutes,* i, 149.   The passage is quoted in Stubbs, *Const. Hist.,* ii, 162, n. 2.

In the same Ordinance of 1306, the king admitted that the misdeeds of the foresters had not ceased. " By

The existence of abuses admitted by Edward

the reports of our subjects and the frequent complaints of those oppressed, whereby our mind is sensibly moved and troubled, we have learned that the people of the realm are miserably oppressed by the officers of our forests." He declared that correct legal procedure was not observed; accusations were presented, not by the " good men " of the country, but by one or two foresters or verderers, and the innocent were condemned. He ordered that the regular procedure should be followed, that the juries of presentment should not consist of officials, and that oppressive and corrupt foresters should be punished.[1]

Edward I recognised the evil and promised mere palliatives. The opposition had demanded a potent remedy in vain. Their long struggle seemed to have ended in defeat.[2]

The extravagant, unsystematic, and oppressive rule of Edward II and his favourites was naturally by no means

The question of disafforestment under Edward II

beneficial to the inhabitants of the Forest. Gaveston regarded it merely as a field for profitable speculations in the leasing of land.[3] The question of the Forest was not raised again until the opposition took concerted action and imposed reforms on Edward. Then, as before, it was the barons who led the movement.[4] In the famous

1. *Statutes,* i, 147 sqq. There was no real jury of presentment for forest offences. See above, p. 163.

2. It has sometimes been questioned whether the disafforestments were really annulled. There is, however, no doubt of it. At the Parliament of 1316 the lords and commons asserted that the perambulations of Edward I had not been put into effect : "Perambulationes ille non sunt hiis diebus observate." (*Parl. Writs,* ii, pt. 2, 159).

3. By letters-patent of 11 Dec., 1310, he was authorised to enclose and let certain estates in the Forest (*C.P.R.,* 1307–13, p. 295).

4. There is nothing about the Forest in the eleven articles presented in 1309, which, as Stubbs says (*Const. Hist.,* ii. 339), represent in particular the wishes of the commons (*Rot. Parl.* i, 443 sqq.). Nothing more can be inferred than that the commons did not venture to touch upon the question of the Forest.

Ordinances of 1311, the twenty-one bishops, earls and barons who drew them up denounced the illegalities committed by the forest officials, and tried to put an end to them. The authorised procedure for the punishment of criminals was, they said, continually violated by " the wardens of the forests on this side Trent and beyond, and by other ministers"; the innocent were condemned, and the people dared not complain : all the officials of the Forest were, therefore, suspended from their functions, and all complaints against them might be brought before commissioners, "good and loyal men," who should be empowered to hear and determine them before the following Easter : and guilty officers should be permanently removed from their posts. As for the future, the officials were ordered to act in strict conformity with the rules laid down in the Charter of the Forest and in the Ordinance of 1306. Nothing was said about perambulations, but it was ordered that the charter should be observed " in all points."[1]

The Ordinances of 1311

Edward II, of course, refused for some years to give effect to the Ordinances, which had been won from him by force. The " two French jurists " commissioned to prove their illegality, went so far as to affirm that "they were in almost all points contrary to the Great Charter and the Charter of the Forest, to which no prejudice might be done, because this would be contrary to the oath taken by the king at his coronation."[2]

The king's resistance

One of those who urged the king to resistance was Hugh le Despenser the elder, who had been justice of the Forest under Edward I, and who had obtained from the pope the bull of 1305.[3] As a result of the parliament which sat from January to March, 1315, Hugh le

1. *Statutes,* i. 160-1 ; *Rot. Parl.,* i. 282-3.
2. See the text of the *Objections* in the *Annales Londinienses* (Chronicles of Edward I nd Edward II, ed. Stubbs, i. 212).
3. See above, p. 223 ; and Stubbs, *Const. Hist.,* ii, 352, 355.

Despenser had to resign his seat on the council,[1] and
Edward II, yielding to a request of the commons, made
proclamation in every county that he proposed to enforce
the Charter of the Forest and the findings of the perambulations, and that he had appointed commissioners to
this end.[2] The king probably forgot his pledges, for
various people refused to pay the twentieth granted by
parliament in return for the promised reforms, declaring
that the king should have had the Charters and
Ordinances executed, besides instituting new perambulations, and that he had done none of these things.[3]

Finally, at the parliament which was held in January,
1316, at Lincoln—a notable place in the history of the
Forest—the opposition party among the
nobles seized control of the government,
and the work of disafforestment was resumed.

The
parliament
of 1316

It is proved by letters patent sent to the sheriffs on 20
February that the triumphant party had determined to
put an end to the conflict, and to execute
the promises of the Charter of 1217,
though not to go beyond them. The prelates, earls, barons, and commons had
declared that the perambulations of the time of Edward
I had not been put into effect, and the king had agreed
that they should be. Nevertheless, the royal council was
to investigate the matter thoroughly.[4] The foresters-in-
fee were summoned to give evidence. All official documents likely to furnish clear information were to be
produced.

Disafforestment
entrusted to
the Council

There was no intention of departing from the lines of
policy laid down by Henry III and Edward I : neither

1. Stubbs, *Const. Hist.,* ii, p. 355.
2. The writ was dated 20 April, 1315 (*C.C.R.,* 1313–18, p. 224).
3. We know of this resistance to the tax from the royal protest of
8 June, 1315 (*C.P.R.,* 1313–17, p. 324).
4. It will be remembered that parliament had just given extraordinary
powers to the council and had appointed as president Thomas of Lancaster, the leader of the opposition.

the forests in the royal demesne, nor those which existed before the reign of Henry II, were to be disafforested; and, if necessary, the results of the perambulations under Edward I were to be revised according to this principle. The final word would rest with the council : and every county court was to elect two knights, who within the fortnight after Easter should appear before the council, empowered to consent, on behalf of the community of the shire, to whatever the council might ordain regarding the limits of the Forest.[1]

There is strong reason to doubt whether the delimitation of the forests was carried out in the way indicated by this writ, and whether the aristocratic government of Thomas of Lancaster fulfilled promises which the crown had succeeded in evading for a century. The first article of the second statute of Edward III, which enjoins the execution and completion of the perambulations made under Edward I, would have been differently worded if the bounds of the Forest had been definitively fixed by Edward II.[2] It seems certain that the indolent Thomas of Lancaster lacked the consistency of purpose necessary to carry out the laborious inquisition initiated by the writ of 1316,[3] that partial results were indeed attained,[4] but that the monarchical reaction of 1322 brought the process of disafforestment to a stand. Letters close, addressed in 1323 to Aymer of Valence, Earl of Pembroke, Justice of the Forest south of the Trent, ordered him to restore to the Forest all the woods of the royal demesne which

Lack of substantial results

1. *Parl. Writs*, ii, pt. 2, pp. 158–9.
2. " Et qe la puralée qui estoit chivauché en temps le roi Edward, ael le roi q'or est, se tiegne en la forme q'ele estoit chivachée et bundée ; e qe sur ceo soit chartre faite a chescun countée ou ele fust chivaché. Et par la ou ele ne feust my chivachée, le roi voet q'ele soit chivauché par bons et loialx e qe chartre sur ce soit faite come desus est dit" (*Statutes*, i. 255).
3. See the letters patent of 21 Nov., 1318, which show that the commissioners entrusted with the perambulation in Devonshire had done nothing (*C.P.R.*, 1317–21, p. 240).
4. It was officially stated, in letters patent of 1341 that the Forest of Dean was reduced by a quarter under Edward II (*C.P.R.*, 1340-43, pp. 190 sqq.).

had belonged to it at the date of the issue of the Charter, and which had been disafforested by the perambulations made during the reigns of Edward I and the present king.[1] We have here, it is true, the principle laid down in the writ of 1316, but effect was given only to the restrictions of this writ and not to its promise that all lands should be disafforested which ought to be. Edward was trying, in fact, by a revision of the concessions, to diminish their value.

It is not surprising that after dethroning Edward II Isabella and Mortimer should have sought to make themselves popular by a complete change of policy. In the statute of 1327, to which reference was made above, they say nothing of any work that may have been accomplished by the council of 1316, and pass over in silence Edward I's repudiation of his promises. They declare that the Charter of the Forest is to be kept in all points; that the perambulations made under Edward I are to hold good, and that others are to be set on foot in counties where none have as yet been made; so that every county containing a forest is to have a charter declaring its limits.[2] Three years later, on 12 July, 1330, Edward III warned the Justice of the Forest south of the Trent not to allow regarders and verderers to charge with offences against the vert and the venison those who dwell in districts disafforested by the perambulations under Edward I and Edward II: these perambulations were to be strictly observed.[3]

Policy of Isabella and Mortimer

---

1. The document is dated 18 March, 1323 (*C.C.R.*, 1318–1323, p. 634).
2. *Statutes,* i. 255, art. i, quoted above; cf. the letters patent of 13 March, 1327 (*C.P.R.*, 1327–30, p. 39) and the letters close of 10 May, 1327 (*C.C.R.*, 1327–30, p. 124).   The inhabitants of Surrey demanded a perambulation : their request was granted, and on 26 Dec., 1327, Edward III entirely disafforested the county; afterwards, on 4 Aug., 1333, he went back on this concession and declared that there had been a mistake.   His good faith cannot be questioned, since in 1300 the jurors had declared that the afforestments in this county were made before the reign of Henry II (*Select Pleas,* pp. 117–8; *Introd.,* p. cvi).
3. *C.C.R.*, 1330-33, p. 147.

We think, therefore, that if a precise date is to be assigned to the end of the long struggle for disafforestment, it is not the reign of Edward II, but **The question settled** the beginning of the reign of Edward III that must be chosen. In later times, notably in 1347 and during the first years of the reign of Richard II, the commons are found complaining because the royal officers "of their malice have afforested, and strive from day to day to afforest, what had been disafforested," and the king replies that he wishes the Charter to be respected.[1] Officially, as the records of these incidents prove, the dispute was settled.

1. *Rot. Parl.*, ii, 169b, 388a; iii, 18a; cf. ii, 311b, 335a, 367b; iii, 62a, 116a. In 1376 the king even replied that he would order a " chivachiée," that is to say, a perambulation to fix the disputed boundaries.

7

SOME REMARKS ON THE ORIGIN OF THE PURLIEU.

Whatever date historians choose to mark the actual accomplishment of the disafforestments, they are **The purlieu** generally agreed that from this time begins the institution of the *purlieu*—that is to say, the disafforested districts were subjected to a special code of law for the protection of the beasts of the Forest. The inhabitants of these districts might hunt only on certain conditions, and they were under the oversight of special officers called " rangers " (*rangiatores, rengiarii*).[1]

On this subject I wish to limit myself to two remarks : (1) The institution of the purlieu was not established at the time of the great disafforesting perambulations;[2] and (2) the laws of the purlieu were not, for the most part, peculiar to the disafforested districts of England.

The fourth and sixteenth articles of the Assize of Woodstock prove clearly that in the time of Henry II **Articles 4 and 16 of Henry II's Assize** there already existed a sphere in which the king's venison had its "peace," but which was outside the Forest properly so called, where the vert also was protected by special laws and under the surveillance of the regarders. This sphere was under the oversight of foresters ; and if the land did not form part of the royal demesne, the owner had to appoint a forester pledged by oath to pro-

---

1. See Manwood, *Treatise of the Lawes of the Forrest,* chap. 20.
2. We are speaking of the institution, the laws of the purlieu, not of the word itself, for this (under the forms poralée, pouralé, puralé) appears in the rolls of parliament as early as the fourteenth century. From this time *Poralée,* the French word for *perambulatio*—an inquisition for the delimitation of the Forest—acquired also the meaning of a disafforested region.

tect the king's beasts.[1]   Article 16 prescribes a severe punishment—a year's imprisonment and fine at the king's mercy—for those who hunt by night, not only in the Forest, but also in those regions outside the Forest where the king's venison has its peace.   The same penalty was imposed on whosoever should make " a *forstallatio,* living or dead, for the king's beasts, between his Forest and the woods or other places disafforested by him or his ancestors." [2]   That is to say, it was unlawful to use obstacles or beaters on the borders of disafforested land to prevent game from taking refuge in what was left of the Forest.

In the time of Henry II, then, there were (1) lands outside, but of course near the Forest, where the king's beasts had their " peace " and where poaching by night was as severely punished as when it was practised in the Forest; (2) disafforested lands, adjoining the Forest, where it was permissible to hunt by day, but where it was contrary to law to hinder beasts that were making for the shelter of the Forest.

Nothing more is known.   We cannot say whether the first class of protected lands was the outcome of disafforestment, or whether it had been instituted round certain forests to prevent the destruction of game that wandered beyond their limits.   In any case, however, it is evident that the twelfth century kings strove to maintain control over lands adjoining the Forest; and that two of the rules afterwards imposed on the inhabitants of the purlieu—those against hunting at night and

1. " Et illi qui extra metas reguardi boscos habeant in quibus venatio domini regis pacem habet, nullum forestarium habeant, nisi assisam domini regis iuraverint et pacem venationis suae, et custodem aliquem ad boscum eius custodiendum " (*Sel. Charters,* p. 187, art. 4).

2. " Item rex praecipit quod nullus de cetero chaceat ullo modo ad capiendas feras per noctem infra forestam neque extra, ubicunque ferae suae frequentant vel pacem habent aut habere consueverunt, sub poena imprisonamenti unius anni et faciendo finem et redemptionem ad voluntatem suam, et quod nullus sub eadem poena faciat aliquam forstallationem feris suis vivam vel mortuam inter forestam suam et boscos vel alia loca per ipsum vel progenitores suos deafforestatos " (Art. 16 : *Sel. Charters,* p. 188).

The right of the
chase in lands
disafforested
during the 13th
century
hindering the game from entering the
Forest—were already in existence under
Henry II.[1] It might be thought that the
kings of the thirteenth century, who
carried out or promised much disafforestment, would have quickly completed the system which
had already been outlined. This, however, was not the
case. It seems that two opinions were held, one assign-
ing the right of free chase to the inhabitants of disafforested regions, the other giving to the king the
power of disposing as he would of all game found in
them : and the kings halted between them. John
seems to have acted on no fixed principle. In his
charters of disafforestment he sometimes stipulated that
the inhabitants of the disafforested country might hunt
every kind of game on it, sometimes he said nothing on
the point.[2] Henry III made warrens on disafforested
land for the benefit of his favourites, and in 1258 the
barons protested, asserting the principle that the chase
was free in disafforested country.[3] Even Edward I,
with his zeal for making laws, established no rules for

Edward I did
not establish
the purlieu
the purlieu, doubtless because he always
had the secret intention of taking back the
disafforested lands. In his ordinance of
1305 he confirmed the principle that per-
sons " put outside the Forest " ought to be free from all
" the things which the foresters demand of them," and in
regard to the venison, he merely specified that he intended to reserve for himself all the hunting in lands
which were part of the royal demesne.[4]

1. On these rules see Manwood, *loc. cit.*, and Fisher, *Forest of Essex*,
p. 167.
2. See the authorities cited above, p. 155, n. 5.
3. See the petition of the barons at the parliament of Oxford, art. 9 :
" Item petunt remedium quod forestae deafforestatae (*sic*) per cartam regis
et per fidem eidem per communitatem totius regni factam, ita quod
quisque ubique possit libere fugare, dominus rex de voluntate sua pluribus
dedit de predicta libertate warennas, quae sunt ad nocumentum praedictae
libertatis concessae " (*Sel. Charters*, p. 374).
4. *Statutes*, i, 144.

The measures taken by Edward II's council, when they wished to carry out the disafforestments, seem equally to prove that at this time there was no intention of establishing in the disafforested districts any extraordinary jurisdiction to protect the king's venison. The ancient Assize of Woodstock, which they need only have applied to the new situation, was apparently forgotten. Only one method of ensuring the peace of the game seems to have been thought of—namely, to get it back into the Forest. By two writs of 5 August 1316, the king ordered the Justice of the Forest south of the Trent to drive the game of the disafforested regions into the Forest within forty days, and reserved to himself, during this time, the right of hunting in the aforesaid districts.[1] It was no doubt hoped that when once restored to the Forest the game might be kept there, and it was perhaps now that with this end in view the authorities began to appoint, in certain forests, a special class of foresters called *rangiatores*.[2] Naturally, however, it was impossible to prevent the game from straying, and the forest officials soon took to prosecuting those who hunted beasts that had wandered into the purlieu. In 1372, 1376 and 1377 parliament protested, and demanded "that every man might hunt in the purlieu without hindrance." The king each time replied that the Charter of the Forest should be observed, an answer which meant nothing, since the charter made

Measures of 1316 to keep the game in the Forest

Possible origin of the rangers

1. *C.P.R.*, 1313–17, p. 532; cf. the letters of Edward III (26 Dec.. 1327) cited by Manwood (chap. 20).

2. In the seventeenth century the ranger undertook in his oath to drive back to the Forest all beasts which left it for the purlieu (*Book of Oaths*, 1649, cited by Fisher, *Forest of Essex*, p. 166). Mr. Turner quotes a document of the twelfth year of Edward III where mention is made of a person " nuper rengiarius " of the Forest of Braden (*Select Pleas*, p. xxv, n. 3). He states, however, that he has rarely found references to rangers in the fourteenth century. Mr. Fisher has discovered none in Essex before 1489. Manwood (chap. 20, § 13) gives no precise information about the institution of these officers.

no provision for such cases.[1] All these incidents show
that the kings of the fourteenth century were anxious to
secure their venison from any harm with which the disafforestments might threaten it, but they also show that
no fixed rules and no administrative system had as yet
been set up for the purlieu.

Gradually fixed rules arose : but they were neither
peculiar to the purlieu nor new. As we have seen, the

The rules of
the purlieu not
peculiar
to England

laws against hunting by night and *forstallatio* are already to be found in the
Assize of Woodstock. In order to enjoy
the right of the chase, the inhabitants of
the purlieu had to possess no other qualifications than
those demanded by the Ordinance of Richard II from
every sportsman in the country.[2] Moreover, the restrictions placed on their hunting were no more severe than
those which had to be observed in France by the lords
of lands adjacent to royal forests : they were even less so.
In France, no one might hunt deer or other large game
within a tract two leagues[3] broad around the royal
forests,[4] and in some districts the woods in this zone
might not be sold except by permission of the king.[5]

In a word, then, the institution of the purlieu was
established in England at the very end of the Middle
Ages, but the germs of it already existed before the

1. *Rot. Parl.,* ii, 313, 368 ; iii, 18.
2. See below, pp. 247 sqq.
3. Cf. the *distancia duarum leucarum* in the passage cited above, p. 190,
n. 3.
4. See in the *Ordonnances,* v, 210 sqq., a very interesting dispute concerning the hunting-rights of the bishop of Albi, whose sport had been
interfered with by the king's officers in forests " a Forestis regis per
duas leucas vel circa distancium." In 1368 the Master of Waters and
Forests for the sénéchaussée of Toulouse confirmed the hunting-rights of
the bishop in these forests, and authorised him, for special reasons, to
hunt in a forest which he possessed within a distance of two leagues from
the royal Forest. Cf. the great "Ordonnance des Eaux et Forêts " issued
by Louis XIV in 1669, titre xxx, art. 14.
5. In 1232 the *bailli* of the Gâtinais held an inquisition to discover
whether " boscus Brissi, qui distat a foresta domini regis per unam leucam
vel circiter, qui est domini Brixiacensis . . . potest vendi sine licentia
domini regis." (The document is published by L. Delisle : *Historiens de
France,* xxiv, pt. i, p. 298*, no. 98).

thirteenth century, and the kings of France, on their side, had instituted a sort of purlieu around their forests.

Theory of the French origin of the purlieu It seems possible that the English purlieu and the analogous institution in France had a common origin in a Norman custom. According to a petition addressed to Lous IX. by Henri d'Avaugour, Philip Augustus had confiscated a *haie*,[1] situated in the *bailliage* of Verneuil, because in this *haie* the huntsmen of the Lord of Laigle had hunted game which had come from the royal forest of Evreux, even following it into the forest. The confiscation had been made on the report of the king's huntsman, Roger de Bémécourt, a Norman knight.[2] Philip Augustus no doubt had precedents for his action : and it is not un-reasonable to suppose that the powerful dukes of Nor-mandy had created round their forests a protected zone, and that the rules on this subject in the Assize of Wood-stock date from a time before the Conquest. Perhaps, indeed, they were known as far back as the Carolingian period.[3]

1. A *haie* was an enclosed hunting-preserve [corresponding, therefore, to the English " park "] It appears that this particular *haie* was not entirely enclosed.

2. *Querimonia Henrici de Avaugor* (A.D. 1247), in *Historiens de France,* xxiv, pt. ii, p. 730.

3. See the charter of 26 March, 800, by which Charles the Great allows the abbot and monks of St. Bertin to send their men to hunt in the abbey woods, " in eorum proprias silvas," in order to provide the house with skins and leather, on condition, however, that the forests of the king be respected : " salvas forestes nostras, quas ad opus nostrum constitutas habemus " (*Monum. Germ., Diplom. Karolin.*, vol. i, p. 256, no. 191). It was perhaps because their woods were near a royal forest that the monks of St. Bertin needed this special permission.

8

THE DECLINE OF THE FOREST. CONTRARY DEVELOPMENT IN FRANCE.

We cannot undertake to pursue further the history of the English Forest,[1] and shall be content with explain-

Lack of evidence

ing, in a few words, why it ceases henceforth to be connected with the history of the constitution. There are no printed judicial records to serve as authorities for this concluding chapter. The rolls of parliament, the collections of writs and statutes, the numerous and valuable calendars of the patent and close rolls, cannot supply those characteristic and vivid details which are essential to a picture of the actual effects of legislation and of the working of the administrative system. They enable us, however, to form consistent and fairly definite conclusions of a general nature.

It will not be until all the extant " perambulations " of the reigns of the three Edwards have been published, that historians will be able to determine, even approximately, within what limits the forest law was subsequently ad-ministered. In the present lack of printed evidence, we can only say that the forest law remained in force throughout the fourteenth century—not infrequently with the distortions and abuses that had disgraced it during the previous two hundred years—though in some respects its severity was diminished.

State records prove that the administrative machinery remained almost exactly as before. The chapters of the

1. Elaborate researches among original records would be necessary for the accomplishment of this task. Many unpublished documents concern-ing the Forest in the 14th and 15th centuries are no doubt in existence. It is remarkable, however, that Mr. Fisher was unable to find any forest pleas for Essex between 1324 and 1489 (*Forest of Essex*, p. 89).

Maintenance of the administrative and judicial machinery
regard were in essentials identical with those of the thirteenth century.[1] We have numerous writs concerning the judicial eyres, and the handing over of offenders to their twelve "mainpernors," who must undertake to produce them on the appointed day before the itinerant justices.[2]

The king's writs make continual reference to the Assize of the Forest, along with the Charter of 1217, and all offences against the assize were punished. Royal justice did not spare even the archbishop of York.[3]

Up to the end of the century there were loud complaints against the foresters. At a time when the government was short of money and oppressive, it was natural that the foresters should have the same evil reputation as the sheriffs and escheators. Printed records being rare, we have few details as to their exactions. Some echoes of popular grievances reach us through the petitions of the commons in parliament.[4]

Continuance of abuses

Complaints in Parliament

The people did not venture to complain of the forest system itself, and they showed unusual boldness when in 1372 they pointed out that the game destroyed crops and pastures and forced the peasants to abandon certain villages.[5] They likewise feared that complaints against the officials would prove useless or injurious to themselves.[6] There was probably much

1. See in the *Calendars of Close Rolls* the writs ordering the holding of the regards before the arrival of the justices; e.g., *C.C.R.*, 1307–1313, pp. 174–5, where the *capitula* are all quoted.   2. *C.C.R., passim.*
3. A park held by the archbishop in Sherwood Forest was confiscated by reason of an offence against the Assize of the Forest.   On 14 Feb., 1355, the king pardoned him, and ordered Ralph de Neville, justice of the Forest south of the Trent, to restore the park.   Ralph de Neville ignored the command, and on 20 Nov., 1356, the king had to repeat it, mentioning that the archbishop [Thoresby] was his chancellor (*C.C.R.*, 1354-60, pp. 113, 288).
4. Protests from important men are rare; the complaint of the bishop of Salisbury, who at the parliament of 1325 asserted that his "free chase" had been confiscated, is an exceptional case (*Rot. Parl.*, i, 440b).
5. *Ibid.*, ii, 313a.   6. *Ibid.*, iii, 18a (A.D. 1377).

oppression. The officers of the Forest punished people for offences committed outside the limits fixed by the perambulations.[1] The innocent were unjustly condemned, without regular inquisition, and by means of false witnesses.[2] William de Claydon, Justice of the Forest in the days of Edward II, threw people into prison and otherwise maltreated them, sometimes forcing them to accuse " certain who were in no wise guilty."[3] Other officers, to secure a conviction, would bring forward strangers who knew nothing of the matter.[4] Notwithstanding the Charter, inhabitants of the Forest were summoned to the swanimotes, and fined if they failed to appear.[5] The foresters demanded contributions to which they had no claim.[6] Sometimes the chancery refused to issue writs against officers who were violating the Charter of the Forest.[7]

Edward III and Richard II repeatedly showed a desire to protect their subjects against such abuses. They ordered inquisitions,[8] and issued minute reminders of the correct procedure for the punishment of forest offenders.[9] In the statute which provided safeguards against purveyors, Edward III also ordered the foresters to content themselves with the levies " due according to ancient

Intervention by the kings

1. *Rot. Parl.*, ii, 311b, 335a, 367b ; iii, 62a, 116a (A.D. 1376, 1377, 1379, 1381).
2. " Pur ceo qe plusours gentz sount desheritez, reintz et destruz par les sovereins gardeins de forestes de cea Trente et de la, et par les autres ministres, encountre la fourme de la chartre de la Foreste . . . . " (First statute of Edw. III, art. 8 : *Statutes*, i. 254). Cf. *Rot. Parl.*, iii. 164b (A.D. 1383). 3. *Rot. Parl.*, ii, 10a ; cf. p. 380b.
4. *Ibid.*, ii, 169b (A.D. 1347). 5. *Ibid.*, iii, 18a (A.D. 1377).
6. *Ibid.*, ii, 24 (A.D. 1328) and 239b (A.D. 1351–2).
7. *Ibid.*, ii, 203b. The records of the inquisitions (*P.R.O., Forest Proceedings, Treasury of Receipts*) would no doubt furnish many instances of the crimes and exactions of the foresters. See the inquisition of 1369 published in Turner, p. xlix.
8. *C.C.R.*, 1343–6, p. 257.
9. In 1327 Edward III set forth in detail all the rules of procedure (*Statutes*, i. 254, art. 8). In 1383 Richard II forbade forest officials to put any pressure on juries to make them accuse the innocent, to imprison anyone " without due indictment," or to impose fines contrary to the Assize of the Forest. (*Ibid.*, ii. 32.) As was pointed out above (p. 163) there was no jury for forest offences in the 13th century.

R

law." [1]   Like their brethren in France, the kings of England saw clearly that it was their interest to defend their subjects against the exactions of officials, even when these sprang from an excess of zeal in the service of the crown.   In the fourteenth century, as before, they knew quite well that they had many unscrupulous foresters who pocketed arbitrary amercements and sold wood without accounting for it. [2]

But it was hard for a fourteenth century ruler to secure the obedience of his officers, and to check or even to discover their extortions.   Matters were still **Inadequate** worse when the throne was occupied by an **repression of** incapable king like Edward II, or by an **abuses** extravagant and pleasure-loving warrior like Edward III : as for Richard II, it is scarcely necessary to mention that he succeeded to the crown as a child, at a time when the authority of the government was weak and discredited.   It is, therefore, very probable that the suppression of abuses committed by the foresters was of a mild and ineffectual nature.

In the fourteenth century, nevertheless, the Forest was no longer one of the chief grievances of the nation.   It is **The Forest** remarkable that, with the exception of Essex, **no longer a** the counties most profoundly affected by the **national** revolt of 1381 were precisely those where no **grievance** forest existed : and in Essex itself, the forest law seems to have had as little to do with the rising as elsewhere.   The peasants demanded the abolition of hunting privileges, but not the abolition of prosecutions for assart, purpresture, and waste, though these were an essential feature of the forest code in England.   Their attitude is very significant.

---

1. *Statutes*, i, 321, ch. 7 (25 Edw. III); Thomson, *Magna Carta*, p. 356.
2. It is significant that in an act of amnesty, of which we shall speak below, Edward III expressly excludes from the operation of its benefits the justices ; head wardens ; wardens of forests, parks, and chases ; foresters ; verderers ; regarders ; agisters ; deputy-wardens ; under-foresters ; and sellers of wood.   (*Statutes*, i, 392, ch. 4).

In the present state of knowledge, it is difficult to say with certainty to what extent the position of the inhabitants of the Forest had improved. It is **Modification of the forest law** clear, however, that the severity of the forest law had been considerably relaxed. In all replies to petitions concerning the Forest, the king repeats that he means to follow the Charter of 1217. The trees were no longer regarded as sacred : at his accession Edward III gave permission to landowners to take from their woods within the Forest whatever they needed for their houses or fences.[1] The well-being of the population was set above the preservation of cover for the game : and this alone was a revolutionary change. Moreover, a very welcome alteration was gradually made in the method of conducting inquisitions. In the thirteenth century, when a trespass against the venison was discovered, the inquisition, as we have seen, had to be conducted by the four nearest townships, and they were collectively amerced if they failed to supply satisfactory information. By the end of the reign of Henry III this oppressive system was beginning to fall into disuse, and its place was taken by general inquisitions, which were concerned with all offences, against both the venison and the vert, recently committed in the Forest. The Ordinance of 1306 established them on a firm footing, and in the fourteenth century they occurred very frequently, sometimes even twice in one year.[2] Mr. Turner has published, as an example, the record of a general inquisition of 1369 " on the state of the Forest of Rutland." It was

1. " Item qe chescun homme qi eit boys deinz forest, poet prendre en son boys demeigne housbote et heybote sanz estre attaché par ministres de la foreste, issint q'ils le face [sic] par veue de forester." (*Statutes,* i, 255, chap. 2). Compare the corresponding article of the *Consuetudines et Assise de Foresta,* published forty or fifty years before : " Liberacio housbote et haibote fiat prout boscus pati potest in statu quo est, et non ad exigenciam petentis " (*ibid.,* p. 243).

2. See the tables drawn up by Mr. Turner, p. xlvii. It should be noted that the regards, which dealt with other offences than the destruction of game, continued to be held, as is proved by the close rolls of Edward II and Edward III.

conducted by the deputy-justice of the Forest south of the Trent : and the deputy-warden of the Forest of Rutland, six foresters, two verderers, twelve regarders, twelve freeholders of the Forest, and twelve freeholders from outside, appeared as jurors.[1] The authorities, then, had abandoned the special inquisition on injuries done to the game, which was in reality a means of raising money. Furthermore, trespasses against the vert and venison were leniently treated by the king : a statute of the forty-third year of Edward III granted indemnity to all private individuals who were guilty of such offences.[2]

In the fifteenth century, thanks at first to the policy of the Lancastrian kings,[3] and afterwards to the anarchy which almost suspended the operation of the

Decay of the forest system forest law, the forest system became weaker and weaker. The rolls of parliament no longer contain complaints against the Forest. According to English legal authorities, however, it was during the second half of the sixteenth century that the decline of the system became most rapid. The pleasure of the chase, declared the attorney-general of Charles I in 1628, "being not so much esteemed by the late King Edward the Sixt (by reason of his minoritie), and by the two succeeding Queenes (by reason of their sexe), the lesse care of the due execucion of the forest laws consequentlie ensued, and the keeping of the Courts of Swainmote and Justice Seate became almost totallie neglected

1. Turner, p. xlix.
2. *Statutes*, i, 392. It is, however, stated that the commons had demanded this amnesty, and that the king was rewarding them for the assistance they had so often given him.
3. Pierre de Fenin's Chronicle (ed. Mlle. Dupont, *Soc. d'Hist. de France,* 1837, p. 187) contains a curious passage concerning the pity felt by Henry V—in France, at any rate—for the people who were oppressed by the owners of warrens : " Le povre peuple l'amoit sur tous autres ; car il estoit tout conclu de preserver le menu peuple contre les gentis hommes des grans intortions qu'ilz faisoient en France et en Picardie et par tout le royaume : et par especial n'eust plus souffert qu'ilz eussent gouverné leurs chevaulx, chiens, et oyseaulx sur le clergié ne sur le menu peuple, comme ils avoient a coustume de faire ; qui estoit chose assés raisonnable au roy Henry de ce vouloir faire, et dont il avoit et eust eu la grace et priaire du clergié et povre peuple."

and disused."[1] A large amount of forest land was at this time enclosed without authority.[2] When, under Elizabeth, John Manwood took up his pen to write the " Treatise and Discourse of the Lawes of the Forrest," it was in the hope of reviving laws of which " verie little or nothing " remained.[3] James I and Charles I tried to recall them to life, and the famous Justice Finch even demanded that the perambulations of Edward I should be revoked.[4] But the Great Rebellion prevented the realisation of such worthy ambitions.[5]

Lamentations of Manwood

The restraints which in the twelfth and thirteenth centuries had pressed so heavily on so many English peasants had, in short, largely disappeared at the end of the Middle Ages. It was no longer a crime for a landholder to cut down a branch or clear a piece of the Forest which belonged to him. But it must not be inferred that everyone was free to take the game : and a sketch of the development of the English game-laws will perhaps not be without interest.

Lenient treatment of trespasses against the vert

During the fourteenth century the venison was still eagerly coveted. Whenever circumstances were favourable, organised poaching on a grand scale became prevalent, and the foresters themselves were not the least guilty. When the lands of Thomas of Lancaster were seized by Edward II, the great forest of

Origin of the game-laws. The right of the chase eagerly coveted

1. Cited by Fisher, *op. cit.*, pp. 294-5.
2. *Ibid.*, pp. 323 sqq.
3. " . . . Seeing that so many do daily so contemptuously commit such heynous spoiles and trespasses therein, that the greatest part of them are spoiled and decayed, and also that verie little, or nothing, as yet is extant concerning the lawes of the Forrest . . . " (Ed. 1598, dedication to Lord Howard, Justice of the Forests).
4. S. R. Gardiner, *Hist. of England, 1603-1642*, vii, 362 sqq.   Cf. J. Nisbet, *Hist. of the Forest of Dean, Eng. Hist. Rev.*, 1906, p. 449.
5. Interesting details concerning the Forest in modern times will be found in Mr. Fisher's book.   See also J. Nisbet and G. W. Lascelles, *Forestry and the New Forest*, in the *Victoria County History of Hampshire*, ii, 428 sqq.

Pickering[1] was the scene of hunts arranged by the inhabitants and the foresters.[2] At the beginning of the Hundred Years' War Edward III had scarcely sailed for France when a general attack was made on the game in the forests, parks, and chases belonging to the crown.[3]

At the end of the Middle Ages, however, the question of hunting-rights had changed its character. The two parties to the controversy were no longer the king and the baronage. On the one side were the king, the barons, and the wealthy landowners who owned warrens; on the other, the peasants, artisans, and lower clergy. These classes wished for permission to hunt and fish on Sundays, partly for the sport, partly to supplement their incomes. It infuriated them to see the multiplication of warrens swarming with game, to the damage of the crops and the exclusive advantage of the rich and their servants. The whole of the royal demesne was treated as warren. In disafforested districts, many estates where game was plentiful had been made warrens for the benefit of one or two people. The regions where all might hunt doubtless consisted of little save fields and moors where neither fur nor feather was to be found. The rebels of 1381 insisted that hunting and fishing should be made entirely free. Assembled at Smithfield, they demanded from the king by their spokesman, Wat Tyler, " that all warrens, as well in fisheries as in parks and woods, should be common to all; so that throughout the realm, in the waters, ponds, fisheries, woods, and forests, poor as well as rich might take the venison and hunt the hare

Demand for the abolition of game-preserves

Claims of Wat Tyler

---

1. The Forest of Pickering in Yorkshire, and the forests of Lancashire, were held by the earls of Lancaster, who, by an exceptional privilege, enforced all the forest laws for their own advantage (Turner, p. ix).

2. Letters close of 22 Aug., 1323 (*C.C.R.*, 1323–7, pp. 15-16).

3. Letters close of 26 July, 1339 (*C.C.R.*, 1339–41, p. 258). See the inquisitions published by Greswell, *op. cit.* pp. 104–9. The clergy were still conspicuous among the poachers. Cf. what Chaucer says of the sporting monk in the prologue of the Canterbury Tales.

in the fields." Richard hesitated, and if we are to believe the continuator of Knighton,[1] it was then that Tyler seized the bridle of his horse and was slain by the king's followers.

During the disturbed years which followed the rising, the lower classes acted on the principle for which their leader had suffered. In a petition of the **The Parliament of 1390 opposed to popular demands** parliament of 1390 it was stated that "artificers and labourers, that is to say, butchers, sewers, tailors, and other varlets, keep greyhounds and other dogs, and on festivals, at times when good Christians are in church hearing divine service, they go hunting in the parks, rabbit-preserves, and warrens of lords and others, and ruin them utterly." The commons proceeded to declare that "under colour of such chases," these wicked people encourage one another in the deplorable spirit of revolt, the effects of which have been seen, holding "at these times their meetings for debate, covin, and conspiracy, in order to stir up riot and sedition against your Majesty and the laws." To prevent a social upheaval, it was obviously necessary to bestow special hunting-rights on landed proprietors and the rich : " May it please the king to ordain in this present parliament, that no kind of artificer, labourer, or any other who does not possess lands or tenements to the value of forty shillings a year, or any priest or clerk, if he has not a preferment worth ten pounds, shall keep any greyhound or other dog, unless he be bound or led, hobbled or lawed, on pain of imprisonment for a year; and that every justice of the peace shall have power of enquiry and to **The Statute of Richard II** punish all offenders."[2] " Le roi le veut," was the answer; and a statute was issued forbidding, on pain of a year's imprisonment, every

1. Knighton, *Chronicle,* ed. Lumby (R.S.), ii. 137.   Cf. the letters-patent of 12 May, 1381 (*C.P.R.*, 1377–81, p. 634).
2. *Rot. Parl.*, iii, 273, cap. 58.

layman who did not possess landed property worth forty shillings a year, and every clerk with an annual income of less than ten pounds, to keep hunting-dogs or to use ferrets or any snares whatsoever to catch deer, hares, rabbits, or any other game. This, said the statute, was " the sport of the gentle." [1]

The crown, then, resisted the encroachments of the people by establishing special privileges in favour of certain classes of society. Exactly the same course was adopted in France. Seven years later, the statute of Richard II was followed by an ordinance of Charles VI conceived in the same spirit.[2] The same motives were alleged on both sides. The artisan must stick to his craft and the peasant to his plough, or else order would vanish.[3] The only difference was that in France the privilege of the chase was limited to the nobility, whereas in England it was conferred on all who held a moderate amount of landed property. The game-laws, as is usually the case, were symbolical of the state of society.[4]

In the fifteenth and sixteenth centuries the struggle between the privileged and the poachers continued. In 1417, when Henry V was engaged in the conquest of Normandy, parliament complained that armed bands were laying waste the chases of the lords, beating and wounding the keepers.[5] During the Wars of the Roses, disguised and masked brigands stole the

The struggle for the right of the chase in the 15th and 16th centuries

1. *Statutes* ii, 65, cap. 13.
2. Ordinance of 10 Jan., 1397 (*Recueil des Ordonnances,* viii, 117 sqq.) : " . . . Lesdits non nobles, en faisant ce que dit est, delaissent a faire leurs labourages ou marchandises, et commettent plusieurs larrecins de grosses bestes et de connins, etc. . . . " Falling into idleness, they " deviennent larrons, murtriers, espieurs de chemins."
3. This theory was put forward again, in the 17th and 18th centuries, by French and English legal writers. Cf. Blackstone, *Commentaries,* bk. ii, c. 27 ; and Pothier, *Traité du droit de domaine et de propriété,* pt. I, ch. ii, art. 28.
4. In Germany also, at the end of the Middle Ages, the nobles claimed that they alone had the right to hunt. See A. Schwappach, *Grundriss der Forst-und Jagdgeschichte Deutschlands,* p. 52.
5. *Rot. Parl.,* iv, 113-4.

deer and committed murders in the forests and game-preserves.[1] In the sixteenth century Henry VIII ordained savage punishments for poachers; and for some years the death-penalty appears again in the forest law.[2] It was a time when hunting-parties on a magnificent scale were arranged by the king and nobility.

As the rural aristocracy grew in power, they gradually threw off all restrictions on their right to hunt on their own estates. When, in the eighteenth century, Blackstone wrote his Commentaries on English Law, he conscientiously stated the theory that the king, by virtue of his prerogative, had exclusive hunting-rights over his whole realm, no subject having the right to hunt without the express permission of the king : but he himself confesses that " this exclusive prerogative of the king is little known or considered."[3] As a matter of fact, the right of the chase was exercised by every landowner on his manor.

Victory of the landed aristocracy

In France, at the same period, the theory of the royal prerogative had triumphed. There the history of the English Forest had been exactly inverted. In France, during the collapse of the Carolingian Empire, the royal Forest, like other prerogatives of the crown, had been dismembered and seized by the nobles, and up to the thirteenth century, the king enjoyed no peculiar privileges in regard to the chase. He acquired one by constituting himself the protector of the weak, not only against his own officials, but also against the owners of warrens. After the accession of St. Louis, the Parlement was rigidly opposed to any extension of the warrens, which were ruining agriculture, and suppressed even royal warrens if they were of recent date. In the course of the thirteenth and fourteenth centuries, the

Inverse process in France

Growth of the royal prerogative in France

1. Statute of i Henry VII (*Statutes*, ii, 505).
2. Statute of 1539, art. 5 (*Statutes*, iii, 731).
3. *Commentaries*, ii, c. 27.

principle was established that a warren was legal only if it was very ancient, and that the king alone might authorise the creation of new ones. Moreover, the extensive rights which the monarchy now claimed in this sphere, were used not only to protect agriculture against the mania of the nobles for sport, but also, as we have seen, to take away the hunting-rights of the common people.

Towards the end of the fourteenth century, at the time when Richard II and Charles VI published their ordinances restricting the chase to the nobility, the growing rights of the king of France and the declining rights of the king of England met, so to speak, and stood side by side at the same height. In the fifteenth century, the monarchy became considerably weaker in England, while Charles VII and Louis XI revived and strengthened it in France. In questions of the chase, Louis XI maintained his prerogative with particular severity. With him, hunting definitively became a royal sport, and no one might hunt save by royal favour. In France after his reign, and in England after the accession of the Tudors, the two opposite movements did not continue regularly. In England Henry VIII was a despot and a keen sportsman, and James I and Charles I tried to restore the Forest to its former state : while in France the anarchy of the sixteenth century afforded an opening to the pretensions of the nobles. Eventually, however, the two processes ended as might have been anticipated from the political experiences of the two nations. While in England the landed aristocracy acquired the right of the chase, in France the king seized it to his exclusive advantage. He allowed the nobles to hunt : but merely for his own pleasure, and at the cost of untold sufferings on the part of the peasantry, he established vast " capi-

The situation at the end of the 14th century

Louis XI

Effect of political changes

The "capitaineries"

taineries " which in many respects recall the English
Forest of the Middle Ages.   On the eve of the French
Revolution, the damage done to cultivation
Exasperation by the king's game and huntsmen was one
of the French of the causes of the exasperation of the
peasantry peasantry, and it is from the English
traveller Young that we have the most vigorous description of the distress and indignation caused by the king's
hunting-rights.   It might almost be said that the institution of the Forest, born among the Franks and transported to England, had afterwards returned from England
to France.   In both countries it was one of the most
odious fruits of arbitrary power.

CAUSES AND GENERAL CHARACTERISTICS
OF THE RISING OF 1381.

STUBBS' account of the rising of 1381 has been more completely superseded than any other part of his second volume. An entirely new light has been thrown on the history of the rebellion and its causes by researches in English records, particularly the judicial and financial collections of the Record Office. The pioneer in this work was a Frenchman, André Réville. This young scholar, who died in 1894 at the age of twenty-seven, presented, in 1890, to the examiners of *l'Ecole des Chartes* a dissertation on the rebellion in Hertfordshire, Suffolk, and Norfolk. To the end of his life he continued his elaborate researches in preparation of the general work in which he hoped to describe the causes and the various aspects of the movement. Two years after the death of Réville, Mr. Edgar Powell published a little book on the rebellion in Cambridgeshire, Suffolk, and Norfolk,[1] and in 1897 an American student of the University of Leipsic, Mr. T. W. Page, wrote an essay on the commutation of the labour services, and refuted the theory of Rogers concerning the causes of the rising of 1381.[2] Réville's manuscripts were entrusted to me, and on them I based a volume which appeared in 1898, and which still remains the most valuable source of information on the rising as a whole.[3] But I cannot be satisfied with merely

1. *The Rising in East Anglia in 1381*, with an Appendix containing the Suffolk Poll Tax Lists for that year.
2. *Die Umwandlung der Frohndienste in Geldrenten in den œstlichen, mittleren und südlichen Graftschaften Englands* (1897). I did not know of Mr. Page's essay in time to make use of it in my work of 1898. [Mr. Page subsequently published an English edition of his study : *The End of Villainage in England* (New York, 1900). Cf. *Eng. Hist. Rev.*, xv, 774.]
3. *Le Soulèvement des Travailleurs d'Angleterre en 1381*, by André Réville. Studies and Documents published with a preface and an historical introduction by Ch. Petit-Dutaillis.

referring my readers to this work. In the first place, the book is out of print, and moreover in the last fifteen years fresh documents have been discovered, and certain parts of the subject investigated more thoroughly.

A chronicle of intense interest, which was used by the Elizabethan historian, Stow,[1] and which I had known only through the somewhat unsatisfactory medium of this writer, has been found at the British Museum and edited by Mr. G. M. Trevelyan.[2] This account of the rebellion, written in French very shortly after the tragic events in London, contains exceedingly precise and, in the main, trustworthy information. In addition Mr. Trevelyan has published with Mr. Powell a number of documents hitherto unedited,[3] and has devoted to the rising of 1381 a chapter in his striking work on England in the time of Wycliffe.[4] Mr. G. Kriehn has examined the sources and certain details of the subject in an article which seemed to foreshadow a more elaborate publication.[5] A book by Mr. Oman, put together somewhat hastily, uses most of the works which we have just mentioned, and contains some interesting remarks on the collection of the Poll Tax.[6]

The causes of the rising have been made clearer by monographs or articles on the fourteenth century

1. See my *Preface* to Réville's work, pp. xii sqq.

2. *An Account of the Rising of 1381* in *Eng. Hist. Rev.*, 1898, pp. 509 sqq. Compare Kriehn's Memoir cited below, n. 5.

3. *The Peasants' Rising and the Lollards, a Collection of Unpublished Documents.*

4. *England in the Age of Wycliffe*, 1899. About the same time there appeared in Russian a book which it would be well to translate for the use of western historians : *Vozstanie Uota Tailera*, by Professor D. Petrushevsky. In the first part he deals with the rebellion ; in the second with its causes and with the fourteenth century manor. See the review of the second part by M. Savine in the *Eng. Hist. Rev.*, 1902, pp. 780 sqq. I much regret my inability to make use of Mr. Petrushevsky's work.

5. *Studies in the Sources of the Social Revolt in 1381*, in *Amer. Hist. Rev.*, vol. vii, 1901-2.

6. *The Great Revolt of 1381.* The reader should refer to the critical review of Mr. Tait, especially in regard to Mr. Oman's study on the Poll Tax (*Eng. Hist. Rev.*, 1907).

manor,[1] and by an excellent study by Miss Putnam, showing how the Statute of Labourers was put into force.[2] Finally, books and essays on political, municipal, religious, and economic history have given us more exact knowledge of the conditions in which the rebellion arose.[3]

With the assistance of these new authorities I have attempted a second sketch, necessarily much shorter than my first. I have fortunately been able to follow the main lines of my previous study; but I have modified and corrected it where necessary, made some important additions, and abandoned one or two theories.[4] I hope, however, that on the whole my readers will recognise the soundness of the main conclusions which the documents collected by Réville enabled me to publish fifteen years ago.

1. F. G. Davenport, *Economic Development of a Norfolk Manor*; A. Clark, *Serfdom on an Essex Manor, 1308-78*, in the *Eng. Hist. Rev.*, 1905; K. G. Feiling, *An Essex Manor in the Fourteenth Century*, in *Eng. Hist. Rev.*, 1911.

2. Bertha H. Putnam, *Enforcement of the Statutes of Labourers during the first decade after the Black Death, 1349-59*, in *Columbia University Studies in History*, vol. xxxii, 1908. Compare the same author's *Justices of Labourers in the Fourteenth Century*, in *Eng. Hist. Rev.*, 1906.

3. For example, C. T. Flower, *The Beverley Town Riots, 1381-2* (*Trans. Royal Hist. Soc.*, New Series, vol. xix); J. Gairdner, *Lollardy and the Reformation in England*, vol. i; E. P. Cheyney, *Disappearance of English Serfdom*, in *Eng. Hist. Rev.*, 1900.

4. Especially that in regard to the feelings of the lower classes concerning the exactions of the Papacy. See below, p. 272, n. 2.

CAUSES OF THE RISING.

Stubbs wisely laid stress on the complex character of the movement of 1381, and on its strange and somewhat inconsistent features; but he gave a very

Questions to be answered insufficient explanation of it, and certain inferences which he derived from Rogers are now shown to be unsound. Why in this particular year did the rural population of certain counties rise in a general rebellion? Why do we find among the rebels many artisans and merchants? Why were the boldest and most violent leaders often ecclesiastics—country priests and chaplains? Why was popular hatred directed against the most influential counsellors of the young king, such as John of Gaunt, Sudbury the archbishop of Canterbury, and Hales the treasurer? What were the grounds of the hatred shown against the judges and the sheriffs, the escheators and the tax-collectors? What was the reason of the massacre of foreign merchants or of the attacks on the municipal authorities in certain towns? How can we explain the unrestrained and unresisted pillage in vast districts? From whence did these armies of brigands suddenly appear, as if they had sprung out of the ground? How was it possible for such diverse movements to occur simultaneously? Were there general causes which operated in all parts? Had the rising on the whole a political character, or must we regard it as a social upheaval provoked by communistic agitators? Had it religious causes, and did Lollardy, then in its infancy, contribute to it? The events of 1381 suggest these questions, and we believe that the documents which have been published will enable us to answer them.

On a careful examination of the records, it appears

that, in order to explain most of the features—sometimes
Initial very astonishing ones—which we have just
causes enumerated, we must go back to two conspicuous facts of general history which dominate the
second half of the fourteenth century in England,
namely, the Black Death, and the war with France.

The Black Death, which ravaged England from
August 1348 to the end of 1349,[1] and made another visit
in 1361, carried off perhaps a half of the
The
Black Death population, caused a remarkable disturb-
and the ance in production, wages, and prices, and
French War led to profound changes in the relations
between employers and workmen, sellers and consumers.
The war with France drove the crown to lavish expenditure and the raising of heavy taxes. It moreover
occasioned an increase of disorder and a decline of morals.
From the plague and the war issued economic calamities
and revolutionary sentiments which explain the rising
of 1381.

We shall first examine the effects of the plague in the
rural districts. As Mr. Ashley justly observes, " to
understand the rural life of England
i. The Black during this period is to understand nine-
Death: tenths of its economic activity." [2] More-
its results in the over, it was in the country villages that the
rural districts
rebellion took its rise.

In his great *History of Agriculture and Prices* Thorold
Rogers argues that in the fourteenth century the villeins [3]
had " almost all " been released from the
Thorold Rogers' burden of forced labour, for which money
theory payments had been substituted. He was

1. And not from May 31 to Sept. 29, 1349, as Stubbs asserts, vol. ii,
p. 418 n. See Charles Creighton, *History of Epidemics in Britain,* vol. i,
chap. iii ; F. A. Gasquet, *The Great Pestilence.*
2. *Introduction to English Economic History,* 2nd edit., vol. i, pt. i,
p. 6.
3. It must not be forgotten that in England at this time " villein " and
" serf " were synonymous. See my study on the *Origins of the Manor*
⟨*supra,* i. 1 sqq.⟩ ; cf. Stubbs, *Const. Hist.,* ii. 475.

led from this to an inference regarding the origins of the rebellion. According to him, the landed aristocracy, compelled, by the abolition of villein services, to employ hired labourers to cultivate their own demesnes, found their interests threatened by the rise in the price of labour after the Black Death, and wished therefore to return to the old system. This reaction infuriated their tenants and was one of the chief causes of the revolt of 1381.[1] Stubbs accepted this theory, [2] which Rogers himself maintained very positively in later works.[3] It was rejected—though rather too hastily—by Mr. Ashley. [4] As far as it concerns the substitution of money payments for labour dues, Rogers' theory is not false; it is merely exaggerated : but in regard to the restoration of the previous system, it is based on mere conjecture, and even if the theory should be confirmed by the discovery of new documents, it would explain to only a small extent the grievances of the peasants. It is evident that the main causes of their discontent must be sought elsewhere.

In my analysis of the manorial records collected principally by Réville, I have shown that the substitution of money rents for labour services had only
Objections to
Rogers' theory just begun when the Black Death came and reduced by one-half the supply of labour and raised all prices. [5] At the same time, Mr. Page was also studying the question, and after extensive researches he arrived at identical conclusions. [6] Up to 1348, in fact, labour services seem to have been rendered in the majority of manors, and in those where money payments existed they had been instituted for special

1. *Hist. of Agriculture and Prices in England,* i. 81 sqq.
2. See Stubbs' *Const. Hist.*, ii. 476-7.
3. *Six Centuries of Work and Wages,* edit. 1908, pp. 253 sqq. ; *Economic Interpretation of History,* p. 29.
4. *Op. cit.* i, pt. ii, pp. 265 sqq.
5. See my *Introduction historique* to Réville's book, pp. xxiii sqq.
6. *Umwandlung der Frohndienste,* especially pp. 22 sqq. See also Miss Davenport, *Economic Development of a Norfolk Manor,* p 52.

s

reasons, varying according to place and circumstance, but unconnected with a desire to improve the villein's lot. In the first half of the fourteenth century, it sometimes even happened that the system of commutation operated to the evident disadvantage of the villeins, and that while continuing to perform week-work, they were thenceforward compelled to pay a pecuniary compensation whenever their services were not actually required.[1] In short, it is true that labour dues had begun to disappear, but the institution of money rents was not always a gain for the peasant, and it was far from general. A return to the old system, therefore, cannot be, as Rogers urges, "the key to the insurrection of Wat Tyler." Rogers, moreover, cites no document which proves that this reaction occurred, and the researches of Mr. Page have convinced him that, on the contrary, in the years immediately before the revolt the tendency towards the substitution of money payments for labour became stronger rather than weaker.[2] No doubt in manors where the change had taken place disputes may have arisen in the way that Rogers suggests; but there is no reason to believe that such cases were frequent.

" The key to the insurrection " must therefore be found elsewhere. We have to discover what happened as a result of the plague, and how the lords came into conflict with the peasants.

The Black Death had been most fatal to the lower classes, who lived in very insanitary conditions.[3] Whole villages were depopulated. Of those able to work, a great number of free tenants and villeins perished. The agricultural labourers, farm servants, road-menders, and the reapers

Rise in wages after the plague

---

1. Maitland, *Hist. of a Cambridgeshire Manor* (*Eng. Hist. Rev.*, 1894, pp. 418 sqq.). Compare my *Introd. Historique*, p. xxiv.
2. *Umwandlung*, pp. 40 sqq.
3. See the preamble of the Ordinance of 1349, in *Foedera*, Rec. ed., iii, pt. i, 198 ; or in Miss Putnam's *Enforcement of the Statutes of Labourers*, Appendix, p. 8*.

who came from the towns for the harvest season, were also decimated; and the survivors profited by the situation to demand higher wages. Rogers has calculated that after the plague rural wages rose 48 per cent.[1]   The judicial documents recently published by Miss Putnam confirm those used by Rogers. They show that reapers frequently received 5d. or 6d. a day instead of the 2d. or 3d. which they earned before the plague. Haymakers, instead of 5d., demanded 9d., 10d., and even 1/- or 1/2d. an acre. [2]

The small holders, and especially the villeins, observing this rise of wages, strove to benefit by it; and many left their holdings to offer themselves as hired labourers. This is a notable fact, the importance of which cannot be exaggerated.   Villeins fled from their manors much more frequently than before. With this exodus following so closely on the plague, the landowners saw their manors becoming devoid of workers.[3]   All the manorial records show us that vacant holdings were very numerous and that tenants could not be found to occupy them. The landlord was already unable to cultivate his own demesne by means of labour services. We may mention, for example, the state of things described by Miss Davenport in her valuable study on the manor of Forncett in Norfolk. Out of 3,219 day's works in winter, summer, and autumn, 1,452 in 1376-77, and 1,722 in 1377-78, could no longer be obtained. It was not that the labour services had been converted into a pecuniary tax; there was in the manor only one holding where this change had been carried out; but the tenants had disappeared in large numbers, whether through the extinction of whole

Small holdings deserted

---

1. *Hist. of Agric.*, i. 265 sqq., 687.

2. Miss Putnam, *Enforcement*, p. 90.

3. For examples, see Maitland, *History of a Camb. Manor*, pp. 423 sqq.; Miss Davenport, *op. cit.*, pp. 72 sqq.; Page, *op. cit.*, pp. 38 sqq. and note 27.

families or through departures from the district.[1]   If the demesne was to be cultivated on the same lines as before, it was therefore necessary to have recourse to agricultural labourers; but their claims had doubled.   And what was to be done with deserted holdings outside the demesne?

To avoid ruin, certain lords no doubt took up sheep rearing, which required few hands.   English sheep, moreover, had a high reputation, and their wool had for long been famous.   But this policy involved a revolution which could not be rapidly accomplished, and in fact it was mainly after the beginning of the following century that it was very gradually carried into effect.

Remedies. Sheep-breeding

Most of the landholders continued to practise agriculture as best they could.   Often they went so far as to lease both their demesne and also the empty holdings, and in this way serfs as well as free peasants received land on advantageous conditions.   It was perhaps in order to keep their villeins that the lords of certain manors abandoned the system of labour services after the plague.[2]   At any rate it is evident that in many cases they thought it wise and profitable to make concessions. In France, in the same way, the calamities of the Hundred Years' War forced the nobility and the church to enfranchise the serfs in a body.   It is also certain that the English landowners were often driven to pay their hands very high wages, and that they fought amongst themselves for a supply of labour, seeking to attract villeins from other estates and enticing labourers who were working in the neighbourhood.   The legal cases of

Concessions made to obtain labour

1. Miss Davenport, *op. cit.*, pp. 51 sqq.; see also Page, *op. cit.*, p. 35 and note 22.

2. Thus in 1352 all the labour dues were changed into pecuniary rents in the manor of Castle Combe (Page, *op. cit.*, p. 33, n. 18).   The motive of this substitution is not quite clear: the rise in the price of food may have made it to the lord's interest to abolish the labour services, for a meal was generally given to those performing them.   See the examples of these meals in my *Introduction*, p. xxvi, n. 4; p. xxvii, n. 4; p xxviii, n. 1.

which we are about to speak prove this clearly. Con-strained by circumstances, the aristocracy thus helped to develop the class of free-tenants, farmers, and well-paid labourers who, after repeatedly raising their demands at the expense of the higher orders, turned against them in 1381.[1]

Besides these landlords of opportunistic temperament, there were others more tenacious and strong-willed, who

Resistance of certain landowners

were eager to maintain their rights and their ancient methods of cultivation. It is not surprising to find among them a number of churchmen. In England, as in France, ecclesiastical landlords administered their estates during the Middle Ages with scrupulous and severe vigilance. [2] At this time, they took the earliest opportunity of undoing any changes they had made. Thus the court rolls of the manor of Hutton, which belonged to Battle Abbey, show the abbot driven to lease vacant holdings in 1349 and the following years, but letting them for only a short term—twelve years at most. After 1355 he con-cluded new arrangements for one year only, raising the rents and returning to the old system of tenure whenever he had a good chance to do so.[3]

A number of manors, especially those in the hands of monasteries, had lords of the same temper as the abbot

The burdens of villeinage maintained

of Battle. A certain number of manorial records dating from the years immediately before the revolt bear witness to the rigor-

1. It should be noticed that in England the plague only assisted a development which the disastrous famines of the reign of Edward II had rendered necessary. Wages had begun to rise as early as the first half of the fourteenth century and an increase in the numbers of free holdings and farms had already appeared before 1350 (see my *Introduction*, pp. xxix sqq.). But the decline in population caused by the plague accelerated the movement, and gave rise to new ambitions.
2. Their covetousness was a theme of reproach. In the Year Books of Edward II (iv. 69) there appears this gibe of Justice Bereford at the bishop of Hereford : '' Gentz de seinte Eglise ont une merveillouse manere : s'ils eient le pée en la terre a akun homme, il volont avoir tut le corps.''
3. K. G. Feiling, *Essex Manor, Eng. Hist. Rev.*, 1911, p. 335.

ous maintenance of the burdens of villeinage, and to the differences which were thus caused between the lords and the villeins. The dispute over labour services did not arise in the way Rogers supposed; no attempt was made to revive an obsolete institution; the lords merely desired the continuance of obligations which were still in existence, although no longer compatible with the progress of the labouring class. Dues of various kinds were sternly exacted, and the personal disabilities of the villeins inexorably maintained. The manorial courts showed no mercy to the villein who without leave had married his daughter, sent his son to school, or sold a fowl.[1] Fifteen years after the plague the villeins of the manor of Hutton saw the lord abbot buy for their benefit such instruments of correction as a pillory and a ducking-stool; and from 1366 to 1368 the number of fines inflicted in the manorial court increased three-fold. [2] We have numerous proofs of the severity shown by certain lords. Men of moderate views like the pious William Langland were horrified, and offered the unsuccessful advice: " When you inflict a fine, let mercy fix its amount." In his sermons, Wycliffe vainly rebuked the lords for ruining the poor with fines. [3] The victims had no legal means of escape. The villeins were still at the mercy of their lord, with the sole protection of manorial custom. The courts of common law were more strictly closed to them than ever; no villein could bring an action against his lord. And when they ran away, they were pursued and put in prison.

The contrast between their legal condition and the new prosperity which the economic crisis had brought to the

1. See my *Introduction historique,* pp. xxxvi, sqq. ; and Réville's essay on the rising of the peasants at St. Albans, pp. 5 sqq.

2. Feiling, *op. cit.,* p. 335. See also in the *Chronica Monasterii de Melsa,* ed. Bond. (R. S.), iii. 126 sqq., the account of the troubles between the abbot of Meaux and his villeins about 1358.

3. See my *Introduction historique,* p. xxxvi.

The law
and economic
changes
    labouring class in general, was for the villeins a source of continual irritation. Even those who were badly treated by their lords had benefited through the general rise of prices. At least up to the death of Edward III, they could make large profits on the sale of their produce, for the price of corn and cattle did not decline till the last quarter of the century. [1] But the burden of serfdom seemed to them only the more insupportable.

Nothing was therefore more natural than the efforts they made to free themselves by means of concerted action. The movement became so general

The villeins
combine
that in 1377 the matter was put before the king by parliament. According to the lords and the knights of the shires, the villeins were conspiring to refuse their " customs and services " and claimed that they were " free from every kind of serfdom." They threatened with death the officers of their lords, and refused to obey the decisions of the manorial courts. They supported their claims by passages from Doomsday Book.[2] They gathered on the roads, and joined in " confederacies " to make resistance to their lords.[3] The statute of 1377, which authorised proceedings against the conspirators, failed to overcome their obstinacy.[4] The general refusal of " works, customs, and services," in the counties which rebelled in 1381, was thus only the extension of a movement already in existence.

The statute of 1377 was not the only weapon which the landowners obtained from the crown and from parliament. Another had been given at the very beginning of

1. See the lists of prices in the first vol. of Rogers' *History of Agriculture and Prices*.
2. Without doubt because the services were not expressly mentioned. See the very sound remarks by Mr. Tait in his review cf Mr. Oman's work (*Eng. Hist. Rev.*, 1907, pp. 161 sqq.).
3. See the text of the statute of 1377 in *Statutes*, vol. ii, pp. 2 sqq. ; or in my *Introduction historique*, pp. xxxvii-xxxviii.
4. For an instance of a league of villeins in 1380 to withhold from a lord his " consuetudines et servicia," see my *Introduction*, p. xxxix, n. 4.

the crisis to employers and consumers as against workmen and vendors of commodities, namely, the ordinance and statutes " to restrain the malice of servants " and to obviate " the outrageous dearness of victuals."

While the plague was still raging and it was impossible for parliament to assemble, the royal council had taken vigorous measures. An ordinance had been published on 18 June, 1349.[1] It compelled men and women under sixty, having no means of support, to work when they should be required; they and all other labourers had to accept the wages usually paid in 1346, or in the five or six years before. Breaches of contract were forbidden. Penalties were imposed on all those who should violate the ordinance, including employers who offered wages above the legal rate. Retailers of food and innkeepers were to charge reasonable prices.

The Ordinance of 1349

The statute of 9 February, 1351, made the law more precise, and fixed at a definite amount many kinds of wages. It was afterwards re-issued and made more severe. A statute of January 1361 ordained that labourers who went from county to county seeking higher wages should be branded on the forehead with a red-hot iron. The commons, especially from 1377 to 1380, were continually clamouring for the enforcement of the law.[2]

The Statutes of Labourers

In certain respects this legislation was a complete novelty. Of course mediæval notions concerning the regulation of labour easily led to intervention of this kind. In the towns, it was usual for wages and prices to be controlled by the municipal authorities. The local courts, whether of the county, the hundred, or the manor, had for long concerned themselves with the relations between employers, workmen, and consumers; but agri-

1. In the *Foedera* it is dated 1350, and the mistake has passed into my *Introduction* to Réville's book. The exact date is to be found in *Statutes,* vol. i, pp. 307 sqq. ; and in Miss Putnam, *Appendix,* pp. 8*–12*.
2. *Statutes,* i. 311 sqq., 366 sqq., etc. ; Miss Putnam, pp. 12*–18*.

cultural wages had never been subjected to an official limitation, and free labourers had never been forced to reside in a certain district. It was natural that the government should listen to the complaints of employers and consumers, and seek remedies for an unprecedented crisis which threatened to ruin the whole nation[1] ; but it could not reconcile interests diametrically opposed to each other, and its policy excited furious indignation.

This policy was persistent and vigorous. On the enforcement of the ordinance and the statutes, Miss Putnam's solid work has thrown an entirely new light, and one can only regret that, as regards the greater part of the subject, the researches of this scholar come to an end at the year 1359. The ancient
Enforcement of the Statutes popular courts sometimes dealt with offences against the statutes of labourers; but it was to the advantage of the lords, who were granted the fines paid by their tenants, that such cases should come before the royal tribunals. As a rule, offenders were tried by special commissions of " justices of labourers," or by commissions charged at the same time with the conservation of the peace.[2] The statute of 1368, in fact, entirely transferred to the justices of the peace the functions of the justices of labourers. The class from which these guardians of public order were chosen was

1. The English government was not the only one to take such measures. In France, and in particular at Paris, the Black Death also caused a rise in wages, and the king published an ordinance (30 Jan., 1351) which it is interesting to compare with the English ordinance. See *Ordonnances*, ii. 352 sqq. ; R. Eberstadt, *Das französische Gewerberecht vom dreizehnten Jahrhundert bis 1581*, pp. 163 sqq. ; Fagniez, *Docum. relatifs a l'hist. de l'Industrie et du commerce en France*, ii. xxviii sqq.

2. It was natural that the same commissioners should be charged with the keeping of the peace and the execution of the statutes of labourers. Even during the period when special commissions were appointed, that is to say, from 1352 to 1359, out of 501 commissioners who were nominated as " justices of labourers," there were 299 who in the preceding years had been justices of the peace. Among these 501 there were a few lawyers and municipal officials, but most were rural landowners. Parliament made constant efforts, which were generally in vain, to obtain control of the appointments.

the most conservative in the country—the class which already controlled local administration and furnished the members of the house of commons, and which had the greatest interest in the maintenance of the old economic conditions—namely, the middle class of the rural districts.

Each " commission of labourers," appointed at fixed salaries, exercised jurisdiction in a single county, or more commonly in a subdivision of a county, and tried cases with the assistance of a jury of presentment and a petty jury. As far as can be gathered from the reports which are still extant, " excesses " of wages and prices were the offences with which the commissioners had most often to deal, but they concerned themselves with almost all the cases provided for in the statutes. They sometimes even turned their attention to dividing the supply of labour among the employers. The abbot of Pipwell complained that they compelled his tenants to work for those in competition with him, and that at a time when he had land lying fallow through lack of labour; and the king pointed out to the justices that it was not reasonable to deprive the abbot of the help of his tenants when he had need of them, and was ready to pay legal wages.[1] It is evident that the commissioners were very active and very tyrannical.

The commissioners often inflicted sentences of imprisonment, but they generally imposed fines, or else simply condemned the offender, whether labourer or employer, to pay the *excessus*—that is, the difference between the legal wage and the wage given. Every year the fines and the *excessus* amounted to a sum large enough to be coveted. During the first years it was used, at the request of parliament, to relieve taxation. Subsequently the lords succeeded in securing for themselves the sums which their respective tenants were condemned to pay.

1. Miss Putnam, *Appendix*, p. 218.*

Cases more difficult to decide were the actions for breach of contract. These were generally brought either before the King's Bench, or more fre-

Action of the supreme courts quently before the Court of Common Pleas. Miss Putnam conjectures that from 1351 to 1377 the two supreme courts dealt with 9,000 of these actions, brought by employers against men who left their work before the end of their contract, or against other employers who had enticed their labourers from them. Here again we see that the statutes were very widely interpreted, and that schoolmasters, chaplains, bailiffs, and esquires were regarded as bound to their masters by the terms of these laws.

It was in such ways that the statutes were put into force. The royal council watched narrowly over their adminis-

Aims of the government tration, and often recalled commissioners and suppressed abuses. There can be no doubt that the advisers of Edward III and Richard II were honestly trying to avert a catastrophe, without any intention of oppressing the labourers, of filling the treasury with the produce of the fines, or of increasing the authority of the crown. They did not succeed in stopping the increase of wages and prices, for in the years immediately before the revolt the commons were continually complaining that the statutes were not observed; but it is beyond question that they retarded the rise of rural wages, and the break-up of the manorial system. [1] The object which the government persistently and honestly pursued was the maintenance of the old social organisation.

For this very reason the execution of the ordinance of 1349 and of the subsequent statutes exasperated the small-

Unpopularity of the justices holders and labourers of the country districts. It was not unknown for every workman within the jurisdiction of a

---

It is impossible to accept Stubbs' assertion that the statutes pro-duced no effect whatever (*Const. Hist.*, ii, 473).

commission of labourers to refuse the oath to obey the statute; and sometimes the commissioners were attacked and threatened with death.[1] In 1381 the rebellious peasants seized the justices and broke open the prisons. All of whatever degree who were connected with the administration of the law became objects of the same hatred, and were regarded as enemies of the people.

The results of the Black Death were equally striking in the towns. In the fourteenth century town life was beginning to assume some importance. At the accession of Richard II, London had 40,000 inhabitants, York and Bristol 12,000, Plymouth and Coventry 9,000, Norwich, Lincoln, Salisbury, Lynn, and Colchester between 5,000 and 7,000.[2] Industries were multiplying and becoming more specialised. The gilds of artificers (craft gilds) were developing by the side of the merchant gilds. There were forty-eight of them in London at the end of the reign of Edward III. The woollen industry was bringing much wealth to the towns of Norfolk. [3] The plague carried off hundreds in the narrow streets of the towns as it did in the cottages of the peasants, and in the towns also the high price of labour gave to the survivors an unprecedented prosperity. The records show a house-painter, a weaver, and several tailors obtaining three times as much as their previous wages. [4] Moreover, these demands, though greatly to the disadvantage of the consumer, did not necessarily occasion trouble between masters and workmen. Most of the masters worked with their own hands, and lived on very intimate terms with their workpeople, taking counsel with them as to means of increasing their profits. Often

Effects of the Black Death on the industrial classes

1. Miss Putnam, pp. 76, 93 sqq.
2. Ashley, *Economic History*, i, pt. ii, p. 11, based on the Poll Tax Rolls of 1377.
3. *Ibid.*, i, pt. i, pp. 86 sqq., pt. ii, pp. 70 sqq. and 209 sqq.; Gross, *Gild Merchant*, i, chap. 7.
4. Miss Putnam, p. 90.

indeed the journeyman was paid directly by the customer, and his work brought in nothing for his employer. As a rule, therefore, masters and workmen had the same interests, and the public suffered accordingly. The artisans offered a violent resistance to the statutes of labourers. They refused to serve those who would not give them high wages.[1] They broke their contracts in order to work for those who offered more.[2] They formed " leagues, confederacies, and conspiracies " to keep up the price of labour.[3] They forcibly opposed the execution of corporal punishments imposed by the justices of labourers.[4] They supplied to the rebel hordes of 1381 numerous recruits and several leaders. In London the participation of the artisans gave the rising a character of ferocious brutality.

The germ of the revolt in the towns was the same as in the country. In both, those of the working classes who had survived the plague had greatly benefited by the economic crisis which it had caused, and they wished to maintain and even increase their prosperity. Froissart, who was much better informed concerning these events than has generally been supposed, acutely says : " This rebellion was caused and excited by the great ease and plenty in which the meaner folk of England lived." Gower and Langland re-echo the lamentations of the middle classes over the demands of servants and workmen. They must have good fare of flesh or fish, dishes well cooked, " *chaude* or *plus chaud*"; [5] and in a judicial document recently published we actually

The Statutes resisted by artisans

Attitude of the labouring class in general

1. " Rogerus de Melbourne, faber, renuit servire vicinos et servit extraneos causa excessivi," Putnam, *App.,* p. 165.*
2. Even when they were employed in the service of the king. See *Foed.,* Rec. ed., iii, pt. ii, 613 sqq. (A.D. 1361).
3. *Statutes,* i, 367.
4. Putnam, *App.,* p. 167.*
5. See the passages cited in my *Introd.,* pp. xl and xlviii sqq. ; also Stubbs, *Const. Hist.,* ii. 476, n. 1.

read of a carter who left a town because his employer would not pay him by the day or give him fresh meat. [1] In town and country alike the workers were now conscious of their strength, jealous in defence of their comfort and their pleasures, and ready to attack the lords, the rich, and the king's officers, who were endeavouring to deprive them of their new prosperity. Where serfdom still existed, the villeins ran away to offer themselves as journeymen, or else they formed unions to refuse their services.

The merchants and tradesmen were also affected by the laws of Edward III, which punished on the one hand retailers of food and innkeepers if they raised their prices, and on the other hand those who adulterated goods or strove to create monopolies. This class, divided by terrible feuds, was profoundly affected by the rebellion. It provided the rebels with victims as well as leaders; for English capitalists,[2] and still more foreigners under the protection of the crown, like the Flemings and the Lombards, were persecuted, robbed, and murdered. During these days the small traders had their chance of revenging old wrongs and gratifying their jealousy.[3]

The trading-class

Hatred of foreigners

To anyone unfamiliar with the history of the English Church at this period, it must seem strange to find many priests and chaplains among the most dangerous of the popular leaders of 1381. The anarchist preacher, John Ball, was listened to as a " prophet " by the rebels of the south-east. In Essex, in Hertfordshire, Cambridgeshire and Suffolk—almost everywhere in fact— the lower clergy were deeply involved in the rising.

Share of the lower clergy in the rising

Clerks with small benefices and the stipendiary clergy, the two classes which furnished these rebels, had been

1. *Putnam*, App., p. 196.*.
2. See the article by Alice Law, *The English ' Nouveaux Riches ' in the Fourteenth Century* (*Trans. Royal Hist. Soc.*, New Series, ix, 49 sqq.).
3. See the documents cited in my *Introd.*, pp. xlvii sqq., li sqq.

greatly affected by the Black Death.[1]   Obliged by their
duty to come into contact with the sick, the parish priests
were perhaps of all Englishmen the most hard hit by
the pestilence.   In East Anglia more than eight hundred
parishes were deprived of their priests in a single year.
Eighty-three lost two in rapid succession, and ten saw
three perish in a few months.   In some districts no one
could be found to administer the sacraments to the dying.
Extraordinary measures had to be taken.   The bishops
ordained young clerks who had not reached the canonical
age and men without learning or of doubtful antecedents.
As a result of this difficulty in filling their ranks, the
boorishness of the rural clergy, already
Effects of the notorious in normal times, became still
Black Death on
the clergy worse.   In addition, the dearness of food
made them more wretched and greedy than
ever.   Very often they failed to obtain the increase of
income which they needed in order to exist.   Sooner
than accept a cure and fast there for ever, many clerks
adopted a wandering life, selling their ministrations to
the peasants, accepting posts as private chaplains or
chantry priests, and demanding stipends which were
sometimes large enough to bring them before the justices
of labourers.   So even in the Church the Black Death
gave rise to a wages problem, and drove on to the highways, by the side of labourers in quest of good pay,
bands of vagabonds in holy orders, disposed to share
and excite the bitter feelings of the people.[2]

The higher clergy, consisting of younger sons of the
nobility, worldly, greedy, corrupt in morals, did nothing to
relieve the miseries and mollify the con-
Indifference of cealed indignation of this ecclesiastical
the higher
clergy proletariate.   By their insensibility they suggested themselves as an object of attack.

1. For what follows see especially A. Jessopp, " The Black Death
in East Anglia " in *The Coming of the Friars and other historic Essays.*
2. See the documents printed by Miss Putnam, *App.*, pp. 147*, 171*,
194*.

Whereas a parish priest could no longer live on less than ten marks a year, archbishop Islip ordained the suspension of all those who demanded more than five or six marks; and this great prelate drew up a grandiloquent invective against the covetousness of the priests, "gorged with excessive revenues."[1]   It is not surprising that one of his successors, Sudbury, who was among the best prelates of the time, should in 1381 have paid with his head for the accumulated sins of the higher clergy.   It is not surprising that the despised and starving priests, the wretched holders of chantries, and the wandering clerks, should have led the peasants to the assault of episcopal manors and wealthy monasteries.[2]

It has been shown that the events of 1381 owed their origin in particular to the Black Death and its economic and social consequences.   To a less but still important extent the French war had also prepared the way for a revolution.   In the first place, it had made the English discontented.   It necessitated heavy exactions, especially the Poll Tax, which proved to be the exciting cause of the rising.   It rendered unpopular a government which, despite such heavy subsidies, had lost all its French possessions, and could not even protect the English coasts from the descents of French privateers, or the border counties of the north from the raids of the Scots.[3]   When taxes grow and security

ii. Results of the French War

Unpopularity of the government

1. The document is cited by W. W. Capes, *English Church in the Fourteenth and Fifteenth Centuries,* p. 78.   Islip was archbishop of Canterbury from 1349 to 1366.
2. I have abandoned the theory that the exactions of the Papacy may have contributed to the popular discontent (cf. my *Introduction,* p. 1).   It does not appear that the insurgents complained of them.   It is remarkable that where they meddled with disputes as to the tenure of benefices or prebends they supported clerks who had received a papal provision. At Bury the people took the side of Edmund Brownfield, who, being provided by the pope to the abbey, had been imprisoned by the king in accordance with the Statute of Provisors (see Réville, pp. 65-6 ; Powell, pp. 15 sqq.).   At Salisbury and Bridgewater the people likewise supported a provisor (see my *Introd.,* p. cix).
3. See my *Introduction,* pp. lv sqq.

declines, the government always receives the blame. The costly and disastrous war with France produced a hatred of "traitors." In 1381 the English saw traitors everywhere, like the French republicans in 1793.

The war had also tended to brutalise the nation. In the years immediately before the rising, the rolls of parliament, the statutes, and the royal letters leave the impression that great disorder prevailed in the country. Crimes of violence were very frequent. Armed bands were organised, not only for robbery, but to gratify private ambitions, to abduct heiresses, to take possession of a manor, or to terrorise the justices. During the campaigns in France the nobles had acquired lawless habits. They had retainers whose interests they maintained by force; they kept troops of swashbucklers; and in Nov. 1381 parliament pointed to this custom of "maintenance" as one of the causes of the revolt.[1]   Moreover, these armies of lawbreakers were easily recruited, for many of the brigands of all countries who had formerly served under Edward III and the Black Prince, had come to England since Charles V and Du Guesclin had driven them from France. A few, like the sometime weaver, Robert Knolles, had made their fortunes and become pillars of the throne. Knolles helped to suppress the rebellion in 1381; but others who had been less lucky were tramping the highways, [2] ready for any desperate enterprise, and sharing the lot of fugitive villeins, labourers wanted by the authorities, and wandering

1. *Rot Parl.*, vol. iii, 100, sect. 17.
2. They were a subject of complaint as early as the time of the Treaty of Brétigny. According to a statute of 34 Ed. III the justices of the peace were to " informer et enquere de touz ceux qi ont este pilours et robeours *es parties de dela, et sont ore revenuz* et vont vagantz et ne voillent travailler come ils soleient avant ses hours." In 1363 the king wrote to Warin de l'Isle that horrible robberies had been committed in Wiltshire, Berks, and Hants by " malefactores . . . qui nuper de pillagio et latrocinio *in partibus exteris* vixerunt" (see the documents published by C. G. Crump and C. Johnson, *The Powers of Justices of the Peace, Eng. Hist. Rev.,* 1912, pp. 234, 236-7).

T

or excommunicate clergy. There can be no doubt that in 1381 bands of rebels were frequently led by old soldiers, both English and foreign, accustomed to pillage and bloodshed, whether for gain or for the gratification of their brutal passions. The exploits of these bands, their daring, their sudden raids, strongly remind one of the great Companies—a name, indeed, by which they sometimes called themselves.[1]

Certain events of 1381 must be ascribed to causes of a much less general character. They might have occurred at other times even if the great rebellion **Secondary and** had never broken out, and they were often **local causes** episodes in long local quarrels which had begun many years before. They were connected with the revolt, however, by more than mere coincidence. Thus, in several towns, the news of the insurrection in the south-eastern counties stimulated the common people to rise up against the oligarchy who held the municipal government. Other towns, like St. Albans and Bury St. Edmunds, renewed their previous efforts to shake off the strict control of their lords. Others, again, which were jealous of their neighbours, used the opportunity to gratify old grudges. Yarmouth, for instance, on which commercial privileges had been conferred by the king, was invaded by the inhabitants of the adjacent districts, and its charter was torn up.[2] Finally, numerous people made use of the insurrection to revenge themselves on their personal enemies.

Whether one considers its principal or its secondary causes, it is true to say that the revolt of 1381 was, so to **The rising** speak, a settlement of old scores of every kind. **lacking** It was above all an eruption of long-cherished **in unity** envy, hatred, and malice—feelings which had every excuse—towards the selfishness of the rich. It is

1. " Dixit quod ipse est nuntius *magne societatis* et missus est ad villam Sancti Edmundi predicti ad faciendum communitatem eiusdem ville surgere " (Powell, *Rising in East Anglia*, p. 127).

2. Réville, *op. cit.*, p. 109.

consequently most instructive to the historian.   But for the same reason it altogether lacked unity, it was not inspired by a single noble idea, and it was directed by demagogues of only mediocre ability.   It had some of the characteristics of a political movement, of a religious movement, and especially of a social movement; but none of these terms defines it sufficiently, and even if one uses all three to describe it, there is still a danger of giving a false impression.

We cannot call it a political rising unless all manner of qualifications are at once added.   It was, in fact,

The rebels without a political programme

inspired by very different sentiments in different regions, and there were districts where the rebels showed no desire for a change of ministers.   Nowhere was there any thought of a dynastic revolution. In several counties, it is true, " kings of the commons " made their appearance; but they were incendiaries without any programme —mere leaders of rebel bands.   Even in the south-eastern counties, where the government was very unpopular, the rebels affected a high regard for the person of the king.   A careful distinction was drawn between him and the " traitors " who surrounded him.

Several " traitors " atoned with their lives for the humiliation and the misfortunes of England, but these murders

Hatred of traitors

were not the outcome of a calculated policy. They were inspired by childish hatred.   This naïve feeling had no connection with any political scheme.   No one suggested any way of doing better than the men in power, and there was no reasonable motive for substituting new ministers for those in control of affairs.   Neither the king, nor as a rule the very persons who were insulted with the name of " traitors," were at all responsible for the evils under which the realm was suffering.   Sudbury and Hales were honourable men.   The Duke of Lancaster, in regard to whom the rebels were by no means in agreement,[1] was rather foolish than dangerous.   All of them were involved in extraordinary difficulties.   Disorder had for many years been general.   The financial problem was insoluble.   Unpopular as the taxes were, they were yet indispensable, since parliament itself was not ready to take the responsibility of making peace with France.   The luxury of the Court, of which so much was said, was not peculiar to England.   The king of France and the duke of Burgundy, in particular, were certainly no less extravagant than Edward III and Richard II. The difficulties would not have been solved by reducing the staff of the king's household.   The truth was that England was paying for Edward III's ambitious policy and careless administration.   It was not by cutting off the heads of several ministers without suggesting anybody to take their place that the prestige and prosperity of England were to be restored.   The political situation was certainly serious, and contributed to the general discontent ; but for many reasons, and especially because they had no clear idea of the reforms which were needed, the rebels were incapable of effecting any improvement. Their very leaders had no political programme.

Nor were the rebels of 1381 heretics.   It may be regarded as proved that Wycliffe had no influence on the revolt.[2]   Lollardy was still in its infancy.

Were religious influences at work? The insurgents were not Lollards ; they nowhere denied the spiritual powers of the clergy ; they nowhere injured the statues or pictures of the saints.   But this does not exclude the possibility that very revolutionary notions about a Christian democracy were in the air, and that many felt a strong contempt for the vices of the higher clergy and

1. See Stubbs, ii. 472.
2. See my *Introduction,* pp. lxiii sqq. ; Trevelyan, *England in the Age of Wycliffe,* pp. 195 sqq. ; Gairdner, *Lollardy and the Reformation in England,* i. 14 sqq.

of the profligate rich. While preaching resignation to humble folk, Wycliffe fiercely denounced the excessive wealth of the prelates and the monks. Men of moderate views, friends of the existing order, were scandalised by the prevalent corruption, and made no effort to hide their virtuous indignation. Langland's " Vision of Piers the Plowman," which was already famous, bears striking witness to this state of mind.[1] Like Wycliffe, Langland had no wish for a revolution, but the puritan fervour which inspired both might easily give birth to fanaticism in less well-regulated minds, and it did in fact exert a strong influence on certain leaders in 1381. Letters couched in obscure and grotesque language,[2] which were passed from hand to hand for the encouragement of the rebels, bear the impress of mysticism. It is also remarkable that during the destruction of the palace of the Savoy in London, the rebels were forbidden to steal anything on pain of death. It is, however, true that elsewhere, and even in London, the lowest greed was often the motive of the crimes they committed, and in many places the insurgents were nothing more than vulgar robbers. The ideas of the religious reformers had widespread influence only in so far as they provoked attacks against the property and the temporal power of the clergy.

To speak of a social rising would be more correct. It was not merely that the distribution of the lands of the clergy, the abolition of serfdom, the repeal of the statutes of labourers, were explicitly demanded by the rebels of Kent and Essex in their interviews with the king; but most of their doings were acts of social warfare. The nobles were terrorised and humiliated; the rich were attacked; manorial customs

Social aspects of the rising

---

1. See J. J. Jusserand, *L'Epopée mystique de W. Langland.*

2. The text of these mysterious letters is given in *Knighton* (R. S.), ii. 138 sqq. ; Walsingham, *Hist. Ang.* (R. S.), ii. 33 sqq. ; and translated by Oman, *op. cit.,* pp 43 sqq.

were repudiated, and all record of them was as far as possible destroyed; prescriptive rights were enlarged; there was much pillaging and many evictions. Nevertheless, even this campaign was lacking in unity. In one county, the rebels thought only of filling their pockets without care for the morrow; in another, they respected the forms of law, and their sole concern was to obtain from their lords charters duly sealed. Nowhere did they suggest that the land should be made common property.

In a word, the political, religious, and economic crisis explains the revolt of 1381; but no definite theory—political, religious, or social—suggested to the rebels a consistent and logical line of conduct. The fire broke out in 1381 not because great agitators, men with principles and a programme, kindled a flame which little by little covered the realm, but because, if I may use the expression, England was full of inflammable material and at the mercy of a spark. It must not be supposed, however, that there was any lack of agitators to excite popular passion. A statute of May 1382 tells us of the activity of wandering preachers who raised their voices at fairs and wherever they could find an audience, preaching " divers matters of slander, to make discord and dissension between the divers estates of the said realm, as well temporal as spiritual, to the disturbance of the people." It is probable that wandering monks and clerks had for long excited the people against the rich. One of them indeed is well known. For twenty years before the revolt the itinerant preacher John Ball[1] advocated in town and country the overthrow of the government and society. [2] But it was not he or, it seems, any other agitator of note who led the first rebels. When Essex and Kent rose up he was in prison.

Lack of principles and leaders

Agitators

John Ball

1. Cf. a note of Stubbs, *Const. Hist.*, ii. 473, n. 1.
2. See my *Memoir* on *Les Prédictions populaires, les Lollards et le soulèvement des travailleurs anglais en 1381* in *Etudes d'Hist. du moyen age dédiées à Gabriel Monod*, pp. 373 sqq.

The brand which suddenly kindled the fire was the Poll Tax, voted by the Parliament of 5 Nov. 1380 to raise money for an expedition to France. With **The Poll-tax** the exception of beggars, every lay person of the realm over fifteen years of age had to pay a shilling (three groats). In each village the strong were to help the weak, but no one should pay less than a groat or more than twenty shillings. [1] This impost fell very severely on the poor, much more so than the Poll Tax of 1379. [2] The object of the government was to conciliate the rich, and to make humble folk contribute more largely than before. Moreover, there were villages where it was impossible for the strong to help the weak, because no one was strong : and thus in adjacent districts, according as they possessed wealthy inhabitants or not, the poor might be taxed at quite different rates. Everything, therefore, tended to excite opposition. Finding the people in an ugly temper, the collectors often allowed the village constable to supply them with false lists, which estimated the population at a figure much lower than the actual one. But the government quickly perceived the fraud, and as early as 2 January 1381 the sheriff and the escheator of each county were ordered to supply the exchequer with exact information as to the number of those liable to contribute. [3] Finally, on 16 March, the king set up in sixteen counties commissions empowered to revise the assessments and to exact payment from every one who had hitherto evaded the imposition. This measure was suggested by the sergeant John Leg. It was shown, for example, that in Norfolk 8,005 names, in Suffolk 12,904, had been omitted.[4] Even the corrected lists which were then drawn up gave a total much inferior to what might

1. See the passage cited in Stubbs, *Const. Hist.*, ii. 470, n. 3.
2. *Ibid.*, 468. In 1379 the rich were taxed at a much higher rate, and those in humble circumstances all paid a groat.
3. *C. P. R.*, 1377-81, pp. 627-8.
4. Powell, *Rising in East Anglia*, p. 6.

have been expected,[1] a fact which proves that many people had fled to avoid the tax and had joined the army of vagabonds and outlaws.

The doings of these commissions put the last straw on the patience of the people. The sixteen counties where they had been set up were all, or almost all, affected by the rising. It is absolutely certain that the weight and the unjust assessment of the tax, coupled with the foolish determination of the government to get the full amount, were the direct cause of the revolt. Wherever they could, the rebels burnt the poll-tax rolls, maltreated the collectors, and sought out the sheriffs and escheators who had been commissioned to revise the assessments and to arrest those who resisted. One of their victims in London was John Leg. The evidence of the facts, the assertions of the chroniclers, and the admissions of the parliament of Nov. 1381 [2] all point in the same direction. The peasants rose on a question of taxation; and, to repeat what was said above, they rose at this time because they were in a state of revolutionary excitement [3] for the various reasons which we have mentioned.

General irritation

1. The lists of the Poll Tax of 1377 furnish a total of 1,355,201 persons over fourteen years of age, and the list of 1381 a total of 896,451 persons above fifteen. In Essex and in Kent, the counties where the revolt first broke out, the figures fell from 47,962 (1377) to 30,748 (1381), and from 56,557 to 43,838 (Powell, *Rising, App.* I). In an otherwise interesting chapter on the Poll Tax, Mr. Oman (*op. cit.,* pp. 22 sqq.) has, in dealing with these figures, made mistakes which have been pointed out by Mr. James Tait (*Eng. Hist. Rev.,* 1907, p. 162).

2. See my *Introduction,* pp. lvii sqq.

3. " Plures ligei . . . in comitatibus Cancie et Essexie insurrexerunt et ut mala per eosdem *longe ante precogitata* facilius ad finem ducerent in diversas et magnas turmas se congregaverunt " (Inquisition of 1382, in Réville, *op. cit.,* app. II, no. 10, p. 196, n. 4).

GENERAL CHARACTERISTICS AND RESULTS OF THE RISING.

This is not the place for a detailed history of the revolt : and we shall limit ourselves to pointing out its character in each district and emphasising certain features which are passed over by Stubbs.

The chancery of Richard II fixed 1 May as the approximate date of the beginning of the rising,[1] and there is in fact every reason to believe that very early in the month the collection of the poll-tax occasioned disturbances in Kent and Essex. The first documents bearing a precise date refer to Essex.

Disorders in the south-east during May

Essex was a poor county, which, as we have seen, was for long subject to the oppression of the forest law. The burdens of serfdom were heavy,[2] and bitter discontent prevailed. The people of Essex rose in a body, villeins, artisans, and rich landholders. They played a prominent part in the movement. It was they who remained longest in arms; and they worked enthusiastically to spread the revolt, sending emissaries to distant parts with instructions. In this county the first signal of rebellion seems to have been given by the villagers of Fobbing, led by one Thomas, surnamed Baker from his trade. In conse-

The outbreak of the rising in Essex

---

1. ". . . Ipse fuisse debuit unus illorum qui Fflandrenses in Colchestre tempore rumoris, videlicet inter primum diem maii, anno regni nostri quarto, et festum Omnium Sanctorum extunc proxime sequens, interfecerunt" (Réville, *op. cit.,* App. II, no. 61). ". . . In insurrectionibus a primo die maii anno regni nostri quarto usque festum Omnium Sanctorum tunc proxime sequens qualitercumque factis . . . " (*ibid.,* no. 219).

2. See especially Clark, *Serfdom on an Essex Manor, 1308-78* (*Eng. Hist. Rev.,* 1905, pp. 479 sqq.).

quence of the second assessment of the poll-tax, a supplementary contribution was demanded of them. They declared that they would not pay a penny more. On being " sternly threatened " by the royal commissioner, they sought help in the neighbouring villages. Certain justices of the peace were sent to Brentwood to restore order : but they were driven away on 30 May by bands from the villages along the Thames between Barking and Corringham. This was unquestionably the first centre of the insurrection.[1]

These events were at once reported in London, and caused great excitement. London was a restless city, a field of frequent agitations, whether political, social, or religious. In 1377 and 1378 the attempts to bring Wycliffe to trial had occasioned serious riots, and men's tempers had not been soothed by the news which for the past year had been arriving about the disturbances in Flanders and Paris. Several aldermen were hostile to the government and to William Walworth the mayor.[2] Some of the inhabitants[3] considered that the book of the constitutions of the city was only fit to be burnt. Others were awaiting an opportunity to settle personal quarrels : among these was Thomas Faringdon, a citizen of good family, who thought he had a grievance against Robert Hales the treasurer.

Effect on London

1. See the inquisition published *Trans. Essex Archæol. Soc.,* New Series, i. 218-9. Also the anonymous chronicle published by G. M. Trevelyan (*An Account of the Rising of 1381, Eng. Hist. Rev.,* 1898, p. 510). Cf. the other documents cited in my *Introduction,* pp. lxx-i. The anonymous chronicler gives very full information, which corroborates what was put forward in my *Introduction* as to the starting-point and cause of the rising in Essex ; but I cannot agree with Mr. Oman in his opinion that we should adopt this account in its entirety and prefer it to that of the inquisition.
2. William Walworth, fishmonger, was mayor from March to October, 1381. See A. B. Beaven, *The Aldermen of London in the time of Richard II* (*Eng. Hist. Rev.,* 1907, p. 525).
3. As, for instance, the brewer Walter atte Keye, who on 14 June was looking for " liber de constitucionibus civitatis Londoniarum, vocatus le Jubyle," in order to burn it, and who wished to set fire to the Gildhall (Réville, *op. cit.,* App. II, No. 32).

At the end of May or beginning of June, some of the Londoners—among them Thomas Faringdon and two butchers—went to the assistance of the bands which had just gathered in Essex to drive off the collectors and the justices. At the instigation of the new-comers, a number of Essex men set out for London, burning on their way the house of Robert Hales, and those of the sheriff and the escheator of the county.[1] Others crossed the Thames to lend help to the rebels in Kent.

Kent was not unprosperous, and villeinage was rare in the county : but, like the lower orders in London, the people were of a revolutionary temper, no doubt
Kent because it was in Kent that all military adventurers landed on their return from France. On 2 June a mob which had gathered on the right bank of the Thames, at Erith, began its exploits by invading the abbey of Lesnes;[2] and on the following days it marched through Dartford, Rochester, Maidstone, and Preston, forcing the monks and gentry to follow it, destroying and pillaging the houses of certain rich men, throwing open the gaols, and burning all repositories of official records. The systematic destruction of the records of the justices of the peace and the tax-collectors shows what strong feeling had been aroused by the administration of the Statutes of Labourers and the imposition of taxation. After being repeatedly reinforced by the malefactors whom they everywhere set at liberty, the rebel force reached Canterbury on 10 June. They began to seek for archbishop Sudbury, whom in their ignorance they regarded as largely responsible for the country's misfortunes. He was away, and they had to content them-

1. Réville, no. 10 ; *Essex Archæol. Soc. Transactions, New Series,* i. 217 sqq.
2. According to the author of the anonymous chronicle edited by Mr. Trevelyan (p. 511) the initial cause of the rising in Kent was the arrest of a serf, alleged to belong to a knight of the king's household, who had him imprisoned in Rochester Castle. The rebels, if we are to believe this authority, besieged the castle in order to set him free. It is a fact that, according to one of the judicial records found by Réville (*op. cit.,* p. 187, no. 3), a band under Robert Cave, a baker, released and carried away a certain Robert Bellyng, who had been imprisoned in the castle in question.

selves with sacking his palace and the houses of certain others whom they mistrusted, and with cutting off the heads of three " traitors." [1] At this date, the whole of east Kent was in a state of insurrection ; and the district was overrun by hordes of rebels, plundering, burning the records of collectors and escheators, and breaking open prisons.   In Thanet, where serfdom still existed, the services and customary dues of the villeins were declared to be abolished. [2]

On 11 June, the rebels of Kent and Essex who on the previous day had entered Canterbury, set out for London,

March on London

headed by John Ball, whom they had just released from prison,[3] and by two new leaders, Jack Straw and Wat Tyler.

Jack Straw was regarded by contemporaries as one of the chief popular leaders ; but we know very little either of him or of the part which he personally played.[4]   As for Wat Tyler, he suddenly appears in history during the march to Canterbury.   According to the anonymous chronicler, it was after the taking of Rochester (6 June) that the men of Kent "chose as chieftain Wat Teghler of Maidstone to maintain and counsel them." [5]   The rebels passed through Maidstone on 7 June,[6] and Tyler may have joined them there : but it is doubtful whether he was a native of Maidstone, since juries from various places in

1. The executions rest on the authority of the anonymous chronicle.
2. Flaherty, *The Great Rebellion of 1381 in Kent* (*Archæologia Cantiana*, 1860, vol. iii) ; Réville, *App.* II, nos. 1 sqq ; Powell and Trevelyan, *Peasants' Rising*, pp. 4 sqq. ; cf. the anonymous chronicle edited by Trevelyan, p 512.
3. He was in the archbishop's prison at Maidstone (*Chron. Hen. Knighton*, ii. 131), which was forced on ,his same day, 11 June (Powell and Trevelyan, *Peasants' Rising*, p. 9).
4. The confession put into his mouth by the chronicler Walsingham (see Stubbs, *Const. Hist.*, ii. 474) is, I think, almost certainly spurious. F. W. Brie (*Wat Tyler and Jack Straw, Eng. Hist. Rev.*, 1906, pp. 106 sqq.) has tried to prove that the two names are applied in the records to one and the same person.   This theory, however, cannot be accepted. The best chronicles and the rolls of parliament distinguish clearly between Wat Tyler and Jack Straw.   It is likely that the latter name was a corruption of Rakestraw, and that the rebel leader was called Jack Rakestraw.
5. P. 512.   6. Réville, *App.*, ii, nos. 1-3.

Kent—Faversham, Downhamford, and Maidstone itself —asserted that he was born in Essex.[1] Nor is it certain that he was a tiler, as a chronicler affirms,[2] for at this time the name no longer necessarily denoted the profession of its owner.   It is tempting to suppose that Wat Tyler was a wandering adventurer,[3] who had served in the French wars, and now put his military experience at the service of the rebels.   His resolute spirit, his daring, the authority which he acquired over his companions, would be adequately explained by this hypothesis. Froissart, moreover, states that Tyler had served as a man-at-arms in France;[4] and whatever may have been said of his trustworthiness, Froissart, though certainly guilty of much inaccuracy and confusion in his account of these events, had nevertheless collected much precise information, which is often confirmed by official documents.

Such were the beginnings of the rebellion.   It arose almost simultaneously in Essex and Kent, on the shores of the Thames, the occasion being the collection of the poll-tax.   The irritation felt by so many against the great landholders, the justices, the royal officials, the " traitor " ministers, added to the inflammatory advice of certain daring leaders, transformed a riot of tax-resisters into a revolution.   After ten days the flames were blazing in so many places at once that very vigorous action would have been necessary to quench them.   But the government seemed paralysed by the failure of the feeble measures it adopted at the beginning of the trouble.   The great lords and military commanders who

Conclusions concerning the beginning of the revolt

---

1. The authorities are printed by Flaherty, *loc. cit.*, pp. 92 sqq., and by Powell and Trevelyan, *op. cit.*, p. 9.
2. " Unus tegulator de Estsex " (*Eulogium Historiarum*, (R.S.), iii. 352).   Cf. Kriehn, *op. cit.*, pp. 459 sqq.
3. The vagueness of the statements as to his origin supports this conjecture.   At Smithfield, a "valet" in the king's train declared that Wat Tyler was the greatest thief in Kent, and that he recognised him as such (*Chron. anon.*, ed. Trevelyan, p. 519).
4. Ed. Luce-Raynaud, *Soc. Hist., Fr.*, x. 108.

were then with the king hesitated to call the nobles to arms. Helped by treachery, the rebels had everything their own way for several days.

Thanks to the accounts of the chroniclers, historians have long been familiar with the tragic events which came to pass in London and the neighbourhood from 12 to 15 June :[1] the pillaging of the archbishop's manor at Lambeth and the marshal's at Southwark; the rescue of the prisoners in the King's Bench and the Marshalsea (12 June); the abortive attempt at a meeting between the young king and the rebels at Blackheath;[2] the entry of the rebel bands into London ; the burning of the Savoy, the palace of the duke of Lancaster, and of the property of the Hospitallers, whose prior was the treasurer Hales, one of the "traitors" (13 June); the interview between Richard and the insurgents at Mile End, and his promise to enfranchise all the villeins in the realm ; the murder of the archbishop and the treasurer at the Tower, and massacres in the streets of the city (14 June); Wat Tyler's meeting with the king at Smithfield, followed by his death and the dispersion of the rebels (15 June). The documents discovered since Stubbs summarised the history of these events throw no fresh light on the apparent desertion by Richard of the archbishop and the treasurer : and it is still impossible to explain how and why they fell into the hands of the angry mob in a stronghold which was evidently capable of successful defence against the rebels.[3] Nor has greater certainty been

London and the suburbs, 12—15 June

1. See my Introduction, pp. lxxx–xcvi ; Oman, Great Revolt of 1381, pp. 46 sqq.

2. The Anonymous Chronicle (pp. 513 sq.) confirms most of Froissart's account of this episode, and adds a few details of its own.

3. The author of the Anonymous Chronicle tries to justify the king, but his account clearly shows that when Richard left for Mile End nothing was done to ensure the safety of the Tower. The chronicler says that before setting out, Richard advised the archbishop and those with him to make their escape by the river. Sudbury tried to do so, but the notice of the rebels was drawn by the cries of a woman who recognised him, and he went back to the Tower. Realising that he had no hope of escape " l'archevesque chanta sa messe devotement en la Toure

attained regarding the events of 15 June. Notwithstanding Froissart's evidence, it is certain that the interview at Smithfield was desired by the king and his advisers, but the development of the action and the death of Tyler still seem to have been the result of chance.[1] The field thus remains clear for theories.[2]

et confessa le prior de la Hospitall de Clerkenwell et autres ; et puis oya deux messes ou trois et chanta la *Comendacione* et *Placebo et Dirige* et les VII salmes et la latinée et quant il fust a *Omnes sancti orate pro nobis,* le comens entreront et [traierent] le archevesque hors de sa chapelle en la toure " (ed. Trevelyan, pp. 516-7). The rebels wandered at will through the Tower : " Thomas at Sole, ville de Gravesend, se cognovit esse infra cameram domini regis in Turri Londoniensi in crastino Corporis Christi et cum gladio suo lectum domini regis fincit " (Powell and Trevelyan, *op. cit.,* p. 10).

1. According to the Anonymous Chronicle, the king replied personally to the demands put forward by Wat Tyler, all of which he granted, with a reservation of the rights of the crown. At this stage none of his train dared to speak. Tyler, however, aroused the anger of the king's followers by rinsing his mouth and drinking in the king's presence. As he was remounting his horse a " valet " of Kent who was present cried that he recognised Tyler, who was the greatest thief in the whole of his county. Wat Tyler rode at him to kill him ; but Walworth, interposing, exchanged blows with Tyler, and wounded him, while another valet of the king's household, coming to the mayor's aid, cut at him several times with his sword. Tyler spurred his horse and fled ; but he soon rolled from his saddle and fell to the ground. Warned by his shouts, the rebels were preparing to help him, when Richard put himself at their head and succeeded in persuading them to follow him. Walworth went to seek reinforcements ; and the insurgents were surrounded. Tyler was found in a room of the hospital of St. Bartholomew ; Walworth had him carried out into Smithfield, and he was beheaded in the presence of his associates (ed. Trevelyan, pp. 519 sqq.).

2. Mr. Kriehn argues (*op. cit.,* pp. 472 sqq.) that Tyler's death is best explained as one of the political murders " that darken English history." The various precautions taken before the meeting at Smithfield (Richard II's prayers at Westminster ; the selection of a place quite close to London ; the cuirass worn by Walworth under his cloak), and the speed with which the London loyalists arrived to surround the rebels—these facts, he thinks, show that Tyler's murder was premeditated and that he walked into a trap. It may have been so : but the facts relied upon by Mr. Kriehn can be explained on other grounds.

Mr. Powell thinks that a secret understanding, based on common enmity towards John of Gaunt, existed between Richard and the rebel leaders (*Rising in East Anglia,* pp. 58 sqq.). This, he says, would explain the readiness with which, on the death of Tyler, " the rebels transferred their allegiance to the king." His language, however, is misleading ; for Richard had never ceased to be regarded as king by the insurgents. It is moreover difficult to think that such tortuous schemes could have been planned and carried out by a mere youth. For our part, we are disposed to accept the account of the Anonymous Chronicle, and to assign to chance a large share in the events of the day.

On the other hand, the causes of the temporary success of the movement have been more clearly revealed, and the mental attitude of the insurgents in south-east England can be described with some confidence. If the conduct of the king's supporters remains mysterious and suspicious, the records have now shed a very clear light on that of the rebels and their accomplices.

The judicial documents discovered by Réville establish the complicity with the insurgents of a number of Londoners who played a very active part **Connivance of certain aldermen** during the time from 13 to 15 June. "The London mob," says Stubbs, "sympathised with the avowed purposes of the rebels." Sympathy was felt not only by the mob. At least three aldermen played false to Walworth the mayor. One of them, the fishmonger John Horn, was sent to meet the rebels. They were wavering, and half disposed to go home. Horn's mission was to strengthen this inclination. So far from doing so, however, he urged them to push on to London, where, he said, they would be given a hearty welcome and good cheer; and during the next night he in fact admitted several of the leaders to the city and put them up at his house. Finally, on the 13th, he went to Blackheath displaying a royal standard, and declared to the rebels that in the capital they would find none but friends. They accordingly set out, intending to cross the Thames at London Bridge. The defence of the bridge had been entrusted by the mayor to another alderman, Walter Sybyle; he, however, hindered the citizens from preparing resistance, and when the rebels arrived from Blackheath, let them pass without even a pretence of opposition. A third alderman, William Tonge, flung open Aldgate, on the east of the city, to the bands from Essex. In short, London was delivered to the insurgents by aldermen hostile to the mayor.[1]

1. Réville, Document no. 10; cf. Froissart, x. 110. On the subsequent acquittal of the aldermen, see my *Introduction*, p. lxxxiii, n. 3. Cf. a document printed by Powell and Trevelyan, *Peasants' Rising*, p. 30.

Once the rebels were inside the walls, Londoners made use of them and directed their movements. John Horn set himself up as redresser of wrongs, and pronounced sentences. It was certainly at the instigation of Londoners that the insurgents destroyed the Savoy and the Hospital.[1] Many victims of the massacres of 14 June must have been pointed out to their murderers by citizens. Thomas Faringdon and his friends had spent the previous night drawing up proscription-lists.[2] Particular animosity was shown towards those in the service of the duke of Lancaster, who was an object of hatred to a whole party in the city, his surgeon and one of his esquires being slain. A large number of Englishmen and Flemings[3] were beheaded in the streets : some of these were considered " traitors," as for instance the financier Richard Lyons ; but very often the sole motive was personal enmity or jealousy of foreign competition. Along with many tragic episodes, the judicial records narrate mean and almost humorous incidents, which are yet very significant ; and we can see Londoners terrorising their creditors, holding worthy citizens to ransom, and, by a turn of the hand, bringing long actions-at-law to a favourable termination.[4] During this time, as Froissart well puts it, the peasants from Kent and Essex, crowded in the narrow streets, " knew not what they wanted or what they were seeking, but followed one another about like cattle."[5]

Misdeeds of the Londoners

---

1. Réville, Documents, nos. 10 sqq.

2. " Recepit secum noctanter plures principales insurrectores, videlicet Robertum de la Warde et alios, ymaginando illa nocte et cum aliis sociis suis conspirando nomina diversorum civium que fecit scribi in quadam cedula, quos vellet decapitare et eorum tenementa prostrare " (Réville, no. 10, p. 195).

3. That Flemings were murdered is attested by documents of all kinds, and by the Anonymous Chronicle (p. 518), which also mentions the pillaging of the houses of Lombard merchants. [Chaucer's one allusion to the rising concerns the massacre of the Flemings (*Nonne Prestes Tale*, lines 573 sqq.)]

4. Réville, nos. 10, 32, 33, 34, 36.

5. Froissart, x. 98.

U

When on 15 June Walworth came from Smithfield to collect reinforcements, Sybyle and Horn strove by spreading false reports to prevent the Londoners from leaving the city.[1] This time, however, they failed : and the citizens, exasperated by the disorder and violence they had witnessed or endured, brought help to the king.

The reaction of 15 June

Inhabitants of London, urged by political or private hatred, or merely by self-interest, were therefore largely responsible for the murders and other misdeeds committed in the capital. Without their intervention, it would be impossible to understand the demoralisation of the government during the four days or the violence shown towards foreigners.

But it was not only the Londoners who were bitter against the "traitors." The Anonymous Chronicle shows how widespread was this feeling, by which indeed, at times of disturbance, the popular imagination is nearly always inflamed. The malcontents of Essex and Kent were convinced that everything would be well if only they could rid the world of John of Gaunt, the archbishop and the treasurer, the bishop of London, and some of the chief officers of finance and justice. From Blackheath they sent a naïve message to the king, demanding the heads of these traitors. Next day the peasants gathered outside the Tower, refusing to move when urged to go to Mile End ; and the mob on St. Catherine's wharf declared that they would not go away " before they had the traitors in the Tower " : and, as we know, they kept their word. The removal of the " traitors " they associated with the welfare of the king, which they professed themselves anxious to promote. Before entering London they had told a messenger from the king that they were coming " for his salvation and the destruction of those who were traitors to him

Attitude of the rebels of Kent and Essex

Loyalty to Richard

1. Réville, no. 10, p. 194.

and the realm." [1] They had as watchword : " With whome haldes you ?" and anyone challenged had to reply, on pain of death : " With Kinge Richarde and the true comons." When they met the king at Mile End, they knelt, protested their loyalty, and forthwith demanded the death of the traitors. At Smithfield, they showed the same respect for the king's person. Even Tyler seems to have used no threats against Richard himself. At the beginning of the interview, he assumed the demeanour and tone of a demagogue who knew his manners and was anxious to put his sovereign at his ease. He took the young king by the hand and shook it, saying, " Brother, be of good cheer and merry, for within the next fortnight,[2] you shall have more joy of the commons than ever you had before, and we shall be good comrades." [3]

The men of Kent and Essex, however, did not confine themselves to demands for mere personal changes in the government. They wanted large social
Tyler's demands reforms, and on this head the Anonymous Chronicle gives information which seems worthy of belief.[4] At Smithfield the rebels declared that they would not go home without a charter of liberties. When asked to explain what his followers wanted, Tyler said that every law except the statute of Winchester must be repealed, that outlawry must be abolished, that villeinage must cease, and that the property of the church must be divided among the people, except what was necessary for the maintenance of the clerks and of a single bishop, one being quite enough for the whole

1. The statements of the anonymous chronicler on this attitude of the rebels of the south-east are moreover confirmed by other documents of high authority, notably by John Malvern's most valuable continuation of the *Polychronicon Ranulfi Higden* : " Hi quidem de Cantia . . . praetendentes se defensuros regem et regni commoditatem contra suos traditores " (Higden, ed. Lumby (R. S.), ix. 1).
2. Mr. Kriehn (*art. cit.*, p. 471) strangely misinterprets this phrase : *quinsane* means " fortnight," and not the tax known as a fifteenth.
3. *Anon. Chron.*, ed. Trevelyan, pp. 513 sqq.
4. *Ibid.*, pp. 519 sqq. ; cf. Kriehn, pp. 477 sqq.

country. The rebels thus demanded the abandonment of every measure taken since 1285 for the maintenance of public order and the regulation of labour : above all, it seems, they wanted the Statutes of Labourers repealed. The reason for their objection to outlawry was that this sentence was pronounced on wandering labourers who refused to obey the statutes. The demand, already put forward at Mile End, for the abolition of villeinage was only to be expected, for Tyler was speaking on behalf of peasants, many of whom still laboured under the burdens and humiliations of serfdom. Another chronicler adds that the peasants also claimed liberty to hunt and fish, and this too was very natural. As for the reform of the church, it was urged by religious agitators, and especially by John Ball, who had been with the rebels for several days. According to the anonymous chronicler, Ball preached the very doctrine that Tyler put forward in his speech : there was to be no bishop in England except one archbishop, who should be Ball himself ; no religious house might have more than two monks or canons ; and ecclesiastical property should be distributed among the laity. "Wherefore," continues the chronicler, " he was held among the commons as a prophet." [1] The charter of liberties which Tyler wished to dictate to the king may therefore be taken as a faithful summary of the hopes which the leaders had excited in the breasts of the insurgents from Essex and Kent.

When the rebels lost their chief and dispersed to their homes, nothing more was heard of this programme of reforms. For some weeks still, the peasants of Kent and Essex committed robberies, held their enemies to ransom, plundered game-preserves, and burned legal documents : while in Thanet villeins who continued to " do services " were threatened with death.[2] But all this was mere

Essex and Kent after 15 June

1. *Chron. Anon.*, p. 512.
2. *Archæologia Cantiana*, iii. 71 sqq. ; *Trans. Essex Archæol. Soc.*, New Series, i. 218 ; Réville, nos. 59 sqq. ; Powell and Trevelyan, *op. cit.*, pp. 3 sqq.

vulgar lawlessness, and soon ceased in the face of repressive measures.

Notwithstanding the speedy collapse of the ambitious schemes of Wat Tyler, Jack Straw, and John Ball, the rising spread far and wide. Stubbs recog-
Spread of the rising nised that it had a wide range : but he lacked the evidence necessary to form an accurate estimate of the extent of the revolt. The documents collected by Réville, however, show that the greater part of the realm was affected.

Middlesex and North Surrey were as profoundly disturbed as Essex and Kent, and supplied some of the
Surrey and Sussex bands which invaded London or sacked the suburbs. The Essex rebels, who were particularly daring and enthusiastic, sent emissaries as far as the middle of Surrey, and both in this county and in Sussex, there were risings of the peasants, which occasioned serious disorder, though unfortunately little is known about it. Nearly all the south-western counties—
Berkshire, Hants, Wilts, and Somerset—
The rising spreads towards the south-west were influenced sooner or later by the wave of revolution. The towns of Winchester, Salisbury, and Bridgewater witnessed violent disturbances which evidently sprang from local jealousies, though we know that the people of Bridgewater went to seek inspiration in London.[1]

In Hertfordshire the revolt broke out on the evening of 13 June, at the news of the success of the rebel-
Hertfordshire lion in London; but as Réville has shown, the rising in this county had a distinct character of its own.[2] The insurgents were almost all peasants, most of them free and many in comfortable circumstances. In Hertfordshire much land was held by

---

1. Réville, *App.* II, series A and F. Cf. my *Introduction*, pp. xcviii sqq., cvii sqq. On the rising in Surrey, see also Powell and Trevelyan, *op. cit.*, p. 17 : on that in Sussex, Page, *Umwandlung der Frohndienste*, p. 41, n. 37.
2. Réville, pp. 3—49.

the church, especially by the powerful abbey of St. Albans, and the tenants were severely treated. The ecclesiastical landlords refused to enfranchise their serfs, to abandon their monopolies, to renounce their privileges of hunting and fishing, and to extend the customary rights of the peasantry. The town of St. Albans had repeatedly demanded certain liberties, but in vain.[1] Stimulated by both the example and the precepts of the rebels of the south-east, the peasants rose in rebellion, but their object was merely to obtain a few specific reforms.

After receiving a message calling on them to take their weapons and join the men of Kent and Essex in London, St. Albans the inhabitants of St. Albans set out for the capital on the morning of the 14th. In the presence of Jack Straw, they took the oath of obedience to the king and the people, received instructions and promises of aid from Wat Tyler, and obtained from Richard a letter urging Thomas de la Mare, the abbot, to gratify their wishes. They had no thought of demanding the distribution of the abbey lands among themselves. As defined in the charter which the abbot granted them on 16 June, their requests were modest and practical. In the first place, rights of passage, Charters pasture, hunting and fishing were conceded them. The monopoly of the abbey mill was abolished, and it was agreed that the abbot's bailiff should no longer interfere in the government of the town. With these concessions they declared themselves satisfied. The other tenants of the abbey had assembled from all parts of the county, and they also demanded charters. Thomas de la Mare granted about a score, conceding the enfranchisement of the villeins, rights of hunting and fishing, rights of pasture, and the abolition of certain rents and monopolies. At Dunstable, in the same way, the tenants of the priory made no attempt to assert their independence, but they

1. See Stubbs, *Const. Hist.*, ii. 477, n. 1.

Dunstable forced the prior to grant them a charter. Criminal offences were comparatively rare. The peasants of Hertfordshire had listened to the appeals and the advice of the rebels of London and Kent, but on reflection they regarded the whole rising as nothing more than an excellent opportunity for settling old differences with their lords, and they showed folly only in believing, even after the death of Wat Tyler and the dispersion of the rebels at Smithfield, that charters and seals would secure them in the possession of the liberties they had won at so little cost.

The whole of west Hertfordshire had been involved in the rising. The neighbouring counties of Bucks and Beds were also disturbed. Tenants repu-
The midlands diated their services, and furnished recruits to the army of rebels which invaded London. Oxfordshire, Warwickshire, and Leicestershire, and perhaps even the counties bordering on Wales, did not escape the infection.[1] Even in the Wirral peninsula the serfs of the abbot of Chester rose up against their lord, though this seems to have been an ill-timed and isolated outbreak.[2] In general, the intensity of the movement declined rapidly as it spread westwards. Towards the north-east, on the other hand, it retained its strength as far as the limits of East Anglia, and stopped only in the distant county of York.

In Cambridgeshire the revolt was general on 15 June. It lasted only four or five days, but was very
Cambridgeshire violent.[3] The first outbreak was excited by messages from London, brought by a

1. See the documents in Réville, *App.* II, series E and G; cf. my *Introduction,* pp. cii, cvi sqq. and notes.
2. We know of this revolt from documents published by Powell and Trevelyan, *Peasants' Rising,* pp. 13 sqq. According to royal letters of 1 Sept. and a statement of the juries, the abbot's serfs took arms on 29 July in the hundred of Wirral, after the reading of a royal proclamation forbidding assemblies and riots. It is not known if they had already rebelled in the month of June.
3. For the rising in Cambridgeshire and Hunts see Powell, *Rising in East Anglia,* pp. 41–56; Réville, *App.* II, series B.

small landholder of Bottisham, John Greyston by name, who had witnessed the murders in the Tower, and by a London saddler, John Staunford, who had lands in the county. Conspicuous among the leaders were two rich landlords, John Hanchach and Geoffrey Cobbe. The rebels copied the exploits of Wat Tyler's followers, burned manorial and royal records and the Poll Tax rolls, drove away lawyers and tax-collectors, and threw open the prisons; but, as in the neighbouring county of Hertford, and for similar reasons, their hatred was principally reserved for the great ecclesiastical proprietors. The peasants were forbidden to pay dues and to perform their services. The houses of the Hospitallers, the monastery of Ely, Barnwell Priory, and Corpus Christi College were entered and plundered. As the burgesses of Cambridge were jealous of the privileges of the University, it had to promise to abandon them. At the same time its archives were in great part destroyed. In Huntingdonshire the wealthy abbey of Ramsey was attacked by rebels from Cambridgeshire and the south, and in
Hunts and Northants. Northants the abbot of Peterborough narrowly escaped death at the hands of his tenants. This last county was one where, in recent years, the villeins had formed unions to refuse labour services.[1]

In Suffolk and Norfolk[2] different economic and social conditions prevailed. Both counties were rich. Villeinage was not unknown; but there were
Peculiar conditions in Norfolk and Suffolk numerous freeholders, many estates held on lease, and even villages without lords. The independence enjoyed by a large section of the peasantry only stimulated feelings of jealousy and irritation towards the wealthy landlords, especially such as were not ready to abandon the ancient

1. For the rebellion in Northants, see my *Introduction*, pp. xxxix, cvii and the notes.
2. See Réville's account, *op. cit.*, pp. 53—128; also Powell, *Rising in East Anglia*, pp. 9—40.

methods of cultivation.   Among these was the abbot of
Bury St. Edmunds, one of the most powerful lords in
England, who resolutely maintained the burdens of serfdom on his enormous estates, and refused to grant privileges to the inhabitants of Bury.   A large number of
people, moreover, were engaged in manufacture, especially in Norfolk.   The artisans complained of the
execution of the Statutes of Labourers, and chafed at the
competition of the Flemish workmen who had come to
teach them the textile crafts and had afterwards settled in
their midst.   The rebels of Suffolk and Norfolk were
rural tenants, craftsmen, and small traders.   A good
many discontented priests, and a few gentlemen with an
eye to plunder, like Sir Roger Bacon and Sir Thomas
Cornard, threw in their lot with them.   They took arms at
the instigation of messengers sent by the men of Essex,
but it is improbable that they followed instructions from
Wat Tyler.[1]   Their revolt developed on lines of its own,
and had no real connection with any other movement
save that in Cambridgeshire.   Nevertheless it was very
violent.

The East Anglian rising broke out on 12 June on the
borders of Suffolk and Essex.   On that day a priest
fallen on evil times, John Wrawe by name,
gathered a band of men and plundered a
manor belonging to the financier Richard
Lyons, who two days later was to be executed by the
rebels in London.   The Suffolk insurgents had other
leaders, but John Wrawe was the most daring and the
most influential.   He organised plundering expeditions,
which he directed in person or entrusted to lieutenants,
and the booty gathered was divided among the rebels.
Apparently his sole object was to fill his own pockets.[2]
The chief scene of his exploits was Bury St. Edmunds,

The rising in
Suffolk

---

1. See on this subject the remarks of Réville, *op. cit.,* pp. 61 sqq.
2. See the *Declarations of John Wrawe,* published in Réville, *App.* I,
pp. 175—182.

and the inhabitants, while anxious not to compromise themselves, cunningly urged him on to subvert the authority of the abbey. The abbey was then under the provisional rule of a prior, John of Cambridge, who had done his best to maintain the interests of the house against the townspeople. He and another monk were murdered. The monastery was compelled to grant a charter of liberties to the people of Bury. Another band sought out and seized a high dignitary, Sir John de Cavendish, the chief justice of the King's Bench, whose estates were in Suffolk, and who had been commissioned to superintend the execution of the Statutes of Labourers. Cavendish was beheaded.

Bury St. Edmunds

As early as 14 June the south of Norfolk had been infected by the revolt. Three days later the whole county was involved. It was one of those which suffered most severely.

The rising in Norfolk

In the western part of Norfolk the innumerable misdeeds revealed by judicial documents were in general only acts of pillage or revenge, perpetrated by bands or by isolated individuals. So great was the panic they created, that the rebels were allowed to drive off the cattle, carry away money and food, and dismantle houses. At Lynn they hunted out the Flemings and put them to death. Except in two cases, however, there was in this district no attack on manorial rights. In east Norfolk, on the other hand, the revolt took the form of a social war, conducted with a definite plan of campaign by one daring leader. A dyer of Felmingham, Geoffrey Listere, succeeded in securing his recognition as "king of the commons" by all the rebels of this region. He created a war-chest by setting apart a proportion of the plunder and by levying "customs." His aim was to overthrow all existing authority and to abolish all privileges. Tax-rolls and title-deeds were burnt; lawyers were held to ransom, or

Uncontrolled pillage in West Norfolk

Social war in East Norfolk. Geoffrey Listere

even set in the pillory and executed; the nobles were forced, on pain of death, to follow the "king of the commons" and obey him. The charter of privileges possessed by Yarmouth market was torn up, and several Flemings were executed to please the English craftsmen. For some ten days Norfolk was turned upside down.

The agitation spread from there into Lincolnshire, and even into Yorkshire.[1] On 23 June, at the news of what had been happening "in the regions of the south," a revolutionary government was set up in the remote town of Scarborough. The royal officers were driven away, and the property of the rich was seized. Beverley[2] and York[3] had long been in a disturbed state, and it is difficult to decide how far the disorders which broke out in these towns during July should be regarded as a result of the great rising. According to the juries, however, the hostility of the parties who were contending for the municipal government of York revived at the news of the rising in the south, and the central authority asserted the existence of a link between the troubles in this town and the "diabolical revolt in Kent and Essex."[4]

Yorkshire

Though the rising was disconnected, though its leaders were of mediocre ability, we see that it spread from its birth-place in the south-east far towards the Scottish and Welsh borders without meeting any serious obstacle. A kind of bewilderment had paralysed the king's council and all those whose class interests were imperilled. The monks did little but bemoan their fate. The men of Huntingdon, who shut their gates against the rebels, were regarded as heroes; elsewhere people allowed themselves

No resistance to the rising at first

1. See the documents in Réville, *App.* II, series C and D.; C. T. Flower, *Beverley Town Riots* (*Trans. Royal Hist. Soc.,* New Series, vol. xix, pp. 91 sqq.).
2. See Mr. Flower's account, *loc. cit.,* pp. 79 sqq.
3. Cf. Stubbs, *Const. Hist.,* ed. 1903, vol. iii, chap. 21, sect. 488.
4. Réville, Documents nos. 152 and 180.

to be robbed, except those who tried to gain some advantage from the general disorder. The high-born set the example of cowardice, though Sir Robert Salle, who lost his life for protesting against the crimes of the Norfolk mob, must be excluded from this reproach. But in all parts men of gentle blood submitted to be led about by the rebels, joined in their demands, and obeyed their leaders.

It was only on the death of Wat Tyler that courage returned to the king's advisers. Helped by the mayor and the loyal aldermen of London, the veteran Robert Knolles and the other military leaders with the king at last succeeded in organising resistance, their efforts being seconded in another sphere by lawyers like Bealknap and Tressilian.[1] From 18 June onward the chancery despatched letters to the royal officials for the re-establishment of peace in the disturbed counties. The disturbance had been so profound that order could not be restored as quickly as it had disappeared, and up to the month of November the outlook remained troubled. Nevertheless at the end of June it was already clear that the government had the upper hand.

Military measures were necessary in Essex and Kent. The peasants, though defeated, continued to demand liberties, and in the month of October they again tried to kindle a general insurrection.[2] In Suffolk, William of Ufford, who had formerly fled in disguise, had his revenge, and undertook the pacification of the county from which he

1. For what follows see the documents in Réville, especially series G; cf. his account of the suppression of the revolt in Herts., Suffolk, and Norfolk, pp. 129—172. The repressive measures of the government have received general treatment in my *Introduction,* pp. cxii–cxxviii, to which the reader may be referred.

2. See the documents published by W. E. Flaherty, *Sequel to the Great Rebellion in Kent of 1381 (Archæologia Cantiana,* iv. (1861), pp. 67–86).

derived his title.   The warlike bishop of Norwich, Henry Despenser, marched with an armed force through North-ants, Hunts, Cambridgeshire, and Norfolk, and fought a regular battle with the insurgents at North Walsham.   In every county the local gentry took their vengeance for the fright they had been given ; but there was little slaughter, and the sum-mary execution of Jack Straw has few parallels, even in the cases of very conspicuous leaders.[1]   Legal proceed-ings were everywhere instituted.   In a writ issued imme-diately after his return from Smithfield on 15 June, the king ordered that the guilty should be proceeded against according to the ordinary forms of law.   If we remember the barbarous brutality with which the Jacquerie had been punished in France twenty-three years before, this respect for law and legal forms will appear highly to the credit of mediæval England.

The bishop of Norwich

The forms of law observed

The attitude of the courts was on the whole reasonable and impartial.   With the aid of juries of presentment and petty juries, both civil and criminal cases were investigated and tried by commis-sions which included, on the one hand, the sheriffs and the justices, with Tressilian at their head, and, on the other, persons who had taken the lead in resisting the rebels, like Walworth and Robert Knolles, together with several great lords, like John of Gaunt and the earls of Buckingham, Kent, and Oxford, whose interest it was to display their loyalty.   The government kept an atten-tive eye on the proceedings, for the impartiality of the juries was not above suspicion.   It modified certain sen-tences and sometimes granted pardons. On 12 September the commissioners charged with the investigation of thefts of movable goods were recalled for abusing their powers.   Finally, by a series of writs issued in August

Attitude of the government

1. Cf. *Rot. Parl.*, iii. 175, no. 1.   Even John Ball was formally tried ; see Réville, p. 150.

and September, the king suspended the prosecutions and called all cases before the King's Bench.

Parliament, which met in November, and again in January, 1382, was of the opinion that a general amnesty ought to be granted, though it excepted two hundred and eighty-seven offenders. The amnesty was conceded, but the royal officers often disregarded its terms. Certain leaders, though excluded from the amnesty and even condemned by juries, were released. Others, who should have been protected by the general pardon which parliament had obtained, were prosecuted or obliged to buy letters of protection. The pleasure of the king, therefore, determined the fate of many.

Amnesty granted

All things considered, however, we must repeat that the measures of repression were mild. If the victims on both sides be counted, the revolt, according to Stubbs, may have cost the lives of seven thousand persons [1] —a figure derived from the chroniclers. Official records furnish scarcely a hundred and ten names of rebels who were hanged or beheaded. This number is evidently below the truth, but cannot be very far from it. There is clear proof that many who were guilty of most serious offences escaped the penalty of death.

Moderation of the government

On the other hand, the royal council and the parliaments which met after the revolt, were unanimous in their desire to annul all the acts of the rebels and all the concessions which they had obtained. [2] Apart from damage which could not be repaired, they would leave no trace of the violent effort which the lower classes had made to gain greater independence. Such was the will of king and parliament alike.

Results of the revolt. The concessions annulled

Was this intention realised? Rogers asserts that it was not. In his opinion, the victory, though apparently

1. *Const. Hist.,* ii, 482, and n. 5.
2. *Ibid.,* ii. 482 sqq.

Mistaken view
of Rogers it had fallen to the king and the nobles, really remained with the peasants, and the social war of 1381 had as a result the virtual extinction of villeinage.[1]   This view was accepted by Stubbs.   But the records prove that the events of 1381 caused no change in the condition of the peasants. [2] Serfdom continued on the manors where it previously existed.   The problem of wages remained The
old problems
remain as before, and the workmen of the towns, like those of the country, complained of the same evils.   The insurrection had only one appreciable result : it had let loose popular passions which retained their violence for many years. The labourers had gained nothing by the revolt; but they drew from it a more bitter consciousness of their grievances.   They continued to combine for the increase of wages and the repudiation of services.   Every now and then, bands would be formed to burn records, plunder mansions, threaten the justices, or break Leagues and
risings of the
villeins into prisons ; and there was continual fear of the renewal of a general rising. [3]   This profound unsettlement of society increased the influence of revolutionary ideas, and the spread of the Lollard heresy was greatly helped through the envy excited by the wealth of the clergy.   The desire for the division of ecclesiastical property was now fixed in the popular mind.   On the other hand, the great shock of 1381 had inspired those whose privileges were threatened

---

1. Rogers, *Hist. of Agric.,* i. 8, 26, 89 sqq., 476 sqq., iv. 4 sqq., 71, 92.

2. See my *Introduction,* pp. cxxvii and cxxix sqq. ; cf. Feiling, *Essex Manor* (*Eng. Hist. Rev.,* 1911), pp. 334, 336. According to this scholar, the great changes in the manor of Hutton took place between 1424 and 1470. On the real causes of the disappearance of villeinage, see especially E. P. Cheyney, *Disappearance of English Serfdom* (*Eng. Hist.-Rev.,* 1900), pp. 25 sqq.

3. Besides the examples which are cited in my *Introduction,* pp. cxxx sqq., see a document concerning a rising of the villeins of the bishop of Bath and Wells in Somerset in 1398 (Powell and Trevelyan, *Peasants' Rising,* pp. 21-23).

with new energy in their defence. During the whole of the following period the reaction was as vigorous as the previous attack. The anxiety to check the current of revolution appears even in the repressive policy adopted against the Lollards. They were persecuted chiefly because they were regarded as instigators of social unrest. The events of 1381, therefore, left profound marks on men's minds. It was long before the privileged classes forgot the fear which they had felt, long before the people forgot their lost opportunity of winning a little more prosperity.

Resistance of the privileged classes

The conclusions which we have just sketched may one day be stated more fully, perhaps modified, although they are based on a solid foundation of evidence. Whether the investigation of records will reveal new details concerning the little-known movements which took place, for instance, in the midlands, it is impossible to say : but it is certain that much may still be learned as to the causes, the nature, and the results of the rising by a thorough examination of the judicial documents of the second half of the fourteenth century; for this great task is by no means accomplished. Such researches cannot fail to give much satisfaction to those who undertake them, if the rebellion of 1381 is not only, as Stubbs says, "one of the most portentous phenomena in the whole of English history," but also, as I believe, one of the most significant and most interesting events in the whole history of the middle ages.

INTRODUCTION TO THE FRENCH EDITION.

The King of England and his Parliaments in the Middle Ages.

THE volume that we present to the student public completes the French edition of William Stubbs' *Constitutional History of England*. Thirteen years have passed since the appearance of the preceding volume : this delay is explained by the Great War, and later by stress of work, caused in my collaborator's case by the necessity of finishing an extremely important work of his own; in mine, by increasingly heavy duties. We have never, for a moment, thought of leaving our enterprise unfinished. The *Constitutional History* is still to-day a fundamental book and will long remain so; and never has the necessity of thoroughly understanding the formation of political society in England appeared more clearly than to-day.

The French reader will not, I think, be in any way disappointed by the third volume. The English chronicles of the XVth century are wretchedly meagre, a defect which still remains insufficiently compensated by the publication of parliamentary and administrative documents, of which indeed, Stubbs was familiar with only a limited portion ; nevertheless he has given a very interesting narrative account of the Lancastrian and Yorkist period. In accordance with his general plan, he devoted the second part of his volume to institutions; but he has often trespassed beyond his chronological limits, and no one will complain of this. His study of the relations of Church and State is the fruit of a peculiar competence in these matters. The chapter on the Antiquities of Parliament is rich in information on elections, procedure, and debates; thanks to the prudent and scrupulous method of the author, we can make use of these facts even now, when sources inaccessible to him have been brought into use, and some of his valuations have been rejected. In the final pages on English society at the end of the Middle Ages, there are some parts out of date, since municipal and economic history have made great progress; but the picture that Stubbs traced of the English nobility retains the liveliest interest.

A considerable number of new bibliographical references, and some rectifications of the text will be found suggested between brackets in the notes to the French edition. We were not, however, able to leave it at that. A profound change has taken place in the historical appreciation of the great conflicts which ranged the King of England and his subjects against each other from the XIIIth to the XVth century. It was necessary to apprize our readers of it. With this end in view, my collaborator M. Georges Lefebvre, has written some important additional studies on the transformations of the Curia Regis, the monarchical bureaucracy, and the origins of the Council, the House of Lords, and the House of Commons. He has set himself the task of summarising clearly the work of contemporary scholars, a task not always easy in so complex and fluctuating a subject. He has not refrained from correcting judgments which were too absolute, and has even reinstated certain of Stubbs' views which, by excessive reaction, are now being undeservedly neglected. Finally, when there was occasion, he has compared English and French institutions which throw light upon each other mutually.

I am anxious to state here, that all the honour of this careful exposition, which demanded much reading, experience, and reflection, is due to my collaborator. All I have done has been to provide him with certain notes and suggestions, and to play the part of an agent for publication.

I.

Without encroaching upon his *Study*, I wish to consider here the origins and character of the *Parliamentum* as it existed in the time of Edward I, from a point of view not generally taken by twentieth-century medievalists. I shall not bring forward a single new document, but by bringing out more clearly certain connections between the known facts, perhaps I may help the reader to reconstruct the hostile atmosphere in which there developed, very slowly and precariously, what the perspective afforded by the intervening centuries now allows us to regard as the germ of the English parliamentary system.

I call it a hostile atmosphere. This is precisely the opposite of the impression which Stubbs would convey, at least in the passages where he moralises and draws conclusions. He had a mystic conception of the origins of the English constitution. With the patriotic pride of a man of the Victorian era, imbued with ideas whose spirit still seems perceptible to the guest of an Oxford college, he believed, or almost believed, that the English people had had a mission, that of establishing parliamentary government. Despite the reserves which his honesty as a historian imposed upon him, he projected into the past the image of the constitutional monarchy which he saw working under his own eyes, and to which he attributed the greatness of his country. He believed sincerely in an outburst of national enthusiasm, which had imposed the Charters of Liberties, whereas, in the medieval vocabulary, "liberty" or "franchise" means privilege.[1] He believed that the thirteenth-century barons

1. Cf. a characteristic text in *Rotuli Parliamentorum*, ii, p. 166b, ad ann. 1348. The Commons complain that the King has granted so many *franchises* that almost the entire kingdom has been *mis en franchise*, to the great detriment of the Common Law and the great oppression of the people. This should be interpreted as " so many privileges of jurisdiction granted to the lords." See A. F. Pollard's shrewd study *The Evolution of Parliament* (1920),—a book which should be read in its entirety,—Chapter IX, "Parliament and Liberty," especially p. 168 sq. There is nothing more productive in history than the study of semantics.

were heroes who laboured for the future. He believed that the great king Edward I had, by an act of considered judgment, and with the insight of genius, definitely founded the parliamentary monarchy. Finally, having had to renounce the task of working through a huge mass of archival documents still unpublished, he had not been able to see the building up, around the throne of the last Plantagenets and Lancastrians, of the bureaucratic power, admirably adapted to ensuring a regular administration, but, for that very reason, unfavourable to parliamentary development, and embarrassing even to royal absolutism. He had not thrown into relief the absolutist tendencies of Edward I and his circle. He had not perceived the tentative endeavours of certain kings to loosen the grip of the great formalised administrative departments, and to throw off these new fetters.

It is the honour of the present generation,—at the head of which we must place a scholar of genius, the regretted F. W. Maitland—to have tackled courageously the searching of unpublished documents, and to have discovered two fundamental truths.[1] Firstly, the constitutional history of England can only progress side by side with administrative history; this latter will demand much patient research, but it has been begun, and we already observe that the King (or the group of favourites who ruled him) ceaselessly tried to maintain monarchic absolutism, and to defend himself against every institution calculated to limit it; even if that institution was created to serve his authority, he began to distrust it as soon as it adopted principles foreign to his good pleasure. In the light of this observation, not only are many palace revolutions explained, but the alliance of the King with

1. In M. Georges Lefebvre's *Studies* will be found the bibliography of these researches, and the means of following the development of parliamentary institutions, the Council, and the Household. Sensational as certain recent discoveries of documents have been, as, for example on the origin of the House of Commons, I will not repeat here what he says of them. I merely wish to give some personal impressions, resulting from a now lengthy acquaintance with the principal sources.

the nation for the establishment of a system of limited monarchy appears, at any epoch whatever, highly improbable. Secondly, we have gone astray in seeking precise dates for the birth of Parliament, and especially of what the English have called, from the XVIth century onwards, the "House of Commons." Nothing is more misleading than the idea that in 1295 a "Model Parliament" was constituted. The adage *Natura non facit saltus,* remains true as far as concerns medieval history. Like the assemblies of the Three Estates in France, the English parliament is an institution useful above all to the Monarchy, but it is not a conception peculiar to a king of genius. Parliament is merely a development of the *Curia Regis* and it emerged from its matrix only very slowly. The history of its origins is complicated, and by trying to reduce it to a simple formula, we distort it beyond remedy.

II.

We distort that history equally if we neglect the psychological data. From this point of view, the published documents contain many unexploited riches which must be explored anew, without prejudice and with a mind completely fresh. The actors of the drama have not been observed with sufficient curiosity. The fact that we are dealing with the history of institutions is no reason for neglecting to picture to ourselves the men concerned. If we do not succeed in reconstructing a concrete image of the past, the risks of vain hypotheses are multiplied. Thanks to recent works on administrative history, some forgotten personages, who nevertheless played a considerable part, have stood out from the hazy distance in which we could not distinguish them :[1] but it

1. See, for example, the account of the career of Peter de Rievaux, who held simultaneously several very important offices in the reign of Henry III : T. F. Tout, *Chapters,* i, p. 214 sq.

is sometimes the most illustrious whom we have failed to approach sufficiently. Stubbs, who was shrewd, did not fail to show for each period the chain of facts and the historic figures. But, like many Englishmen, he had little imagination, and I wonder whether he fully understood such characters as Henry II, John Lackland, Edward I, Henry V, and what manner of men the chiefs of the baronial opposition were. We ought to examine, in the feeble light which has reached us, what was the temperament, even the physical temperament, of these men. I believe that by application to this question we shall sometimes make strange discoveries.

From the Norman conquest to the Tudors, not to speak of modern times, there was, on the throne of England, an almost uninterrupted succession of champions of personal power, passionate and lustful men, who loved domination, strife, war, and the chase. All these men either tried to retain the great lordships in France, or to be at once kings of England and France. Some were almost driven to distraction by excess of ambition, excess of cares, or excess of pleasure. Henry II, whose Empire stretched from Scotland to the Pyrenees, was neurasthenic : his agitation was the talk of his contemporaries. John Lackland, as I shall presently attempt to prove, was troubled by a psychic excitation which has been defined by our alienists. Richard II was unbalanced. In the midst of this series of tragic figures there occur some ludicrous personages, muddle-headed, unstable, and unintelligent, like the frivolous Edward II or his grandfather Henry III, whose senseless piety irritated even the devout Louis IX. These men were under the yoke of a rapacious court, and the consequences were the same as if they had been formidable tyrants. As for the "heroic kings", Edward I and Henry V, it is scarcely necessary to recall that both were conquerors, who undertook tasks beyond the resources of the England of those days.

How can we suppose that any one of these princes had

a conscious desire to "seal a compact" with the nation, to create a parliamentary monarchy ?

They entertained this idea all the less as their courtiers and officials formed a screen between their subjects and them, save during the short sessions of the assemblies. They had beside them knights attached to their person by the feudal conception of honour, ready for anything in their service : such were those who, upon a thoughtless word from Henry II, went and assassinated the Archbishop of Canterbury ; and the "Chamber" of the kings, their "Wardrobe," and the public services which were gradually organising themselves, were staffed with clerks who had not the slightest desire to be submitted to an external control, or to have anyone haggling with them for the means of government. The hidden action of this circle of attendants is naturally somewhat difficult to discern. But we know what were the ideas of the king's servants concerning the royal power, and what political doctrine they professed in their treatises on administration and law.

This is how the *Dialogue of the Exchequer*, written in the reign of Henry II by the treasurer Fitz-Nigel, begins :

"It is necessary to submit ourselves in all fear and to obey the powers ordained by God. All power, in fact, comes from our Lord God. . . But although abundant riches may often come to kings, not by some well-attested right, but perhaps by ancestral customs, or perhaps by the secret counsels of their own hearts, or even through the arbitrary decisions of their own will, nevertheless their deeds must not be discussed or condemned by their inferiors. For their hearts and the workings of their hearts are in the hand of God, and the cause of those to whom the care of subjects has been entrusted by God himself depends on divine judgment and not on human judgment.[1]

1. *De necessariis Observantiis Scaccarii Dialogus*, ed. A. Hughes, C. G. Crump and C. Johnson, 1902, p. 55.

After the Great Charter this extremely peremptory affirmation undergoes some attenuation. When the jurist Bracton, a counsellor of Henry III, wishes to define the royal prerogative, he speaks of the necessity of conforming to the "laws of the realm," but with what reserves, and in what confused and contradictory terms! Fundamentally, Bracton's doctrine is that, if the king refuses to set right an injustice, God alone can punish him.[1] When divine origin is attributed to monarchical power, it is impossible to escape the conclusion that the fear of God is its sole limit.

This theory of divine right is of ecclesiastical origin, and is found in Capetian France. The English Church confirmed it by its rites and legends. On both sides of the Channel the clergy practised this dangerous policy of exalting the Monarchy, which was certainly profitable to both powers, but which entailed the risk of ending some day in the subjection of the national Church. From the Anglo-Saxon period, the king was crowned and anointed. Once the consecration was complete, he was regarded as a being superior to the rest, to be loved and served. The laws of Ethelred, and, later, the laws of Canute, imposed obedience to the king as a religious duty. The counsellors of the Anglo-Saxon and Scandinavian kings were evidently inspired by the Carolingian tradition, and later on, the Norman kings introduced into England the useful observances of the monarchical cult, invented by the clerks of the Capetian court.[2] The son of Hugh Capet, the pious king Robert, cured the sick with the sign of the cross, and thus in his reign was founded the

1. See *Bracton's Note Book*, ed. Maitland, 1887, i, *Introduction*, p. 30 sq., and a note of Mr. C. H. McIlwain, "The Fundamental Law in Bracton," in *The High Court of Parliament and its Supremacy*, 1910, pp. 101–103. Cf. on *rex* and *lex*, a Latin poem published in Wright's *Political Songs* and cited by M. Bémont, *Simon de Montfort*, 1st edit., p. 219.

2. For all that follows, see H. F. Delaborde. "Du toucher des écrouelles par les rois d'Angleterre," in *Mélanges d'Histoire offerts à M. Ch. Bémont*, 1913, p. 173 sq., and Marc Bloch, *Les rois thaumaturges* 1924, p. 41 sp., 82 sp., 159 sq., and *passim*.

thaumaturgical power of the kings of France, which took
the specialised form of the healing of scrofula.   Now
Henry I of England probably claimed the same privilege,
and in any case, the tradition was founded by the time of
Henry II, and Peter of Blois writes; "The king is holy,
he is the Lord's anointed ; it is not for nothing that he has
received the sacrament of unction, the efficacity of which
is fully demonstrated by...the curing of the king's evil."
Edward I touched in this way one thousand seven hundred and thirty-six sufferers from this disease during the
eighteenth year of his reign alone; Edward II, made
anxious by his unpopularity, tried to claim new thaumaturgical powers; in his reign, and for more than two hundred years afterwards, there were distributed rings which
the royal hands, sanctified by unction, had touched, and
which, from that moment, cured cramp.   Edward II
also wished the oil with which he had been anointed
to be held miraculous, like the holy phial of Rheims;
but the legend of the oil given to Thomas Becket by
the Virgin was not accepted by the Church until 1399,
at the time of the accession of Henry of Lancaster : the
acceptance of this new article of faith for the use of
loyal subjects coincided with the contestable accession of
a new dynasty which required legitimation.

How could English royalty have had the idea of limiting in practice, of its own accord, this power which its
flatterers and its grave counsellors declared to have come
from God, and to be capable of miracles?   It would not
even endure—this point should be insisted on—a bureaucracy too slow to execute its will.   The ingenuity of the
kings (or rather, to make a qualification which is almost
always necessary, of their advisers) was spent, during the
last centuries of the Middle Ages, not in preparing the
parliamentary *régime,* but in maintaining their prerogative, and especially in freeing themselves from the shack-
les of any regular administration capable of thwarting a
policy of megalomania.

Recent work has thrown a vivid light on these palace wars. They are very curious. We already knew that the episcopal chancellor, a great and almost irremovable personage, was with difficulty endured by the king; Henry II had tried, for several years, to solve the problem by entrusting the chancellorship to one of his bastards; John Lackland rewarded the services of Archbishop Hubert Walter by speaking of him, after his death, with the most brutal insolence. But these obscure conflicts become much more clear for us when diplomatists like Eug. Déprez, T. F. Tout, H. C. Maxwell Lyte,[1] give us the history of the small seal, which appears in the XIIth century; it is the king's personal seal, the instrument of his prerogative; its use loses this character only when the king has a chancellor of whom he is sure; and when the office of the "privy seal" ceases to be a household office and becomes an institution of State, then Edward III makes for himself a new private Chancery, and new secret seals appear. Similarly, the Exchequer does not keep for long its financial supremacy. John Lackland, whose reign in many respects marks a turning-point in the history of England, has sums paid directly into his "Wardrobe", in order to be able to pay with ease the mercenaries who uphold his tyrannical power. The "Wardrobe" becomes, for over a century, one of the most important organs of the personal power. When Edward II can no longer use it in this way, he employs another household service, the "Chamber", to procure resources for himself. Lastly, the prince remains the source of justice, despite the royal tribunals which are created in succession, and he reserves to himself the power of judging in equity and of taking cognisance of causes which affect his prerogative.[2] In the fortified

1. See the bibliography and the summary of the question below, p. 373. M. Lefebvre was not able to use Sir H. C. Maxwell-Lyte's work which has just appeared : *Historical Notes on the use of the Great Seal of England*, 1926 (Ch. II : " The Privy Seal ").
2. See the *Studies* of M. Lefebvre, p. 364 sq., and p. 385 sq.

place in which the king defends himself, the Household and the Council are the donjon in which he can take refuge when the rest of the castle has been wrested from him; in this retreat, he finds auxiliaries who are always fertile in stratagems and substitutions, little inclined to advise him to surrender, since they know what it will cost them in their own persons.

Is it then to the baronage and to the national Church that England owes the germs of the parliamentary system?

No one has thought of proclaiming the political spirit of the barons of the eleventh and twelfth centuries; they were too patently lacking in it. But Stubbs praised the generous and farseeing disinterestedness of the "patriotic barons" of the XIIIth century, who "placed themselves in the vanguard of liberty", and he has contrasted it with the selfishness of the barons of the fourteenth and fifteenth centuries.[1]

We certainly must not depreciate to excess the effort made in the era of the "charters of liberties", the era of *Magna Carta,* of the *Provisions,* and of the *Articles of* 1297. It put an end to the hateful tyranny of John Lackland, it did useful service in thwarting the ruinous enterprises of Henry III, and gave Edward I cause for reflection. But I have sought in vain, in the history of this baronial opposition, any manifestation of a real political intelligence, and I am pleased to find my doubts confirmed in this criticism of the judicious historian of Edward II, Mr. T. F. Tout: "With all his caution and all his wisdom, Stubbs goes too far," he says, "when he teaches that the barons and bishops of the early fourteenth century were cast in a meaner mould than the heroes of Runnymede or of the age of Simon de Montfort or even of the opposition to the declining years of Edward I. As far as the rank and file goes, the barons

---

1. See Stubbs' *Const. Hist.*, i, p. 571, 579, 583; ii, p. 655–656, etc.

who won the Great Charter and their grandsons who laid low the power of the Crown in the Mad Parliament[1] were every whit as stupid and as greedy, as narrow and as self-seeking as were the mass of the lords ordainers."[2]

Twenty years after writing, on the subject of the Great Charter, a little study which even to-day sometimes raises protests, I confess that I see nothing to change in it.[3] I said there, and I can only repeat, that the Great Charter was essentially an act of feudal reaction against the progress of an encroaching royal administration and an arbitrary fiscal system. The barons, naturally, could not avoid presenting, along with their own grievances, those of the knights and of the Londoners who supported them, and without whom they would have been delivered up to the vengeance of John. But, from the point of view which concerns us here, they added very few seeds to the sowing which was one day to produce the parliamentary system. Article 12, concerning consent to scutages and aids, was aimed at a definite abuse, and established no new rule of public law. We are told, "It was in 1215, for the first time, that a precise text explicitly established a connection between the payment of an imposition and the consent to that burden."[4] Let us avoid playing upon mere words. There was no need for a precise text to create a connection which was the rule in feudal law. By this interpretation, the customs of the Middle Ages would date only from the period when they were reduced to writing. Excepting the three customary cases (four

1. *Insane Parlamentum* of June 11th, 1258.
2. *Place Edward II*, p. 22–23.
3. M. Léon Leclère, "*La Grande Charte* de 1215, est-elle une illusion?" in *Mélanges offerts à Henri Pirenne*, 1926, p. 279 sq., has recently taken me to task. He contradicts scarcely one of the details of my argument, and yet he concludes that we must return to the traditional interpretation. I leave to the public the task of deciding between us. My study was published as an appendix to t.i. (of the French translation of *Stubbs*) and, in an English translation, in *Studies and Notes Supplementary to Stubbs' Constitutional History, down to the Great Charter*, 1908, p. 127 sq.
4. Léon Leclère, op. cit. p. 287.

in France), the vassal "gave" the aid; it was not raised without his consent. *"Auxilium quod barones mihi dederunt,"* said Henry I.[1] The Great Charter merely recalls this principle. As for article 14, concerning convocations *ad habendum commune consilium regni,*[2] a very badly drafted article, drawn up in great haste, how can we give credit for it to the barons, when it is not found in their Petition ?[3]

The barons did not show any more inventive or perspicacious a spirit in the measures which they imposed for the application of the Charter. The Committee of Twenty-five and the Commission of Four constituted in article 61 formed a supervising Directory whose only weapon against the return of the abuses was rebellion ; the king himself had to require his subjects to swear to rise against him when the Twenty-five, according to the accepted procedure, should summon them to do so. It appears clearly that the barons lacked the greatness to oppose a political organisation worthy of the name to a monarchical administration already powerful and intelligently directed, and aimed resolutely at absolutism. They

1. Stubbs, *Const. Hist.*, i, p. 400, 618; see also ii, p. 253 sq.

2. Translate : " to have the common counsel of the realm," not " to hold the *commune consilium.*" See p. 451, n. 2.

3. As is well known, the *Capitula que barones petunt et dominus Rex concedit* served as the basis for the drafting of the Great Charter. Article 14 makes is easy to reconstruct a discussion which undoubtedly took place between the commissioners of the barons and the agents of the king. The end at least, evidently reflects a wish of the latter; " . . . *Negocium ad diem assignatum procedat secundum consilium illorum qui presentes fuerint, quamvis non omnes summoniti venerint.*" This meant putting an end to the individual claims of prelates and barons who, not having appeared and not having consented personally to the aid, refused to pay it. This is clearly an important point. But article 14 disappeared in the confirmations. The matter seemed *"grave et douteuse"* (Bémont, *Chartes des libertés anglaises*, p. 58, n. 4). They would have had to clear up the obscurities presented by this text, and especially to solve the problem of convoking all the tenants-in-chief, a practical impossibility, and also to distinguish the impositions submitted to the consent of the assembly from the resources which the king claimed to exact at will. In practice, during the thirteenth century, the feudal rule was applied summarily, and the assent of the prelates and the barons was asked for the aid. But the King had many other resources, even outside the issues of his demesne.

had been able to define in detail the abuses of the system, and to demand a return to feudal law, but they were incapable of creating a new public law. Their mediocrity appeared clearly throughout the rest of the crisis and the years which followed. The Committee of Twenty-five after having foolishly enough exasperated the pride of John Lackland, and contributed to the rupture, did not even attempt to govern; the baronage appealed to a foreign claimant and could not even range itself in its entirety on his side; England was saved from anarchy only by the Holy See. We must remember, that in the confirmations of the Great Charter granted by the advisers of the young Henry III, the famous articles 12 and 14 disappeared. The confirmation of February 11th, 1225, bought by the barons and forming the definitive text of *Magna Carta*, says only that scutage shall be taken as in the time of Henry II, and that the "liberties and free customs" of all persons, clerks or laymen, shall be preserved.[1] The moderate rate of the ancient scutage, and the privileges of each individual having been assured, all concern with the most suitable procedure *ad habendum commune consilium regni* was given up.

The great war of the barons at the end of the reign of Henry III repeated in many respects—this fact has not been sufficiently noticed—the crisis of the Great Charter, doubtlessly because the conditions were almost identical, and the new generation of English nobility had scarcely any more capacity than the one preceding.[2] The deeper causes were the same : the king was surrounded by foreign advisers, bled his subjects, and oppressed the national clergy or allowed them to be

1. Article 37 : Bémont, *Chartes des Libertés anglaises*, p. 57–58.
2. The only great figure of this revolution is that of a noble of French origin, Simon de Montfort, a son of the leader of the Albigensian crusade. M. Bémont has just finished a second edition, revised and brought up to date, of his *Simon de Montfort*. I wish to thank him here for his kindness in lending me his manuscript, which has been of great value to me.

oppressed. The deciding factor, in both cases, was a check in foreign policy. In 1258 as in 1215, the barons, fully armed, sought out the king, and demanded satisfaction, and *Magna Carta* was parallelled by the legal sections of the *Provisions of Westminster* which were to be incorporated finally in the statutes of the kingdom. As in 1215, the barons had as allies the Londoners and part of the English Church. As in 1215, they excited the king to resistance by their pride,[1] and the king, supported by the Pope, broke with them. The aristocracy was at first victorious, but it was divided and finally it was beaten and lost part of the fruits of the revolution. Moreover, in both cases, it was the members of the national clergy, partisans of the barons, who suffered the most severe punishment; the barons came off more lightly.[2]

We must not exaggerate the closeness of this parallel. The crisis in the reign of Henry III offers many new aspects. Anti-papal feeling, almost non-existant in 1215, had been developed in certain monastic orders, among the lesser clergy, and in part of the episcopate; and Simon de Montfort, full of sympathy for the evils suffered by the English Church,[3] was considered a defender of ecclesiastical liberties and a saint. On the other hand, the baronage saw more clearly than in 1215, the necessity of securing to themselves the control of the monarchical administration. They did not dream of being content with the barbarous system of the Twenty-five barons

1. See the "Grevancez dont le Roy se pleynt de son Conseil," publ. by E. F. Jacob, in *E. H. R.*, 1926, p. 564–571. The King declares that he cannot tolerate the attitude taken by men who have sworn homage and fidelity to him (art. 24); they say " *Nous volons que issy soit* et autre resoun ne mettent" (art. 4). Cf. for the grievances of John Lackland, the *Histoire des ducs de Normandie et des rois d' Angleterre,* (Soc. de l'Hist. de France) p. 151.

2. The proceedings against the opposing clergy have just been studied by E. F. Jacob, *Studies in the Period of Baronial Reform and Rebellion, 1258–67,* 1925, p. 293 sq.

3. See, on the relations of the reforming bishop Robert Grosseteste and the Franciscan Adam March with Simon de Montfort : F. S. Stevenson, *Robert Grosseteste,* 1899, p. 269 sq.

instituted in the Great Charter. They claimed actually to reduce the king to a nominal power, to seize control of the great offices, and to supervise the central and local administration. But by what means? They only thought of substituting for the rule of the king and his favourites an aristocratic government.[1] The complicated organisation adopted in 1258 became still more narrowly oligarchic in 1264. In short, England was ruled by committees of barons and prelates. There was no question of establishing anything which resembled the parliamentary system. A Parliament was to meet three times a year. In the intervals a permanent Council of Fifteen sat. Now the parliament was composed simply of this Council of Fifteen sitting with a Commission of Twelve.[2] It is true that, in the most critical moments, each of the two parties had to concern itself with securing wide support. As early as 1254, before the great crisis began, Queen Eleanor and the Earl of Cornwall, regents of the kingdom, had summoned to the Easter Parliament two knights from each county. In 1261 the Council summoned to St. Albans three knights from each county, and the king replied by calling upon the knights to meet before him at Windsor.[3] Four knights from each county were present at the Parliament of June 22nd, 1264. Finally, at the famous Parliament of January 1265, Simon de Montfort summoned not only two knights from each county, but two or four deputies from a certain number of towns. This is an interesting fact, but we must understand its character. And indeed scholars are fully agreed on that point; it was a tactical move imposed by the circumstances. Simon de Montfort made no claim to

1. The theory of government by the *Magnates* is set out with interesting precision in a Latin poem of the period, [the *Song of Lewes* (ed. C. L. Kingsford, Oxford, 1890)].

2. See F. M. Powicke, "Some observations on the Baronial Council, 1258–1260," in *Essays presented to T. F. Tout*, 1925, especially p. 127.

3. A letter of Henry III, Sept. 11th, 1261, in *Select Charters*, 9th edit., p. 394.

secure the adherence of the whole nation for his work;
he convoked only those bishops and barons of whom
he was sure, and, (this is evident), the deputies of the
towns in which he had warm supporters. His appeal to
the elements of the lesser nobility and the townsmen who
supported him surprised no one. Moreover, this expedient was not again resorted to; only barons and prelates
were summoned to a Parliament which was to have met
in the following June.

In short, during this serious twelve years' crisis, which
plunged England into disorder and distress, the baronage, aided by part of the episcopate, seized the power for
a time, and, like every class which brings about a revolution, was obliged to seek allies, but had no idea of setting
up a parliamentary machine. It merely created a multi-
plicity of councils of aristocrats and clergy. There is nothing in common between the conceptions of a Simon de
Montfort, moved by mystic ideas, by feudal pride, by
personal grievances, and by the feeling—quite legitimate,
after all— of his superiority over his pitiable brother-in-
law, and the views of an Etienne Marcel who in his case
held—a hundred years later, but in rather analogous
circumstances—the idea of governing France by the
Assembly of the three Estates.[1]

The heir to the throne, Edward, had contributed to the
defeat of the aristocracy. The baronage, after the death
of Henry III, found a master in him. Edward I was a
jurist, and a great administrator, who retained full control
over the governmental machine. The prerogative of

1. I allude to the ordinance of March 1357. We know that Etienne
Marcel and his friends denounced, with the violence of a Simon de
Montfort, the abuses committed by evil counsellors; the regent was
attacked for the same general causes as those which had provoked the
crisis of the reign of Henry III; advisers who were suspect, waste, and
ruinous policy. We may further agree that if monarchical institutions
in France were far behind those of England, the same was by no means
true of social and economic evolution, and it is easy to understand
how a French townsman of 1357 should have had less ill-defined political
ideas than an English baron of 1258.

Y

English royalty, during the Middle Ages, was never stronger or better justified than at that moment. The barons checked the king only by seizing the opportunity offered by his foreign policy. They played a game which might have been useful to England, in opposing an excessive ambition; but to place this opposition in a true light, it suffices to compare it with that of certain barons of St. Louis who rightly advised against the Tunisian crusade. The nobility had no part in the development, of a very special character, taken by Parliament—or rather, by the Council in Parliament—at the end of the reign of Edward I. In the introduction to the volume in which he edited the *Memoranda* of 1305, Maitland considers that the barons of Edward I found very few attractions in the sessions of Parliament, apart from the quite definite cases which affected them, and for a long time afterwards it is necessary to speak of the duties, not of the rights, of those whom the king summons. Later, when the House of Lords is definitely constituted, the barons will claim their right to be summoned to it; but, in the time of Edward I, many of them must surely be not too well pleased "when they receive a writ which tells them that, leaving their homes and affairs, they must journey and labour in the king's service, and all this at their own cost, (for they were paid no wages). Thus for many years one great constitutional question can remain in suspense. It is not raised; no one wishes to raise it. So long as the king does not impose taxes or issue statutes without the consent of the baronage (which is content to agree to them) the baron hopes that the king will mind his own business—and it is his business to govern the realm—and allow other folk to mind theirs."[1]

Stubbs, who lacks the positive, realistic sense of Maitland, weaves illusions for himself concerning the

1. Maitland, p. lxxxvii. See the bibliographical reference below.

thirteenth century barons; nevertheless he admits that the "heroes of 1297" upheld "their own class interests" and were "greater in their opportunity than in their patriotism."[1] Amongst the adversaries of Edward I he attributes exceptional worth only to Archbishop Winchelsey.

Was the English Church capable of supplying the political movement with leaders? It had, from the beginning, the theoretical idea of the limits of monarchical power. From the Anglo-Saxon period, it imposed on the king, in consecrating him, an oath whose formula was perpetuated; as if in payment for the religious prestige which consecration gave him, he had to promise to keep the Church and all the people in peace, to prevent rapine and injustice; sometimes precise engagements were exacted from him. The clergy certainly played a part of first importance in the history of the oldest charters of liberties. It was the clergy who gave the first examples of resistance to unratified taxes. But the Church had, to a much higher degree than the nobility, a real corporate feeling. Unarmed, ceaselessly in fear of the brutal forces which growled around it, it already had that attitude of suspicious autonomy which it has kept throughout the centuries. It acted for itself, to save its own dignity, to defend or regain freedom of elections, and to keep the material means of independent existence. It is a delusion to ascribe patriotic sentiments to the Church of the thirteenth century. The "liberty of the English Church" forms the first of the articles of Magna Carta; but King John adds:— the greatest of these liberties, freedom of election, "we have already granted of our free and unforced will, before the discord which has arisen between us and our barons."[2] And in fact the Church had obtained this private charter on November 21st, 1214.

1. *Const. Hist.*, ii, p. 312.
2. Magna Carta, art. 1. See Bémont, *Chartes des libertés*, p. 27, and the note.

If Henry III had not committed the enormous blunder of concluding a political alliance with the Pope, of accepting the throne of Sicily for his son and of allowing the Roman Curia to vex and oppress the English clergy, it is highly probable that Simon de Montfort would have found little support in the Church. In any case, from the fourteenth century, it abandoned the common way of opposition and ceased to send proctors to Parliament.[1]

It is clear that we cannot attribute any initiative to the Commons in the development of the parliamentary idea. An English Third Estate with a "real share . . . in the reformed and remodelled constitution"[2] is a myth. The knights of the shire and the burgesses, who led a fairly comfortable life as rural proprietors and merchants, had only one desire, to attend to their affairs in peace and

1. Need I add that the idea of parliamentary control is not found in germ in the treatises of scholastic writers? The ecclesiastical conception of the State found in England its most brilliant expression in the *Policraticus* of John of Salisbury (1159). The doctrine of John of Salisbury is almost that which Abbon and Suger formulated in France : monarchy is a power instituted by God for the good of all : the *respublica* is an organism having its life and its members; the soul of the body is the clergy, the sacred and inviolable intermediary between God and man; the head is the prince, who receives his character and his authority from an election, in which God himself, the judgment of his priests, and the approval of his people all concur The prince receives the temporal sword from the hand of the Church, and exercises his power to bring about the reign of peace and justice, following the counsels of the clergy, for the clergy has the mission of informing him of the law to be followed. If he violates the law, he is a tyrant, he must lose his kingdom, and regicide becomes lawful. But who shall decide whether the king has violated the " law "? The author does not say. He entangles reason and metaphor, and though he mixed in the affairs of his time and knew them, one would say he is separated from the real world as by a window. He scarcely makes allusion to feudalism, and does not imagine that the great meetings of the *Curia*, full of barons, can become a means of limiting the royal power. He speaks of a *senatus* which must keep from venality : this naturally refers only to the permanent entourage of the prince. It is very probable that, had the author lived in the thirteenth century. he would have formulated practically the same theory.—The best edition of the *Policraticus* is that of C. C. J. Webb, 1909. The bibliography is given by E. F. Jacob, in *Social and Political Ideas of some Great Medieval Thinkers*, (1923), pp. 83-84. An article by J. Dickinson, "The Medieval Conception of Kingship as developed in the *Policraticus* of John of Salisbury," in *Speculum*, July, 1926, p.368 sq., should be added.

2. Stubbs, *Const. Hist.*, ii, p. 318.

to pay as little in taxes as possible.   Outside London, the
horizon of the townsmen, in those medieval English
towns, which were very small places, was extremely
narrow; Stubbs indeed has noted the insignificance of
their part in Parliament.   The knights of the shire had a
less narrow political spirit, and among them were people
who took an interest in public affairs; but it was in the
circle of the interests of the shire that they acted, and it
was only in the fifteenth century that they began to show
any liking for the commission of deputy to the Parliament.   Until then they showed as little eagerness as the
Third Estate in France, and that was very little indeed,
when they were brought together to elect representatives,
and often the persons chosen turned a deaf ear.   Stubbs
himself has given numerous examples of the moderate
quality of their zeal.   The only advantage that the men of
the communities of shires and boroughs saw in the
meetings of Parliament, was that one could take grievances there and solicit favours; but in this respect, a
reply of the Council sufficed.   They were naturally
reluctant to grant subsidies, and were rarely interested
in legislation and general policy.   One cannot help being
struck by the fact that, during the Hundred Years' War,
they constantly refused to give their advice on the
expediency of prolonging hostilities.   Let no one say
that in the Middle Ages the Commons of England contributed to the foundation of the constitutional monarchy.

In short, at the period when Stubbs[1] is describing
Parliament as the union of the Three Estates of the
nation—in the second part of the thirteenth century and
at the beginning of the fourteenth,—there are in reality,
not three Estates of the nation, but several opposing
forces with conflicting interests and tendencies.

There are the king and his private counsellors, who

1. Stubbs, *Const. Hist.*, ii, chap. XV : " The System of Estates.'   Cf,
A. F. Pollard, *Evolution of Parliament*, chap. IV : " The Myth of the
Three Estates."

maintain as far as possible the rule of the King's good pleasure, or at least, of the prerogative.

There are the officials, who administer the demesne, obtain funds and an army for the king, do justice in his name, perform the bureaucratic tasks, and serve the State faithfully after their own fashion, but who, in general, form companies, hold traditions, and cannot but feel some ill will, or a certain ironical pity for initiative taken by outsiders or for the agitation of incompetent persons; to understand this official state of mind, we have only to watch our own administrations in action.

There are the barons, who respect their lord the king when he is strong, love him when he is generous towards them and can obtain for them fine *guerredons*, and become discontented when he stupidly vexes them and wastes his money without allowing them to profit thereby : when they react, they demand the observance of the Great Charter; when they rebel, they try to govern in the king's stead, and to lay hands on the important offices.

There is the Church, which is more intelligent and better armed for the political struggle. But, in theory at least, it lives apart from the world, save for some prelates who live in the style of barons; it claims independence, and desires that the Crown, which owes to the Church its semi-religious prestige, shall respect its privileges and secure it peace. Besides, the Church is itself badly divided and contains, alongside of an aristocracy, some demagogic elements : it will reserve its critical faculties and its combative tendencies more and more for itself.

There are the knights of the shire and the burgesses. We see clearly that they are capable of resistance to oppression, and we see in the towns factions at strife, where the Crown and the Opposition can both find support; but almost throughout the Middle Ages, these knights and burgesses seek to evade the burden of going to Parliament or of sending there proctors whom they will have to pay and who go there to consent to taxes.

All these forces act separately, for purposes rarely harmonising. It is certainly not at the time of Henry III and Edward I that they unite to create a constitutional monarchy.

In reality the constitutional monarchy was not "founded" at any definite period. The English Parliament was merely the development of an ancient usage. One could almost say it has developed like a natural growth, with the aid of circumstances. Let us go back to the time of its infancy, let us follow it rapidly in its progress, and see, at the end, to what stage of growth it has attained by the time of Edward I.

III.

As far back as we can see in the mists of Anglo-Saxon history, far back in pagan days, we discern the chief of each little kingdom surrounded by a *Concilium*, which corresponds to the *Concilium* described in the *Germania* of Tacitus, and resembles it in many respects. The most ancient law of England, that of Ethelbert, king of Kent, was given "with the counsel of the Witan." Bede assures us of this, and cites another example of a Witenagemot of pagan times, that of Northumbria.[1] When the kingdom of Wessex completed the unification of the Anglo- Saxon principalities, its *gemot* became the "assembly of Wise Men" of the whole of England. It kept its ancient Germanic character. There were many analogies between the system of Anglo-Saxon assemblies and the system of Frankish assemblies; but the Witenagemot evidently played a more considerable, and, above all, a more regular and continuous part.

Like the Carolingians and the first Capetians, the Anglo-Saxon king has around him *ministri*, permanent counsellors, who assume increasing importance according

1. F. Liebermann, *The National Assembly in the Anglo-Saxon Period,* Halle, 1913, p. 2–3. For all that follows, I draw upon this excellent memoir, which exhausts the question.

as the influence of French and Norman institutions grows. About this nucleus of counsellors the other Wise Men are grouped whenever the king convokes assemblies. No more than in Gaul have they any representative character; the king calls to his person the prelates, the ealdormen, and the thanes, whom tradition decrees he must call, or whom it pleases him to summon. They are not very eager to come, nor very numerous. An assembly like that of 933, where we see eighty-nine persons sitting together, exceeds the usual figure. It is almost always an aristocratic gathering, in which the churchmen direct the debates. Sometimes, however, if the *gemot* is held at London, the men of that town are present.

The Witenagemot meets at least once a year: in the eleventh century the king seems to choose the occasion of a great feast, such as Easter, Whitsuntide, or Christmas, according to a practice which the Capetians also adopted. To describe its powers, scholars have been obliged by the scantiness of sources to take the sum of all the information provided by four centuries. Having made allowances for the uncertainty of such a method, we can admit that the Wise Men attend to all sorts of questions, make and unmake civil and religious laws, do justice, name certain ealdormen; they are consulted for taxes, though we cannot say that this consultation was the rule; finally they elect the king, and, in certain cases, depose an unworthy king.

There exists no constitutional guarantee. There are no rules for the frequency of meetings, nor for the choice of members summoned; there are no records; there is no vote constraining the king's will, for we have no example of a law established against his wish. Finally, the king dismisses the Witan at pleasure, and leaves them no right of control in the interval between the sessions, and, when he wishes, he contents himself with his permanent Court instead of convoking his Witan. In short, the assembly of Wise Men is not an independent institution, capable of a regular constitutional opposition.   Still, without speaking of the disagreements, the violent quarrels, of which we have evidence, between the king and the Witan, and the crises when they rid England of a bad prince, the assembly seriously limits and tempers the monarchical authority.   The formula "I and we all" that is found at the head of a law, is quite characteristic.

The Court of the Anglo-Norman kings is a continuation of both the Witenagemot and the Court of the Dukes of Normandy, for William the Conqueror, before 1066, had a Palace, officers, and a Council, and held assemblies.   We have little information about the *Curia Ducis* at this period, but, as far as we can tell, it has almost the same permanent officers and the same varying personnel of bishops and barons, and the same powers and character as the Court of Edward the Confessor or that of Robert the Pious.   When it takes the form of a solemn assembly, it appears now as a gathering of judges, warriors, or political counsellors, and again as a semi-council with power to treat of ecclesiastical affairs.[1]

In one country and another, the institution of the *Curia*, whether princely or royal, is practically the same in the eleventh century, because it has nowhere yet become defined.   It is vague, indeterminate, and of changing aspects, but it is indispensable, and it exists everywhere.   It is admitted that the prince cannot govern without the council of his faithful men ;[2] the sentiments and ideas from which the French feudal system and Anglo-Saxon commendation have alike grown, do not agree with the monarchical idea, without some such modification.   The individual contract which binds the man to his lord, even though the lord were king, obliges

1. L. Valin, *Le duc de Normandie et sa cour*, 1910, p. 102 sq., 171 sq., and, especially, Ch. H. Haskins, *Norman Institutions*, 1918, p. 54 sq.
2. The texts are innumerable. For England, see especially Glanvill, *De legibus Angliæ*, ed. Philips, i, p. 237.

the man to come and make an agreement with his lord when he is summoned, and binds the lord to consult his men. The epics, even more vividly than the historical documents, reflect this state of mind. Take the *Chanson de Roland*,[1] which was doubtless written by an Anglo-Norman poet at the time of the sons of William the Conqueror; Charlemagne, before replying to king Marsila, "summons his barons to hold his council," for "in all things he wishes" to act through them; at the end of the poem, this council judges the traitor Ganelon, for one of the essential attributes of the *Curia* is to aid the prince in doing justice.

This being so, we need not wonder whether William the Conqueror planned to keep the Witenagemot after he had got himself elected king by it, or whether he desired to substitute for it a feudal *Curia* according to the French way. The question is useless. It is enough to say that the generalisation of the system of tenure simply strengthened the old conception of the duty of counsel.[2]

The Court of the Norman kings, like that of the Anglo-Saxon monarchs, is sometimes large and formal, and is sometimes reduced to a small group of familiars and competent persons. The king summons to it whomsoever he wishes; relatives, personal friends, officials, churchmen, lay lords, and passing guests. But, since he is very powerful, the Court, in the narrow sense of the word, has much more importance than in France. It has no need to enlarge itself into pompous assemblies where the barons and prelates fulfil the duty of counsel, when it desires to extend its action outside the royal domain. The Norman clerks who surround the king of England rapidly create a general administration of justice and finance; it would be vain to seek an equivalent in Cape-

---

1. Lines 166–167, 3699 sq.
2. Some modern historians have strongly insisted, but to excess, on the feudal character of the English royalty. See M. Lefebvre's *Studies*, p. 449, note 2. See also the posthumous work of G. B. Adams. *Council and Courts in Anglo Norman England*, 1926, p. 2 sq.

tian France, which is in reality an agglomeration of principalities. The *Curia* of the Plantagenets is thus, in fact, something quite different from the *Curia* of a Louis VII, even though the origin of the institution is the same.

Here again a knowledge of administrative history is indispensable, if we wish to appreciate the part played by the *Concilium generale*. The enlarged *Curia* can be understood only in relation to the restricted *Curia*. The *fideles et familiares regiis specialiter assistentes secretis, in quorum manu consilia regis et regni negotia diriguntur,*[1] the high functionaries who have created the Exchequer and the Benches, drawn up the assizes, worked out the system of writs, extended that of the inquests and the juries; the itinerant justices who travel about the realm, showering it with fines and then returning to sit wherever the king may be; the officials who apply the harsh forest-law, and those who, on the king's behalf, exercise the oppressive rights of purveyance, relief, wardship, marriage, and the *regalia*; all these cannot consider the *Concilium generale* as a "national assembly." From the standpoint of feudal law, as from that of the divine right of kings, the *Concilium generale* of the twelfth century, and *Parliamentum* of the thirteenth *are not an organ of control: in the eyes of the king's men, they are an instrument of government.*

It is therefore clear why the assemblies do not meet regularly at fixed times, and why the highly elastic attributes of the general courts vary. They vary according to the authority enjoyed by the king and according to his character. The Court is primarily a court of justice, and the great cases, and business of a public character, must be reserved for it; but the king retains his prerogative of

1. A letter addressed to the Pope in 1166, by the clergy of the province of Canterbury; quoted by J. F. Baldwin, *The King's Council in England during the Middle Ages*, 1913, p. 12.

judging. It is almost always consulted on questions of war and peace, alliances, and royal marriages; nevertheless, the barons complain that they were not sounded on the subject of the marriage of Matilda with Geoffrey of Anjou, and later Henry III accepts the crown of Sicily after a mere meeting of his private Council. On rare occasions only do the great men take the initiative in a legislative measure, and from an early date the kings publish important edicts without consulting them.[1] The question of taxation is the cause of more difficulties for the Monarchy; yet it is very remarkable that, before the abuses committed by John Lackland, the refusals of taxes of which we have no knowledge are individual refusals, and come from the Archbishops of Canterbury and York. Besides, if the king's counsellors fear that the barons and prelates will not agree to too heavy an aid, they have many ways of obtaining money for him; the judges, the sheriffs, and the escheators give another turn of the screw, the Jews disgorge, the Italian bankers lend money. If the assembly is not docile, it can be dispensed with. The prince, except during revolutions, has almost always the last word.

The opinion which the king's men certainly hold concerning the part of the assembly must also be considered if we wish to avoid all illusion on the nature of an innovation which has struck, if not contemporary writers—they scarcely mention it—at least modern historians; I refer to the summoning of proctors of the communities of the shires and towns, and of proctors of the lesser clergy. All these summonses, during the

---

1. Henry I's edicts on shire courts and on false money;—Henry II's assize of arms;—Ordinances of the thirteenth century. The absence of all constitutional mechanism in the Anglo-Norman period has been indicated in detail by G. B. Adams, *Origin of the English Constitution*, 1912, p. 23, 28 sq., 150 sq., etc. The characteristic feature of the period, he says, is the coincidence of absolutism after the Carolingian fashion with feudalism. It is a good definition.

thirteenth century, are explained by the circumstances. Let us take an example. The first that we know—the medievalist must always take care not to say "Such a thing begins at such a date"—is that of the 7th November, 1213; four discreet knights of each county were urgently summoned for the 15th. It goes without saying that John had not the least idea of assuring the lesser nobility of a permanent part in politics, and it is absurd to see in that summons (or in the August summons, the authenticity of which is highly doubtful)[1] "the first hesitating and tentative step towards that great act in which Church, baronage and people made their constitutional compact with the king."[2] The gravity of the political situation at this time, November 7th, has not been remarked. John had made submission to the Pope, but was not reconciled with the bishops, and two days earlier he had been unable to reach agreement with them on the compensation he was to give them. The barons, in an assembly held on the 3rd at Reading, had accepted the kiss of peace from the legate, but the king had not appeared at Reading, and this reconciliation appeared illusory. Moreover, a great war seemed imminent. French troops were in the act of ravaging the domains of the count of Flanders, the ally of John Lackland, and his arrival, as well as that of the Count of Toulouse, was expected in England. In December John was to give orders for assembling vessels and troops.[3] His attendants evidently judged it necessary, on November 7th, to consult the knights of the shires; they wanted to feel their way.

I need not stress the point any further. The entire

1 See a note by M. Lefebvre in his additional study on the "Origins of the House of Commons," p. 461, n. 1.

2 Stubbs, *Const. Hist.*, i, p. 567.

3. Kate Norgate, *John Lackland*, p. 191 sq.—A. Cartellieri, *Philipp II August*, iv, 397.

history of the thirteenth-century assemblies needs re-statement. But M. Lefebvre has sufficiently shown, especially in reference to M. D. Pasquet's fine essay on the origins of the House of Commons,[1] that at these origins no " constitutional pact " is to be found, but the will of the king's men to utilise the new social forces for the advantage of the Monarchy, and for well-defined ends.

IV.

That this was equally the intention of Edward I, does not seem to us in the least doubtful.[2] We have, for one Parliament of Edward I's reign, an admirable collection of documents, a model for future publications.[3] For many editions of texts will be necessary for a true under-standing of the evolution of the English Parliament in the Middle Ages : the six great volumes of the *Rotuli parliamentorum* (1278-1503), published in the eighteenth century, are a compilation as incomplete as they are incorrect. For the meeting of February-March 1305 we luckily possess the original *Memoranda*, transcribed by F. W. Maitland, and enriched by him with highly valuable appended documents. What is the impression left by reading this collection ?

In 1305 the aged Edward I is at the height of his power. The serious dispute which for several years had

---

1. I would point out here that the English edition of this book, *An Essay on the Origin of the House of Commons*, trans. R. G. D. Laffan, 1925, contains interesting additions and corrections.

2. On the whole question, see M. Lefebvre's *Studies*, p. 476 sq. He has dealt with the part of Edward I. in the constitutional evolution, and has given a bibliography.

3. *Memoranda de Parliamento. Records of the Parliament holden at Westminster*, A.D. 1305, edit. F. W. Maitland, R. S. 1893. Mr. Pollard, *Evolution of Parliament*, Preface p. vi, states that this collection, "buried in the Rolls Series," is usually unknown to English teachers; but he himself has not used it as much as his Preface leads one to hope.

separated him from part of the baronage, the clergy, and even the commons, is over; he has confirmed the Charters, and no one dreams that he is thinking of asking the Pope to revoke the " concessions made at the expense of his honour and to the detriment of the royal supremacy," and to annul the Charters.[1] He has subdued Wales, made peace with France, regained possession of Gascony and of Scotland, and is busy establishing order there. He has great financial embarrassments, and is harrassed by his creditors,[2] but for the moment he is not asking for a subsidy. No stormy session can be foreseen. The session will be wholly normal, and that is one more reason why it should attract our attention.

What strikes us first is that the assembly which met on February 28th, at Westminster, was very numerous, and that, nevertheless, it was merely an enlargement of the Council, a momentary extension, which the king was free to renounce, and which, in fact, he did renounce, as soon as it suited him. If the writs of summons, Maitland tells us, were all obeyed (though this is entirely doubtful) there were present 95 prelates, 145 proctors of the lesser clergy, 9 earls, 94 barons, 74 knights of the shires, 200 burgesses, 33 members of the Council summoned individually, and also other persons specially qualified for certain affairs. No particular name is given officially to this assembly. Such an omission has an important significance. Human institutions do not really exist until they have been given a name. The word *Parliament* is not used by the recorder of the *Memoranda* in the modern sense; it means " colloquy," " conference." No more is the assembly a political gathering resembling our own: with the aristocracy

1. Bull of Pope Clement V, December 29th, 1305 : Bémont, *Chartes des libertés anglaises*, p. 110 sq.
2. See M. Lefebvre's *Studies*, p. 392, p. 478.

and the proctors of the middle classes sit all the great
functionaries, as though in our Parliament it were usual
to summon the most competent men of the Court of
Appeal, the Court of Accounts, the Council of State,
and the Ministries. Finally, after three weeks, on
March 21, the king " *remercie moult* " the prelates,
barons, and people of the commons, and ordains " that
they shall return home quickly and without delay."
John de Kirkby will give to the knights of the shire and
to the burgesses writs by which they can recover their
wages in their own districts. But order is made to the
" bishops, earls, and barons, justices and others of the
Council of our lord the king " to stay until they are
specially dismissed.[1] The session is thus prolonged,
probably until April 18th, by the deliberations of the
Council; the king is said to sit, as before, " in full
Parliament," " in general Parliament,"[2] for there is
full Parliament, full meeting, as soon as all those whom
the king has gathered or kept around him are present.
What was the composition of this Council which was
held from March 21st to April 18th ? According to the
statistics built up by Maitland[3] on rather fragile bases,
it seems to have included four bishops, five earls, seventeen barons, and forty or fifty persons who exercised
the highest judicial, financial and administrative functions, or were the confidants of Edward I. We must add
that on September 15th there was held at Westminster

1. Maitland, text no. 2.

2. Nos. 459, 464.

3. Matland, p. cvi sq. See M. Lefebvre's *Studies*, p. 391, on the
highly important place of the Wardrobe clerks among Edward I's
counsellors in 1305.—Maitland counts the Archbishop of Canterbury
among the counsellors in 1305; as we shall see below, his continual
presence is scarcely admissible.—On April 5, the Bishop of Byblos
appeared "*coram episcopis et aliis praelatis, comitibus, baronibus,
justitiariis, et nonnullis aliis nobilibus, clericis, et laicis, consiliariis
magnifici Principis domini Edwardi regis, . . . generali parliamento
tunc existente*" (text no. 464). These counsellors, who are enumerated,
number thirty-six.

a second *Parliament,* which was merely a much-reduced
gathering of the Council.[1]

The king's agents who prepared the business of the
assemblies had determined what we to-day would call
an important order of the day. But what did Edward I
gain from the gathering of the five or six hundred
faithful men who were with him from February 28th to
March 21st?

The part of these good men in legislation was very
modest. It is evident that the *Ordinatio de Trailbastons,*[2]
transcribed in the *Memoranda,* was the work of the royal
jurists, and that the statute relating to the challenge of
jurymen by the king's officers, drawn up on the occasion
of the petition of a prisoner,[3] was conceded without
difficulty, so that the Commons had no need to insist.
The Forest Ordinance of 1305, in which the king takes
back with one hand what he grants with the other, bears
no trace of collaboration with Parliament.[4] The sole
measure which could have been the common work of the
king and his loyal men is the statute forbidding the
export of ecclesiastical capital; it was claimed by " the
community of England " against the orders of Cîteaux,
Cluny, Prémontré, and others;[5] but the statute *de ap-
portis religiosorum,* which was to be inserted in the
roll,[6] was not published until long afterwards;[7] Edward
I was playing a double part, and did not wish to quarrel

1. Twenty counsellors and ten Scots (Maitland, p. xliv–xlv).
2. Instructions of procedure for the pursuit and punishment of
marauders. See Maitland, Introd., p. liii.
3. Maitland, text, no. 10.
4. See my study on the " Forest," in Vol. ii, of the *Studies and Notes
Supplementary,* etc., pp. 225–226.
5. Maitland, text, no. 486.
6. A blank space of half a membrane follows in the roll the declaration that the king " *ordinavit et statuit certum statutum in hoc casu
in forma que sequitur.*" Cf. no. 485 : the Abbot of Cîteaux asks that
the Cistercian abbots of England may help him to make up the sum
which he has to pay every year to the Holy See : reply "*Le roi ne purra
otroier a la priere le dit abbé santz offendre la ley et les bones gentz de
son roiaume.*"
7. *Statutes,* i, 150.

z

with the Pope, on whom he counted for the cancelling of the Charters.—Was the administration of Scotland and of Gascony the object of a general debate? It is very improbable. It was on March 26th, after the departure of the people who were not part of the Council, that three Scotsmen, the Bishop of Glasgow, the Earl of Carrick, and John Mowbray appeared to state how, in their opinion, Scotland should be represented in the Parliament at which the government of that country was to be organised;[1] and the important ordinance *super stabilitate terrae Scotiae* was prepared during the Parliament of September 15th, which was only a session of the Council.[2] Likewise, it was the Council which, from March 24th to 30th, nominated the high functionaries of Gascony.[3]—If we examine finally the great judicial affairs brought before the Parliament, we observe that it was the Council which, after the closure pronounced on March 21st, judged Nicholas Segrave, a baron accused of treason;[4] the Council which, on March 28th, judged the dispute between the citizens of Salisbury and their bishop;[5] the Council which condemned to a fine the citizens of Winchester, guilty of allowing a hostage to escape;[6] and so on. "The King," it is written in *Fleta*, "has his Court in his Council in his Parliaments, in the presence of the prelates, earls, barons, great men, and other experienced persons; the cases are determined there, and new remedies are found

1. Text no. 13, also very interesting in showing how representation in Parliament was then understood. The three Scots declare that ten persons will suffice, two bishops, two abbots, two earls, two barons, and "*deus pur la commune*," all ten chosen by "*la commune d' Escoce*." These are not deputies sent to Parliament, but proctors, and their number matters little.

2. See Maitland's Introduction, p. xlviii–xlix.

3. Maitland, Appendix II, p. 328 sq.

4. "*Nicholaus Segrave venit in pleno parlamento in praesentia domini regis, archiepiscori Cantuariensis et plurimorum episcoporum, comitum, baronum, et aliorum de consilio domini regis tunc ibidem existentium,*" (text. no. 449). The pledges appeared on March 29th.

5. Text no. 451.

6. Text no. 456.

for new wrongs as they appear; justice is done to each according to his deserts."[1]   The king's Court, in its judicial aspect, keeps all its authority despite the successive creations of the " Benches "; it keeps its ancient character as the supreme court and the tribunal of equity, which is not bound by the Common Law, and has power to make innovations. But, as the complicated formula of the *Fleta* well indicates, the judicial " Court " is held in the " Council " during the meetings called " Parliaments."

From this analysis we may conclude that Edward I had no wish, in 1305, to associate the lay and ecclesiastical aristocracy as a whole, and the proctors of the lesser clergy and of the commons in the legislative, administrative and judicial work which had to be done. Before the meeting of the general assembly, the work of the session was prepared, and prepared very carefully ; now, we have the proof that beforehand it was decided to reserve the solution of this or that matter for the Council, held after the closing of the full assembly ; on the back of a petition concerning a rather delicate matter in the law of wardship, one of the king's clerks had written in 1305, "To be dealt with at the end of Parliament, before all the judges. . . ." Another hand has added that the Council has asked for further information.[2]

All this being so, since the king asked for no subsidy, what was the use of the full assembly? To present petitions, and, through the opportunity which they afforded, to keep the Council informed of what was happening in the kingdom. Later, in the course of the fourteenth century, when the Chancery organises itself as a court of justice and can hear most of the petitions, the business of the Council will be lightened. But about 1305, it is encumbered with an enormous number of complaints

1. Cited in Maitland, p. lxxxi, note 2.   See Maitland's important observations, p. lxxix sq.
2. Text no. 251.

and requests, even though only the most important are reserved for it.[1] Maitland has published several hundreds of petitions presented at the Parliament of 1305, and he estimates that a large number must have disappeared from the archives.[2] The usage of the petition is derived from the recognised right of the subject to complain of the king,[3] and is reinforced by the fact that the king's agents are tyrannical, interfering in everything in the land, so that it is necessary to solicit all sorts of permissions, and that, on the other hand, the high functionaries are very jealous of their authority;—the Chancery cannot do anything of importance without the Council's authorisation, while, in general, courts of law and of finance can deal only with cases introduced by a writ issued from the Chancery.[4]

All the petitions are addressed " to our lord the king," or else " to our lord the king and to his council." About a third come from collective bodies; religious houses (the most frequent source), the Universities of Oxford and Cambridge, towns, communities of counties, communities of merchants, groups of foreigners, of soldiers, of royal officials, of prisoners, etc. . . The most general petition, to which we have already called attention above, is the *Petitio Comitum, Baronum et Communitatis regni Angliae* against the relgous orders which export capital.[5] Another comes from those who hold " knights' fees," and who have furnished service during the war or paid compensation, and from whom the Exchequer unduly claims scutage. In another, they ask power to

1. They were much more numerous still at the beginning of the reign. See Maitland, Introd., p. lvi, on the measures adopted for sorting them out.

2. Maitland, p. xxxii.

3. A text of the jurist Bracton, cited by Stubbs *Const. Hist.*, ii, p. 250, note 1: "*Contra ipsum (regem) non habebitur remedium per assisam, immo tantum locus erit supplicationi ut factum suum corrigat et emendet.*"

4. See the details of procedure in Maitland, p. lxviii sq.

5. Text no. 486.

raise a scutage of 40 shillings from their subjects.[1] A very curious collective petition is that of the *Pauperes homines terrae Angliae*, claiming " a remedy in the matter of men placed on inquisitions, juries, and assizes, commonly corrupted by the presents of the rich," and in the matter of ecclesiastical judges who encroach on the royal jurisdiction and exact fines.[2] The king's Council had, and we also have, thanks to these complaints and requests, a picture of the life of the king's subjects, of the manner in which they governed themselves and were governed by the local officials. Thus we can hear the University of Oxford groan against the disorderly behaviour of the town, and the greed of the retailers, and expose to the king all its petty grievances. The democratic faction at Newcastle accuses the faction of the rich of impeding the freedom of trade. The communities of the shires and the towns and all classes of society count on the king's help and, indeed, are strongly bound to inform him of their wishes, so imperious and well-respected in his prerogative. In the far-off county of Cumberland, the burgesses of Cockermouth need the king's authorisation to raise a tax with the object of repairing three bridges carried away by a flood.[3] No less interesting, for the government of Edward I as well as for the historian who studies them, are the individual petitions. From Mary, the king's daughter, from a merchant plundered by the Norwegians, down to a gaoler who has allowed a prisoner to escape,[4] all subjects, great and small, have recourse to the petition when they solicit the king's goodwill or justice, for he is the dispenser of good things and the redresser of wrongs. The officials themselves

1. Nos. 203, 198.—Request for raising a tallage on the lands of the Ancient Demesne : no. 87.
2. No. 472.
3. Oxford, nos. 66 to 76.—Newcastle, no. 166.—Cockermouth, no. 8, See also no. 78.
4. Princess Mary, no. 7.—Merchant, no. 174.—Gaoler, no. 57.

employ this method to obtain the settlement of matters of administration,[1] or to try to obtain payment of their wages, for the king has on all sides complaining creditors.[2] Claims against the excesses of royal officials are not many,[3] whether because they fear their master too much to serve him badly, or because men are too much afraid of them to complain : both explanations are doubtless valid. On the other hand, violence, novel disseizin, usurpation, pressure or intimidation exercised by the powerful are often denounced; manners and morals are gross and appetites brutal; one feels that as soon as the king's hand weakens, the disorder will be terrible.[4]

The replies made to the petitions presented in the Parliament of 1305 are very remarkable. They are the work of expert jurists, with clear minds, dry and precise, and free from passion. One has only to compare the style of the replies, concise and clear, with that of the petitions, written in diffuse and obscure French. Often further information is demanded, involving searches into the archives, or an inquest by the sheriff or the escheator ; enquiry will be made whether the favour asked will be to the advantage or disadvantage of the king; but, in most cases, the answer is given at once. It is given in a manifest spirit of justice, with a care for equity and for public interest which spares no one. Mary, the king's daughter, who asks a financial favour, namely that she might have the profits of the escheats, wardships, and marriages in the manors which the king has given her, is refused. John, Duke of Brittany and Earl of Richmond, obtains rights which cannot harm the king, but is refused permission to export specie issuing from his

---

1. Nos. 90, 110, 173.
2. Nos. 58, 80, 175, 272, 275, etc.
3. Nos. 61, 182, 255, etc.
4. See especially the petition of Richard Gykel, no. 181. He has been violently dispossessed of his inheritance; the assize-men have been the object of such threats that they have pronounced against him.

English lands.[1] Sometimes a difficult case is brought forward before the king; or sometimes the reply takes the general character of an ordinance. Most often it is considered sufficient to point out to the petitioner the way to be pursued in order to obtain a solution.[2]

If all the work is done by the Council, what occupies the time of the hundreds of persons who form no part of it? Evidently, they must have held discussions, at the beginning of the session, in order to establish certain collective petitions and to gather support. But above all they must have had business to transact in the administrative departments. They must not return empty-handed. The baron, the bishop, or the proctor of an ecclesiastical or a lay community must prosecute to the end the business in which he is interested. This is amply proved when the king, in dismissing them on March 21st, specifies that " *ceux qui ount a busoigner* . . . *demoergent a siwre lour busoignes.*" Of the two duties which our present-day deputies perform, that of exercising their political mandate and that of watching over particular interests, I fully believe that, from February 28th to March 21st, 1305, the persons summoned by Edward I were concerned almost entirely with the second.

The impression we obtain from the *Memoranda de Parliamento Regis* of the thirty-third year of Edward I is, then, that at this time England had a very powerful king, very ably served, anxious for good administration, but with an uncompromising love of authority. In his eyes this mob of six hundred persons was not the Witenagemot; the real *Concilium* which by ancient custom must attend the king to inform and serve him, is that body which he in practice calls his *Conseil*, that is to say, the people whom he retains around him after

1. Petition of Mary, no. 7; of Duke John, nos. 161–165.
2. Cases resulting *coram rege*; nos. 238, 241; ordinance, no. 17: method of prosecution, nos. 59, 135, etc.

344 STUDIES IN CONSTITUTIONAL HISTORY

the mass of the prelates, barons, and proctors has been
dismissed. Now we have seen that the majority of them
are high functionaries. Edward I appoints as a counsellor
whomsoever he wills; he must be a "good man," and one
whom he " loves,"[1] and he must go straight. I doubt
whether the Archbishop Winchelsey regularly attended
the sessions of the Council, as the list drawn up by
Maitland would have us believe; we see the king, on the
occasion of a complaint brought against his great ad-
versary , cite him to appear in a letter of extraordinary
brutality.[2] He was, like Louis XI, a terrible king.

In this land where a lord could not raise a tax from
his subjects nor establish a warren, where a University
could not found a college, nor a town establish a tax
without the prince's authorisation,[3] why does the King
summon a great Parliament, when he does not intend to
ask for a subsidy and when no danger threatens the land?
Firstly, it is because a long tradition, which, as we have
seen, goes back in the mist of ages until it is lost, enjoins
him to do so. He has no thought of breaking it,
especially as it does not seriously inconvenience him.
It troubles him only when he wants money, and at that
point he is fully obliged, by the feudal law still in full
force, to ask consent to the aid. And then this great Parliament is useful to him; he is too intelligent not to
realise this. Just as, long ago, the Witenagemot amalga-
mated the small Anglo-Saxon principalities, so now the
gathering of five or six hundred men coming from every
corner of the land cements the unity of the kingdom.
It is an excellent chance for the barons of Cornwall or
Northumberland to listen to the best English jurists and
to understand matters of law. And finally, at West-

1. See the writ nominating a counsellor which I have reproduced in
t. ii, of the French edition of Stubbs, p. 311, note 2.
2. Petition against the Archbishop, and the king's letters; text no.
204.
3. It should be stated that most of the important towns were in the
royal domains.

minster the king gets into touch with his subjects and learns what is going on. M. Lefebvre very aptly reminds us,[1] in his treatment of the English Parliament, of that text of Hincmar in which we see so clearly the advantage reaped by Charlemagne from his great assemblies.

In short, I agree entirely with the eminent historian T. F. Tout when he holds that Edward I, far from having been the founder of the free constitution of England, had not, any more than Philip the Fair, any conscious intention of sharing his power with the people. " Had he been " he adds, " a younger man, had he had ten more years of life, he might have combined the humiliation of the baronage and episcopate with the real subjection of the Scots. In that case, who can doubt but that he would have dealt as roughly with constitutional freedom as ever French autocrat had done?"[2] I will go further than Mr. Tout. In the Parliament of 1305, Edward I, sitting in his Council, seems to me an autocrat.[3] The turning-point of English constitutional history is not there. It needed the great upheavals of the fourteenth and fifteenth centuries to check and weaken the powerful Monarchy founded by William the

1. See his *Studies*, p. 453.
2. *Place Edward II*, p. 32.
3. Stubbs' conclusions concerning Edward I, and the character of his reign, rest on interpretations of texts which are astonishing in so great a scholar. Speaking of the summonses to the famous Parliament of 1295, he says that we might see, in the form of the summonses addressed to the prelates, a prophetic inauguration of the representative system, and that the citation of Justinian's code, *ut quod omnes similiter tangit ab omnibus approbetur*, was transformed by Edward from a simple legislative maxim into a great political and constitutional principle. (Vol. ii, pp. 133-134). Now in this summons to the prelates, it was merely a case of employing their habitual phrasing. Edward's Chancery was using a comonplace preamble in accordance with the usual scholastic forms. Compare, for example, Abbo's text concerning the consultation of the *episcopi et primores regni*, cited in Luchaire, *Inst. mon.*, t. i, p. 249. If there was any definite purpose in expressing this idea in the particular summons to the prelates, it was at most because the clergy had often exacted respect of the right of consent, and even of individual consent.

Conqueror. There was certainly in England, an embryonic political society before that; not only the already remarkable unity of this small and vigorous state, but further, very ancient and solid local institutions, whose importance Stubbs most judiciously declared,[1] disposed this people to move in the direction of constitutional liberty; and Edward I, by his frequent assemblies of Parliaments, by his frequent summonses to proctors of communities, by the conscientious treatment which his counsellors gave to the petitions, did much to strengthen this political education. But it was the disorders of Edward II's reign, the growing need for money resulting from the war with France and the prodigality of living among the knights, and the social progress hastened on by the shock of the great plague, which opened the new phase, in which the outlines of parliamentary institutions were sketched. It was then that the House of Commons, the House of Lords, and the Council were to become distinct entities.

In this Introduction we have considered only the phase of remote origins. If the formula of Bracton's continuator, " The king holds his Court in his Council in his Parliaments " remains fixed, with its significance, in the memory of the reader; if he has seen that the Parliament of 1305 is yet little removed from the old Anglo-Norman assemblies, and that it owes its new features to the perfecting of monarchical centralisation, my purpose is accomplished. I will merely recall, in closing, that after the eclipse suffered during the civil wars, the House of Commons was definitely consolidated only by the despot Henry VIII; he might have broken it; but being well advised, he preferred to make use of it.[2] He followed, consciously or not, the policy of Edward I and of the medieval kings, who, for their own advantage and

1. Cf. M. Lefebvre's *Studies*, p. 490.
2. See Henry VIII's declaration to the Commons, quoted in Pollard, *Evolution of Parliament*, p. 231. Cf. p. 322 sq

without thinking of paving the way for a future which could not be foreseen, preserved the feeble germs of the parliamentary system.

Stubbs, at the end of his monumental work, asks permission to moralise, and counsels his readers to be just and sympathetic towards their ancestors. We too will ask the same permission, to request that no one should attribute to them ideas which they could not have held, since they were still very near to nature. Political liberty is not a natural thing. These are the natural things : violence, oppression, and despotism. Liberty can only be the conquest of a refined civilisation. Its conception requires guidance by a moral idea which is slow to form. To find the practical means of crushing down evil instincts and the spirit of domination, there is necessary a great effort of observation, reason, and measured wisdom, and of this the men of the Middle Ages were not capable.

CH. PETIT-DUTAILLIS.

ADDITIONAL STUDIES.

By G. Lefebvre.

The Transformations of the " Curia Regis " at the end of the Middle Ages.

Introduction.

As early as 1894, in his *Etude sur la vie et le règne de Louis VIII*,[1] M. Ch. Petit-Dutaillis showed

Recent works on constitutional history

that Stubbs' views on the constitutional evolution of England had grown out-of-date. This observation has since been confirmed by the remarkable studies of Messrs. G. B.

---

1. Page 57. See also his " Additional Study," on the " Great Charter," (*Studies and Notes Supplementary*, i, p. 127). Since then the most notable works published have been :— *Magna Carta: Commemoration Essays*, edited by E. Malden, London, (Royal Hist. Soc., 1917) : (studies by Messrs. W. S. McKechnie, J. H. Round, P. Vinogradoff, F. M. Powicke, H. Jenkinson, C. H. MacIlwain, G. B. Adams, R. Altamira; Messrs. Vinogradoff and Powicke examine anew the meaning of article 39, " *Nullus capiatur liber homo*"; G. B. Adams, the attitude of Innocent III regarding the Great Charter. Cf. the observations of J. Tait, *E. H. R.*, 1918) ; two notes by A. B. White on the name of the Charter (the epithet *Great* was attributed to it to distinguish it from the Charter of the Forest) in *E. H. R.*; 1915, p. 472, and 1917, p. 554; Fox, *The Originals of the Great Charter, E. H. R.*, 1924; Miss Faith Thompson, *The first century of Magna Carta*, Minnesota U. P., 1925; articles by M. Leclère in the *Revue de l'Univ. de Bruxelles*, 1913 and in *Mélanges d'Histoire offerts à Henri Pirenne*, 1926, t. i, p. 279 sqq. In the works cited below (notes 2 and 3), Messrs. Adams and MacIlwain adopted the "feudal" interpretation of the Charter, formulated in 1907, by M. Petit-Dutaillis, who accepted the views set out by Mr. McKechnie in *Magna Carta*, 1905,(2nd edit., 1914).

Adams,[1] C. H. MacIlwain,[2] D. Pasquet,[3] and A. F. Pollard,[4] on the origins of Parliament and particularly of the House of Commons.[5]

It must be observed that we have new documents at our disposal. In 1893, F. W. Maitland published the **New Documents** roll of the Parliament of 1305,[6] and it was the discovery by Mr. H. Jenkinson[7] of a part of the writs of the Parliament of 1275 which contributed chiefly to take from the Model Parliament of 1295 part of the importance which Stubbs attributed to it. It is true that the great scholar was so prudent, and so attentive to the texts, that in describing the composition and the attributes of the *commune concilium* or " national assembly," he frequently observed that they remained almost entirely theoretical, and were realised or exercised only by exception.[8]

1. *The Origin of the English Constitution*, Yale Univ. Press, 1912.
2. *The High Court of Parliament and its Supremacy*, Yale Univ. Press, 1910.
3. *Essai sur les origines de la Chambre des Communes*, 1914 (Thèse Lettres). (English translation, revised, 1925.)
4. *The Evolution of Parliament*, London, 1920.
5. We recall at this point that the reaction against Stubbs' views on the origins of the House of Commons , and the part of Edward I, goes back to the works of M. Ch. Bémont (*Simon de Montfort*, 1884, and, for Edward I, *Chartes des libertés anglaises*, p. 108) and to those of L. Riess; *Geschicte des Wahlrechts zum englischen Parlament im Mittelaiter*, Leipzig, 1885, and "Der Ursprung des englischen Unterhauses "; *Hist. Zeitschrift*, 1888. Stubbs cites these works in his last edition, but does not adopt the conclusions.
6. *Memoranda de Parliamento; Records of the Parliament holden at Westminster*, A.D. 1305; *R. S.* 1893. Maitland searched for the petitions mentioned in the roll and found about 500; he also found, in the Chancery and the Exchequer rolls for 1305, some of the writs given for the execution of the decisions taken on these petitions. He published part of both series. This roll is incomplete; particularly, it contains nothing for Gascony. Mr. R. G. Atkinson has added to Maitland's publication in an article in the *E. H. R.*, 1921, on the petitions addressed to this parliament by the Channel Islands.
7. Published in *E. H. R.*, 1910, " The First Parliament of Edward I." Mr. G. O. Sayle's discovery of the summons, to the 1268 parliament, of the representatives of 27 cities and boroughs, also helps to connect the parliament of Edward I with that of Simon de Montfort (*E. H. R.*, 1925).
8. See for example *Const. Hist.*, i, p. 617. " The advice and consent of the Assembly may have been, no doubt in many cases was, a mere formality."

Still, we cannot read his work without obtaining the conviction that, unconsciously, he postulated, as pre-existent in law, the English constitution such as it functioned in his own time, and which he considered the ideal constitution.[1] The common effort of the different classes of the nation to make a reality of it was, in his eyes, the essential feature of the medieval history of England. It is possible that political sentiment and national pride were not the sole causes of this optical illusion; Stubbs was writing a constitutional history, and, from 1215 onwards, he left administrative history almost untouched, though he had made a brilliant study of it up to that date, because he rightly saw in Henry II's reforms one of the origins of constitutional progress. If he could have devoted part of his researches to the history of the Council and of the Household in the thirteenth, four-teenth, and fifeenth centuries, as did Messrs. J. B. Baldwin[2] and T. F. Tout,[3] he would perhaps have modi-fied his conclusions; but it is unlikely that he would have agreed entirely with those of Mr. Tout.[4] In any case, we see how the *commune concilium* never ceases to be, in his eyes, a " national assembly,"[5] to such a point that he denied to the Capetian assemblies any resemblance to

The completion
or rectification
of Stubbs'
work

1. See *Const. Hist.*, i, p. 617. " Legislation was one of the nominal rights that belonged to the whole council as the representative of the nation," and especially ii, p. 262. " It is probable that the theory of the constitution was somewhat in advance of its actual progress."
2. *The King's Council in England during the Middle Ages*, Oxford, Clarendon Press, 1913.
3. *The Place of the Reign of Edward II in English History*, Manches-ter Univ. Press, 1914; *Chapters in the Administrative History of England*, vols. i and ii, Manchester U. P., 1920; "Some Conflicting Tendencies in English Administrative History during the XIVth cen-tury " (*Bulletin of the John Rylands Library*, 1924).
4. Tout, *Chapters*, ii, p. 146 : The Council is a reinforcement of the Household, the Parliament a reinforcement of the Council. The Council and the Parlament give advice; the king decides; the House-hold, *i.e.*, the administrative services, execute; ii, p. 190 : "The parliamentary system grew up in obedience to the royal will. It was no yielding to a people crying for liberty."
5. See, for example, *Const. Hist.*, i, pp. 604 sq.

it ;[1] we see also how he mistook the real nature of the Great Charter; we understand how Edward I appears to him a national hero, as having realised the wish of the English people in organising at length the Parliament of the " Three Estates," and admitting it to a share in the government of the country.

These views are abandoned to-day, even by the historians who, like Mr. Pollard, fully recognise the eminent services which Parliament has rendered, **New theories of the origins of Parliament** and continues to render to England.[2] Mr. Adams has set himself to prove that the *commune concilium* or so-called national assembly was merely a feudal court. Messrs. MacIlwain and Pollard have denied it almost any legislative and financial importance; they see in it essentially a high court of justice, where knights and burgesses rarely appear save as pleaders or petitioners. M. Pasquet has shown that the sovereigns, and especially Edward I, saw in the summoning of the commons merely an administrative and political expedient, a form of royal government which would strengthen their authority without in the slightest degree disintegrating it. The reaction has been so strong that some English scholars seem to judge it excessive. Indeed, in our view, some modification is necessary.[3]

1. See *Ibid.*, ii, p. 269.
2. Mr. Pollard, *Evolution of Parliament*, pp. 3 et seq., attributes as much importance, if not more, to Parliament, as did Stubbs himself, but for a different reason as far as the Middle Ages are concerned; the progress of Parliament did not result, during this period, in making England a constitutional state, but in contributing essentially to creating national unity and the English state. He agrees with Stubbs for the modern and contemporary periods; the parliamentary system is the only expedient able to reconcile the existence of a national state with self-government, and it incontestably constitutes the most important contribution of the English people to the progress of universal civilisation.
3. In their essays on the Great Charter, cited above, Messrs. Vinogradoff and Powicke react against the exclusively feudal thesis of Mr. Adams, in that they see in the *liber homo*, not the *baron* or *tenant-in-chief*, but the *freeholder*. Mr. Tait seems equally inclined to find this thesis too absolute (see the review cited above, p. 348, note 1); he too brings some modifications, in favour of Edward I, to M. Pasquet's conclusions (*E. H. R.*, 1914, p. 750).

Whatever the result, if the facts established by Stubbs remain fixed, with due allowance for complementary discoveries and for reservations imposed here and there by further enquiry, it is certain that the historical perspective has been transformed. It appears to us to-day that the Middle Ages, in respect of the constitutional and parliamentary system, were only a period of very slow gestation, and that even in 1485, nothing foreshadowed the brilliant part in store for it.

The historical perspective has been transformed

The struggle of the king against the barons who wish to wrest the government of the kingdom from him, appears to us to-day as the essential factor in the history of England from the thirteenth to the fifteenth century. Stubbs held the fourteenth-century barons in paltry esteem : at this time it is indeed the activity of the Commons which provides the interest in the history of Parliament; it is owing to them that Parliament is organised and its attributes extended. But Stubbs accorded the highest eulogies to the thirteenth-century barons who, at Runnymede and at Oxford had made the rights of the nation triumph. We think now that neither group was better or worse than the other; the barons never thought of anyone but themselves.

The principal theatre of this struggle was the Council, which thus becomes the centre of medieval history. But, as Mr. Tout has shown, this history is enlightened and enriched in a singular fashion by the study of the administration. The Council, whether in deliberation or in judging, did not, contrary to current ideas, dispose of a single executive agent of its own. The application of its decisions required a writ or a warrant which only the administrative services of the *Curia* could issue. It was therefore useless for the barons to control the Council

The Council as the centre of medieval history.

unless they controlled these services also; that is to say,
the great offices to which they were subordinated; that is
why they are seen demanding the nomination, in Parliament, of the ministers as well as of the counsellors. But,
for a long time, the Household, and, still more the
Chamber, remained the inviolable domain of the king;
when, therefore, the ministers had been removed from his
authority, he found in these services endless means of
inventing administrative expedients which weakened or
even annulled the action of the older administrative departments; he could thus take back with one hand what
he had been forced to yield with the other. It is by the
history of the Household that we can explain in particular the long resistance opposed to the barons by the
kings of the thirteenth and fourteenth centuries.

Mr. Tout has further shown that this administrative
history, the study of which is made particularly difficult
The importance and even forbidding by its technical char-
of administra- acter, is destined to reconstruct the aspect
tive history of medieval England. It is very true that,
in the daily life and for the material prosperity which is
the principal preoccupation of the English, as of all
other men, the good functioning of an adequate administration is more important than political questions, so
that the latter do not come before public opinion unless
the chiefs of the administration turn it from its proper
purposes and make of it an instrument of oppression.
It is equally certain that an administration quickly
acquires a corporate feeling, an expert knowledge, and a
tradition which give it an independent strength by
making it the framework of the state, so that political
changes scarcely affect it, and, in consequence have less
influence than might be expected on the obscure and
vital life of the country. Mr Tout has shown that the
barons, as well as the king, worked to perfect the
administration : they merely disputed with him its direc-

AA

tion.[1] And even in the ordinary course of things, it depends on the administration whether a decision of the royal power or a law of Parliament shall be effectively put into excution. It is now a commonplace truth that an order of the central power cannot be executed if it does not correspond to the sentiments of the great majority of the population or to its needs, as understood by them. But it must be added that this order is even more surely condemned to remain a dead letter if the administration is not interested in it or if it lacks the means and the zeal. Thus, as Mr. Tout has said, Parliament,—and also the Council—are put back to their correct importance in the history of the Middle Ages.[2]

We must therefore pursue, for the succeeding centuries, the story of the administrative transformations of the *Curia* which Stubbs admirably summarised up to the end of the twelfth century. We must reconstruct the history of the Household, of which he spoke only incidentally, because the chroniclers say little about it, and long and patient researches into the archives have been necessary to reveal its importance. We must also take up again the history of the Council, which assumes a new aspect now that we know more of the *Curia* and of the Household. Finally, the origins of the House of Commons deserve to be examined once more, for the study of administrative needs throws a new light upon them.

Object of these studies

1. Mr. Tout has recalled, in relation to this point, that in the nineteenth century, the political parties in France contended for the power, i.e. the direction of the administration, without essentially modifying the organisation given to it by Napoleon.
2. *Chapters*, i, pp. 6–7. Stubbs himself recognised that with respect to the fifteenth century, the incapacity of the administration provoked an eclipse of constitutional opinion (*Const. Hist.*, iii, p. 280 sq.) and he insisted on the state of weakness into which constitutional custom had fallen at the time of Edward IV (*Const. Hist.*, iii, pp. 285 sq.)

Exchequer, Benches, and Chancery.

It seems to us to-day that the dismemberment of the *Curia* resulted from causes much more complex than was formerly thought. It was attributed to the **Dismemberment of the "Curia"** necessity of specialising functions, and that necessity has undeniably exercised a certain influence. Still, to be really effective, the specialisation of functions presupposes a corresponding specialisation of personnel; now we find that in fact the latter usually takes place after the former; the Exchequer, the Benches, the Chancery, though grown out of the *Curia* keep a common personnel for a long time. Moreover, once constituted, these sections of the *Curia* are rather opposed than otherwise to the perfect specialisation of functions; they even enter into conflict with each other and encroach upon each other's competence, as their personnel becomes more stable. Messrs. Baldwin and Tout have shown that they owe their particular individuality to many other factors; judicial procedure, administrative methods, the drafting of records and deeds, and the use of different seals.[1]

But, at the same time as they differentiate themselves from each other, their characteristic aspect is gradually **The original nature of the Council and of the Household** marked by a common feature which opposes them all together to the *Consilium regis* and to the " Household "; their procedure and their methods of administration grow fixed and assume a routine, whereas these two cores of the *Curia* continue to escape, in great measure at least, from this sort of senility. From the judicial point of view, it is in relation to the *Consilium regis*, that unstable assembly of heads of the *Curia* in the king's presence, that they are principally differentiated; from the administrative point of view, the distinction operates mainly in relation to the " Household,"

1. Baldwin, pp. 39, 47.

where there remain permanently the clerks and the educated laymen who ensure the execution of the king's wishes. The three sections of the *Curia* with which we are to deal, then, gradually lost their capacity for renewal and invention, while from age to age new tasks were imposed upon them, proportionate to their acquisition of an individuality of their own. The Council and the Household, on the contrary, preserved this power. Juridically this fact is expressed by saying that the king, in delegating part of his authority to the Exchequer, to the Benches, and to the Chancery, by this time grown out from the *Curia,* still kept it none the less intact in his own hands; the Council and the Household therefore retained a universal competence. From the historical, or even from the social point of view, this fertility of resources justifies the royal prerogative—which excited so keenly, and often so justly, the distrust of contemporaries—because, without it, the perfection of judicial procedure and of administrative methods would have been very difficult, if not impossible.

I.

The Exchequer.

We know which section was the first to organise itself in the *Curia*, and that it had, from the beginning, a well-defined administrative personality. Since **New researches on its origins** our first volume appeared, the much-disputed question of its origin has been examined anew by Mr. R. L. Poole,[1] whose work Mr. Tout has summarised.[2] The Anglo-Saxon kings had a Treasury which was at first part of the Chamber, that is, of the service which was the most intimately attached to the very person of the king; the Treasury was placed in the king's bedroom or in the adjoining wardrobe. It was next fixed at Winchester, and it remained there after the Conquest; but, up to Henry II's reign, its personnel was not completely separated from the Household; under William Rufus and Henry I, the treasurers, Herbert, Geoffrey de Clinton, and Guillaume du Pont de l'Arche, were also chamberlains, *i.e.* heads of the Chamber; in the *Constitutio domus regis*,[3] the Treasury is a branch of the Household, as is the Chamber, even though it has ceased to be itinerant. Guillaume du Pont de l'Arche is the last lay magnate to be at once chamberlain and treasurer. It is probable that he was treasurer in 1135, and we find him as chamberlain under Matilda and under Stephen. After him, Nigel of Ely does not seem to have been chamberlain, and the separation became final when the

1. R. L. Poole, *The Exchequer in the Twelfth Century*, 1912; see also Ch. H. Haskins, *Norman Institutions*, 1918; G. H. White, " Financial Administration under Henry I," in *Transactions of the Royal Hist. Soc.*, 1925.
2. Tout, *Chapters*, i, pp. 72 sq.; Baldwin, pp. 8, 41 sq., 209 sq,
3. See *Const. Hist.*, i, p. 373, n. 2,

last-named, in 1159, had bought the office of treasurer
The Exchequer for his son Richard fitz Nigel, bishop of
separates from London, who held it forty years. Thus, at
the Household the beginning of Henry II's reign, the
Treasury became a clerical office having nothing more
to do with the Chamber and the Household.[1] A
single feature recalled the origins of this administration;
there survived two chamberlains of the Treasury whose
offices became herditary, and returned to the king, by
extinction, only in the time of Edward I and Edward II.[2]
But the titular holders had themselves replaced at an
early date by deputies whom they nominated; this was
probably why the other members of this department, the
Exchequer barons, whose nomination the king retained,
found their importance increasing.

Moreover, in 1156, this administration, which had
taken the name of Exchequer, was already fixed at
London.[3] The Treasury of Winchester is subordinated
to it in the famous *Dialogue,* and it was probably, from
that moment, no more than a place of deposit.[4] Mean-
while, the use of the *abacus* which gave to
The "abacus" the old Treasury the name of "Exchequer,"
and whose origin is the principal subject of dispute, had
been introduced. Mr. Poole holds that this system of
accounting was borrowed from France and was working
as early as 1118. Nigel may have been one of those who

1. Tout, *Chapters,* i, pp. 83 sq.
2. Edward I resumed the heritage of the Redvers, Earls of Devon,
and Edward II himself nominated the deputy of the Warwicks at the
death of Guy whose heir was twelve years old (1315). The weighers,
melters, and ushers also made themselves hereditary. It is possible
that the later tendency to nominate clerks as chamberlains, is due to
the king's desire not to let their offices become hereditary again. (Tout,
Place Edward II, pp. 48 sq.)
3. It is useful to remember that in the XIIIth and XIVth centuries,
the Exchequer was transported to York several times, notably after the
conquest of Scotland. (Miss D. M. Broome, "Exchequer Migrations to
York in the XIIIth and XIVth centuries," in *Essays presented to
T. F. Tout*).
4. On this, see Tout, *Chapters,* i, p. 95.

made it known, and its introduction must have contributed to the transformation of the old administration of the Treasury.[1] In any case, by the time of Henry II, the financial competence of the Exchequer was well-defined, its technique was organised, and it had its records, the Pipe rolls.[2]

Still it was a long time before its personnel was entirely its own. The barons of the Exchequer sat, by other titles, in every section of the *Curia*,
Specialisation
of personnel
and their specialisation was obscurely effected during the thirteenth century. At the beginning of the fourteenth century, one of the four or five Exchequer barons takes the position of chief; one of the best administrators of the time, Walter Norwich, spent a great part of his career as chief baron, and was, as far as we know, the first to bear that title.[3]

On the other hand, the Exchequer long remained a

1. See *Const. Hist.*, i, pp. 406 sq., and M. Petit-Dutaillis' additional note in *Studies and Notes Supplementary*, p. 45; Poole, *op. cit.*, pp. 42–69. Mr. Poole cites three treatises on the *abacus* composed at the end of the tenth century by an abbot of Fleury, an abbot of Lobbes, and Gerbert; he knows two more dating from the beginning of the twelfth century; one by Raoul of Laon, the other by Adelard of Bath, also written at Laon (Adelard had left England at the end of the eleventh century); yet another was written in England by one Turchill, and mentions, as though he were still alive, a sheriff who is believed to have died in 1115. Nigel, the future treasurer, whom Henry II ordered in 1155 to reorganise his finances, had studied at Laon and was working in the *curia* in 1126–7 at the latest. John, bishop of Lisieux, who gives a judgment in the Exchequer of Normandy in 1130, began his administrative career in England, whither he had fled in 1103, being archdeacon of Seéz; he became chaplain and counsellor to Henry I, and the collaborator of Roger of Salisbury. We must clearly distinguish between the knowledge of the *abacus* which the Anglo-Saxons may well have acquired by the eleventh century, by means, for example, of the first three treatises cited by Mr. Poole, and its generalisation, as a means of accounting in the administration and in current usage, the introduction of which by Norman clerks the facts quoted by Mr. Poole would tend to prove. These facts would be decisive only if we had proof that the Norman Exchequer is earlier that the English Exchequer. The question still remains open. But there seems to be an increasing probability of simultaneous introduction, in England and in the duchy, of this method of accounting, in the administration of one and the same sovereign, by clerks of Norman origin, taught in France.
2. See *Const. Hist.*, ii, p. 409.
3. Tout, *Place Edward II*, p. 54 sq.

simple session of the *Curia,* and, in consequence, at any
moment the great officers, the justices, the
magnates, and the king himself, came to
sit there. During the minority of Henry
III, an attempt was made to bring as many
barons there as possible.[1]

(margin: But the Exchequer remains a session of the "Curia")

We thus see that, if the financial competence of the
Exchequer distinguished it from the rest of the *Curia,* it
had, at the beginning, many other attributes which, at
any instant, made it once more either the Council or a
department of the Household. The king held Council in
his Exchequer and issued writs of summons to that effect.
Under Edward I the same thing still went on, and not
only in matters of finance; deliberations are held there
on a statute, on treaties, on the affairs of Gascony.[2]
However, Mr. Tout has suggested that the formula
consilium in scaccario could be interpreted in the material sense; it may have met in the place where the
Exchequer was installed, for lack of another, or because
it was convenient to have at hand the personnel of that
department in order to consult it at need; it would not,
then, result that the Exchequer was reabsorbed under
such circumstances into the Council; and, in consequence, it would have lost all political competence much
sooner than we are apt to think.[3]

On the contrary, it is certain that it long retained the
same judicial competence as the *consilium regis, i.e.* it
judged not only financial causes, but suits
of all sorts, without being submitted to the
common law. Under Henry III, it kept a special roll as
a tribunal, and it took cognisance of suits
directly without a writ of chancery. But,
on one hand, it thus came into conflict with
the courts;[4] the statute of Rhuddlan (1284)

(margin: Its jurisdiction)

(margin: The Exchequer specialises and becomes a court of common law)

1. Baldwin, pp. 8, 41 sq.
2. Baldwin, pp. 211–217.
3. Tout, *Place Edward II*, pp. 56–57.
4. Baldwin, pp. 46, 217.

forbade it to judge any case save those of the king and his officers, and thus claimed to take from it cognisance of common pleas.[1] On the other hand, its procedure became rapidly formalistic, *i.e.* it adopted the formal procedure of writs and judged like the law-courts. At the time of Edward II, it had become a court of common law to such a point that appeal was made to the Council for error of judgment in the Exchequer. It resisted on this point, and in 1357 obtained the creation of a " Statutory Court of Exchequer," which received the appeals of error, and, in principle, decided without appeal. But no longer judging in equity, the Exchequer had ceased to be, in this respect, a session of the Council.[2]

From the administrative point of view, the Exchequer was also in the beginning the executive secretariat of the **The Exchequer** *Curia;* the chancellor, keeper of the great **as the** seal, sat there. At the end of the twelfth **secretariat of** **the "Curia"** century this situation begins to be modified. A *scriptorium* of the Exchequer tends to be instituted; in 1189 the summonses which it issues are drawn up by the clerks of the chamberlains.[3] The royal seal being

---

1. This statute was more than once evaded, the pleaders acquiring, for purposes of the suit, the status of servant to the treasurer or some other such officer. Mr. Baldwin points out many suits of all sorts which were judged in the Exchequer under Edward I or Edward II (pp. 218–223).

2. Baldwin, pp. 228 sq. He admits that the Exchequer was robbed of its equitable jurisdiction by the Chancery as a result of the political events of Edward II's reign, and especially of the fall of Walter Langton, whose unpopularity it shared. Mr. Tout has contested this interpretation (*Place Edward II*, p. 183). Besides, Mr. Baldwin shows, p. 231, that the decline of the Exchequer's jurisdiction resulted also from the formalistic character of its procedure. In the first year of Edward III, the Exchequer having summoned a man by reason of a suit relating to lands held of the crown, so that the statute of Rhuddlan was not broken, the king forbade it to issue such writs without his permission. In consequence, the Exchequer had become a court of common law, and could not receive pleas except on writ of chancery. Mr. Baldwin notes, however, that it continued to judge a few isolated cases. Finally the Exchequer became once more a court of equity, but by imitating the Chancery, and this jurisdiction did not develop until modern times, though its beginnings go back to Edward III, (pp. 223–224, 227–228).

3. Tout, *Chapters*, i, p. 140; Baldwin, p. 209.

insufficient, since it had to follow the king, Henry II,
who felt this inconvenience very keenly on account of
the extent of his French domains, ordered the making
of a duplicate which was entrusted to the Exchequer and
served as a seal of absence; but this replica of the great
seal çeased to be indispensable for the execution of public
business when, in the thirteenth century, there was developed the use of a private or small seal which ended by
being employed, at need, instead of the great seal. The
The Exchequer Exchequer nevertheless retained the dupli-
Seal cate of the great seal which had been
entrusted to it: it was the Exchequer seal, the use of
which was purely administrative.[1] On the other hand,
at the end of the twelfth century, the Chancery developed rapidly as a particular section of the *Curia,*
included moreover in the Household, and became at once
the general secretariat for all offices.[2] The
The Secretariat chancellor was not long in leaving the
of the "Curia"
passes to the Exchequer: from the 18th or the 20th year
Chancery of Henry III, he had himself represented
there by a clerk who became, in the middle of the
century, the chancellor of the Exchequer.[3] The separation was accentuated by the disappearance of the justiciar
after 1265; the chancellor then became the rival of the
treasurer; under Edward I, the precedence belongs first
to one, then to the other; in the end the chancellor
obtained it. After the fall of Walter Langton the Chancery registered another success: it seized upon the roll
of Parliament and on the nomination of the sheriffs.[4]

But, since the Exchequer was, above all, a council for
finance and a treasury, it is in this field that the rivalry
Financial of the sections of the *Curia* and the House-
function of the hold's capacity for invention showed them-
Exchequer selves most clearly. It is important indeed

1. Tout, *Chapters,* i, pp. 121 sq.
2. On the Chancery, see below, p. 372, sq.
3. On the Chancery, see below, pp. 372 sq.
4. Baldwin, p. 228.

to observe that its financial monopoly had never been absolute : the king's Chamber held his purse and never accounted before it.[1] The Exchequer had been organised principally to receive the sheriffs' farm,[2] and the feudal revenues of the king : it kept Domesday book, and in the eleventh and twelfth centuries, the tours of the barons were sufficient for corrective inquests and local negotiations. When Henry II had reformed the land tax by instituting carucage, and still more when taxation of movable goods had been substituted for assessment on land, it was not to its antiquated methods that recourse was had to establish the new taxes; in any case, its personnel would not have sufficed. The assessment was entrusted to juries and the collection to knights; now, the returns of the sheriffs became insignificant compared with the new resources. As,

It is restricted by the "Consilium" — on the other hand, the Exchequer gradually separated from the *Consilium* in which the financial deliberations took place,[3] it was reduced to a mere Treasury and a Court of Accounts. But in this respect too its part decreased. As the Treasury, it was largely ousted in the thirteenth century by the Temple of London.[4] Moreover, the expenses of the

1. Below, pp. 382 sq.
2. We recall here that the office of sheriff has been the object of new researches since our first two volumes appeared. In addition to those of Mr. Ch. H. Haskins (*Norman Institutions*) we mention those of which Mr. W. A. Morris has published the result in *E. H. R.*, 1916 (Anglo-Saxon period), 1918 (beginning of the Norman period), and 1922 (Henry I) [and also in *The Medieval English Sheriff to 1300.* 1927]; also Miss M. H. Mill's articles. "Adventus Vicecomitum," *E. H. R.* 1921 and 1923.
3. Baldwin, p. 230. Even if we admit that the Council continued to sit in the Exchequer under Edward I, the separation in any case is complete under Edward III; the Council decides the raising of subsidies on wool, and on this occasion sends its orders to the Exchequer by writ of Chancery. Even the contracts for the coining of money appear on the Chancery's Close Rolls.
4. See Miss Sandys, "The Financial and Administrative importance of the London Temple in the XIIIth century " (in *Essays presented to T. F. Tout*, 1925). The Temple played the same part in France. (L. Delisle, "Mémoires sur les opérations financières des Templiers," in

state were acquitted in the Exchequer on a writ delivered
in the Chancery according to an order or warrant from
the king. As long as the chancellor was part of the
Exchequer and of the Household, the connection remained sufficient; but it was strained when he had left
the Exchequer and commenced to organise a service
distinct from the other sections of the Household. The
necessity of avoiding the formalities which delayed the
service doubtless explains in part the development of the
financial side of the Household, and more particularly
of the Wardrobe : as it had charge of the
purchases on the king's behalf, it was
natural that it should have the disposal of
money ; as it accounted to the Exchequer, unlike the
Chamber, there was no objection in principle, on the
part of the Treasury, to making advances to it. But it
was even more simple to have funds paid directly to the
Wardrobe, on condition of its rendering account, and
that is what was done. These vagaries seem to go back
to the time of John Lackland, and chiefly to the government of Peter des Roches, who put at the head of the
Wardrobe his relative Peter of Rivaux; they rooted
themselves deeply at the end of Henry III's reign and
followed an extraordinary development under Edward I;
the Wardrobe then received from the Exchequer
£10,000 or £20,000 at a time, and, often, these payments were not half the funds at its disposal. It seems
evident that the king and the Household bureaucracy
must have seen in these methods a means of increasing
their power : in the thirteenth century, the barons tried to
impose a treasurer of their own choice, and, in consequence, to control the Treasury; but when they
achieved this, the advance of the Wardrobe robbed them

And by the Wardrobe of the Household

Mémoires Ac. Insc., 1889; Borelli de Serres, Services publics, i, p. 237,
iii, p. 5; Viollet, Hist. des Inst. pol. et admin., ii, 125). On the
Templars of England see also A. Perkins, "The Wealth of the Knights
Templars in England," Amer. Hist. Rev., 1910.

of their advantage. But, under Edward I, the treasurer was the king's man, so that administrative exigencies more probably played a dominant part; what proves this further, is the fact that these methods were vastly extended in times of war.[1]

Nor is that all. During hostilities, the ordinary resources of the treasury became insufficient; the expedients employed to replenish it were probably not devised at the Exchequer, which, in any event, was not entrusted with their practical application. From the time of Henry III, it was the Wardrobe which contracted loans. Italian bankers were introduced in the Council; they treated with the Wardrobe, under Edward I, or the Chamber under Edward II, refusing to furnish any document to the Exchequer. The Wardrobe began to pay its creditors with recognitions of debt or " debentures." It made use of the sheriffs to obtain many objects which were necessary to it, notably for the upkeep of the fortifications and the equipment of the county forces; the sheriffs received writs which authorised them to deduct the expenses from the sums which they had to pay into the Exchequer; these *praestita* were not strictly an innovation : the novelty was in their extension.[2] But the most

New financial technique under Edward I.

1. On the whole of this question we cannot do better than to refer the reader to the different chapters on the Wardrobe in Mr. Tout's *Chapters*, and particularly to ii, pp. 85 sq. Though Mr. Tout insists strongly at the beginning of his work on the importance of the administrative point of view, his account leaves a final impression that he principally attributes the financial innovations, and also those concerning the privy seal, to the despotic tendencies of the kings, notably Edward I. We cannot doubt that they favoured the changes referred to, and especially in the case of the privy seal. But it seemed to us necessary to bring into full light, according to the spirit of Mr. Tout's work, the administrative necessities, the action of which cannot be contested.

2. On this point, see Miss M. H. Mills' articles, "Adventus Vicecomitum," *E.H.R.* 1921 and 1923. Until 1276 the allowances made to the sheriffs, on presenting the king's warrants ordering them to pay his expenses in anticipation of the payment of their farm, are relatively rare. After that date they multiply rapidly until 1284, but they are not found for all counties. They become general from 1298. For the " debentures," see Tout, *Chapters* ii. p. 101.

Wooden money curious expedient, apparently dating from Edward I's time, was the use made of " tallies "[1] of the Exchequer to obtain funds or credit at the Wardrobe. The tallies served as receipts to the sheriffs and collectors. There was nothing to prevent their preparation in advance; the Wardrobe had them delivered and the Exchequer debited it with them; the Wardrobe then negotiated them exactly like modern cheques or obligations on the receivers of revenues, or else gave them in payment. This expedient was, probably, the only one which made it possible not only to obtain the resources, which were immediately indispensable, but even to mobilise wealth, so as to feed the State loans and discharge part of the ever-growing taxes; it was a system of " wooden money," which, to some extent, played the part of paper-money.[2]

It is clear that, by all these means, the part hitherto played by the Exchequer as State Treasury was greatly reduced; this part became largely fictitious. To contemporary eyes, the more easily the king found means of obtaining money, the more he squandered; besides, the barons realised that it was quite useless to place one of themselves at the Treasury if his control became illusory; that is why they repeatedly demanded that all the issues

1. On the tallies, see *Const. Hist* i. p. 410 The tally is a piece of wood in which notches are cut recording the pounds, shillings and pence received. J. F. Willard, "An Ancient Tally of the Exchequer," (*J. R. B.*, 1923).

2. This use of tallies has been brought to light by Mr. H. Jenkinson, "On Exchequer Tallies," in *Archeologia* 1911. See also Tout, *Chapters*, ii, p. 99. In 1297, at the Easter-term, the Wardrobe received from the Exchequer £39,566, of which £7,582 was in tallies; in 33 Ed. I, Michaelmas-term £16,633, of which £10,395 was in tallies; Easter-term, £26,086, of which £10,079 was in tallies. It will be observed that, in these new financial methods, one at least, the extension of loans, coincides with the progress of the commercial operations of the Italian merchants who thus disposed of liquid capital, and with the decline of the financial character of the Temple, the banking capacity of which, founded on landed revenues, did not lend itself to new developments. (Miss A. Sandys, "The Financial and Administrative importance of the London Temple in the XIIIth Century" in *Essays presented to T. F. Tout*, 1925).

of the state should be paid into the Exchequer; but they could not prevent the borrowings nor the anticipations. Their grievances were certainly well-founded in part, but on the other hand the State could not have lived without these technical inventions. Under Edward II an expedient of more clearly despotic character still further weakened the position of the Exchequer : the Chamber

The Exchequer and the Chamber received the administration of the enormous domains confiscated from the Templars and from the *contrariants* or rebels of 1321.[1]

The Exchequer, however, never ceased to receive part of the public funds.[2]   But throughout this period, it undeniably tended to become a mere *Chambre des Comptes*. Even as such, it lost much

The Exchequer accounts of its real authority, because the Wardrobe produced its accounts only very irregularly, and often after enormous delays.[3]

It is in this sense that we can speak of the decadence of the Exchequer in the thirteenth century, but, from the technical point of view, its accounts made some progress. From the beginning of the thirteenth century there appeared new rolls; notably the *Memoranda* and *Issue Rolls*. At the beginning of the fourteenth century, bishop Stapledon, being treasurer, had decreed, by the ordinances of Cowick (1323) and of Westminster (1324), certain measures for auditing accounts in arrears, and for relieving the Pipe Roll, which had reached extravagant dimensions.   He entrusted the control of the domains to a special personnel with a particular roll for this purpose. The second ordinance of York for the reform of the Household (1323) obliged this section to prepare itself for presenting its accounts at convenient times.[4]   But

1. Below, p. 398.
2. Below, pp. 388, 392, 396.
3. Below, p. 392.
4. The *Memoranda Rolls* were kept by special officers, the *remembrancers* of the Exchequer, who appear distinct from the chancery clerks in the first third of the thirteenth century. The progress of education

still, we know that the Exchequer, under Edward III,. had not perfected its accounting to the point of being able to establish an exact balance-sheet of the expenses and receipts of the State.[1] The confusion of loans and anticipations of all sorts enregistered in its rolls, jumbled in along with the effective receipts and expenses, make them very difficult to study, and it is clear that the Exchequer had not succeeded in overcoming the difficulties of accounts which the development of financial technique had progressively engendered.

tended to suppress the distinction between the lay *sergents* of the chamberlains, who worked in the Exchequer of Receipt by means of tallies, and the treasurer's clerks, who were employed in the Exchequer of Accounts. At the beginning of the fourteenth century, the receipts themselves were reckoned by rolls and records; the tallies served for control, or as a means of credit. The barons of the Exchequer, specialised from the beginning of Henry III's majority, and numbering five or six, were indifferently clerks or laymen. Some officers, however, remained clerks; the chancellor, the remembrancers, the clerk of the rolls of issues and receipts. (later *Clerk of the Pells*) and the clerk of receipts or cashier (Tout, *Place Edward II* pp· 47 sq.). On the Exchequer personnel, see also Miss D. M. Broome, "Auditors of the Foreign Accounts of the Exchequer" *E. H. R.* 1923, and the addendum, 1924. On the technique of accounting, see J. F· Willard "The Memoranda Rolls and the Remembrancers'" (1282-1360), in *Essays presented to T. F. Tout;* Richardson "The Exchequer Year" in *Trans. Roy. Hist. Soc·*, 1925. (It commences as a general rule on September 29th); Miss M. Mills "Experiments in Exchequer Procedure" (1200-1232) *ibidem..* On the Exchequer archives, V. H. Galbraith, "The Tower as an Exchequer record office in the reign of Edward II," in *Essays presented to T· F. Tout.*

1. On this point, see Tout and Miss D. M. Broome, "A National Balance Sheet for 1362-3" (*E. H. R.* 1924).

II.

The Benches.

The origin of the judicial Benches is clearly connected with the introduction of the formal procedure by writs, and with the organisation of eyres of the justices which was the result.[1] In 1178, Henry II appointed five justices to sit permanently *in Banco*. This Bench had competence to hear the pleas of the crown, but it also received all the cases which the itinerant justices had not dared to decide, and these very quickly obtained so great a place in its vacations that at the beginning of the thirteenth century the court was called " Court of Common Pleas "; it is under this name that the Great Charter ordered it to be fixed at Westminster.

The Bench, or Court of Common Pleas

This first Bench, the origin of the Court of common pleas, was, from the beginning, subordinated to the king's tribunal, the *Placita coram rege*, which were one of the essential functions of the *Consilium regis*. But the judges of the Bench could sit in the *Consilium* assembled to hear the pleas; so that the two courts remained at first ill-defined. We even find, at the time of John Lackland, that, if a pleader claimed to be judged *coram rege*, the judges *in Banco* replied that their tribunal must be regarded as held *coram rege*, and thus they rejected the exception.[2] The differentiation, however, seems to have come about fairly quickly. Even in the reign of this

It is separated from pleas "coram rege"

---

1. Baldwin, pp. 47 sq.; Maitland pp. lxxix sq.; *Select Pleas of tne Crown*, introduction; *Bracton's Note Book*, introduction.
2. *Curia Regis Rolls of the reigns of Richard I and John*, edited by Mr. C. T. Flower, (1923), p. 462: *Cum omnia placita que corum justiciariis de banco tenentur, coram domino rege vel capitali justiciario teneri intelliguntur.*"

same John, the *Placita coram rege* were separately en-rolled,[1] and as they followed the king, the installation of the Bench at Westminster meant yet another difference. The specialisation of personnel was much more slow, and cannot be dated precisely. But the differentiation was essentially a result of procedure. The judges of the Bench applied the formal procedure as they found it; they created no new writs, and when the jurisprudence seemed to them obscure, they sent the case *coram rege, i.e.* to the *Consilium regis.* This latter therefore formed a court of appeal;[2] it dealt in first instance only with the suits which were directly brought before it by great persons or with suits in which great persons were implicated, so that the king alone seemed to have sufficient authority to impose on them respect of the sentence.

The procedure differs

The Court *coram rege* was therefore distinguished from the Bench in that it created a jurisprudence in doubtful or new cases; the capacity of invention was preserved in it;[3] this is why the exercise of justice in the *Consilium* was not distinguished from the power of legislation. The *Consilium* performed its functions either in its narrow, ordinary form, or for the more important causes, in its enlarged form, *i.e.* in the general Parliaments to which the barons were summoned in numbers; thus were petitions in Parliament multiplied.

The court *coram rege,* by reason of the disorders at the end of Henry III's reign, had to judge an increasing number of cases

Origin of the King's Bench

1. One of the rolls published by Mr. Flower (see preceding note) con-tains the pleas held before the king in the year 2 John. The continuous series of rolls of pleas before the king and of pleas of the Bench at Westminster begins with Henry III, who held the pleas in person after his majority. This document is therefore of great importance. Richard had never stayed long in England, and this was John's first stay of any considerable length; it is thus possible that this roll is the first of this kind which had ever been kept.

2. The first writ of error is mentioned in 1256 (Baldwin p. 66).

3. Particularly the creation of new writs (Baldwin p. 64).

at first instance, and of criminal suits; its authority was needed to re-establish public peace.[1] Thus, at the time of Edward I, a second Bench began to be instituted. The Court *coram rege* shrank from day to day to a few professional judges, and then took the name of " King's Bench." At first there existed, between this ordinary session and the wider session of the Court, the same confusion which, a century earlier, had existed between the first Bench and the Court *coram rege*; the judges of the new Bench are members of the *Consilium regis* or judicial session; thus, when they judge separately, they regard themselves none the less as *coram rege*; a suit can be begun before them and continued before the Council, or vice versa, without any change of instance. Yet Bracton knew two courts only; the treatise known as the *Fleta* mentions three. A new class of rolls appeared. The King's Bench received, in the fourteenth century, actions of trespass, and became the great crim-

It becomes a a court of common law also

inal court.[2] But above all it quickly became a court of common law.[3] By the time of Edward III, it had long been working in conformity with the system of writs, and according to fixed rules. Once more, differentiation had been principally brought about because the Council, which was now beginning to take shape as a definite institution, continued, in keeping the pleas *coram rege*, to exhibit a creative force, to institute new writs, and to face the new juridical needs by means of its jurisprudence exempted from all restrictions, and also by its ordinances.[4]

---

1. Baldwin, p. 63.
2. Ibid, p. 262.
3. This characteristic was acknowledged by Edward I in 1291, Mr. Baldwin says. But in reality, some time had to elapse before the King's Bench ceased to judge in equity. (p. 63).
4 On the general characteristics of the Council's jurisdiction, see below pp. 406 sq.

III.

The Chancery and the Office of the Privy Seal.

From the remotest origins, the chancellor had been as it were the general secretary of the *Curia;* he directed **The Chancellor in the Exchequer and in the Household** the office of charters and was the head of the clerks who formed the *scriptorium regis;* he also kept the royal seal.[1] But this secretariat had no separate existence. It was as a member of the Exchequer, which was then the chief executive office of the *Curia,* that the chancellor directed it. It was also part of the Household; its clerks worked not only at the Exchequer, but also in the Chapel, which was part of the Chamber, and in the Wardrobe which, at the time of John, appears as a service independent of the Chamber. The chancellor paid into the Wardrobe the money he received, and it was to it that he returned his accounts. Thus at the beginning of Henry II's reign, he enjoyed no great prestige, and ranked considerably lower than the justiciar and the treasurer; the Chancery was given up for a bishopric; this was what Thomas Becket did. When the prestige of the office had began to grow, the chancellor no longer gave it up on becoming a bishop, but delegated the administrative duties to a *sigillifer*; this is what Longchamp and Walter did.

The chancellor saw his importance grow as a result of

---

1. Tout, *Chapters,* i, pp. 14-16, 121 sq., ii, pp. 63, 156 sq.; Baldwin pp. 206 sq.; 236 sq. Mr. Tout's chapters on the Wardrobe contain further indications. The Chancery has been far less fully studied than the Exchequer. Mr. Tout announces that Miss L. B. Dibben is preparing a work dealing with the subject as a whole.

the institution of formal procedure;[1] is was he, naturally,

Growth of the importance of the Chancellor who issued the writs, the drafting of which became an absorbing task. The great profits resulting to the king were bound to enhance the prestige of the chancellor. From the reign of Henry II, he has an assistant, the *magister* or *protonotary*. The minority of Henry III marks a certain weakening of the office, but immediately afterwards the chancellor reappears as a great person; he is nominated for life and buys his office; the royal seal becomes the great seal; the profits from it are given to the chancellor, on condition that he maintains a staff of clerks directly under his orders. Henry III's voyage to France in 1230 seems to have made it clear that the clerks of the chapel must, to avoid inconvenience, be distinguished from those of the chancellor; from 1232, men speak of the clerks of the *cancellaria* and of the *cancellaria regis*, though, for a very long time afterwards, the chancellor's

He ceases to sit at the Exchequer clerks continued to go and work in the Household. At the same time the chancellor ceases to sit in the Exchequer.

Before the end of the twelfth century, the Chancery had developed its technique and fixed it in formulas. It

Acts and rolls of the Chancery had distinguished between the royal acts: the charters, the letters patent and the letters close, themselves subdivided into several categories; each kind of act had its long, rigid formulas, phrased in Latin and using a great amount of parchment, so that, under Henry II, in order to economise, they began to simplify and shorten by abbreviations those acts which had no great importance, particularly the warrants that the king addressed to the chancellor to authorise him to issue writs. Nor was the fixing of the seal accomplished without formalities, and it was particularly troublesome to be obliged to use it for

1. For the judicial reforms of Henry II, see below, p. 456.

unimportant acts which, further, on account of their smallness, could not support the seal. We must add that the Chancery enrolled all the acts which it sealed; at the end of the twelfth century, in addition to the roll prepared for it at the Exchequer, there appear others of its own which, at that time, are so well kept that we can believe they must have had antecedents.[1]

At the same time as the Chancery was thus making itself into a separate office, though still dependent on the Household, its chief tended to escape from the king's authority : he was a bishop, and therefore a baron; he could not be removed. Therefore the king set about the creation of a new Chancery which should be closely subjected to himself. While the State Chancery was fixing its technique in complicated forms, it was its rival which found expedients for saving parchment and for speeding-up the execution of the royal wishes.

Origin of the privy seal

As early as the reign of Henry II, it is probable that the king used a signet, and Richard I had a small seal. Under John, there existed a small seal and a private seal which were probably identical. This seal was at first used to seal letters close when the king had not got the great seal at hand, but it ended, in this very reign, by being affixed on letters patent. The king used it particularly, as was natural, to authenticate the warrants which he addressed to the chancellor. At first, these warrants were enrolled like the other acts, but as their contents were repeated in the writs, this double labour was speedily abandoned. Such was the beginning of a new Chancery, whose expeditious methods, during the thirteenth century, constituted an administrative advance. The

---

1. *Rotuli cartarum* (beginning in 1199), *Rotuli litterarum patentium* (1201), *Rotuli litterarum clausarum* (1200), *Rotuli de liberate, de misis, ac praestitis*. For the further perfecting of the rolls, see below, p. 400, note 2.

acts under the private seal were recorded on
Acts under the private seal paper or on small pieces of thin parchment, in a more cursive hand, stripped of the archaic formulas, and often abridged; they were not enrolled, but kept as they were in " files." In the eyes of the lawyers, their most essential characteristic was perhaps that they could be written in French, and, in the fifteenth century, in English.[1] This new Chancery,

by its origin, was naturally that of the
The Chancery of the Chamber Chamber.[2] In all probability, it contributed even more than financial necessity, to the sudden progress of the Wardrobe, which had been hitherto only an obscure department of the Chamber.

The Household having thus its own Chancery, it was natural that the State Chancery should complete its
The Chancery is separated from the Household separation from the Household. But this required a long time. During the minority, of Henry III, the private seal disappeared, because it was the personal seal of the king and not a seal of the State. It was, however, so necessary to the administration that Hubert de Burgh used his own personal seal to replace it. It reappeared after 1230. But Henry III, having once quarrelled with Ralph Neville, disposed of the great seal at will, and later appointed as Neville's successors chancellors who were under his control.[3] After that the royal prerogative had not the same interest in distinguishing between the two seals. In 1242, Henry, departing for France, left the small seal

1 On the seals : Baldwin, pp. 255 sq.; E. Déprez *Le sceau privé*, 1908; and, most important, Tout, *Chapters*, *passim*.

2. *Ibid;* i. p. 153. The first examples of letters under the small seal are some letters close of 1206 and of 1208. But we cannot yet call the small seal the seal of the Chamber, because the chancellor was still part of the Household; perhaps, even, the small seal was at this time entrusted to him. The first example of letters patent under the small seal is of 23rd May, 1211; they were enrolled in Chancery.

3. Mr. Tout says (*Chapters* i. 285) that Miss L. B. Dibben has worked out a complete list of the chancellors from 1244 to 1258.

at the Exchequer and took with him the great seal, which was entrusted to the Wardrobe; in 1253, on the contrary, he took with him the small seal. Still there is no doubt that, despite this confusion, the private seal was regarded as the particular instrument of the prerogative. It seems that it was under the private seal that Peter des Roches and his confederates obtained from the king the order for Richard Marshal's assassination in Ireland,[1] and, in 1258, the barons reacted violently against the impotence to which the Chancery had been reduced, and demanded that its chief should be of independent status, nominated by themselves. On the other hand, although Henry III had kept the Chancery in obscurity, the tendency towards differentiation persisted none the less. After the death of Neville, the free disposition of the revenues of the office was taken from the chancellor; then there appeared in his

The "Hanaper" service the *hanaper* department, authorised to receive these revenues and to account for them to the Wardrobe. The barons took the separation one step further; they granted a salary to the chancellor.

Edward I had a chancellor of high worth, bishop Burnell, who had his full confidence and to whom was given back the full administration of the revenues of the office; but the system inaugurated by the barons was re-established for his successor John Langton. Both exerted their action over the Wardrobe and their own office at once, for under Edward I, the vigorous authority of the master maintained the co-ordination of the departments and in practice re-established a sort of unity of the Curia. It is thus only the more characteristic that

The private seal used as a seal of State the private seal should become incontestably a seal of State: its administrative utility merely appears the more clearly. From 1279 at the latest, Edward I used it to seal acts

1. Tout *Chapters* i. pp. 224-5; see *Const. Hist.*, ii, p.49.

which bore no relation to the ordinary work of the Household, and even for charters. In his lifetime the barons and the commons complained that in this manner, under the privy seal, writs were issued contrary to the common law. The *Articuli super cartas* forbade this abuse, but it persisted, and the Ordinances of 1311 were an effort to remedy it once more.[1]

The Chancery and the Household completed their separation during Edward II's reign. From 1275 there

The keeper of the privy seal becomes a minister of State (1311)

was in existence a keeper of the private seal among the Wardrobe clerks; the Ordainers of 1311 secured his nomination by the barons; the keeper thus became a minister of State on the same footing as the chancellor and the treasurer, though of somewhat lower dignity. Finally, in 1324, the *hanaper* ceased to account to the Wardrobe and was attached to the Exchequer.[2]

The keeper of the privy seal rapidly developed his office in the fourteenth century. He became the special

The privy seal escapes from the Household and is attached to the Council

chancellor of the Council and under Edward III was empowered to summon the *Magnum Consilium*, while the chancellor sent out the summonses to the Parliament. The clerks of both offices served the Council until Richard II's time: then those of the privy seal

---

1. Tout *Chapters* ii, p. 153. In the *Articuli super cartas*, the barons explain that writs of the small seal must not be granted so frequently, because they often are so granted in violation of the common law, "concerning things which, by course of law, belong to the great seal." In the text sealed by the king they have contented themselves with saying "*Desutz le petit seal ne isse desoremes nul bref qe touche la commune lei.*" (Bémont, *Chartes des libertés anglaises*, p. 104). Another article decrees that the chancellor shall always follow the king, evidently so that he shall not have the pretext of being without the great seal. These articles specially annoyed Edward I because they affected the Household. But they were never executed. In 1306, setting out for Scotland, he ordered the chancellor and the Exchequer to remain in London. (Tout, *Chapters* ii, p. 75). The ordinances of 1311 declared anew null and invalid those letters of privy seal having as object the delaying or disturbing of the course of the law. (Baldwin, p. 256).

2. Tout, *Chapters* ii. p. 77. Stubbs dates the Chancery's autonomy from the reign of Edward III only (See *Const. Hist.* ii. p. 282).

gained the day.[1] Having thus become the secretariat of the Council, the office of the privy seal was separated from the Wardrobe, and, in its turn, ceased to be the exclusive instrument of the prerogative. Edward III therefore made use of two new seals; the *griffin*, which disappeared in 1355, and the secret seal or signet. Once more a private chancery or personal secretariat of the sovereign was being set up.[2]

The "griffin" and the signet

Thus in the fourteenth century the Chancery ceased to be the general secretariat of the State; the Exchequer, the Council, the Chamber, each had its own staff of clerks and its particular seal. This is one of the features which best distinguish the administrative history of England from that of France. In the fourteenth century, the French chancery, on the contrary, retained all its attributes; the chancellor sent his notaries and his secretaries to work in the Council, in the Household, in the *Parlement* and in the *Chambre des comptes*, but he kept them under his authority. The *Parlement de Paris* had no perfectly distinct chancery before the fifteenth century. The difference is slighter with regard to the private seal and the signet: St. Louis had both; the private seal belonged to the Chamber and was entrusted to a chamberlain; the signet was the king's personal seal. But the keeper of the private seal did not become an officer of State as in England, and the signet appears to have had no political importance.[3]

The Chancery in England and in France

1. Baldwin, p. 257-8. Under Edward III, the keeper employed five clerks; under Henry IV, nine.

2. Below, pp. 401, 404.

3. Viollet, *Hist. des Inst. pol. et admin*, ii, pp. 102 sq.; O Morel, *La grande chancellerie royale de l'avènement de Philippe de Valois à la fin du XIVe siècle*, 1900 (especially pp. 120-1, 267). Baldock, Edward II's chancellor, seems to have tried to submit the rising office of the privy seal to the Chancery, so as to re-establish, in some degree, the unity which existed in France at that time. (Tout, *Chapters* ii. p. 312).

The English Chancery, like the Exchequer, became also a court, and it is as such that it has hitherto attracted the attention of most historians. But the development of its jurisdiction was late; it was a sort of compensation for the losses which the Household had inflicted on it. The chancellor issued the writs, and it is through this that he became a judge: in granting the suitable writ, he determined the action; petitions which it was desired to submit to the Council were thus addressed to him, as well as to the treasurer. In the thirteenth century the Chancery supplied the " triers " and the " receivers " of the petitions in parliament. When no writ seemed applicable, the chancellor created a new one; it was an enormous power; the provisions of 1258 forbade him to act thus without the approval of the king and of the Council; Edward I renewed this prohibition.[1] But the same king adopted the habit of sending to the chancellor a part of the affairs submitted to the Council, evidently for consultative purposes, and so that he might indicate the suitable writ: in reality, the chancellor seized the opportunity to judge the case completely.[2] After the reign of Edward II, Parliament, ceasing to deal with private petitions, began to send them

The Chancery becomes a court

Issue of new writs in Chancery

Restriction of this power

The chancellor's jurisdiction

1. On all this, see Baldwin pp. 238 sq.; Edward I's prohibition was in 1285.
2. Baldwin p. 242: Tout, *Chapters* ii, p. 16. In 1315, we find a very clear case of equitable jurisdiction (Tout, *Chapters* ii. p. 311). In 1340 the Chancery is designated as a court in a statute, and, in 1349, a celebrated proclamation of Edward III to the sheriffs, announces that he is sending back to the Chancery certain questions touching the common law and the king's special grace, which, hitherto, he had decided in person (See *Const. Hist.* ii. p. 282 note 2). A little afterwards, the judicial records of the Chancery began. Various statutes of Edward III gave to it the causes relating to the sheriffs' and purveyors' abuses, and to *praemunire* (27 Ed. III). Under Richard II the transformation of the Chancery into an ordinary court made rapid progress. On the jurisdiction of the Chancery, see W. Paley Baildon, *Select Cases in Chancery* (1364–1471), (Selden Soc. 1896).

to him in the main.[1] The pleaders were in connivance with the chancellor for the widening of his competence : his jurisdiction was popular, because at that period it was simply a form of pleas *coram rege,* and thus, in consequence, it was outside the common law ; it was an equitable jurisdiction.

The differentiation is foreshadowed in the fourteenth century, but dates mainly from the fifteenth ; it was due **The Chancery** likewise to dissimilarity of procedure, of **as a court of** the records, and of the seal. The forma-**common law** lism of its rolls, of its acts, and of the use of the great seal, inclined the Chancery to formalism of procedure : it quickly created for itself a jurisprudence and a fixed procedure ; it became in its turn a jurisdiction of common law.[2]

We have set ourselves to study principally the dismemberment of the Curia from the administrative point of view. But we have been unable to avoid frequent allusion to the political character which its transformations did not fail to assume. Accordingly as the offices of state acquired a tradition, the king could keep his liberty of action only by weakening them to the benefit of his intimate counsellors and of his servants. This

1. We must remember that the roll of Parliament was kept by the Chancery, and that the Chancery clerks classified the petitions in Parliament. We must also note that it had always been a custom to present petitions through the medium of a minister.

2. Baldwin, pp. 246 sq. Even under Richard II there was no separation as regards staff ; the justices sat in Chancery and in the Council. But under Edward III we begin to distinguish the pleas "before the king and his Council," "in his Chancery," and "before the justices." (i.e. before the court of Common Pleas and the Bench). Under Edward III and Richard II the chancellor is allowed to decide alone, but only in a few cases. In the fifteenth century, e.g. under Henry IV, the presence of one or two justices is still necessary ; but henceforward there are "masters in Chancery." Under Richard III, it is admitted that, in certain causes, the chancellor is competent to judge alone. The separation of the Chancery and of the Council is thus achieved from the point of view of procedure before it is complete as regards the personnel.

explains the development of the administrative and political functions of the Household, as we shall shortly see.[1]

1 We regret our inability to use the interesting studies of the late G. B. Adams : *Council and Courts in Anglo-Norman England*. The volume reached us when the printer had finished the setting-up in page of the chapters just read.

[See also Mr. B. Wilkinson, *The Chancery under Edward III*, Manchester U. P. 1929. This work contains, in addition to an analytical description of the office in the fourteenth century, a brief summary of the development of the Chancery before 1327, and two appendices on the earlier period.]

The Chamber and the Wardrobe of the Household.

The King's Household, *domus regis*, comprised in England as in France, the entire group of services attached to the person of the prince.[1] It **The Household** was early divided into *ministeria, métiers*, or *offices*. The chiefs of the Household were the stewards.

In England, at the end of the twelfth **The 'Seneschals' or stewards** century, there were two and they were hereditary; but at the coronation of John, the claims of Roger Bigod were rejected and there remained only one, the Earl of Leicester. But, at this period, the steward had become merely a court official. The effective functions had been abandoned by these great lords to stewards who were simply royal functionaries : in 1230 there seem to have been two : a little after, one rose above the other and became " chief steward."[2]

In the eleventh century, alongside the domestic *ministeria* we can distinguish in the Household a *camera* or king's Chamber. In France, a *chambrier* **The Chamber under Henry I** of Henry I is known (1047). In England the *camera* appears in the *Constitutio domus regis* :[3] is has its chief, *magister camerarius*, and its purse, although the Treasury is not yet clearly separated from the Household.[4] The Chamber remains thus under Henry II, but is better known to us, **Under Henry II** thanks to the *Dialogus de Scaccario* and to

---

1. See Luchaire, *Manuel* pp. 531 sq.; *Inst Mon.* i. p. 159 sq.
2. See *Const. Hist.* i. pp. 382-385; Tout, *Chapters* i. pp. 158 sq. On the Steward : L. W. Vernon Harcourt, *His Grace the Steward and Trial of Peers*, (1907).
3. See *Const. Hist* i. p. 372 n. 2. This document was written about 1135. In France, we have no account of the Household before 1231, and no rules before those of St. Louis.
4. Tout, *Chapters*, i. pp. 83 sq.

the " Roll of the Pipe." It appears as a second Treasury into which the king, by means of writs, orders direct payment of the revenues of certain manors and even of a part of the sheriffs' farms; it proceeds to purchases for the king's service; it is absolutely independent of the Exchequer, even for accounts, which it returns to the king alone. It is an administrative body; in 1164-5 there is a roll of the Chamber; we know some clerks of the

The clerks of the Chamber
Chamber; Walter of Coutances was one, in 1175; William of Sainte-Mère Eglise, in 1183; one of these clerks was " king's clerk ", for example, Richard le Breton in 1176-7; Richard I also had his clerk. As we have seen, these clerks were not specially or exclusively attached to the Chamber, but were classed as a single body along with the Chapel and Chancery clerks. Still, at the end of the twelfth century, the *Camera regis* appears as a clearly

The chamberlains
characterised branch of the Household.[1] In the twelfth century it had at its head a chamberlain, whose office had, in practice, several holders at the same time. These chamberlains were barons, who made their dignity hereditary. Thus at the time of Henry II, distinction begins to be made between them and the active chamberlains, and, under John Lackland, these latter are clearly distinguished from the court chamberlains and those of the Exchequer : the Chamber has its own officers.[2]

Up to the time of Henry II, the Wardrobe is of no

1. Tout, *Chapters*, i. pp. 100 sq.

2. Similarly in France, from the reign of Louis VI, the Chamberlain begins to play an active part : at the end of the XIIth century, the title of *chambrier* is honorary. The chamberlain played a more important part than in England, because the *Chambre aux deniers*, later the *Chambre des comptes*, was still not separated from the Household in the XIIIth century : the chamberlain accounted for the treasure, which was deposited at the Temple, at least, for the greater part, for there was also a chest of the Household at the Louvre, under Louis VIII and Saint Louis.

importance : it is simply a dependency of the king's
The Wardrobe Chamber, in the material sense of the word,
a room adjoining the bedchamber, where,
in addition to the king's clothes, his treasure and his
private archives are kept. But, under
Under Henry II Henry II, it emerges as a particular department; it has its staff, though its purpose has not
changed, and it remains a place of storage. It develops
visibly under John Lackland : we find that
Under John it has a clerk, an usher who attends to
provisions when the king goes on a journey, and a carter
who has the important duty of transporting the royal
equipment at such times. This personnel still does not
seem to be separate from the Chamber; it serves indifferently in either. But, at the end of the reign, the
Wardrobe stands out suddenly as an important administrative department : it draws up acts and keeps rolls : it
also has a treasury, but it is fed by the Exchequer, to
which it makes account. From that time the payment of
the troops seems to be its business.[1] We know the
importance of the mercenaries in John's struggles against
the barons; it seems, then, that at the origin of the
Wardrobe as an administrative service we find simultaneously, as we have already noticed, both the need of
a more pliable instrument, and the king's will to exercise
uncontrolled power. During the minority of Henry III,
the Wardrobe recedes from view; but it reappears from
Under Henry III 1219, and, during the reign of Henry III it
becomes the essential branch of the House-
hold, and one of the great administrative services of the
state; the Chamber falls into obscurity for a century.
This is another of the features which distinguish England from France; in France, the Chamber
The Chamber in France always kept the predominance, whereas
the English Wardrobe eclipsed the service

1. Tout, *Chapters* i. p. 167 (letter close of Jan 24th, 1215)

of which it was, in origin, merely an adjunct, and played, for over a century, the part filled by the Chamber on the Continent. But this is merely a difference of form rather than of substance. Chamber or Wardrobe, it was always the Household, and these domestic and intimate names signify that we are concerned with an organ of the personal power.

We have indicated above the administrative reasons which seem to explain how the Wardrobe became, on the one hand, the principal treasury of the State, and, on the other, a new chancery.[1] We must add that the service, once created, offered a promising career not only to clerks, but to those educated knights who became less rare in the thirteenth century : the steward, who took part in the auditing of the Wardrobe accounts, was always a layman. As usual, the ambition of the staff was bound to help in extending its competence and functions. Now this extension served perfectly the absolutist tendencies of the monarchy, and when Henry III came into conflict with his barons (partly as a result of this very progress of the Wardrobe) the new administration was admirably qualified to serve him as a fulcrum, and so its importance grew.

The Wardrobe becomes a treasury and a chancery

Its staff

Causes of its advance

It seems to have been the Poitevin Peter des Roches who worked systematically to develop the Wardrobe.[2] He set there as clerk Peter de Rivaux, who was either his nephew or his son; Rivaux acted from 1219 to 1223; then he disappeared, but came back in 1230. These two men were, along with the steward Geoffrey de Croixcombes, the engineers of Hubert de Burgh's fall in 1232, which involved in practice the disappearance of the office of

Peter des Roches and Peter de Rivaux

1. Above, pp. 364-366, 374-375.
2. For the reign of Henry III : Tout, *Chapters* i. pp. 180 sq.

CC

justiciar; thus we have, in the origins of the advance of the Wardrobe, an administrative rivalry, a struggle between two court factions, and a conflict between an English minister and foreign adventurers.[1]

The accounts of Brakley and Kirkham, clerks of the Wardrobe, for the years 1224-1227 have been kept.

Wardrobe staff and expenses (1217-1227) Their immediate chief seems to be the chaplain Luke, who bears the title "king's treasurer":[2] henceforth, therefore, the Wardrobe treasury is sharply distinguished from that of the Chamber. Its chief subsequently took the name of "keeper of the Wardrobe." In 1218, the Wardrobe had spent £30, in 1219, £35. In 1223, Rivaux had already increased its out goings to £1,993. Under his successors they reached, for ten months of the year 8 Hen. III, the total of £9,000, on account of the siege of Bedford and Richard of Cornwall's expedition to Poitou. They dropped to £2,000 in the eleventh year. The domestic expenses of the Household remained moderate, about £2,000, and did not justify the recriminations of contemporaries. Administrative necessities alone can explain these sharp variations of expenses.[3] Rivaux also developed the direct payment of revenues into the Wardrobe: the Exchequer provided for only a little more than half of his needs. At last,

1.Mr. Tout (*op. cit.* i, p.230), thinks that Rivaux may also have imitated the papal administration. Honorius III, (1216-1227), as we know, exerted a great influence over England during the early years of the reign : now it was he who, as chamberlain of the Pope from 1187 to 1189 had had the *liber censuum ecclesiae romance* written in 1192 by Guillaume Rufio de Saint Jean d'Angély, *clericus camerae et cancellariae domini papae.* The Pope had thus organised a *Camera* which was at once a Chamber and a Chancery; and the constitution of a chancery of the privy seal in the Wardrobe is one of the essential features of the history of the Wardrobe in the thirteenth century.

2. In Stubbs, the treasurer of the Wardrobe is not always clearly distinguished from the treasurer properly so called, or treasurer of the Exchequer (See *Const. Hist.* ii, index, under this word). Luke warranted the accounts which the clerks presented at the exchequer; he therefore fulfilled rather the functions of the future controller of the Wardrobe. The treasurer was for some time indifferently styled clerk of the Wardrobe, or keeper; the latter prevailed in the end.

3. Tout, *Chapters,* i. pp. 190 sq.

after 1230, when the private seal reappeared and at the same time Rivaux returned to the Wardrobe, the latter became a Chancery, and after Neville's fall, the great seal itself was sometimes entrusted to it.

After the fall of Peter des Roches, Rivaux was again driven out (1234) and the Wardrobe staff again became exclusively English, but the institution was not thereby weakened. Moreover, after the king's marriage, a new invasion of foreigners, Savoyards and Provencals, as

Brother Geoffrey well as Poitevins, was experienced. Brother Geoffrey of the Temple, clerk of the Wardrobe, forbore with them for a long time; then, in 1240, he tried to resist their demands and was at once dismissed.[1] Then the Wardrobe fell back into foreign

The Wardrobe and the foreigners hands. Peter of Aigueblanche, a Savoyard (1240-1), Peter Chaceporc, a Poitevin (1241-1252), Artauld de Saint-Romans, a Provencal or else a Burgundian (1255-7), and finally, once more, Peter of Rivaux (1257-8) held it in turn. Chaceporc, whose accounts we have, had to pay the expenses of the king's campaigns in France; he disbursed £10,000 in 1243-4, £5,000 in 1244-5.[2] He was called king's treasurer.[3] The Wardrobe purchases have

Origin of the Great Wardrobe become so important that we see developing within it a section specially charged with this service : it is the Great Wardrobe, which is soon to acquire autonomy.

The Wardrobe had become a fashionable institution, and each of the members of the royal family wished to

Wardrobes of the queen and of Edward have his own : the queen, Eleanor of Provence, was the first to possess one ; another was then created for the lord Edward ; it accompanied him on the crusade and financed it as well

1. *Const. Hist.* ii. p. 58, (Geoffrey is not named) ; Tout, *Chapters* i. p. 251.
2. *Ibid*, i. p. 264
3. *Ibid*, i. p. 266

as it could. It was still an institution depending so closely on the king that at the death of Henry III the staff of his Wardrobe was dispersed; the lord Edward's now became the royal Wardrobe, and there was no Wardrobe in England until he had returned to his kingdom.

The barons, in 1258, made scarcely any changes in the Household, but they struck at the Wardrobe indirectly by restoring to the Chancery its glory, and by forbidding the payment of public reven-ues elsewhere than at the Exchequer. But this last provision was only very incompletely carried out : before 1258, three fifths of the Wardrobe's re-sources came from the Exchequer; Mr. Tout places the proportion at two-thirds, *i.e.* a fifteenth more, during the baronial domination. Moreover, the king kept his private seal. But after Lewes the reduction was severe : the Wardrobe now spent only £4,500, over half of which came from the Exchequer.[1] Nevertheless it seems clear that the barons, with their usual incapacity, had not yet clearly realised the importance and methods of the Wardrobe. They needed more than fifty years more to conceive the idea of tranforming it into an office of State.

The Wardrobe and the barons (1258-1265)

The rest of Henry III's reign was a period of stagna-tion.[2] But under Edward I the Wardrobe assumed an extraordinary importance. The ordinance of Westminster, which Mr. Tout has published,[3] shows that by 1279 its organis-ation had realised great advances. The whole Household is placed under the authority of two stewards and two marshals; they have command of the guard of sergeants-at-arms and archers, and of the knights of the Household; but,

The Wardrobe under Edward I

The Ordinance of Westminster (1279)

1. *Ibid*, i. pp. 295 sq
2. On the end of Henry III's reign, see Ehrlich "Exchequer and Wardrobe in 1270," *E. H. R.* 1921.
3. Tout, *Chapters* ii. pp. 158-163. It is analysed on pp. 27 sq.

above all, the chief steward, a great personage who is
The chief steward at least a knight, has the policing of the
Household, and exercises civil and criminal
jurisdiction within a day's distance from the court. The
Household clerks are divided between the Chapel (which
has five), the domestic offices, and the Wardrobe. The
ordinance says nothing of the Chamber and does not
mention the chamberlain; but both existed, though they
did not emerge again from their obscurity until the end
of the reign.

The Wardrobe is a small group of eight clerks, each
having, however, his assistants and servants; the low
The Wardrobe clerks number partly explains their importance,
for they were fully informed of all business;
but they were not enough to perform the
work, and often it was necessary, as before, to send
clerks from the Chancery to help them. They were
badly paid: eight marks a year, and a grant for robes;
this salary was temporary: when the king had been able
to get them a benefice, they received nothing more, unless the benefice was insufficient. They dined in the Hall.
But in 1300 the statute of St. Albans gave the steward
and the treasurer £200 each, to maintain their staff; the
same had been done in 1293 for the Chancery.[1]

The real chief of the Wardrobe was the keeper or
treasurer. But he acted in concert with the stewards.
The keeper One of them recorded each evening, with
the keeper, all the expenses of the day:
these day-books have been kept. Every year they drew
up the Wardrobe account, which was, in practice, that of
the whole Household, which it had to finance.

The controller, despite his name, had long been an
archivist. From 1275 there was also a keeper of the
The controller private seal. We do not know when the
two offices were combined, but in 1296-7

1. The Statute of St. Albans seems to have been revoked in 1310 at
Woodstock (Tout, *Chapters*, ii. p. 248).

Benstead occupied both. As he was also attached to the king's person as *secretarius*,[1] the controllership had become, at that moment, one of the most important offices in the state.

In the ordinance of 1279, another feature shows the importance of the duties of the keeper or treasurer : a third clerk, the cofferer, appears to assist him ; charged with the keeping of the accounts, he soon assumed the habit of effecting receipts and payments, and thus performed by the fourteenth century, the functions of the treasurer, who therefore was free, even in the reign of Edward I, to attend to the king's service.

The cofferer

There were in addition to these clerks, the usher, the sub-usher, and the surgeon and the doctor of the king, all clerks, who were supposed to sleep at the Wardrobe, thus perpetuating the memory of its domestic origin.

The other clerks

In Edward I's political system the Wardrobe was at once a nursery for administrators and the pivot of the governmental organisation.[2] Nearly all the notable servants of Edward I, and especially his chancellors, were first of all Wardrobe clerks, passing thence to the Exchequer or to the Chancery. The exceptions came from the Chancery, which at that time was not yet completely detached from the Household, and functioned in complete accord with it.[3]

The Wardrobe as the pivot of the administration

The Wardrobe and Chancery clerks who were thus being prepared for the great offices were generally of obscure origin : such were the keepers, G. de Louth, W. Langton, John Droxford, (or of Drokensford) (these last two had at

The origin of the clerks

1. That is "confidant ;" the word does not designate a particular function.
2. Tout, *Chapters*, ii. pp. 10 sq :
3. Of the five chancellors, Burnell and Greenfield were from the Household ; John Langton and Hamilton were plain clerks of the Chancery ; Baldock alone had but recently joined the Household. Edward I was less strict in the choice of his treasurers : two were monks.

first been controllers), the keeper of the privy seal, Benstead, and nearly all the others. The principal exception is in the case of the two Becks, sons of a great Lincolnshire baron, who were both keepers, and then became bishops : they then left the service and one of them became, from 1283, one of the most zealous leaders of the opposition. This fact throws some light on Edward I's administrative policy : it helps to explain his preference for functionaries of low birth, and his unwillingness to appoint the chancellor and the treasurer to bishoprics while they were still in office.[1]

Together with the Household knights, the Wardrobe clerks supplied Edward I with his familiar advisers, the *secretarii,* to whom he added barons only in exceptional cases; naturally, they were summoned to Parliament. Maitland has noted, in that of 1305, the existence of this little circle of intimate counsellors around Edward I. This observation becomes even more instructive when, by the light of Mr. Tout's researches, we identify them with the Wardrobe clerks : for example, Droxford, and better still, Benstead, the king's personal secretary. In 1305, there was amongst them scarcely anyone, except the chancellor, who had not been of the Wardrobe, but he had been drawn from the Chancery itself. The ordinary Council was therefore essentially a council of officials.[2]

They are the chief counsellors of Edward I

Under Edward I, the different sections of the Curia functioned in perfect accord. In practice Burnell directed the Chancery and the Wardrobe simultaneously. Similarly, Walter Langton had full control of the Wardrobe at the same

Unity of the administration under Edward I

1. Edward I made bishops of his old friend Burnell and of Baldock, at the end of the reign. But Greenfield and John Langton left office on becoming bishops, and Hamilton died without having received this reward. He was more indulgent towards the treasurers : three became bishops and retained their office. But Walter Langton was the first treasurer under Edward to play the part of first minister : in fact, no one had held such a position since Burnell's death.

2. Tout, *Chapters,* ii, pp. 60, sq., 82-4.

time as he ruled the Exchequer.[1] Thus there is no occasion for saying that Edward I intended to annul the Exchequer for the benefit of the Wardrobe: it was enough for him to have control of both.[2] This even explains why the differentiation of the sections of the *Curia* was not hastened under Edward I: he was undoubtedly a man of action first, and the systematic perfection of institutions did not interest him much.

But the same does not apply to the technical amelioration of methods when it became a question of supplying **The function of the Wardrobe under Edward I** the indispensable means of action for his policy. Two periods have accordingly been distinguished in his reign; during the government of Burnell, who died in 1292, the Wardrobe remains practically as it was before; it is a conservative period. But after that the wars rapidly bring about a financial difficulty which continually grows worse, and Edward resorts to the Wardrobe, giving it the duty of finding the money, and from 1295 it employs all its activities and its inventive talents in the manner we have described.[3] In particular it has been noticed that there is no question of " wooden money " before 1295, and that this expedient is in full use in the course of the financial year 1297.

Droxford, during six years of the reign, handled some £70,000 a year, while from 1274 to 1280 the Wardrobe **Receipts and expenses of the Wardrobe** received only £24,000. Now the expenses were even higher, so that the deficit became permanent. In 1295, in fact, W. Langton left £15,000 of debts and his accounts were not rendered in 1300. Droxford had a deficit of £13,000 for the year 1296-97, of £40,000 for 1297-8; his accounts for 1307

1. *Ibid*, ii. pp. 107-8. He takes as lieutenant, at the Exchequer, Droxford, keeper of the Wardrobe; in 1305 Benstead, controller of the Wardrobe, becomes chancellor of the Exchequer, and he also is assisted by Droxford.

2. Above, p. 365, note 1.

3. Above, pp. 365-366. Tout, *Chapters*, ii, pp. 85 sq.

were only presented in 1322, and were not audited until 1334. It is clear that the Wardrobe, in spite of all its efforts, was completely swamped by the rising tide of expenses. This capital fact shows that Edward I's enterprises were beyond the strength of the kingdom; it explains his final check; it accounts also for the violent irritation which favoured the baronial attack almost immediately after the king's death, and, to return to the Wardrobe, it helps us to understand why, in spite of the efficiency and the hard work of its members, they were accused of waste.

The responsibility of the Wardrobe was all the heavier in that it had been trusted with the military administration, the needs of which were always in excess of the available resources.[1] At first the Household could mobilise an appreciable number of horsemen and of infantry, and the Wardrobe had to provide for them. Its clerks themselves went to the army with their followers. Ralph de Manton, cofferer, was taken and slain by the Scots.[2] Also, the Wardrobe was required to maintain and provision the king's castles. But further, it had also to give orders for the raising of the county contingents, and similarly to attend to the requisition of ships. The clerks valued the horses, paid and assembled the troops, and led the infantry to the mustering-place. Those of the Great Wardrobe bought the provisions and the clothing, and for this purpose used the right of *prise*, usually without being able to pay, so that protests were very lively even under Edward I,[3] and provoked one of the ordinances

Its military functions

---

1. *Ibid*, ii. pp. 135 sq.
2. In the campaign of Carlaverock, in 1300, Mr. J. E. Morris has shown (for his researches see the French edition of *Const. Hist.* ii. p. 346, n. 2.) that the Household supplied 552 horsemen out of about 2,000. According to the *Liber quotidianus* of the Wardrobe, which Mr. Morris did not use, Mr. Tout thinks the proportion was nearer a third than a quarter (*Chapters* ii. p. 140).
3. See *Const. Hist.* ii. p. 176 (1300).

of 1311. Although the Wardrobe continued to follow the court, these duties resulted in the fixing of a part of its services. The cofferer often stays at London: a

The privy Wardrobe

new Wardrobe, that of the arms, or the king's privy Wardrobe, is created at the Tower; it manufactures and repairs the weapons; the Tower also becomes the chief magazine or store-house of the Wardrobe.

One last feature finally shows the importance of the Wardrobe under Edward I and allows us to measure the

Wardrobes of the queen and of the royal children under Edward I

responsibility which rested on it : the separate wardrobes of the queen and of the royal children were closely subordinated to it; it provided their personnel, passed on money to them at the king's orders, and received

their accounts. This close centralisation assumed a political importance when the Prince of Wales, under the influence of his favourites and principally of Gaveston,

The Wardrobe of Edward of Carnarvon

attempted to get rid of this tutelage. In reality, it is partly explained by administrative needs. The prince's appanage in-

cluded three parts; Cheshire, North Wales, and South Wales; each was a separate unit, with its justices, its Exchequer, and its Chancery. It was the Prince's Wardrobe which assured the unity of the principality.[1] We

Its political purpose

see that Edward I could not cease to take an active interest in an administrative organism of such great importance on the

morrow of the conquest of Wales. He put at its head clerks from his own Wardrobe, e.g. Walter Reynolds, who had been his keeper up to 1297, Meldon, and Ingelard de Warley, who played important parts in Edward

1. Edward of Carnarvon, like the king, had a great seal and a privy seal; but the two offices are not clearly distinguished; the head of the prince's administration was a chancellor. The differentiation of his *Curia* was less advanced than that of the *Curia regis*, and the *Wardrobe* of his Household included all services.

II's Household. But the prince's Household was the terror of the country, so many exactions did it commit, and in spite of this it went hopelessly into debt. In 1305, the king having refused any subsidy, a **Conflict of the two Wardrobes** violent conflict broke out; the prince found his means of existence cut off and had to capitulate : Gaveston was exiled. In his eyes it was Walter Langton who was responsible for this insult, and he paid for it as soon as his master was dead. As at the time of Hubert de Burgh, the political history was in reality shaped by the conflict of two court factions constituted of favourites and officials; they were, this time, entrenched in their two rival Households.[1]

After the fall of Walter Langton, those old servants of Edward I who had achieved any notoriety were not long in departing, and the favourite clerks of **The Wardrobe under Edward II** Edward II replaced them.[2] But the destiny of the Wardrobe was soon to take a new departure, which, while raising its dignity, put an end for ever to its progress.

The ordainers of 1311 did not interfere with the organisation of the Household, but they determined to make of the Wardrobe an office of State, the **The Wardrobe in 1311** chief of which should be nominated, as in the case of all the others, with the consent of the barons, and they claimed, at the same time, to put its activities into harmony with those of the other departments. The steward was forbidden to hold common pleas, and was reduced to judging offences committed in the court and the lawsuits of its members. The Wardrobe was forbidden to receive any sum except from the Exchequer; the "accustomed" prises alone were allowed to it. As for the privy seal, it remained as it was, but a special keeper was appointed for it, distinct from the

1. Tout, *Chapters*, ii. pp. 41, 165 sq.
2. *Ibid*, ii. pp. 191 sq. Benstead and Droxford left the Wardrobe. Warley became keeper and Reynolds chancellor.

controller, and the new keeper of the privy seal, North-burgh, was nominated, for the first time, in the following year. The Parliament of London proceeded to the pro-mised purging and replacements : the Wardrobe officers, including the steward, were submitted to the process.[1]

We know that Edward II, in concert with Gaveston, tried to go back on these resolutions. Fleeing to York, **The Wardrobe during the troubled years** he summoned the Chancery there, but it showed the greatest unwillingness to serve his designs ; he sent Walter Langton, re-called for the purpose, to sit at the Exchequer : but the barons drove him out, and seeing to it that the revenues were paid into that department, they deprived the king of resources and brought about Gaveston's fall.[2] In the midst of the disturbances which followed, the part of the Exchequer in the Wardrobe receipts went on de-creasing, and the Wardrobe could find only very little money elsewhere. In 1312-13, it received **Receipts and expenses** only £8,462 instead of £78,000 in 1307-8. The civil war thus ended in paralysing the state, and it is lack of money which, in part at least, explains the defeat of Bannockburn : it was regarded as the defeat of the Household.[3] The Parliament of York (1314) provoked a new purging of the Wardrobe, and for a little time it functioned almost as the ordinances of 1311 decreed. In fourteen months it received £60,000 of which only £3,000 came otherwise than through the Exchequer.[4] But the incapacity of Thomas of Lancaster once more loosened the vice : in the second half of 1316, the sums which had not come through the Exchequer rose from 5 per cent. to 40 per cent., and the proportion remained at 15 per cent. for the two years following.

1. Tout, *Chapters*, ii. pp. 145 sq. 228 sq.
2. *Ibid*, ii. pp. 149, 232.
3. *Ibid*, ii. 201.
4. *Ibid*, ii. pp. 202, 237-8.

At the same time the deficit reappeared.[1] Then· the
general situation brought about the forma-
The reform
of 1318
tion of a reforming coalition which is one
of the curious features of the reign, and
which has been brought to light by Messrs. Conway
Davies and Tout.[2] It was set up by a few well-intentioned
barons such as Pembroke, Badlesmere and the younger
Despenser on the one hand, and on the other, by professional officials, such as Northburgh, the keeper of the
privy seal. The king and Lancaster were obliged to
accept, at Leake, the organisation of a Council which
Ordinance of
the Household :
decline of the
Wardrobe
was proclaimed at the Parliament of York.
Badlesmere became steward and Despenser
chamberlain : an ordinance of December
1318 reformed the Household. The organisation it described shows that the Wardrobe, having
become an office of State, had already lost its preponderance. Each sub-division of the Household, especially
the Chapel, henceforth accounts separately, no longer to
the Wardrobe, but to the Exchequer ; the privy seal has
become a separate chancery which no longer belongs to
the Wardrobe. The Wardrobe once more becomes
simply one of the Household services ; it has only four
herbergeurs or provisioners, whereas the rest of the
Household has thirty-six.[3]

But the baronial interference with the Wardrobe had
for it yet another fatal result. The king, no longer able
Development of
the Chamber
to rely on it to resist the barons, brought
the Chamber from the obscurity in which it
was vegetating, and set about restoring it
as an instrument of the prerogative. From the beginning
of his reign, he had shown himself inclined to make use
of it, probably because the Wardrobe was not yet rid

1. *Ibid*, ii, pp. 203, 240.
2. Conway Davies, *Baronial Opposition to Edward II*, 1917.
3. Tout, *Chapters*, ii. pp. 246 sq. The ordinance of 1318, along with
that of 1323, is published in *Place Edward II*, pp. 270 to 318.

of his father's clerks; the Chamber had contracted loans from Italian bankers who refused to return any account of them to the Wardrobe; we must conclude that the Chamber had been for the king a secret treasury. He had entrusted the administration of Langton's possessions in 1307, and those of the Templars in 1308, to keepers who were clerks of the Chamber, and several of them accounted to it only.[1]

The Ordainers, fully occupied in submitting the Wardrobe to their control, had not observed that it was being revived under another form; they had not claimed the power to nominate the chamberlain. Yet, since they had decreed the payment of all revenues into the Exchequer, a commission had been nominated to restore to the Exchequer the administration of the domains entrusted to the Chamber; the king had suppressed the commission, and, after his break with the Ordainers, the Chamber had not been troubled any further. At the same time, the king, deprived in principle of the privy seal, had felt the desire to create a new one, whether to authenticate warrants addressed to the keeper of the privy seal, or for his personal correspondence; thus there had appeared the secret seal, the custody of which had been given to the Chamber, which had thus in its turn become the king's special chancery.[2]

The seal of the Chamber

At last, in 1318, at the parliament of York, the barons laid hands on the new institution also; they made the chamberlain a minister of State and appointed to this post one of their own number, the younger Despenser.[3] But he quickly went over to the king's party, and his victory in

The Chamberlain a minister of State, 1318

1. On the Chamber under Edward II : Tout, *Chapters*, ii. pp. 315 sq. The most important of these clerks was Wingfield, called "clerk of the king's Chamber" in 1309, and "general keeper of the lands of the Templars" in 1314.

2. Tout, *Chapters*, ii. pp. 282 sq.

3. *Ibid*, pp. 326, 331.

1321-2, took the power of the Chamber to its greatest height.[1] In 1313, it had been forced to give up, in theory, the domains of the Templars to the order of St. John, but it forced the latter, by innumerable quibbles, to leave it a considerable share. The con-

The manors of the Chamber fiscations decreed against the *contrariants* (Lancaster had five counties) put enormous territories at the disposal of the Chamber. If this government had lasted, the Chamber would have made Edward II far more powerful than the Wardrobe could ever have done, and, most important, it would have assured him complete independence of Parliament.

But the reforming party of 1318 had not disappeared, in spite of Pembroke's death and the execution of

Permanence of the administra- tive staff Badlesmere, and it became evident that its strength was derived less from the barons than from the officials.[2] It is a remarkable fact that the baronial reforms had spared many of these men, who took care to keep to the edge of the political conflict, and to continue their administrative work whatever the party in power. As for the subordinate personnel, it had not been touched. It thus tended to develop into a bureaucracy serving the State rather than the king.

Many of these men were capable and conscientious workers who took their profession seriously. They had no sympathy for the favourites. They could

The party of the officials have no taste for despotic whims which upset administrative traditions, multiplied institutions, and, by opposing these to each other, put their mechanism out of order, and reduced them to impotence. When they served in the Chancery or in the Exchequer, they were, moreover, quickly infused with the corporate spirit which had developed there. Now

1. *Ibid*, pp. 207 sq.
2. Tout, *Chapters*, ii. pp. 189, 217 sq.

the best of them generally ended by being rewarded with bishoprics. Some of them even preferred now to remain laymen, or to return to that status, such as Walter Norwich, who is the best type of this kind of functionary :[1] having risen in the hierarchy, they succeeded in worming themselves into the ranks of the aristocracy, and in founding baronial families. Thus they became independent, and, joining with those of the magnates who had a little sense of politics, they were able to form a kind of third party. They desired the king to be master, but wished him to respect the great departments of the *Curia* and to govern through experienced officials, not through favourites. This third party had won an initial success in 1318. Against all expectation, it gained even more important victories under the younger Despenser's government. Bishop Stapledon, the treasurer, and Robert Baldock, the chancellor, set about curbing the ambition of the *familiares* of the Chamber, and reforming the great departments of State, and restoring their prestige.[2] And it is remarkable that Despenser offered no opposition ; probably he had kept, even in becoming a favourite, something of the principles of the opposition of which he had at first been a member. It is true that, once the barons were crushed, the Chamber became less useful, and that, in any case, it did not lose all its power ; but still, it seems that Stapledon and Baldock took the initiative in the ordinances of Cowick and of Westminister against the king's wishes.

1. *Ibid*, ii. p. 220. The son of a Norfolk squire, he began as an Exchequer clerk, became Walter Langton's secretary, fell with him, and then returned to favour. He renounced his clergy, married, and became a knight in 1312 : baron of the Exchequer in 1311, treasurer in 1314, he was, after 1317, the first chief-baron of the Exchequer, and he remained so all his life. His grand-daughter became Countess of Suffolk.

2. For their reforms : Tout, *Chapters*, ii, pp. 258 sq., 260, 304, 311, 340 sq. For the Exchequer reforms, see above, pp. 367--368. Mr. Tout shows that the Chancery too had, under Edward II, some very capable clerks, notably the two Ayermins, one of whom, William, became bishop and chancellor. The rolls were much improved. William Ayermin gives for the first time, in 1316, a satisfactory Parliament Roll (*Place Edward II* pp. 62, 184).

The Chamber was forced to give up to the Exchequer the domains of the *contrariants* (1322). It kept the

Ordinances of Cowick and Westminster 1322 possessions taken from the Templars and those confiscated before 1321; many more were allotted to it, in addition to certain escheats, without counting the movables and the jewels of the *contrariants*. In spite of all, at the end of the reign, it scarcely handled more than £2,000, which it devoted to the personal needs of the king and the Despensers. This sum was enough for the Chamber to discredit itself by its bad administration, and so to do harm to the government, without being sufficient to allow the Chamber to play any part in politics at a time

Household reform: ordinance of York of crisis. The Household, too, underwent a new reform, the Wardrobe being included by the second Ordinance of York (1322), when it took the form which it kept until 1782.[1]

When Edward II had been dethroned, the Chamber returned into obscurity; but a few years after Mortimer's

The Chamber under Edward III fall Edward III revived his father's policy.[2] Manors were again reserved for the Chamber, and when the Hundred Years' War began and the king had sequestered the goods of alien priories, they were entrusted to the Chamber. A complete hierarchy of officials was organised to administer these domains, in the Chamber and in the counties; justices, escheators, stewards, auditors, and receivers.

The "griffin" A new seal, the *griffin*, was created to give the Chamber its own chancery. The receivers refused to account at the Exchequer.[3] As Mr. Tout says, these Chamber manors were " royal fran-

---

1. Tout. *Chapters*, ii. pp. 344 sq.
2. Tout, "Some Conflicting Tendencies" (cited above, p. 350, n. 3).
3. The receiver Hatfield accounts to the king, who orders him to burn the rolls and schedules so that the Exchequer shall have no knowledge of them. The Wardrobe, on the contrary, continues to account to the Exchequer.

DD

chises '' taken out of the control of the Chancery and the Exchequer.

When Edward III wished to prepare for the war against France, the Wardrobe, too, resumed its activity : **The Wardrobe and the Hundred Years' War** it fulfilled the same military and financial functions as under Edward I.[1] The officials of the Chamber and Wardrobe provided the real ministers of Edward III from 1337 to 1341.

Kilsby Kilsby, one of the receivers of the Chamber became keeper of the privy seal, so that this office fell back under the king's discretionary authority. When he left England, Edward left the Exchequer and almost the entire Chancery there; he took with him the office of the privy seal, the greater part of the Chamber, all the Wardrobe, and the Great Wardrobe, **The Household in the Netherlands** which took up its quarters in Antwerp. He set up in the Netherlands, with the chiefs of the *curiales,* a government which embarked on a conflict with that which he had left in England, and in which the third party dominated, under the leadership of Archbishop Stratford.

After the crisis of 1341, Edward III, in spite of his apparent victory, gave up his system of personal rule. **Edington's reforms** He let Kilsby go to Palestine,[2] and the treasurer Edington, bishop of Winchester,

---

1. It was under Edward III that the cofferer acquired all his import-ance. (Tout, *Chapters,* ii- p. 23). The financial needs of Edward III were no less than those of Edward I. In 1362-3 the annual expenses were £66,666; the hereditary revenue £10,000; customs produced £30,000, leaving a deficit of £26,666. (T. F. Tout and D. M. Broome, "A National Balance Sheet for 1362-3." *B. H. R.* 1924). The Great Wardrobe and the Privy Wardrobe, installed at the Tower, then underwent a great extension. Their archives and those of the Chamber provide the first information on the beginnings of firearms. See T. F. Tout "Firearms in England in the XIVth century" E. H. R. 1911 : Edward III was using powder in 1333-4, and on 1st Feb. 1345 he ordered the repairing of his cannons and the making of a hundred *ribaldos* or mortars for his expedition to France : it is therefore likely that they were used at Crécy.

2. See *Const. Hist.* (French Edition) t. II. p. 472 n. 2. Edington's part has been brought to light by Mr. Tout, ("Some Conflicting Tendencies").

was allowed to strike the same blow at the Chamber as

The writ of 1356 Stapledon had struck in 1322 : by writ of Jan. 21, 1356, the Chamber manors were restored to the Exchequer. The *griffin* disappeared.

The Chamber and the Wardrobe disappear from history The Chamber again became a simple Household department, fed by the Exchequer and placed under its control. It disappeared for ever from history : even Richard II never tried to restore its political and administrative importance. The influence of the Commons also contributed to this. Their financial control slowly deprived the Chamber of the greater part of its financial expedients. For the same reason, the Wardrobe also dropped back into obscurity.[1]

In exactly the form in which it had been organised under the Edwards, the Household survived itself in the Households of the royal princes, which had been formed in its image.[2] The Black Prince had a household almost from his birth ; that of John of Gaunt, who had become one of the greatest lords of the kingdom by his marriage with the heiress of the Lancasters, was scarcely less important. These households were installed in London, like that of the king, and so helped to make that town the capital of realm.[3] But, most important, they gave unity to the appanages and made them States within the State.

1. Tout, *Place Edward II*, p. 174 sq. The Wardrobe again became a privy service; see W. Paley-Baildon, "A Wardrobe Account of 16-17 Richard II" (1393-4) in *Archæologia*, 1911, and the extracts of accounts published by Mr. Wylie, *Henry IV*, iv, pp. 193, 219, 230. But its expenses continued to excite complaints from Parliament; *Const. Hist.* iii. pp. 44, 55. See also Wylie, *Henry IV* iii. p. 315; *Henry V* i. p. 26.

2. Mrs. M. Sharp, "The Administrative Chancery of the Black Prince before 1362" in *Essays presented to T. F. Tout*. The household of the Black Prince fulfilled the same functions as that of Edward of Carnarvon (later Edward II). But he had no great seal, nor, it seems, any chancellor before becoming prince of Aquitaine (1362) ; John of Gaunt, on the contrary, had one, like Edward of Carnarvon. On the latter's Household, see p.

3. Tout, "The Beginnings of a Modern Capital," (*Proceedings of the British Academy*, xi).

Edward III found that it paid : his sons were thus more easily able to raise troops and obtain money to pay them. But this power could be turned by the princes against the king or against one another : the solid administrative organisation of the appanages was in part the cause of the civil wars which broke out in the fifteenth century.

Moreover, the king's Household had not exhausted its creative power. Under Edward III, it re-established once more a secret seal, the *signet*, and supplied the king with clerks specially attached to his person. Under Richard II, the name of " secretary," which hitherto had been generally employed in the sense of " confidant," is reserved for one of these clerks and assumes a precise administrative sense : he is the clerk of the secret seal.

The office of the signet and the secretary are found again under the Lancastrians, but for a long time they played no part in politics. But between 1437 and 1443, Henry VI opposed his office of the secret seal to the Chancery and to the privy seal, which were in the hands of the magnates, and Edward IV employed his secretary, William Hatclyffe, on numerous embassies between 1464 and 1480.[1] Still, it was only under the

1. On the Office of the secret seal and the secretary, see Miss L. B. Dibben, "Secretaries in the Thirteenth and Fourteenth Centuries" (*E. H. R.*, 1910); Mrs. F. M. G. Higham, "A Note on the Pre-Tudor Secretary," in *Essays presented to T. F. Tout* [and T. F. T. Plucknett, "The Place of the Council in the Fifteenth Century," *Trans. Roy. Hist. Soc., Fourth Series*, i. 1918]. In 1347 the keeper of the privy seal is still called *secretarius*. Henry IV mentions "one of the clerks of our signet." After 1437, the Council had to recognise that the affixing of the privy seal could not be refused on the production of a warrant under the signet and in 1444, the king proclaimed that all gifts made since 1432 in virtue of letters under sign manuel, signet of the Eagle, or signet of arms, "as well as those sealed by the chamberlains and the clerk of the council," were as legal as if the chancellor had received a warrant under the privy seal. The secretary was then Thomas Beckington, the most notable secretary of the Lancastrian period. It is therefore remarkable that no mention is made of him : we conclude that the signet was then at the

Tudors that this last creation of the Household assumed full importance, when Thomas Cromwell, after the fall of Wolsey, made the secretary the political heir of the chancellor.

Like the administrative history of the sections detached from the Curia, that of the Household, which is, as it were, its counterpart after the last years of John Lackland, cannot be completely isolated from political history. If the Household became the executive agent of the royal will, it owed this mainly to the fact that the barons had succeeded in placing the Exchequer and the Chancery under their control. The rivalry of these administrations was thus in large measure provoked by the struggles which set the king and the barons at grips with each other. But, in its turn, it throws a vivid light, as we are now about to try to prove, on the history of the Council, which was the principal theatre of that strife.

disposal of all the clerks of the office, that the secretary was not yet its exclusive keeper, and that his official situation was still inferior to that of the chamberlain and of the clerk of the Council. Hatclyffe was a layman, the king's physician; nor are his numerous journeys abroad compatible with the custody of the signet. In this reign the organisation of the office still seems little advanced.

The Council and the Origins of the House of Lords.

From the beginning the Council was the centre of initiative and co-ordination in the *Curia* : the Exchequer and the Chancery merely carried out its orders, and when these departments failed to obtain its confidence, the Council did not hesitate to create others drawn from the Household, as we have seen. To be able to deliberate there was no need for the Council to be a permanent and closed body ; and moreover, the king wished to consult whomsoever he pleased. As a particular section of the *Curia,* the Council did not begin to appear until the thirteenth century and did not finally obtain a separate individuality until the reign of Richard II. Having no fixed personnel and no bureaucratic organisation, it did not let itself become imprisoned by tradition. Even when it had become an organised body, it kept the liberty of decision and the faculty of innovation, because it shared in the sovereign power, whose business it was to redress grievances and remedy the insufficiency and the imperfection of common law and administrative custom. It kept in this way a strong hand upon the government and administration of the kingdom.

Importance of the Council from the beginning

It always kept the right to decide and to innovate

This is shown in a most curious manner in the domain of justice. Whereas the Exchequer and the Chancery became courts of common law, the Council remained the master of its procedure, because it set up for itself a special chancery, first the privy seal, then the signet. It never used juries; it either enquired by writ and by administrative means, or it questioned the pleaders and even obliged the accused to give evidence against him-

It creates a procedure differing from the common law

self by putting him upon oath. The Chancery having

Writs created, in 1346, a writ *quibusdam de causis,* and, later, a writ *sub poena,* which cited the person named to appear without indicating the charge, the Council seized upon them and issued them in French, under the privy seal. It kept no judicial record and proceeded in secret. From the end of the thirteenth century it nominated extraordinary com-

Extraordinary commissions missions (commissions of *trailbaston* and commissions of *oyer et terminer*) to re-establish order in the counties, employing the same procedure. It was contrary to the common

Dangers and advantages of the jurisdiction law and offered no guarantee to property and to individual liberty, and this explains the protests of Parliament. But since it was expeditious and less costly, and, in troubled times, more effective than the regular tribunals, Parliament often resigned itself to shutting its eyes. The Council was not content with continuing to judge on appeal, with re dressing errors, and with declaring the law in order to cope with the new needs of society : it received criminal complaints directly, when the courts of common law dared not take cognisance because of the high position of the offenders, or when they had been powerless to have their sentences carried out. Thus it kept the supreme control of police in the realm, an essentially political attribute, since the great problem was always that of bringing the barons to reason, and the commissions were thus a good means of attacking their franchises.[1]

1. See *Const. Hist* iii, pp. 259, 261, 288. Mr. Baldwin has studied at great length the features of the Council's jurisdiction and the extent of its competence (pp. 64, 260 sq., 280 sq.). On the commissions of *trailbaston* (against marauders or "staff-trailers") and of *oyer et terminer,* see *Const. Hist.* ii, p, 284-285. Parliament frowned upon them. The second statute of Westminster (1285) forbade the issue of further commissions except under urgent necessity, and then to regular judges only. Mr. Baldwin (p. 267)remarks that as a result of this method of choice, the commissioners were led to judge according

Similar observations can be made concerning finance and legislation. We have seen how the Council created

The Council and the finances

for itself in the Wardrobe and the Chamber treasuries distinct from the Exchequer, and how it employed these departments to evolve new financial methods. In the fourteenth century, Parliament gradually brought under its control both the receiving and the appropriation of taxation, but the Council's part still remained considerable. Firstly, the customs were levied without the consent of Parliament until about the end of Edward III's reign; then, in the matter of impositions, the initiative belonged, after all, to the Council: it decided whether they were necessary and whether it was desirable to summon a Parliament: and finally, through the agency of the Household, it continued to employ expedients of all sorts to obtain resources; the Commons obliged it to give up tallages and scutage, but had far more difficulty in limiting the abuses of the right of purveyance or the commissions of array, and were never able to prevent the Council from borrowing on all sides.[1]

Similarly, when, in the course of the fourteenth century the distinction between the statute and the ordinance

Council and legislation

had been worked out, the king in his Council still retained a great part of the power of legislation; he modified bills of Parliament before ratifying them; he paid members of Parliament to have bills presented; he took it upon himself to suspend statutes; he granted letters of dispensation or of remission; above all, he issued ordinances to complete the provisions of statutes or to take their place,

to the ordinary forms, and to entrust the execution of their decisions to the sheriffs. These commissions played the same part as the French *justices prévôtales* of the *ancien régime* who judged without appeal, without regular forms, and had their decrees enforced forthwith. Their regularisation prevented them from committing abuses, which had sometimes been monstrous, but their efficacy was greatly diminished.

1. See *Const. Hist.* ii pp. 545 to 599. In the fifteenth century, Parliament began to guarantee in each session, the future borrowings of the Council; (*Ibid* iii, pp. 260-261)

provisionally at least. The Commons fought their hardest to obtain the sanctioning of their bills without alteration, and to protect their statutes from the Council's enterprises, but with incomplete success. And, in spite of their distrust, they were themselves obliged to grant to the Council the right of making ordinances for particular circumstances, or to shut their eyes to actions which necessity had decreed.[1]

As for general policy, it was not within the competence of the Commons, who even showed unwillingness to express an opinion in this matter, when the Council consulted them to oblige them to assume their responsibility.[2]

The Council and general policy

The government of the kingdom therefore remained in the hands of the Council, and throughout the whole of the Middle Ages, Parliament's part appears to have been very mediocre in comparison.

It is master of the government

Besides, nobody dreamt then of a permanent Parliament controlling governmental action day by day; still less would anyone have thought that this control could come to the Commons.

The real question, the stake in the political struggles, was to know what should be the composition of the Council. In the eleventh and twelfth centuries the king called to his *Consilium* whomsoever he pleased; usually, his *familiares*, the principal personages of the *Curia*, especially the great officers : occasionally, some barons. If these latter were numerous, the "Council" which was later called "ordinary," "continual," or "restricted" could become an enlarged *Curia* : this is what was called, at the time of Edward I, the Council in Parliament.

The choice of counsellors: the real stake in medieval political struggles

The system of tenure introduced by the Norman conquest had made service of court an obligation of the

1. See *Ibid* ii, pp. 426-427, 599 sq.; iii, pp. 260, 261-2.
2. See *Ibid* ii, pp. 633 sq.; iii, pp. 267-8.

tenant in chief, but not a right.[1] In the thirteenth century the barons maintained the opposite. They claimed that, in virtue of their tenure, they were the natural counsellors of the king. Pride and interest impelled them to drive the *familiares* from the *Consilium*, or rather, to reduce them to the position of technical auxiliaries. Nevertheless they almost always proved incapable of assiduous session in the ordinary Council. Therefore the choice of the great officers of the *Curia*, the first among the *familiares*, was of capital importance. Would they be chosen from the barons? Or would the the king choose them from the common people, the favourites, and the functionaries?

From the thirteenth century the king and the barons contended, in the Council, for the government of England: this is the true drama of medieval history.[2]

II.

Up to the thirteenth century we perceive no rivalry between the two elements of the *Consilium regis*. The

Agreement between the barons and the "familiares" up to the end of the twelfth century

solidarity of the conquerors as opposed to the vanquished was probably responsible for this state of affairs under the first Norman kings; on the other hand the king, though very powerful, asked little of his barons, beyond service in the host, and did not encroach upon their rights, so that they were not very anxious to come to the Council. But, above all, the great officers were barons; the *miles litteratus* was an exception, and, in consequence, the administration did not produce any upstarts; when a clerk rose, he became

1. On this question, see below, p. 449.
2. The question arose in France also. The *familiares* of the Capetians were the object of the hostility of the royal family and the nobles. Everyone knows the fate of Pierre de la Broce and of Enguerrand de Marigny. But there are several earlier examples of palace revolutions: the murder of Hugh de Beauvais, under Robert II; the disgrace of Etienne de Garlande, under Louis VI, and that of Gille Clément under Philip Augustus (Luchaire, *Manuel*, pp. 537 sq.).

a bishop, that is, a baron. Now the feudal barons did not dream of excluding the professionals from the Council; it was axiomatic that the task of pure administration was their business; it was enough that they should keep their place, have no political influence, and, above all, should obtain but the smallest portion of the liberality which the king could dispense.

The situation changed entirely from the reign of Henry II. Royal policy began to undermine the feudal edifice; the development of the administra-
Causes of their
conflict
tion and the decadence of the feudal army multiplied financial requirements : judicial reforms increased the number of lawsuits : the importance of the *consilium* of *familiares* grew in proportion, and quite naturally began to excite the distrust of the barons. Now, its composition underwent a like modification. The part of the professionals grew in it, not only because they were indispensable, but also because they proved docile instruments. Under Henry III we find, for the first time, lawyers, Segrave and Passelewe, reaching office : when the French domains had been, for the greater part, lost, under John Lackland and Henry III, foreigners arrived to seek their fortunes in England : both groups monopolised the king's favours and became bishops, whilst others were soon to found families of lay barons.[1]

It was then that, in the course of the thirteenth century, the baronial reaction directed its attack against the king's regular counsellors. The outcry against foreigners supplied a popular catchword, but, in reality, the movement was directed against all the upstarts who were taking the place of the feudal barons and threatening to invade their ranks;[2] behind them doubtless, the

1. See above, p. 400.
2. For example, in 1341, one of the grievances is formulated thus : "The same men now make themselves governors and counsellors more than their estate warrants" (Baldwin p. 80).

progress of the royal power attracted some attention, but it is highly probable that the material favours heaped upon the *familiares,* and feudal pride, hurt by the elevation of these upstarts, excited the spirit of sedition much more than purely political considerations.

The barons maintained that service of court made them the king's natural counsellors. But the practical realisation of their claim was never satisfactory. Their political

The barons incapable of assiduity

spirit was very feeble, and personal selfishness was rapidly dissolving class solidarity which had for a moment been aroused. They wished to form the ordinary or continual Council, but it was never possible to make them assiduous in this matter. Either they confined themselves to placing a few

Attempts to remedy this.

of their number in the great offices, and these men found their influence counterbalanced by the personal following of the king; or else they imposed on the king counsellors who quickly yielded place to the *familiares* : and it was in order to remedy this insolvency that the plan was devised of imposing an oath on the counsellors, and later, of paying them. But the barons were no less jealous of each other than of the upstarts, so that these aristocratic councils were always very unstable and had but a mediocre authority. In order to govern they had constantly to call the other barons to their side : and so, during the periods of aristocratic reaction, the government belonged less to the *Consilium,* in the narrow sense of the word, than to the enlarged *Curia* which was called Parliament in the thirteenth century, *Magnum Concilium* in the fourteenth and fifteenth centuries, and which in the sixteenth century became the House of Lords.

This is why its history is characterised by great instability and extreme confusion. When the king was

Instability of the Council

popular, fortunate, and strong, the Council of the *familiares* became preponderant, and baronial assemblies were rare; when the

king was a minor, or proved incapable, or could not
resist a rising, the magnates invaded the ordinary Council and assemblies of barons were multiplied. It was
altogther an exception when Edward III, after 1341,
and particularly Henry V, succeeded in governing personally though surrounding themselves with great
barons : their victories in France assured their success,
but the equilibrium did not survive them.

These conflicts do not concern political history alone.
They contributed to the definition of the membership
and function of the Council, and to the making of it into
an organised body.

III.

When the barons denounced the " evil " counsellors
of John Lackland, the *Consilium regis* was not yet an
organised institution, The same holds true
The Council for the minority of Henry III. No Council
during the
minority of of Regency was appointed. But William the
Henry III Marshal endeavoured to strengthen his
power by bringing as many barons as he could, not only
to the assemblies which were soon to be called Parliaments, but also to the restricted *Consilium*. They were
never present regularly. The first professional lawyers,
Stephen Segrave and Martin Pateshull, were constantly
associated with them.[1] No essential change can be dis-
cerned under Hubert de Burgh's rule.[2]

1. Stubbs (*Const. Hist.*, ii, p. 270) and Bémont (*Simon de Montfort*
p. 111) have suggested that the formation of the Council might go
back to the beginning of Henry III's reign, and especially to a
Council of regency. Mr. Baldwin opposes this opinion (pp. 16 sq.)
and his conclusions are here reproduced. There is no trace of the
nomination of a Council of regency ; the official documents do not
take cognisance of any "councillors" as members of a particular
institution ; at the most, the rolls mention here and there "the
magnates of our Council." Mr. Baldwin, however, admits that the
circumstances increased the importance of the *Consilium*, because
William the Marshal and, later, Hubert de Burgh, lacking the
authority of the royal dignity, were obliged, far more than a sovereign,
to secure the co-operation of the *Curia* and the barons.

2. Baldwin pp. 22 sq.

When he had taken over the government, Henry III quickly surrounded himself with foreigners, mostly Poitevins, amongst whom were many capable men who developed the administrative organisation of the *Curia* and the Household, for example, Peter des Roches and Peter de Rivaux.[1] But not all his favourites were foreigners : Segrave and Robert Passelewe were English. Henry III clearly sought to exclude from the government the barons who had conquered his father. Segrave became justiciar ;[2] the seal was taken from Ralph Neville, and after his death the Chancery was constantly changing hands, and was given to subordinates.[3]

The Counsellors of Henry III

As early as 1234 the attacks began, and in 1237 the king had to allow the nomination, in Parliament, of twelve counsellors, on whom an oath was imposed for the first time.[4] Henry III quickly got rid of them. In 1244, to avoid being forced to accept a plan of reform, he himself presented to the Parliament four counsellors of his choice.[5] From that moment we find many references to a Council of limited and definite personnel. The conflict between the king and the barons thus seems to have precipitated the setting up of the Council as a particular institution.

Institution of the oath, 1237

Progress of the institution

1. Baldwin, p. 23 sq. See above, pp. 385-386.

2. See *Const. Hist.* ii p. 51. Re-established by the barons in 1258, the office finally disappeared in 1265.

3. Above, p. 375.

4. Baldwin, p.26. Stubbs (*Const. Hist.*, ii, p. 54) does not mention the appearance of the oath in 1237. In France it exists under Philip III.

5. Baldwin, p. 29. The plan of reform is noticed by Stubbs (*Const. Hist.*, ii, p. 62), but he does not mention the king's stratagem described by Mr. Baldwin. The latter observes that Henry's plan of creating a privy Council from which the barons would be entirely or almost entirely excluded, appears in the plan of government established for Apulia when Henry's son, Edmund, was candidate for the Silician throne in 1256 : this plan contained a Council in which only two barons were to sit.

Its composition played an essential part in the great crisis which began in 1257. In that year the plan of reform did not attempt to regulate the composition of the Council, but it claimed to subject its members to the oath.[1] This expedient later seemed insufficient, and the Provisions of 1258 set up a Council of Fifteen controlled by committees. But these rules were not strictly observed, for the barons did not serve regularly.[2] New attempts were made in 1263 and in 1264. After Lewes, the barons delegated to three of their number the nomination of a Council of Nine, who were to take oath, and it was stipulated that three at least should always be present. The king in particular could not choose the great officers without their consent. We know little of the functioning of this Council, but Mr. Baldwin regards it as, beyond doubt, irregular and disorganised.[3] The principal result of all this upheaval was that the necessity of a permanent Council of stable organisation became clear to the minds of all. Henry III himself remembered the lesson. In truth, as soon as the king was once more able to choose his counsellors, the Council again became what it had been in the twelfth century, a temporary assembly of variable composition, in which the *familiares* were subordinated to the barons. But in 1271, when Henry III was ill and impoverished, and Edward was setting out for the Holy Land, he

The Council 1257-1265

Results of the crisis

1. Baldwin, p. 30. This claim occurs in the list of grievances mentioned but not analysed by Stubbs (*Cont. Hist.*, ii, p. 73).
2. But see Mr. F. M. Powicke's study, "Some observations on the baronial council, etc." in *Essays presented to T. F. Tout*, which throws some remarkable light on the history of the crisis and rectifies the views of Stubbs (*Const. Hist.*, ii, pp. 83-84) on the Provisions of Westminster. Mr. Powicke shows that the Council of Fifteen was the real master of the government, and that the Provisions of Westminster tended, not, as Stubbs thought, to diminish its authority over local administration, but on the contrary to strengthen it, with the object of repressing the abuses of franchises, he believes, and of re-establishing order.
3. See *Const. Hist.*, ii, p. 94; Baldwin, pp. 33 sq.

named a Council and made it take oath : for the first time this expedient, invented by the barons, was incorporated in the king's government.[1]

Naturally it suited Edward I admirably. From the first year of his reign we have to deal with *jurati de consilio*.[2] The oath became a regular practice. But Edward did not fix the number of his sworn counsellors and he reserved the right of adding to them counsellors who had not taken the oath. Moreover, the sworn counsellors were not always present : the king sent them on missions and employed them for all purposes, at long distances. Thus the effective composition of the Council always remained variable. But of course so strong-willed a king jealously kept to himself the nomination of the Council, and allowed the barons only a very small part in it.[4] The permanent nucleus was composed in the main of the chiefs of the *Curia* and of the Household : the chancellor, the treasurer, the chamberlain, the steward, the keeper and the controller of the wardrobe, some justices, some Exchequer barons, and some Chancery and Wardrobe clerks : all told, from thirty to thirty-five persons.[5] Edward added to these a few confidential agents : a Franciscan, a Dominican, and some foreign bankers. It is certain that many of them were sworn.

The Council of Edward I; sworn members

1. Baldwin, p. 37. Stubbs does not appear to have known of this precedent.
2. Baldwin, p. 71 : the barons, the bishops and the chancellor (not sworn) *cum juratis de consilio*.
3. Stubbs thought (*Const. Hist.*, ii, p. 273) that the permanent Council had all taken oath.
4. For Edward I's Council, see Maitland, pp. xxxvi sq. ; Baldwin. pp. 71 sq. ; Tout, *Chapters*, ii, pp. 148 sq. Mr. Baldwin cites examples of sworn barons : in 1296 the archbishop of Dublin and Hugh le Despenser; in 1306, John Salmon, bishop of Norwich (he prints the writ on p. 91).
5. Maitland takes from the acts given during the Parliament of 1305 the names of the persons attesting them, (Maitland, pp. xl, xli), but we cannot conclude that they were all members of the Council. Mr. Pollard says that at the end of the reign the Council must have included some 70 members—including 5 earls, 4 bishops and 17 barons, 31 officials and judges, and 6 *magistri*. (*Evolution of Parliament*, p. 30).

Most of the time, they alone were present : many acts, including gifts, sentences, and even statutes, bear their attestations alone. However, at all times there were a few sworn barons. But we have proof that they were rarely anxious for this, because the oath obliged them to be assiduous in attendance, and this seemed to injure their dignity.[1] Most frequently the magnate who attends the

Counsellors summoned by writ of privy seal

Council is summoned to it expressly, by a writ resembling that which would summon him to Parliament, but issued under the privy seal.[2] For Edward I the "continual" council is essentially the assembly of his *familiares*. He speaks, in 1289, of those who are *de consilio nostro seu familia nostra*.[3]

Still, it remained established that a baron summoned to Parliament became a member of the Council for the occasion, and the addition of the Com-

The Council in Parliament

mons in no wise changed this custom. The *consilium regis* thus once more became the enlarged *Curia*, and that is why Mr. Baldwin maintains, after Maitland, that there was under Edward I only one Council.[4] In this sense, then, we can say that Edward I innovated less than at first appears : like all his predecessors he attempted to govern with his *familiares*, but he did not cease to associate with them a more or less considerable number of barons at the great feasts or according to circumstances.

It is, however, none the less true that Edward I had

---

1. In 1386 the archbishop refused to swear because it was the privilege of his church to be present at all Councils, "secret or not." (Baldwin, p. 100).

2. M. Petit-Dutaillis reproduced in the French edition of the *Const. Hist.*, t. ii, p. 311, n. 2, a writ of this kind, from M. Déprez, *Le sceau privé*.

3. Tout *Chapters*, ii, p. 150, note 1 : by letters patent of 13 June, 1289, Edward authorises Itier d'Angoulême, constable of Bordeaux, to keep with him those whom he wishes "*de consilio nostro seu familia nostra.*"

4. Baldwin, pp. 67 sq.

three sorts of counsellors: the sworn members, those

who were summoned under privy seal, and those summoned under the great seal. From one assembly to the next, the composition of each of these three categories of counsellors varied at his discretion, and he cared little about fixing the organisation of the *Consilium,* but he evidently held three sorts of Councils.

1. Those to which he called the sworn counsellors, of whom some might be barons; this is the "ordinary" or "continual Council."

2. Those to which he called in addition a more or less considerable number of barons by writ of privy seal; at this period, this kind is not distinguished from the "ordinary Council", but it will later become the *Magnum Consilium.*

3. Those which he convoked by writ of the great seal;[1] it is before this Council that the Commons appeared from time to time; soon the name of "Parliament" will be reserved for the assemblies of which they

---

1. The difference between the Council and the Council in Parliament appears clearly in 1305; on March 21, all those who were not of the king's Council, *including the barons*, were authorised to withdraw; the Parliament still continued, however, for the sense of the word was not yet restricted, and it continued to apply to the meeting of a council: even the epithet "general" was still used for it. But it is evident that, in the terminology which was soon to prevail, and which has become classic, the assembly, from March 21st, 1305, was no longer a Council in Parliament or a Parliament, but an ordinary Council. On April 5th the bishop of Byblos produced there a papal bull inviting the king to put him in possession of a priory. Maitland, has reproduced the names of the counsellors who were present that day. They numbered 36, of whom 21 were members of the Curia; among the others were 2 bishops, 3 earls, and 10 knights, who in reality, had been personally summoned to the Parliament. (Maitland, pp. xlii sq.; no. 464, p. 297). Now there had appeared in Parliament 95 prelates, 9 earls, and 94 barons (*ibid*, p. xxxv). In consequence, setting aside the special competence of the Council in Parliament respecting the vote of the aid, it is clearly distinguished from the ordinary Council: to one, as to the other, the king only admitted those barons whom he had summoned, but the ordinary Council was open only to a very small number of persons expressly designated. The assembly of April 5th, 1305, corresponded to the second of the categories which we have distinguished in the text.

form a part : in this "Council in Parliament" the sworn members did not sit as of right; they were summoned to it under the great seal, like the other members.[1]

IV.

The preponderance of the men of the *Curia* in the Council was felt all the more strongly by the baronage

Irritation of the barons against the 'familiares' of Edward I

since they were increasingly developing the Household services, especially that of the Wardrobe : the king governed and administered by means of the same low-born agents whom he then thrust into the great offices and provided for at the expense of the Church.[2] Accordingly, the attempts of the thirteenth century were

Edward II

resumed under Edward II. During the first months of the reign, it is true, Edward II seemed to live on good terms with the barons;[3] in reality he had the same idea as his father concerning the extent of his authority. But he had no capacity for government, and did not distinguish between his royal authority and his individual caprice : he distrusted his ministers, if they were capable and independent, almost as much as if they had been barons, and he would have no one with him but his favourites. He aggravated the

1. It is certain that not all the sworn members were present at each meeting of the ordinary Council, nor were they all summoned to Parliament, though many of them attended. (33 in 1305; Maitland, p. xxxvi). Edward's Council greatly resembles that of Philip the Fair. In 1303 there exists a *"Grand Conseil," "Conseil étroit ou secret"* whose members are nominated by letters patent and take oath; Philip the Fair also holds solemn Councils at which there appear the unsworn barons; finally, he calls together assemblies which later will take the name of States-general.

2. See above, pp. 390-391.

3. On Edward II's reign, see Tout, *Place Edward II* and Conway Davies, *Baronial Opposition to Edward II,* 1917. In France the feudal reaction of 1314 was similarly directed against the Council of the *curiales.* Under the last three Capetians, at least under Louis X and Charles IV, the chief of the Council was Charles of Valois in reality : Luchaire, *Manuel* pp. 537 sq.; Petit, *Charles de Valois,* (Thèse Lettres, 1900), pp. 144 sq.

position by his blind devotion to Gaveston, whose boasting and free talk mortally wounded the barons; now he was a Gascon, and again the out-cry against foreigners served as a pretext for sedition. Stubbs has passed severe judgment upon the fourteenth century barons because he had a high idea of the national sentiment and disinterestedness of those of 1215 and of 1258. Mr. Tout has put the facts back into their true perspective; it was neither better nor worse in 1311 than under John or Henry III.[1] The Ordinances of 1311 required the expulsion of the "evil" counsellors and the appointment of fit and proper persons to the great offices and to the Council. But the Ordainers established no plan for choosing them. They did not seem anxious for the creation of a permanent Council such as that of 1264; they rather inclined to summoning the barons frequently, and decided that Parliament should be held once or twice a year. In consequence, after their departure, the Council again became just what it had been before.[2] In 1316, at the parliament of Lincoln, a Council of magnates was appointed with Thomas of Lancaster as its chief. But he had no capacity at all, and this Council quickly vanished. Another check came in 1318: the new Council did not last a month.[3]

The outcry against the foreigners was merely a pretext

The Council in 1311

in 1316

in 1318

In fine, Edward II could always return at once to his Council of *familiares* whom he drew from the Household, as his father had done; he ruined himself, but the question of the Council remained unsettled.

Edward II governs with his "familiares"

But the formation of a class of professional adminis-

1. Tout, *Place Edward II*, p. 22.
2. Baldwin, p. 93.
3. *Const. Hist.*, ii, pp. 355-361; Baldwin, pp. 95 sq.

trators, of which we have already spoken,[1] began to

A reforming party grows up among them

exercise during this reign an influence which Edward I, in spite of all his distrust, had doubtless not forseen. It was their alliance with Pembroke which assured the momentary success of the reforms of 1318, imposed at once upon the king and upon the Lancastrian party. Under the Despensers, two of these men, the chancellor Baldock and the treasurer Stapledon, checked the progress of the Chamber and restored and reformed the Chancery and the Exchequer.[2] Even so, they perished with their masters. But the coalition which overthrew Edward II included several members of this third party, notably Stratford and Ayermin : personal interest had allied them with the friends of the queen and of Mortimer and with the partisans of Henry of Lancaster, but they still remained faithful to their views, as Stratford's attitude proved later on.

Mortimer and Isabella did not profit by the lesson : their first Parliament named fourteen magnates of the

Mortimer and Isabella

Council under the direction of Henry of Lancaster, but they got rid of them and governed with their creatures.[3] A coalition of the third party, the Lancastrians, and Edward III's friends overthrew them in their turn.[4]

For some ten years, Edward III showed his intention

1. Above, p. 390. The constitution of a class of royal functionaries is evident in France also as early as the thirteenth century. It is characterised by a more marked lay element. Edward I still employed many clerks, whereas in France, under Philip the Fair, the personnel becomes entirely lay. The difference arises from the much later beginning of the teaching of Roman Law in England. But, in the fourteenth century, the Household itself became a school of administration for laymen, and in London schools of customary law were created. Then the official body was to some extent laicised. Cf. Tout, "Some Conflicting Tendencies."

2. Above, pp. 367, 400.

3. See *Const. Hist.*, ii, p. 386 ; Baldwin, p. 98.

4. For the history of the Council during the reign of Edward III ; Tout, "Some Conflicting Tendencies."

of securing the co-operation of the magnates,[1] whose leader was still Henry of Lancaster, and of the families which had risen through the discharge of public services, above all, of the Stratfords, who included three bishops in their family. John Stratford, made archbishop of Canterbury in 1333, and his brother Robert, bishop of Chichester in 1337, were chancellors in turn. In reality, the former was also master of the Treasury. But little by little Edward III freed himself and returned to his father's policy. The Wardrobe and the Chamber assumed new developments, and Kilsby, the keeper of the privy seal, became the king's right hand.[2]

The opening of the reign of Edward : the Stratfords

On the eve of embarking for the Netherlands in 1338, Edward III set up a Council, of which the chancellor and the treasurer were the principal members, in order to exercise, in reality, the regency in the name of the little Duke of Cornwall ; it was a council of administrators attached to traditions. He took away with him almost the entire Household, and attached to his person another Council composed of *familiares* and of barons who were a party to his designs against France, and therefore entirely docile. Now by the ordinance of Walton he subordinated the Council of regency to his own ; he even took away the great seal and entrusted it to Kilsby who thus became the real chancellor. The conflict between the two Councils soon began. Under Stratford's direction, the administrators left in England gained the victory : they sent so little money to Edward III that he yielded : he gave the presidency of the Council to the archbishop and left him in control

The Council of 1338

The council in the Netherlands

The ordinance of Walton
The conflict between the two Councils

1. Baldwin, p. 99 : in 1332 Edward declares, in Parliament, that he will have certain named magnates to counsel him.
2. Tout, "Some Conflicting Tendencies ;" this is the man whom Stubbs calls Kildesby, *Const. Hist.*, ii, pp. 406 and 411.

of the government.[1] But the evil was done and the campaign failed. Edward returned in a rage on November 30th, 1340, and set out to avenge himself.

He at once dismissed the great officers and most of the justices. For the first time, the jealousy of the lay functionaries showed itself officially and provided the pretext with which the king coloured his action : it was pointed out that he ought not to appoint to the great offices men who were sheltered from all responsibility by benefit of clergy. For the first time, England had a lay chancellor and a lay treasurer. We know how the magnates refused to let the archbishop be excluded from the Council in Parliament, and obliged the officials, with Kilsby at their head, to leave instead, and demanded that the great officers and the justices should be nominated in their presence; in case of vacancy the king should consult, in Parliament, the lords "whom the king, in his privy Council, should no longer oppose." We also know that when Parliament was dissolved, the king revoked his concessions.[2]

The crisis of 1341

Rivalry of the clerks and the laymen

But in reality, though he resumed the choice of his counsellors, Edward III gave up imitating his father. The privy counsellors were mostly members of the Curia and of the Household. It was enough to add to them a few lords or bishops;[3] but magnates con-

Edward III restores agreement between the "familiares" and the barons

1. For this purpose Edward made a short stay in England in 1340; he made in Parliament other far-reaching concessions in return for a vote of fairly large subsidies, which were, moreover, raised by collectors wholly independent of the administration. See *Const. Hist.*, ii, pp. 408-409 and 597.

2. On the crisis of 1340 to 1341, see *Ibid*, ii, p. 409; Baldwin, p. 99; and chiefly Mr. Tout's article cited above, p. 421, n. 4; this article has entirely reconstructed the story, and brought out the importance of the Ordinance of Walton [See also Tout, *Chapters*, iii, pp. 69-150].

3. Baldwin, pp. 100 sq. He gives examples of lay lords and "retained" bishops, *i.e.*, bishops nominated to be permanent members of the Council. In his opinion, the oath, under Edward III, does not aim at forming an exclusive body or at giving a personal right to sit in the Council, but at imposing on the lords an obligation to attend.

tinued to be summoned to the Council, and those who were willing to attend were well received; some showed themselves more assiduous than others in the "small" or "secret" councils which Edward adopted the practice of calling twice or three times a year. And above all, the great officers were usually bishops who had the confidence of the barons; in 1343, the Chancery was restored to a bishop, and the treasury soon had the same fate.[1] The most influential of these new officers was Edington, treasurer in 1345, bishop of Winchester in 1346, and chancellor from 1356 to 1362; he it was who, in 1356, ended for ever the power of the Chamber, in favour of the Exchequer and the Chancery. It was, therefore, the third party which triumphed. Edington had played, with greater success, the same part as Baldock and Stapledon under Edward II. The *familiares* of the Household continued to serve in the offices, but they showed themselves conservative and prudent; the bishops who directed the great public services behaved in the same manner and in no wise opposed the king. Unity was restored in the administration and the Council, as at the time of Edward I, but this time by a common agreement between the king and the barons.

Edington

This tranquillity was partly due to Edward III's character and to his foreign policy. The barons undeniably yielded to the seduction of the *roi chevalier*, all of whose tastes and faults they shared. The French war attached them to him by interest and by lure of adventure. But it is probable that neither the king's dominance nor warlike passions would have sufficed to make them forget their interests; if they consented so easily to the compromise which ended the crisis of 1341, it was because Edward loaded them with all sorts of individual

Causes of the agreement: Edward's concessions to the baronage

1. See *Const. Hist.*, ii, pp. 432-33.

favours; in particular he did not refuse them immunities or franchises, and he abandoned the local administration to them.[1] Edward III thought only of the present moment : he needed the barons to make war, and he won them no matter how, in the same way as he secured the co-operation of the Commons by yielding gradually to their demands. Moreover he believed that the Crown was sufficiently strengthened against any baronial counter-attack by the gathering of many great fiefs into the

The appanages hands of his children;[2] he did not foresee that the appanages, as soon as he died, would bring about the ruin of the royal power by their rivalry developing into civil war. In this respect, his policy recalls that of the Valois, especially John the Good, whom he resembles in character.

As long as he was successful and active, internal peace continued. But, after 1370, circumstances became threa-

The Council in 1371 and in 1376 tening. In 1371 Parliament again asked for lay officers;[3] in 1376 the Good Parliament demanded that the Council should be "strengthened" by ten or twelve lords "to remain continually" : at least, six or four were always to be present for current business. The king was not asked to give up the right of choosing them, and in consequence he agreed to name nine, who took the oath : but he stipulated that the three great officers (chancellor, treasurer, and keeper of the privy seal) should perform their duties without the Council's advice : Parliament was thus duped. Besides, when it had gone, the king dismissed the nine and took back his ordinary counsellors.[4] But in reality, Edward himself played no great part in the crisis. It was not he who was concerned : in 1371 he

1. See below, p. 433. It is also owing to this complaisance on the king's part that the summoning of the great barons to the Council in Parliament became a hereditary right.
2. See *Const. Hist.*, ii, p. 436
3. See *Const. Hist.* ii, p. 411.
4. See *Ibid*, ii, p. 448 sq. ; Baldwin, pp. 116 sq.

426 STUDIES IN CONSTITUTIONAL HISTORY

does not seem to have looked unfavourably on the fall of his counsellors; in 1376, the question was that of driving John of Gaunt's party from the Council, and in **The aristocratic** 1377, it was John who annulled the work **factions in the** of the Good Parliament.[1] A new period **Council** had begun; the aristocratic factions, putting the king out of play, were now to contend for the power.

This is the spectacle presented by the minority of Richard II : the aristocracy ruled.[2] The Council became, in fact, a council of regency designated **The minority of** "on the advice of the lords in Parliament." **Richard II** In July 1377, twelve counsellors were added to the great officers : for the first time, the whole Council received its commission by letters patent **The Council** and thus took on the character of a definite- **becomes a** ly determined institution. Moreover, a **closed body.** salary was allotted, also for the first time, **Councillors'** **salaries** in order to strengthen the guarantee of attendance which the oath had not been able to secure.[3] But John of Gaunt and his adversaries contended for the pre-eminence : in October 1377, the Lancastrians were driven out. Thus remodelled, the Council sat until

1. The faction of John of Gaunt was able to rely upon the Lollard opposition. Mr. Tout thinks, however, that too much importance has been attached to the so-called anti-clerical movement which came into prominence in 1341 and in 1371 through the demand for lay officers. In 1341 it was a pretext : Kilsby himself was a clerk. In 1371 it was a question of dismissing ministers unsuited to conduct the war on account of their estate. Rivalry certainly existed from the fourteenth century onwards between the clerks and the educated laymen (see above, p. 421, n. 1), but England still continued to be governed mainly by churchmen until the Reformation, and their right to the lower positions was never disputed.

2. Under Richard II the Council begins to be better known. The *Proceedings*, sparse, it is true, published by Nicolas, begin in 1386, and a journal of the Council for the years 1392 and 1393 has been found (Pollard, *Evolution of Parliament*, p. 281). We have seen that at this time the privy seal became the seal of the Council and that one of the clerks of this office became "the clerk of the Council" (above, p. 404, n. 1).

3. *Const. Hist.*, ii, p. 462; Baldwin, p. 120.

October 1378 : it was the first time that a Council designated by the barons sat for a whole year.[1]
Government by the magnates It was then reconstructed, and functioned
under the same conditions until the Parlia-
ment of January 1380.[2] This time demand was made in
Parliament merely for the nomination of the five great
officers.[3] The financial administration of the aristocracy
had been bad and left a deficit of £22,000. The rivalry
was redoubled. For the next seven years the king
became more or less master of the Council once again.[4]

The cause was, in part at least, that there had grown
up around Richard a group of favourites who encouraged him to take advantage of the divisions
The "familiares" of Richard of the aristocracy to give them the Council.
Richard did not attempt to revive the
Wardrobe and the Chamber, but he relied upon the
office of the signet and he filled the Council with his
friends and his officials. The magnates were no longer
summoned to the Council except occasionally.

1. *Const. Hist.*, ii, pp. 463-4 ; Baldwin, p. 122.
2. *Const. Hist.*, ii, pp. 466-467 ; Baldwin, p. 122.
3. *Const. Hist.*, ii, pp, 468-470 ; Baldwin, p. 124.
4. Baldwin, pp. 124 sq. He observes that during this period other
methods were tried for controlling the administration. Already in
1379 a commission had been nominated to examine the Household
accounts. (*Const. Hist.*, ii, p. 469). In 1380 another was appointed ;
petitions were also sent to a commission ; these parliamentary committees were also in fact elected councils, but for a definite purpose.
Judicial channels were also used : Ferrers, a member of the Council,
was accused of treason in the interests of France, on the production
of letters which were discovered to be false. After the revolt of 1381,
Parliament returned to its direct attacks ; it observed that the king
should have with him "the best lords and knights of the realm."
The king conceded the establishment of a council of enquiry to seek
out abuses ; its members are said to have sat several days "in private
council." (See *Const. Hist.*, ii, p. 485). The king announced in
Parliament that Arundel and de la Pole were "nominated and sworn"
of the Council. In 1385 the Commons asked to know the names of
the counsellors : the king replied that he had enough and did not
wish to change any of them. (See *Ibid*, ii, p. 494). In another
petition they demanded those of the lords of the Council, and the
king named only two bishops and two bannerets (though Mr. Baldwin
observes that the roll is damaged). The growing tension has been
noted by Stubbs (*Ibid*, ii, pp. 486- sq.).

After the departure of John of Gaunt, the aristocracy re-formed its ranks under the direction of Thomas of Woodstock and Henry of Derby and the crisis began. After the condemnation of Michael de la Pole, a great and "continual" Council was nominated in Parliament; it was put on oath and given precise instructions; the king was forbidden to add other members to it (1386).[1] Richard and his friends prevented it from functioning. The Merciless Parliament (1388) struck at the evil counsellors.[2] It was decided anew that only those who were nominated in Parliament should be counsellors.[3] But on May 3rd 1389, Richard, having reached his majority, dismissed them.

The dispositions adopted in 1386 had been put into the form of a statute, and Parliament would have had a right to protest against any pretension on the king's part to choose his Council henceforth. But Richard, at first, upset nothing: the duke of Gloucester, eight lords of the earlier councils and four of the *appellants* entered the Council, and everyone seemed satisfied.[4] Thus the

The aristocratic opposition

Richard II's Council after 1389

1. See *Ibid*, ii, pp. 495 sq. ; Baldwin, p. 126. The Council received, in addition to its usual powers, an extraordinary commission to reform the Household and the finances.. Councillors were forbidden to give the king advice contrary to their opinions. Their decisions for reform were to have the validity of a statute. If they did not continue to act, the king's gifts were to be void.

2. See *Const. Hist.*, ii, pp. 500 sq. ; Baldwin, p. 128.

3. The officers and counsellors swore not to permit the repeal or annulment of any of the acts of Parliament. Their names were not announced in Parliament, but the five appellants were predominant. They controlled grants and had £20,000 given to themselves : this anticipates the greed of the counsellors of Gloucester and of Bedford.

4. See *Const. Hist.*, ii, pp. 508-510; Baldwin, pp. 130 sq. At a meeting of the Council in 1390 the councillors refused to approve certain expenditure for fear that Parliament should make them responsible : the example of 1388 had borne fruit. Stubbs has shown that in the Parliament of 1390 the officers and councillors resigned in order that Parliament should be free to put them on trial : the Commons declared that they were guiltless, and they resumed their offices (*Const. Hist.*, ii, p. 508).

crisis which followed appeared obscure to Stubbs.[1] Its cause and its mechanism are now very easily explained. A series of ordinances which do not seem to have been voted by Parliament but which were certainly imposed by it, had strengthened the Council's power to the detriment of the king, especially in the matter of grants : as these were one of the principal attributes of the prerogative, these restrictions seemed intolerable to Richard.[2] Moreover, since Parliament had not exacted the observance of the statute of 1386, he had only to introduce new members into the Council little by little, nearly all of them being officials, to make himself master of it.[3] With the exception of the lords created or promoted by Richard himself, the magnates ceased to appear in the Council, unless by special summons. Finally, since the second year of the reign, the payment of salaries had been discontinued.[4] Richard rewarded the counsellors by individual grants : those of the lower rank received money, some in the form of life annuities ; the lords were provided for by means of confiscated lands.[5]

Richard's absolutism was attributed to a design syste-

1. See *Const. Hist.*, ii, pp. 509 sq.

2. No gift was to be granted by the king except on the advice of the Council and with the individual consent of the dukes of Lancaster, York, and Gloucester as well as that of the Chancellor and two at least of them. This ordinance is mentioned by Stubbs (ii, p. 510, n. 3). In 1392, or a little earlier, other ordinances lay it down that the king shall give full confidence to the Council in all things relating to the government, and will allow them to govern according to their duty, without ordering them, by message or by letter, to do anything contrary. (Baldwin, p. 131).

3. Instead of twelve or fifteen councillors, we now find as many as thirty-four. But we find the king issuing a series of ordinances in a Council of thirteen members of which seven knights were his men. In the journal of 1392-3 for most of the time, only the officers sat, and they in small numbers.

4. An ordinance of 1390 had re-established them, but Richard did not observe it.

5. Mr. Baldwin (pp. 132 sq.) has been able to make our knowledge precise, thanks to the record of 1392, which Stubbs did not know. The most assiduous bishops were those of Winchester, Durham and Chester, the lay lords were fewer. (Cobham, Lovell).

matically planned by him. In reality, his supporters

were bound up in his enterprise to such an extent that one cannot truly say whether he really was the originator of it. These officials were neither foreigners nor base adventurers, but highly capable administrators.[2] The nature of the conflict is quite clear, as in 1341. It was a question of knowing whether the Council, and therefore the government, was to be in the hands of the Household bureaucracy, or whether the administration should receive its leaders at the hands of the assembled barons. It is probable that the latter were preparing to impose once more upon Richard a Council of their own choosing. He forestalled them in 1397, but in 1399 his adversaries got the better of him, and in the accusation justifying his overthrow, they reproached him with having made up his Council of favourites, and with having prevented its annual renewal.[3]

Richard's check was decisive: under his successors, the magnates remained masters of the "ordinary" or "permanent" Council. They had thus

Definite check
to the monarchy
Exclusion of the
"familiares" succeeded in excluding from the ordinary or continual Council, at least in the capacity of deliberating members, the function-

1. Mr. Baldwin has shown that the complaints of Parliament (especially in 1390) concerning ordinances which transgressed the statutes, and conciliar decisions which infringed the common law, were completely ignored by Richard's Council. Thus a statute of 1390 had brought back the staple from Calais to England: an ordinance of Feb. 13th, 1392 authorised merchants to transport wool to Calais, on giving security of paying the dues there instead of in England, so that they were no longer obliged to cross through the ports designated by Parliament; in addition, the ordinance added several ports to those which Parliament had named (p. 137).

2. Baldwin, pp. 139-142, has given the names of many of Richard's servants during this period. We find among them some cadets of good family, Stafford, Scrope, Clifford, Thomas Percy, Guy Mone, king's clerk: some knights, Bussy (the speaker of 1397), Greene, Bagot, Russel; a squire, Lawrence Drew; Master R. Salby, doctor of law, and, among the lords, the dukes of York, Albemarle, Exeter, and Surrey and the earl of Wiltshire.

3. Baldwin, p. 143. This last grievance was not legally justified, as this demand had never been put in statutory form. It would have been more legitimate to have invoked the violation of the statute of 1386.

aries of the Curia and the Household, who had for so long formed the permanent element in the Council. Almost at the same time they succeeded in excluding from it the lesser nobility, the knights or bachelors, whom, it is true, Edward I and Edward III had summoned on rare occasions only, but whom Edward III had often preferred to the clerks. They had provided him with the first lay chancellor and the first lay treasurer, Bourchier and Parning. Towards the end of the reign, many had played an important part in the Council and had been specially aimed at in 1376; Parliament had admitted a few more of them in 1377. They finally disappeared in the fifteenth century.[1]

and of the knights

V.

The magnates worked in the same way to exclude the *curiales* from the Council in Parliament, and finished by transforming it, to the detriment of the lesser barons also, into a closed and hereditary body, which became the House of Lords.

The Council in Parliament

In the course of the conflicts whose history we have summarised, the magnates never failed to use the meeting of Parliament to show their hostility towards the *curiales,* and in this they could count on the support of the Commons, who were little inclined to allow officials the right of taking

Exclusion of the "curiales"

1. See *Const. Hist.* , ii, p. 463 : in July 1377, the Council includes 4 knights and 2 bannerets (Mr. Baldwin says 4 bannerets in all,; p. 120) ; in October, 2 bannerets (*Const. Hist.*, ii, p. 465) or bachelors (Baldwin, p. 122). On the knights of Edward III, see *Ibid*, p. 88 ; the most important is Bartholomew Burghersh : in the 27th year of the reign he is paid for 249 days service at London. Richard Stury and Richard Stafford, brother of the earl, were particularly denounced in 1376. In 1404 there are still some knights and squires in the Council (below, p. 437. n. 2). Under Richard II and the Lancastrians, we find no foreigners, either, in the Council, though Edward III still had several in his ; in 1377 one of them, Guiscard, seigneur d'Angle, (in Poitou) was made Earl of Huntingdon (Baldwin, p. 83).

part in the voting of taxes and the control of their
employment.[1] From Edward III's time the justices,
the Exchequer barons, and the officers of similar rank
were no longer admitted to the Council in Parliament
save for consultation, though in practice they were often
allowed to be treated in the same way as the sworn
counsellors. In the fifteenth century, they themselves
declared that they appeared in Parliament to do justice,
and not to take part in politics. After 1376 it is clear that
they are no more than the assessors of the lords. Their
number continued to diminish. Edward III rarely had
more than ten in session, and sometimes seven, five, or
even fewer. In 1375 only the chancellor, the treasurer,
and the keeper of the privy seal were admitted; under
Richard II the chamberlain and the steward of the
Household were added. However, it was only in 1539
that the right of voting in Parliament was officially withdrawn from them.

Left alone in the Council in Parliament, the magnates
gradually transformed into an herditary right the primitive obligation of appearing there upon
royal summons. There is no doubt at all,
in spite of interminable controversies, that
at the time of Edward I the king kept the
right of calling to the Council, by individual writ, such barons as he wanted. Their number
varied greatly: it continued to decrease
during the fourteenth century: from an
average of 74 under Edward II, it dropped
to 43 under Edward III.[2] It is true that many families

Summons to the Council in Parliament becomes hereditary

The number decreases

1. Pollard, *Evolution of Parliament*, pp. 74-75, 123, 316 sq.; Baldwin,
p. 122: the views of Parliament in this matter are clearly shown by
a petition of the Commons, July 1377, asking for decisions on the
interpretation of the Great Charter to be made "by those who are
ordained to be of the continual Council with the advice of the justices,
serjeants at law, and such other men as they shall think fit to summon."
See *Const. Hist.*, iii, p. 409.
2. .See *Const. Hist.*, ii, p. 425; iii, pp. 16-17, 20, 200, 457.

died out, but we recognise that certain houses ceased to be summoned, and that others were summoned only intermittently. Nevertheless it is certain that, during the fourteenth century, convocation by writ of the great seal tended to become hereditary.[1] The decrease of the number of great families certainly contributed, by restricting the king's choice. But it is also a proof of the power acquired by the great barons, thanks to primo-

Heredity results from the social power of the great barons

geniture and to the statute *Quia emptores*, which prevented the division of their lands ; thanks also to the seizing of waste land and to seignorial abuses which the king could never entirely uproot and which flourished anew in times of trouble. The local administration fell gradually into the hands of the magnates. The sheriffs were chosen from among them, and they dominated the hundred and

Edward III abandons the local administration to them

shire courts, whose decadence was now evident. At first Edward III tried to remedy this by means other than the extraordinary inquests which the twelfth and thirteenth century kings had used. While re-establishing exclusively royal central administration by reviving the Wardrobe and the Chamber, he also attempted to set up a local administration which should directly represent the Crown, so he created the "justices of the peace", nominated by him and appointed to reform the abuses.[2] But after 1341, when he had changed his policy and decided to govern in agreement with the barons, he chose the justices of the peace from among the local magnates themselves, and thus the new institution helped to complete the dispossession of the traditional courts. He even allowed himself to go to the length of appoint--

1. When Richard II created lords of a new sort, the lords by patent (*Ibid*, iii, p. 452), he granted them the right in heredity, but usually limited it to males.
2. See *Const. Hist.*, ii, p. 286 and C. G. Crump and C. Johnson, " The Powers of the Justices of the Peace," *E. H. R.*, 1912.

FF

ing sheriffs for life or at farm, and made liberal concessions of immunities and franchises. It is natural that he
should have regularly summoned to Parliament the great
barons whom he needed, and that he should have
avoided offending them by putting upstarts to sit with
them. Thus the Council in Parliament became a restricted and closed body of hereditary great

The House
of Lords

barons, although the name of "House of
Lords" is not anterior to the Tudors.[1]

The king, however, had not renounced the right of
summoning, at his discretion, any baron whom he desired. But under Edward II men began to

The "Magnum
Concilium"

reserve the name "Council in Parliament"
for the assemblies in which the barons summoned to the Council sat conjointly with the Commons,
and to reserve that of *Magnum Concilium* for the assemblies in which they sat without any summons of the
Commons.[2] Accordingly as heredity tended to triumph
in the Council in Parliament, the difference grew more
marked : but both assemblies were still summoned under

1. On the peerage, see *Const. Hist.*, ii, pp. 185 sq., iii, pp. 452 sq. :
Mr. Pollard has reviewed the present state of the question (*Evolution
of Parliament*, pp. 81 sq.). He is definitely hostile to the idea of an
hereditary peerage in the Middle Ages, and places it in Tudor days.
Mr. L. O. Pike (see French edition of *Const. Hist.*, t. ii, p. 211) defends
the opposite opinion. Mr. J. H. Round (*Peerage and Pedigree*, 2 vols.
1910) also places heredity at a much earlier date than Mr. Pollard
believes. Mr. Pollard gives some figures (p. 99) which incline one
to think that heredity was far from secured in the fourteenth century :
there were summoned to the Parliament of 1295, 41 barons; in 1300,
99; in 1321, 90; in 1322, 42; in 1333-4, 63; in 1346-7, 30; in 1347-8, 56;
now, says Mr. Pollard, extinctions cannot make the number of lords vary
so greatly. See *Const. Hist.* iii, p. 454. To the question of barony by
writ there is naturally attached the question of barony by tenure,
which continues to arouse much controversy (Round, "Barons and
Knights in the Great Charter," in *Commemoration Essays* : on this
work see above, p. 348, n. 1; "Barons and Peers," *E. H. R.*, 1918;
Miss R. R. Reid, "Barony and Thanage," *E. H. R.* 1921).
2. See above, p. 418 n. 1. In the Parliament of 1305, the King
dismisses the Commons and those Barons who are not part of his
Council, and then continues the session with the barons he has retained.
But in 1305 the restricted assembly, according to the roll, keeps the
name *Parliamentum generalissimum*. On the *Magnum Concilium* cf.
Const. Hist., ii, pp. 429-130; iii, pp. 261-2, 102.

the great seal.[1] Now from the 27th or from the 45th year
of Edward III, the writs for the *Magnum*

It is convoked
under the privy
seal *Concilium* were given under the privy seal,
while the Council in Parliament continued
to be summoned under the great seal.

Henceforth, the assemblies called *Magnum Concilium*
are clearly distinct from Parliament. Nothing, on the
contrary, distinguishes them any longer from the assemblies to which Edward I and his successors summoned
their sworn counsellors and a certain number of barons,
convoked under the privy seal : the *Magnum Concilium*
thus becomes the heir of Edward I's enlarged Council.[2]

In consequence, Mr. Baldwin holds that it was merely
an enlarged session of the ordinary Council, and he

Is it distinct
from the
ordinary
Council? refuses to allow it a separate existence as
distinct from the latter :[3] in the fifteenth
century, he says, both were summoned
under the privy seal; it seems certain that
there was never any permanent and sworn *Magnum
Concilium*, constituting an organised body :[4] the epithet
itself was emphatic, for there was such a thing as a
Magnum Concilium in which those present were fewer
than in an ordinary Council.

Nevertheless, we can object that, without the existence of any general rule, the ordinary Council was, in
the fourteenth century, more habitually called "privy",
"secret" or "continual".[5] In Edward II's time,
we hear of "secret councils and *others*". It is also
difficult not to admit some distinction between the ordinary Council and the *Magnum Concilium* when we
see Wykeham, in 1377, styled *"capitalis secreti consilii*

---

1. Both constitute the third sort of *Concilium* described on p.. 418.
2. The second type of *Consilium* (p. 418).
3. Baldwin, pp. 103 sq.
4. Contrary to the opinion of Mr. L. O. Pike.
5. Baldwin, pp. 103-106.
6. *Ibid,* p. 106.

et magni consilii gubernator".[1] From the reign of
Richard II, every time a sworn council of definite composition was nominated, other lords could not be summoned to it without transforming it into a *Magnum
Concilium,* and the distinction became even more clear.

In fine, without forgetting, we repeat, that contemporaries were not concerned with any such classification,
we can say that henceforth there existed
three sorts of Councils : (1) the "ordinary",
"restricted", "privy", "secret", or "continual Council", of which the barons, with the intermittent help of Parliament, succeeded in making a sworn
body of defined composition, in which the Household
functionaries were no longer anything more than their
auxiliaries; (2) the *Magnum Concilium,* an assembly
of barons summoned under the privy seal ; and (3) the
"Council in Parliament",—now separated from the
House of Commons,—from which the technical element,
made up mainly of Household functionaries, was elim-
inated, and which was transformed into an hereditary
House of Lords.[2]

**The three
Councils**

VI.

Under the Lancastrians the ordinary Council never
recovered the form which Edward I and his successors
had striven to give it. Brought to the
throne by the aristocracy, they never attempted, even at the highest point of their
power, in the reign of Henry V, to oust it from the

**The ordinary
Council under
the Lancastrians**

1. Pollard, *Evolution of Parliament,* p. 279. In 1415 Bedford also
stated the opinion that the *Magnum Concilium* differed from the
Council and from Parliament (Baldwin, p. 108).
2. It is necessary to observe that the more preponderating the power
of the lords became, the more did the *Magnum Concilium* tend to be
confounded, as regards composition, with the House of Lords, since
the number of the latter was very small and the king had scarcely
any choice.

government. It is true that bureaucratic influences did not completely vanish. It was not positively decided whether the Council should be nominated by Parliament and whether the Household should be entirely excluded from it. On the other hand, it was always a problem to secure the presence of the magnates nominated at the Council, and the functionaries could take advantage of this. But the characteristic of the Lancastrian period is that it put the government under the strict control of the aristocracy. In Stubbs's eyes, the Council of the Lancastrians is the germ of the parliamentary system. For us it represents essentially the triumph of an oligarchy of barons who, from the time of John Lackland, had been striving to seize control of the State and who had at last succeeded, with the complicity of the princes to whom appanages had been given.[1]

The Lancastrian period marks the triumph of the oligarchy

At first Henry IV could name the Council at will, and his weakness did not immediately appear : the kingdom was very disturbed, and the magnates, busy in conquering or defending their lands, were less than ever disposed to stay in attendance on the king : at first even the offices were entrusted to men of secondary rank. Generally, unless they were summoned to it, the magnates sat in the Council only by accident : their number did not always reach four, and sometimes there was only one.[2] Before

The Council of Henry IV

1. Baldwin, p. 147; *Const. Hist.*, iii, p. 259
2. Baldwin, pp. 147 sq. Parliament asked that gifts should be made "by the advice of the Council." The king evasively replied that he "would be advised by the wise men of his Council in the things touching the state of the king and the realm, saving, however, his liberty." We find in the offices, after Arundel's withdrawal, John Northbury, esquire, treasurer; Erpingham, a knight, chamberlain; master R. Clifford, keeper of the privy seal; and in the Council, John Prophet, dean of Hereford, John Duward, an esquire of Essex, John Cheyne, speaker of the first Parliament of Henry IV, and three citizens of London summoned for financial questions. For the Council of 1399, see Wylie, *Henry IV*, i, 27 ; it comprised 26 persons of whom 24 were present at the session of December 4th, 1399.

the end of the year 1400, it is true, the offices passed
into the hands of more important personages, and the
Council gradually regained its administrative activity.[1]

**Weakness of the
Government**
But it seems to have had no influence on
the policy of Henry IV. Still, it was
reproached with its inability to keep order,
and this was attributed to its bad composition. In 1403
the Percies, revolting, invoked among other motives
the necessity of reforming the government "to set up
wise counsellors to the advantage of the king and the
realm."[2] The Parliament of January 1404 manifested
exactly the same sentiments. We do not know its
demands but the king submitted to it the list of his
counsellors; not one was new, and all were his friends;
but what the "Unlettered Parliament" wanted was
merely that their names should be known in order to
impress upon them the sense of their responsibility.[3]
The failure was complete: the magnates served irregularly; one session was reduced to twelve members
without any lord. Still the Parliament of October 1404
voted subsidies "for the great confidence which it had
in the Council." But, in 1406 the attack was very
sharp, and a return was made to the tradition begun

**The Council
again
nominated in
Parliament**
by the Good Parliament in 1376: the king
had to nominate his Council in Parliament:
the lords were much more numerous in
it; they were pressed to take oath before
the Commons, and in the end they consented, after having extracted a grant of salaries and a promise that
Parliament would vote reasonable subsidies. Parliament
brought about a great number of ordinances regulating
the Council's activities, and drew up a list of 31 articles

1. Baldwin, p. 152.   On the changes brought about in 1402, see Wylie,
Henry IV, i, p. 301.
2. Baldwin, p. 153.
3. *Ibid*, pp. 153-4; Wylie, *Henry IV*, i, pp. 410-1; *Const. Hist.* iii
pp. 45, 255.

to be observed.[1] These measures were not all applied,
but the lords worked with sufficient zeal, and as the
king was ill, almost the whole government was given
up to them; the burden seemed heavy to them, and in
1407 they obtained release from their oath.[2]

A little later, discord broke out in the royal family,
and naturally extended to the magnates and the Council.
The aristocratic factions The Prince of Wales and his friends put
themselves at the head of a faction and
triumphed;[3] the Parliament of 1410 de-
Government of the Prince of Wales manded a new Council; the king named
seven lords, including the prince and the
bishop Beaufort : three officials only were added to them.
This was therefore a very aristocratic and very homogeneous body, drawn from a single party; they accepted
the same obligations as in 1404. They were capable
men : the success was complete; almost all served the
whole year without change, and with regularity. We
cannot doubt that the ascendency of the Prince of Wales
contributed greatly to this result : this year of government already belongs to the reign of Henry V.[4]. In
The King recaptures the Council November 1411 the king dismissed this
Council; Arundel and Thomas of Lancas-
ter, now Duke of Clarence, regained con-
trol.[5] But Henry IV died soon afterwards, and the new
king recalled his associates.

Henry V wished to renew the war in France. The

1. Baldwin, pp. 155-8; Wylie, *Henry IV*, ii, pp. 427-463; *Const. Hist.*,
iii, pp. 55, 255.
2. Baldwin, pp. 159-60; *Const. Hist.*, iii, p. 62
3. *Const. Hist.*, iii, pp. 66-67; Baldwin, p. 161; Wylie, *Henry IV*.
iii, pp, 313-4.
4. *Const. Hist.* iii, pp. 67-68, 255; Wylie, *Henry IV*, iv, p. 50;
Baldwin, pp. 162-3. The Council included no knights or squires, so
that the lesser nobility had disappeared. The prince was excused
the oath. The king was entirely pushed aside : the Council even
disposed of gifts. Also, on March 19, 1411, the prince assembled the
Magnum Concilium to examine the project of an expedition in aid
of the Burgundians; he summoned 32 lords and knights.
5. *Const. Hist.*, iii, pp. 69-70. This change of government altered
the foreign policy : the new government upheld the Armagnacs (1412).

necessity of obtaining the assistance of the magnates was imposed on him, as formerly on Edward III. Besides, his ideas, his preferences, and his connections were all aristocratic; this, above all, was what determined him to govern with the lords. He surrounded himself with a small chosen Council, of a dozen members, great officers, prelates and temporal lords who were at the same time his personal confidants. Except the bishop Beaufort,[1] he did not pay them, but relied on their loyalty. He seldom raised men of mediocre rank, and never admitted subordinate officials to political deliberations. The justices and the clerks were summoned to the Council, but only to expedite administrative and judicial affairs; never indeed was the public peace better respected. The same thing happened when Bedford, in 1415 was guardian of the kingdom and the king had nominated a Council for him. The lords, satisfied with this attitude, occupied in the war and full of deference to a victorious king, returned to their usual indifference to the routine work of the Council: they rarely attended. Often the chancellor, the treasurer, and the keeper of the privy seal found themselves the only ones present, whereas the ordinances required the presence of four or six counsellors. Proclamations and even gifts were successfully issued on the sole authority of the king, the Council's advice not even being mentioned for form's sake, and no one ever protested.[2]

But this system could only be ephemeral. The harmony was entirely personal, and, but for the victorious war which he was conducting abroad, it is even doubtful that Henry V could have prevented a counter-attack from the lords

Henry V governs with the lords

His Council

This accord cannot survive Henry V

1. He continued to receive £200 a year.
2. Baldwin, pp. 164-8; *Const. Hist.*, iii, p. 255. Henry V also summoned the *Magnum Concilium* in 1414 and in 1415 to consult it on the declaration of war against France; *Const. Hist*, iii, pp. 86-87.

who were not his confidants. Now it was his ascendency alone which had been able to give to the aristocratic government the stability and unity which were indispensable to the conservation of the State. After his death, the oligarchy was the sole master of the realm during Henry VI's minority, and, left to itself, it split up once more.

At the Parliament of 1422, it was the lords who nominated Bedford Protector, with Gloucester as deputy in his absence: the Council was not only nominated in Parliament, it was expressly elected thereby, that is to say, by the lords. It was given a sovereign power, namely, the nomination to the offices and benefices, and the control of the Treasury. There were included in it the same men who had served Henry V; but it was much more numerous than in his time; it comprised 21 members in 1422, and 23 when the Commons asked for the communication of the list in 1423. We are certain that they took no oath.[1] Afterwards, a great number of regulating ordinances was promulgated, reproducing and developing the arrangements of 1390 and 1406. In particular, salaries were re-established.

The Council of Regency

The influence of this Council was beyond question. In fact, the whole royal prerogative was in its hands. The Protector could give no letters patent, nor perform any act of government save with its consent. Added to the profits that could be secured by sitting in the Council, this consideration explains why the attendance of the lords was more regular then than at any other period. The Council was irremovable: it filled its own vacancies.[2] In 1430 it was decided in Parliament that no great official or member of the Council should be nominated or dismissed except with the consent of the Council.

Government of the oligarchy

1. Baldwin, pp, 169-172; *Const. Hist* iii, pp. 99 sq.
2. The bishop of Durham alone was nominated in Parliament, in 1426.

The government of the oligarchy had pitiful results. The judicial activity of the ordinary Council withered away; in other words the oligarchy ceased to redress grievances and repress violence; it allowed each of its members to abuse his authority in the counties.[1] The war increased the deficit to a disastrous extent: in 1429 it was £20,000 a year. The councillors nevertheless voted themselves, in addition to their salaries, enormous sums under the name of gifts or of expenses of embassies and missions.[2] As nothing could be obtained without their support, favouritism and corruption displayed themselves shamelessly in the full light of day. They could not fail to quarrel over the sharing of spoils, and thus the Council was quickly rent into factions, of which Gloucester and Beaufort were the principal leaders. Until their deaths in 1447, the Council became the theatre of the quarrel of these two men, and so remained the centre of political history.[3]

Its results

Quarrels of Gloucester and Beaufort in the Council

From 1435, the king's influence began to be felt: the Council warned him "not to give a small office to a great man and a great office to a little man." When Henry VI took over the power in person, on November 12th, 1437, a few modifications accordingly resulted, but Mr. Baldwin has shown that they were not as profound as Stubbs

Henry VI and the Council

1. The same thing happened to the judicial activity of the Council in Parliament, which had played so great a part in the thirteenth century. It was reduced to nothing in the fifteenth: the suits went mainly to Chancery. The jurisdiction of the lords was scarcely exercised save in political matters at times of crisis; the factions used it to wreak vengeance. The civil jurisdiction was reorganised in the sixteenth and seventeenth centuries. See *Const. Hist.*, iii, pp. 494-5.

2. The Dukes had £8,000 a year each, the others £200. Deductions were made in cases of absence, but on the declaration of the councillors themselves. The Exchequer could not bear the expenses: its payments were sometimes twelve years in arrears. Some councillors advanced money or gave guarantees for borrowings. This is chiefly what gave so much influence to Beaufort.

3. Baldwin, pp. 172-183; *Const. Hist.*, iii, pp. 104 sq., 256.

would have us believe in saying that the Council became simply the instrument of the king and of the court. Firstly, the personnel did not change : Henry confirmed the councillors in their office and for six years only the normally necessary replacements were effected. Further, the Council retained its attributes, except the nomination to offices and the donations : the king, being of age, resumed the most important of the royal prerogatives.[1] But this was really a matter of form, for the councillors did not hesitate to interfere with the king, both individually and collectively, in order to impose their will on him, especially as salaries ceased to be regular and fell within the king's discretion.[2] In fact, it was the same oligarchical " junto " which remained in power. The principal difference was that the unfortunate Henry VI, incapable of resisting solicitation, took over the responsibility for the waste and disorder.[3]

The situation changed with the rise of de la Pole, earl of Suffolk. Unlike Gloucester and Beaufort, he rarely appeared at the Council : he made his way through the support of the king and queen, independently of his colleagues. The deaths of Beaufort and Gloucester made him master of the State. Against this all-powerful minister, this upstart of merchant origin, the aristocracy banded themselves together. The magnates almost entirely ceased coming to the Council; no more salaries were paid : in case of need, the government was obliged to have recourse to summoning a *Magnum Concilium*. The ordinary Council now performed unimportant duties only, and the administration became extremely weak. When Cromwell led the attack which overthrew Suffolk,

Suffolk and the Council

1. *Ibid*, iii, p. 256.
2. As early as 1433, the bishops had renounced them and only received them under exceptional circumstances, as did the great officers, except the treasurer and the chancellor. The other councillors received rewards at the king's pleasure, usually for life.
3. Baldwin, pp. 184 sq.

the latter was charged with having been "sole counsellor", and on the occasion of the revolt of 1450, Cade
invoked as his motive the dismissal of the lords and the
appointment of men of low origin to the Council (1450).[1]

The Duke of York made the king re-establish the old
oligarchical Council.[2] Then, under the Duke of Somerset,

The Duke of York and Somerset

the Council fell back to impotence. In 1453
it could not stop the private war between
the Percies and the Nevilles; hundreds of
pardons granted by the Council prove that justice was
suspended and that its authority was defied with im-
punity. After the fall of Guienne, the Yorkists had a
Magnum Concilium of twenty-five members summoned.
They called in Duke Richard : he observed that not as
many lords had been summoned as was possible, and
demanded a new meeting. It was thus that he secured
Somerset's overthrow and his own preponderance. The
Magnum Concilium requested him to summon a Parliament, and as the king had become mad, the Duke was
made chief of the King's Council and Protector. A
Council was nominated, but it was not proclaimed in
Parliament.[3] The Council and its chief again received
the sovereign powers, including that of making grants.
For a year, the government exercised its power in the
same forms as before 1437 ; but it was now in the hands
of a party. Henceforward it was always so. When the
king recovered, a *Magnum Concilium* set Somerset at
liberty (4th March, 1455) and he returned to power, with
a Council whose composition we do not know, but from
which York was excluded. The battle of St. Albans
restored the preponderance to the latter and he declared
that he would act in agreement with the lords : the

1. Baldwin, pp. 189-193; *Const. Hist.*,iii,.pp. 136-138, 147, 151-152, 156.
2. He made no reform in the Council. The act of repeal of 1451
annulled the king's gifts if not signed by the chancellor, the treasurer,
the keeper of the privy seal, and six lords (Baldwin, p. 194).
3. *Ibid*, pp. 195 sq. The list of councillors is given on p. 198; See
Const. Hist., iii, pp. 171-2.

Parliament of June 1455, gave back to the Council the nomination to offices and benefices. The duke was dismissed on February 26th, 1456, and this time the Council ceased to play any part : the conflict was removed to the battlefields. Doubtless, the Council was never so powerless. The lords scarcely came to the Council any more, and even summonses could not bring them. They were therefore replaced by men of lower rank. In 1455 we find an ordinary chancery clerk at the Council. The sessions lost all regularity ; pleaders were dismissed without any decision ; sentences, moreover, remained without effect.[1]

Unimportance of the Council during the civil war

Mystery hangs over the Council during the reign of Edward IV. It is probable that it was not nominated and that the king limited himself to designating individually the persons with whom he wished to work. The Council again became a body of officials to whom the king added the lords who had his confidence. In general, nominations and donations are the acts of the king alone : there are very few *per concilium*. The weakness of the Council remained obvious, as far as justice and the maintainance of peace were concerned. And the same was true under Richard III.[2]

The Council of Edward IV

To sum up, the reign of Henry IV was a period of groping during which the magnates progressively re-established the system for which they had fought under Richard II ; then Henry V, succeeded in reconciling the preponderance of the oligarchy with the needs of the State because, thanks to his personal ascendency, he could impose discipline on it ; finally the lords, some sixty great families, seized control of the government : some made up the Council ; the

Summary

1. Baldwin, pp. 199 sq.; *Const. Hist.*, iii, pp. 174 sq., 178 sq., 256.
2. Baldwin, pp. 419; *Const Hist.*, iii, p. 257.

others were joined to that body in the *Magnum Concilium* which naturally included, with a few exceptions, all those who were usually summoned to Parliament, so that, on the eve of the War of the Roses, it was scarcely more than an extra-parliamentary session of the House of Lords; Parliament, completely dominated by them, found itself an accomplice, and moreover, without any authority. The oligarchy exploited the State for its own profit and quite naturally split up, the appanaged houses taking the direction of the factions whose support could bring them the supreme power. The most ambitious of the lords or the upstarts sought in their turn to win the king's favour and to revive, under this protection, the ancient Council of the *familiares* : but they came to grief against the social and military power of the oligarchy. It was necessary that the anarchy which resulted should exhaust itself by the progressive destruction of those who were its artisans. Then Henry VII organised the privy Council, doubtless such a body as Edward I would have wished to possess. The *Magnum Concilium* disappeared, and, heredity having definitely prevailed in the House of Lords, that body became the last refuge of the aristocracy.

THE ORIGINS OF THE HOUSE OF COMMONS.

I.

The appearance of the knights summoned from the shires, and of the burgesses summoned from the good towns, the boroughs, before the *Consilium* of the king, held in Parliament, was the origin of the House of Commons.[1] Before enquiring why they were summoned

---

1. What does the word *commons* mean in the expression *House of Commons*? In the ordinary language of to-day, *commons* means "lower people." For a Frenchman, the term *communes*, applied to the history of the Middle Ages, simply evokes the idea of towns which have obtained a charter perpetuating their political independence. *House of Commons* admits of neither of these two meanings. Historians who have some experience of teaching and of the errors made by students and even by some teachers, will understand why we insist on this, since the present publication was undertaken for students, not for specialists. The term presents its difficulties; it is one of the innumerable vague words of the Middle Ages. M. Pasquet, in his excellent *Essay on the Origin of the House of Commons*, declares on the first page of his book that *commons* meant the "representatives of the communities of the shires and the communities of the towns," that is, of the freeholders of the country and of the burgesses of the towns, and he does not think it necessary to justify a definition which, to him, seems assured. In fact he provides (p. 35, 36, 55, 80, 86, 92, 93, 103, 109, 137, 140, 148, 152 etc.) many examples proving that the knights represent the *communitas tocius comitatus* and the burgesses represent the community of a town. But it is by no means true that *commun, communa* and *communitas*, if we confine ourselves to the texts of constitutional and parlimentary history cited in M. Pasquet's book and elsewhere, have this meaning exclusively, and that is why we must put students on guard against the disappointments and misunderstandings which these contradictory meanings may provoke. Medieval men were not troubled by confusion of terms. *Communitas regni, communauté de la terre*, ought always to mean the whole nation (as in the texts of 1258 and 1270 cited by Pasquet, pp. 37-38, and p. 73). Now in the Great Charter (art. 61) *communa tocius terre* certainly has not this wider meaning, and beyond doubt, as Mr. McKechnie suggests, it refers to the barons only. In the statute of 1275, *communauté de la terre* means the knights and burgesses summoned to Parliament (see Pasquet, p. 75 et sq). In the statute of 1322, which will be discussed at the end of this study, *communauté du royaume* seems also to have this sense. Similarly, *communitas, commune*, by itself signifies sometimes the nation, (text of 1301: Pasquet, p. 113), sometimes the baronage (constitution of 1258, cited and discussed *ibid* p. 50), sometimes the deputies of the towns (text of March 1322: *ibid*, p. 227, n. 1), *and sometimes the whole body of elected deputies, as opposed to the "great men" summoned personally* (texts of 1339 and 1341: *ibid*, p. 227, n. 2). Although *commune*, and *communauté*

there, it is necessary to obtain a precise idea of the nature of this enlarged *Curia,* for it has given rise to much discussion.

It does not seem that there is anything to amend in what Stubbs has said of the *Consilium* for the Norman period.[1] As we have already recalled, the king governed by means of a permanent *Curia,* at the head of which were placed the great officers, bishops or barons, chosen by him; he held counsel with those of these *familiares* whom it suited him to consult, without the *Consilium Regis* being a particular institution : in the eleventh century it is styled indifferently *Consilium* or *Curia regis.* However, the Normon king could not, any more than the Anglo-Saxon king, dispense with the support of the great landed proprietors; he therefore summoned them to his presence, whether on the occasion of the great religious festivals, or as circumstances required; the ordinary *Consilium,* the small *Curia,* was then enlarged in a highly variable degree, though its nature was not changed. In Anglo-Saxon eyes, it cannot have been distinct from the witenagemot. Nevertheless, the system of tenure introduced by the Norman conquest had modi-

The "consilium" of the Norman kings

still have very divergent meanings in the fourteenth century (see the texts cited *ibid,* p. 227, n. 1), *it is the last meaning which, in the reign of Edward III, is clearly tending to prevail.* The expression *House of Commons* does not exist yet, but in the text of 1341 taken by M. Pasquet from the *Rot. Parl.,* ii, p. 127, the distinction is clearly made between the *grands* and the *commune,* namely *les chivalers des counteez,, citeyns, et burgeys, i.e.* the elected representatives of the communities of counties, episcopal towns (*civitates*) and boroughs. So we return to M. Pasquet's definition : but it was useful to justify it. It is understood that, outside texts of parliament history, *communa* and *communitas* can have other meanings, though they all share the idea of collectivity with common interests. For example, in 1275, Edward I, wishing to establish a tax, consults the *communes de marchanz de tot Engleterre* (cited by Pasquet, p. 80). In municipal institutions, we find the *commune* in the French sense of the word (See French edition of *Const. Hist.,* t. i, p. 96); as to the word *communitates,* in urban charters, its meaning is obscure and debatable; it often seems to mean the ancient free urban community prior to the oligarchical municipal government . (Note by M. Petit Dutaillis).

1. See *Const. Hist.* i, p. 385 sq.

fied the position of the great proprietors, direct vassals

Influence of the feudal system of tenure of the king, with respect to the *Curia.* They now owed service of Court, in the same way as service of the host. But if they were thus qualified, by their tenure, to become part of the *Curia,* if it was enough to be "tenant-in-chief" to be summoned to the *Consilium,* this quality was not

Service of court does not imply the right to be summoned necessary : the king retained the power to summon other persons to it also.[1] In this sense, the *Consilium* or *Curia* was not an exclusively feudal assembly.[2] It is, in fact, because the king's choice was not limited that he was later able to summon to his court the knights, who were not all his direct vassals, and the burgesses, who were no part of the feudal hierarchy at all.

Nevertheless Stubbs thought that at the time of Henry II, all the tenants-in-chief could be present, not indeed

Stubbs' views on the "Commune Concilium" at the ordinary *Consilium,* but at the enlarged *Curia* which he calls the *Commune Concilium.*[3] He probably admitted that, little by little, the obligation of service of court had finally, in the minds of the barons and in custom, entailed as counterpart the right to fulfil that service. Though his exposition is very circumspect, it seems

1. The English *Curia* thus had the same character as the French *Curia,* contrary to Stubbs' opinion. (See *Const. Hist.* ii, p. 269), Cf. Luchaire, *Inst. mon.,* i, 253 sq.

2. This is a feature which Messrs. Adams and Pollard seem to leave in the dark, so strongly do they insist on the feudal character of medieval England. At the time of the Great Charter, says Mr. Adams (p. 149), England is "the most perfectly logical feudal kingdom to be found in Christendom." For Mr. Pollard "This English national constitution is a direct growth of the earlier feudal constitution of the State" (p. 6) ; in consequence, he regards it as derived from the Conquest and the Norman organisation ; every link between Anglo-Saxon and Norman England seems broken ; the king seems never to have been more than the head of the feudal hierarchy ; he had no longer any subjects, but only vassals. But it seems very difficult to ascribe the liberty of the king's choice exclusively to the feudal character of royalty. The idea of sovereignty never completely vanished.

3. See *Const. Hist.,* i, pp. 608 sq.

capable of being summarised thus: the king had kept the faculty of bringing his *familiares* into the enlarged *Curia*, but he was obliged to summon to it all the tenants-in-chief. It is against this interpretation that scholars of to-day have vigorously protested.

To appear in the *Curia* was not, they say, a right for the vassals, but an obligation, instituted in the sovereign's interest to permit him to secure their collaboration; to them it appeared burdensome and annoying, even to the greatest, unless ambition or interest brought them into the royal circle. In the thirteenth and fourteenth centuries, every time the magnates had imposed on the king an ordinary council of their own making, the utmost difficulty was experienced in obtaining a satisfactory attendance from its members. On the other hand, in the ordinary run of things, it was enough for the king to consult those vassals whose adherence would bring with it that of the rest. Without any doubt, he summoned them personally, though no writ of this kind earlier than 1205 has survived;[1] and for most of the time, it is even probable that he contented himself with associating with his *familiares* the barons who, for some reason or another, were temporarily staying at the court. In the twelfth century as in the eleventh, there was, therefore, no fundamental difference between the ordinary *Consilium*, or *Curia* of the *familiares*, and the great *Curia* which gathered together a more or less considerable number of tenants-in-chief: both are the *Consilium regis*,[2] and when the word *Parliamentum* appears in the

Objections of modern scholars

1. *Ibid.*, i, p. 609
2. See especially Baldwin, pp. 10, 11; Adams, p. 345. "All the functions of the state were exercised by a single institution, and this institution existed under two forms, which were distinguished from each other only by size and manner of meeting." Pollard, *Evolution of Parliament* p. 24, cites the famous text from *Fleta*, ii, 2. "*Habet enim rex curiam suam in consilio suo in parliamentis suis.*" Compare the formulas *Scaccarium in parliamento regis; placita coram rege in parliamento; placita coram consilio in parliamento.*

thirteenth century, it is applied to both.[1] The king's right to consult whomsoever he will remains intact, and for contemporaries these assemblies differ, at the most, in the numbers present. Thus the *Commune Consilium*, or national assembly, of Stubbs, imagined as a particular institution, does not exist. It is even contested that, in the texts, the expression *Commune Consilium* designates an assembly, the word *concilium* requiring to be translated by "counsel," and not by "council."[2] As for supposing, with Stubbs, that in its most extended, though almost theoretical form, this so-called *Commune Concilium* could have included all the landed proprietors of the realm,[3] it is objected that the feudal conception of service of court was opposed to it; even supposing that the king had kept the right to summon them, the

There was no "Commune Concilium"

---

1. On the use of the word *parliamentum* see *Const. Hist.*, i, pp. 514, note 611, and Maitland, pp. lxvii, lxxxi sq.; the Parliament is a session, a full meeting of the Council; Edward I still does not distinguish several Councils; in his time the word does not yet apply specially to the assembly in which the Commons appear, or assembly of three estates; the *rotulus parliamenti* of 1305 is a roll of the Council. See also Pollard, *Evolution of Parliament*, pp. 32, 46 sq.

2. Pollard, *Evolution of Parliament*, pp. 28-37 : article 12 of the Great Charter says that scutage and aid cannot be raised *nisi per commune consilium regni nostri;* the text should be interpreted in the light of two others drawn from article 14 : *Et ad habendum commune consilium regni . . .; procedat secundum consilium eorum qui presentes fuerint.* According to Mr. Pollard it is not a question of holding a common council, but of obtaining the common *counsel* or consent. The clerks wrote in Latin, but they thought in French; whether they wrote *concilium* or *consilium*, in both cases it is the word *conseil (counsel)* and not the word *assemblée (council)* that they had in mind. Mr. Pollard makes a similar observation regarding the expression *plenum parlia mentum*; it may mean a parliament of which all the component parts are assembled, but also a very much reduced *parliamentum* deliberating in public : in French the clergy thought *en plein parlement (i.e., in open debate)* an idea analogous to that expressed in the words *en plein air* (in open air), (*E. H. R.* .1915). W. A. Morris, moreover, thinks that in the expression *plenus cimitatus*, the adjective indicates publicity rather than the number present. (*Ibid.*, 1924). The interpretation is certainly ingenious. We can compare with the articles of the Great Charter, the text given by Maitland (no. 20, p. 19) : "*cum, de communi consilio ordinatum sit quod . . . .*" Mr. Polladr's explanation would allow its reconciliation with Maitland's statement that, under Edward I, we cannot distinguish several Councils (*Ibid.*, p. xvii, note.).

3. See *Const. Hist.*, i, p. 606.

assembling of so great a mass of men was evidently impossible.

Nor is there any difference in so far as concerns competence. The *Curia* of *familiares* and the enlarged *Curia* both deal with all governmental matters.

The enlarged "Curia" had no special attributes Messrs. MacIlwain and Pollard have brought into full light the essentially judicial character of the "terminal courts,"[1] but they nevertheless treated of questions of general policy and finance, just as the small Curia. On the other hand, both assemblies seem purely consultative. Stubbs himself agrees that there is no trace of resistance on the part of the barons in matters of taxation before the end of Richard I's reign,[2] and M. Pasquet rightly observes that in the eleventh and twelfth centuries "the ecclesiastical order alone was at that time organised and able to offer some resistance to the arbitrary will of the king."[3]

This interpretation does not seem to express the entire reality. There is no doubt that the the king of England

These views perhaps too absolute believed himself free to summon to his *Curia* such barons as he pleased, but the first question is to learn whether it was not in his interest to summon them all to it. However powerful, the Norman or Angevin king could not treat the advice of his vassals as negligible, and if the latter officially kept silence in the courts of the eleventh and twelfth centuries, it is hard to believe that this tacit approval did not result, on the essential matters at least, from a preliminary understanding. When we attempt to imagine what went on in these meetings, we must go

1. The four judicial terms of the year were Hilary (14th Jan.), Easter, Trinity, and Michaelmas (Sept. 29).
2. See *Ibid.*, i, p. 618.
3. Pasquet pp. 5–6 (This opinion must admit some limitations. In the conflict between William Rufus and St. Anselm, which by a strange omission, Stubbs has not described and to which M. Pasquet makes allusion, the archbishop of Canterbury was upheld, not by the bishops, but by the barons). (Note by M. Petit-Dutaillis).

back to the Carolingian assemblies described by Hincmar.[1] We must not forget that in feudal times absentees

The King had reason to summon the tenants-in-chief. Article 14 of the Great Charter

often held themselves free to refuse their
concurrence in the measures adopted; in
times of crisis, above all, it was therefore
of paramount importance to summon all
the tenants-in-chief who could not legally
decline the summons. Some think that the
famous article 14 of the Great Charter, which regulates
these general assemblies, was set down in the exculsive
interest of the king himself.[2] We are nevertheless inclined to think that it must have had antecedents. It is
true that there remains no writ of any such convocation,
and it is likely that no one attempted to secure its exact
fulfilment. But its very possibility was sufficient to make
the great *Curia* tend to be distinguished from the lesser
one.

Moreover, the opinion of the king and the lawyers
ought not to be the only thing to receive our attention :

The opinion of the barons

that of the barons has also its value. It
cannot be denied that in the thirteenth
century they regarded the tenant-in-chief
as the natural counsellor of the king. They had therefore come to regard service of court as a right. Was
this a new idea? It is hard to believe so, for there was
at least one case in which all the tenants-in-chief had to
be summoned to the *Curia,* according to feudal custom.

The question of the general convocations is, in fact,
closely bound up with that of the competence of the great

The voting of an aid requires their presence

Curia, as articles 12 and 14 of the Great
Charter precisely show. When the king
wished to raise an aid, apart from the customary cases, we cannot contest that he had to ask for

1. Hincmar's text is reproduced in the French edition of the *Const.
Hist.* t. i, p. 158, n. 1, according to Pron's edition. See Viollet's
commentary, *Hist. des inst. pol. et adm.*, i, pp. 211 sq.
2. M. Petit-Dutallis in his additional note on the Great Charter :
Studies and Notes Supplementary; i, pp. 142-143.

the consent of his vassals; in this sense, the obligation
to appear became a right for the tenants-in-chief, because
it was impossible to dispense with them. Moreover the
Curia of the *familiares* could not make a binding decision in such a case, and, in consequence, this was a
feature which distinguished it from the enlarged *Curia.*

At the beginning this right was not greatly appreciated It is true that at the beginning this distinction had no great importance. The
barons doubtless admitted that from time
to time, when circumstances urgently demanded it, they could not escape granting some subsidy
to the king, especially as long as his power remained
intact. As long as aids were rare and were assessed at
a modest rate, it mattered little to them that they should
be regularly granted, and, if they were summoned by
a general writ, many of them had no desire to incur the
expense and trouble which service of court entailed, in
order to go and consent to what they would not have
dared to refuse. They had no political spirit, and remained strangers to juridical theory. Nevertheless, it
does not follow that the right of granting the extra-
feudal aid, and the faculty of coming to the *Curia*, which
was, in this case, the counter-part of service of court,
were without importance; it all depended on the point
at issue.[1] So long as the king respected

It becomes important from the end of the twelfth century the jurisdiction of the barons over their
men and his exactions remained customary,
service of court remained an obligation;
but, when the judicial reforms of Henry II

1. Pasquet, pp, 9 sq. admits the distinction, but not before the
reign of Henry III, when it "begins" to appear. It seems difficult,
however, to admit that article 12 of the Charter is an innovation in
law, even though M. Pasquet's observations on the practical unimportance of the voting of the aid at this time are full of historical sense.
Mr. Tait, in his review of Mr. Pollard's book, even though he has
provided yet another argument (*E. H. R.*, 1912, pp. 720-728) for dis-
allowing the existence of a *commune concilium*, also thinks that the
importance of consent to the aid has been too much reduced (*E. H. R.*,
1921, p. 254).

undermined seignorial authority, and when scutage tended to become an aid without consent, the barons regarded it in a different light and it appeared to them as a right. It is regarded as settled that Henry III never raised an aid without their consent.

The enlarged *Curia,* therefore, was not a national assembly, as Stubbs would have it; it was, in reality, only very slowly distinguished from the ordinary *Curia.* Still, it seems that Stubbs was right in establishing a distinction in principle between them. This is no unimportant point, if we ask ourselves in what atmosphere the House of Commons can have begun to develop. When the knights appeared in the *Curia* in the capacity of representatives, not all were tenants-in-chief, but several of them were; it will doubtless be admitted that in this case, they would not be inclined to renounce, as representatives, the prerogatives which they could have exercised as tenants-in-chief; the distinctions of the lawyers counted for nothing in this. And this confusion implied a state of mind which was bound to be communicated to the whole body of knights acting collectively as one of the Estates of the realm.

The enlarged "Curia" can be distinguished from the ordinary "Curia"

Importance of this point in the history of the House of Commons

We can now seek the motives which determined the king, and the barons themselves, to bring into the *Curia* knights without distinction of tenure, and burgesses, as representatives of all the freemen of the kingdom.

II.

The scholars whose works we have cited have shown that the English kings acquired the habit of summoning before the Council, in their Court in Parliament, knights and burgesses in order to facilitate the government of the country for judicial, administrative, and financial purposes. Thus a new element was added

Causes of the calling of the knights and burgesses to Parliament

to the *Curia*. These persons did not appear in their own personal title, and as a result, the representative principle made progress hand in hand with the future House of Commons.

The king, holding his Court, has always been the supreme recourse of the freeman, but we must attribute the importance of the judicial function of Parliament to the institution of formulary procedure by Henry II. Henceforward, by obtaining a writ, every freeman was able to escape from the customary procedure, the judicial duel, and the ordeal, and especially to assure himself of the royal protection against seignorial abuses. Stubbs has shown not only the pecuniary interest which prompted Henry I, for the writs were bought in chancery, but also the anti-feudal and centralising character of his measures.[1] In the thirteenth century, the royal jurisdiction was ceaselessly undermining manorial jurisdiction in this way : under Henry III the number of types of writs rose from 60 to 450. In principle it was for the itinerant justices to act upon the writs; but appeal could be made to the king, and further, in doubtful cases, the justices referred the matter to him; the permanent *Curia* and its different sections, when it had split up, sent difficult cases, in the same way, to the reinforced *Curia,* so that Parliament became a court of equity. Besides, the visits of the justices were irregular, and many cases came at first instance before the Courts

I. The judicial functions of the Parliament

1. See *Const. Hist.* i, ch. xii and xiii; ii, pp. 267-268. (The date of the Great Assize is uncertain, as Stubbs notes; but Mr. Round has reduced the field to a choice among these three dates : April 1170, October 1175, and April 1179; *E. H. R.* 1916).On the judicial reforms of Henry II and their development under his successors, besides F. Pollock and F. W. Maitland, *The History of English Law before the time of Edward I,* often cited in the notes of these chapters, and the treatise of Mr. W. S. Holdsworth, *A History of English Law* (2nd edn. : Vols. i, ii, and iii deal with the period before 1485) ; see M. Jouon des Longrais' work *La conception anglaise de la saisine du XIIe au XIVe siècle,* (Paris, Jouve, 1924, Thèse de droit) especially pp. 45 sq.

or before the Parliament, at least until the institution
of commissions of *Nisi prius* by Edward I; at this time
the knights and burgesses had long been accustomed to
appear before the Council in Parliament, in order to
represent their communities there, whether as procura-
curators or as members of juries.[1]

The counties and the boroughs wishing to complain
of a lord, or of some agent of the king, or of some other
Knights and community, pleaded in Parliament, like
burgesses as individuals, deputing knights or burgesses
procurators for the purpose. Thus the judicial reforms
indirectly called before the Council attorneys of the
counties and the boroughs.[2]

These procurators acted for local purposes, we may
say, and their missions did not affect public order. But
As jurymen Henry II's reforms have another feature,
the systematic employment of the jury.
Now, as soon as cases came before the Council, the
juries of knights, appointed in conformity with the
assizes, were summoned there; in particular, in cases of
an appeal, chosen knights were cited to give an account
of the decision returned in the first instance: they "defended" the county, which, if the sentence were altered,
might be condemned to pay a fine. Thus, by the development of this institution, the representation of the
county in Parliament was incorporated in the administration of the kingdom.[3]

The extraordinary importance of judicial affairs in the
activities of Parliament appears fully in the roll of 1305,

1. Pasquet, pp. 26-27. For the commissions of *Nisi prius*, see *Const.
Hist.*, ii, p. 284.

2. Maitland, p. 353, notes approximately, in 1305, 8 petitions of
communities of shires, 29 of communities of boroughs, 2 of Scottish
boroughs, 3 of other local communities, 4 of merchant-communities;
63 come from religious communities and 16 from the Universities. See
also p. lxxiii sq.; the knight of the shire or the burgess moves the
petitions of his county or his town.

3. Pasquet, pp. 23 sq.

Importance of judicial affairs in Parliament published by Maitland, and has been well exposed in the works of Messrs. MacIlwain and Pollard. The session of Parliament is preceded by a proclamation of the king, who calls upon all his subjects to present their petitions : the work begins with the nomination of the "triers" and the "receivers" charged to examine them, and to send some to the Courts which can take cognisance of them, and others to Parliament. In 1290 the Michaelmas Parliament received 250, even though one Parliament had been held in January and another in April; in 1305, one of the two Parliaments of that year had 500 lodged. A great number of Parliaments seem to have been entirely occupied in examining petitions, and thus we see why, under Edward III, for example, the Commons demanded more frequent Parliaments, and why the kings from time to time took measures to hasten the presenting and classifying of petitions, in order that the assembly might find time to deal with other matters.[1]

These facts have induced Messrs. MacIlwain and Pollard to regard Parliament as being essentially a court

1. Maitland, pp. lxviii sq. ; MacIlwain, p. 51; Pollard, *Evolution of Parliament*, pp. 34 sq. Generally parliament is a court of first instance : *high court*, a name given to it in the XVIth century, signifies "open and common to all," *le plus frank leu d'Engleterre;* perhaps it was also less costly : writs had to be paid for, but not, apparently, the expenses of a suit in Parliament. Nevertheless, Parliament was also a court of appeal (Pollard, *Evolution of Parliament*, p. 40). Regarding measures taken in the time of Edward I, for expediting the petitions, see *Const. Hist.*, ii, p. 276 and Pasquet, p. 197. In the fourteenth century misgivings were caused by the election, as representatives, of the *mainteneurs* of cases, and of lawyers. (See *Ibid.*, iii, p. 413). In 1404 Henry IV excluded the lawyers from parliament because they gave more time to their clients' suits than to public business (*Ibid.*, iii, p. 47). Under Henry VII the session of Parliament was once more largely devoted to judicial affairs : in 1485 the *triers* and *receivers* were named *ut justitia conqueri volentibus possit celerius adhiberi* (Pollard, *Evolution of Parliament*, p. 61). In 1311 the Ordainers laid it down that Parliament should meet at least once a year in order that lawsuits should not be delayed. The Commons again made similar demands under Edward III; if it had been a question of taxation, they would have been less eager (*ibid.*, pp. 34, 42-3).

The high court of Parliament of justice, "the high court of parliament," to follow the expression of Tudor days. Mr. Pollard distinguishes, in the thirteenth century, two sorts of Parliament : the Terminal Parliaments, in which Stubbs recognised judicial sessions of the king's Council,[1] and the Parliaments to which the knights of the shire and the burgesses were summoned at the same time as the barons ; the chief innovation of Edward I would therefore lie in making the meetings of both coincide : it was natural that the knights and burgesses who were present at the first, to bring the petitions of their communities, should also be instructed to represent them, at the king's order, to hear what was to be asked of them in the matter of taxation or administration. In this sense the Parliament of November 27th, 1295 would not be the real model Parliament, for it does not seem possible that the "Terminal Parliament" of Michaelmas should have lasted to that date. The **The Parliament of 1298** model Parliament would become that of May 25th, 1298, for the Exchequer and the Common Pleas were summoned for the 2nd and 9th of June, and, like it, to York ; from that moment the judicial sessions and the sessions of general interest would have coincided.[2] But Mr. Tait has rightly objected that the "terminal sessions" were not entirely devoted to the despatching of judicial business. Mr. Pollard himself recognises that it was in one of these sessions that the statute *Quia emptores* was promulgated, and the *aide pur fille marier* granted, in 1290.[3]

It is none the less clear that the judicial function of Parliament contributed greatly to accustoming the knights and burgesses to attendance there, **Petitions in Parliament** and that it continued to attract them long after they had begun to be summoned

1. See *Ibid.* ii, p. 275 ; iii, pp. 309 sq.
2. Pollard, *Evolution of Parliament*, pp. 50 sq.
3. *Ibid.*

regularly to it for quite different reasons. They would have come much less willingly if it had only been a question of voting taxes, and it is in its judicial form that Parliament was able to contribute to the development of centralisation and unity in England on the one hand, and, on the other, to preparing the members of the future Commons for collective action.[1] For long years, it is principally as petitioners that they appear in Parliament.[2] Even in 1305, it does not seem that any of their number could be found among the "triers" and the "receivers," though these persons may nevertheless have consulted them on occasions. Nor did they take any part in the *placita*, which, under Edward I, sometimes took place after their departure. The greater number of the complaints were of an individual nature, could not give rise to a debate in an assembly, were submitted to the king's Council only to obtain from it a solution of a difficulty of juridical nature, and called for no other settlement beyond the issue of a writ. But

Collective petitions

there were also others which, emanating from communities, bore witness to abuses of a general nature, which could be brought to notice by a collective complaint and which it could be proposed to redress by a legislative measure of common interest. It is through this channel that the Estates of the realm came to present to the king, at the same time as the grievance, a bill which he had only to sanction to make a statute of it. In 1305 five petitions of the Estates already figure in the list drawn up by Maitland : the Commons associate themselves with one and present another.[3] Messrs. Baldwin, MacIlwain

1. "In this sense the origin of parliaments must be traced back to Henry II." (Pollard, *Evolution of Parliament* p. 36).
2. Pasquet, pp. 201 sq. This explains why the Commons never claimed the judicial power in Parliament, a fact which Stubbs thought strange. (*Const. Hist.*, ii, pp. 261, 641).
3. Maitland, pp. 353 sq. : the barons presented three petitions to obtain discharge of scutage and to be authorised to raise scutage and tallage from their vassals : No. 486, p. 313-4, is directed against the

and Pollard rightly remark that in the Middle Ages justice was not separated from legislation and from administration, and that a statute was little more than a judicial decision to which a general application was given by means of an appropriate wording. Thus, thanks

Consequences of the right to petition

to the extension of their right of petition by intervening in the administration and before the Council, the Commons ended by acquiring, in fact, a right of initiative in matters of legislation. Mr. Pollard has, moreover, related to the Commons' right of petition, the complaints against the officers of the king, and he sees in it, consequently, the origin of ministerial responsibility.

Great as were the numbers in which the king's Council in Parliament saw the knights appear, sent by their communities or summoned as juries by the

II. The control of the local administration: general convocations

king himself, they did not represent the whole of England and their powers had always a local and fragmentary character. But, in certain circumstances, they were summoned from all the counties at once. The first of

1213

these general convocations known to us goes back to 1213; the writ of November 7th ordered the sheriffs to send to the king four discreet knights.[1] We do not know whether this assembly ever

---

Cistercians *"ad petitionem comitum, baronum, et communitatis Angliae :"* (margin, *Communitas Angliae contra abbatem Cisterciensem"*) ; No. 472, p. 305, is aimed against the corruption of juries *ad petetionem pauperum hominum terrae Angliae."*

1. Stubbs (*Const. Hist.*, i, p. 565) attached great constitutional importance to an earlier convocation which is known to us only through Roger of Wendover : on July 21st, 1213, John Lackland is said to have summoned, for August 4th to St. Albans, the reeve and four men from each of the *villae* of his domains. This text has given rise to many discussions. M. Pasquet (pp. 38 sq.) has summarised the hypothesis to which it has given rise and has proposed a new one which seems satisfactory (Mr. J. Tait seems inclined to adopt it : *E. H. R.* 1914, p. 750; see *Ibid.*, the correction, proposed by Mr. H. W. C. Davis, to the interpretation he suggested in *Ibid.*, 1905).

effectively met, and, in any case, its object remains unknown. But we are better informed on other general 1226-27 convocations which took place in 1226 and in 1227 : their purpose was to return the results of an inquest on the administration of the sheriffs. Perhaps that of 1222 was concerned with an enquiry on the forest.[1] In October 1258 it was 1258 certainly concerned with a new inquest on the sheriffs.[2] And perhaps there were many others. The control of the sheriffs was always one of the essential preoccupations of the kings : it formed a part of that duty of justice which was, in the eyes of the monarch as in those of his subjects, the *raison d'etre* of royalty, and, in this way, the judicial parliament naturally became administrative. The preoccupation of securing this control is so evident, especially among the kings who care for their authority, such as Edward I, that Riess has seen therein one of the essential reasons for the constitution, by that king, of the House of Commons : one of the purposes of the regular convocations of the knights was, it is suggested, to give the central power regular information on the provincial administration. It has rightly been objected that, according to this plan, the summoning of the burgesses is hardly explained, for

It takes away all constitutional importance from this summons. In any case, we can build nothing on so controversial a text. Stubbs (*Const. Hist.* i, p. 666) has given an inexact text of the summons of Nov. 7th, 1213, mentioned above; he has printed *quatuor discretos homines* and has put them on the same footing as the four men of the *villa* : but the correct reading is "*milites.*" Miss A. E. Levett has examined anew the discussions relating to this writ (*E. H. R .* 1916).

1. For the first general convocations, see A. White, "Some Early Instances of Concentration of Representatives in England" (*Amer. Hist. Rev.* Vol. xix); "Was there a Common Council before Parliament. ?" (*Ibid.*, vol. xxv). On August 13, 1227, the king summoned the representatives of 35 counties out of 37. Westmoreland, one of the two shires omitted (the other is Cornwall), had been cited in 1226.

2. Pasquet, pp. 30 sp.. Stubbs (*Const. Hist.*, ii, p. 232) thinks that the knights of October 1258 were not representatives. In the modern sense of the word they were not, for it is doubtful that they were elected, but they appeared in the name of the counties.

it is admitted that the boroughs had few dealings with the sheriffs.[1] But if this reason, in practice, is insufficient to account for all the general convocations, it does not seem doubtful that it is to it that we must look to explain the oldest of them, and that it must have weighed heavily in the mind of Edward I. In any case, the intermittent summoning of the knights of the shire from administrative motives must have increased the importance of the part they played in the shire court and in the transaction of local business;[2] it must also have encouraged petitions of public interest, and in consequence, collective petitions. Without this summoning, it is likely that the petitions to the judicial Parliaments would have kept, as in France, an individual and local character.

Consequences of these convocations

Thus the judicial reforms of Henry II had as a natural result, the intermittent appearance, in Parliament, of knights and burgesses who represented their communities, and the desire to control the local administration induced the Angevin kings to summon, from time to time, to the same Parliament, the delegates of all the counties.

But the financial needs of the monarchy also occasioned general convocations, and, in the end, were the chief cause of their multiplication. We know that financial problems became very pressing under the Angevin kings. The financial innovations of Henry II were scarcely less important than his judicial reforms.[3] Scu-

III. Financial needs multiply the general convocations

---

1. Pasquet, pp. 183-186.
2. G. Lapsley, having studied the representation of five counties under Edward II, concludes that, among those elected, there is a little group of knights who are present at more than one Parliament; some even appear often; now we observe that they are particularly active in local administration ("Knights of the Shire in the Parliaments of Edward II," *E. H. R.*, 1919).
3. See *Const. Hist.*, i, pp. 622 sq. On the origins of royal taxation, see Stephenson, "The *firma unius noctis* and the Customs of the Hundred," *E. H. R.*, 1924; and the Studies of Miss Demarest on the same subject, *Ibid.*, 1918, 1920, 1923.

tage[1] tended to become a sort of aid without consent,
Reforms of Henry II. exacted from the military holdings, while
on the other tenures there lay the burden
of carucage, substituted for danegeld, which had fallen
into disuse and no longer yielded anything. We are
justified in believing that, but for the baronial rebellion
against John Lackland, these taxes, gradually becoming
annual and raised without consent, would have ended
in the institution of a national imposition taken at the
king's discretion. The attempt failed. Moreover, during the thirteenth century the product of scutage became
insignificant. By the end of the twelfth century the rise
of prices, and the progress of sub-infeudation, which
made the fiefs smaller and smaller and transformed the
vassals into simple rural proprietors, strangers to military life, did not permit of the rigid exaction of the
service due. Henry II and Richard I had
Disappearance of scutage to be content with a fraction. From John's
time, the reduced service became custom-
ary. The preponderance of the barons fixed the custom,
and, by the middle of the thirteenth century, this reduced
service was all that the barons recognised as due. The
loss was enormous. For example, the Courtenays of
Okehampton in Devon, who owed 92¾ knights' service
under Henry II, admitted only 3 under Edward I. In
1315 the barons refused to pay scutage on the old basis,
saying, without mincing matters, that the king's vassals
did service for a much smaller number of fiefs than they
really held, so that a tenant-in-chief of 40 or 50
fiefs provided 4 or 5 knights only. Again, by the end
of the twelfth century, a distinction was recognised
between scutage and the "fine." Summoned to the host,
the tenant could arrange the payment of a compensation
or "fine;" if he did not do this, and yet did not come,
he had to pay scutage, after the campaign, at the usual

1. We note here that W. A. Morris has found a mention of scutage
in 1100 (*E.H.R.*, 1921).

rate of 20 or 40 shillings, it being admitted that he could recover the total sum from his own vassals. As this rate had become ridiculous, the king attempted to multiply the fines. At this time, moreover, zealous sheriffs sometimes attempted to take scutage from the under-vassals although the tenant-in-chief had already paid a "fine." But, during the thirteenth century the "fine" also became customary; in consequence, the raising of scutage properly so-called fell into disuse, for there was no longer any reason for preferring it: it was abandoned after 1257 and henceforth the "fine" alone was exacted. Only the "fine", having become customary and being calculated according to the reduced service, became almost valueless. Military tenure was thus rid, or almost rid of the duties which were its *raison d'etre* and which constituted one of the fundamental resources of feudal royalty.[1]

The natural consequence was the development of the aid which the tenants-in-chief granted, on behalf of all who held of them, and which tapped all the resources of the realm, the king being able, for his part, to tallage his domain, of which most of the towns were part, at the same, or more usually, at a higher rate. The military tenants made no difficulty in admitting this transformation, because it substituted for the old service of the host, the weight of which they had borne alone, an imposition which weighed on the other tenants also, and on the townsfolk too.

Development of the aid

It seems that Henry II had at first wished to adopt

1. On financial history, see S. K. Mitchell, *Studies in Taxation* under *John and Henry III*, 1914 (and Mr. Powicke's observations *E. H. R.* 1915, pp. 530 sq.). The question of scutage has been taken up by Miss H. Chew in two articles in *Ibid.* "Scutage under Edward I" (1922) and "Scutage in the XIVth Century" (1923), which we follow here. On the taxation of movables, see the studies of Willard for the reigns of Edward I (*Ibid.*, 1913, and also 1914, p. 317, note 1) and of Edward II (*Ibid.*, 1914).In 1284, the revenue of Edward I for the Easter term was £26,828 3s. 0¼d. (Miss M. Mills; *Ibid.*, 1925).

an assessment on land. Carucages were still raised in the first half of the thirteenth century,

The assessment of the aid usually according to the area ploughed, sometimes according to the number of yokes, and surveys of the communities were undertaken with this purpose, especially in 1198 :[1] the church lands were included in the task. But Henry II came to adopt concurrently assessment of movables, for example in the assize of arms (1181) and notably for the Saladin tithe. It was just and advantageous not to tax the land alone, but the reason which brought about the abandonment of carucage remains obscure; nevertheless the fact is established : during the thirteenth century assessment on movables became the rule; the landed revenue was included in it.[2] The assessment of carucage and the survey were established by the royal

It is made by the juries and passes into the hands of the knights officers; but, in practice, naturally enough, they could only operate according to the information supplied by the taxpayers or their representatives : for this purpose, use was soon made of the procedure of juries of knights, which had become common in the shire courts.[3] It was even more indispensable in the assessment of taxes on movables, the cataloguing and valuation of which were much more difficult.[4] The assessment of the aid there-

---

1. See *Const. Hist.*, i, p. 548.
2. Assessment on movables could have co-existed with carucage, of which it would have been the complement. But doubtless it was preferred to draw up one roll only, not merely to simplify, but because the value of movables was probably estimated by comparison with the revenue from a measure of land.
3. See *Const. Hist.*, i, p. 665 (1198).
4. See *Const. Hist.*, i, p. 627 (assize of arms) : and ii, pp. 53,,223-4. M. Pasquet (pp. 189 sq. and also pp. 167-168) has described with greater precision than Stubbs the conditions of assessment. The highly detailed enumeration of the goods to be valued, and the standard of valuation were determined by the central power. But the juries had to make the census of the goods, and the standard included either a maximum below which the juries might go, or perhaps several headings under which they had to classify any given article. We have the rolls for Colchester for the subsidies of 1295 and 1301 (*Rot. Parl.*, i, 228 and 243) and the roll of a Bedfordshire village for 1297 : H. Hall, *Formula Book of English Historical Documents* ii, 46, (1908).

fore passed rapidly into the hands of the knights. The
The levying of the aid same thing often happened as regards the collection, and this was a very heavy task for the knights. Riess has even partly attributed the constitution of the House of Commons by Edward I to the desire to put himself in touch with the collectors of the tax, and it is certain that these collectors were often included among the deputies : in 1295, in 21 counties out of 35, the collector is a deputy, and, most usually, for the same county in which he is commissioned to collect the aid. But there are many Parliaments in which the proportion is the very reverse. We must therefore be content to see, in the question of collection, one of the many motives which decided the kings to take into more and more serious consideration the opinion of the knights, and we must not try to give it an almost exclusive importance. In Riess's hypothesis, moreover, the summoning of the burgesses would go unexplained. The question of the assessment, as M. Pasquet has very ably shown, was much more important.[1]

It is an essential fact that in the thirteenth century, the aid, in England as in France, was not a lump sum
The aid a tax by quota divided out over the country, (*impôt de répartition*), but one in which everyone paid a fixed quota proportionate to his holdings. (*impôt de quotité*). Perhaps this fact has not been given all the importance it merits. It seems that it would have been in the king's interests to get a lump sum voted, and, in any case, if this had been done, it is probable that the part played by the knights would have been much less important.[2] The amount of the carucage was

1. A discussion of the thesis of Riess will be found in Pasquet, pp. 183 sq.
2. In dividing a lump sum among the communities, as was the case in France from the fifteenth to the eighteenth century, the central power no longer had much interest in regulating the assessment, for the community as a whole was responsible for the amount due ; therefore there were many local variations in the manner of sharing

fixed per unit; therefore the yield of the tax depended on
the enumeration of taxable units by the juries. But once
the enumeration of the carucages was made, their freedom of valuation was necessarily very much restricted
subsequently. It was quite otherwise when, for the
carucage, there had been substituted the raising of a
tenth or some other fraction of the value of the goods,

**Its yield
depends on
the knights**
and this is why the change is of such great
importance. From that moment, the yield
of the aid depended largely on the juries of
knights, without taking into account the fact that, as
collectors, they could hasten the payment to a greater
or a less degree.

Hence we see why the king thought it useful to come
to an agreement with them, both regarding the expediency and the rate of the aid. The first

**Necessity of
consulting them**
general convocations of the county knights,
for the purpose of such consultations, date
perhaps from 1225, 1232, and 1237; there may have
been many others. But the first certain example goes
back only to 1254: we must probably add to it the
Parliament of April 1258, and it is remarkable that in
this way the necessity of conciliating the knights should
have imposed itself upon the barons as well as on the
king.[1]

among the taxpayers, and especially a great number of abuses to
which little attention was paid because the yield of the tax was secured
in advance. With the tax by quota it was very different: the yield
depended on the assessment; as the medieval kings had not at their
command a vast and competent bureaucracy, we see why the English
kings gave a great impetus to the development of juries, the use of
which was familiar to them. The evolution, in fact, seems to have
been the same in England as in France : in the fourteenth century, the
tenth and the fifteenth on incomes was a fixed sum divided among
the communities according to a valuation of 1334 (See *Const. Hist.*
iii, pp. 350, 572).

1. Pasquet, pp. 31 sq. Regarding the Parliament of 1258, Stubbs
thinks that the knights were summoned for local affairs only, taking
the terms of the writs *de expensis* in a literal sense, (See *Const. Hist.*
ii, p. 232, note 1), whereas M. Pasquet, considering that we must
regard this as a formula only, concludes that they were summoned,
as in 1254, for financial reasons (p. 37).

In their mind, according to what has just been said, it was not a question of asking the knights for their

Did the knights consent to the aid? consent to the principle of the aid : that of the tenants-in-chief alone was necessary. But it is a question which has been much discussed. The writs which order the collection of the aid in 1225, 1232 and 1237 associate the knights with the barons in the consent which makes the aid lawful : it is very difficult to see in this anything more than a formula when in 1225, they go so far as to include the villeins !¹ However, it is perhaps not impossible that this formula itself bears witness to the desire to gain the goodwill of the population. Moreover, Stubbs main-

Negotiations in the county courts tained that, before the time of the general convocations, the shire courts, where all the freeholders owed suit and service, dis-cussed the principle of the tax with the king's officers and could refuse their consent.² There is no proof of this.³ But, remembering what happened in France, we are led to think that the officers who, in the reign of Henry II, came to assess and collect the aid in the county courts, may well have been able to negotiate and conclude local agreements with the county knights, whose collaboration they knew to be indispensable : we must confess that the general convocations are much easier to explain if we admit this hypothesis.⁴ In law, these agreements could be concerned only with the as-

---

1. *Const. Hist.*, ii, p. 254.
2. *Ibid.*, i, p. 626-627; ii, pp. 223, 225-226.
3. Pasquet, pp. 31, 179; Stubbs quotes only one example of 1220, and M. Pasquet shows that this example has not the significance which Stubbs attributed to it.
4. The example given by Stubbs (*Const. Hist.*, i, p. 627) of the men of Horncastle who in 1168 make a payment for an aid "*quod ipsi assederunt inter se concessu justitiarum aliter quam justitiae*" seems fully to confirm this. See also the texts cited in *Ibid.*, i, pp. 425 and 431, from which Stubbs infers that the judges arranged the details of the aid with the barons in the county court at the time of Henry II, and even asked for their consent there, in the reign of Henry I (this latter text seems inconclusive).

sessment and the collection; they were of an administrative character. But the payment of the tax was no less important than its concession, and, in practice the county knights found themselves invested with a real power of consent which, by custom, must have become in their eyes a right, according to the conception of the Middle Ages. The way of constitutional progress was thus prepared by an ambiguous situation, and, perhaps the knights were confirmed in their view by the example of the clergy, who, during the thirteenth century, claimed the right of consenting to the aid by their proctors summoned side by side with the bishops.[1]

The knights consent in fact, if not in law

This is why Mr. Adams seems to have been too absolute in denying the county knights any representative character before 1264, on the ground that they had no right to refuse the aid asked for; they were, he says, proctors with full powers to consent to what would be commanded them, in fact, proctors with a mandate understood to be imperative. But, in reality, they discussed the rate of the tax. M. Pasquet has given proof of this for 1254, and has wisely compared this Parliament with the assembly of clergy of 1226.[2]

The necessity of consulting the burgesses was, from

1. E. Barker, *The Dominican Order and Convocation, a Study of the Growth of Representation in the Church during the XIIIth Century,* 1913. According to Mr. Barker, the application of the representative system to Parliament was imitated from the ecclesiastical assemblies, whose practice was itself derived from Dominican usages. M. Pasquet refutes what is exaggerated in this thesis (pp. 19, 20), but recognises that the clergy, long before the laity, defended the principle of representation against both Pope and king, to wit that no engagement, especially of a pecuniary nature, can be valid unless it has been freely undertaken by those concerned or by their representatives (pp. 21 sq.). The knights and burgesses certainly never demanded, as did the clergy, to be represented, so that we cannot agree with Mr. Barker that there was imitation; but the example of the clergy may have influenced the manner in which the knights understood their part in the general assemblies, and this, it seems, is the chief conclusion which we can draw from the comparison, made also by M. Pasquet, of the Parliament of 1254 and the assembly of the clergy in 1226.

2. See the entire discussion in Pasquet, pp. 63-70.

the same motives, bound to come soon. Henry III made
The burgesses arrangements with the merchants more than
once, and when Edward I wished to give
a definite assessment to the customs, he consulted them.[1]
For the boroughs of the domain, it would be vain to
allege that tallage was not granted like the aid: the
conditions of assessment were of the same nature, and
from the administrative standpoint, there was in this
respect no difference between the various taxes.[2]

The origin of the appearance of the county knights
and the burgesses before the Council in Parliament
Characteristics completely explains the features of this
of shire and representation. The knights came to pre-
borough
representations sent a petition, to serve as members of a
a jury, to bring the reply to an inquest,
to learn what the king had decided with his barons,
without having the right to judge, to counsel, or to
consent in the juridical sense of the word: it was there-
Number of fore of no importance to fix their number. In
representatives 1275, Edward I asks for 4 or 6 burgesses;
not fixed in 1290, two or three knights. From 1295
the rule is to summon two knights, but for the burgesses
it is later: in 1306 the king summons one or two, at
will.[3] In the same way, it mattered little that they
should be elected. The electoral body was certainly quite
ready to hand; it was the county court. It has been

1. See *Const. Hist.*, ii, pp. 549 sq. The origin of the customs has
been studied anew by N. S. Gras, *The Early English Customs System*
(Harvard Economic Studies, vol. xviii; 1918). It is a collection of
texts preceded by a long introduction. According to Mr. Gras, the
customs do not appear, in the twelfth century, as a form of the right
of purveyances, as was the view of Hall, whose theories Stubbs seems
to have adopted (*Const. Hist.*, ii, p. 549, n. 4); there is no trace of
this toll in kind on merchandises leaving the kingdom. The customs
were, then, a right, of royal institution, over foreign trade, and were
taken in money. Nevertheless Mr. Gras recognises that there was
an exception: the prise of wine, paid to the king's butler, actually
represented the value of the wine taken, at first, in kind. It seems
that the problem is merely put back to an earlier date.
2. See *Const. Hist.*, ii, p. 201; Pasquet, pp. 193-4.
3. Pasquet, pp. 195-6.

claimed that the county knights represented the tenants-in-chief only; they are supposed to have performed in their name, the service of court, with the prerogatives attached thereto, so that, in spite of their appearance in **They are chosen in the county court** it, Parliament, according to this theory, kept its feudal character. But it is certain that they truly represented the county court to which all freeholders were summoned in principle.[1] Still, it is beyond doubt that this court was a very imperfect electoral body. It was an obligation and a burden to be present in it, and no one was eager to assume these or to claim them as a right. Tenures were conceded conditionally on fulfilling the obligations of the grantor at the court. In 1236 the statute of Merton authorised the tenants to have themselves represented by an *attorn-atus*. Generally, the shire court was attended only by a **Unwillingness to accept the charge** very small number of persons, and in the beginning it is likely that there were no elections. In 1264 the knights were elected, and probably in 1265 again. But very often, doubtless, the sheriffs themselves chose the delegates, and no one thought of protesting.[2] On the one hand, the example of the boroughs under Edward I and after him, is peremptory. Not one ever claimed the right to be represented. On the contrary, in 1368, Torrington asked to be exempted from this obligation.[3] On the other hand,

1. Pasquet, p.217; see *Const. Hist.*, ii, pp. 194, 240-241.
2. Pasquet, pp. 139 sq. See *Const. Hist.* ii, pp. 237 sq., 243, 453; iii, pp. 417 sq., 424.
3. Pasquet, pp. 170-171; *Const. Hist.*, iii, p. 467. Colchester, Maldon and Hull also obtained temporary exemption in the fourteenth century. Since Riess, when it is desired to show the unwillingness of the boroughs to be represented, the many returns in which the sheriffs declare their inertia are also invoked : *nihil responderunt; nullum dederunt responsum*. Mr. J. G. Edwards studying "The Personnel of the Commons in Parliament under Edward I and Edward II" (in *Essays presented to T. F. Tout*) shows in the first place that the returns have not always been used correctly. Thus M. Pasquet cites Yarmouth as "habitually" refusing to answer (p. 159). Mr. Edwards states that we have the returns of this town for 24 parliaments out of 28 between 1290 and 1327. But, above all, he has proved that a negative return

The
"manucaptor" the chosen knight had to provide a *manu-captor* who guaranteed his appearance. Electors and candidates, therefore, were both lacking.[1] The reason for this is not hard to understand. Unless a collective petition was to be presented, the delegates were attending at the king's request, to bind themselves, in the name of the county, to undertake some charge; from the personal point of view the journey, more often than not, held no attractions for them; while as for the electors, not only did the king's appeal presage a tax, but they had also to pay the expenses of their representatives, and these were very high.[2]

The representation of the Commons in Parliament was therefore the work of the monarchy; it was suggested by the needs of the State, so much

Representation
of the commons
results from
State
necessities

so that the very barons, whenever they made themselves masters of the government, as in 1258, adopted the same expedients as the king. It clearly tended to break up the feudal framework of society, but nobody was aware of this; neither the knights nor the burgesses, in fact,

does not prove that no election was made. Thus, in the Parliament of Feb. 1305, the return states that Colchester has not replied; yet a writ *de expensis* exists for its representative. In reality we can draw one certain conclusion only from the words *Nihil responderunt* namely, that the sheriff did not receive the borough's reply at the right time. It has also been noted that the restriction of the electoral franchise, finally settled in 1432, was sought by the counties. But this fact does not seem to prove a desire not to be represented. It is a fact of social significance : its purpose was to exclude the poor from the electorate. The unwillingness of the shires and the boroughs to send representatives still remains, however, none the less certain. Cf. below, p. 497, note 2.

1. Pasquet, pp. 145-6, 156, 165; *Const. Hist.*, iii, p. 439.
2. *Const. Hist.*, ii, pp. 241, 247; iii, pp. 501-503; Pasquet, pp. 166-171. In 1315, the indemnity was 4s. per day for the knights and 2s. for the burgesses. In 1305, the Northumberland knights received 100s. for the session, which had lasted from Feb. 28 to March 20. In the valuation of movables at Colchester in 1295 and in 1301, a cow is valued at 5s.; in the maximum rates of 1305, "the best cow" is valued at 12s.; a fat sheep with its wool, at 20d.

were asking to appear, except as petitioners, when they wished to have recourse to the king's justice; they had neither the quality of royal advisers, nor the power of consent, which were baronial prerogatives : finally, their presence favoured the raising of the aid, which was being substituted for the burdens of military tenure, the barons themselves reaping the greatest profit thereby. Neither the knights, nor the burgesses, nor the chroniclers attached any importance to these convocations, because their development was gradual, because the use of the jury and of the petition had made the idea of representation familiar, and because there was no need to create an electoral body, the county court being an institution of immemorial antiquity.[1]

Contemporaries attach no importance to it

But the representation of the Commons is not, to our eyes, merely the work of the king, a development of the royal administration. Quite apart from its constitutional importance, which later events alone have brought to light, it is a social fact of fundamental interest: it proves that the tenants-in-chief, by the end of the thirteenth century, were no longer the only rich and considerable persons in the kingdom. The progress of sub-infeudation had strengthened the lesser nobility. The knights were not all, or even nearly all, tenants-in-chief, and even those who were had been able to increase their domains by becoming under-vassals of a baron. Henry II's reforms had made them the basis of the local administration and had obliged them to acquire judicial and financial experience : in reality, they governed the counties. This is why the king and

It is proof of the social importance acquired by the knights

1. Under Henry III and Edward I, the chronicles mention only the barons in the Parliaments. At the Parliament of 1265, the burgesses are mentioned only by the *Chronicle of the Mayors and Sheriffs of London;* this work omits the knights and is, moreover, mistaken in the number of burgesses sent by the towns, there being two, not four. See *Const. Hist.* ii, p. 97, note 2; and Pasquet, p. 14.

the barons were induced to consult them. The same thing happened in the case of the burgesses during the thirteenth century: their appearance in Parliament bears witness to the progress of the commercial class, which, under Edward II, led the younger Despenser to attempt to conciliate the merchants by the organisation of the Staple.[1]

Not only had the co-operation of these classes become indispensable to the administration of the kingdom, but

Their political support was of value their support was not negligible when a great crisis set the barons and the king at strife, though, from the feudal standpoint, these two alone were qualified to exercise the power, to the exclusion of the Commons. Perhaps it was to gain their support that John Lackland summoned the knights in 1213. In any case, there can be no doubt that this was the intention of the barons in 1261 and 1264. And M. Pasquet, following M. Bémont, has clearly shown that, in proceeding to the first joint convocation of the county knights and the burgesses,

Simon de Montfort Simon de Montfort had planned to rely upon them in order to hold in check the great barons who were deserting him. Thus was the social impulse manifested in the purely political field. Certainly, in the eyes of Simon himself, this was merely an expedient which was to have no repetition. But recent discoveries have proved that his initiative had really had an unparalleled constitutional importance.[2] The writs published by Mr. H. Jenkinson have shown us that in April 1275, at his first Parliament, Edward I, summoned knights and burgesses, as had Simon de Montfort, but in greater numbers: four

1. Tout, *Place Edward II*, pp. 241-266.
2. Pasquet, pp. 50 sq.—We note here that M. Ch. Bémont is preparing a new edition of his book on *Simon de Montfort* (1884) brought up to date by reference to the documents published during the last 40 years.

knights from each county and four or six burgesses from each borough, instead of two. Another document, discovered by Mr. G. O. Sayles, shows that Henry III, too, summoned to the Parliament of 1268 the representatives of twenty-seven cities and boroughs. For the first time, to our knowledge, he ordered that the names of the deputies should be officially "returned," and that they should be given full powers. It is at least probable that in summoning the burgesses, he did not forget the knights, whose appearance in Parliament was already familiar. If this conjecture is some day verified, Edward I will no longer even have the merit of having been the first to renew Earl Simon's experiment; even at present, it is already clear that the memory of it was never effaced.[1]

III.

In the light of these facts, the part of Edward I in the constitutional evolution seems much less original than Stubbs thought. The Parliament of 1295 was not the outcome of a series of experiments deliberately undertaken; it was not a real innovation, introduced after an

Misrepresenta-
tion of the part
played by
Edward I.

1. The articles of Messrs. Jenkinson and Sayles are cited above p. 349, n. 7. Mr. Sayles has discovered a fragment relating to a deliberation of an assembly held at the end of March 1268, ordering the addressing of summonses to 27 cities and boroughs for April 22nd; probably use was being made, for the holding of this Parliament, of the gathering of a council by the legate Ottobono. Stubbs does not mention it (for 1268 he cites only the Parliament of Northampton, June 4th, where Edward took the cross; *Const. Hist.*, ii, p. 101, n. 5). Stubbs wondered whether the burgesses gave consent to the aid in the Parliament of 1269. The formula "the most powerful men" of the cities and boroughs did not even make it possible to affirm that they were representatives. We can measure by this the importance of Mr. Sayles' discovery. The return of the towns in 1268 is not addressed to the sheriffs: the cities and boroughs must give to their representatives letters patent showing their names. Full powers (*"ut nos quicquid in premissis nomine nostro fecerint ratum habebimus et acceptum"*) are not asked for by the writs of 1254, 1264, 1265. Those of 1275 also do not mention full powers; the Parliament of 1268 is therefore ahead of that of 1275. Full powers re-appear in 1284 and become the rule from 1290 onwards.

interval of thirty years, when that of the great Earl had been forgotten, even if we admit that Edward himself could ever have lost the memory of him who had once been his friend and whom he had had to strike down on the field of battle. Henry III himself perpetuated, in part at least, the tradition of the Parliament of 1265, and as early as 1275, Edward I revived it. The Parliament of 1295 is distinguished from that of 1275 only by the simultaneous appearance of the proctors of the lower clergy, whose representation also was no novelty.[1] Edward I, then, was sufficiently clever to take up again, for the benefit of the monarchy, the experiment of Simon de Montfort, but the so-called conception of the "Model Parliament" is not personally attributable to him.[2]

Moreover, the rising of the barons against Edward appears to have been no more "national" than those of 1215 and 1258; there is no indication that they demanded the summoning of the Commons to associate them in the consent to taxes; on the contrary they are found, in 1305, asking permission to tallage their domains, as the king tallaged his own.[3] Nor did the Commons themselves, any more than previously, demand to be represented in Parliament. As has already been said, the attitude of the counties, and, still more, of the boroughs, is conclusive, and the number of boroughs represented never ceased to diminish throughout the fourteenth century.

Indifference of the barons

and of the Commons

In short, the administrative motives which made desirable the summoning of the knights and burgesses

---

1. In his third chapter, M. Pasquet reviews anew all the Parliaments of Edward I, examined by Stubbs (*Const. Hist.*, ii, pp. 111-165). The discovery of the writs of 1275 by Mr. Jenkinson is mentioned in the French edition of the *Const. Hist.*, ii, p. 129.

2. Cf. *Const. Hist.*, ii, pp. 305-306.

3. Maitland, no. 87, p. 54.

imposed themselves on Edward I as on his predecessor, and with much greater force, if that is possible. The number of petitions went on increasing. Edward exercised a close supervision of the sheriffs. And, above all, his financial needs exceeded all measure because of his policy of expansion. The roll of 1305, as Maitland has observed,[1] shows his inextricable embarrassments; Mr. Tout arrives at the same conclusion by a study of the functioning of the Wardrobe during this reign,[2] and we know that his unreasonable demands set him at strife with the clergy and the barons. Now the feudal taxes no longer yielded anything.[3] It was not that Edward I had renounced them; on the contrary, while accepting the customary "fines" for the reduced service, he put forward the claim to raise scutage for the service effectively due, but abandoned for nearly a century; moreover, he attempted to levy it directly on the undervassals. But the studies of Miss H. Chew have shown that he failed, that his successors were no more successful and that in the end, Edward III had to sanction, in 1339, the disappearance of military commutation, and in consequence, of the service of the host. The extra-feudal aid, therefore, became the sole extraordinary resource of the State, and in consequence, the goodwill of those who were charged to assess and collect it became more indispensable than ever. The general summons to the

Edward I obeyed the same motives as his predecessors

His financial needs

1. Maitland : petitions of the king's creditors, nos. 58, 59, 275, and p. 321 ; in no. 175 the king makes a general reply to them : he promises to pay them as soon as possible (pp. 133-4) ; in no. 80, the justices of the two benches, and the barons and clerks of the Exchequer claim their wages; similarly as to no. 272, for the archers and *balistarii.*
2. Above, pp. 392-393.
3. In 1300, though no extraordinary tax had been raised, and though expenses had not been exceptional, Edward I received £58,155 and spent £64,105 (See *Const. Hist.* ii, p. 575). Now we can obtain an idea of the yield of a scutage at 40s. per fief from that of the aid *pur fille marier* in 1290, taken at the same rate, and yielding, according to J. H. Ramsay (*Dawn of the Constitution,* p. 527) £3,061.

boroughs without distinguishing, as Stubbs has already shown,[1] between those which were of the domain and those which were not, had the advantage of increasing the yield of the aid : the boroughs of the domain paid more than the counties, whereas the others were treated like the latter; but in gathering together the representatives of both, the more favoured boroughs were induced to pay at the higher rate, and this is probably one of the reasons which explains the unwillingness of certain boroughs to appear in Parliament.[2]

If, therefore, certain Parliaments of Edward I mark an advance in constitutional evolution, his will counted for nothing in this; it was an administrative perfection which he desired to realise, and he yielded to the necessities which had already constrained his predecessors. Nevertheless, it would be extravagant to reduce him to the level of Henry III and to deny any personal character to his policy.

There is no doubt that Edward I, after more than fifty years, resumed the systematically anti-feudal policy of the first Angevin kings. The inquest of

His anti-feudal policy

Quo warranto and the statute of *Quia emptores* are well-known testimonies to this.[3]

---

1. See *Const. Hist.*, ii, pp. 244 sq. ; Pasquet, pp. 217 sq.
2. *Const. Hist.*, ii, pp. 545-6 ; Pasquet, pp. 218-220. Regarding the boroughs which were not of the domain, M. Pasquet seems to put the first summons to them in 1296; cf. the writs he publishes, p. 101, n. 2 and p. 103, n. 2; the first relating to the aid granted in 1295, speaks of the '*burgenses et alii probi homines de dominicis nostris civitatibus et burgis ejusdem regni;*" the second, relating to the Parliament of 1296, mentions the "*burgenses et alii probi homines de singulis civitatibus et burgis regni nostri de quorumcunque tenuris aut libertatibus fuerint et de omnibus dominicis nostris.*" Mr. J. Tait has observed that, in the later writs, *dominicis* is always a noun, and that, in the first of these texts, a comma should be placed after the word *nostris*. (*E. H. R.*, 1914, p. 750). Further, M. Pasquet himself points out (p. 218), that Lynn, which belonged to the bishop of Norwich, was represented in the Parliament of 1283.
3. *Const. Hist.*, ii, pp. 115, 189. It is true that in practice this statute also benefited the great vassals, and that is why they accepted it without objection; but the principal advantage was to the king. Moreover, it destroyed one of the principles of feudal organisation, and the king alone could congratulate himself on this.

Nor was manorial jurisdiction safe from his enterprises.[1] Of course Edward I had no intention of renouncing the profits which he could still obtain from the feudal system, and we have seen him trying to revive scutage. But the main tendency of his policy was to ruin the feudal hierarchy and to treat all Englishmen as subjects : the taking of scutage from the under-vassals led stealthily in this direction; more significant still, he imposed knighthood on and summoned to the host, without distinction of tenure, all those having a certain landed revenue : he doubtless found in this yet another pecuniary advantage : but the judicial reforms of Henry II had also resulted in increasing his revenues by the sale of writs. We may always doubt, and with reason, that these kings attempted to ruin feudalism in order to realise a political ideal : their ambition, their needs, and the circumstances are more satisfactory explanations for the historian. But it does not follow that the final result escaped their attention, or that they did not take it into consideration. Now if this is so, there is a

The summoning of the Commons is in accordance with it

parallelism between the direct summoning to the host, in their quality as knights, of all who possessed a sufficiently large holding, whether it was or was not of military origin, and whether they were or were not tenants of the king, and the summoning, before the Council, of the county knights, representing all freeholders, without distinction of overlordship, and of the burgesses of all the boroughs, whether on the domain or not.[2] The habit of summoning the whole body of the future Commons marks the importance of the new social classes, the decadence of the

1. See Maitland, *Select Pleas in Manorial and Seignorial Courts* (Henry III and Edward I), 1889, (Selden Society); and T. F. Tout and Hilda Johnstone, *State Trials of Edward I*, (1289-93), 1906 (*Roy. Hist. Soc.*).

2. *Const. Hist.*, ii, pp. 290 sq., and 295; Pasquet, pp. 208 sq.

feudal state, and the progress of national unity : Edward

He believed it would strengthen the royal power
I might well think that the royal power would be strengthened thereby. Even if one doubts that he had such far-reaching views, it cannot be contested that the conflict which ranged against him the barons, the Church, and the Pope, was very likely to remind him of Simon de Montfort's expedient, especially as, in 1275, he had already resuscitated the Parliament of 1265 : Simon had opposed the Commons to the barons; why should Edward I not have thought of doing likewise?[1] And since Philip the Fair summoned them in 1302 and in 1308, to obtain their support against Boniface VIII and in the affair of the Templars, is there not occasion to think that in 1307 they may have compensated, in Edward's mind, for the absence of the clergy? From all this we may conclude that Edward I's policy was sufficiently coherent to allow us to recognise in him a real statesman.

In the same way, if the Parliament of 1295 was not the innovation that Stubbs, in his ignorance of the writs of

Importance of the Parliament of 1295
1275, saw in it ; if, after as before it, Edward continued to hold Parliaments differently constituted, there is still no occasion to lower its importance too far. After all, as M. Pasquet has remarked, it is the first Parliament in which we find together the enlarged *Curia*, the knights of the shires, the borough representatives, and the proctors of

---

1. We should add that Edward I attempted to govern through the clerks of his Household, from whom he chose his Council, as Mr. Tout has shown (above, pp. 391-392, 416-417). Mr. Tout observes that his reign falls into two periods : until 1290 he is relatively conservative (though we must not forget the *Quo warranto*) ; after 1290, his financial needs give an exceptional importance to the Wardrobe, and financial expedients are multiplied (above, pp. 392-393), with the result that the opposition of the barons is aroused ; this observation seems to throw some light on the convocation of 1295 ; feeling the storm approaching, Edward I might have been induced to resort to the expedient of 1265, which he had used in 1275.

the lower clergy. On this ground, it remains true that afterwards it is to this Parliament that men looked back as being the "model" of the most general convocations.[1]

But, if Edward I thus keeps an eminent place in constitutional evolution, we see that his part was very different from what Stubbs thought: he never dreamt of becoming a constitutional king; he never entertained the idea that his power might become stronger if he shared it with his people; that is a modern conception which he could not attain. He believed that he could use the Commons as an instrument of government, to make his personal power unchallenged, or, if it is preferred, absolute.[2] In his eyes, Parliament remained what it was, the enlarged Council:[3] sometimes he called to it, as of old, only the barons in greater or less number; sometimes, when it seemed to him opportune, he summoned knights and burgesses at the same time, at his good

Edward I was not a constitutional king

His Parliament is still an enlarged "Curia"

1. Mr. Tait remarks that at the end of the reign there is an indication that the assembly of the three Estates, on the model of 1295, was beginning to be regarded as the "Parliament" properly so-called. The preamble of the statute of Carlisle, 1307, says that it was passed in the Parliament of Feb. 1305, but that its publication and proclamation have been adjourned "*a parliamento proximo praeterito usque ad presens parliamentum apud Karliolum*"; this "last Parliament" can only be the one which passed the statute; from which it would result that the name of "Parliament" was denied to the assembly of Sept. 1305, in which the Commons did not figure, and to that of May 1306, which included two knights from each county and two burgesses from each borough, but in which the lower clergy were not represented. (*E. H. R.*, p. 750).

2. For Stubbs' conception, see esp. *Const. Hist.*, ii, p. 324. But we recall that he has nevertheless here and there made numerous qualifications of his thesis; *e.g.* ii, pp. 266-268; Edward I left intact "the vital and prolific power of the prerogative;" ii, pp. 309-310; it is probable that he would have wished to leave to the Estates only the voting of taxation, and to keep policy and legislation to himself. See below, p. 484, n. 2, and p. 485, n. 1. There is no cohesion between his partial conclusions, founded on the texts, and his general conception.

3. On the *Curia* in its relations with the Parliament of the three estates, see Baldwin, pp. 307, 308. Stubbs recognises that men had long persisted in applying the name "Parliament" to the meetings of the Council and of the *Magnum Concilium*. (*Const. Hist.*, ii, p. 236).

pleasure. But, strictly speaking, they were not part of

The Commons have no power in it

the enlarged *Curia* : the Commons appear before the Council, but do not enter it ; they have no judicial authority and have never acquired any ; not only are they not always present, and in consequence, cannot form an essential part of a Parliament, but also, when they are summoned, they are dismissed as soon as possible, very often before the close of Parliament, which, after their departure, attends to its traditional occupations, to the settling of the petitions, and the examination of the most important matters.[1]

At the most, we can say, with Mr. J. Tait, that towards the end of the reign, the name "Parliament" was begin-

Meaning of the word "Parliament"

ning to be reserved for the assemblies of the *Curia* in which knights and burgesses figured : this fact would prove their growing importance, but it cannot prevail against the general trend of the other facts which characterise the work of Edward I.[2]

We have not, then, to examine whether Edward I wished to set up a House of Commons : the question

The question of the three Estates

could not even be raised, in fact. In practice, even when the Commons were represented, they did not in any way form a body. Stubbs has described Edward I's Parliament as an assembly of the three Estates or orders. But it really appears composed of six Estates : the king's counsellors, the barons, the bishops, the lower clergy, the knights, and the burgesses ; further, in certain circumstances, the merchants are added. In the time of Edward I it was impossible to foresee how these Estates would group themselves or even whether they would not remain isolated from each other.[3]

---

1. Pasquet, chap. iii and iv.
2. See above, p. 482, n. 1.
3. Pollard, *Evolution of Parliament*, pp. 61 sq. He has set out to show that Stubbs was wrong in using the term "Parliament of the

Moreover, Edward I never thought of allowing to the Commons the right of participating in the legislation : the Commons have only the right of peti-

Edward I did not recognise the right of the Commons to legislate

tion : they have not even the right of counsel ;[1] when their consent is mentioned —which is only in the statutes of 1275 and 1307—it is a pure form, and the writs of execution mention the barons only. Edward claimed to legislate by his sole authority, and he saw no constitutional difference between the statute and the ordinance : at the most, men were perhaps beginning to concede to the first a permanence, inferior, it is true, to that of the common law, but one which the ordinance, purely adapted to circumstances, did not possess; there was, however, nothing absolute in this distinction.[2] In the same way, he did not think of conceding to the Commons the right of consenting to taxation. We must not forget that after confirming the Great Charter, he had his oath annulled by the Pope; that by unanimous consent, he always kept the

three Estates" or "system of Estates." The constitution of the House of Commons is really the antithesis of such an organisation. He presumes that the system of Estates involves the right of veto for each of them, so that the religious reforms of the XVIth century would have required a political revolution if England had had such a system. Such a veto is not inherent in the system of Estates. But it is evident that the English organisation was much more supple. On the political part of the merchants under Edward III, see *Const. Hist.* ii, p. 398 and iii, pp. 608 sq.

1. The writs of summons never recognised it in them : see *Const. Hist.*, iii, p. 410

2. On the attributes of the Commons at the time of Edward I, see Pasquet, ch. v. Some indications brought out by Mr. J. Tait lead us to think that about the end of the reign, a distinction was growing up between ordinance and statute : the statute *de false moneta*, passed in the absence of the Commons in 1299, is treated as an ordinance in the Wardrobe accounts; similarly the act *de conspiratoribus* of the Parliament of Sept. 1305, in which the Commons did not figure, is called an ordinance, not a statute (*E. H. R.* 1914, p. 750). Stubbs (*Const. Hist.*, ii, p. 260) admits that the Commons had, in fact, only the right of petition, but on p. 259 his argument tends confusedly to a contrary conclusion. [See also T. F. T. Plucknett, *Statutes and their Interpretation in the first half of the Fourteenth Century.* (Cambr. Univ. Press, 1922).]

right of tallaging his domains, and, therefore, the greater part of the boroughs; that the so-called statute *De tallagio non concedendo* was never admitted by him, and that, in the French text of the *Confirmatio cartarum* which he sealed, he only admitted the necessity of consulting the Common Council for raising the traditional *aides, mises, et prises*, the definition of the Common Council and that of the *aides, mises, et prises* remaining at his discretion. If he thus evaded the demands of the barons, how shall we believe that he was disposed to grant anything to the Commons?[1] It goes without saying that he never imagined that he could be obliged to ask their advice or consent in the direction of his general policy.

At the time when Stubbs' ideas prevailed unquestioned, there appeared to be a striking contrast between

Comparison between England and France

the constitutional history of England and that of France. The English barons had obtained the Great Charter under John Lackland, and had had it confirmed under Edward I, not for themselves alone, but for the whole nation; on the contrary, the French nobles, who were, besides, less persevering and less united, had never thought of anyone save themselves. "The difference of their attitude from that of the English barons under John Lackland, Henry III and Edward I is striking," remarked a French scholar.[2] Before the national coalition

1. Stubbs holds that from 1295 taxation must be voted by the Commons (ii. pp. 255-257, 264). He is clearly unwilling to take all the value from the so-called statute *de tallagio non concedendo*, but he is fully obliged to recognise that it was the French version which bound Edward I (ii, pp. 148-149). He also recognises that Edward kept the right to tallage his domain, and that in 1303 he raised a scutage without any consent in Parliament so far as we know (ii, pp. 544-546). The right to tallage the domain reappears under Edward II and Edward III (and is abandoned only after 1340 (ii, pp. 546-547). We know that Edward I acted in no better faith regarding the forests. (See M. Petit-Dutaillis, *Studies and Notes Supplementary* ii, pp. 270).

2. *Histoire de France* published under the direction of M. Lavisse, t. iii 2e partie p. 270.

Edward I had to bow, though with a fairly good grace, and to organise the House of Commons; on the contrary, it was of their own accord, and only because they thought they saw in it a means of government, that the Capetians, and more particularly, Philip the Fair, had summoned the States General. "The States General," said the same historian "were not imposed on the last Capetians of the direct line, as were the Parliaments on the Plantagenets of England."[1] On several occasions Stubbs opposes the constitutional plan of Edward I to the absolutist policy of Philip the Fair.[2]

The new interpretation which results from the works we have tried to summarise has caused this contrast largely to disappear. This has certainly been seen already : the policy of Edward I, and his Parliament, as described for us by Messrs. Pasquet and Pollard, closely resembles the policy of Philip the Fair and his States General, as we know them by the classic accounts of Messrs. Langlois, Luchaire, and Viollet.

There are more similarities than contrasts between Edward I and Philip the Fair

For Edward I, as for Philip the Fair, the king is not merely the head of the feudal hierarchy. Without renouncing the rights which he has in virtue of this position, he regards all the inhabitants of the kingdom as his direct subjects, and he attempts to make a reality of this conception. Like his predecessors and like the Capetians, he undermines seignorial jurisdiction. He seeks to replace feudal obligations by a national taxation. He attempts to attach the under-vassals directly to himself. Philip the Fair, in 1308 and in 1313, attempts to raise from these latter the feudal aid for the marriage of his daughter and for the knighting of his eldest son,

1. *Ibid.*, p. 272
2. *Const. Hist.* ii, pp. 305, 310 But on p. 309, Stubbs admits that Edward I would probably have wished to limit the function of the Parliament of the Three Estates to voting the aid, and likens him, in this respect, to Philip the Fair.

just as Edward I tried to raise scutage from them. He opens direct relations with them by summoning them to general assemblies. He seeks to make them contribute directly to the extra-feudal aid. Certainly, the efforts of the French monarchy came later and encountered different obstacles; but, at the end of the thirteenth century and at the beginning of the fourteenth, England and France, in this respect, resembled each other more than they ever have at any other period. Stubbs, it is true, has remarked this, but the resemblance was closer than he thought.

The same is true of the assemblies. Those of the Capetians were, in all points, comparable to those of the Norman and Angevin kings. The king of France holds council in his *Curia* with his *familiares,* to whom he adds, when necessary, the vassals who owe him service of court, who have obeyed his call, or whom circumstances have brought to him, though they never all appeared at once. At the end of the thirteenth century, the permanent *Curia,* the division of which is now taking shape, holds judicial session *in parliamento* at the great festivals of the year, under the presidency of the king or his representative, and is then reinforced with lords and bishops.[1] *Requêtes* are presented to him from all parts of the kingdom. At the beginning of the fourteenth century, the nobles and the communities of the provinces often send their deputies to the *Curia* to put their grievances and complaints before him. As in England, the king experiences the

And between the assemblies

1. On the *Curia* in the XIVth century, see Viard, "La Cour (Curia) au commencement du XIVe siècle (*Bibl. de l'Ec. des Chartes,* 1916 pp. 74 sq.); "La Cour et les parlements au XIVe siècle" (*Ibid.* 1918, pp. 60 sq.). Until the ordinance of 1345, the word *Parlement* does not indicate a distinct autonomous institution; the *Parlement* is only a judicial session of the *Curia.* Moreover, when summoned to the assembly of 1303, the prior of Reuilly describes it thus : "convocatio in *vestra regali curia* Parisius proximum celebranda" (Picot, *Documents relatifs aux Etats Généraux et assemblées réunies sous Philippe le Bel (1302-1308)*, 1900, p. 68).

necessity of acting with the subjects who, he claims, owe him taxation; his envoys negotiate with the local communities before fixing the rate. Philip the Fair thus "decreed" a large number of subsidies which his commissioners had "demanded" or "obtained" : his lawyers recognised his right to impose them, but in practice there were discussions and reciprocal concessions. In 1314 it seemed to him opportune, probably in order to hasten the raising of the aid, to consult his subjects as a whole. In 1302 and 1308 the necessities of general policy had already caused him to assemble them in the same way. There was nothing to prevent collective petitions from developing in France as in England, and they were not so numerous at the Parliament of 1305 that the States General could not have made up the time lost.

In France, as in England, the accession of the Third Estate to the traditional assemblies did not constitute an innovation introduced at a definite date and attracting attention to itself. The French archives give us no information on the antecedents of the assembly of 1302, but beyond the fact that the burgesses had already been summoned, it is not even certain that it saw for the first time a regular representation of the Third Estate; it was remarkable only in the circumstances under which it was held, and, perhaps, by the numbers present.

In short, the character of the representation of the Third Estate scarcely differs at all from what we know of the English Commons. The documents published by M. Picot[1] show clearly that the Third Estate was summoned to be notified of the king's decisions, and to do what he should ask of them. In 1314, when the aid was desired, they had not to discuss the principle itself.[2]

1. Add to these the letters to the *bailli* of Senlis, 17th Feb. 1302, reprinted in the *Bibl. de l'Ec. des Chartes,* 1906, p. 468, by M. Jusselin.
2. The documents published by M. Picot show that appearance at the assembly of 1302 was obligatory and was definitely imposed by the king; the absentees are threatened with penalties (Picot, No. 1). The deputies are proctors equipped with full powers, carrying, in

Contemporary English historians[1] insist strongly on the fragility of Edward I's work. In Scotland, in Wales, in Guienne and in Flanders, he had under-

The reaction of the nobility in England and in France taken too much : the resources of England were too small. This, to a great extent, was what had induced him to strain the resources of government to the uttermost, and by a necessary consequence, to enter into a conflict with the tenants-in-chief and with the Church. A formidable reaction broke loose as soon as he was dead. It will not escape notice that, though the work of Philip the Fair was more solid, the feudal aristocracy was nevertheless in rebellion when he died in 1314; it also attempted to wrest charters of liberty from the last Capetians. But in the end it failed, whereas the English barons succeeded in the long run in ruining all the attempts

It triumphed in England made by Edward II and his favourites to continue the enterprise of Edward I.[2] Further, Edward I had not foreseen, any more than had Philip the Fair, the political development of the repre-

The middle class also developed its part in politics sentation of the middle class : the collective petitions, the effective consent to the aid, and the claim to subordinate the aid to the redress of grievances. In England the middle class finally obtained the recognition of its claims, thanks to the financial embarrassments of Edward III ; in France, the attempts of the bourgeoisie, more audacious, at least after Poitiers, received no permanent sanction.

advance, consent to whatever shall be asked of them, but having no power to ask to refer anything back to their constituents : it is an imperative mandate (Picot, nos. 1, 27, 30, 42, 46). In 1302 the representatives of the towns played an altogether secondary part : everything was done by the king and the nobles. In their declaration of April 9, 1302, the prelates of Tours do not speak of the towns : *"pro eodem (rege) aliis que prelatis et ipsius regni proceribus tractaturi"* (*Ibid.*, no. 4). The reply of the cardinals to the representatives of the towns gives them the same refutation as to the nobles, but much more briefly. (*Ibid.*, no. 8).

1. E.g., Mr. Tout, (*Place Edward II*, p. 36).
2. They have been minutely studied by Mr. Tout in the works cited above.

It would be too ambitious to seek in this work the deeper causes which brought about this divergence between the constitutional history of England

Why the Commons succeeded when the Third Estate failed

and that of France. But it seems that we are justified in noticing in the origins of the House of Commons certain features which would call for reflection if one were to attack the problem, and which, though fully brought to light by Stubbs, do not seem to have been rated by his successors at their true worth. When we follow in Stubbs the history of the English Parliaments, or, in M. Pasquet's study, that of the assemblies of Edward I, it clearly appears that the knights of the shires formed the first element of the English Commons, and were for long the principal element; the originality of the future House of Commons, and nearly all its force, came to it because the lesser nobility was charged with the representation of the freeholders, and because they possessed a certain administrative capacity. Both of these features were already obvious at the time of Edward I, and their origin is found in the county court.

Importance of the county court

Because that institution was kept alive, in spite of the Norman conquest and the feudal reorganisation of England, the knights kept in touch with all the free tenants, who, like them, owed suit and service there. Since the great feudatories never attended, and, at the most, sent their agents to represent them there, the lesser nobility naturally took the lead. The monarchy, from the time of Henry II, found in it a means of governing and a fulcrum against feudal organisation; by the use of the jury, this lesser nobility found itself representing the freemen, and was forced to acquire judicial and financial competence. But doubtless it will be thought that the solution of the problem is merely pushed back by this method.

The lesser nobility would never have taken up this function had not the king been strong enough to impose it

Why the lesser nobility represented the freeholders

on them, and that strength was his in virtue of the Conquest. Doubtless again, they would never have been able to fill the part, had they not, at a fairly early date, lost their military character : the strength of the monarchy and the insularity of the kingdom may have contributed to this.[1] Doubtless again, the smallness of England must have counted for much in the rapid advance of monarchical centralisation; on the other hand, it must also have favoured concerted rebellion by the magnates, and subsequently, the collective action of the Commons : in 1315 the French nobles did not demand a Great Charter, but a number of provincial charters; France, unlike England, was not yet a kingdom, but a collection of "nations."[2]

But, when due weight has been given to all these hypotheses, it will still stand that the existence of the

The county court is a link between Anglo-Saxon and medieval England

shire court forced itself on the monarchy and on its subjects, though no one even dimly saw the importance of the fact, as the instrument of government they required, whereas in France the later Capetians found nothing of the kind. There had been in France something resembling that court, but among the new barbarian invasions which marked the ruin of the Caro-

1. See *Const. Hist.*, iii, pp. 563-4. We are inclined to believe, with Stubbs, that the strength of the monarchy was the chief reason. From the eleventh to the fourteenth century, the kings did not, in theory, tolerate private war. To be knighted was simply to undertake to serve the king or to pay him scutages and fines. When the aristocracy again took the lead, from the middle of the fourteenth century, knighthood enjoyed a new lease of popularity.

2. We would call attention here to the study by M. Artonne, *Le mouvement de 1314 et les chartes provinciales de 1315,*" 1912. See also J. Petit, *Charles de Valois,* 1900. The smallness of England, and its resulting unity, helps also to explain why Parliament was not, like the States General, split up into provincial Estates, a fate with which it was at certain times threatened. Thus, in 1360, Edward III summoned five provincial assemblies (*Const. Hist.*, ii, p. 429).

lingian Empire, all trace had disappeared of what might have become a national institution.[1] The *prévôtés* and *bailliages* of France were for a long time nothing more than institutions of the domain, and the *bailliages* developed under the form of purely royal institutions, without the active participation of the nation. It has been thought that Stubbs and the historians of his generation had too easily insisted on the part played by the county court. They clearly tended to exaggerate the importance which it had for Englishmen in the Middle Ages, and the numbers which attended, and the regularity of its electoral operations. But they were right in seeing in it, as an element in constitutional evolution, a fundamental feature of primitive history, a link between the old England and the new. In this respect—and it is essential—Stubbs' work remains intact, and this does not seem to have been sufficiently remarked.

IV.

As we have observed, the occasional summons of the Commons to Parliament did not in the least, to Edward I's mind, involve the subdivision of that assembly. Parliament was one; the Chamber, where all its members met in the king's presence, was the only House of Parliament, and remains so in law, even though in the sixteenth century it became the House of Lords: it is there, still, that the Commons appear to hear the speech from the throne

The unity of Parliament under Edward I

---

1. See Viollet, *Hist. des inst. pol. et admin.*, i, pp. 307 sq. The capitularies distinguish the ordinary pleas of the county and the extraordinary pleas. To the first, all freemen are summoned; the count appoints, for judging, certain important men or *scabini*, with the assent of the assembly; the *scabini* alone are bound to attend the extraordinary pleas. In the *bailliage* of Vermandois, studied by M. Waquet, (*Le Bailliage de Vermandois aux XIIIᵉ et XIVᵉ siècles*, 1919), the *bailli* did not judge; he simply appointed men to judge. This seems to be a trace of the ancient Frankish institution. It survived in the law of the "Belgic" provinces (Flanders, Hainault, Artois, Cambrésis) until the French revolution: in theory, the seignorial *bailli* did not judge, he merely appointed judges.

and to receive notification of the royal sanction which transforms the bills into statutes; it is to this House that the Clerk of Parliament was and still is attached, and in the beginning, there was no other; the Roll of Parliament enregistered only what took place in that House, and only there were the Commons "in Parliament."

As has been said, they did little there and their position was very humble. Nevertheless, when the king **Necessity for** addressed a precise request to them, it is **separate** probable that, from the first, it must have **deliberation of** been necessary, to ask them to deliberate **the Commons** apart, in order to obtain a reply from them. In any case, it does not seem doubtful that this was so by the reign of Edward II. In certain cases even the barons held meetings outside the parliament chamber. The clergy did so too, and this is why in the end they ceased to appear, excepting of course, the bishops and the abbots, who were summoned by special writs.[1]

Mr. Pollard, invoking the right to supply from the imagination the definciencies left by the silence of the rolls has traced a vivid sketch, not without **Description by** humour, of what a session of Parliament **Mr. Pollard** probably resembled at the time of Edward I.[2] "The king in council clearly met the lords and commons in parliament in common session, when the chancellor or some other member of the council, usually a judge, explained to the assembly the purport of its summons and the requests for assistance and advice that would be laid before it. The advice was mainly a matter for the lords, the assistance for the commons. There is reason to believe that from Edward I's time the king's council sat in the midst of this assembly on four woolsacks (of which only one remains) facing one another,

1. Pollard, *Evolution of Parliament* p. 121.
2. *Ibid.*, pp. 120-121.

and that Fleta's phrase about the king holding his council in his parliaments has a literal and material, as well as a figurative meaning : no one would have arranged the four woolsacks in that way unless their occupants were normally engaged in confidential deliberation.[1] Outside this inner ring there sat, to the right of the throne, the spiritual lords, and to the left the temporal lords, and facing the throne there stood the commons. To them the demand for aid would be particularly addressed, and then the problem of how and what to answer would arise. Probably there would be a division of opinion, and possibly discordant murmurs ; courageous commons at the back might urge in whispers to their colleagues in the front the exhorbitance of the king's demands and the necessity of refusal ; timid members at the fore might tell their daring but half-concealed advisers at the back to speak for themselves ; and then, amid the muttering and murmuring the chancellor or other member of the council might suggest that not much progress was being made, and that the commons should go and talk it over among themselves, and then come back with an intelligible answer. On some such occasion it must have been suggested that they should choose some one of their members to be their Speaker, and that his answer, whether representing unanimity or but a small majority, should be considered equally binding upon all. The commons then trooped out of parliament to discuss in some more private place their domestic differences. They only reappeared in parliament when they had reached a resolution which was reported by the Speaker ; and he alone had liberty of speech in parliament."[2]

Under Edward II the Commons met in this way, it

1. *Const. Hist.*, iii, pp. 441, 487.
2. For the deliberations in the time of Edward III, see *Const.Hist.*, ii, p. 623-624.

appears, in the refectory of Westminster Abbey; later,
they met in the Chapter-House; the fact
is noted in 1352 and is stated to be of long
standing in 1376.[1] But concerning their
deliberations we know nothing. Whatever
the Commons did outside the Parliamentary Chamber,
having no legal value at all, goes unrecorded in the rolls
of Parliament. The progressive development of the
power of the speaker in the meetings of the Commons,
which is closely bound up with the progress of their
aptitude for deliberation, escapes us completely. In Parliament the speaker alone spoke : all the liberty of speech
which he claimed tended to be taken back from him if
he happened not to express exactly the opinions of his
colleagues; this modest liberty is not claimed by him
even for those in whose name he speaks, for, in Parliament, it is not for them to speak.[2] Moreover, as Mr.
Pollard rightly remarks, the Commons had not to appear
in Parliament either for long or often. Beyond the
king's demand and the reply that it involved, their collective presence had no justification. Almost the whole
mass of the petitions, under Edward I, had still no more
than an individual or a local interest; in 1305, out of
500 petitions, only five are of public interest, and three
of these concern the feudatories alone.

At first these deliberations have little importance

The organisation of a House of Commons, and the
growth of its importance in Parliament depended on the
fusion of the knights and the burgesses,
on the development of the collective petition, and on the relation which had to be
established between the redress of grievances and the favourable reception given to the demand
for financial assistance.

Causes of the progress of the House of Commons

1. Pollard, *Evolution of Parliament*, pp. 113, 125; *Const. Hist.*, iii,
pp. 396-399, 445. [See also V. H. Galbraith, *The Anonimalle Chronicle*,
Manchester Univ. Press, 1927, pp. xliii-xlv].
2. Pollard, *Evolution of Parliament* p. 126; *Const. Hist.*, iii, pp. 471-
473; 477-484.

Now, there is an important reservation which must be introduced into Mr. Pollard's description, and he himself has made it elsewhere : at first, knights and burgesses deliberated apart; there are examples of this separation under Edward III. Mr. Pollard has found one even in 1523.[1] And it is difficult to follow the progress of their fusion because of the obscurity of the words *communitas, commune, gens du commun*. In the fourteenth century their meaning is still obscure in the rolls : the *commun* is sometimes opposed to the knights; for example, in 1322 we have mention of the *chivalers des countez et les gentz du commun;* and similarly in 1340. In 1343 the roll speaks of the *chivalers des countez* and of the *communes;* on the next line, *des prelats, grantz, et communes,* and, a little further on, *des chivalers des countez et autres communes.*[2]

It is evident that from the social and moral points of view, the knights differed greatly from the burgesses. The knights belonged, in theory, to the military class, and the obligation of knighthood put a gulf between them and the burgesses; in the fourteenth and fifteenth centuries the knight is still counted a baron and *nobilis* : now there was no social distinction between the greater and smaller barons : there was, therefore, much in common between the county knights and the future Lords; at Lincoln, in 1301, the first county knight whose activities are known to us, Henry of Keighley, spoke not for the Commons, but for the barons.[3] It was the persistence of the barons in creating an hereditary peerage on the

Marginal notes:

Separate deliberations of the knights and the burgesses

Superiority of the knights over the burgesses

---

1. Pollard, *Evolution of Parliament*, p. 113.
2. *Const. Hist.*, ii, pp. 395-396, 411 (note 3), 621-622; iii, pp. 444-446; Pollard, *Evolution of Parliament*. p. 114; Pasquet, pp. 226-228. See also above, pp. 447, note 1.
3. Pollard, *Evolution of Parliament*, p. 115. On the relations between the barons and the knights, see *Const. Hist.*, iii, pp. 548-549, 563, 567-568. [See also Tout, *Chapters*, iii, pp. 137-139].

basis of the royal writ which brought about the definite separation. But the name "House of Lords" appears only under Henry VIII. On the other hand, the knights performed administrative functions in the country, which placed them far above the burgesses. That they were of much higher consideration is proved by the fact that they were summoned regularly, long before the burgesses, and the difference of their parliamentary wages bears further witness: a burgess received only half that paid to a knight. Moreover, the boroughs paid the aid at a higher rate than the counties: this inequality did not tend to develop solidarity.[1] The ascendency of the knights, moreover, survived the fusion, and until 1533 the speaker was always chosen from among their number.

Mr. Pollard attributes the preponderance of the knights partly to the indifference of the burgesses: most of the 74 knights were usually present in Parliament, whereas only about a score of burgesses appeared. This assertion, founded on the examination of the writ *de expensis* has been with good reason contested by Miss May MacKisack and by Mr. J. G. Edwards. Their researches prove that the kings of England saw to it that knights and burgesses were regularly "returned" and were present at the sessions with more regularity than we have been in the habit of believing, since the appearance of the work of Reiss. It is to the social rank and administrative capacity of the knights that we must attribute their preponderance in the Commons. But, with this reservation, it remains true, as Mr. Pollard says, that if fusion came about, it was because the lesser nobility deliberately consented to it.[2]

The burgesses were regularly represented in Parliament

1. Pollard, *Evolution of Parliament*, p. 124; Pasquet, p. 150; see *Const. Hist.*, i, p. 605; ii, p. 193.
2. Pollard, *Evolution of Parliament* pp. 127, 317-8; *Const. Hist.* iii, pp. 612 sq.; Miss May MacKisack, "Borough Representation in Richard II's reign," *E. H. R.* 1924; J. G. Edwards (study cited above,

KK

Facts were not lacking, however, which tended to draw together the two categories of representatives. Edward I, involuntarily, no doubt, had contributed to it in having both summoned by the sheriff, whereas Simon de Montfort had summoned the burgesses directly.[1] Figuring on the same return, both represented communities, whilst the other members of Parliament were present as individuals; in the Middle Ages, this resulted in a striking inferiority in the case of the knights as well as for

Reasons for the fusion of the knights and the burgesses

p. 473, n. 3). Since Riess, it has been held that many representatives did not appear in Parliament, because their names do not figure in the writs *de expensis*. It is true that Mr. Pollard admits that a certain number of towns paid their deputies themselves : he cites eight such, as well as the Cinque Ports. But Mr. Edwards has shown that the accounts of several other towns mention the payment of delegates who do not figure in the writs *de expensis*; so that one cannot trust in the latter to deny the presence of a representative at the Parliament. Thus the accounts of Leicester show that the borough was represented in 13 Parliaments between 1301 and 1324, and in 23 others under Edward III; now we have for Leicester only 3 writs of the first period and 5 of the second. Though we have not the same check on the counties, Mr. Edwards has been able to show that in their case, too, the writs are not complete. In 1301, Henry de Keighley, member for Lancashire (*Const. Hist.*, ii, p. 158), does not figure in them. For the Parliament of March, 1340, we have these writs for 33 out of 37 counties : Oxford and Surrey are among the counties whose writs are missing; yet a deputy from each of them was nominated "trier" of the petitions. But as the practically regular presence of the knights is not contested, the chief importance of Mr. Edwards' study is that it shows that the boroughs, though unwilling, obeyed the king's orders much better than we have been ready to admit. It presents yet another interest. The progress of the Commons depended largely on the experience of the deputies and therefore on their re-election. Mr. Pollard thought they were almost always changed at each Parliament. The tables drawn up by Mr. Edwards for the period of 1290-1324 prove that this is quite wrong. For the counties, the deputies who have been elected one or more times previously are in a majority in ten Parliaments : they are in a minority in eleven; and they balance the number of the others in 12; 657 members were elected only once, 507 were elected more than once, and go to make up 1612 elections. For the boroughs, deputies previously elected form the majority in six Parliaments, the minority in fifteen, and balance the others in six; 634 deputies were elected once, 346 more than once, accounting for 1108 elections. Re-election was thus far from being an exception; one deputy was 13 times re-elected. But it will be noticed that the proportions are less favourable for the boroughs : the superiority of the knights, though lessened, still exists.

1. Pasquet, p. 55.

the burgesses : both were convoked only exceptionally ; they were dismissed together, generally before the barons; they took only a slight and subordinate part. Finally, we can add that the knights did not represent in Parliament their own class alone, but all the freeholders of the county court, socagers as well as the rest. Whatever their own feelings may have been, this quality must have lowered them beyond remedy in the eyes of the barons by writ, and by way of reaction, must have driven them slowly towards the burgesses. Here again does the importance of the county court appear.[1] The fusion was favoured by the practice of the collective petition which the king unconsciously encouraged by consulting knights and burgesses in common. Reciprocally, the fusion multiplied these petitions in proportion as it became more intimate. English historians seem now to agree in placing its rapid progress in the reign of Edward II, and this is one of the reasons for which Mr. Tout gives that reign a great importance in the history of England. From 1314, Mr. Pollard discovers debates *ad petitionem Communitatis Angliae;* from November 1325, he observes that the rolls begin to distinguish the petitions *pur tote la commune* from the rest. For 1326-7 he cites the formulas *prient les chevaliers et la Commune, prie la Commune;* in 1325 a passage from the roll : *"et auxint, sire, prient vos liges gentz"* seems to him to indicate a speech from the speaker. Complaint is also made that when petitions are presented, they are adjourned before the king or the chancellor *"dount nul issue n'est fait";* in 1327, the Commons ask that their petitions should be transformed into statutes in Parliament. In 1340, six burgesses and twelve knights are elected to join with prelates and barons as triers and receivers of petitions and to put them

The collective petition

---

1. Pasquet, p. 150 ; Pollard, *Evolution of Parliament*, pp. 115, 117.

into the form of statutes. The collective petition is thus
hallowed by custom, and, since it presup-
poses deliberation, we may say, in that
sense, that under Edward III there is a
House of Commons.[1]

A House of
Commons
exists under
Edward III

We may add that at the same time there appears the
first sign of a distinct corporate organisation : the Commons have their clerk. In all probability
they must have been allowed a clerk from
an early date, in order to help them draft
their petitions and their replies to the king, and probably
also to set up a record which would make possible the
issue of the writs *de expensis*. From the fact that this
attribute is fully established under Edward III, we
should perhaps be justified in concluding that separate
deliberations go back to the time of Edward I. In any
case no trace has survived of any minutes prior to the
Journal which was undertaken in 1547, and perhaps none
were recorded before that date.[2]

Beginning of
its corporate
organisation

As far as the progress of the Commons is concerned,

---

1. Pollard, *Evolution of Parliament*, p. 119. For the first texts
recording the separate deliberation of the magnates and the Commons,
see *Const. Hist.*, ii, pp. 395-396, 411-412, 621-622; iii, pp. 444-446;
Pasquet, pp. 227-228 reproduces several of these texts. He calls attention
to the fact that in the Parliament of Sept. 1332, it is not certain that the
knights deliberated with the burgesses :the prelates deliberated "*par eux
mesmes; et les ditz countes, barouns, et autres grauntz par eux mesmes;
et auxint les chivalers des countés par eux mesmes*"; but the burgesses
are not mentioned until the moment of the concession of the aid : "*les
ditz prélats . . .etc. . . et les chivalers des countes et toute la Commune*"
grant the aid. In Dec. 1332 the doubt is lifted : the prelates deliberated
separately, the earls and barons by themselves, and "*les chivalers et
gentz de countez, et gentz de la Commune par eux meismes.*" The text
of Jan. 1333 is very precise : it is decided in Parliament that there shall
deliberate by themselves a certain number of lords who appear to be
counsellors of the king, the other lords and the proctors, the knights, and
people of the Commons. In 1341, at the Parliament of the quinzain after
Easter the king charges "*les ditz grantz et les aultres de la Commune
qu'ils se treissent ensemble et s'avisent entre eux; c'est assaver les
grantz de par eux et les chivalers des countez, citeyns et burgeys de
par eux.*

2. Pollard, *Evolution of Parliament*, p. 114; *Const. Hist.* iii, p. 468.

the reign of Edward II presents an importance which we
must neither exaggerate nor depreciate, and
The Commons under Edward II which must be focussed correctly. It must
not be exaggerated : the Parliaments of
1322 show, for example, that the Commons were treated
in a very casual fashion. The Commons met on March
17th, and five days later the king sent them a message
that they might go away, that he had no time to receive
They are treated casually with unconcern their petitions, nor to reply to them, and
that he would hold another Parliament for
this purpose. In September, when an aid
had been voted, the barons were asked whether the king
ought to march against the Scots or to reply to the petitions; they replied in favour of the first alternative, and
the Commons were again dismissed. On December 4th,
at York, only five prelates came, and the petitions were
once more adjourned to a Parliament which was to be
held in January.[1]

The interpretation given by Stubbs to the famous
statute of York 1322 gave to the Commons far too strong
a constitutional position : according to him,
The Statute of York (1322) this statute confirmed and strengthened
that assertion, formulated in the writs sent
to the clergy in 1295 by Edward I, that what concerns
everyone must have the consent of all, in other words,
that a true law or statute should be established in Parliament with the approval of the three Estates.[2] Since it
is certain that after 1322, just as before, the king continued to issue legislative measures of every kind, whatever name may be given them, this theory can hardly
be maintained. It is possible that the *Communauté du
royaume* was nothing but a redundant formula. But
if we hold that this *Communauté* here refers expressly
to the Commons, as opposed to the prelates, earls, and

1. Pollard, *Evolution of Parliament*, p. 116.
2. *Const. Hist.*, ii, pp. 258-9.

barons, Mr. G. Lapsley suggests that the statute of
York must have had as its object to prevent the barons
from having subsequent recourse to their expedient of
1311. They had then entrusted the reform of the kingdom to a commission nominated by themselves and taken
from their own ranks. While annulling the ordinances
which this commission had issued, the statute simply
laid it down that henceforth all measures concerning the
power of the king and the "estate" of the realm, in fact,
all constitutional modifications, could be established only
in full parliament, and not by a committee of barons
acting on behalf of a narrow oligarchy. The statute, in
fact, confirmed the statutes and establishments promulgated by Edward II and by his predecessors before 1311,
and the clause under discussion does not seem to have
envisaged ordinary legislation. Moreover, the practice
of subsequent times shows no change at all. Constitutional alterations having more importance than ordinary
legislative measures, we can scarcely see, in the statute of
1322, anything more than an emergency
measure directed against the most troublesome barons, and, to the minds of its
promotors, powerless to modify in the slightest degree
the situation of the Commons in Parliament.[1]

An emergency measure

Yet we must not excessively depreciate the importance
of the Commons at the time of Edward II either. In
addition to the wholly practical reasons of
an administrative nature which we have
already enumerated, the summoning of the
Commons corresponded increasingly to the
desire to obtain their adhesion to political
measures of a certain importance. Mr. Lapsley, having
studied the representation of five counties in the Parliaments of this reign, concludes that interference of a

But the influence of the Commons grows under Edward II

1. G. Lapsley, "The Commons and the Statute of York." *E. H. R.*,
1913.

political nature influenced the choice of the knights for Essex and Hertfordshire in 1311 and 1322, and for Bedfordshire in 1318, 1321, and 1322. This does not prove that the barons considered the consent of the Commons as being legally necessary, but we may think that when important measures were in the field, the goodwill of the Commons seemed to them desirable. Without their being called upon to express consent, their approval resulted from their presence and was not negligible; in particular, it was thought useful to show them the opportuneness of the measures adopted : the knights exercised a great influence in their counties, and their opinion easily became public opinion; therefore it was prudent to set aside those from whom systematic opposition was expected. It is evident that the social progress which was the basic origin of the summoning of the Commons, continued in this way to show its results, and that in fact, if not in law, their moral influence was developing.[1]

From Edward III's reign onwards, the ground becomes firmer, and Stubbs' account regains full credit.[2]

1. G. Lapsley, "Knights of the Shire in the Parliaments of Edward II." *E. H. R.*, 1919.

2. For the fourteenth and fifteenth centuries, see Pollard, *Evolution of Parliament*, pp. 129, 263-4, 327. Mr. Pollard's book re-opens the discussion on the authority of the *Modus tenendi parliamentum;* Stubbs refuses to recognise it, and rightly, as it seems (*Const. Hist.* ii, pp 174, 266, 625) whereas Mr. Pollard thinks that there is no reason for denying it for the period at which the treatise was written. (p.68). Mr. Tait, (*E. H. R.* 1921) agrees with Stubbs' view. The date of this tract has been the object of a minute examination, based on the study of the 47 manuscripts at the British Museum (Hodnett and White : "The manuscripts of the Modus tenendi parliamentum," *E. H. R.* 1919). Most scholars, (see the bibliography in Gross, p. 447), placed it at the end of the fourteenth century; Stubbs, in the last quarter; Riess in the second half of Richard II's reign; M. Bémont at the beginning of the reign. This recent study puts it back to a much earlier date, perhaps to Edward II's reign. Before the end of the fourteenth century there are two distinct versions occurring in two manuscripts. one which also contains accounts of the period of Richard II, and the other, in which the *Modus* is found together with documents of the period of Edward II. Mr. Tait has put forward some facts in support. It is possible that the *Modus* was revised at the time of Richard II.

Their subse-
quent progress Moreover, during the fourteenth century
the sensible progress of the townsfolk and
even of the villeins, gradually prepares the
way for the transformation of national representation.
Mr. Pollard thinks that about the middle
But their
importance of the fifteenth century a new evolution is
remains slight being outlined : men are beginning to take
until the XVIth
century an interest in Parliament, to solicit the
candidature, and to regard the franchise as
a privilege and not merely as a duty. This does not
alter the fact that Fortescue finds nothing to say of the
constitutional function of the Commons, and that in
practice, their part still remains very humble. Stubbs
himself recognises that all the great crises in the political
history of England in the fourteenth and fifteenth centuries were decided without the Commons, so that this
history remains the work of the feudal aristocracy. The
progress of collective petitions even contributed to make
the frequent meeting of Parliament much less necessary.
By the end of Edward III's reign, the Commons have
lost interest in the individual petitions which increasingly go to swell the activity of the Council and of Chancery : thus, from the constitutional point of view, the
judicial Parliaments are falling into insignificance.[1] But,
this being so, the king had scarcely ever to summon the
Commons now except to ask money from them, and they
were not eager for this. "What can the people desire,"
says Sir Thomas Smith, "if not few taxes and few Parliaments?" And in fact, in the fifteenth century they
became much more rare, which was bound to injure the
political education of the Commons. It might even have
happened that Parliament almost disappeared and'
the king of England might, like the king of France,
have gone so far as to ask provincial assemblies for the
voting of the aid : in 1282, Edward I assembled in this

1. Pollard, *Evolution of Parliament* p. 128.

way two Parliaments, just as there were two Convocations; in 1360 Edward III formed five provincial assemblies. These expedients were not followed up, happily for the Commons. Perhaps we must conclude from this that national unity, in a form at once administrative and moral, was now too far advanced. In any case, at the end of the fifteenth century, the Commons were not yet associated in the government of the kingdom; still less could it be foreseen that they would one day enter into conflict with monarchy. Mr. Pollard's work has shown that it was the Tudors who, by calling the Commons to vote the statutes to bring about the religious revolution and to strengthen the monarchy itself, associated them at last in the government of England.

INDEX.